Latino/a Literature in the Classroom

In one of the most rapidly growing areas of literary study, this volume provides the first comprehensive guide to teaching Latino/a literature in all varieties of learning environments. Essays by internationally renowned scholars offer an array of approaches and methods for the teaching of novels, short stories, plays, poetry, autobiography, testimonial texts, comic books, children's and young adult literature, films, performance art, and multi-media digital texts, among others. The essays provide conceptual vocabularies and tools to help teachers design courses that pay attention to issues of:

- form across a range of storytelling media
- content such as theme and character
- historical periods, linguistic communities, and regions
- institutional classroom settings.

The volume innovatively adds to and complicates the broader humanities curriculum by offering new possibilities for pedagogical practice.

Frederick Luis Aldama is Arts and Humanities Distinguished Professor of English at the Ohio State University, USA, where he is also Director of the Latino Studies Program and founder and director of Latino and Latin American Studies Space for Enrichment and Research (LASER).

Latino/a Literature in the Classroom

Twenty-first-century approaches to teaching

Edited by
Frederick Luis Aldama

Routledge
Taylor & Francis Group

LONDON AND NEW YORK

First published 2015
by Routledge
2 Park Square, Milton Park, Abingdon, Oxon OX14 4RN

and by Routledge
711 Third Avenue, New York, NY 10017

Routledge is an imprint of the Taylor & Francis Group, an informa business

British Library Cataloguing-in-Publication Data
A catalogue record for this book is available from the British Library

Library of Congress Cataloging in Publication Data
Latino/a literature in the classroom : 21st century approaches to teaching / Frederick Luis Aldama [editor].
pages cm
Includes bibliographical references and index.
1. American literature--Hispanic American authors--Study and teaching.
2. Latin American literature--Study and teaching--United States. 3. Hispanic Americans in literature--Study and teaching. 4. Hispanic Americans--Intellectual life--Study and teaching. I. Aldama, Frederick Luis, 1969- editor. II. Title.
PS153.H56L38 2015
810.9'868073071--dc23
2014036770

ISBN: 978-0-415-72420-3 (hbk)
ISBN: 978-0-415-72421-0 (pbk)
ISBN: 978-1-315-85752-7 (ebk)

Typeset in Times New Roman
by Taylor & Francis Books

Contents

Illustrations

Figures

Tables

Notes on contributors

Frederick Luis Aldama is Arts & Humanities Distinguished Professor of English and University Distinguished Scholar at the Ohio State University, where he is also founder and director of LASER—Latino and Latin American Space for Enrichment Research. He is the author and editor of over 20 books. He co-edits several book series, including Cognitive Approaches to Literature and Culture, Global Latino Americas, and World Comics and Graphic Nonfiction. He also edits several additional book series, including the Latino Pop Culture and Latin/o American Profiles.

Jesse Alemán is a Professor of English at the University of New Mexico, where he teaches courses in nineteenth-century American and Chicano/a literatures. His scholarship focuses on nineteenth-century American and US Latino/a literary histories and national identities. He has over a dozen articles in journals and edited collections. In 2003, he edited and reprinted Loreta Janeta Velazquez's 1876, *The Woman in Battle*, and in 2007, he co-edited *Empire and the Literature of Sensation* with Shelley Streeby. He is working on *Wars of Rebellion*, a book about nineteenth-century Hispanic writings about the U.S. Civil War, and he is co-editing *The Latino Nineteenth Century* with Rodrigo Lazo. He is the recipient of three teaching awards; has twice been named Outstanding English Faculty member at the University of New Mexico; and as a summer faculty member of Middlebury College's Bread Loaf School of English, he's also been awarded the Ruth and Lillian Marino Endowed Chair for teaching excellence.

Heather Alumbaugh is Associate Professor of English at the College of Mount Saint Vincent, where she is the Director of the Honors Program and the Co-Director of the Women's Studies Program. Her scholarship and teaching focus on Latino/a literature, Women's literature, and American Modernism. She is a member of the Board of Directors of LifeWay Network, a non-profit organization that provides "safe housing for women who have been trafficked and [offers] education about trafficking to the general public."

Magdalena L. Barrera is Associate Professor of Mexican American Studies at San José State University. Her primary research agenda, situated at the intersection of literary/visual studies and cultural history, is the textual recovery of Mexican American experiences in the early twentieth century, particularly around narratives of citizenship, gender, and cultural adaptation. She also writes about the mentoring and retention of first-generation students and students of color in higher education. Her essays and reviews have appeared in the *Journal of Latinos and Education*; *Aztlán: A Journal of*

Chicano Studies; *Bilingual Review*; *Women's Studies*; *Revista Camino Real*; and *Sexualities in History: A Reader*.

David A. Colón is Associate Professor of English and Latino/a studies at Texas Christian University. He is the editor of *Between Day and Night: New and Selected Poems, 1946–2010* by Miguel González-Gerth (2013). His criticism has appeared in numerous journals, including *Jacket2*, *Transmodernity*, *Cultural Critique*, *The Journal of Latino/ Latin American Studies*, *The Journal of Philosophy: A Cross-Disciplinary Inquiry*, *MELUS*, *Studies in American Culture*, and *How2*, among others. He is a contributor to *The Princeton Encyclopedia of Poetry and Poetics* and the forthcoming *Cambridge History of Latina/o Literature*. His first novel, *The Lost Men* (2012), was nominated for the Arthur C. Clarke Award, and his second novel, *The Reckoning of Bárbaro Soto*, is forthcoming from Aignos.

Sheila Marie Contreras is Associate Professor of English at Michigan State University, where she is also Director of the Chicano/Latino Studies Program (CLS). Her book, *Blood Lines: Myth, Indigenism and Chicana/o Literature* was published by the University of Texas Press in 2008. She teaches courses in Latino/a Literary and Cultural Studies and Women's Studies at the undergraduate and graduate levels at Michigan State. Her current research project explores mestizo@ and Métis identity and comparative indigeneities. Contreras resides in Lansing, Michigan, where she has been an active community participant in the Lansing School District's restructuring process, as well as a member of the Chicano/Latino Advisory Committee to the Lansing Board of Education.

María Acosta Cruz is Professor of Language, Literature and Culture at Clark University. She teaches and conducts research in the areas of Caribbean and Latino cultures. She is the author of numerous articles and the book *Dream Nation: Puerto Rican Culture and the Fictions of Independence* (2014).

Marivel T. Danielson is Associate Professor in the School of Transborder Studies at the Arizona State University. Her research and teaching focus on Chicana/Latina literature, sexuality, gender, performance, and race/border/diaspora theory. She is the author of many articles and the book, *Homecoming Queers: Desire and Difference in Chicana Latina Cultural Production* (2009).

Stephanie Fetta is Assistant Professor at Syracuse University. Currently, Dr. Fetta is working on a book addressing the issue of shame and U.S. Latin@ Literature. Hegemonic forces shame racially and gendered bodies as an instrument of social control. In Latin@ literature, authors illustrate the consequences of shaming on the individual while they demonstrate shame as a social dynamic. Dr. Fetta is the editor of *Chicano/Latino Literary Prize: An Anthology of Award-Winning Fiction, Poetry, and Drama* (2008).

Elena Foulis teaches Latina/o literature at The Ohio State University and currently serves as coordinator of outreach and service learning in the Department of Spanish and Portuguese at The Ohio State University. She is currently engaged in a statewide initiative to collect, catalog, and preserve oral narratives of Latinos in Ohio in collaboration with the Ohio Hispanic Heritage Project and the Center for Folklore Studies.

Michael Nieto Garcia is Assistant Professor of literature at Clarkson University in upstate New York. His essays have appeared in *Prose Studies*, *Social Analysis*, and *a/b: Auto/Biography Studies*, as well as in the critical collections *Identifying with Freedom* and *The Culture and Philosophy of Ridley Scott*. He is the translator of *They Say I'm a Monkey* (2005), and the author of *Autobiography in Black and Brown* (2014).

Ellen M. Gil-Gómez is Professor of English at California State University, San Bernardino where she teaches primarily Chicano/a Cultural Studies and literature, as well as comic narratives, graphic novels, and Feminist and LGBTQ Theories. She has published mainly in the area of Chicano/Latino and Women of Color Studies, which includes her book *Performing La Mestiza* (2001) and numerous articles and chapters. Her most recent publications are focused on comics and online pedagogy.

Jennifer Carolina Gómez Menjívar is Assistant Professor at the University of Minnesota Duluth. Her research interests include sociolinguistics, languages in contact, bilingualism, and language policy. Her work on language attitudes and varieties of Kriol in Belize has appeared in the *Proceedings of the 40th Annual Berkeley Linguistics Society* and the *Journal of Pidgin and Creole Languages*.

Christopher González is Assistant Professor of English at Texas A&M University-Commerce where he teaches twentieth- and twenty-first-century literature of the United States. He received his PhD from the Ohio State University, specializing in narrative theory and Latino/a narrative across media. Junot Díaz and Gilbert Hernandez are the subjects of two forthcoming books González has authored, and he has recently published essays on the comic artists Wilfred Santiago and Jaime Hernandez, filmmakers Alex Rivera and Robert Rodriguez, and novelists Jonathan Lethem and Philip Roth. Along with Frederick Luis Aldama, González is co-author of *Latinos in the End Zone: Conversations on the Brown Color Line in the NFL* (2013).

Lisa Sánchez González is Professor of English at the University of Connecticut. Along with many essays on Puerto Rican, American, and Caribbean literary history, Sánchez is the author of *Boricua Literature: A Literary History of the Puerto Rican Diaspora* (2001) and *The Stories I Read to the Children: The Life and Writing of Pura Belpré* (2013). She recently published her much anticipated first collection of short stories, *Puerto Rican Folktales/ Cuentos folclóricos puertorriqueños* (2014).

Monica Hanna is Assistant Professor of Chicana and Chicano Studies at California State University, Fullerton. Her research focuses on literature of the Americas, genres including historical fiction and literary journalism, and nationalisms. Her work has appeared in journals including *Callaloo*, *Metamorphoses*, and *Label Me Latina/o*.

Tace Hedrick is Associate Professor of English and Women's Studies at the University of Florida. Her research and teaching focus on Chicana/o and Latina/o literature and theory as well as on Women's Studies and feminist theory. She is the author of *Mestizo Modernisms: Race, Nation, and Identity in Latin American Culture, 1900–1940* (2003) and *From Dirty Girls to Dirty Blonde: Chica Lit and Americanization for the Twenty-first Century* (2015).

Paloma Martinez-Cruz, PhD is Assistant Professor at The Ohio State University where she teaches and publishes on contemporary hemispheric literature and culture, women of color feminism, performance, and alternative epistemologies. She is the author of

Women and Knowledge in Mesoamerica: From East L.A. to Anahuac (2011) and the translator of Afro-Brazilian author Conceição Evaristo's debut novel, *Ponciá Vicencio* (2006). Martinez-Cruz is also the editor of *Rebeldes: A Proyecto Latina Anthology* (2013), a collection of stories and art from 26 Latina women from the Midwest and beyond. Martinez-Cruz is at work on a book examining the resistance fronts found in Chicano/a popular culture.

Ellen McCracken is a Professor of Latina/o American literature and cultural studies at the University of California, Santa Barbara. She is the author of *From Mademoiselle to Ms.: Decoding Women's Magazines* (1993); *New Latina Narrative: The Feminine Space of Postmodern Ethnicity* (1999); and *The Life and Writing of Fray Angélico Chávez: A New Mexico Renaissance Man* (2009). She is editor of several volumes, including *Guitars and Adobes and the Uncollected Stories of Fray Angélico Chávez* (2009) and has published numerous articles on U.S. Latina literature and culture. She is also the recipient of the James Phelan Prize for Best Contributions to the journal *Narrative*.

Cruz Medina is an Assistant Professor of English at Santa Clara University. His writing has appeared in *College Composition and Communication, Reflections: A Journal of Public Rhetoric, Civic Writing and Service Learning*, and *alter/nativas: latin american cultural studies journal*. His book titled, *Poch@ Pop: A Latin@ "Cultural Traitor" Resists Deficiency Rhetoric in Popular Culture*, is forthcoming in Frederick Luis Aldama's Latino Pop Culture series with Palgrave.

Julie Minich is Assistant Professor of English at The Center for Mexican American Studies at the University of Texas, Austin. Her research and teaching focus on Chicana/o studies and disability studies. She is the author of numerous articles and the book *Accessible Citizenships: Disability, Nation, and the Cultural Politics of Greater Mexico* (2014).

Amelia María de la Luz Montes is Associate Professor of English at the University of Nebraska, Lincoln. Her research and teaching focus on late nineteenth and contemporary Latina/Latino and hemispheric literature as well as LGBT literature. She has published numerous articles, edited and introduced a new edition of Ruiz de Burton's first novel, *Who Would Have Thought It?* (2009), and is currently working on a book entitled, *Corazon y Tierra: Latinas Writing on the Great Plains and Midwest* as well as finishing a fictional memoir entitled *The Diabetes Chronicles*.

Paula Moya is Associate Professor of the Department of English at Stanford University. Her teaching and research focus on twentieth-century and early twenty-first century literary studies, feminist theory, critical and narrative theories, American cultural studies, and Chicano/a and U.S. Latina/o studies. She is the author of *Learning from Experience: Minority Identities, Multicultural Struggles* (2002) and the co-editor of *Doing Race: 21 Essays for the 21st Century* (2010), *Reclaiming Identity: Realist Theory and the Predicament of Postmodernism* (2000) and *Identity Politics Reconsidered* (2007).

Urayoán Noel is Assistant Professor of English and Spanish at New York University. His essays have appeared in journals such as *Contemporary Literature, Latino Studies*, and *Small Axe*, as well as in a number of books. He is the author of *In Visible Movement: Nuyorican Poetry from the Sixties to Slam* (2014) and of various books of poetry, including the forthcoming *Buzzing Hemisphere/Rumor Hemisférico*.

Randy Ontiveros is Associate Professor of English and affiliate in Women's Studies and U.S. Latina/o Studies at the University of Maryland, College Park. He is the author of *In the Spirit of a New People: The Cultural Politics of the Chicano Movement* (2013). He is currently writing a book about the suburbs in Latino/a history and culture.

William Orchard is Assistant Professor of English at Queens College/City University of New York. He is co-editor of *The Plays of Josefina Niggli* (2007) that the American Library Association named one of 24 "Best of the Best Books Published by University Presses." He is currently working on a book entitled *Graphic Educations: Politics, Pedagogy, and the Latino/a Graphic Novel*.

Marilyn Patton teaches literature and writing at De Anza College in Cupertino, California. She has also taught at Stanford and at the University of California, Santa Cruz. She has attended performances of El Teatro Campesino since 1973 and has invited staff members to speak to her classes. Her main non-academic involvement in theater has been political street theater.

Ana Patricia Rodríguez is Associate Professor in the Department of Spanish and Portuguese and U.S. Latino/a Studies Program at the University of Maryland, College Park, and the author of *Dividing the Isthmus: Central American Transnational Histories, Literatures, and Cultures* (2009).

Richard T. Rodríguez is Associate Professor of English and Latina/Latino Studies at the University of Illinois, Urbana-Champaign, where he is also affiliated with the Department of Gender and Women's Studies and the Unit for Criticism and Interpretive Theory. He is the author of *Next of Kin: The Family in Chicano/a Cultural Politics* (2009). He is currently finishing a book on queer Latino representation in film and literature and the politics of social space.

Brant M. Torres is Assistant Professor of English at the University of San Francisco. He teaches American literature from the colonial period through the twentieth century, LGBTQ literature, and literary theory. He is currently working on a book tentatively titled *Occult Feelings: Esotericism and Queer Relationality in Nineteenth-Century U.S. Literature*, which investigates how the literary use of occult language, images, and philosophies encouraged the exploration of new forms of erotic attachment in nineteenth-century America.

Nan Tynberg is a recently retired adjunct professor of English at California State University, San Bernardino, Palm Desert. She taught a wide range of literature courses, directed the Palm Springs Library's video history project, produced two documentaries, and published several articles. She is currently writing a book tentatively titled *Shape: Reading in Three Dimensions*, which explores the relationship between visual/sculptural artistry and literature.

Jennifer Harford Vargas is Assistant Professor of English at Bryn Mawr College. Her teaching and research interests include Latino/a cultural production, hemispheric American studies, theories of the novel, undocumented migrant imaginaries, and testimonio forms. She is working on a book manuscript tentatively titled *Forms of Dictatorship in the Latina/o Novel*, is co-editing a volume of essays on Junot Díaz, and is author of "Dictating a Zafa: The Power of Narrative Form in Junot Díaz's the Brief Wondrous Life of Oscar Wao" (*MELUS* 2014).

Juan Velasco is Associate Professor in the Department of English at Santa Clara University, where he teaches courses in creative writing, autobiography, and Latina/o literature. He is the author of fiction and nonfiction, including *Enamorado* (2000), *Moving Borders: Tradition, Modernity and the Search for "Mexicanness" in Contemporary Chicano Literature* (2003), and *Call Me When I Am Gone*—published as a DVD in 2008. He has articles in the *Chicana/o Cultural Studies Reader* and the *Latino/a Popular Culture*. He is currently finishing up the scholarly book, *Automitografía: A Study on Contemporary Chicana/o Autobiography* that examines contemporary Chicana/o autobiography from 1959–2012.

Jackie K. White is Associate Professor of English at Lewis University where she teaches young adult literature and poetry, among other areas. She is also a former 6–12 grade teacher. She is a former editor for the literary annual *RHINO* as well as the author of three chapbooks of poetry: *Come Clearing* (2012), *Petal-Tearing & Variations* (2007), and the Anabiosis Award Winning, *Bestiary Charming* (2006). She co-translated (with Frances Aparicio) César Miguel Rondón's *The Book of Salsa* (2008). She has completed a translation of Sherezada Vicioso's *Algo que decir: Essays on Feminist Caribbean Literature*.

Introduction

What are we teaching when *teaching* Latino/a literature?

Frederick Luis Aldama

What is Latino/a literature?

As the multitude of teachers brought together in this volume demonstrate, there is much conceptual work that goes into deciding what texts to include in courses on Latino/a literature—and how to frame their teaching. When we choose our texts (from novels, short stories, autobiographies, *testimonios*, comic books, films, and much more), we begin by asking: What ingredients must be present for a given Latino/a literary text to be considered? What is the ethnic heritage of the author: Dominican, Cuban, Mexican, Puerto Rican—or is he or she of Central and South American descent? Do the authors use Spanish, Spanish and English, *caló*—or just English? What content should the texts have: themes, events, and characterizations that gravitate around issues, occurrences, and people of the Latino/a Americas—or something else? What literary historical period should be covered?

All these questions and more are further considered within larger institutional contexts of the teaching itself. Teaching Latino literature in an English department necessarily means that one can't include Spanish-only texts, for instance. Teaching Latino/a literary texts within survey courses on multicultural literature means that one's selection of texts might be even more constrained and precious. Within the institutional context we also consider the likely student demographic that will fill our classrooms. This demographic is shaped by many factors, including socioeconomics, race, gender, ethnicity, region of country. We consider our higher education settings such as two-year community college, four-year university as well as private, public, and online environments.

All these questions, contexts, and much more shape our teaching of Latino/a literature. As you'll discover reading the chapters that make up this volume, there is a living, breathing multidirectional flow of conceptual work taking place as we design and then put into practice twenty-first-century approaches to teaching Latino/a literature in the classroom.

This volume shares many pedagogical strategies used by teachers around the country that one way or another give shape to this entity called Latino/a literature. We might take pause here and ask, what is this category Latino/a literature? Carlos Gallegos identifies how this is a flexible category because it grows out of the always in flux identity of Latinos generally. Suzanne Bost and Frances Aparicio succinctly sum up the history of the various Latino/a identity terms as "contested, sometimes fluid, and always relational" (*Routledge Companion to Latino/a Literature* 2013: 2). Grown from the fluidity of Latino as an identity category, however, can be both "a blessing and a curse to this literary tradition" (1–2), Gallegos remarks. And, when Ilan Stavans tries to put his finger on the category in the Introduction to *The Norton Anthology of Latino Literature* (2010), it seems to enlarge and make it even more impalpable. He defines it as concerning "the tension between double attachments to place, to language, and to identity" (*Norton* liii). Accordingly, Latino/a literature grows from and is attached to a common Hispanic linguistic and cultural ancestral heritage. It is shaped by our experience of the movement of national borders and migration flows.

Putting our finger on Latino/a literature to get an exact (replicable) pulse might be difficult. Practically speaking, in our designing and teaching of Latino/a literature it is certainly the case that there is fluidity. In some courses I include Arturo Islas, and in others I don't. In courses I taught a decade-plus ago I did not include Junot Díaz because he had yet to arrive on the scene. Today I include more comics, when yesterday I did not. Where we decide to make our slices into the ever-growing corpus of Latino/a literature we necessarily move in and move out of different texts. Within this movement, however, we do establish solid ground—within a given course, and across courses taught in long stretches of time. That is, there is Latino/a literature in the classroom that is at once impermanent *and* permanent. We determine this movement of texts chosen (and those not) in our pedagogical designs and practices. We identify for our students the corpus of texts chosen as: Latino/a literature. This is to say, the category of Latino/a literature is a pedagogical construct. In a more general sense, it is a practical way of identifying for our students that we will not be reading a similarly chosen set of texts from Russia or Japan or Argentina. It is a way for us to indicate that the body of texts we choose to teach are a mere slice out of a planetary republic of letters—and this slice we call Latino/a literature.

With this in mind, Latino/a literature is an artificial construct used to best serve our pedagogical aims. It is a category we place over that movement of texts in and out of our twenty-first-century classrooms that cut roughly but productively into the larger corpus that makes up world literature. This allows us not only to choose texts to teach as constrained by limitations of time (one-day, one-week, ten-week, 15-week modules), but also to choose texts (and methods for teaching them) that are reproducible from one generation of teachers to the next.

As the authors of the chapters herein attest, there are myriad ways that we determine how to make such slices into the planetary republic of letters. For instance, I base my decisions on factors that include consideration of how well a given author (or author-artist in the case of comic books) uses the formal narrative tools, structures, and devices to give shape to texts as *new* objects not only jettisoned into the world for our consumption, but that make *new* our perception, feeling, and thought toward all aspects of the lived experience of Latinos, including migration, the dangers of border crossing, and middle-class suburban existence, and more.

Who is a Latino/a? … who is a Latino/a author?

No matter the group of students, when teaching a Latino/a literary course or text the first thing they ask me is: What is a Latino/a author? This is an excellent question, of course. I use it as a springboard to get the class to explore more deeply what's at stake with such a question. That such a question presupposes a specific sequence of DNA that makes an author Latino. To get them to think critically about this I put on the table the well-known poet William Carlos Williams, asking them what we might do with him given that he was born to an English father and a Puerto Rican mother and received, what Lisa Sánchez González identifies as, "a bilingual, bicultural formation in the U.S." ("Modernism and Boricua Literature" 243). His poetry doesn't deal directly (if at all) with this bilingual, bicultural heritage, but does that mean we don't include him in the Latino/a literary fold? (For more on William Carlos Williams, see Sheila Contreras's chapter herein.) I mention other authors such as: Poet Marie-Elise Wheatwind (Mexican, Swedish, and Russian Jewish), novelist Francisco Goldman (Jewish American and Catholic Guatemalan), short story authors such as Dagoberto Gilb (German and Mexican ancestry), essayist Gustavo Pérez Firmat (he playfully self-identifies as a "*cubanzo* redneck, spic and hick in equal parts") (6), and playwrights such as Sandra María Esteves (Puerto Rican and Dominican), Caridad Svich (Cuban/Argentine and Spanish/Croatian). With these and many other mixed-heritage authors discussed who self-identify or are identified as Latino/a, the students come to understand that this cannot be a determining category for who is included and who is not. As the course unfolds, they begin to see that it is not because of ancestry that one writes texts to be included in the Latino/a literary canon. Rather, it is that certain individuals have decided to commit time, energy, and resources to recreate in their writing (short stories, novels, poetry, plays, performances, and comic the experiences of that part of the population identified as Latinos/as). What they learn over the course of the class is that the identification of the Latino/a that makes up "Latino literature" is less about *attachment* to place, language, or nation and more about recreating in new and engaging ways a history of survival—on the part of both the writers and their subjects. This history of survival includes not only long-experienced racism and prejudice within the United States, but the increased difficulty of migratory flows from proximate Hispanophone countries: Mexico, Guatemala, Honduras, Nicaragua, El Salvador, Cuba, and the Dominican Republic, for instance. It also includes the socioeconomic push of Latinos out from rural, self-sustaining communities to the less hospitable urban environments. They learn that the authors included in my courses on Latino/a literature choose to distill, reconstruct, and give particularized shape to these past and present experiences of Latinos—a people with this history of survival.

This history of survival includes the forced movement of people across borders from countries where exploitation, oppression, and acts of genocide occur. It includes the dangerous crossing of borders internal to the United States, such as those borders imposed on sexuality recreated by authors like Arturo Islas, John Rechy, Ivan Velez, Cherríe Moraga, and others. It includes the recreation of movement of people within countries where official government policy has systematically eradicated agricultural infrastructures, forcing farmers and their families to relocate to urban centers. (See, for instance, Daniel Alarcón's *Lost City Radio*.) It includes the recreation of migratory flows that result from dictatorships that crystalize in a novel like Junot Díaz's *Brief Wondrous Life of Oscar Wao* and that gives shape to Latino/a "transnational identities and experiences" (Vargas, "Dictating a Zafa," 2014: 25).

The survival of Latinos stretches across time (history) and place (region, country, and continent). Within this history of survival and displacement exist a number of authors who willfully choose to give shape to these experiences in the form of novels, poems, films, comic books, short stories, performances, drama, and the like. For this reason we see in each chapter included in this volume a move to expand the boundaries of what authors and texts are included in the teaching of Latino/a literature in the twenty-first century.

Other identifiers

Today, Latino is a term that is ***panethnic*** in orientation. It's an umbrella term inclusive largely of those with Mexican, Cuban, Dominican, Puerto Rican, and Central American ancestry; its orthographic variants Latin@ or "Latino/a" reflect "a widespread political gesture against the gender power of the noun's masculine form to signify all Latinos, irrespective of gender, and to acknowledge Latinas as an essential component of the panethnic designation" (Allatson 2007: 141). Latino/a captures a history of the struggle of Latinas to fight for gender equality and sexual discrimination within and outside the Latino community. Hence, Latino/a reflects the struggle to broaden the Latino category to be inclusive of the whole Latino population. And, *Latinidad* or Latino-ness is used for the cultures and histories of national origin that inform the lives of Latinos/as. Notably, there is also the more academic (and arguably more clunky) category "Latin/o American" used to identify the hemispheric, continental links between the culture, language, and history of those inhabiting the North, Central, and South Americas— as well as those with African origins and indigenous roots (see Aldama and Stavans *Muy Pop!*).

Clearly, as discerned from the title of the volume, I choose the identifier "Latino/a" to capture shared transnational Hispanophone historical legacies and to foreground an all-inclusive (gender and sexuality) worldview. As you will see, the different contributors to the volume will variously break down and make visible the identities that make up this umbrella category: Mexican American, Hispano, Chicano, Nuyorican, Boricuan, Cubano, Dominican. Future generations of teachers will likely break this down even more by making visible literature produced by authors who choose to recreate the experiences of PortoMexes, Cubolivians, Mexistanis, Blatinos, LusoLatinos, among others. That is, each of the chapters in the volume keep centrally in mind that the elements that make up identity categories such as the one used for the volume are fluid.

The different histories of migration and policies toward Latinos (or of borders moving over populations as in the case of those living in the northern Mexican territories known today as the Southwest) have led to different experiences with access to education and literacy. The use of English (and less and less Spanish) by Latino/a authors is largely socioeconomically and historically determined. For new émigrés without formal education in English, its everyday use (spoken and written) can be and is very difficult. For those who have had access to education, movement in English and Spanish can become a choice. For others, where Spanish is no longer spoken at home or in their proximate environs, Spanish becomes the second tongue. And, unlike other groups that have given shape to the general population of the United States, Spanish is still alive and present. Many families have contact with relatives that have crossed land and sea from Hispanophone countries. This said, it is a fact that English as the lingua franca of the book-publishing marketplace does put certain pressures on authors. Even if they have the ability to write and shape their stories in Spanish or entirely bilingually, they tend not to. (See Christopher González's chapter in this volume.) All this impacts the choices Latino/a writers make when creating their novels, poetry, plays, comic books, and the like. Lourdes Torres (2007: 92) identifies strategies used by Latino/a authors that incorporate Spanish in unexpected ways, including the reworking of Standard English so that it "conveys the linguistic reality of [the Latino] multilingual population".

Latinos in time and place

The history of Latino/a literature is a trace-marker of the sorts of people (identified as Latinos/as) living in time and place as a historical, sociological entity that has become the *majority* minority population in the United States. According to the U.S. census data from April 1, 2010, one out of every six people in the United States is Latino. Those of Mexican origin represent the largest group: approximately 31 million. Those of Puerto Rican origin: 4 million. Those of Central American origin: 4 million. Those of Cuban origin: 1.6 million. These numbers do not account for the undocumented Latinos living in the United States that number in the 10–12 million.

We live in a country where people migrate from all over the world; this mainstream is decisively mixed and multicultural. It is a country where Latinos/as and all other groups that make up the general population have grown a rich and diverse appetite for a wide variety of cultural products. Satisfying this diversified demand creates new needs and new demands. And this satisfaction of new appetites implies the education of the senses (tastes, smells, touch, sounds, sights) as well as the education of the cultural needs with respect to these appetites. It implies the education of aesthetic capabilities and interpretations. That is where teachers like those included in this volume enter the picture. In our pedagogical capacity we function as guides to show how Latino/a literature can and does educate the senses of our students.

The various chapters that make up this volume and Latino/a studies scholarship generally shine a light on the different historical conditions that have led to respective Latino groups' push-pull toward urban centers. For instance, the post-World War II Great Migration of Puerto Ricans to U.S. cities was fueled by policies such as Operation Bootstrap, whereby many Puerto Ricans left to find jobs in urban centers in the United States. This led to, as David Colón writes, an "economic disturbance on the island, and a massive wave of migration, sustained over decades and often operating in two directions, to New York City in particular" (2001: 272). For Colón, this was the moment of the birth of the Nuyorican—and eventually the growing of those who would become the politicized, Nuyorican poets of the 1960s and 1970s. Such poets as Miguel Algarín, Pedro Pietri, Victor Hernández Cruz, Miguel Piñero, Sandra María Esteves, and Tato Laviera penned poetry that crossed all linguistic, social, cultural, linguistic boundaries. As Urayoán Noel further identifies, they explored "the complexities of identity and belonging at multiple levels: family, community, city, nation, and beyond" (*In Visible Movement*, xiii–xiv). It is this urban demographic that eventually led to, as Vanessa Pérez Rosario (2010) remarks, "a shift in this literature from a rural to an urban focus" (8). The same can be seen with the explosion onto the scene during this epoch of other Latino/a authors of Mexican, Cuban, and Dominican descent that grew abundantly from an urban worldview—and that increasingly satisfied the ever multiplying tastes of Latino (and other) readers.

As the Latino population has increased, so too has its socioeconomic diversity, yielding a sufficiently large number of urban educated, middle-class individuals who, in turn, yield a sufficiently large number of cultural producers, consumers, and interpreters: authors, filmmakers, intellectuals, readers, critics and academics, scientists, and the like. One professor in this volume, Cruz Medina, reflects on his experience earning a PhD to become a professor (now at Santa Clara University) that enabled him to change "the family trade of mowing lawns to instead teaching English at the college level" (2013: 35). And another, Monica Hanna, talks about how she literally read her way into college and to ultimately earn a PhD—a very different path taken by her mother and grandmother. (See Monica Hanna's "In the Stacks.")

So over the course of two centuries of literary production that from the earliest literature (as seen with courses taught by Alemán and de la Luz Montes, for instance) to the most contemporary (as seen with courses taught by Tace Hedrick, Randy Ontiveros, and Martínez-Cruz, for instance) to all those in between (all the other courses mentioned by all the other professors in this volume), we see how Latino/a literature is linked to the history of Latinos. Those working under conditions that made it difficult to have the free time to do anything other than sleep to those today who have more of a chance to become authors. For instance, those Mexican workers and immigrants of the 1930s who constituted the majority of the labor force in Texas's cotton industry did not have the time or energy to write novels—or any document for that matter. (See Magdalena Barrera's "Domestic Dramas.") Under these conditions, even if the will to write or to read was present, there was little time for either a readership or an authorship to grow. Once socioeconomic and political conditions began to change for some of the population of Latinos/as then we see a growth in a series of authors writing for a growing body of Latino readers with increasingly varied appetites for all kinds of texts—novels, poetry, autobiographies, biographies, and the like. (See Christopher González's chapter herein that talks about Latino/a authors writing for readers present and *future*.) As Manuel M. Martín-Rodríguez succinctly states, Latino/a literature "has no existence beyond the materiality of its physical components without a reader or a group of readers who would respond to, interact with, and make their own the precise formal arrangement of materials that a text or a book offers them" (2003: 2).

Today we see all variety of authors writing, including the more commercial Chica lit that Hedrick describes teaching in her chapter in this volume. From yesterday to today we have a literature that moves (like our demographic patterns) from the few able to write to a greater number today—some even make a living as authors. And with this we also see a greater range of styles and techniques being used to give shape to stories to satisfy all kinds of audience appetites.

This seeming abundance of varied literary artifacts, however, does not mean that Latino/a authors and their Latino/a readership have arrived. We have a diversified body of readers satisfied by a diverse corpus of literary texts. In *Gritos*, Dagoberto Gilb puts it succinctly: "It seems impossible that so many of the writers I have known—and yes, me, too—with a decent record of publications by usual standards, still fight a battle for acceptance, that we are a product of an ongoing American story that is not foreign, not only about a dark exotic people, not only fascinating as so much is 'south of the border,' not just about the poor and dangerous other side of the tracks" (2003: x). Just as demographic weight does not dissolve walls enforced by socioeconomic and racist behavior and policy, neither does the weighty presence of Latino/a literature guarantee its automatic public inclusion.

Specifics of design

I have organized the volume in five major sections. While there are no prescriptive ways to read the chapters that make up each section, there is a certain trajectory and flow present. Appearing in section I are chapters that focus on teaching Latino/a literature within different foundational categories: historical periods such as the nineteenth and early twentieth centuries as well as post-civil rights era; linguistic and trans-national anchors; queer and differently bodied practices; and fundamental generic configurations. Section II presents chapters that focus on the teaching of clusters of texts demarcated by authors with Mexican, Hispanophone Caribbean, and Central American ancestry. Moving to section III, the volume telescopes more toward its center, presenting focused approaches to the teaching of specific genres such as poetry, theatre, and performance art. With the chapters that make up section IV the volume begins to move back out toward general approaches to all variety of formats. These include the teaching of comic books, ebooks, young adult and children's literature, and some films. Section V concludes the volume, presenting a medley of snapshot approaches to teaching specific Latino/a authors and their texts.

I choose to open Part I, Teaching Foundational Moments, with Jesse Alemán's chapter, "Recovered and recovery texts of the nineteenth century." Here Alemán offers an approach to the teaching of some foundational texts that engage with, reproduce, and critique the colonial history in the Americas. After identifying how to overcome certain institutional obstacles in the teaching of literature from this period, Alemán presents a method and approach that at once unpacks the aesthetic components of these texts and that considers how these artifacts are "constituted by and simultaneously constituting its cultural moment." That is, he demonstrates how one might teach these early Latino/a texts in ways that work within and against American literary history *and* within and against histories of "governance, slavery, expansion, colonialism, and capitalism." Sheila Contreras's Chapter 2, "Modernism, modernity and US Latino/a literature" follows. Contreras moves us into the early twentieth century, offering an approach that will call into question literary genealogies that have one way or another pushed Latino authors and their literary products outside of modernity—and the cultural movement of modernism. She provides us with a map that places Latino/a cultural producers throughout the twentieth century as very much shapers of modernity and modernism, including its primitivist variants. In Chapter 3, "Latino/a queer expressions," Richard T. Rodríguez sets us down firmly in the latter part of the twentieth century, insisting that we pay attention to the extensive body of work produced by LGBT Latino/a authors. He offers an approach for us to bring gender and sexuality front and center to our teaching of Latino/a literary texts as well as for adopting a queer reading practice of non-LGBT Latino/a literary texts. In Chapter 4, "Spanglish in the classroom," Jennifer Carolina Gómez Menjívar presents the theories and methods she has used to teach native, heritage and non-native speakers about Spanglish in Latino/a literature. She covers a range of genres over a long stretch of time (from 1848 to the present) as well as introducing students to sociolinguistic research methods. For Gómez Menjívar, a linguistic approach to teaching Spanglish can transform the classroom into a space of resistance against linguistic prescriptivism. In Chapter 5, "Crisscrossed languages," Heather Alumbaugh shares with us how one might guide students to attend nuances of language (English and Spanish) as a formal device used by Latino/a authors to shape stories that crisscross identity, history, national boundaries, and much more. She provides a methodology that includes a Narrative Discourse Map and Character Log, which will help us guide students to a more nuanced reading of Latino/a literature. Monica Hanna and Jennifer Harford Vargas's coauthored Chapter 6, "Transnational forms," shares with us ways that we might have students identify and explore texts that cross-pollinate the genres of the chronicle and dictator novel. By having students attend to formal matters (genres) and sociohistorical circumstance students are able to deepen their understanding of what it means to exist and to create as a Latino/a within the

Americas. Michael Nieto García's Chapter 7, "Latino literary nonfiction" closes this first section. He offers us a model for ways that we might approach the teaching of Latino/a memoirs, essays, historical narrative, and journalistic books. After laying out how nonfiction works to establish readerly contracts that differ from fiction, he identifies formal and stylistic tools that students might use to explore the various ways that Latino/a nonfictions transgress strict fact-versus-fiction divides and readerly expectations. Ultimately, he shares a model to instill in our students "a love of close reading with all the social and cognitive benefits that this entails."

I begin Part II, "Teaching Parts That Make up the Latino/a Whole," with Christopher González's Chapter 8, "Mexican American/Chicano authors." After identifying the need to put pressure on higher administrators to create courses on Mexican American literature, he offers a multi-pronged approach that attends to formal techniques used by authors as well as sociohistorical and political contexts of production and consumption. González is also sensitive to different students' environments, including those who might not take readily to studying Mexican American literature carefully and deeply. He thus offers practical tips for transforming such a classroom into a positive learning environment. With María Acosta Cruz's Chapter 9, "Teaching the Hispanophone Caribbean" we shift focus to Hispanic Caribbean authors and their "migrating brethren." Acosta Cruz offers a linguistic, cultural, and historical approach to teaching texts (film included) by first, second, third generation Cuban, Dominican Republican, and Puerto Rican authors. Under her tutelage, students learn to analyze how authors use linguistic and other formal devices to create engaging and eye-opening texts with themes of belonging and not belonging to family, community, and nation. In Chapter 10, "Teaching Boricua literature," Lisa Sánchez González, a self-identified pedagogical alchemist, shares ingredients she uses to create a vital, dynamic classroom setting for teaching Boricua authors. Her alchemical model includes: (1) the teaching of the colonial history of Puerto Rico and the social history of the colonial diaspora in the continental United States; (2) the unlearning of misinformation about these histories and any misconceptions about Latino culture; (3) the identification of humor as a tool for creating positive, socially empowered classroom discussions. I end this section with Ana Patricia Rodríguez's Chapter 11, "Central American U.S. Latinos." She shares with us a "student-centered," "community-based," social-justice approach to teaching Central American US Latino/a texts (literature and film especially). Building on her theory of **"transisthmus"** as formulated in her other scholarship (see *Dividing the Isthmus*), she identifies an approach that leads students to question too-easy formulations of culture, politics, history, region, and nation.

Part III "Teaching Poetry, Theatre, and Performance Arts" begins with Urayoán Noel's Chapter 12, "Teaching U.S. Latino/a poetry in the age of social media." Here Noel shows us how a "performalist pedagogy" can be used to teach students not only a grammar for close-reading poetry (figures of speech, sound, and tone) but also how meaning is generated by how it is performed. For Noel, the formal matters that give shape to any given poem (or *corrido*) and its performance form an inseparable unit of meaning. With this model in place, we see how students learn to analyze the poetry of "decentered" Latino/a authors who increasingly use social media venues such as YouTube to perform their work. William Orchard also shares a pedagogical approach that places the performance front and center. His focus, however, is theater. In Chapter 13, "Theater in the Latino/a literature classroom," Orchard not only teaches students the history of Latino/a theatre production and the nuts and bolts concepts for analyzing it, but also enlists "the creative energies of students" by having them imagine how any given play might be staged. His approach is interactive and collective. By having the students examine the choices made in the realizing of a play, Orchard shows us how students learn first hand how different technical devices can and do have dramatic consequences in the realization of a play from print to stage production. Like Orchard (and Urayoán Noel before), Marivel Danielson identifies a pedagogy that's especially attuned to performance practices. In Chapter 14, "Teaching US Latino/a performance," Danielson shows us how she creates a learning environment where concepts learned (orchestrations of gesture, posture, gait, spinal alignment, and gaze) enable students to reflect on the creating of their own "critically informed performance pieces." I end this middle section with Paloma Martínez-Cruz's Chapter 15, "Performance pedagogy in the Latino literature classroom: Guillermo Gómez-Peña's La Pocha Nostra." Martínez-Cruz shows us how she builds her approach to teaching performance art in her study (and work with) La Pocha Nostra. By showing us how she teaches a variety of La Pocha Nostra texts (video performances, live performances, and print performances such as Gómez-Peña's *Dangerous Border Crossers*) as well as sharing with us the types of performance-based assignments she gives her students, we learn of ways for students to develop critical insights into performance art and how it can be a space for interrogating restrictive identity categories.

I open Part IV, "Other Latino/a Forms and Spaces," with my chapter on teaching comic books by and about Latinos. Here I outline the importance of teaching students about the genealogy of Latinos in comics and comics made by Latinos as well as considerations of the material conditions that shape the making and consumption of Latino comics. Additionally, I offer a model for teaching students how to identify the devices used to *geometrize* Latino/a stories in this visual and verbal format. I follow this with Ellen McCracken's Chapter 17, "Crowdsourcing Latino literary study: participatory learning and enhanced e-books." McCracken uses non-Latino/a iBook/enhanced teaching environments as a model for creating a Latino/a iBook/enhanced and digitally interfaced classroom. Such a classroom would allow for the making of "crowd sourced" networks whereby students would combine their "efforts of research, design, and implementation" to create enhancements to print books. Sharing her experience of creating such a digital environment she demonstrates how one might use this model for deep, collective learning. Whereby the creating of a "network of multi-medial augmentations" (timelines and maps as well as photos and film clips) to enhance printed editions of Latino/a literary texts (she mentions Junot Díaz and Julia Alvarez, for instance) will enrich the student's understanding of social and historical contexts as well as "democratize knowledge in a wider public arena." Jackie White's Chapter 18, "Latino/a young adult and children's literature" shows us how the inclusion of young adult (YA) and children's literature in our college classroom curricula can and does expand students' sense of what can be learned and taught in the Latino/a literary classroom. Moreover, she warns that by not teaching Latino/a YA and children's literature, we deny the younger generations of scholars and teachers the necessary tools to grow an "empathic, informed, and critically thinking citizenry." The two chapters that follow focus on the rather recent rise of a middle-class and upper middle-class Latino/a demographic that is variously embraced or interrogated by Latino/a authors (and film directors). Tace Hedrick's Chapter 19, "Teaching matters of class and style with chica lit" shows us how an "intersectional framework" can be used to teach a growing body of Latino/a literature that focuses on middle-class characters—and characters that aspire to be middle class. Her intersectional framework offers students the conceptual tools to be able to see how a given text puts front and center class and race categories; these are tools that allow students to interrogate how Chica lit reproduces middle-class (coded as white) privilege. Randy Ontiveros's Chapter 20, "Teaching the suburbs," provides a model for teaching texts by and about Latinos in the suburbs. With a series of examples and reading strategies grown from teaching a variety of storytelling formats (film included) he shows us how we might get students to think about other ways that Latinos/as experience class (spatially configured as suburban life) contradictions in the United States. And, Julie Minich's Chapter 21, "Defamiliarized bodies: disability studies in the Latino/a literature classroom," offers a pedagogical practice that seeks to expand students' sense of what Latino/a literature is. She does so by bringing disability studies into the Latino/a literature classroom. Having students explore "the sociopolitical, epistemic and ethical implications of bodies" also provides ways for them to critically think about how Latino/a bodies have been reduced to the "value of the labor their bodies perform."

In the fifth and final part of the volume, "Snapshots: Case Studies in Action," I include 15 short entries that focus on the teaching of only one or two Latino/a authors and their respective texts. Authors covered include: Ana Castillo, Oscar "Zeta" Acosta, Sandra Cisneros, Jimmy Baca, Junot Díaz, Alejandro Montoyá, Cristina García, Arturo Islas, Pat Mora, Denise Chávez, Gloria Anzaldúa, Cherríe Moraga, Luis Valdez, María Ruiz de Burton, Richard Rodriguez, and Helena María Viramontes. The short snapshots bring together a range of pedagogical approaches and practices. Each approach is different and grows out of a wide range of experiences within specific institutional settings: from online to urban campus environments, from first generation Latino college students to older return students. Some identify a digital pedagogy that uses Twitter/Instagram and others an educational praxis of resistance. Others identify a comparatist approach, and others a feminist, queer model. Finally, it includes a model for teaching a Latino/a author within a region of the United States (Arizona) where censorship policies are formally in place.

Means to ends

This volume offers teachers in all variety of institutional contexts ways in which they can design courses on Latino/a literature that can include particular topics and themes, periods, linguistic communities, regions, and conceptual vocabularies and tools. It offers teachers ways in which they can teach *across* such topics and themes, periods, linguistic communities, regions, and conceptual vocabularies and tools. It offers teachers insight into how to situate the teaching of Latino/a literature within time (history) and place (geography). It offers teachers insight into how issues of linguistic, cultural, and ancestral difference inform Latino/a literature. It offers teachers the tools by which they can have students analyze the devices (style, voice, perspective) and content (theme and character) used by Latino/a authors to reframe and make interesting experiences, people, and environments anchored one way or another to the experiences and identities of Latinos. It offers insights into how twenty-first-century technologies can be used to open up new pedagogical practices. Finally, with a general assault on the teaching of the humanities—and even more so subjects like Latino Studies in places like Arizona—there's a powerful urgency to our teaching of Latino/a literature in the twenty-first-century classroom.

Part I
Teaching foundational moments

1 Recovered and recovery texts of the nineteenth century

Jesse Alemán

Since it was founded in 1992, the Recovering the U.S. Hispanic Literary Heritage Project, headed by Nicolás Kanellos and Arte Público Press, has transformed U.S. literary history to the point that we can no longer approach modern and contemporary Latino/a writings in the United States as a recent phenomenon born out of twentieth-century political conflicts, population booms, or demographic changes. Rather, the recovery of earlier Latino/a literature offers a corpus of work that troubles the usual expectations of **minority writing** (i.e., that it tells the story of identity, class, or cultural conflicts) but also reveals the historical formation of the conditions that produce such conflicts for U.S. Latinos/as in the first place. This is what Ramón Saldívar means when he explains that:

> *history* is the subtext that we must recover because history itself is the subject of [Chicano narrative's] discourse. History cannot be conceived as the mere "background" or "context" for this literature; rather, history turns out to be the decisive determinant of the form and content of the literature.
>
> (1990: 5; italics in original)

Saldívar's statement rings true for all U.S. Latino/a literature—history is the "determinant of the form and content"—but history is also the greatest detriment when it comes to teaching recovered texts to contemporary students trained in English Departments, which usually plot American literary history along the rise, fall, and reconstruction of Anglo America.

Language is also a high hurdle when it comes to fully understanding early U.S. Latino/a writings, the majority of which were penned in Spanish. At the graduate level, we should encourage students to gain Spanish language fluency if recovered texts are central to that student's future research and scholarship, but outside of Spanish Departments, undergraduate classes on U.S. Latino/a literature are conducted in English with no Spanish language fluency required or even expected. This holds true even at my own institution, the University of New Mexico, with an undergraduate population of native Spanish speakers, bilingual learners, and a number of students who gained Spanish as a second language through high school or undergraduate curricula. Our English Department remains "English only," while literature in Spanish is more likely to be found in our Spanish and Portuguese Department, taught within a curricular framework of Iberian, Peninsular, and greater Latin American literatures. While language is lost in one department, the specific historical formation of Latinos/as in the United States might be occluded in the other. Fortunately, though, a number of nineteenth-century recovered texts are available in translation, and for undergraduate classrooms,

I have no qualm teaching these texts in English, because I think what we lose in translation is offset by what we gain in literary knowledge.[1]

Besides reprinted texts available through Arte Público, there are two main anthologies to use in survey courses on recovered nineteenth-century U.S. Latino/a writing. *Herencia*, edited by Kanellos, brings together a large collection of U.S. Hispanic writings from colonial times to the contemporary, and many of the texts are products of the Recovery Project's efforts. The collection is not without its flaws: its structuring organization of "Native," "Immigrant," and "**Exile**" literature doesn't hold up well as a method of organization, and its headnotes are unevenly penned, with some offering biographical and publication history and others offering not much instructive information at all. However, the collection also brings together editorials, letters, speeches, poems, short stories, histories, chronicles, and excerpts from novels that showcase the diversity of U.S. Latino/a print culture over the last 400 years. Ilan Stavans's *Norton Anthology of Latino Literature* (2011) also offers a swath of texts, and while its headnotes and footnotes are very helpful, the collection's organization, as Kirsten Silva Gruesz notes, produces a text "fundamentally at odds with itself, contradictorily espousing a transnational and a United States nation-based perspective without allowing either one enough oxygen to sustain itself" (2012: 336). This dilemma dislocates U.S. Latino/a literature, and while this might be Stavans's point—that U.S. Latino/a literature resides somewhere in between two nations—it deterritorializes Latino/a literature from specific historical moments within what I would suggest is its most strategic pedagogical category: the United States. After all, for undergraduate English students, early U.S. Latino/a literature gets its pedagogical power from the fact that much of the writing occurred *within* the United States when, presumably, such populations and print culture didn't exist for students familiar only with canonical American letters or contemporary U.S. Latino/a writing.

I use *Herencia* in my undergraduate survey classes because I want to support the Recovery Project; at the graduate level, I use individual texts because I want advanced students to focus on specific forms of early U.S. Latino/a writing rather than consume short, excerpted pieces. I also teach to different ends when it comes to undergraduate and graduate pedagogy. At the graduate level, I teach in seminar style, so I select narratives across the nineteenth century and allow discussion to carry the direction of our analysis. I maintain several key investments. First: that all early U.S. Latino/a narratives are historical in their form, content, and aesthetics. Second: I chart an alternative literary history to the canonical nineteenth-century American focus on romanticism, realism, and naturalism to demonstrate that these categories are neither natural nor representative of all the nineteenth-century literature produced in the United States. Finally, I cultivate analysis that views narrative as both art and artifact; something created but also something constituted by and simultaneously constituting its cultural moment.

In this vein, there's little difference between how I teach early Latino/a literature and other graduate classes, such as the nineteenth-century American novel, so it's more informative for me to chart my undergraduate pedagogy, which is thematically organized. At the undergraduate level, I focus on coverage, content, and the place of Latino/a literature within and against American history to demonstrate how Latino/a print culture engages with U.S. historical matter already somewhat familiar to students (i.e., governance, slavery, expansion, colonialism, and capitalism to name a few) but does so through political and literary discourses not so familiar to them (i.e., Cuba's insurgent movements; Mexico's *reforma*; or the poetic longings for the homeland by writers exiled in the United States). In other words, I select texts that take up historical themes or ideas with which our students are most familiar to examine how U.S. Latinos/as engage with, depart from, or reproduce with a difference those ideas.

For instance, the 1812 pseudonymous book, *El amigo de los hombres*, appeared in Philadelphia as an appeal to the people of the Americas to throw off Spanish monarchical rule and establish their independence. "On Behalf of Mankind," as *Herencia* has it, is a prime example of the political rhetoric that circulated and fomented revolutionary discourses throughout the Americas, and its place of publication necessarily invites students to understand the American Revolution as one of a series of independence movements sweeping across the Americas. As the narrator declares, "the welfare of the people is the supreme law and the only sacred one; all pacts or contracts that offend it are null by nature. No one can renounce the rights that are afforded him by the social contract" (2002: 515). Echoing Paine's *Common Sense*, mouthing Lockean theory of social contract, and sounding like the Declaration of Independence, "On Behalf of Mankind" introduces students to the rhetoric, context, and history of Spanish American revolutionary discourses, and because it's written as a polemic, the pamphlet also affords the opportunity to teach the historical debates surrounding Spanish American independence.

One point vexing independence was the question of slavery. As with the U.S. Declaration, slavery troubled the distinction between political independence and freedom from slavery, shoring up the fact that independence, liberty, and freedom were not always understood synonymously and were not extended universally, despite proclamations otherwise. In the history of the Americas, the Spanish crown often kept independence movements in check by way of slavery; after all, the Spanish colonial system and military presence in the Americas provided whites with a sense of security following the violence of the **Haitian revolution**.[2] However, "On Behalf of Mankind" directly addresses this issue, offering a response to the problem of slavery by noting that (1) the population disparity between blacks, whites, and people of color is not as exaggerated as the Spanish crown presents it and that (2) republican independence would "try to make men of all classes and conditions happy" (2012: 514). Indeed, the pamphlet offers a pedagogically informative narration of race in the early nineteenth-century Americas, with its distinctions between blacks, mulattos, and whites and a theory of racial interaction at odds with the history of race relations in the United States: "The blacks aspire to the esteem of the whites, they want to be mistaken for them and in the second or third generation they are already tied together by blood and interests in such a way that they form one caste with the whites" (514). In short, the pamphlet's answer to the threat of black rebellion against whites is simple—racial mixing, because black and white "blood and interests" would then be commingled in a way that tied their collective interests against the Spanish crown.

I use this pamphlet to introduce students to U.S. Latino/a literature's historicity—its political discourse; the nature of the debates about independence; and the way the pamphlet articulates a language about slavery and race relations that marks a paradigm different from the U.S. discourses about race and slavery. Félix Varela's 1820s "Essay on Slavery" (2002) is especially instructive on this point. His essay offers a primer for students to understand slavery's history in Cuba and the cautious way Varela advocates for its abolishment on political, economic, and social grounds. Slavery is antithetical to a free government, Varela maintains, and it also creates unstable social class relations, but most importantly, slavery inhibits free labor, economic development, and the diversification of the market. Varela concludes:

give liberty to the slaves in such a way that their own owners do not lose the capital they spent on their purchase, or the people of Havana do not suffer new burdens, or in a way that free blacks in their first unexpected [freedom] do not want to extend themselves beyond what has been granted to them, and finally by helping agriculture in whichever form possible so that it won't suffer.

(2002: 528)

Implicit in Varela's argument against slavery are also the historical reasons the island was reluctant to end it: owners would lose capital; whites might suffer from the influx of free blacks; the number of free blacks might threaten the social balance of power; and the island's agrarian economy would collapse. However, I also use Varela's essay to teach students about the social construction of race in terms of blacks, mulattos, "people of color," and whites:

The introduction of Africans on the island of Cuba gave origin to the class of mulattos, many of whom have received their freedom from their own fathers, while others suffer in slavery. ... The slaves are employed in agriculture and in domestic service, while the freemen are almost all dedicated to the arts, mechanical as well as liberal; it is estimated that for one white artist there are twenty of color.

(2002: 525)

The snapshot Varela provides of racial identity in relation to genealogy and the division of labor invites the class to examine how slavery in Cuba and across the Caribbean resonates with the problem of slavery in the United States but produces a different way of understanding its significance for independence movements, republican rhetoric, and revolutionary momentum that swept across the Americas (including the United States) throughout the nineteenth century.

While it sounds like I teach early U.S. Latino/a literature as history, I'm rather explaining a pedagogy that highlights the historicity of these early texts. It's a fine distinction but one that maintains that history is not just the context for the literary text but also the content of it. Yet, even though many early U.S. Latino/a writers were politicians, I don't presume history to be only political; we also see the development of different literary forms as part of Latino/a political history. "On Behalf of Mankind" is a polemical pamphlet like the scores of pamphlets that debated the American Revolution; Varela's piece is a persuasive essay, with a main argument supported by examples that advance his position through proof and critique of the opposition. These literary forms also generate a political rhetoric that, because it's fanning the flames of revolution, sounds much like the contemporary rhetoric of activism. Students tend to find José Alvarez de Toledo y Dubois's manifesto, for example, strikingly relevant to modern and contemporary struggles against oppression. "Mexicans," Toledo y Dubois asserts, "signaled by Providence, the time has arrived for you to throw off the barbaric and shameful yoke with which the most insolent despotism has ignominiously oppressed you for 300 years" (2002: 518). In New Mexico, at least, Toledo y Dubois's statement rings as true now for some as it did when he penned it to critique the tyranny of the Spanish crown.

The first part of the class, then, introduces students to early forms of U.S. Latino/a literature through a rubric of revolution, republicanism, and slavery, with attention to how republican revolutionary discourse uses the language of slavery to link chattel slavery to political slavery under the yoke of monarchy. The anonymously published 1826 historical novel, *Jicoténcal*, brings these ideas together within the context of the conquest of Mexico through a literary style we might call *republican romanticism*.[3] As the first historical novel to be published in Spanish in the United States (Philadelphia), the narrative invites close attention to the way the novel, as a genre, handles the polemics of independence. Characters debate republican ideals through staged conversations in the backdrop of romance, seduction, and rape, and instead of direct attacks on the ruling Spanish government, the novel displaces its critique of empire to the days of **Hernán Cortés**, the **Aztecs**, and **Doña Marina**. Already familiar with the debates by way of pamphlets, essays, and manifestos, undergraduates tend to find the novel a little melodramatic for their contemporary tastes, so I focus their attention instead on its form, on the idea that, as a novel, it is crafting a historical allegory that turns the history of empire, conquest, and colonialism into a multivalent narrative form. It is ostensibly about the sixteenth-century conquest of Mexico, but, as allegory, it could also be about Spain's colonial rule over Cuba, the struggle for Mexico's budding republic, or even a critically attuned narrative about the U.S. emergence as an empire in the Americas.[4]

My attention to history, form, and content (or better put, the form of historical content) establishes a tripartite rubric with which to understand the boom of Cuban writings during the mid-nineteenth century, when exiles and ex-patriots penned poems, editorials, pamphlets, plays, and novels about the island's history, politics, and fate. I focus on lyrical exile poetry, collected most famously in the 1856 *El laúd del desterrado* [*The Lute of the Exile*] and written in the United States by Cuban politicians, newspaper men, and men of letters. Beginning with José María Heredia's 1825 "Hymn of the Exile" and ending with Martí's 1890s *Versos sencillos*, Cuban exiles penned paeans to their beloved island, turning the political content of pamphlets, manifestos, and essays into the stuff of poetry, and for this sequence, *Herencia* shines as an anthology, for it provides bilingual versions of their poetry selections. Poems in Spanish alongside their English translation allow bilingual readers to hear the force of the exile's critique without excluding monolingual readers from the form and content of lyrical language.

While the "Hymn of the Exile" establishes the tone, voice, and political concerns of the exile poet, Miguel Teurbe Tolón's "Siempre" ["Always"] is as moving in English as it is in Spanish in its articulation of the interior conflict the poet feels so far away from home: "Eso, eso noche y día, / y momento tras momento / es pensar que como harpía / se posa en mi pensamiento / y devora el alma mía" ["All that, night and day, / And moment after moment, / Makes me think that a harpy / Has settled in my thoughts / And devours my soul"] (2002: 550). Similarly, Pedro Santicilia's "A España" ["To Spain"] seemingly begins as an homage to Spain but ironically works through Spanish history as a form of disillusionment for the speaker, who ends by affirming that, "Y en vez de admiración, sentí en el alma/Un sentimiento, España, de desprecio" ["And instead of admiration, I felt in my soul / A sentiment, Spain, of contempt"] (556). The swath of Cuban poetry doesn't necessarily depart from the political rhetoric of the earlier tracts. Lola Rodríguez de Tió's 1896 "10 de Octubre" ["Ode to October 10"] (2002), for example, sounds as polemical as the treaties of the early nineteenth century: "Con llanto y sangre está escrita / En cada pecho cubano, / Y aunque se ensañe el olvido; / ¡que el llanto nunca es perdido / ni se hace el crimen en vano!" ["With tears and blood it is written / On the heart of every Cuban, / And despite the tyrant's wrath / It will never be forgotten. / For tears are never shed in vain, / Nor does crime forever prosper"]

(2002: 561). However, the poem also invites examination of how, as a form, poetry expresses the speaker's interiority, an internal conflict that works as metaphor for the mediation of a divided self. Rodríguez de Tió's speaker goes on to articulate a kind of patriotic awakening that literally refers to the poet's native Puerto Rico but figuratively suggests a coming to consciousness about the very revolution the poem memorializes:

"Hay otra tierra ... ¡la mía! / Que con ardoroso empeño, / Despierta del torpe sueño / Que alargó la tiranía. / Tal vez, tal vez llegue el día, /—en época no muy lejana—/ en que a la patria cubana / siga en virtud y en valor, / ya que en su inmenso dolor / ¡el mismo Dios las hermana!"

["There's another country ... mine! / Which with an arduous effort / Awakens from the deep sleep / too long imposed by tyranny. / Perhaps the day will come, I hope /—In the not too distant future—/ When brave and pure she will dare / To follow Cuba's example, / Since by the great pain they share / God Himself has made them sisters!"]

(2002: 563)

The exile poems set the stage for reading Martí's *Versos sencillos*, an 1891 collection that seems almost belletristic were it not that students have already been prepared for reading the way exile poetry mediates through metaphor internal turmoil with external political struggle. From the start, students sense that there's nothing simplistic about Martí's simple verses; that, from the opening stanza of his first poem, he's crafting a conceit already recognizable from earlier exile poetry: "Yo soy un hombre sincero / De donde crece la palma / Y antes de morirme quiero / Echar mis versos del alma" ["A sincere man am I / From the land where palm trees grow, / And I want before I die / My soul's verses to bestow."] (575–76). As students learned from the exile poets before Martí, the speaker expresses the distance from home as a rift in the soul that poetry can imaginatively and formally mend. It's a telling lesson about poetic form that begins with Heredia and finds full aesthetic expression with Martí—namely that the exile poets are not only expressing a longing for home from an alien nation (the United States), but they are also giving early expression to Latino/a alienation in the United States.

The literature of early Mexican America travels a different trajectory in terms of form. Beginning with *testimonios*, early nineteenth-century Mexican American literature is largely narrative, and from the start, it recounts cultural contact, colonial conflicts, and racial identity. Interestingly, much early Mexican American writing is narrated through a first-person "I" that invites students to examine Mexican American history in relation to questions about identity, credibility, and literary self-fashioning. Juan Seguín's 1834–42 *Personal Memoirs* (2002) and Juan Cortina's 1859 "Proclamation" (2002), while not first on my reading schedule for this sequence, are nonetheless instructive examples for the way Mexican American narratives emerge from a combination of *testimonio*, autobiography, political tract, and call to arms. Seguín sets out to clear his name by untangling his military, political, and governmental affiliations during the 1836 Texas revolution, when he fought for Texan independence, and the 1846–48 U.S.–Mexico War, when he was impressed to serve in the Mexican army against the United States. His story of binational conflict sounds contemporary to students, for Seguín writes his memoir "as a foreigner in my native land" (2002: 107). However, I also encourage students to analyze Seguín's rhetorical self-fashioning, for he is very deliberately setting out to correct his public reputation as a person, politician, and a Texan. I ask students, for instance, to examine how Seguín narrates his life in a way that de-mythologizes the Texas revolution:

> Many a noble heart grasped the sword in the defense of the liberty of Texas, cheerfully pouring out their blood for our cause, and to them everlasting public gratitude is due; but there were also many bad men, fugitives from their country, who found in this land an open field for their criminal designs.
>
> (2002: 107)

The pronouns alone here indicate that Seguín doesn't view himself as a foreigner but in fact as part of a Texan cause helped and hindered by outsiders; they are the foreigners who are the audience to whom he's writing his account.

Cortina's 1859 "Proclamation" is a cross between an *apologia*, a manifesto, and an open call to arms against Anglo Americans in Texas. After leading several guerilla skirmishes and raids, Cortina finds himself having to explain his actions to the Spanish-speaking citizens of Texas: "You do not have to fear," he assures them, "because orderly people and upright citizens and their interests are inviolable to us. Our objective, as you are aware, and whose record you cannot deny, has been to punish our enemies' shameless behavior, which thus far has gone unpunished" (2002: 113). I ask students to consider how Cortina balances the justification of his actions through a combination of upholding moral values, presenting himself as a protector of Mexican American people and their interests, and threatening with a promise of more violence to come:

> the time has come, there are no more than six or seven oppressors. Hospitality and some other noble feelings protect them, for now, from our rage, and the laws of humanity are to us inviolable, as you have seen. ... Our personal enemies will not possess our land, except by paying for it with their own blood.
>
> (2002: 115)

Students also notice in both language and content a revolutionary rhetoric that sounds different from Cuban writings, so I spend time working through those differences: What accounts for them historically? How are those differences related to different forms of colonialism? And what does it mean in literary culture for Mexicans to be writing as "strangers, begging for a haven in their former homeland," as Cortina puts it (2002: 115), rather than Cubans writing about their homeland from exile?

These questions allow us to tease out the differences within U.S. Latino/a history. For instance, we don't hear as vocally the appeal to republican independence in early Mexican American writings as we do in Cuban literature, and instead of the poetry of exile, we have proclamations vowing to oust oppressors and take back "our land" (Cortina 2002: 115). Early Mexic American writings, then, unfold the historicity of cultural conflict between Mexico and Anglo America. In Francisco P. Ramírez's 1855 prescient critique of the United States in his July 24, 1855 editorial, for example, he maintains that the U.S.'s "much-lauded freedom is imaginary" to "all individuals of color" who either have no protection under the law or who find themselves subject to laws, such as the so-called 1855 Greaser Act, that target Mexicans for disenfranchisement (2002: 110). What is poignant about Ramírez's editorials is his use of ironic tone to point out the hypocrisy of U.S. proclamations of democratic freedom. He writes in another editorial:

> Since the year 1849 a certain animosity (*so contrary to a magnanimous and free
> people*) has existed between the Mexicans and Americans, to such an extent that
> the Americans have wished with all their heart that all the Mexicans put together
> had no more than one head to cut off.
>
> (111; italics added)

Ramírez's irony—"so contrary to a magnanimous and free people"—not only captures
his disdain for the rhetoric of U.S. democracy but also expresses the way such hypocrisy
manifests itself historically: he directly references the decapitation of Joaquín Murieta,
the infamous California Mexican bandit, as a fate Anglo Americans wish on all Mexicans.

Published in 1854 by the Cherokee writer, Yellow-Bird (John Rollin Ridge), *The Life
and Adventures of Joaquín Murieta* (1977) is for this reason a central component of my
syllabus. The narrative articulates the cultural clashes, violence, legal hypocrisy, and fantasy
of racial rebellion that make the Murieta narrative essential for studying nineteenth-century
Mexican America. An amalgamation of hyperbolic news reports, adventure tales, sentimental writing, and sensational literature, *Murieta* is a novel par excellence—it is an
uneven narrative populated by different literary forms that bespeak to Rollin Ridge's
attempt to write a history of conflict from multiple sources. When teaching it, I don't
make a case for its aesthetic quality; in fact, just the opposite—as a form, the narrative
is not coherent. It has an impossible narrative perspective that is both omniscient and
first-person limited; it incorporates a very bad romantic Ode to Mt. Shasta early in the
narrative; and while Murieta sets out to enact revenge against Anglo America, he and
his band end up killing Chinese laborers. However, it's precisely its unevenness that's
instructive, for it shows the way cultural conflicts produce conflicted narratives that, in
this case, give rise to the first Native American novel and one of the most important
early Mexican American narratives as well.

Murieta marks the turning point in the class as we move to one of two of María
Amparo Ruiz de Burton's novels. I have taught both of her texts often, and nearly every
time, undergraduates respond more productively to *Who Would Have Thought It?* than to
The Squatter and the Don. It's possible *Who Would Have Thought It?* contains more
recognizable literary forms—it's part seduction tale, part passing narrative, part sentimental and domestic novel, and part historical romance. *Squatter* too is part sentimental,
domestic, and historical narratives, but there is something about the way it hedges its
political critique that students tend to reject its literary value because the novel sounds
too overtly polemical. I think this is a function of genre expectation, the idea that a
"good novel" shouldn't be openly political, and I have in the past worked to unravel
such an aesthetic position, but I have discovered that *Who Would Have Thought It?* for
some reason invites more student interest, participation, and interaction than *Squatter*.
Put simply, undergraduates tend to find the first novel "better" than the second and are
thus willing to engage it more critically.

Students tend to linger on the novel's most intriguing dilemma, for while it critiques
Yankee America, its political hypocrisy, racism, vapidity, and lack of morals, culture,
and intelligence, the narrative also idealizes Mexican whiteness, which students find
baffling at best and racist at worst. I teach this conflict because it affords the opportunity
to discuss the historical formation of race, the way racial identity is not a fixed category
but tied to class, gender, sex, language, and religion. Lola Medina, discovered in Indian
captivity in the southwest and dyed dark, gradually becomes lighter as she spends more
time in the northeast, and by the end, she's more white than the Anglo Americans in

the novel and opts to return to Mexico. Her racial transformation occurs through a Spanish-Mexican caste system in the Americas that troubles the U.S. binary hypo-descent racial logic, but as students often note, both paradigms end with the valorization of whiteness. What I help them to see, however, is how the novel shows this whiteness to be a social construct rather than a biological given. Of course, the narrative would have us believe that Lola's whiteness is natural, but what it also reveals is that whiteness is socially produced by related categories of class and culture as well as strategic differences from Native, African, and Anglo American identities. In other words, *Who Would Have Thought It?* teaches us the historical formation of Mexican American whiteness as both a response to Anglo American racism and an articulation of a similarly racialist Spanish-Mexican *casta* system.[5]

After selections from *Squatter*, we end the semester and syllabus with Martí's "Nuestra América" to bring together the themes, content, and historical pressures that early U.S. Latino/a literature narrates from the start of the nineteenth century. There are other late pieces to consider, but with his essay, Martí returns the class to questions about independence, revolution, and republicanism. This time his critique of Yankee America sounds much more layered, especially after students have read early Mexican American narratives of conflict and culture clashes. Students are quick to recognize that, while Martí uses flowery rhetoric, his critique is still in league with early Cuban tracts against Spain, but they also notice that Yankee America, rather than Spanish imperialism, has become precisely what Spain was to Cuba at the start of the century: a colonial presence from which Latinos/as must break to establish independence. For me, this is why teaching the historicity of early U.S. Latino/a literature is so important, for it not only demonstrates that Latinos/as engaged with, reproduced, or critiqued colonial power, but from its early essays to its later writings, it charts how the United States went from being a model of republicanism to becoming a new world colonial power far greater than Spain's empire, and instead of being on the outskirts of it, Latinos/as in the nineteenth century grew up in the belly of this beast. And lived to write about it.

Notes

1 To borrow Kirsten Silva Gruesz's phrasing, however: "This is not to imply that the field should be the province of the English department: to the contrary, its greatest vitality as an intellectual project derives from its unique status as an institutional free radical, whose driving research questions are discussed and disseminated in multiple departments, each offering students distinctive but overlapping narratives and canons. (Language, of course, helps drive this multiplicity.)" (2012: 339).

2 Ferrer explains that revolutionary leaders "were men conversant in the principles of Enlightenment and convinced, in theory and—to a certain extent—in practice, of the justice of abolition. They shared the conviction that they could not declare freedom for themselves while enslaving their neighbors; and they criticized past Cuban patriots for having advocated the continuation of racial slavery on the island. At the same time, the men of 1868 were also members of a traditional land- and slave owning class, accustomed to the economic, political, and social advantages that came with slave ownership in a slave society" (1999: 9).

3 *Herencia* attributes *Jicoténcal*'s authorship to Varela, with good reason. However, Anna Brickhouse explains that, given its political allegory, an unknown Mexican author, José María Heredia, or Vicente Rocafuerte Bejarano could have written it (2004: 53–54).

4 My article, "The Other Country," unpacks this point further.

5 This racial logic helps to explain why slavery is not such a pressing issue in early Mexican American literature as it is in Cuban writings. Aside from the fact that Mexico abolished

slavery in 1824, early Mexican American writers tended to see their struggle as against Anglo America but not quite alongside the oppression of blacks and Native Americans.

Resources for teaching recovered and recovery texts of the nineteenth century

Alemán, Jesse. "Assimilation and the decapitated body politic in *The Life and Adventures of Joaquín Murieta.*" *Arizona Quarterly: A Journal of American Literature, Culture, and Theory* 60.1 (Spring 2004): 71–98.

——. "Wars of rebellion: US hispanic writers and their American civil wars." *American Literary History* 25.1 (Spring 2013): 54–68.

Alemán, Jesse, and Shelley Streeby, Eds. *Empire and the Literature of Sensation: An Anthology of Nineteenth-Century Popular Fiction.* New Brunswick, NJ: Rutgers University Press, 2007.

Facio, Elisa, and Irene Lara. *Fleshing the Spirit: Spirituality and Activism in Chicana, Latina, and Indigenous Women's Lives.* Tucson, AZ: University of Arizona Press, 2014.

Goldstein, David S., and Audrey B. Thacker. *Complicating Constructions: Race, Ethnicity, and Hybridity in American Texts.* Seattle: University of Washington Press, 2007.

González, John Morán. *Border Renaissance: The Texas Centennial and the Emergence of Mexican American Literature.* Austin: University of Texas Press, 2009.

Gruesz, Kirsten Silva. "Authors, readers, and the mediations of print culture." In *The Routledge Companion to Latino/a Literature.* Eds. Suzanne Bost and Francis Aparicio. Abingdon, Oxon; New York: Routledge, 2013: 485–94.

Kanellos, Nicolás. *Hispanic Immigrant Literature: El Sueño del Retorno.* Austin: University of Texas Press, 2011.

McMahon, Marci R. *Domestic Negotiations: Gender, Nation, and Self-Fashioning in US Mexicana and Chicana Literature and Art.* New Brunswick, NJ: Rutgers University Press, 2013.

Ontiveros, Randy J. *In the Spirit of a New People: The Cultural Politics of the Chicano Movement.* New York: New York University Press, 2013.

Padilla, Genaro M. *The Daring Flight of My Pen: Cultural Politics and Gaspar Pérez de Villagrá's Historia de la Nueva Mexico, 1610.* Albuquerque, NM: University of New Mexico Press, 2010.

Poyo, Gerald E. *Exile and Revolution: José D. Poyo, Key West, and Cuban Independence.* Florida: University Press of Florida, 2014.

Rivera, John-Michael. *The Emergence of Mexican America: Recovering Stories of Mexican Peoplehood in U.S. Culture.* New York: New York University Press, 2006.

Rodríguez, Jaime Javier. *The Literatures of the U.S.–Mexican War: Narrative, Time, and Identity.* Austin: University of Texas Press, 2010.

The Latino-Hispanic American Experience: The Arte Público Hispanic Historical Collection Series I. Available from: www.ebscohost.com/archives/featured-archives/latino-hispanic-series-one (accessed May 23, 2014).

Nineteenth-century U.S. Latino/a literature: undergraduate

Republicanism, revolution, and slavery

Anonymous, "The friend of men."
Anonymous. *Xicoténcatl.* Trans. Guillermo I. Castillo-Feliú. Austin: University of Texas Press, 1999.
Bejarano, "Necessary ideas for all independent people of the Americas."
Toledo y Dubois, "Mexicans."
Varela, "Essay on Slavery."

Exile's lute: poetry

Byrne, "My Flag" (2002)
Heredia, "Hymn of the Exile" (2002)

Martí, *Simple Verses* (2002)
Santicilia, "To Spain" (2002)
Teurbe Tolón, "Always" (2002)
Rodríguez de Tió, "Ode to October 10" (2002)

Mexican America: conflict and contestation

Briones, "A Glimpse of Domestic Life in 1827"
Cortina, "Proclamation" (2002)
de la Guerra de Ord, "Occurrences in Hispanic California"
Ramírez, "Editorials" (2002)
Seguin, "Personal Memoirs" (2002)
Tafolla, Santiago. *A Life Crossing Borders.* Houston: Arte Público Press, 2009.
Vallejo, "Letter to William Heath Davis"

Novel form and narrative history

Martí, "Our America."
Rollin Ridge, John. *The Life and Adventures of Joaquín Murieta.* Norman: University of Oklahoma Press, 1977.
Ruiz de Burton, María. *Who Would Have Thought It?* and selections from *The Squatter and the Don.*
Velázquez, Loreta Janeta. *The Woman in Battle.* Ed. Jesse Alemán. Madison: University of Wisconsin Press, 2003.

Nineteenth-century U.S. Latino/a literature: graduate

Anonymous. *Xicoténcatl.*
Alemán, Jesse and Shelley Streeby, ed. *Empire and the Literature of Sensation.* New Jersey: Rutgers University Press, 2007.
Seguín, Juan. *A Revolution Remembered.* Denton: Texas State Historical Association, 2002.
Rollin Ridge, John. *The Life and Adventures of Joaquín Murieta.* Norman: University of Oklahoma Press, 1977.
Ruiz de Burton, María. *Who Would Have Thought It?* and *The Squatter and the Don.*
Tafolla, Santiago. *A Life Crossing Borders.*
Velázquez, Loreta Janeta. *The Woman in Battle.*
Villaverde, Cirilo. *Cecilia Valdés.* New York: Oxford University Press, 2005.
Zavala, Lorenzo de. *Journey to the United States of North America.* Houston: Arte Público Press, 2005.

2 Modernism, modernity, and U.S. Latino/a literature

Sheila Marie Contreras

There is a distinction to be made between **modernity** as a period of historical transformation, and **Modernism** as an artistic and cultural movement associated with artists and writers engaged in particular techniques of expression. As a historical period, modernity can be said to span a few hundred years, associated with **conquest** and **colonization** (also known as the "age of exploration") and, eventually, industrialization and mechanization. As a cultural movement, Modernism suggests thematics of individual alienation, stylistic challenges to accepted conventions of language and visual imagery, fragmented representation, and an emphasis on form over content. While many Modernist works communicate an overall disenchantment with the condition of society, others exhibited an enthusiasm for the new and the innovative, especially in the field of representational technologies as theorized by Walter Benjamin. The emphasis on form over content, however, restrains direct political and social critique, a tension that is documented by David Weir in his analysis of French poet André Breton. Weir identifies Breton as a surrealist *and* a socialist who was "forced" to accept that "innovative, progressive art is no guarantee of social progress" (1997: 1). Evidence of this conclusion is supported by the fact that the famous texts of European and American literary Modernism depend upon classically trained readers familiar with the educational imperatives of the elite classes; thus, these texts are perceived as deliberately inaccessible to the masses.[1] Critic Raymond Williams, however, has famously argued against certain conventions of understanding Modernism, particularly with regard to its historical emergence and a reliance on "the modern absolute," a new universalism that represses the influence and specificity of immigration and the metropolis.

In terms of teaching "Latino" literature, studies of Modernism focus on Latin American literature and the development of "**modernismo**," associated with Nicaraguan poet Rubén Dario and his publication of *Azul* in 1888. Major influences on Latin American modernismo are to be found in Spanish lyric poetry, French symbolism, and the work of nineteenth-century U.S. Anglo-American writers such as Ralph Waldo Emerson, Edgar Allan Poe, and Walt Whitman. Literary critic Iris Zavala, however, has made the argument that modernismo inverts the image of the heroes of modernity—the "explorer," the missionary, the soldier—and instead renders them as the violent, the conqueror, and the colonizer. The historical moment of 1898 and the **expansionist** imperial projects of the United States in the Caribbean (Cuba and Puerto Rico) and in the Pacific (Guam, Hawai'i, the Philippines) are forecast by the prescient Cuban revolutionary and writer José Martí in his famous essay "Nuestra América" (1892). Martí is a forerunner to the anticolonialism that Zavala locates in Latin American modernismo.

Against this very brief and quite general backdrop of Anglo-American, European, and Latin American modernisms, we (students and teacher) can take up issues of U.S. Latina and Latino literatures and histories. In considering the place of U.S. Latin@s in thinking about modernity as a historical period and Modernism as a cultural movement, it is beneficial to first establish with students who are U.S. Latin@s and how they are different from Latin Americans.[2] The simplest explanation would be that U.S. Latins@s are people with ancestors in Spanish-speaking Latin America, and who were born, raised, and educated in the United States. The realities of immigration, and the fact that many migrate as children and grow into adulthood in the United States, however, expands that definition. Many people who were not born in the United States should be and are considered U.S. Latin@s.[3] Secondly, most, but certainly not all, U.S. Latin@s are also "mestiza" or "mestizo," which translates from the Spanish to "mixed," and refers to intermixing between European (specifically, Spanish) and Indigenous peoples that began with the Conquest of the Americas in the sixteenth century. Thus, most Latin@s are distinct from Spaniards in that they also have Native American ancestry.[4]

The case of Mexican American subjectivity helps us understand this phenomenon. On the one hand, people of Mexican descent have a distinct experience within U.S. Latinidad as many families have lived in the United States since before its modern political borders were established. The disenfranchisement of this population, as individual families and as communities, can be directly linked to Euro-American land grabs and the subsequent exclusion of Latin@s from institutional power in the United States. Particularly for Mexican Americans, the link to Latin American traditions, literary or otherwise, may not be fully-fledged, existing only as vague references and without any sense of patriotic loyalty to a Latin American nation, especially when one can trace their presence in the U.S. Southwest to the mid-nineteenth century or before. In contemporary times, however, Mexicans more than any other group are figured as im/migrant, even as the migration from our neighbor to the south has been forced by the neocolonial and neoliberal practices and foreign policies of the United States. People of Mexican descent travel to and within the United States for work and sustenance, leaving hinterlands in Mexico and the periphery of the United States to work in the fields of agriculture and the factories of the metropolis. We can think back here to Williams' work that I referred to earlier, and his argument about the unacknowledged role of immigration and the place of the metropolis in definitions and theories of Modernism. We could say that the narrative techniques of Modernism are well-suited to representations of Latin@ life: experimentation with languages; the alienation of the individual transformed into alienation from the artificially constructed nation-state; outsider perspectives on accepted conventions and traditions because of marginalization from them. While conventional Modernism positions travel as a privilege of leisure and luxury—one cannot travel and have the time to write memoirs or short stories full of local color when one has to report to a workplace five days a week or more—the realities of Latin@ travel create the conditions in which Modernist sensibilities of the nonelite have flourished.

As a population in the United States, Latin@s are predominantly viewed as recently arrived, having just immigrated from Latin America. But this is a vast oversimplification as Spanish-speaking and mestiz@ people have been in what is now the United States since the earliest stages of colonization and settlement by Europeans. Wherever there were Spanish settlements—and those pre-date English-speaking European settlements in North America—there was also the presence of mixed-race people.[5] The truth is that if we think in terms of the "modern era," rather than in terms of the host of cultural expressions known as "modernism," Latin@s have been present since the very beginning, having come into existence with the conquest and colonization of the Americas initiated in the sixteenth century. The racial mixing that produced conquest-era mestiz@s and led to present-day U.S. Latinidad is very much indicative of a modern condition in which the known becomes elusive, borders and definitions cease to communicate stability, and the very definition of "humanity" both expands and contracts. Thus, mestiz@s, or Latin@s, have always been "modern."

I have mentioned that Latin America has its own expressions of what may be called "modernist sensibility." But since U.S. Latin@s are generally believed to have come into existence only very recently, they are not often considered in the Modernist context, which dates to the latter part of the nineteenth and first part of the twentieth centuries. Moreover, U.S. Latin@s are figured in the popular imagination as impoverished and undereducated, associated with simpler modes of existence and unceasing work, while Modernist aesthetics and sensibilities have always been the province of the bourgeois elite. The case of William Carlos Williams is particularly interesting. Williams was half Puerto Rican, and incorporated his cultural knowledge, in terms of language and a critical cultural perspective, into his writing. He has been included in the canon of American Modernism, but his Latinidad has rarely been acknowledged. Issuing from the islands of Puerto Rico and Cuba and their exile communities in the United States, a discourse of resistance to the threat of U.S. incursion contributed to the formulation of Latin@ modernism and its precursors. Anticolonial intellectuals in Puerto Rico and Cuba shared a struggle against annexation of their island nations by the United States. These collective efforts enabled literary figures such as José Martí and Sotero Figueroa of Cuba, and Lola Rodríguez de Tío and Luis Muñoz Marín of Puerto Rico to voice their projects of self-determination and national sovereignty in powerful pre-Modernist moments.

A trenchant Modernist theme that one should explore with students is that of return. Seemingly connected to the idea of travel, the "return" in Modernist literature is sometimes figurative, sometimes literal, and is sought due to an alienation from the present. Disillusioned with their own cultural contexts, including the advent of industrialization and the social tragedies that came with it, Modernist writers tried to imagine not cures for the current conditions, but eras that preceded their own impoverished times. The early twentieth century in which they wrote was also a period in which the academic fields of anthropology and archaeology were being consolidated. Descriptions, exhibitions, histories, and theories of "ancient" and "primitive" societies began moving from the private drawing rooms of wealthy amateur explorers and collectors, to museum halls and, finally, to university classrooms. The circulation of this material provided a wealth of information upon which writers could ruminate to create idealized images of social organization in which shared divisions of labor and power, nonviolent social relations, and relaxed, unpoliced sexual relations allowed individuals to live free of inhibition and legal constraint.

Private individuals and, later, university researchers, had continued a tradition begun by sixteenth-century missionaries, colonial administrators, and soldiers of illustrating and commenting upon **Indigenous cultures**. These communities were perceived by the writers and by their audiences as less "civilized" than the Western contexts that produced the chroniclers. Even if these "primitive" societies were characterized by their alien distance (in terms of history as well as geography), the Modernist construction found in its own romantic depictions hope for a freer and more sustaining existence. In the world of art, "primitive art" (the art of Africa, Mesoamerica, and the Pacific), introduced Western practitioners to artistic skills and practices that were thought to contain deep complexity in their apparent simplicity. In the context of "Western" or European art and literature, this movement is known as Primitivism; in the context of Modernism, it is called Modern Primitivism. Notable European Modern **Primitivists** include English author D. H. Lawrence, French painter Pablo Picasso, and English sculptor Henry Moore. Avant-garde writers and artists such as André Breton of France and Sergei Eisenstein of Russia, like Lawrence and Moore, were captivated by Mexico, in particular.

At the same time that Europeans and Anglo Americans were becoming fascinated with so-called primitive themes and peoples, Mexico was emerging from the **Revolution of 1910**. The post-Revolutionary Mexican state was in the midst of defining itself against the past dictatorship of President Porfirio Díaz, as well as its past status as a colony of Spain. **Pre-Columbian Mesoamerican** cultural patrimony, specifically through the Aztecs, gave the Mexican state a strategy for defining itself as a modern nation with a unique and monumental history. A cultural movement known as *indigenismo*, or "indigenism," took hold as artists such as Diego Rivera glorified the Aztecs and Maya in mural depictions of Mexico's past commissioned by state officials, such as Secretary of Education José Vasconcelos. Together with Manuel Gamio, an archaeologist and anthropologist considered to be the "father of Mexican *indigenismo*," Vasconcelos developed social policies under its banner. These policies, such as rural education initiatives, had the stated purpose of acculturating Native Mexicans, with the intent to incorporate them into modern Mexican mestiz@ society. These programs diminished Indigenous affiliation and encouraged identification with the mainstream Mexican population, imposing free market ideology and severing cultural ties, as John Brading argues.[6] It is a sad irony of *indigenismo*, a Mexican Modernist endeavor, that apparent attempts to valorize the Indigenous in Mexico involved the deracination of Native people and communities.

From the U.S. side, journalists such as John Reed and John Kenneth Turner traveled in Mexico, documenting the Mexican Revolution for their reading publics, who could not get enough. John Kenneth Turner famously rode with Pancho Villa, chronicling his exploits and humanizing his mission. Writers such as Katherine Anne Porter also went to Mexico, drawn by the socialist principles of the Revolution, and seeking to make a name for themselves in the literary sphere. Photographer Edward Weston, who achieved the great respect of important Mexican artists of the period, spent an important part of his career in Mexico. Italian photographer Tina Modotti documented the art and the people of the period, beginning her career as a model and student of Weston's, but quickly becoming an artist in her own right. All were part of a community of European and American Modernist expatriates in Mexico, some with deep connections to artists of the Mexican Renaissance, the name given to the period of artistic revival associated with the production of state-sponsored murals that followed the Revolution. A few of the most well-known Mexican muralists of this period include Diego Rivera, David Alfaro Siqueiros, and José Clemente Orozco. Frida Kahlo was one of the most influential Mexican Modernist painters of this period. Her self-portraits, for which she is best known, offer uncompromising representations of women's subjectivity based upon her own life experience. An unrivalled feminist icon in Latin America and beyond, Kahlo continues to attract critical attention and acclaim.

The reclamation of Pre-Columbian Mexico also captured the imagination of U.S. Latin@ artists and writers, specifically Mexican Americans, many of whom chose to call themselves Chican@.[7] As the Mexican state and Modernist Mexican artists and writers had glorified their ancestral past, Chican@s in the late 1960s and early 1970s began projects of Indigenous recovery, thus developing their own versions of *indigenismo*. The symbolic power of the Aztec and Maya as ancestral civilizations that could rival Greece and Rome was not lost on people of Mexican descent in the United States. Chican@ activists at this time were organizing agricultural fieldworkers to campaign for fair wages and improved working conditions and launching campaigns for educational justice and inclusion in the public schools. These activists, artists, and writers drew upon the Mexican Renaissance tradition to develop their own cultural iconographies that could challenge the negative representations of Mexicans in U.S. popular culture and revitalize community pride and empowerment in the face of oppressive and marginalizing material conditions. People looked to the ancestral past—one of technological sophistication, cultural achievement, and spiritual certainty—to help them visualize a future of recovered connection to their own indigeneity. As a population perceived solely as immigrant, U.S. Mexicans could draw upon that heritage to advance the community as a whole and argue for their own right to reside within the modern borders of the United States. Furthermore, this knowledge—based upon recovered pre-Columbian histories and mythologies—provided empowering counterpoints to unflattering media portrayals and the lack of representation in social and political systems of power.

Prior to the development of Chican@ *indigenismo*, the most available narrative of community pride was one that emphasized *Hispano* heritage and the link to Spain as a marker of a "civilized" identity. This line of argument unconsciously accepted the conventional and Eurocentric assumptions that the non-European was not culturally evolved or intellectually sophisticated. The advent of *indigenismo* challenged that thinking and gave working-class and darker-skinned mestiz@s ways to visualize their own achievements based upon the very images that had in the past been used to degrade Mexicans. If we consider Modernist techniques of representation as culturally, rather than historically, grounded, then we can recognize these artistic and literary endeavors by Chican@s as explorations of thematics associated with the cultural movement of Modernism, as well as post-Revolutionary Mexican muralism. Rather than focusing on an argument that European Modernism influenced Chican@ indigenism, however, I want to emphasize the influence that worked in the other direction, from the Americas back to Europe. Mexican post-Revolutionary *indigenismo* impacted European Modernist expression and, later, Chican@ cultural nationalism.

At this time in history, we are just beginning to see U.S. Latin@s entering higher education in larger numbers, although challenges remain with respect to retention and graduation rates, and representation among faculty and administrators. The second generation of Mexican American students—the children of college-educated Mexican American parents—are also starting to appear. It is commonly understood that curricula acknowledging the diversity of students, including their community histories and cultural production, help to engage students from those backgrounds in the life of the university. Many students, however, whether or not they are Latin@ or specifically of Mexican descent, will find the material here to be fascinating.

It is important to remind students that in 1920, the end of the Mexican American War in 1848 and the signing of the Treaty of Guadalupe-Hidalgo (in which Mexico ceded more than half of its territory to the United States) were a mere 72 years in the past. The knowledge of that loss, along with the memory of Spanish colonialism and the immediate realities and challenges of managing a post-Revolutionary cultural and political context, were etched in the Mexican national psyche. Thus, Mexican artists, writers, and politicians were attempting to establish a unique and unified national character in relation to the United States, as well as with regard to their history as a Spanish colony and as a people recently engaged in a revolution.

Mexico has been represented in the U.S. popular imagination over and over and for a very long time. When teaching classes on this history of representation, one cannot help but intersect with the historical epoch of modernity and the cultural patterns of Modernism. The themes of exploration and travel, **conquest** and **colonization**, **industrialization** and **urbanization**, migration and removal, abound. The earliest texts of travel in the Americas, those produced by missionaries, explorers, soldiers, and administrators, provide students with the first depictions of Native and mestiz@ subjects, even if not told from their own perspectives. Miguel León-Portilla's collection of Indigenous accounts of the Conquest, *The Broken Spears: The Aztec Account of the Conquest of Mexico* (1966), offers a partial corrective to this absence, although the lacunae can never be fully remedied.

The time period in which U.S. literary and filmic genre of the Western is set is also the time of Mexican removal from land. As Euro-American settlers moved westward, they occupied lands inhabited by Indigenous people and mestiz@s. This conflict over land is depicted in popular film and television repeatedly. One might consider teaching María Amparo Ruíz de Burton's *The Squatter and the Don* (written in 1885 and published in 1992), which tells this story from the perspective of an elite class of *Californio* Mexican landholders, who were themselves situated at the cusp of Modernism. Or, one might consider teaching Elena Zamora O'Shea's *El Mesquite* (1935), which fictionalizes the Anglo-American settlement of Texas land from the perspective of an ancient tree that witnesses Native, then Mexican, and, finally, Anglo occupation of the territory. Teaching Américo Paredes's *With His Pistol in His Hand: A Border Ballad and Its Hero* (1958) and his analysis of the Mexican American folk ballad *corrido* can alert students to the working and underclass perspective on this land loss handed down through oral traditions.

The period of Revolution and ensuing immigration to the United States, coterminous with the Modernist period, can be accessed through the teaching of a number of different vantage points, and through texts produced at the time. Journalist Daniel Venegas's *The Adventures of Don Chipote, Or, When Parrots Breast-Feed* (1928) provides an early depiction and analysis of immigration and the treatment of Mexican migrants in the United States. Leonor Villegas de Magnón's recovered text *The Rebel*, originally written in the 1920s, is an autobiographical account of the Revolutionary period in Mexico and is known for its representation of the role of women during the war. A committed revolutionary, the author documents her work founding *La cruz blanca*/The White Cross, a medical corps that served injured soldiers on both sides of the conflict. Maria Cristina Mena's *The Collected Stories of Maria Cristina Mena* (1997) offers examples of post-Revolutionary fiction directly influenced by Modern Primitivist trends and the presence of expatriates in Mexico City, such as D. H. Lawrence. Mena, like Villegas de Magnón, left Mexico with her family at a young age to escape the conflict. She later returned and wrote for English language magazines, in which some of her short stories were published.

The period of Chicano nationalism, which saw the emergence of Chican@ indigenism, yields a good deal of interesting material for students to explore Modernism and U.S. Latin@ literature. Luís Valdez's play, *Dark Root of a Scream* (1967), signals his early foray into the area of Mesoamerican theatrical symbolism, a theme that would be explored throughout the work of Teatro Campesino, the theatre group with which he worked for years. *El Plan de Aztlán/The Plan of Aztlán*, a political manifesto produced at a youth conference in 1969 and based upon a text penned by the poet Alurista, provides another strong example of the marshaling of pre-Columbian myth and iconography to advance a social critique of Mexican American marginalization in the United States. Carmen Tafolla's groundbreaking feminist poem, "La Malinche," takes on the male representations of Chican@ pre-Columbian ancestry by rewriting the story of **La Malinche**, translator and advisor to Hernán Cortés. La Malinche, also known as Doña Marina, has been historically represented as a traitor for her work with the Spanish occupiers, a negative depiction that feeds the patriarchal suspicion and denigration of women more broadly in Mexican and Chicano societies. Tafolla critiques directly this narrative trend, at the same time calling into question male leadership in activist circles of the time. The publication of Gloria Anzaldúa's *Borderlands/La Frontera: The New Mestiza* in 1987 was deeply influential in reminding readers of the power of the pre-Columbian archive, as she recharged it to advance a feminist critique of male power and domination in Chican@ communities.

There would be many ways to approach teaching students about the relationship between U.S. Latin@ literatures and Anglo American and European Modernisms. My own training and specialization in Chican@ literature prompt my exploration of the connections between Mexican *indigenismo*, European and Anglo American Modernist Primitivism and Chican@ cultural nationalism. Because the writers and artists of post-Revolutionary Mexico were so engaged with European Modernists of the time and then had such influence on Mexican American nationalist cultural production of the 1960s and 1970s, we have a rich terrain for study. Other approaches can and do emphasize how Latin American political writings and works of *modernismo* anticipated and preceded the thematic and political concerns of later European Modernists, and also talk back to celebrated Anglo-American writers. Increasingly, studies of modernity and Modernism from a U.S. Latin@ perspective highlight previously unrepresented experiences of modernity that emerge in the writings of mestiz@s and complicate accepted definitions and terminologies.

Notes

1 In American Modernism, T.S. Eliot's "The Wasteland" stands as a most notable example. Poet and critic Ezra Pound's influence on the development of U.S. Modernism is without question. Major works of European literary Modernism include James Joyce's *Ulysses* (1922) and Virginia Woolf's *To the Lighthouse* (1927).

2 The use of the ampersand at the end of "Latin@s" is a strategy to acknowledge the presence and influence of women and to resist the reproduction of a Spanish grammar in which the masculine form is taken to represent the collective whole, that is, the masculine grammatical form "Latino" stands in for all people of Latin American descent, whether they are men or women. We have equivalents in English, where, for example, "man" or "men" stands in for "people" or "humanity." The use of "man" or "men," however, is at this point obsolete and considered to be sexist language according to standard grammar and usage handbooks used at the college and university level. Initial attempts to make the presence of women explicit in the transcription of Latin@ identity used the slash instead: "Latina/o." More recently, that more cumbersome form has given way to the use of "Latin@," which has become a convention in Latina and Latino cultural and critical discourse. Further testament to the depth and pervasiveness of the tradition of masculinist language is the fact that the word processing spell-checker consistently changes "Latina" to "Latino" every time I type the word as I write this document.

3 Adult immigration is a more complicated matter. I hold to the definition that "U.S. Latin@" refers to a person who was socialized, educated, and emerged into adulthood in the United States. A key distinction is that adults who migrate from Latin America to the United States

leave cultural contexts in which mestiz@s occupy positions of power and influence throughout society. U.S. Latin@s do not have that experience.
4 European immigration to Latin America complicates this even further. A case in point is the recently installed Pope Francis, widely considered to be Latino. Born and raised in Buenos Aires, Argentina, the son of Italian immigrants, he is not racially mestizo as the term has been conventionally understood in Latin@ Studies.
5 St. Augustine, Florida was established in 1565, and is generally thought to be the first European settlement in the United States. That accepted truth has come into question as Florida State University researchers Fletcher Crowe and Anita Spring in 2014 claimed that they have discovered the long-sought French settlement of Fort Caroline, founded in 1564, in Georgia. See "Oldest fortified settlement ever found in North America? Location of Fort Caroline may be in Georgia," *Science Daily*. February 21, 2014. Retrieved July 20, 2014; and Soergel, Matt (February 22, 2014), "Scholars say ancient Fort Caroline nowhere near Jacksonville," *The Florida Times-Union*. Retrieved July 20, 2014. Crowe and Spring have been challenged by colleagues and local historians. See "LAMP disputes new Fort Caroline claims," *Keepers Blog*, St. Augustine Lighthouse & Museum. February 22, 2014. Retrieved July 20, 2014, and "Local archaeologist defends history of Fort Caroline," *Historic City News*. March 15, 2014. Retrieved July 20, 2014.
6 Gamio played a central role in the excavation and reconstruction of one of the world's most famous archaeological sites, the pyramids at Teotihuacan, outside Mexico City. See Brading.
7 "Chicana" and "Chicano" are terms specific to people of Mexican descent born and/or raised in the United States.

Resources for teaching Modernism, modernity, and U.S. Latino/a literature

Contreras, Sheila Marie. *Blood Lines: Myth, Indigenism and Chicana/o Literature*. Austin: University of Texas Press, 2008.

Delpar, Helen. *The Enormous Vogue of Things Mexican: Cultural Relations between the United States and Mexico, 1920–1935*. Tuscaloosa: University of Alabama Press, 1995.

Díaz del Castillo, Bernal. *The Discovery and Conquest of Mexico, 1517–1521*. New York: Da Capo Press, 1996.

Levins Morales, Aurora. *Remedios: Stories of Earth and Iron from the History of Puertorriqueñas*. Cambridge, MA: South End Press, 2001.

Lomas, Laura. *Translating Empire: José Martí, Migrant Latino Subjects and American Modernities*. Durham: Duke University Press, 2009.

Padilla, Genaro M. *My History, Not Yours: The Formation of Mexican American Autobiography*. Madison: University of Wisconsin Press, 1993.

Paredes, Américo. *George Washington Gomez: A Mexicotexan Novel*. Houston: Arte Público, 1990.

Prescott, William H. *History of the Conquest of Mexico*. New York: Modern Library, 2001.

Ramos, Peter. "Cultural identity, translation and William Carlos Williams," *Multi-ethnic Literatures of the United States* 38.2 (Summer 2013): 89–110.

Saldívar, José David. *Trans-Americanity: Subaltern Modernities, Global Coloniality and the Cultures of Greater Mexico*. Durham: Duke University Press, 2011.

Saldívar, Ramón. *The Borderlands of Culture: Américo Paredes and the Transnational Imaginary*. Durham: Duke University Press, 2006.

Sánchez, Rosaura. *Telling Identities: The Californio Testimonios*. Minneapolis: University of Minnesota Press, 1995.

Stavans, Illan, and Acosta-Belan, E. *The Norton Anthology of Latino Literature*. New York: W.W. Norton, 2011.

Williams, Raymond. *The Politics of Modernism: Against the New Conformists*. Ed. Tony Pinkney. London: Verso, 1996.

Williams, William Carlos. *The Autobiography of William Carlos Williams*. New York: New Directions, 1951.

3 Latino/a queer expressions

Richard T. Rodríguez

Chicana lesbian writer Gloria E. Anzaldúa, in her highly influential book *Borderlands/ La Frontera: The New Mestiza* (1987), insists that "Chicanos need to acknowledge the political and artistic contributions of their queer." "People," she implores, "listen to what your jotería is saying. The **mestizo** and the queer exist at this time and point on the evolutionary continuum for a purpose. We are a blending that proves that all blood is intricately woven together, and that we are spawned out of similar souls" (106). This chapter echoes Anzaldúa's plea by asking that we pay attention to *la jotería* (or queer people) in the classroom for registering the vital interventions Latino/a LGBT (lesbian, gay, bisexual, and transgender) writers have made on the literary scene.[1] Yet it also makes the argument that we equally pay attention to queer representations that often surface within the pages of canonical and perceived heteronormative texts.

Taking a cue from feminist cultural critic Sandra K. Soto, I maintain that a commitment to "reading like a queer" allows teachers and students to "expand the very definition of [Latino/a] cultural production as primarily a set of representations underwritten by oppositional consciousness and cultural maintenance amid the ongoing race- and class-based disenfranchisement of peoples of [Latino/o] descent" (2010: 14).[2] Such an expansive approach facilitates consideration of how gender and sexual politics must inform our understanding of both queer and "straight" literary texts. Attentiveness to Latino/a queer expression, I maintain, must refuse to isolate LGBT concerns by placing the burden of responsibility on self-identified LGBT writers. Indeed, while signaling their remarkable contributions, we must simultaneously challenge the normative tenants of how Latino/a literature has conventionally been taught and understood. This is possible by supporting queer reading practices—of both LGBT and non-LGBT literary texts—to destabilize normative ideologies that often foreclose trenchant appraisals of queer matters in Latino/a communities.

Rather than follow a linear chronology that tracks the evolution of Latino/a queer representations and expressions from a moment of repression to one of openness and visibility, my contribution considers and moves between contemporary and early texts while spotlighting key moments in the history of queer Latino/a literary expressions. I therefore adopt what queer theorist Carolyn Dinshaw calls a "queer historical impulse, an impulse toward making connections across time between, on the one hand, lives, texts, and other cultural phenomena left out of sexual categories back then and, on the other, those left out of current sexual categories now. Such an impulse extends the resources for self- and community building into even the distant past" (1999: 1). The pedagogical value of such an approach cannot be overestimated given how it might promote a more capacious and dynamic understanding of LGBT literary histories and identities.

Building bridges with Latina lesbian writing

The 1980s are often regarded as the years during which queer Latino/a—especially Latina—writers began to break the silence around sexuality and identity. In particular, Cherríe Moraga and Gloria E. Anzaldúa's edited collection, *This Bridge Called My Back: Writings by Radical Women of Color* (1981), is commonly acknowledged as jumpstarting not only the organizing category "women of color" but also the literary reputations of its editors.[3] While many of the contributors to the anthology would go on to become established writers in their own right, Moraga (with *Loving in the War Years: Lo que nunca pasó por sus labios* (1983)) and Anzaldúa (with *Borderlands/La Frontera*) are undoubtedly the most widely recognized and taught Latina lesbian writers. Even so, critics like Catrióna Rueda Esquibel have convincingly argued that we "recognize the contributions made by both Gloria Anzaldúa and Cherríe Moraga while at the same time reading their work in a larger context of Chicana lesbian writing" (3). Writers in this larger context include Chicanas like Terri de la Peña, Naomi Littlebear Morena, Emma Pérez, Sheila Ortiz Taylor, Rocky Gamez, Monica Palacios, Carla Trujillo, Amelia María de la Luz Montes, and Myriam Gurba, and Latinas such as Tatiana de la Tierra, Erika Lopez, Luzma Umpierre, Carmelita Tropicana, and Achy Obejas.

While more often than not duly mentioned in relation to both Anzaldúa's and Moraga's individual works, beginning with key pieces published in *Bridge* provides students with a necessary critical framework to ascertain the predicament of women of color, caught between the Scylla of predominantly white and middle-class feminisms and the Charybdis of patriarchal and homophobic cultural nationalist movements. In particular, Anzaldúa's "Speaking in Tongues: A Letter to Third World Women Writers" (1983) Moraga's "La Güera" (reprinted in *Loving in the War Years*), and their succinct yet pointed introduction are invaluable pieces in *Bridge* for grasping the interplay of racism, classism, sexism, and homophobia.

Although not conferred the same sense of primacy and historical urgency as *Bridge*, numerous edited anthologies would follow in its footsteps and highlight the work of Latina lesbian writers. These include Juanita Ramos's *Compañeras: Latina Lesbians: An Anthology* (1987; reprinted in 1994); Anzaldúa's *Making Face, Making Soul/Haciendo Caras: Creative and Critical Perspectives by Women of Color* (1990); Carla Trujillo's *Chicana Lesbians: The Girls Our Mothers Warned Us About* (1991); Lillian Castillo-Speed's *Latina: Women's Voices from the Borderlands* (1995); and Anzaldúa and AnaLouise Keating's *This Bridge We Call Home: Radical Visions for Transformation* (2002). Charting the emergence of Latino/a literary anthologies while paying attention to the inclusion (or, as it were, exclusion) of LGBT writers might prove advantageous for having students think about the politics of publishing queer narratives in mainstream publications. Additionally, it might behove instructors to consider the role small presses like Kitchen Table Press, Third Woman Press, South End Press, and Spinsters/Aunt Lute, for example—have played in shepherding the work of Latina lesbian writers into print as compared to mainstream publishing houses.

In view of the steadfast autobiographical impulse characterizing Moraga's and Anzaldúa's writing (as well as the work by many other Latina lesbians), it would benefit students and instructors alike to consult published interviews with these writers (such as the informative interview with Moraga in Bridget A. Kevane and Juanita Heredia's *Latina Self-Portraits: Interviews with Contemporary Women Writers* (2000), and Keating's edited collection of interviews with Anzaldúa titled *Interviews/Entrevistas* (2000)). Lourdes Torres's influential essay "The Construction of the Self in U.S. Latina Autobiographies" (1991) is beneficial for comprehending the crucial historical and personal currency of life writing. After Anzaldúa's passing in 2004, Moraga would write and publish "The Salt That Cures: Remembering Gloria Anzaldúa" in her book *A Xicana Codex of Changing Consciousness: Writings, 2000–2010* (2011). The essay is a brutally honest account of Moraga's and Anzaldúa's falling out, and Moraga's attempt to make sense of their respective differences. Moraga's piece is also crucial for underscoring the contingent foundations of solidarity and the ways a shared queer identity and politics do not always result in instantaneous or lasting alliances.

Where the boys are(n't)

A common charge in Latino/a literary circles has been that Latino gay men have not produced a comparable body of work in contrast to the extensive offerings of Latina lesbians because they elect to remain closeted regarding their sexuality. In *Next of Kin: The Family in Chicano/a Cultural Politics*, I argue that this is not the case. Considering the particular historical circumstances of Latino gay men, to

> establish a similarly solid body of work, projects must be pursued which would: 1) recover and compile materials that are out of print, unpublished, or published in obscure journals and periodicals; 2) conduct and amass oral histories of Chicano gay men (perhaps even writing the histories of those lost to AIDS with the help of family and friends); 3) promote and distribute recent writing, visual art, and film and video (for example, through curatorial efforts, festival acquisition, and the publication of literary anthologies); and 4) critically examine the representations of Chicano gay men in various social and cultural contexts (such as literature and film) to unveil their positionings therein.
>
> (139–40)

Before and after the publication of *Next of Kin*, work published or on its way toward publication has adhered to such protocols. For example, a handful of edited anthologies have aimed to follow in the footsteps of *Bridge* by forging communities of likeminded writers. These include Jaime Cortez's *Virgins, Guerrillas, and Locas: Gay Latinos Writing about Love* (1999) and Erasmo Guerra's *Latin Lovers: True Stories of Men in Love* (1999). Furthermore, recent scholarship has made clear that gay Latino men were indeed active in generating literature and other expressive forms before and during the 1980s. An excellent example is the artist-activist Joey Terrill who produced the 'zine *Homeboy Beautiful*, which focused on Latino gay male sexuality and community in Los Angeles in the late 1970s (see Rodríguez 2011). Another example is *Ya Vas, Carnal* (1985)—a collection of gay love poetry by three San Francisco-based poets, Rodrigo Reyes, Francisco X. Alarcón, and Juan Pablo Gutiérrez—published four years after the initial publication of *This Bridge Called My Back*. Hardly silent about their homosexual self-identification and object choices, some of these poets were additionally activists in the Bay Area, mobilizing to cultivate cultural spaces in neighborhoods like the Mission District and raising awareness about the spread of HIV/AIDS in local Latino/a communities (see Roque Ramírez 2009). Important to note when teaching the expressive forms of these writers is that their activist and erotic ambitions were intimately connected to their desire to produce creative work.

In early 1990s Los Angeles (and serving as an excellent comparative example with the work of Terrill), writer Gil Cuadros would publish short stories and poems detailing his struggles as a person with AIDS while negotiating family, homophobia, and racial objectification in the predominantly white gay community. Initially appearing in various periodicals and anthologies, Cuadros's work was compiled as a book, *City of God* (2001), and posthumously published by City Lights Publishers. Cuadros's death in 1996 at the age of 34 speaks to why a substantial body of work by Latino gay male writers pales in comparison to Latina lesbians given the deadly impact of AIDS that cut short their lives and, as a result, their expressive endeavors. The AIDS epidemic also claimed the lives of Puerto Rican writer Manuel Ramos Otero, author of many books written in Spanish focusing on first-generation gay Puerto Rican migrant men in New York City, and Chicano novelist Arturo Islas, whose books *The Rain God* (1984) and *Migrant Souls* (1990) explore interlocking themes of family, masculinity, and sexual repression in the U.S.–Mexico borderlands.

Numerous overlapping thematic and genre-focused threads enable a contrast between Latino gay male writers and their queer Latina counterparts that may pedagogically play well in the classroom. Queer Puerto Rican literary critic Lawrence La Fountain-Stokes argues that while autobiography "can be seen as a straightjacket or prison, for authors such as Ramos Otero it represents an enabling strategy, full of possibility. To conduct autobiographical projection as a form of literary criticism is to challenge norms, mix genres, and surreptitiously stake out a location of creative subversion and affirmation" (24). This makes perfect sense for understanding the autobiographical impulse and the mixing of genres in the work of Anzaldúa and Moraga, as well as Frankie Barrera's *The Diary of Baby Chulo* (1999), Rigoberto González's *Butterfly Boy* (2011), and Richard Villegas, Jr.'s *I ♥ Babylon, Tenochtitlan, and Ysteléi* (2011). Furthermore, family dynamics more often than not wield a significant influence on queer sexualities and loom large in the work of Moraga, Cuadros, and Islas. Earlier, foundational texts might be contrasted with more recent books such as Manuel Muñoz's short story collections *Zigzagger* (2003) and *The Faith Healer of Olive Avenue* (2007); Felicia Luna Lemus's novels *Trace Elements of Random Tea Parties* (2004) and *Like Son* (2007); and Achy Obejas's short story collection *We Came All the Way from Cuba So You Could Dress Like This?* (1994) and novels *Memory Mambo* (1996) and *Days of Awe* (2002).

Well before the 1970s John Rechy took the literary world by storm, first with his bestselling debut novel *City of Night* in 1963 and subsequent novels like *Numbers* (1967) and *This Day's Death* (1969). The son of a Scottish father and a Mexican mother and born in El Paso, Texas, Rechy has been recently embraced as a Latino writer despite recurrent shunning by Latino literary critics given the overemphasis on gay sex and lack of significant ethnic content of his early work.[4] In his 1978 essay, "The Evolution of Chicano Literature," Raymund A. Paredes comments that one "problem related to labeling literary work is simply that authors frequently shift interests from one work to another." John Rechy's essay, "El Paso del Norte" certainly should be considered Chicano literature, but his novel, *City of Night*, which is virtually devoid of ethnic content, should not" (104). Understandably, Paredes has been taken to task for making the argument that *City of Night* should not be considered a Chicano text because foregrounding a gay identity means eclipsing a Mexican American one (Paredes tellingly admits the novel is *virtually*—and not *completely*—devoid of ethnic content). Yet whether one agrees or disagrees with Paredes, his provocative argument might nonetheless serve as a way to ask what counts as Latino/a literature (and by whom) and how queer matters have historically marginalized LGBT writers in order to narrowly define the Latino/a literary canon in normative terms. And categorization aside, with the proliferation of Latino/a-penned queer texts it makes sense to consider Rechy alongside later authors like Cuadros, Ricardo A. Bracho, Lorenzo Herrera y Lozano, Elliot Torres, Emanuel Xavier, Jaime Cortez, and David Caleb Acevedo and Charlie Vázquez, who also unflinchingly write about gay male sex and desire.

Normative canons and queer potentiality

Juan Bruce-Novoa's essay "Homosexuality and the Chicano Novel" is unquestionably one of the first and foremost critical overviews of queer representations in Chicano/Latino literature. Noting the "various attitudes and a willingness to address the topic" of homosexuality, Bruce-Novoa sees the literary realm as "a progressive space of dialogue, an appropriate space in and through which a more androgynous Chicano identity can be forged" (76). Examining foundational texts by presumably straight writers like Jose Antonio Villarreal's *Pocho* (1959), Oscar Zeta Acosta's *The Autobiography of a Brown Buffalo* (1972) and *Revolt of the Cockroach People* (1973), and Floyd Salas's *Tattoo the Wicked Cross* (1967) alongside books by out writers like Sheila Ortiz Taylor's *Faultline* (1982) and *Spring Forward/Fall Back* (1985) and Rechy's *City of Night* (1963) and *This Day's Death* (1969), Bruce-Novoa, although encouraging future projects focused on LGBT representations in Latino/a literature, unfortunately undercuts the possibility of advocating a queer reading practice that not only pines for affirmative representations but rather aims to destabilize the presumption of heteronormative masculinity.

Just as Bruce-Novoa confesses that he "could have mentioned some novels—like [Alejandro] Morales' *Caras Viejas y vino nuevo*, [Sergio] Elizondo's *Muerte en una estrella*, or [Rolando] Hinojosa's *Partners in Crime*—in which homosexual acts or topics appear, but are not central to plot or structure" (76), he also notes at the start of his essay that "the most read texts of the early Movement"—Américo Paredes's *With His Pistol in His Hand* (1958) and Rodolfo "Corky" Gonzáles's *I Am Joaquín* (see Gonzáles 2010) among them—not only stressed the traditional role of the male, but glorified the male hero almost to the point of romantic hyperbole (69). Failing to register a juncture between the masculinist imperatives of Movement-era texts and later works which would explicitly broach queer subjects, Bruce-Novoa misses the opportunity to reflect on how the appearance of "homosexual acts or topics"—no matter how minor or non-central to plot or structure—may serve to generate alternative reading of these texts to assist in destabilizing the "acts and topics" often rendered primary or natural. Surprisingly, Bruce-Novoa excludes Estella Portillo's play *The Day of the Swallows* from his analysis. Although his focus is on the novel, close attention to this key text published in 1971 (and which won the noted Premio Quinto Sol Award) would expose how the protagonist's lesbianism moves from a minor to a major point, ultimately determining the play's narrative outcome. Reading as such helps critically ascertain works like *With His Pistol in His Hand* and *I Am Joaquín*. In this regard, Sandra K. Soto offers a superb example of how to read Paredes's work (and that of Moraga, Castillo, and Richard Rodríguez), as earlier mentioned, "like a queer." For Soto, "the feminist critique of foundations and origins should make it possible not only to foreground nonmasculinist forms of *chicanada* (as [Sonia] Saldívar-Hull compellingly attests) but also to revisit—now from feminist and queer vantage points—the very foundational texts and themes from which they seem to depart" (96–97).

Reading in this vein assists in critically engaging literary texts in which queer characters do appear but in nonaffirmative ways. Indeed, reading peripheral or maligning representations of queers helps shed light on the way their appearance is fundamental for upholding patriarchal, sexist, and anti-LGBT principles. For example, in *Next of Kin* I offer a reading of Joe Olvera's poem "Gay Ghetto District" (1980) that illustrates the impossibility of assimilating gay men into the familiar terms by which the Chicano movement and Chicano poetic discourse had been defined. Lawrence La Fountain-Stokes makes a similar move regarding Puerto Rican writer Luis Rafael Sanchez's short story "¡Jum!" (1966). A "paradigmatic case of the violent expulsion of a queer Puerto Rican subject," La Fountain-Stokes points out that this short story, which "portrays the persecution and harassment that an effeminate black man is subjected by his community, culminating in his death" signals the "[a]ctual or self-imposed expulsion from the social collective (the family, the nation) ... at the core of much of twentieth-century queer Rican migration" (xxv). Queer reading practices such as these can help students unmask the ideologies that necessarily require queers to prop up the logics of heteronormativity and queer phobia.

One might also consider a popular text like Puerto Rican writer Piri Thomas's *Down These Mean Streets* (1967) that similarly depends on queers to uphold heteromasculinist prerogatives while at the same time disclosing the fluidity of sexual desires and practices between men, no matter what their sexual identification. (In a personal conversation, gay Chicano playwright Ricardo A. Bracho confessed that he considers "*Down These Mean Streets* as queer as *City of Night*.") In a classic scene in Thomas's memoir, protagonist Piri and his close male friends enter an apartment to smoke pot and partake in an orgy with the "faggots" who reside there. Fashioned as a pot-induced haze with the narrator's recounting of the scene appearing as italicized text (thereby drawing a line between the reality of the outside world and the hallucinated destabilization of "straight thinking" within the interiority of the apartment), Piri is determined to keep his masculinity and heterosexuality intact even after receiving a blowjob from one of the queens. As African American queer critic Robert F. Reid-Pharr succinctly puts it, "The episode in the gay men's apartment is from the very outset overdetermined by the intense ambiguity that suffuses the extremely homosocial world of the gangs. The faggots, the *maricones*, stand in for the constant danger that the macho young men, with their relentless emphasis on masculinity and the male body, will stumble themselves, inadvertently or not so inadvertently, across the line that separates the homosexual from the homosocial" (115).[5]

An excellent contemporary counterpoint to this scene and *Down These Mean Streets* in general is Pulitzer Prize-winning Dominican American writer Junot Díaz's *Drown* (1996), particularly the eponymously titled story in the collection. In "Drown" we witness the disintegration of the close bond between two young men after two brief sexual encounters. Díaz's story affords the opportunity to discuss sexual desire versus sexual identity in relation to masculinity. Similarly, one might also consider Sandra Cisneros's classic novella *The House on Mango Street* (1984) and Ana Castillo's epistolary novel *The Mixquiahuala Letters* (1986) to signal the queer bonds between women and how these bonds are predicated upon friendship, intimacy, and desire. Catrióna Rueda Esquibel's reading of *Mango Street* in *With Her Machete in*

Her Hand (see the chapter "Memories of Girlhood: Chicana Lesbian Fictions") is an excellent example of reading "on the surface" non-LGBT texts against the grain for tapping queer concerns. The recently "recovered" novel *Caballero* (written in the 1930s and 1940s but not published until 1996) by Jovita González and Eve Raleigh is another excellent case in point. In the novel, Luis Gonzaga, one of the two sons of family patriarch Don Santiago, clearly stands apart from his siblings and peers. Aside from the fact that he is, not surprisingly, an artist who delights in all things aesthetically pleasing, he is also a queer figure of resistance in contradistinction to the masculine authority and compulsory heterosexuality of his father and brother.

Recently, queer Latino/a writers have excavated the past for material for fashioning revisionist histories and identities. Alicia Gaspar de Alba's *Sor Juana's Second Dream* (2007) takes as its focus the seventeenth-century Mexican nun and poet Sor Juana Ines de la Cruz. In Gaspar de Alba's purview, Sor Juana's lesbian sexuality is not merely a subject based on speculation but a possibility within the realm of fiction. Likewise, Emma Pérez's *Forgetting the Alamo, Or, Blood Memory* (2009) undertakes a rewriting of Texas history with a Tejana lesbian protagonist. And Michael Nava's *The City of Palaces* (2014) uses an expanse of transnational Mexican history as a palimpsest for fleshing out the life stories of fictional characters like José Sarmiento, whose experiences reflect those of noted gay Mexican actor Ramón Novarro. Exemplifying how a queer in the present moment might, to borrow from Carolyn Dinshaw, "touch the past," these three novels illustrate the propensity for not only reading like a queer but also writing like one.

Re-reading the literary scene

Akin to novelists' efforts at rewriting historical narratives for queer purposes, various poets have nodded to, while disidentifying with, heterosexual Latino/a writers and their work that often serves as a template for revisionist narratives. José Esteban Muñoz understands disidentification as "the ways in which queers of color identify with ethnos or queerness despite the phobic charges in both fields" (11). While not necessarily "phobic," disidentifying with straight writers and their work sometimes promotes the adoption of particularly effective literary forms and thematic impetuses. For example, Eduardo C. Corral's poem "Variation on a Theme by José Montoya" from his book *Slow Lightning* (2012) manifests as a trenchant rewriting of Montoya's classic "El Louie." Additionally, Lorenzo Herrera y Lozano's "You Bring Out the Joto in Me" from *Amorcito Maricón* (2014) revises Sandra Cisneros's unapologetically feminist poetic anthem "You Bring Out the Mexican in Me" to articulate an unabashed gay male sexual politics. Thus asking students to read these poems side by side would no doubt provoke interesting dialog about queer re-readings of Latino/a literary classics.

The burgeoning field of queer Latino/a poetry—to which Corral and Herrera y Lozano have indelibly contributed—is both dynamic and refreshing, warranting in-depth consideration in the classroom for the range of perspectives it offers. Yosimar Reyes's *For Colored Boys Who Speak Softly* (2009) elegantly engages with themes pertaining to undocumented struggles, racism, unrequited love, and sexual identity. Chicana lesbian writer Verónica Reyes's *Chopper! Chopper!: Poetry from Bordered Lives* (2013) functions as a stunning tapestry of voices and experiences from the East L.A. barrio the poet calls home. (Reyes's poetry also refers to women of color writers and activists like Audre Lorde and Angela Davis, which in many ways mirror the cross-racial/ethnic dialog evident in *This Bridge Called My Back*.) And Guatemalan-American writer Maya Chinchilla's *The Cha Cha Files: A Chapina Poética* (2014) highlights—through, as one of the poem's titles makes clear, a "Jota Poetics"—the personal passions and everyday life experiences of a queer Chapina in California. While many queer Latino/a poets have faced difficulty in the effort to publish their work on mainstream presses, Lorenzo Herrera y Lozano has played a significant role in seeing the work of Chinchilla, Pablo Miguel Martínez, Dino Foxx, Adelina Anthony, and Joseph Delgado reach the printed page. The mastermind behind Kórima Press, Herrera y Lozano, has fought to make writings by queer Latinos/as possible and accessible.

In addition to poetry, the field of children's and young adult (YA) fiction is an arena where queer Latino/a expressions proliferate. Rigoberto González—from his children's book *Antonio's Card/La tarjeta de Antonio* (2005) with illustrator Cecilia Concepción Álvarez to his high school-set novels *The Mariposa Club* (2009) and *Mariposa Gown* (2012)—is an excellent example of a writer who has contributed a plethora of affirming images for younger readers. Along with González's books, Gloria Velásquez's *Tommy Stands Alone* (1995) and *Tommy Stands Tall* (2013), as part of Arte Público Press's Roosevelt High School series, grapple with serious topics like suicide and the growing pains of a gay teen searching for and finding support from family and friends. Furthermore, Alex Sánchez's young adult novels—from *Rainbow Boys* (2001) to *Boyfriends with Girlfriends* (2011)—have tendered hopeful scenarios for teens struggling with their sexual identities in a persistently phobic culture. While books such as Sánchez's point up the demand for queer-affirmative YA literature, they have also been met with resistance as conservative organizations have sought to ban their circulation in schools.

The impossibility of avoiding discussion on the significance of lesbian, gay, bisexual, and transgender themes and concerns in the teaching of Latino/a literature should be clear. And the commitment to teaching gender and sexuality in the context of Latino/a literature not only lies in selecting one or two representative texts by LGBT writers as evidence of queer existence but in actively showing the queer potential of any text, no matter the author or thematic thrust. To read like a queer can mean looking for praiseworthy non-normative representations, but it also means catching the heterosexual blind spots that persist without acknowledging the fact that, to quote a famous queer maxim, we are everywhere. This certainly includes the classroom.

Notes

1 While one must distinguish the term "queer" from "LGBT" given how the latter marks specific identities (either self-embraced or unwillingly assigned) whereas the latter functions as both a noun and a verb (one may be a queer but one can also queer a text by reading against its conventional interpretations), there is nonetheless an overlap that I wish to hold on to given how queer is impossible to ascertain without consideration of the marginalization and empowerment of LGBT people.

2 I have taken the liberty of changing Soto's "Chican@" to "Latino/a," a move I imagine she'd endorse given her call for categorical expansion.

3 Originally published in 1981 by Persephone Press, a white women's press that folded in the spring of 1983, *Bridge* was reprinted in a second edition by *Kitchen Table: Women of Color Press of New York*. When Kitchen Table ceased operation, Third Woman Press (headed by Professor Norma Alarcón, also a contributor to the anthology) reprinted the book in a new format in 2002. As of this writing the book is out of print. It should be noted that the book was translated into Spanish by Alarcón and Ana Castillo and published under the title *Esta puente, mi espalda: Voces de mujeres tercermundistas en los Estados Unidos* (1988).

4 I would argue that Rechy's 1991 novel *The Miraculous Day of Amalia Gómez* assisted in the significant changing tide of his reception by many scholars as a Latino writer.
5 For another excellent reading of *Down These Mean Streets*, see Noel Zavala's forthcoming essay "Racing Boyhood: The Role of Colorism in Latino/a Adolescence in the Mid-Twentieth-Century," in *Perspectives on Latino/a and Chicano/a Young Adult Literature*, co-edited by Norma E. Cantú, Gabriela Baeza Ventura, and Laura López.

Resources for teaching Latino/a queer expressions

Aldama, Frederick Luis. *Brown on Brown: Chicano/a Representations of Gender, Sexuality, and Ethnicity.* Austin: University of Texas Press, 2005. Print.
Asencio, Marysol, ed. *Latina/o Sexualities: Probing Powers, Passions, Practices, and Policies.* Newark, NJ: Rutgers University Press, 2009.
Costa, María Dolores, ed. *Latina Lesbian Writers and Artists.* New York: Routledge, 2003.
Danielson, Marivel T. *Homecoming Queers: Desire and Difference in Chicana Latina Cultural Production.* Newark, NJ: Rutgers University Press, 2009.
Foster, David William, ed. *Chicano/Latino Homoerotic Identities.* New York: Routledge, 1999.
Güido, Gibrán, and Adelaida R. del Castillo, eds. *Queer in Aztlán: Chicano Male Recollections of Consciousness and Coming Out.* Cognella Academic Press, 2013.
Hames-García, Michael, and Ernesto J. Martínez, eds. *Gay Latino Studies: A Critical Reader.* Durham: Duke University Press, 2011.
Perpetusa-Seva, Inmaculada, and Lourdes Torres, eds. *Tortilleras: Hispanic and U.S. Latina Lesbian Expression.* Philadelphia: Temple University Press, 2003.
Rivera-Servera, Ramón H. *Performing Queer Latinidad: Dance, Sexuality, Politics.* Ann Arbor: University of Michigan Press, 2012.
Rodríguez, Juana María. *Queer Latinidad: Identity Practices, Discursive Spaces.* New York: New York University Press, 2003.
Rodríguez, Richard T. "Imagine a brown queer: inscribing sexuality in Chicano/a-Latino/a literary and cultural studies." *American Quarterly* 59.2 (2007): 493–501.

4 Spanglish in the classroom

A linguistic approach to code-switching in Latino/a literature

Jennifer Carolina Gómez Menjívar

"Broken English." "Lazy Spanish." Language attitudes with regard to code-switching abound among students, regardless of their personal or academic backgrounds. After many years of teaching Latino/a literature in the Midwest, I stopped discussing Spanglish as a special unit and instead made it the focal point of my courses on the subject. I realized that my former approach did little to dispel negative perceptions of Spanglish and that students left the class without a nuanced understanding of the processes that languages undergo when they come into contact. I decided that it was necessary to provide students with the linguistic tools they need to understand the rules and grammar of Spanglish from day one so that they could become better readers and critics of Latino/a narratives. I hoped that they would become better literary analysts and, of course, sociolinguists.

Finding a suitable approach to teach students about Spanglish can be a challenge at institutions where many of our colleagues believe that, "Spanglish is primarily the language of poor Hispanics, many barely literate in either language," as Roberto González Echevarría (1997), Sterling Professor of Hispanic and Comparative Literatures at Yale University, once stated. Colleagues who continue to profess such beliefs have not kept abreast of the linguistic research that provides evidence as to Spanglish speakers' fluency in both languages (Gonzáles 1999; Johnson 2000; Zentella 1997). It can also be challenging to teach about Spanglish in a teaching environment where students may have never encountered Spanglish, and it may be equally complex in a classroom full of students who code-switch on a daily basis. Linguistic theories provide scholars we work with and the students we teach with the tools they need to examine code-switching in Latino/a literature.

This essay draws on my pedagogical experience in Spanish- and English-language classrooms in the Midwest, first at a large research institution and then at a regional university. Insofar as readings are concerned, I compile linguistics readings into a course reader that my students use together with literary readings from Ilan Stavans's *The Norton Anthology of Latino Literature* (2011) throughout the semester. I was first drawn to study the interfaces of language and literature when I encountered the work of Roman Jakobson and Roland Barthes, among others, who saw in the vocabulary and methods of linguistics a master science for the analysis of narrative. And, although this perspective might not be fully embraced by literary critics across the board, it holds important weight for those of us who study Spanglish in Latino/a texts. In what follows, I discuss the theories and methods I have developed to teach native, heritage, and non-native speakers about the rich language deployed in Latino/a texts and the cultural heritage of Spanish in the United States.

Language attitudes

We hold attitudes toward language at all its levels, including spelling and punctuation, words, grammar, accent and pronunciation, dialects and languages, and even the speed at which we speak evokes reactions (Garret 2010: 2). Although these attitudes permeate our daily lives, speakers are often unaware of the covert and overt prestige systems across languages. Knowing this, I begin the course by conducting a linguistic experiment with my students. I design a matched-guise test (Lambert *et al.* 1960), which uses 30-second recordings of the same individual telling a story first in Spanglish and then in English or Spanish, depending on the language of the course. After listening to the first clip, students complete a five-level modified Likert survey that lists 16 personality attributes, including "attractive," "intelligent," "trustworthy," and "violent," which I have used in my language attitude research (Salmon and Gómez Menjívar 2014). In addition, the survey asks students to answer five qualitative questions with regard to their perception of the speaker's origin, educational attainment, and professional profile. We discuss the results and what they mean because, invariably, the "speaker" who uses the standardized language receives a better evaluation than the "speaker" who uses Spanglish. They are genuinely surprised to find that they have evaluated the same person differently according to the language they hear.

Standard language ideologies influence ideas about correct and incorrect forms of a language, and the devaluation of some varieties leads to a view of them as nonstandard or substandard (Milroy 2007; Preston 1996). After reading the Treaty of Guadalupe Hidalgo (1848) and the Treaty of Paris (1898), we discuss the place of Spanish in the United States. We observe the importance of language attitudes in the wake of these annexations, discussing the driving forces behind Latino/a writing in English and the Latino/a writing in Spanish. We read excerpts from John Seguín's *Personal Memoirs of John N. Seguín* (1858) and María Amparo Ruiz de Burton's *The Squatter and the Don* (1885) against the Southwestern newspaper poetry written in Spanish. This is a conversation that continues in our discussions of texts by Caribbean writers like Lola Rodríguez de Tió, Julia de Burgos, and Sotero Figueroa, who all wrote in Spanish in order to present a united front against the cultural and linguistic imperialism of English-language United States.

The readings give students a clear idea of the importance of the Spanish language to the newly annexed Latino/a populations and bring to light the language attitudes that color language debates today. In preparation for the group of readings we cover next, we discuss Peñalosa's (1980) list of attitudinal concerns among Latinos/as: attitudes toward one's own speech, other Latinos/as' attitudes toward one's speech, one's attitudes toward other Latinos/as' speech, Anglos' attitudes toward Latinos/as' speech, Anglos' attitudes toward one's speech, one's attitudes toward the speech of Anglos. I then assign two authors at opposite ends of the Latino/a English-Spanish language attitude spectrum: Richard Rodríguez's *Hunger of Memory* (1982) and, at the other end of the spectrum, Ariel Dorfman's *Heading South, Looking North* (1998). Nothing drives the point home better to them than these two very different perspectives.

Why is Spanglish so readily criticized? Why are its speakers considered less educated and less hardworking than monolinguals? I believe that the root cause of such presuppositions lies in the omission of linguistic data from general discourse. As Garrett (2010: 12) indicates, discourse around code-switching is set in terms of "laziness" or "impurity," which extends as much to the speakers as the language. When Mexican and Spanish territories were annexed to the United States, Latino/a writers were subjected to the pressures of proving their literary worthiness and yet remaining loyal to their culture. It wasn't until the mid-1950s that literature in Spanglish made its appearance. The two canonical texts we study—Américo Paredes's *With his Pistol in his Hands* (1958) and José Antonio Villareal's *Pocho* (1959)—provide examples of just how gradually authors incorporated code-switching into their works. No longer suffering from a cultural cringe, writers during this period came to believe that it was possible to code-switch in their writings without being a traitor to their heritage and experience. Code-switching here, as in many other classics of the period, marked a departure from monolingual writing to Spanglish as a marker and assertion of social identity. By the 1970s, pochismos and code-switching were being cultivated by brown writers, especially Chicanos and Puerto Ricans, as indicators of ethnic pride (Tovar 1974). Since it is in poetry and, in parti-cular, the spoken word that Spanglish really acquires a flavor that has a lasting effect on Latino/a letters, we finish the first part of the course by studying the Nuyorican Poets, the San Antonio Women Poets, and the Puerto Rican Young Lords. They leave us with the certainty that despite having its critics, Spanglish is, as Artze (2001) states, "here to stay."

Unpacking Spanglish

After completing the section on language attitudes, we are ready to unpack Spanglish. We begin by examining the goals of its speakers, and for this task, I have found Grosjean's (1982) diagram highly useful because it clearly demonstrates a speaker's awareness of his/her interlocutor's linguistic background when choosing whether or not to employ code-switching in conversation—an observation we can extend to writing. According to Grosjean, a bilingual individual speaking to a monolingual will use either their first (L1) or second language (L2) in their interaction.

However, a bilingual individual speaking to another bilingual individual has the option of using their L1 or L2 as a base. They will then code-switch (or not code-switch) within the language base they have chosen.

This part of the course works brilliantly with Julia Álvarez's *How the García Girls Lost Their Accents* (1991), which provides us with clear instances of the relationships

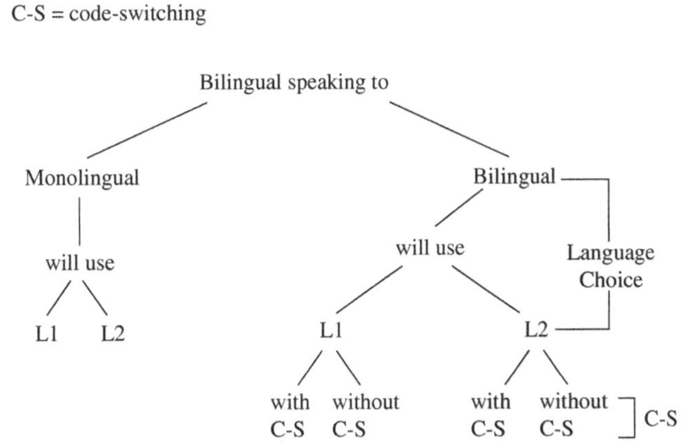

Figure 4.1 Grosjean's language choice and code switching diagram

that are created along these lines. I begin by asking my students to provide linguistic evidence from the texts that describe the relationships between four dyads: Mother-daughters, Father-daughters, Mother-Father, daughters-daughters in this witty novel. An example that often arouses their curiosity is that although her husband insisted that she speak to the girls in Spanish so that they wouldn't forget their native tongue, Laura García used English when it mattered most: "She spoke in English when she argued with them. And her English was a mishmash of idioms and sayings that showed she was 'green behind the ears,' as she called it" (1740). The rapport or lack thereof is evident in the linguistic choices the daughters make with relation to their mother: "her daughters never called her *Mom* except when they wanted her to feel how she had failed them in this country. She was a good enough Mami, fussing and scolding and giving advice, but a terrible girlfriend parent, a real failure of a Mom" (1740). That their relationship to their father is becoming increasingly distant is likewise revealed through linguistic choices: "Yoyo and her sisters were forgetting a lot of their Spanish, and their father's formal florid diction was hard to understand" (1744). There are many examples in this text and students genuinely enjoy discussing how family relationships are structured through language. It is also an opportune moment to discuss the implication of other linguistic concepts, such as conventional and conversational implicatures, on narrative voice.

Covering this terrain allows me to introduce the three types of code-switching identified by Poplack (1978, 1980): tag-switching, intersentential code-switching and intra-sentential code-switching. As an introduction to these terms, I ask them to circle the words in Spanish in the excerpt from *The García Girls* in order to better see their syntactic placement and identify the types of code-switching that occur in the text. For example: "So simple and yet so necessary, eh?" (1741) is an example of tag-switching; "With patience and calm, even a burro can climb a palm" (1742) is an example of intra-sentential code-switching; and, "'¡Ya, ya!' She waved them out her room at last" (1743) is an example of intersentential code-switching. We cover the strategies used by Latino/a authors in Spanglish texts: the use of lexical items that are easily understood by monolingual English speakers, Spanish followed by an English translation and calques (Torres 2007). Having established that these strategies have a direct implication on relationships between author-reader and reader-author, we are ready to pursue analyses of language and identity in key texts such as Luis Valdez's *Zoot Suit* (1978), Pat Mora's *Agua Santa/Holy Water* (1994) and Junot Díaz's *The Brief and Wondrous Life of Oscar Wao* (2007).

Close readings allow us to zero-in on the aesthetic values espoused by Latino/a authors who code-switch in their texts. Take, for example, this passage from Gloria Anzaldúa's *Borderlands/La Frontera* (1987):

> *Mi papá se murió de un* heart attack *dejando a mamá* pregnant *y con ocho huercos*, with eight kids and one on the way. *Yo fui la mayor, tenía diez años.* The next year the drought continued *y el ganado* got hoof and mouth. *Se cayeron* in droves *en las pastas y el* brushland, *panzas blancas* ballooning to the skies.
>
> (1499)

Being able to see the Spanish in italics allows them to quickly perceive the lexical and syntactic choices that Anzaldúa makes in her text. For instance, while "kids" is obviously a lexical option available, Anzaldúa's use of "huercos" not only conveys her mother's voice and dialect, but also sounds graver than most Southwestern English terms or other Spanish terms, like "chicos," "hijos," or "niños." The description of the dying cows has the same effect, for "panzas" sounds much bigger and grotesque than "bellies," and "ballooning" gives us a more horrific image than the more awkward phrase, "montando en globo," in standard Spanish. Such words are more than just images, they are the bedrock of the text's prosody and underlying aesthetics.

An important piece of the puzzle to remember, I tell my students, is that the acoustics of English and Spanish are very different. Working in groups they devise a list of the phonetic characteristics that make both languages unique, often pointing to the *th* sounds that exist in English but aren't found in Spanish, or the *ñ* that doesn't exist in English. After going over the types of syllables permitted by the two languages (Colina 2012), we cover accent and stress in Spanish (Hualde 2012). Since most of them are only familiar with accents as a feature of romance languages, I often explain this feature of language with acoustic analogies. Stress is the part of a word in any language that can literally be heard louder than the unaccented syllables, I tell them, and linguists can actually measure the difference in decibels. I put this to the test by asking a volunteer to choose a multisyllabic word in English. I ask the students to place their hands about an inch over their desks and say the word, hitting the desk when it "feels right to do so." A native speaker of a language will intuitively know where the stress of a word should be and will be unable to hit the desk on any other syllable.

I want my students to understand that working with the acoustic features of two languages is an art. Writers who work with both languages are fully aware of the aesthetics of sound and whether they use a Spanish or English base in their texts, they weave a rich tapestry with the features of the two languages they combine. Before we look for this skill in Latino/a lit, we discuss pitch, a prosodic element that accounts for the highness or lowness of a tone. While it is common knowledge that men and women's voices differ in pitch after puberty, with women's voices being typically higher than men's voices, it is less commonly known that languages differ in pitch distinctions. When we surrender to the idea that those pitch distinctions have linguistically meaningful purposes, we are in the right position to study the contours and tones of Gianna Braschi's *Yo-Yo Boing* (1998) and "Pelos en la Lengua" (2000). Following O'Rourke, we draw conclusions about the role that intonation plays with respect to attitudes and feelings expressed in the text. I ask my students to underline the Spanish in Braschi's bilingual manifesto so that when it is read out loud, they are better able to hear the differences between the two languages:

> El bilinguismo es una estética bound to double business. O, 'tis most sweet when in one line two crafts directly meet. To be and not to be. Habla con la boca llena and from both sides of the mouth. Está con Dios y con el Diablo. Con el punto y con la coma. Es un purgatorio, un signo grammatical intermedio, entre heaven and earth, un semicolon entre la independencia y la estadidad, un estado libre asociado, un maramacho multicultural.
>
> (1977)

The rise and fall of the voice/s in Spanish and English in both of Braschi's texts provide us with a wealth of information that can be used to examine the effects created by the falling and rising patterns we literally *feel* upon hearing the utterances in Spanish or

English. As we progress through our study of aesthetics and prosody with Mariposa María Teresa Fernández's "Poem for My Grifa-Rican Sistah or Broken Ends Broken Promises" (2001), students develop an appreciation for Spanglish as a strategic narrative technique with implications for the author, narrator, and audience.

If it is not yet clear to my students that we are engaging in an increasingly technical understanding of Spanglish and code-switching, it certainly becomes clear when we tie loose ends by going over the grammatical restrictions of Spanglish. Code-switching is a complex strategy that is part of a larger expressive repertoire, instead of a weakness or evidence that the individual lacks command of one or both languages (Zentella 1981). According to Rothman and Bell (2005: 520), the structure of Spanglish can essentially be divided into three subdivisions:

1   the adaptation of lexical units or phrasal constituents from one language into the other on a phonological, morphological, and/or morphophonological level;
2   the adaptation of some lexical elements or phrasal constituents from one language into another semantically;
3   the phenomenon of code-switching or a rule-governed amalgamation of the two languages at the level of syntax.

In order to work with the first of these three points, I provide them with excerpts from the Lexicon in Ilan Stavans's *Spanglish: The Making of a New American Language* before putting them in small groups. I give them a list of ten nouns or ten verbs from among those they have studied the night before and set them the task of devising the grammatical rules that underlie the making of the Spanglish lexicon. This allows students to understand that because the final coda position in a Spanish word is almost exclusively a vowel, nouns like troca, which is derived from "truck" must undergo "phonological adaptations." Or why verbs in Spanglish, such as lonchar, which is derived from "to have lunch" must adopt the infinitival morpheme -ar as a rule when they undergo "morphological adaptations."

Calques abound in English and too often, a monolingual speaker is unaware of the fact. Thus, I begin my discussion of the second point by asking students to guess the origin of common words like Milky Way (Latin), flea market (French), cookie (Dutch) and brainwashing (Chinese). Who knew English speakers devised direct translations from the original language, turning these words into the words of ordinary speech?! The idea is quite out of this world for my students, who have seldom considered the origins of their lexicon with a critical eye. But it is the power of the "tropicalized English," as Frances Aparicio (2007) calls it, that we work with when we examine Ana Castillo's *So Far from God* (1993), Francisco Goldman's *Ordinary Seaman* (1997) and Susana Chávez Silverman's *Killer Crónicas: Bilingual Memories* (2004). Throughout the analyses of these works, we stress the power of doubling in lexical and syntactic choices that place characters and their speech in multiple worlds and realities at once.

The third point discussed by Rothman and Bell allows us to explore grammaticality in Spanglish. Most of my students in the Midwest don't have intuitions about Spanglish, but they often know people in their social networks who certainly do. I create a grammaticality judgment task on Survey Monkey that consists of five questions and asks students whether they would say or not say the sentence listed. In order to eliminate judgments based on prescriptivism, there is a space that allows the participant to re-write the phrase as they would say it. I ask my students to distribute it widely to Spanish-English speakers using Facebook and Twitter and the student who finds the greatest number of participants over the period of two weeks, gets a prize, usually a full copy of one of the Spanglish texts we have studied in class up to that point.

Participants who hold prescriptivist, anti-Spanglish beliefs will indicate that they would not say any of the phrases. We do not examine those responses further. Instead, we focus on the participants who rephrased sentences in "correct" Spanglish. These are the participants whose intuitions about Spanish generally abide by the Free Morpheme Constraint and the Equivalence Constraint first discussed by Sankoff and Poplack (1981). When the results are in, we discuss which sentences were deemed grammatical and ungrammatical by the participants, as well as the alternatives they provided.

I like Montes-Alcalá's (2009) straightforward explanation of the Free Morpheme Constraint, which bans switches within words, and the Equivalence Constraint, which states that both parts in a switch must be grammatical in the languages involved (104). There are more theories about the grammatical constraints of Spanish and ways to account for other instances of code-switching, but at this level, my students only need to know that there is a clear understanding among linguists that code-switching is rule-governed and that speakers of Spanglish show a virtually unanimous consensus when asked to provide intuitions about what is grammatical and what is ungrammatical in Spanglish.

---

1. *Estaba watching TV cuando sonó el teléfono.*

   I would say this.
   I would not say this. Instead, I would say _____.

2. *Stephanie está runiendo with Sonia.*

   I would say this.
   I would not say this. Instead, I would say _____.

3. *I wanted to go to the store pero mi Mom me dijo que I had to wash the dishes.*

   I would say this.
   I would not say this. Instead, I would say _____.

4. *I gave le un libro.*

   I would say this.
   I would not say this. Instead, I would say _____.

5. *Yo siempre pensé that tú were el más guapo de todos.*

   I would say this.
   I would not say this. Instead, I would say _____.

Figure 4.2 Sample Spanglish grammaticality judgment test

Spanglish speakers

I like to dedicate the last weeks of the course to the people that matter—the writers and speakers of Spanglish. I start by covering what we already know: that code-switching has discursive functions, implications for identity construction, and is a reflection of the social networks in which bilingual individuals participate (Auer 2013; Gardner-Chloros 2012; Gumperz 1982). Specifically, Spanglish has stood the test of time to serve as a marker for group membership and solidarity (Rothman and Bell 2005; Gonzáles 1999; Toribio 2002). When we examine its covert and overt prestige in the community, it is clear from this growing body of research that Spanglish is quite often a conscious choice on the part of speakers, and hence, writers. These linguistic findings allow us, students and critics of Latino/a literature, to recognize Spanglish as a strategy to mark quotations, give emphasis to ideas, reiterate and elaborate, and realign the roles of author, narrator, and audience, among other communicative intentions.

Code-switching, as research in linguistics makes clear, is an indicator of bilingual proficiency. And, thanks to psycholinguistics, there is evidence that cognitive mechanisms and neuro-anatomical structures are involved in the simultaneous control of two languages. Although the nature of the course does not allow us to delve too deeply into psycholinguistics, I point out that these scientific findings are tools that provide a unique window into bilingual cognition. Underlying any print, digital or oral Latino/a narrative is a complex psychological and neurological process that is now beginning to be studied in experiments using neurological imaging and eye movement data (Dussias 2003; Kutas, Moreno, and Wicha 2012). The take-away lesson here is that there is not just a political imperative for authors who use Spanglish, but also an *intellectual* driving force that leads them to use this as a form of expression. A text like Gustavo Pérez Firmat's "Bilingual Blues" (1995), for instance, reveals the linguistic prowess of the bilingual poet. Deploying Spanglish as an aesthetic tool ultimately leads him to achieve "multilingual wordsmithing" in his poetry:

> ... psycho soy, cantando voy: contradicciones, You say tomato, I say tu madre; You say potato, I say Pototo. Let's call the hole un hueco, the thing a cosa, and if the cosa goes into the hueco, consider yourself en casa, consider yourself part of the family
>
> ... Soy un ajiaco de
>
> un potaje de paradojas: a little square from Rubik's Cuba que nadie nunca acoplará. (Cha-cha-cha´.)

I seek to instill in my students appreciation for the literary and linguistic aspects of pieces like these, but above all, I provide them with a body of evidence to counter the declarations that Spanglish is indicative of language deterioration. I see the final weeks of my course as an opportunity to revisit those language attitudes (which are always attitudes toward the individuals who speak a given linguistic variety) that my students had when they began the course. By turning my classroom into an intellectual space where Spanglish can be unpacked and dismantled in all its technical glory, I make my classroom a space of resistance against linguistic prescriptivism and linguistic imperialism.

As I write this in 2014, the number of Spanglish intellectuals, speakers, and writers is growing across the South and the Southeast at an exponential rate. The most recent census data available shows a demographic shift away from California, the Southwest and Northeast to states like Arkansas and West Virginia, which have not been traditionally associated with Latino/a experience. This migratory flow has critical implications for the growth of Spanish and hence, Spanglish: "In 2010, 20.6 million Hispanics lived in the West, 18.2 million lived in the South, 7 million lived in the Northeast and 4.7 million lived in the Midwest" (Passel, Cohn, and López 2011). South Carolina, the state with the most rapid growth between 2000 and 2010, saw a 148 percent growth in the Latino/a population. The figures in descending order were 145 percent in Alabama, 134 percent in Tennessee, and 122 percent in Kentucky (Passel, Cohn, and López 2011). There is no doubt that Latinos/as and Spanglish are transforming counties across the South and with time, we will hear more about Spanglish and Latino/a culture in places that dominant discourses have traditionally coded as white spaces—as in the case of Latinos in Appalachia (NPR 2014).

The South and the Southeast is set to become the home of a new generation of Spanglish intellectual activity. Importantly, these regions will soon come to grapple with questions of language policy and its implementation in public schools and other institutions. Generations of speakers of Spanglish stand to lose or gain from a linguistically informed perspective of Spanglish. And lest we forget, there is an emerging body of literature—linguistic and literary—that takes into account the Latino/a experience in the South, most notably represented by Marcos McPeek Villatoro, whose Salvadoran protagonist, Romilia Chacón, a Salvadoran detective from Atlanta living in Tennessee is a magnificent character who negotiates the cultural and linguistic complexities of Latino experience in the New Latino South.

One thing is clear—using linguistic tools to examine Spanglish in the classroom gives us a solid bedrock of research on which to examine, evaluate, and critically assess the complexities of the language and its speakers. And, they have the power to change language attitudes, held by monolingual and bilingual speakers alike, about Spanglish.

Resources for teaching Spanglish in the classroom

Aluma-Cazorla, Andrés. "The gay immigrant and the use of Spanglish in Ángel Losada's *No quiero quedarme sola y vacía*: a linguistic transgression or a struggle to assimilate in the late capitalist city." *Hispania: A Journal Devoted to the Teaching of Spanish and Portuguese* 97.3 (2014): 364–65.

Casielles-Suárez, Eugenia. "Radical code-switching in *The Brief Wondrous Life of Oscar Wao*." *Bulletin of Hispanic Studies* 90.4 (2013): 475–87.

Hernández-Chávez, Eduardo, Andrew Cohen and Anthony Beltramo. *El languAge de los Chicanos: Regional and Social Characteristics of Language Used by Mexican Americans*. Arlington: Center for Applied Linguistics, 1975.

Keller, Garry D. "The literary stratagems available to the bilingual Chicano writer." In *The Identification and Analysis of Chicano Literature*. Ed. Francisco Jiminez. New York: Bilingual/Bilingüe, 1979, pp. 263–316.

Klee, Carol A. and Andrew Lynch. "El contacto del español con el inglés en Los Estados Unidos." *El español en contacto con otras lenguas*. Washington DC: Georgetown University Press, 2009, pp. 193–262.

Montes-Alcalá, Cecilia. "Code-switching in US Latino novels." *Language Mixing and Code-Switching in Writing: Approaches to Mixed-Language Written Discourse*. Mark Sebba, Shahrzad Mahootian, and Carla Jonsson, Eds. London: Routledge, 2012, pp. 68–88.

Montrul, Silvina. "El español en los Estados Unidos." *El bilingüismo en el mundo hispanohablante.* Malden, MA: Wiley-Blackwell, 2013, pp. 104–29.

Moyna, María Irene. "Back at the Rancho: language maintenance and shift among Spanish speakers in post-annexation California (1848–1900)." *Revista Internacional de Lingüística Iberoamericana* 7.2 (2009): 165–84.

Poplack, Shana. "Sometimes I'll start a sentence in English y termino en español: Toward a typology of code-switching." *Linguistics* 18.7–8 (1980): 581–618.

Postma, Regan. "'¿Por qué leemos esto en la clase de español?': The politics of teaching literature in Spanglish." *Hispania: A Journal Devoted to the Teaching of Spanish and Portuguese* 96.3 (2013): 442–43.

Roca, Ana and John M. Lipski, Eds. *Spanish in the United States: Linguistic Contact and Diversity.* Berlin: Mouton, 1993.

Rudin, Ernst. *Tender accents of Sound: Spanish in the Chicano novel in English.* Tempe: Bilingual Press, 1996.

Sánchez-Muñoz, Ana. "Who Soy Yo? The creative use of 'Spanglish' to express a hybrid identity in Chicana/o heritage language learners of Spanish." *Hispania: A Journal Devoted to the Teaching of Spanish and Portuguese* 96.3 (2013): 440–41.

Silva-Corvalán, Carmen. *Language Contact and Change. Spanish in Los Angeles.* Oxford: Oxford University Press, 1994.

Zentella, Ana Celia. *Growing up Bilingual: Puerto Rican Children in New York.* Maiden, Massachusetts: Blackwell, 1997.

5 Crisscrossed languages

Heather Alumbaugh

crisscross, *v.*
1. trans. ... to cross repeatedly.
2. intr. To intersect or cross repeatedly. ("crisscross")

Why does an author write in crisscrossed languages? What does the resulting text look like? What does the text demand of the writer? Of the reader? The multiple openings of Sandra Cisneros's novel *Caramelo* (2002) crystallize the significance of crisscrossed languages in the fiction of Julia Alvarez, Sandra Cisneros, and Cristina García. On the first page of the novel, Cisneros writes the book's dedication in untranslated Spanish: "*Para ti, Papá.*" Next, she presents the dual epigraphs first in Spanish, "*Cuéntame algo, aunque sea una mentira,*" and then in translated English on a separate page, "Tell me a story, even if it's a lie." Finally, Cisneros's authorial disclaimer blatantly crisscrosses, starting with the title, "DISCLAIMER, OR I DON'T WANT HER, YOU CAN HAVE HER, SHE'S TOO *HOCICONA* FOR ME." These specific creative intersections of Spanish and English more largely represent two important aspects of Latina writing: first, they illuminate the conceptual and formal mastery that Latina authors exhibit in order to create narrative discourses that cross "repeatedly." Second, they underscore the complex interpretive work that crisscrossed texts ask of the reader. Because these texts include narrators who are to varying degrees "bigamists of language" and anxiously yet joyfully cross multiple boundaries, they demand a significant skill set from authors and readers alike (Dorfman 2003: 33–34).

Our job as educators is to help students gain the critical ability to interrogate texts on their own terms. One way to teach the crisscrossed discourses in Julia Alvarez's *How the García Girls Lost Their Accents* (2010), Sandra Cisneros's *Caramelo* (2002), and Cristina García's *Dreaming in Cuban* (1992) is to focus on these authors' surprisingly similar treatments of **translation**. Through their uses of translation in all of its multiple forms, they construct the vibrant and repeated intersections of two or more languages, cultures, and histories that comprise their respective novels. Translation is how each author embraces what Jacqueline Stefanko (1996) calls "the power of writing as boundary crossing" (51). In order to grasp *what* these three Latina authors translate/ crisscross in their fictions, we need to teach students to evaluate *how* they do so.

To specify, Alvarez, Cisneros, and García utilize the formal strategies of multiple narrative voices and languages and the conceptual tools of characterization and familial/historical representations to accomplish linguistic, cultural, and historical translations in their works of fiction. Their translations—in other words, their authorial representations of crisscrossed languages and cultures—communicate that "Latinos are a byproduct of the age of empire: transplanted, uprooted, in a constant process of reinvention" (Stavans: lxiv). Linguistically, they use multiple voices and written translations back and forth between Spanish and English; culturally, they transmit, uncover, and reinvent the various myths, practices, and products of their respective Dominican/Dominican American, Mexican/Mexican American/Chicano, and Cuban/Cuban American heritages; and historically, they interrogate and communicate the complex histories of Latino **exile**, **emigration**, and **migration** to, from, and within the United States. These authors employ acts of translation in order to render intelligible to their audiences—to both non-Latino and Latino readers alike—their idiosyncratic fictive worlds. As translation itself occurs precisely because there is a lack of knowledge that the translator attempts to remedy, investigating this topic is an act of knowledge building for writers, students, and educators alike.

I suggest that an effective way to teach the larger topic of crisscrossed languages/translation is to break it up into formal and conceptual subtopics: narrative voice, narrative language, adolescent female character, and familial history linked to national/exilic/migration history. In this way, students can grapple with each of the concepts independently before they apply them to the texts. Additionally, instructors can pick and choose what they need given the ability and analytical maturity of their students. For instance, if teaching to high school students, instructors can focus on one subtopic and one text; if teaching to community college students, instructors can elect a few of the subcategories, primary texts, and secondary texts; and if teaching a semester-long course, instructors can adapt the model syllabus I provide at the end.

Translation

Students need to interrogate what it means "to translate" in order to analyze crisscrossed languages. Most academic institutions have access to the *Oxford English Dictionary Online*. When possible, I ask my students to search for the verb "to translate" instead of the noun "translation" as the verb is where the grammatical action takes place. Working with this source, students will discover that translation means much more than "to turn from one language to another." Indeed, the verb "to translate" can also mean "to use in a *metaphorical … *sense"; "to *interpret, explain*"; "to *transform, alter*"; and "to *transport with the strength of feeling*" ("translate", emphasis mine). Alvarez, Cisneros, and García all creatively use the multiple definitions of "to translate" in their works. Their respective narrative discourses, characters, and plots are all attuned to the Latin root of the prefix "trans" that means literally "across, through, over, to or on the other side of" ("trans"). Providing students with a nuanced understanding of the multiple meanings of translation will enable both bilingual *and* monolingual students to examine critically these authors' translations.

Instructors of more advanced students may want to include a larger context on contemporary translation theory. An accessible starting point is Martha Cutter's *Lost and Found in Translation* (2005) that analyzes the metafictional use of "translation as trope" in contemporary Ethnic American writing and focuses on translations in ethnic fiction that are not only "represented lexically or linguistically" but also "thematically" (5). She asserts, and I agree, that translation as trope operates as a "metaphorical construct utilized to constellate a series of questions about ethnic identities, language practices, and the way tongues from other cultures can (or cannot) be preserved within the linguistic domain of the English language" (5). Cutter's introduction usefully evaluates contemporary translation theories. She underscores in particular the *creative act* in translation, since translation is "not a *literal* transfer of meaning" (16). Like André Lefevere and many other translation theorists, Cutter focuses on theories of translation that understand it as a process of "finding metaphors," "interpretation," and co-authorship (16–17). An additional way to incorporate current translation scholarship is to weave some of the wonderful essays from the anthology *Nation, Language, and the Ethics of Translation* edited by Sandra Bermann and Michael Wood throughout each section of the syllabus (see in particular the selections by Edward Said, Lynn Visson, Gayatri Chakravorty Spivak, Henry Staten, and Sandra Bermann).

Instructors who have more time may want to include a segment on **Malinche**—the Amerindian female slave who was both Cortés's translator and mistress—as she inaugurated the concept of the ethnic female translator in the new world. Although she is specific to Mexican, Mexican American, and Chicano/a cultural histories, her historical reception and reconsideration reveal the importance of women as translators of language and culture and the power that female translators can wield as survivors and creators. Malinche has been the subject of multiple and contradictory interpretations, but all of them focus on her role as a female translator: she has been vilified as a political and cultural traitor to her people (which is why "malinchismo" and "malinchista" are pejoratives), Octavio Paz linguistically sexualizes her and figures his understanding of Mexican cultural inferiority and machismo as her sons, and Chicana writers and theorists have reinterpreted her through the lenses of both post-colonialism and feminism.

Another possible entrée is to have students investigate the authors' discussions of translation. All three writers have readily accessible interviews and official author websites. As an example, Cristina García commented in a 2007 interview about the complicated issue of authorial translations of "minority" languages and cultures as Americans' "literary appetite[s]" continue to increase for "from-the-margins literature":

> Especially with first novels, there is a sense of having to explain, translate, or emphasize the more colorful or folkloric aspects of one's culture to make it palatable to a mainstream audience … You have to strike a balance that incorporates culture but not in this weird, anthropological way.
>
> (quoted in Irizarry 2007: 190)

Here, García helps instructors and students alike ask productive questions regarding translation: How do Latina authors "represent [their] own writing and culture on [their] own terms" without, as García says, "overexplaining it to imaginary audiences"? (191). How do Latina authors perform the crucial yet daunting creative balancing acts that comprise their fictions?

Formal features: narrative discourse

García's comments provide an elegant segue into an analysis of *how* these authors crisscross, of how they translate what they do. Through surprisingly similar formal maneuvers, Alvarez, Cisneros, and García all deftly "strike a balance" between "amplifying a reader's understanding" of their respective Latino/a linguistic and cultural heritages while not over-translating them (Irizarry 191). While wary of over-translation, the fact remains that these authors fashion texts that have multiple audiences. The diverse linguistic and cultural landscapes that populate the contemporary U.S. reading public ensure that their readers—Latino and non-Latino, monolingual or multilingual, native born or immigrant alike—will most likely not share their characters' same experiences. One of the most obvious ways these authors render crisscrossed languages, cultures, and histories intelligible is through their specific constructions of *narrative discourse*.

Multiple narrative voices

H. Porter Abbott's treatment of narrative discourse in *The Cambridge Introduction to Narrative* (2008) offers an approachable starting point for students of multiple levels. He writes, "narrative is the representation of events, consisting of *story* and *narrative discourse*; **story** is an *event* or sequence of events (the *action*); and narrative discourse is those events as represented" (19). Abbot continues, "we never see a story directly, but instead always pick it up *through* the narrative discourse. The story is always mediated—by a voice, a style of writing ... " (20). Abbott illuminates both the paradoxical distinction between and interdependence of narrative event and representation; providing students with this theoretical apparatus equips them to be more sophisticated close readers. I propose that instructors emphasize two similarities in *narrative discourse* that Alvarez, Cisneros, and García employ in their novels: their respective constructions of multiple narrative voices (who tell the story) and of multiple narrative languages (that tell the story). I also suggest that we lead our students to investigate the novels' formal elements as authorial acts of translation. By directing students to the definitions of translation as transportation, transformation, and interpretation, we can help them see how Alvarez, Cisneros, and García create fictive worlds that carry across from history to fiction to audience and back the idiosyncratic experiences of Latina women in the United States. In the process of these translations, the writers produce what Jaqueline Stefanko deftly calls "new ways of telling" (50).

Many critics have noted Alvarez's employment of a "complex of narrators" (Barak 1998: 163), Cisneros's creation of co-narrators Lala and her grandmother Soledad (Alumbaugh 2010: 59), and García's "metafictional use of multiple narrators" (Payant 2001: 165), but none have analyzed together the authors' constructions of multiple narrative voices in these particular novels. A comparative analysis of narrative discourse, then, can become our students' task. When I teach texts with multiple narrators, I ask students to keep what I call a Narrative Discourse Map, in which they document the title of each chapter, who narrates the chapter, a brief summary of it, and the setting(s) (where applicable). This device enables students to take *visual* control of a surplus of narrative information. The maps can be assigned as guided reading journals, can be written on parts or all of the novels, and can be done individually, in groups, or as a whole class.

Alvarez's first novel offers an approachable yet challenging opportunity for student investigations of multiple narrative voices. Although many students identify with the angst of maturing from adolescence to adulthood that the García girls experience or with having immigrant parents, they often struggle with the complexity of Alvarez's narrative structure and voice. Alvarez uses reverse chronological narration in her three-part novel: it begins in 1989 and ends in 1956. Omniscient and limited third-person narrations, moments of free indirect discourse, and first-person narrations (both singular and plural) crisscross in all three parts and at times within chapters. As the daughter Yolanda emerges as the central narrative voice, the novel nevertheless relies on multiple voices to reveal the García family members' exile from the Dominican Republic (because of the father's part in a failed plot to overthrow Trujillo), their various acculturations to the United States, and their migrations back and forth between the two.

Table 5.1 gives an example of a Narrative Discourse Map of the first and last chapters of Part I (1989–1972) of Alvarez's novel. This type of written and visual annotation leads students to more complex analysis about an individual text's multiple narrative voices, when and why individual characters speak, how texts are similar, and how and why texts differ.

Instructors can also stress the remarkable similarities and crucial differences between Alvarez's and García's use of multiple narrative voices. *Dreaming in Cuban* revolves primarily around three generations of Cuban women: Celia (grandmother), Lourdes and Felicia (daughters), and Pilar (granddaughter). Like Alvarez, García composes a crisscross of third- and first-person narrations to communicate to her readers a story of family exile; her first-person narrations also include letters written by one of the primary characters, Celia. As in Alvarez's first novel, a young female first-person narrator, here Pilar, emerges as one of the text's central narrative voices, and she narrates the majority of the first-person sections that are not Celia's letters. The female family members all

Table 5.1 Narrative Discourse Map of Part I (1989–1972) of Alvarez's *How the García Girls Lost Their Accents*

PART I: 1989–1972	
Chapter Title: "Antojos"	
Narrator(s)	Vacillates between omniscient and third person limited narrative perspectives (the later of Yolanda) and includes moments of free indirect discourse (11).
Summary	Recounts Yolanda's return to the Dominican Republic after a five-year period; she has lost her Spanish (she does not know what *"antojo"* means) and craves a "home."
	Demonstrates, through Yolanda's simultaneous freedom to go on a car trip unchaperoned and her desire for *guyaba* (guava), that her exile to the United States has given her comparative gender freedom to that of her Dominican female cousins yet burdens her with a desire for a "home" and less "turbulent life" (11).
	Sets up a primary contradiction: Yolanda both yearns for what she perceives to be missing yet is "just fine on her own" (11).
Where/When	Dominican Republic, presumably 1989 (28 years after Trujillo's assassination), in both the extended family's compound and the countryside as Yolanda makes her way to the beach.
Chapter Title: "The Rudy Elmenhurst Story"	
Narrator(s)	Starts with first person plural "we" but quickly reveals Yolanda as the first person narrator; a retrospective narrative, which allows Yolanda to critique the events she records from a later, and presumably more mature, perspective (98).
Summary	Recounts how Yolanda's immigrant status affected her feelings of linguistic, cultural, and *sexual* belonging: "For the hundredth time, I cursed my immigrant origins" (94).
	Repeated commentary about how she lacked the language to express herself, both literally and figuratively, and was subject to "an immigrant's failing, literalism" (89).
Where/When	Yolanda's second year of a co-educational college somewhere in the northeastern United States, sometime in the 1970s.

Source: Alvarez, J. *How the García Girls Lost Their Accents.* Chapel Hill, NC: Algonquin Books, 2010.

experience Cuba's revolution in, at times, radically different ways: Celia embraces the revolution's potentials, Lourdes flees in exile with her husband and daughter to the United States, Felicia stays in Cuba but experiences no meaningful connection to the new government or to the men who abuse her, and Pilar feels caught between her desire for home and her anger at her family's exile. Despite their differences, each woman considers/"dreams" of Cuba in surprisingly similar terms: as a historical force of separation between and return to self and family.

One of the differences between the two novels exists *not* in the texts' use of multiple narrative voices, but rather in *what* those voices translate. To help students draw out the texts' differences, instructors can guide them to both books' inclusion of first-person narrations told by a knowledgeable, nonfamily member, which in Alvarez is Chucha and in García is Herminia Delgado. Chucha's and Herminia's narrations are both manageable in length but conceptually rich, which make them particularly useful for student interpretation. These perspectives provide outside yet intimate perspectives on the impact of major historical tides on the families in each book. The books differ, however, in the experiences these "external" voices carry across to the reader: while Chucha's voice explains to readers the exilic condition, Herminia's voice reveals the insights of a person who remained in a country from which so many have fled.

In Alvarez's novel, the Haitian female servant Chucha—who was saved by the family patriarch and girls' grandfather Papito during the 1937 Dominican state-sponsored massacre of Haitians—completes the lyrical chapter entitled "The Blood of Conquistadores" that opens Part III (1960–1956). The chapter uses a crisscross of third-person and multiple first-person narrations, so why does Alvarez end with Chucha's first-person musings? One clue is in the events the chapter documents. Taking place mostly on a single, devastating day in 1960 at the family compound in the Dominican Republic, the chapter is a two-part, elegiac, suspenseful, and not overly didactic evocation of the days leading up to the family's exile to the United States. Part I of the chapter opens with the arrival of the *guardias* and Carlos's (Papi's) escape to one of the compound's constructed safe spaces; Part II ends with Chucha's voice. In between, Alvarez crafts a frenzy of vivid and heartbreaking events to conjure those crucial days in the life of the García family. Among the most poignant events in Part I is Yoyo's memory of being beaten by her parents "very hard with a belt in the bathroom, with the shower on so no one could hear her screams" after telling a neighbor "about Papi having a gun" (198). Alvarez uses this memory to transport diverse readers to the realities of a totalitarian regime in which the violence of the state has infiltrated the seemingly sacrosanct space of the family. Because of the text's chronological structure and multiple voices, we already know two important plot details when Chucha's voice takes over at the end of the chapter: Chucha "left [her] country too and never went back" (221) and the girls will be exiled to "a bewitched and unsafe place where they must now make their lives" (223). Students at this point should have the analytical ability to grasp the connections that Alvarez draws between all of the exiled women in the text. Through a combination of plot and narrative voice, Alvarez deftly transports/translates a reality that many readers have not experienced directly: the violence of forced exile.

Herminia's narration appears towards the end of García's novel in a chapter entitled "God's Will" that includes not only her first-person narration, but also that of Ivanito, Felicia's son. Told in 1980 after Felicia's ordination as a *santera* and her descent into madness and death (caused by the syphilis she contracts from her violent first husband), Herminia's short and impactful narration touches on many aspects of post-revolutionary Cuba. It is important to note that like Chucha, Herminia is of African descent and practices *santería*. About Cuban race relations she reveals, "For many years, nobody spoke of the problem between blacks and whites … Things have gotten better, that much I can say" (184–85); about gender relations she exposes, "the men are still in charge. Fixing that is going to take a lot longer than twenty years" (185). Her most poignant commentaries are about Felicia, whom she figures as loving, loyal, stubborn, and color blind: "Felicia is the only person I've known who didn't see color" (184). Her insights about both Celia and Felicia highlight their polarizing fanaticisms: "Celia revered El Líder and wanted Felicia to give herself entirely to the revolution, believing that this alone would save her daughter. But Felicia would not be dissuaded from the *orishas*. She had a true vocation to the supernatural" (186). Herminia's narration functions as a form of lucid translation that explains and interprets; as such, it operates as a model for student analysis and interpretation. It appears towards the end of a novel that encompasses two national settings, multiple decades, diverse characters, and major historical events including pre- and post-revolutionary Cuba, the Cuban revolution, Cuban exiles, the Cuban missile crisis, the advent of the New York punk scene, and the Mariel boatlifts. Despite the novel's complicated historical context (or perhaps because of it), García writes Herminia's narration in an accessible and lucid prose style, with a sprinkling of untranslated Spanish that does not diminish the section's readability. Both Herminia's insights and the brevity and directness of her sentences provide students with a snapshot of Cuba post-revolution and of the del Pino family members who remain.

Instructors can use Cisneros's *Caramelo* (2002) to provide students with a contrast to Alvarez's and García's use of narrative voice. *Caramelo* is told primarily from a first-person narrator, Lala, who additionally co-narrates with her grandmother and (less obviously) the author as narrative framer. The text covers multiple generations of the Reyes clan, and the occasion of the text's narration is an act of translation as transportation: Lala tells Soledad's story in order to help her grandmother's ghost "cross over." Cisneros's novel includes a profusion of linguistic and cultural translations, and the narrative structure itself is littered with translations: the length, the footnotes, the transliterations, the multiple openings, the epilogue all attempt to redress the absence of knowledge that Cisneros's readers most likely have about multiple aspects of Mexican, Mexican American, and Chicano/a culture and history. I have written extensively elsewhere about Cisneros's treatment of narrative voice in *Caramelo*, and I provide the bibliographic information at this chapter's end for instructors' consultation. Still, I offer this suggestion here for students' comparative analysis: Part II of the novel, "When I Was Dirt," includes the text's most sustained use of co-narration, and its opening chapters are particularly concerned with how to tell readers "Just enough, but not too much" (92).

Crisscrossed languages

Each author writes in the crisscrossed languages of Spanish and English; consequently, their texts craft what Ariel Dorfman calls "the many intermediate wonderful full-fledged **patois** that prosper in the spaces in between established linguistic systems" (34). The novels' crisscrossed languages most obviously represent their topical and structural affiliations with the art and practice of translation. In a 1997 interview, Alvarez succinctly articulates the artistic necessity of writing in both languages: "I'm a hyphenated person interested in the music that comes out of the language that hears both languages. My stories come out of being in worlds that sometimes clash and sometimes combine" (qtd. in Suárez 2005: 120). Each text's particular bilingual language evokes the "clash" and possible "combi[nation]" of cultures of its respective fictive world and "represents a culturally specific Latinidad" (Torres 2007: 79). I provide here an overview of how to bring multilingual *and* monolingual students through a rigorous analysis of each text's language use; in the sample syllabus, I offer additional readings that could appeal to instructors of advanced students.

Alvarez and García translate their written Spanish into English more frequently than Cisneros. Two examples from *How the García Girls Lost Their Accents* demonstrate how Alvarez uses moments of translated Spanish to represent the girls' simultaneous removal from and return to their culture and language of origin and to invite different readers in to her novel. The first example appears in "*Antojos*" in an exchange between the Americanized Yolanda and her Dominican aunts:

> "Any little *antojo,* you must tell us!" Tía Carmen agrees.
> "What's an *antojo?*" Yolanda asks.
> See! Her aunts are right. After so many years away, she is losing her Spanish.
> "Actually it's not an easy word to explain … An *antojo* is like a craving for something you eat."
>
> (8)

Anyone who has a competent mastery of Spanish—especially someone like Yolanda whose first language is and was for many years Spanish—would know what *antojo* means. So why does Alvarez translate the word? Alvarez directs this translation to non-Spanish speakers and uses it as an overture to her readers as they join Yolanda on her journey back to the Dominican Republic. (This moment also presents a pregnant opportunity for students to interrogate the class and racial privileges that the de la Torre and García families enjoy even as they were victims of Trujillo's terror.) In contrast, she directs her translation of "Chapita!"—"Trujillo's hated nickname" that Yoyo hurls at her father during a vicious fight—to non-Dominicans, *not* to non-Spanish speakers (146). While most Spanish speakers would understand *antojo*, a Spanish speaker of Puerto Rican, Cuban, Mexican, or Chicano descent, for instance, would not necessarily know the nickname that Dominicans use for the dictator Trujillo.

Although García likewise translates much of the novel's Spanish immediately into English, she uses specific moments of untranslated Spanish to evoke her Cuban heritage and to ask her readers to exercise their own translation skills. Because these moments occur infrequently, however, most of her novel is at least linguistically translatable to her readers (the intricacies of Cuban political history she evokes nevertheless require significant knowledge building on behalf of her readers). In "Translational Backformations," Lori Ween highlights García's choice to keep "*gusano*" in Spanish, a word that literally means worm but that figuratively represents "Castro's vilification of the Cubans who fled the revolution" (Weiss qtd. in Ween 2003: 135). The word *gusano* erupts as a moment of free indirect discourse in Celia's limited third-person narration in the novel's first paragraph; as Celia scans the beach with "binoculars" on watch for potential foreign (read American) invaders, she thinks, "No sign of *gusano* traitors" (3). Ween asserts that "the presence of terms in Spanish within García's texts provide an element of authenticity, while at the same time there is the possibility that some readers will feel alienated by the language" (135). We can add additional commentary about García's use of *gusano* in particular: the word's position at the beginning of the novel in

Celia's perspective unveils Celia's zealous commitment to the politics and integrity of post-revolutionary Cuba and functions as a signpost to readers that they are about to enter a bilingual fictional world. There are other moments of untranslated Spanish that appear in the novel, namely the excerpts from Frederico García Lorca's poems and many of the terms associated with *santería*. Instructors can utilize a Guided Scavenger Hunt to help both monolingual and multilingual students excavate moments of untranslated Spanish. In this assignment, instructors can ask students: Where do these moments appear? In order to translate them and their roles in the text, what do we need to know? After students perform this initial work, instructors can provide them with translations and prompt them with additional questions: What conceptual and historical issues do these moments bear across? Finally, why does García refuse to translate each of these instances?

Again, instructors can use Cisneros's *Caramelo* as a contrast, for the novel includes significantly more moments of transliterated (including often amusing calques), creatively interpreted, and untranslated Spanish. The novel's focus on the interrelationships of storytelling, knowledge, and migration necessitates a particular narrative voice, which I define elsewhere as a "migratory narrative voice that has the ability to cross supernatural, spatial, and narrative boundaries" (Alumbaugh 2010: 54). Cisneros employs, among other formal strategies, crisscrossed languages to craft the novel's migratory and communal narrative voice and to engage readers with different language competencies.

As an example, let us return to the multiple openings of *Caramelo*. The dual epigraphs, which are translated and appear on different pages, provide monolingual and Spanish/English bilingual students with different interpretive opportunities. The English "Tell me a story, even if it's a lie" underscores a number of the text's linguistic and topical concerns. The words "story" and "lie" mirror one another syntactically: they are nouns that come after indefinite articles at the end of consecutive phrases that Cisneros visually separates with a comma. This mirroring underscores the crucial importance of storytelling—whether or not the story is factually true is less important than the fact that it is told. Instructors may also want to emphasize the command form of the verb "tell me" and to encourage students to question who narrates here. The implied subject of the command form in both English and Spanish is "you," so the narrator here demands from readers their immediate participation in the creation of the story and constructs from the novel's beginning a communal narration. Bilingual students with a sophisticated knowledge of Spanish grammar can be encouraged to analyze the creative liberties that Cisneros takes with her translation(s) of the epigraph. In Spanish, Cisneros conjugates the verb "*ser*" (to be) in the subjunctive mood as *sea* (it could be); thus, the verb in Spanish expresses conditionality and desire. Cisneros's English translation shifts that conditionality from the verb to "even if." Why does she make this shift? What would the phrase communicate instead if Cisneros translated it as "even if it *may* or *could* be a lie?" This micro reading demonstrates the type of analysis that students can perform on a text that addresses multiple audiences simultaneously. The Guided Scavenger Hunt would work equally well with *Caramelo*. Because the novel includes so many moments of linguistic translation, instructors can direct students to the translations that occur in the various chapter titles and in the supernatural exchanges between Lala and Soledad in Parts II and III.

As instructors work with *Caramelo*, they should highlight the novel's additional differences from Alvarez's and García's fictions that could account for Cisneros's increased Spanish use. First, Cisneros's novel is about migration, both the specific migrations (not exile) that U.S./Mexican political relationships and policies made possible as well as the specific racial-ethnic-class identities that Spanish migration to the new world created (in Mexico in particular). Second, as a Chicana writer, Cisneros has a larger immediate Latino reading public of around 31 million than either Alvarez or García. Third, Mexican, Mexican American, and Chicano writing in the U.S. has a longer history of production and reception. And fourth, *Caramelo* is not Cisneros's first novel; indeed, it was published 18 years and multiple books after Cisneros wrote *The House on Mango Street*. Calling our students' attention to the different political, historical, demographic, and literary histories that inform these three writers will help them to see how their crisscrossed languages are *different*.

Conceptual features: character and familial/national history

The majority of this chapter focuses on the authors' formal maneuvers because narrative discourse is frequently more difficult for students to analyze than authors' thematic decisions. Still, I would like to highlight more briefly some of the conceptual similarities that the three novels share. It is striking that although these texts were written over 21 years apart by Latina writers of different heritages, they all include female adolescent narrators and/or characters who were very young immigrants to the United States or are children of immigrants. The authors' similar decision to use young female narrators/ characters represents an epistemological choice. Because these characters, like many readers, do not know as much about their histories, cultures, and languages of origin as their parents and grandparents, they serve as potential surrogates for the reader. As the young characters make sense of the world around them, so do readers, and these authors craft their characters as a means to explain, interpret, and transport their fictive worlds to varied audiences. This interpretation explains particularly García's decision to give Pilar the last name *Puente*, which means Bridge in Spanish.

A way to give students a manageable entrée into these unruly, multivocal, bilingual texts is to ask them to keep a Character Log about one of the female adolescent characters in each novel. This type of assignment should reveal to students that Alvarez's "García girls" (Carla, Sandra, Yolanda, and Sofia), Cisneros's Celaya (Lala) Reyes, and García's Pilar Puente share additional similarities beyond their age and Latina ethnicity: they are all in turns funny, angst-ridden, rebellious, and insightful. Lala's humor—as exemplified by her wry question and answer, "Who wants to be called a white girl? I mean, not even white girls want to be called white girls" (354)—reverberates in all of the novels. Yolanda's description of the "García girls" can be applied at different moments to the other female characters: "We took turns being the wildest" (86). And Pilar's insights about art and gender are typical of the type of stunning analytical maturity these characters at times exhibit:

> Even supposedly knowledgeable and sensitive people react to good art by a woman as if it were an anomaly, a product of a freak nature or a direct result of her association with a male painter or mentor. ... As for the women, we're supposed to make extra money modeling nude. What kind of bullshit revolution is that?
>
> (139–40)

Instructors can ask their students to focus on one major similarity instead of the multiple ones I enumerate above; indeed, the texts consistently reveal that the young female characters experience their bi-cultural realities in simultaneously positive and negative ways.

They also consistently underscore the female characters' desire to be artists and to discover, as Pilar declares, "a unique language" that "obliterates clichés" (139). Character Logs can help students additionally discern the texts' differences: whereas Alvarez and García craft multiple narrative voices, Cisneros constructs a co-narrated discourse and hands over to Lala much of the narrative power of the text. These female characters have different experiences of exile, migration, race, and class. Much of the physical violence against women that is explicit in Alvarez and even more so in García does not appear in Cisneros's text.

Finally, these texts offer another topical similarity that instructors can highlight: all three novels link family history to national/exilic/migration histories to demonstrate how private and public histories repeatedly intersect. Andrea O'Reilly Herrera's claims about García's novel can apply equally to all three texts; like García, Alvarez and Cisneros draw "parallel[s] between the private lives" of their characters and "the 'context' or 'larger backdrop'" of historical events (1997: 72). These historical linkages and intersections serve similar translative purposes in all three novels. First, Alvarez, Cisneros, and García use them to provide intimate accounts of the personal consequences of historical forces of exile, immigration, and migration; the intimate accounts encourage readers to engage with the material *despite* their potential lack of historical knowledge. Even if readers do not have an understanding of exile and migration or the histories that produce these experiences, they can feel Celia's loss of family or apprehend that every year Lala crosses the border from the United States into Mexico on her family's annual migration, her "mind forgets" but her "body always remembers" (18). Second, the voices that tell these stories—mostly women, all marginalized in mainstream United States and their respective Latino cultures alternately by their gender, race, class, age, and immigrant/migrant statuses—intervene into the very nature of historical narratives by offering alternative perspectives. Finally, the novels' intersections of private and public histories invite readers to compare and contrast their understandings of U.S. histories and the texts' treatments of the same.

Instructors may want to begin with *Dreaming in Cuban*, as García's novel is explicit about how familial and exilic histories crisscross, and to ask students to examine García's pairing of Celia and Pilar. Celia's and Pilar's historical ruminations abound. For instance, Celia muses in the novel's first chapter on the vicissitudes of history by focusing on the failed American baseball career of "El Líder" (Castro's fictional surrogate): "Frustrated, El Líder went home, rested his pitching arm, and started a revolution in the mountains. Because of this, Celia thinks, her husband will be buried in stiff, foreign earth. Because of this, their children and their grandchildren are nomads" (6–7). With an almost preternatural memory, Pilar echoes her grandmother's propensity to think historically: "I was only two years old when I left Cuba but I remember everything that's happened to me since I was a baby, even word-for-word conversations" (26). Additional moments to explore with our students include Alvarez's chapter "The Blood of the Conquistadores" and Cisneros's treatment of how the Reyes family members experience (frequently on both sides of the U.S./Mexico border) any of these historical periods: that immediately precedes the Mexican Revolution, the Second World War, and the Vietnam War. As an alternative, instructors can ask students to examine the historical and cultural information that Cisneros transmits in the novel's footnotes and in the "Chronology" that closes the book. Again, after establishing the texts' similarities, I encourage a comparative approach: how do Alvarez, Cisneros, and García make *different formal decisions* to represent the crisscrossing of these various histories?

A student originally brought to my attention the moment in *Caramelo* when Lala tells her family in both English and Spanish that her grandparents' ceiling has collapsed, but her family members struggle to understand her: "The wall has fallen … *la pared arriba, es que se cayó. Ven, Papá, ven*" (60). Lala attributes her family's slow response to her own linguistic failure to find the "words for what I want to say" (she says wall in English and *pared* in Spanish, but not ceiling). My student saliently asserted that Lala's interpretation is limited: whether or not Lala uses the word ceiling is irrelevant as she clearly communicates in two languages that a piece of the house has collapsed. The real problem, the student discovered, is not mistranslation but the fact that no one *is listening*.

This lively exchange with my student crystallized to me the very skills that these three novels ask of their readers and that we, as educators, want to impart to our students. Alvarez, Cisneros, and García perform acts of formal and conceptual translation—of transliteration, explanation, interpretation, transportation, transformation, and creation— that bear across to readers their novels' crisscrossed languages, cultures, and histories. As a result, their texts propagate readers who are *creative listeners*, like my student who grasped what Lala communicates even if her fictional family does not. Ultimately, these texts invite our students to adopt the very translation skills that the three authors exhibit in their evocative and lyrical novels. To become "translators," then, students need to be creative, equally attentive to close reading practices as well as audiences, and capable of explanation and interpretation of complex linguistic, cultural, and historical materials. Working with the topic of translation can help our students transform from passive to active learners, from readers to creative listeners to textual co-creators.

Resources for teaching crisscrossed languages

Aldama, Frederick Luis. *Analyzing World Fiction: New Horizons in Narrative Theory.* Austin: University of Texas Press, 2011.

Alumbaugh, Heather. "Narrative coyotes: migration and narrative voice in Sandra Cisneros's *Caramelo.*" *MELUS* 35.1 (2010): 53–75.

Alvarez Borland, Isabel, and Lynette M. F. Bosch. *Cuban-American Literature and Art: Negotiating Identities.* Albany: University of New York Press, 2009.

Barr, Marleen S. *Genre Fission: A New Discourse Practice for Culture Studies.* Iowa City: University of Iowa Press, 2000.

Caminero-Santangelo, Marta. *On Latinidad: U.S. Latino Literature and the Construction of Ethnicity.* Miami: University Press of Florida, 2007.

Cowart, David. *Trailing Clouds: Immigrant Fiction in Contemporary America.* Ithaca: Cornell University Press, 2006.

Cutter, Martha J. *Lost and Found in Translation: Contemporary Ethnic American Writing and the Politics of Language Diversity.* Chapel Hill: University of North Carolina Press, 2005.

Irizarry, Ylce. "An Interview with Cristina García." *Contemporary Literature* 48.2 (2007): iv, 175–94.

Méndez Rodenas, Adriana. "En búsqueda del paraíso perdido: La historia natural como imaginación diaspórica en Cristina García." *MLN* 116.2 (2001): 392–418.

Ontiveros, Randy J. *In the Spirit of a New People: The Cultural Politics of the Chicano Movement.* New York: New York University Press, 2013.

Roca, Ana, M. Cecilia Colombi, and Guadalupe Valdés. *Mi lengua: Spanish as a Heritage Language in the United States, Research and Practice.* Washington, DC: Georgetown University Press, 2003.

Socolovsky, Maya. *Troubling Nationhood in U.S. Latina Literature: Explorations of Place and Belonging.* New Brunswick, NJ: Rutgers University Press, 2013.

Vázquez, David J. *Triangulations: Narrative Strategies for Navigating Latino Identity.* Minneapolis: University of Minnesota Press, 2011.

Ween, Lori. "Translational backformations: authenticity and language in Cuban American literature." *Comparative Literature Studies* 40.2 (2003): 127–41.

Wickelson, Paul. "Shaking awake the memory: the gothic quest for place in Sandra Cisneros's *Caramelo*." *Western American Literature* 48.1 (2013): 90–114.

Appendix: model undergraduate syllabus: 10 weeks

(The Resources section includes additional sources that instructors can use in each section.)

Table 5.2 Model undergraduate syllabus

Week 1	**Translation Theories** Excerpts from *Routledge Encyclopedia of Translation Studies* (ed. Mona Baker); Walter Benjamin, "The Task of the Translator"; excerpts from *Nation, Language, and the Ethics of Translation* (eds Sandra Bermann and Michael Wood); Martha Cutter, excerpts from *Lost and Found in Translation*; Ilan Stavans, "Translation"; Lawrence Venuti, "Introduction."
Week 2	**Crisscrossed Languages** H. Porter Abbott, excerpts from *The Cambridge Introduction to Narrative*; Frederick Luis Aldama, "Language and code-switching"; Gloria Anzaldúa, "How to Tame a Wild Tongue" and other selections from *Borderlands/La Frontera*; Jules Chametzsky, "Reflections on Multilingualism"; Gene Demby, "When Our Kids Own America" from *Code Switch: NPR*; Werner Sollors, "Introduction: After the Culture Wars or, From 'English Only' to 'English Plus'"; Lourdes Torres, "In the Contact Zone"; David T. Vázquez, "Notes on Triangulation."
Week 3	**Malinche** Norma Alarcón, "*Traddutora, Traditora*"; Martha Cutter, "Malinche's Legacy"; Pilar Godayol, "Malintzin/La Malinche/Doña Marina"; Cherríe Moraga, "A Long Line of Vendidas"; Octavio Paz, "The Sons of La Malinche"; selections from *Feminism, Nation and Myth: La Malinche* (eds Rolando Romero and Amanda Nolacea Harris).
Weeks 4–5	Julia Alvarez, ***How the García Girls Lost Their Accents*** (order based on novel's initial publication date).
Weeks 6–7	Cristina García, ***Dreaming In Cuban***
Weeks 8–9	Sandra Cisneros, ***Caramelo***
Week 10	**Wrap-Up:** Finish Cisneros and group presentations on the novels' differences.

6   Transnational forms

Monica Hanna and Jennifer Harford Vargas

Introduction: our American genres

In 1990 Cuban American literary critic Gustavo Pérez-Firmat posed what was to be a field-defining question: "Do the Americas have a common literature?" The question holds particular significance for Latino/a literature and, in turn, invokes further questions: What is the place of Latino/a letters in this literature of the Americas? How is Latino/a literature influenced by both Latin American and U.S. American literary traditions? Moreover, what genres circulate in the Americas and how do Latino/a writers mobilize and modify these narrative forms?

There is a range of answers to these questions as numerous aesthetic influences and genre forms have helped shape Latino/a literary production. One approach to transnational form is a focus on "influence" in which we might trace, for example, how the structure of Chicana writer Ana Castillo's first novel *The Mixquiahuala Letters* draws on the structure of Argentine writer Julio Cortázar's *Rayuela* [*Hopscotch*], or how Peruvian American writer Daniel Alarcón's *At Night We Walk in Circles* (2013) is thematically and narratively indebted to Chilean writer Roberto Bolaño's *Los detectives salvajes* [*The Savage Detectives*]. Shifting the focus from direct influences to genres, we might consider the ways a variety of genres such as *lo real maravilloso* [marvelous or magical realism], *testimonio* [testimony], the historical novel, and the migration novel shape Latino/a literature. Indeed, the two genres that have "emerged from Latin America to go global" and have seen the most substantial creative and scholarly attention in Latino/a studies are magical realism and the *testimonio* (Nance 2012: 239).[1] Although all writers must wrestle with form and choose one that best fits their aesthetic and political designs, the options available to Latino/a writers are multiplied by their transnational linguistic and narrative inheritances.

In this chapter we examine the transnational forms of Latino/a literature through two canonically Latin American genres—the *crónica* [chronicle] and the dictator novel—that are not widely studied or taught in Latino/a studies. We argue that an attention to form and genre adds another layer to the trans-American aesthetic productions and literary relations delineated by scholars such as José David Saldívar, Kirsten Silva Gruesz, Anna Brickhouse, Doris Sommer, Lois Parkinson Zamora, Ana Patricia Rodríguez, Alicia Schmidt Camacho, and Raúl Coronado who have mined hemispheric connections that are not visible through the optic of nationally bounded literary studies. As Paula Moya and Ramón Saldívar articulate it, "an interpretive framework that yokes together North and South American instead of New England and England" is "an alternative and epistemologically valuable way of describing our place in the world and understanding the literature we teach" (2003: 2).[2] It is thus imperative to be attuned to the particular literary forms Latinos/as use to represent their lived experiences and even re-imagine their social worlds. Since most trans-American literary criticism has been archival, thematic, genealogical, and/or discursive, we focus in this chapter on the critical import and pedagogical utility of genre-based hemispheric approaches to the study of Latino/a literature.

We read hemispheric relations of domination and creative resistance through the circulation and modification of Latin American narrative forms and through the aesthetic tactics, discursive tropes, and transnational subjectivities that constitute the imaginative horizon of the Latino/a chronicle and the Latino/a dictator novel. In reading narrative form and hemispheric geo-politics together, we contend that Latino/a literature cannot be fully understood without considering how Latin American literary traditions migrate to the United States and undergo a process of transformation, transculturation, and reformulation through the pens of Latinos/as.[3] An attention to form situates Latino/a novelists in an active role in shaping contemporary literary, cultural, scholarly, and political movements that seek to redefine "Americanness."

Below, we lay out the landscape of two emerging transnational generic traditions in Latino/a literature with roots in Latin American literary traditions: the chronicle and dictator novel. We each first provide brief overviews of the histories of our respective genres (Hanna on the chronicle and Harford Vargas on the dictator novel) and then offer examples for how to integrate these transnational forms in the classroom. We hope that our suggestions for teaching chronicles and dictator novels will serve as helpful resources for faculty and students and will further an understanding of how deeply embedded Latino/a literature is in Latin American literature, and how the two mutually inform each other.

The Latino/a *crónica*

The chronicle is a genre that is well known and studied within Latin American Studies because of the long established tradition of the *crónica* in Latin America, but it is not as well known or recognized in U.S. American Studies, despite the fact that there are many overlaps between the *crónica* and narrative and advocacy journalist traditions in the United States. Modern and contemporary *crónicas* integrate literary techniques usually associated with fiction into nonfiction journalistic writing in order to create narratives that give historical and narrative depth rather than just answering the "five w's" of conventional journalism. Latin American *crónicas* have narrative and interpretive functions that can be political, investigative, ethnographic, historical, educational, consciousness-raising, and/or denunciatory.

Practitioners and theorists of the Latin American *crónica* such as prolific Mexican journalist Carlos Monsiváis and scholar Esperança Bielsa trace its history back to the *crónicas de Indias* produced during the Spanish conquest in which Spaniards documented their experiences in the Americas.[4] The contemporary form of the Latin American *crónica*, however, is more closely related to the *crónica modernista* of the late nineteenth and early twentieth century, which was practiced by politically engaged writers such as statesmen José Martí from Cuba and Rubén Darío of Nicaragua. In the contemporary period in Mexico, the genre has been used by post-1968 heavy-hitters like Carlos Monsiváis and Elena Poniatowska, and continues to be relevant today for writers like Sanjuana Martínez, Anabel Hernández, and Diego Enrique Osorno. Modern and contemporary *crónicas* are marked by techniques such as a focus on quotidian experiences rather than traditional journalistic subjects, the use of a stylized voice, the inclusion of the *cronista* [chronicler] in the narrative itself, and fictionalization (Bielsa 2006: 39).

The chronicle has a transnational and transhistorical genealogy, as a hybrid genre associated with periods of intense social change dating back to the earliest contact between Europeans and indigenous Americans. Latino/a chronicle draws on this Latin American *crónica* tradition and U.S. "new journalism," while also drawing on overlapping genres of life writing such as *testimonio*, memoir, and travel writing. The chronicle is a "liminal genre" (Corona and Jörgensen 2002)—located between generic conventions, geographies, and traditions—that mimics the spaces of the inter-American borders so central to the writings of many Latino/a chroniclers. Contemporary Latino/a writers (including those with a literary formation and those with a journalistic formation) concerned with issues of transnational identity and social justice have adopted the genre in order to represent those realities as fully as possible. As a border- and genre-crossing narrative form, with a history of documenting often-ignored issues related to social justice, it is a genre well suited to contemporary writers seeking to document transnational Latino/a political, economic, and cultural concerns. A partial list of Latina and Latino writers who have published in this genre includes: Daniel Alarcón, Alfredo Corchado, Francisco Goldman, Daniel Hernandez, Sonia Nazario, Mirta Ojito, Héctor Tobar, and Luís Alberto Urrea.

In looking at transnational generic connections, it is important to not view these as simple transfers from one nation to another, but rather to look at the ways in which genres travel. At the same time that U.S. Latino/a chronicle writing shares important similarities with the Latin American *crónica*, it also has differing concerns. Latino/a chronicles offer engaging and generally accessible narratives that immerse students in questions regarding the ethics, politics, rhetoric, and representational aesthetics of contemporary Latino/a realities. They add to the genre an emphasis on the individual and cultural repercussions of lives lived across national borders, which is often expressed generically in explicit referencing of transnational influences and on the level of content with their interest in representing Latinidad as an ethnic formation; on seeing U.S. Latino/a experiences as intimately tied to Latin American phenomena; and on their often increased level of self-reflexivity, which derives from the chroniclers' multiple positionings somewhere between "insiders" and "outsiders" in a variety of national and situational contexts. Latino/a chronicles depict migration as a process that does not end on arrival in and subsequent assimilation into the United States, like the "melting pot" model embraced in the country for so many decades.

U.S. Latino/a chroniclers often make connections across intra-ethnic national borders, drawing similarities between people and experiences across Latin American nations and not just in the United States. Moreover, they often cite a transnational set of writing influences that bridge borders. Daniel Hernandez, for example, a Chicano journalist whose collection *Down & Delirious in Mexico City* (2011) chronicles his experiences as a "pocho" living and working in Mexico City, cites influences that include New Journalists Joan Didion and Hunter S. Thompson;[5] the Italian writer Oriana Fallaci who has a crucial Mexican connection, as she famously and very publicly condemned the massacre at Tlatelolco in 1968; the U.S. historian and writer Mike Davis; U.S. Latino writers and journalists Francisco Goldman, Daniel Alarcón, and Rubén Martínez; and Mexican journalists Alma Guillermoprieto, Diego Enrique Osorno, Laura Castellanos, and Sanjuana Martínez.[6] This list contextualizes Hernandez's work within the productions by young chroniclers across the borders of the Americas, with the strong participation of U.S. Latino and Latina writers. Reading one of Daniel Hernandez's chronicles that takes place wholly within Mexico City and has no explicit transnational referent, such as his "The Warriors" in *Down & Delirious*, next to a chronicle such as "Dancing: The Funky Dive" by Carlos Monsiváis, another chronicler of the megalopolis who influenced Hernandez in his representation of subcultures, reveals the Chicano chronicler's concern with authenticity, belonging, and perspective that is influenced by his transnational experiences.

Because of their generic "in-betweenness" and the range of topics they explore, Latino/a chronicles can easily be integrated into a variety of different types of courses in literature, journalism, ethnic studies, Latin American studies, politics, history, and anthropology. The genre can be studied on its own, or integrated into units that include a variety of generic forms seeking to represent a relevant thematic topic, such as migration, popular culture, media, politics, and ethnic identities across the Americas. Below I offer some suggestions for introducing the genre to students and integrating it into a variety of different syllabus formats.

In the classroom, when studying U.S. Latino/a chronicles, there are several questions I pose to students that help to guide our discussions. Before we even begin our readings, I prepare students for our examinations of the alternative journalistic approach of Latino/a chroniclers by inquiring about their existing understanding of journalism with questions such as:

- What are/should be the goals of journalism as you understand it?
- What topics should the news inform us about?
- In the United States, we tend to place high importance on objectivity in journalism. Why do you think this is? How does this look? Is objectivity possible? To what extent?
- What do you think of the term *literary journalism*? Is this a paradox?

These types of questions help students to articulate ideas they have about journalism coming into their study of Latino/a chronicles, especially since narrative journalism can sometimes be easily disregarded because of its recourse to advocacy at times. One of the key characteristics of the chronicle, for example, is the explicit presence and involvement of the chronicler who uses the first person singular pronoun; this is something conventional journalism (much lilke many English classrooms) often frowns on. As a result, it is important for students to recognize this as a different approach and interrogate how and why these writers might use this strategy. At the heart of this shift is the notion that traditional journalism cannot fully capture the complex experiences that the chronicler attempts to represent, and that notions of "objectivity" can obscure relations of power.

Once we begin our study of the primary texts, which I pair with Latin American examples as well as secondary readings, I ask students more questions about genre. Because the chronicle draws from conventions associated with a variety of different genres, it is difficult to categorize. In fact, Mexican journalist Juan Villoro has called the *crónica* the "*ornitorrinco*" or "platypus" of the prose world since it draws on genres from reportage to short story to modern theater (2012: 578–79). The generic slipperiness of the form can open a productive discussion in the classroom on the boundaries of these various genres. Some questions I use to direct the class include:

- How do the readings differ from the conventional journalism that you are accustomed to reading in U.S. newspapers? Can you make any connections to journalistic and literary genres that you are familiar with?
- How do these writers mix journalistic and literary narrative modes within their work? Why do you think they do this?
- Do you find this hybrid form effective? What does the form inspire in the reader? How might that answer vary by audience?
- How does the work of U.S. Latino/a writers in this genre compare to major U.S. and Latin American practitioners of related genres?

The chronicle as genre cannot be divorced from an intense focus on the content, of course. Latino/a chronicles address some of the most politically contentious issues of our time. And, significantly, the popularity and wide circulation of the form allows these authors to intervene in U.S. public discourse in a way that can be more difficult for fiction to achieve given the literary market. Contemporary Latino/a chronicles of undocumented migration between Latin America and the United States, such as Sonia Nazario's *Enrique's Journey* (2006), Jorge Ramos's *Dying to Cross* (2006), Rubén Martínez's *Crossing Over* (2001), and Luis Alberto Urrea's *The Devil's Highway* (2004), have won awards, become bestsellers, and/or been adopted as part of high school and college curricula, while their authors have been interviewed on national television about their work. These Latino/a chronicles thereby successfully intervene in and reshape the current rhetoric regarding the subject of undocumented migration and immigration reform that is so central to politics in the United States and across the Americas.

When teaching a course in Chicano/a Studies, on literature or on cultural studies, I often discuss representations of migration and since many chronicles center on themes of migration at the heart of U.S. Latino/a identities, organizing a discussion of genre that is linked thematically to this issue is productive. The contemporary boom in U.S. Latino/a chronicle writing has been inspired in part by massive numbers of migrants and an increasingly impermeable and perilous U.S.–Mexico border.[7] As we write this essay, projections suggest that the number of detainments of "unaccompanied minors" migrating to the United States primarily from Central America in 2014, which had already reached over 50,000 in June, could reach 90,000 by the end of the fiscal year.[8] In my courses I link statistical data and media representations of migration with fictional and non-fictional literary representations as well as representations in the visual arts. In integrating chronicles, I might teach the following together: a section of Sonia Nazario's *Enrique's Journey*, a chapter from Hector Tobar's *Translation Nation* (2005), Reyna Grande's (2012) excellent recent memoir *The Distance between Us* (which has been a favorite among my students at Cal State Fullerton), and Patricia Riggen's film *La misma luna/Under the Same Moon* (2007). Though two are journalistic narratives, the other a life writing narrative, and the last a fictional film, these works all represent the undocumented migration of children, and in two cases "unaccompanied minors," from Latin American countries to the United States. These narratives are all linked through a "zoomed in" perspective on a political "hot topic" by looking at individual lives of ordinary people dealing with the consequences of an economically and culturally globalized hemisphere. In examining representations of migration through a variety of genres, students can consider and discuss in class the ways in which these different types of narrative form converge and diverge, what limitations and possibilities each afford, and how these different representations allow for different perspectives on the issue. In classrooms with widely varying political views on issues of migration to the United States, it will be important to note and think through the different reactions to these kinds of texts, including feelings of authorial bias that different audience members might register in relation to some or all of these representations. Such moments, while sometimes awkward or tense, are nonetheless productive. Another issue I like students to consider is the ways in which these narratives imagine divisions and alliances among different Latin American-origin groups, including those between foreign-born and native-born Latinos/as in the United States.

Since quite a few Latino/a chroniclers, such as Héctor Tobar, Francisco Goldman, and Daniel Alarcón, also produce fiction, a study of the chronicle within a literature course could pair works by one of these individual authors in both fiction and literary journalism in order to more closely examine the generic choices made by the authors and analyze the effects of their choices. The three authors mentioned above all produce fiction that is invested in the historical and contemporary realities faced by Latinos/as both within the United States and within Latin America, and their journalistic work represents those interests. A class discussion of Daniel Alarcón's recently published *At Night We Walk in Circles* (2013), for example, would be incomplete without a discussion of his *Harper's* piece, "All Politics Is Local (2012)," in which students consider the shifts Alarcón makes between his journalistic representation of the Lurigancho prison outside Lima, Peru and his fictional take on the aftermath of war in an unnamed South American country that sets a significant part of its narrative action in a prison modeled on Lurigancho. Pairing works by the same author working in different narrative modes allows students to further consider the reasons why authors with multiple "tools" at their disposal might choose one over another, while considering the effects of those choices on the audience.

My final example of a text worth integrating in the classroom also has a connection to Daniel Alarcón. The chronicles of the *Radio Ambulante* podcast present the producers' (including Alarcón's) and journalists' vision of Latinidad that is bilingual, stresses transnational interconnectedness, and views the Latino/a population in the United States as one that constitutes a Latin American country. The program features stories that crisscross Latin American countries. The production also features transnational collaborations between producers and journalists across borders. It is distributed worldwide as an audio program via SoundCloud audio on the *Radio Ambulante* website, and airs on radio stations in the United States, Mexico, Argentina, and Colombia. One classroom exercise is to have students review the first episode, "Moving," for discussion. The episode brings together four stories that span countries (the United States, Honduras, Mexico, and Argentina) and time, but are thematically linked by representations of "moving," including migration, exile, and experiences of acculturation. The episode, which is available on the *Radio Ambulante* website, allows students to discuss issues including: the significance of language and translation, the ways in which new media and "old" media methods of distribution might affect reception, and the connection between technologies like audio recordings and written narratives. Questions to pose to students might include:

- What do you think of the undifferentiated use of English and Spanish between the stories?
- How might your experiences differ if you are monolingual or if you are English–Spanish bilingual?

- Does *Radio Ambulante* bring anything different to our experiences as listeners than a radio program like *This American Life*, which is very similar in format?
- How does the way in which chronicles are distributed affect their content and audience?

Because of the economy of the format, *Radio Ambulante* chronicles are easy to integrate into classroom discussions of Latino/a literature, and can open up the discussion to the many intersections of the short radio journalism pieces with various other types of Latino/a literary narratives.

The Latino/a dictator novel

In February 2013, *Radio Ambulante* hosted a special live show in New York City at the Instituto Cervantes featuring a conversation between executive producer Daniel Alarcón, Francisco Goldman, and Junot Díaz. Perhaps unsurprisingly given that all three writers have written about dictatorship in their respective home countries of Peru, Guatemala, and the Dominican Republic, their conversation turns from the politics of Latino/a linguistic practices and different genre designations across the hemispheres to shared histories of dictatorship. Relating how he tries to render the violent and hallucinatory traumas of Central America's history in his writing, Francisco Goldman recalls how Roberto Bolaño declared Latin America an insane asylum. Daniel Alarcón builds on this, noting:

> If one of the premises of Radio Ambulante is the idea that two things—that political borders may be real but cultural borders are much more fluid and another being that with 55 million Latinos in this country the United States is a Latin American country as well—I was just thinking about it. If what Bolaño says is true, then that would make the United States also an insane asylum. ["It obviously is," Goldman interjects.] And I think that intuitively feels very true. But that reminds me a lot of what I read from you, Junot, where you talk a lot about these traumas that particularly affect our communities and the cultural wounds that we carry with us ...
>
> ("Junot Díaz and Francisco Goldman Live in New York")

Díaz elaborates on both comments as he describes the myriad ways those who flee their "country of horror" carry their trauma to the United States and this trauma, in turn, becomes their children's haunting inheritance. Latinos/as are thus shaped by the twinned insane asylums of Latin American authoritarian regimes and the United States imperialism.

Latino/a fiction and Latin American fiction share a common concern with dictatorial power in its multiple instantiations. The Latin American dictator novel, written in Spanish, depicts authoritarian regimes such as *caciquismo, caudillismo,* dictatorship, and military juntas in Latin America. The tradition is a long and rich one beginning its modern instantiation with Domingo Faustino Sarmiento's influential mid-nineteenth century text *Facundo: Civilización y barbarie* [*Facundo: Civilization and Barbarism*], though some scholars trace the genre's genealogy back to the *crónicas de Indias,* the chronicles documenting Spain's encounters with the Americas. (It is thus not hard to see that the *crónica* and dictator novel have a twinned history and can easily be taught together.) The tradition includes such earlier works as José Mármol's *Amalia,* Miguel

Angel Asturias's *El señor presidente* [*The President*], and Enrique Lafourcade's *La fiesta del rey acab* [*King Ahab's Feast*]. During the 1970s, the Boom generation of writers produced a seminal group of dictator novels: Gabriel García Márquez's *El otoño del patriarca* [*Autumn of the Patriarch*], Augusto Roa Bastos's *Yo el supremo* [*I, the Supreme*], and Alejo Carpentier's *El recurso del método* [*Reasons of State*]. The genre remains vibrant and contemporary in particular due to novelists from the Southern Cone and Central America such as Ariel Dorfman, Luisa Valenzuela, Sergio Ramírez, Gioconda Belli, and Roberto Bolaño who use their creative productions to explore issues such as exile, Latin American feminisms, and truth and reconciliation.

In recent years, the dictator novel has migrated north of the U.S.–Mexico border and into the English language. To invoke the words of Nicaraguan Sergio Ramírez, "the astonishing excesses of dictatorships, crime, torture, the disappeared" do not only haunt the pages of Latin American fiction; for, as Ramírez so eloquently puts it,

> [t]he old ghosts that have come out of the basements of the presidential palaces do not stop the sounds of the chains they are dragging. And these ghosts have crossed the United States border like many other clandestine migrants, hidden in the genes or in the luggage of the immigrants who will one day be first class writers.
>
> (author's translation)

In the past two decades, a wide range of Latino/a novels have been haunted by the ghosts of dictatorships past. Consider, for example, Julia Alvarez's *How the García Girls Lost Their Accents* (2010) and *In the Time of the Butterflies* (1994), Francisco Goldman's *The Long Night of White Chickens* (1992) and *The Ordinary Seaman* (1997), Graciela Limón's *In Search of Bernabé* (1993), Demetria Martínez's *Mother Tongue* (1994), Héctor Tobar's *The Tattooed Solider* (1998), Edwidge Danticat's *The Farming of Bones* (1998), Loida Maritza Pérez's *Geographies of Home* (1999), Achy Obejas's *Memory Mambo* (1996), Salvador Plascencia's *The People of Paper* (2005), Angie Cruz's *Let It Rain Coffee* (2005), Junot Díaz's *The Brief Wondrous Life of Oscar Wao* (2007), Sylvia Sellers-García's *When the Ground Turns in Its Sleep* (2007), Cristina García's *King of Cuba* (2013), and Daniel Alarcón's *Lost City Radio* (2007) and *At Night We Walk in Circles* (2013), among many others.[9]

Unlike their counterparts in Latin America, these Latino/a novels are written in English and infused with a Latino/a trans-American consciousness. Most of the novels are situated in the United States and peppered with references to life under dictatorship or with back-story conflicts and flashback sequences that occur in Latin America. Moving between New Jersey and the Dominican Republic, Massachusetts and Guatemala, Chicago and Cuba, New Mexico and El Salvador, New York and Peru, among other sites, they foreground the transnational afterlife of historical dictatorships on contemporary Latino/a communities and individuals. The authors, along with most of their characters, were born or grew up in the United States so their identity formations are rooted in U.S. Latinidad. At a generational and geographic remove from Latin American authoritarian regimes, they are what Holocaust scholar Marianne Hirsch terms a "post-memory generation" and, as such, they grapple with how to "remember" and write a history they have not lived.[10] Given their different geo-social location, the U.S.-based post-memory Latino/a generation looks to the south and to the past to confront their parents' experiences of dictatorship and the transnational residual traces of that oppressive past in their present.

At the same time, the novels disabuse readers of their stereotypical associations of the United States with democracy and Latin America with dictatorship because modes of domination in the United States echo or mirror those in Latin America.[11] The novels complicate such facile and inaccurate binaries and enact intersectional analyses of domination and privilege. Latino/a dictator novels highlight how the experience of being racialized minorities in the U.S. is marked by oppression and how hierarchies of power—be they racial, gendered, sexual, economic, linguistic, or bodily—dictate subjects' agency. The novels thereby sketch out a complex spectrum of dictatorial power that models for students how to conduct transnational and intersectional analyses of power dynamics.

Dictator novels also provide a lens through which to consider a range of themes shared by Latino/a writers from various national origins. These include different forms of state violence, imperialism, social justice, migration, racial discrimination, economic exploitation, machismo and heteropatriarchy, language politics, cultural identity formation, and transnational history.[12] Dictator novels can thus be easily included not just in Latino/a literary studies courses but also courses in history, political science, sociology, LGBTQ studies, U.S. ethnic studies, and Latin American Studies. They can be incorporated into broader survey courses of U.S. literature, Latino/a cultural studies, literatures of the Americas, or world literature; they can be the focus of discrete genre courses; or they can be taught in individual units on any of the aforementioned thematic topics.

Perhaps most valuably, I use Latino/a dictator novels to teach students how to analyze hierarchies of power, both in terms of sociopolitical relations and in terms of the structure of novels. Dictatorship in Latino/a novels is not just a thematic concern but also an aesthetic concern. That is, the novels do not simply represent dictatorial power; they also strategically use the novel form to critically interrogate dictatorial power. Thus they enable students to engage with formalist analysis, and deepen their understanding of how form shapes content and structures their reading experiences. I ask students to be attentive to the narrative politics of: which characters are granted attention, who has power and agency, whose perspectives focalize the narrative, what languages are privileged, how plots are constructed, how space is used on the page, the significance of paratextual material, how metafiction makes us conscious of the novel itself, why different artistic forms are transculturated in a novel, and so forth. In doing so, I teach students to read power relations at the levels of both content and form. Students can thereby analyze how the novels dictate or tell their stories while attempting not to be dictatorial or, to use another useful word play, how the novels navigate the slippery similarities between authoritarianism, authority, and authorship. What follows are some ideas about how to teach dictator novels with an attention to social hierarchies of power and structures of power in the novel form.

Dominican American public intellectual Junot Díaz's novel *The Brief Wondrous Life of Oscar Wao* (2007) provides a wonderful opportunity for students to read political and narrative power together through the lens of what narrative theorist Alex Woloch calls the character-system. I ask students to track how narrative attention is distributed among characters in a novel, pointing out how the novel reverses the correlation between characters' positions in the sociopolitical hierarchy and their position in the text's narrative hierarchy.[13] Students thereby examine the impact of having the politically powerful dictator Rafael Trujillo be a minor, flat character while socially marginalized Afro-Dominican characters are major, round protagonists. Given the central role of U.S. minority experiences in the novel, students also analyze why structurally and thematically the novel figures a transhistorical and transnational relationship between the Latino/a lives of Oscar and Lola and their Dominican mother Beli, grandfather Abelard, and even their slave ancestors in the sugarcane fields.

Dominican American poet, essayist, and fiction writer Julia Alvarez's *How the Garcia Girls Lost Their Accents* provides the occasion for students to reflect on U.S. ethnic identity formation. As we analyze the novel's reverse temporal structure and its multi-perspectival structure, I ask students to reflect on who has access to survival and self-invention and how the past shapes futurity and the kinds of Latina selves imaginable. Focusing on the novel's various metaphors as well as on the symbolic function of language and naming, I invite students to question the pressures to literally lose one's accent and symbolically lose one's culture, opening up a conversation about the dictatorial mandates of monolingual and monocultural ideology. This gives us the opportunity to debate models of cultural assimilation and transculturation, and to consider them within the context of hemispheric histories of colonization and authoritarianism.

Chicana activist-author Demetria Martínez's *Mother Tongue* provides students with the opportunity to analyze intra-ethnic solidarity across different Latino national origin groups through the Sanctuary Movement[14] and how a novel can function as testimony against trauma. I ask students to track the power dynamics in the romance between María (a Chicana rape survivor) and José Luis (a Salvadoran torture survivor) and compare their different forms of violation. I also encourage them to interrogate what I call domestic dictatorship within the context of María's physical abuse in the domestic space of her home in the domestic United States and to consider how patriarchy dictates female subordination and represses female sexual agency. We also discuss how the novel's incorporation of different genres (such as testimony, poetry, epistles, recipes, and news reports) redefines storytelling as a place of refuge and sanctuary as an aesthetic space.

Guatemalan American journalist and novelist Héctor Tobar's *The Tattooed Soldier* enables students to investigate how plot and narrative perspective can structure comparative visions of racial regimes and state violence in the hemisphere. I point students to the multiple significations of "plot" in the novel: as the main sequence of events, as Antonio's plan to assassinate the military killer Longoria, and as Longoria's attempt to establish order and control over his environment after attending the U.S. Army School of the Americas. I then ask students to consider how the narrative formally fractures the binary between the victim of dictatorship (Antonio) and the perpetrator of dictatorship (Longoria) and between democracy (the United States) and dictatorship (Guatemala), pointing them to look at how the foil characters of Antonio and Longoria are given equal attention as narrators and to the parallels between Guatemalan military brutality and Los Angeles police brutality. Perhaps most valuably, students unpack the relevance of the Rodney King uprisings in Los Angeles that serve as the backdrop for the novel's explosive events. This provides a prime opportunity to discuss contemporary racial profiling and debate whether justice can be achieved given mass impunity and, in the context of the disproportionate incarcerations of Latinos/as and Blacks in the United States, an unequal penal system designed to maintain white supremacy.

Returning to Peruvian American *cronista* Daniel Alarcón, his novel *Lost City Radio* gives students the chance to explore how different technologies from the photograph to the radio can serve as sites of memory and modes of challenging state violence and official history. I ask students how the radio, a technology of aural visibility, is represented in a print novel and how Norma's radio show functions as a form of memory work and a technology of reappearing the disappeared. We then analyze how the state's arbitrary profiling and torturing of potential dissidents is represented as a form of so-called "tadek," illuminating how the spectacle of state power renders its injustices invisible. I also challenge students to draw parallels between the multiple kinds of disappearances in the novel as well as with contemporary kinds of disappearance such as the undocumented migrants who have vanished during their harrowing treks across Mexico and the Arizona desert.

To make a unit on the dictator novel more comparative and transnational, it can also be extremely useful to create Latin American–Latino pairings for students to explore how Latino/a imaginaries differently interrogate dictatorial power. For example, reading Gabriel García Márquez's *El otoño del patriarca* [*Autumn of the Patriarch*] or *La fiesta del chivo* [*The Feast of the Goat*] alongside Cristina García's *King of Cuba* opens up a discussion about the value of narrating from inside the presidential palace from the perspective of the dictator (a technique characteristic of the Latin American Boom generation) as well as what happens when incorporating oppositional exilic and second generation Latina perspectives within the text. Placing Augusto Roa Bastos's *Yo el supremo* [*I, the Supreme*] in conversation with Salvador Plascencia's *The People of Paper* facilitates an analysis of the critical import of metafiction and the trope of the dictator-as-writer; this highlights the differences between using metafiction to undercut the authority of the authoritarian figure or, in the case of the borderlands Chicano novel, to interrogate the novel form itself and the exploitation of characters who are not compensated for their labor and whose lives are plotted by the writer-as-dictator, which is particularly symbolic given the characters are undocumented farm workers. Positioning Manuel Puig's *El Beso de la mujer araña* [*Kiss of the Spider Woman*] alongside Junot Díaz's *The Brief Wondrous Life of Oscar Wao* allows a comparative reading of the function and value of footnotes and popular film in a novel about authoritarian power, as well as a discussion of how the Latino/a imagination is shaped by other modes of popular culture and how Latino/a gender and sexuality is differently policed and embodied.

I often tell my students at Bryn Mawr College that our classroom is not a dictatorship where, as the professor, my singular voice is authoritative and dominant; rather, it is a discussion-based seminar where myriad perspectives and voices collectively generate knowledge and develop varying readings of our texts as we learn from each other. I find that one useful way to enrich the syllabus, encourage a more dialogic classroom, and familiarize students with often unfamiliar political histories is to have Cultural Critics Panels or Dictator Critics Presentations. For the Cultural Critics Panel, I group students into thematic panels and then ask them to find a cultural production that relates to dictatorship. Students are responsible for finding relevant supplementary material to present on, contextualizing and offering their own analysis of it for the class, and posing a couple of discussion questions to engage the class in a communal analysis of their particular text. The cultural product they choose can take any form—a performance, a mural, a poster, a photo, a film clip, a song, a poem, a dance, a *crónica*, a *testimonio*, a memorial site, etc.—as long as it relates to the topic of dictatorial power. My students at Bryn Mawr have come up with creative and fascinating examples. For example, they have done critical analyses of different *altares* [altars] and monuments to the disappeared; the theater group Yuyachkani; the murals in Balmy Alley in San Francisco; the *cueca sola* that the mothers of the disappeared dance alone; the poetry of Pablo Neruda and Roque Dalton; the documentary *Nostalgia de la luz* and the film *Men with Guns*; and the protest songs of Violeta Parra, Victor Jara, and Calle 13.

For the Dictator Critics Presentation, I have students focus on researching important relevant background to deepen the class's contextual understanding of a novel. For example, I have them research the Dominican Republic under Rafael Trujillo's dictatorship, the U.S. Army School of the Americas, the euphemistic discourse used to describe state violence and torture, official and alternative forms of memorialization in the public sphere, truth and reconciliation commissions, or the Sanctuary Movement. I often guide students to useful secondary texts such as Lauren Derby's *The Dictator's Seduction* (2009), Lesley Gill's *The School of the Americas* (2004), Marguerite Feitlowitz's *A Lexicon of Terror* (1998), Diana Taylor's *Disappearing Acts* and *The Archive and the Repertoire*, Macarena Gómez-Barris's *Where Memory Dwells* (2008), Ariel Dorfman's *Exorcising Terror* (2002), or Renny Golden and Michael McConnell's *Sanctuary* (1986). After presenting their research, students pose textually based questions that help illuminate how such issues are depicted in a given novel, with particular attention to the how of representation and to a specific passage in the novel. I find that shifting the power dynamics in the classroom so that students are the teachers during their panels/presentations helps students feel empowered as analysts participating in the project of cultural studies and counter-dictatorial narrative production.

Conclusion: crossing borders, crossing genres

Just as genres cross borders, so do peoples. In order for students to understand contemporary Latinos/as and their cultural production, they must first acquire a historical consciousness about Latin American immigration to the United States. As Juan González makes clear in his landmark history of Latinos/as in the United States, *Harvest of Empire* (now a fantastic documentary integral to any Latino/a studies classroom), we cannot understand Latin American migration without taking into account the U.S.'s countless interventions in Latin America—colonization, annexation, occupation, counter-insurgency campaigns, propping up dictatorships, support for military coups, exploitative trade agreements, foreign policy drug measures, and border militarizations, not to mention its Bracero Program and its incessant demand for cheap labor—all of which constitute the push and pull factors that shape hemispheric migrations.

We have proposed that the chronicle and the dictator novel are two highly useful genres through which we can teach such important historical and contemporary transnational issues. We have focused on Latino/a authors' aesthetic choices, on why they represent transnational realities through the use of forms that originate from Latin American literary traditions and how they adapt and modify these forms to their experiences as U.S. Latinos/as. Finally, we have argued that doing so allows students to understand the ways in which visions of Latinidad have shifted decisively from the model of acculturation prevalent just a few decades ago to one which takes into account the enduring connections (physical, emotional, artistic) that continue to culturally tie citizens of the Americas to each other across borders.

Notes

1 There is an abundance of critical literature on these two genres, especially in relation to their U.S. ethnic, hemispheric, and global migrations and adaptations. The collections on magical realism edited by Lois Parkinson Zamora and Wendy Faris, and by Lyn Di Iorio Sandín and

Richard Pérez and those on *testimonio* edited by the Latina Feminist Group, and by Louise Detwiler and Janis Breckenridge, are particularly useful texts in the classroom.

2 These works by individual scholars—as well as essays included in collections such as those edited by Gustavo Pérez Firmat, Juan Poblete, Jon Smith and Deborah Cohn, Jeffrey Belnap and Raúl Fernández, and Caroline F. Levander and Robert S. Levine—participate in what literary scholar Paul Jay (2010) has labeled the "transnational turn in literary studies."

3 This is not exclusively a South-to-North process; indeed, just as migratory routes are circular, so are generic routes. We can consider, for example, how in 2007 Latinos Daniel Alarcón and Junot Díaz were both named in the highly prestigious and selective Bogotá 39, a list of the top 39 Latin American authors under 39 years of age.

4 Examples include sixteenth-century *crónicas* written by Hernán Cortés, Bernal Díaz del Castillo, and Bartolomé de Las Casas.

5 This connection makes particular sense because of the generic intersections between *crónica* and "New Journalism," one that has been noted by various Latin Americans investigating the genre, including Carlos Monsiváis. New Journalism, which was codified by Tom Wolfe in the 1970s, is characterized by its use of novelistic conventions (free indirect discourse, characterization, symbolism, etc.) in journalistic writing.

6 See Monica Hanna's interview with Hernandez, "Chronicling the New Transnational Migrant Experience: An Interview with Daniel Hernandez" in *Label Me Latina/o* (2014).

7 See Marta Caminero-Santangelo and Ruth Brown for useful scholarly articles on the subject of contemporary chronicles about undocumented migrations. On the ironies of border security, see Wendy Brown. An accessible text to use in the classroom on the subject of transnational Latinidad and its effect on United States cities is Mike Davis's *Magical Urbanism* (2001). Although the data is from the 2000 census and thus not fully up-to-date, his concepts continue to be relevant, such as his discussion of "transnational suburbs."

8 This projection was supplied by the Department of Homeland Security, according to the *New York Times*. See Richard Fausset and Ken Belson (2014).

9 Since shorter forms can sometimes be easier to incorporate into a syllabus than long-form novels, see Helena María Viramontes's "Cariboo Café" (1985), Benjamin Alire Sáenz's "Alligator Park" (1992), Achy Obejas's "We Came All the Way from Cuba So You Could Dress Like This?", Edwidge Danticat's story cycle *The Dew Breaker* (2004), and Daniel Alarcón's story collection *War by Candlelight* (2005).

10 In this sense, we could think of them as doing similar work as African American neo-slave narratives. African American literature and scholarship is highly attuned to the traumas of slavery and to the residual elements of slavery in the present, so reading a neo-slave narrative like Toni Morrison's *Beloved* together with a Latino dictator novel like Junot Díaz's *The Brief Wonderous Life of Oscar Wao* enables students to think intergenerationally and interracially about the afterlife of trauma.

11 In order to get students to articulate their stereotypes about dictatorship, I begin by having them watch trailers for the films *The Great Dictator, Bananas, Moon over Parador, Last King of Scotland*, and *The Dictator* and then ask them to identify the tropes used to portray dictatorship (embodied in the dictator) and democracy (embodied in white savior figures).

12 For example, we can use Latina/o dictator novels to teach about state violence such as repression, torture, disappearance (e.g., *Lost City Radio* and *The Long Night of White Chickens*); social justice in the form of revolutionary and solidarity movements (e.g., *In the Time of the Butterflies* and *Mother Tongue*); imperialism in the form of occupation and interventionism (e.g., *Let It Rain Coffee* and *The Tattooed Soldier*); migration such as exile, undocumented migration, or reverse migration (e.g., *In Search of Bernabé* and *When the Ground Turns in Its Sleep*); racial discrimination and economic exploitation (e.g., *The People of Paper* and *The Ordinary Seaman*); machismo and heteropatriarchy (e.g., *Geographies of Home* and *King of Cuba*); language politics and cultural identity (e.g., *How the García Girls Lost Their Accents* and *The Farming of Bones*); and history's impact on the present (e.g., *The Brief Wondrous Life of Oscar Wao* and *Memory Mambo*).

13 See Jennifer Harford Vargas, "Dictating a Zafa: The Power of Narrative Form in Junot Díaz's *The Brief Wondrous Life of Oscar Wao.*" *MELUS: Multi-Ethnic Literature of the United States* 39.3 (Fall 2014): 8–30.

14 The Sanctuary Movement was a political-religious movement in the United States in the 1980s that sheltered Central American refugees from military dictatorships and imagined itself as a contemporary underground railroad. The New Sanctuary Movement currently aids undocumented migrants in the United States.

Resources for teaching transnational forms

Belnap, Jeffrey and Raúl Fernández, eds. *José Martí's "Our America": From National to Hemispheric Cultural Studies.* Durham, NC: Duke University Press, 1998.

Concannon, Kevin, Francisco Lomelí, and Marc Priewe, eds. *Imagined Transnationalism: US Latino/a Literature, Culture, and Identity.* New York: Palgrave, 2009.

Dowdy, Michael. *Broken Souths: Latina/o Poetic Responses to Neoliberalism and Globalization.* Tucson, AZ: University of Arizona Press, 2013.

Di Iorio Sandín, Lyn and Richard Perez, eds. *Moments of Magical Realism in US Ethnic Literature: Meta-Morphoses and Migrations.* New York: Palgrave Macmillan, 2012.

Levander, Caroline F. and Robert S. Levine. *Hemispheric American Studies: Essays Beyond the Nation.* New Brunswick: Rutgers University Press, 2007.

Parkinson Zamora, Lois. *The Usable Past: The Imagination of History in Recent Fiction of the Americas.* Cambridge: Cambridge University Press, 1997.

Pérez-Firmat, Gustavo, ed. *Do the Americas Have a Common Literature?* Durham, NC: Duke University Press, 1990.

Poblete, Juan, ed. *Critical Latin American and Latino Studies.* Minneapolis, MN: University of Minnesota Press, 2003.

Rodríguez, Ana Patricia. *Dividing the Isthmus: Central American Transnational Histories, Literatures, and Cultures.* Austin: University of Texas Press, 2009.

Smith, Jon and Deborah Cohn, eds. *Look Away: The U.S. South in New World Studies.* Durham, NC: Duke University Press, 2004.

Vigil, Ariana. *War Echoes: Gender and Militarization in US Latina/o Cultural Production.* New Brunswick: Rutgers University Press, 2014.

7 Latino literary nonfiction

Michael Nieto Garcia

It is an annual ritual—following fast on the migratory descent of college and high school students from the soaring heights of summer vacation back to the stooped roost of cramped desks—that sometime during the first few weeks of the fall term the following Socratic exchange, or some version thereof, can be heard in classrooms everywhere:

STUDENT: "What I like [or dislike] about this novel is blah."
TEACHER: "Well, before we go any further, we should clarify—is this a novel?"
    Silence from the entire class.
STUDENT TWO: (in a hesitant voice) "I guess it's not really a novel."
TEACHER: "What is the difference between a novel and work of nonfiction? Anyone?"
STUDENT THREE: "A novel is fiction. And nonfiction is ... *not* fiction."
TEACHER: "And what is fiction?"
STUDENT FOUR: "Fiction is made up. It didn't really happen—in the real world."
TEACHER: "Why does it matter? Why is it important that we make a clear distinction in our minds between fiction and nonfiction?"
STUDENT TWO: (more assured now) "Because you'd be really mad if someone told you it was all true, but it was really just made up."
TEACHER: (supremely self-satisfied at having turned this into a teaching moment) "Well said, all of you. Yes, it is that and more. Wittgenstein said that the purpose of philosophy was to let the fly out of the fly-bottle, to clarify the unwarranted vagueness in our language, and fuzziness in our categories, that leads to woolly thinking. To sharpen your mental concepts is to develop your mind."

The generic confusion (confusion about the book's **genre**) can just as easily go the other direction, as often happens with one of the most iconic of Latino/a texts, Sandra Cisneros's *The House on Mango Street*. Many readers think of *Mango Street* as Cisneros's **memoir**, though the collection of linked vignettes is clearly labeled as "fiction/literature" on the back cover. Marketers of the book, aware that novels sell better than collections of poetry or short fiction, caused a different kind of generic confusion by also promoting it as a "novel." Though inaccurate, the "novel" designation at least signals to readers that the book is a work of fiction, thus evading the type of betrayal perpetrated on readers by James Frey and his publisher in 2003 when calling his *A Million Little Pieces* a "memoir," despite blatant fabrications, including his account of an 87-day jail term. As it turned out, the author hadn't even spent the night in jail.

Another example of authorial deception is Danny Santiago's *Famous All over Town*, a 1983 novel depicting barrio life as told from the perspective of a Chicano youth. A year after publication it was revealed that the author's real name was Daniel Lewis James, an Anglo in his seventies. In both cases, readers felt betrayed by the author's deceptive self presentation.[1] And in Frey's case—because he claimed to have written a memoir—the authorial presentation unequivocally violates the "Autobiographical Pact," as life writing scholar Philippe Lejeune dubbed the tacit understanding between authors and their readers about the rules and conventions of presenting a work as autobiography (1989: 29).

Similar pacts and conventions hold for other genres. Somewhat paradoxically, genres are kept fresh by writers transgressing and otherwise writing against the genre's conventions even as they work within the form, but that does not change the more fundamental truth, as suggested by our astute student, above, that the *genre that we attribute to a text matters because it orients reader expectations and frames interpretation.* Clarity of genre is even more important for nonfiction than fiction because works of nonfiction are presented to us as true, as corresponding, according to the truth standards of that genre, in a particular way with the world outside the text.

In what follows, I wish to both clarify and complicate some of our notions of literature, and of literary nonfiction by or about Latinos/as in particular. We can easily clarify—for example, and as we have just done in distinguishing fiction from nonfiction—the important distinctions to keep in mind when reading or teaching memoir, say, as opposed to history. (By way of settling the matter before moving on, let us say that history is based as objectively as possible on historical facts: the public record, written documents, eyewitness accounts, the internal consistency of such accounts, and cross-checking multiple sources against each other; memoir, in contrast, focuses on subjective experience, beholden to those same historical facts, but refracting them through the viewpoint, emotions, and self-narrative of the author.) In addition to clarifying what can be clarified, we must also complicate, or nuance, what is commonly oversimplified, including an overly simplistic notion of what we mean by *literature* and *nonfiction*. Not all books are literature, and not all nonfiction has the same truth standards.

As our subject is teaching literary nonfiction, proposing a working definition of *literature* might seem like a logical way to proceed. This is no easy mandate to fulfill. Thankfully, we need not, for our purposes here, enchain ourselves to this Sisyphean task. Defining, as we have already done, the *nonfiction* half of the compound term *literary nonfiction* is far easier than defining *literary*—the adjectival form used to designate that which has the quality of literature. In lieu of a procrustean definition, then, I devote a section each to four primary dimensions of literature: the political, aesthetic, ontological, and epistemic. I take this approach because Latino/a literature is frequently taught in non-literature courses, and this is an approach that equips the nonspecialist with some key conceptual tools for teaching literature—and literary nonfiction in particular—in any classroom. First the political.

The politics of prose

The first political reality to note about literature, as Latino/a scholars have long brought attention to, is that canonization and what gets deemed as literary often have as much to do with the dynamics of power in society as with the aesthetic sentiments of the age.

The second political reality about literature, and a particular challenge when teaching minority literature, is this: many students are initially resistant to reading the assigned texts in the first place. Vocationally minded students may not see the value of a literature course at all, while students of a culturally monolithic mindset may resent the diversity requirement at their school. Personally, I prefer to address their reservations directly by beginning the semester with a spirited class discussion about the value of the course, and of the texts we will be reading—and how both are relevant to their own lives.

For art's sake

Having first suggested that all art is political—and that even our artistic sensibilities are influenced by politics, including the politics of our unexamined assumptions and biases—I must now also insist on the aesthetic dimension of texts. Some texts really are more literary (in the formal and aesthetic senses) than others. Even those who are hesitant to generalize, or to make any claims about the literariness of texts that exhibit X quality as opposed to Y quality, concede this point insofar as they agree that there are texts about whose **literariness** there is general agreement among those generally agreed to be the most perspicacious readers. Indeed, there tends to be consensus about the literariness of texts even among those who dislike the content, politics, tone—or even the style—of the text in question.

Richard Rodriguez's *Hunger of Memory* (1982) is a classic case in point. Even those who were initially critical of the book—in particular for Rodriguez's positions on polarizing political issues such as assimilation, affirmative action, and bilingual education—inevitably qualified their criticisms by commending the author's prose style. The book, all agreed, was beautifully written. To take another example, and to widen the scope of the U.S. Latino/a literary tradition to include the long and profound influence of writers from the Americas, the literary merit of Jorge Luis Borges's *Ficciones* (1956) is universally acknowledged—not least of all for its storytelling technique and seminal narrative innovations—and this was so even when fantastic literature was not in vogue with the big publishing houses in New York, London, Madrid, Mexico City, and Buenos Aires. The same can be said of Gabriel García Márquez's *Cien años de soledad* (1969) and magical realism. Making these and related conversations the subject of classroom discussion is a great way to inject needed nuance into our understanding of the politics of canonization, as well as to instill a lifelong appreciation of literature in one's students—literature as art, as narrative, as an essential part of what makes us human.

Thou shalt not commit a social science

In the opening scenario of this chapter, our astute student chastened readers for sometimes failing to distinguish a work of fiction from one of nonfiction. As teachers we must likewise chasten ourselves for too often treating works of literature as sociology. To do so is to commit an ontological fallacy, to discount the full dimensionality of texts in favor of a one-dimensional understanding of literature that is simultaneously overly generalized and overly reductive. Ethnic writers, and ethnic autobiographers in particular, as I have argued elsewhere, have long been marginalized by the sociologizing of literature, specifically in the form of mainstream reader expectations that their characters (in fiction) and life narrative (in autobiographical writing) will be representative—regardless of the particularity of their own experiences—of an entire race or ethnic group.[2] We do, of course—and we should—read works of literature to learn about others and to vicariously experience lives, thoughts, and perspectives other than our own. If doing so invites a **sociological approach** (see Markus and Moya 2010) then let us celebrate and learn from such readings as one of many angles from which to begin to understand the text and its context. But let us do so without ever forgetting that we are trying to understand and appreciate a work of art, and that this is just one of many incomplete and provisional starting points. In all cases, the same caveat applies: *no one approach should be applied to the exclusion of all other interpretive frames.*

A defining quality of literature is its irreducibility. Like consciousness, it arises from emergent properties, meaning that its true essence—its ontological nature—is holistic rather than atomistic. For that reason, we must strive to appreciate works of literature in their totality. At Harvard's 1946 Victory Commencement, the English poet W. H. Auden delivered a somewhat tongue-in-cheek exhortation to graduates: "Thou shalt not sit / with statisticians nor commit / a social science" ("Under the Lyre," in *Selected Poems* 2007: 187). His words serve as a waggish defense of art and the humanities against overly reductive and empirical approaches imported whole cloth from the social and physical sciences. This is by no means to suggest an unbridgeable divide between science and the humanities, or that the two cultures cannot learn from each other. It's just the opposite. However, we must be ever vigilant against reductive approaches that distort more than they illuminate. And, ontologically speaking, we must keep always in mind what level of reality we are dealing with. For what we are really talking about when we call something literature is not the physical book (nor just any instance of writing) but something much more abstract: the artistic expression of written language, and the meaning that people derive from it.

Epistemology of the text

The epistemological dimension of texts boils down to hermeneutics. We derive meaning from texts by interpreting them. This does not mean, it must be stressed, that each text has a single, secret meaning, or that all interpretations are equally persuasive. Literary interpretation focuses on the text in question, but thus circumscribing the object of study doesn't make the task of interpretation any less challenging, since—and this adds yet another qualification to our earlier discussion about how works of literature correspond to the real world—words and texts are only meaningful in context, and part of that context is the world outside the text. Social context matters all the more so for literary nonfiction by Latino/a authors, as their texts tend to be written and read with heightened awareness of the author's social location.

In respect to the multidimensionality of literature we can offer the following summation: every text is a story, and no story is an island. Rather, stories are social, and interpretation—as central to what makes us human as language or consciousness—is driven by context. When we think of stories we tend to think of imaginative fiction. But as I hope to have impressed upon you by now, nonfiction texts are stories too.

Tools for teaching Latino/a literary nonfiction

The remainder of this chapter provides a **literary toolbox** for reading nonfiction—the different assortments of tools presented in fairly schematic form in separate sections. Though the presentation is schematic, the application of these tools should not be. Modeling the use of these tools—noticing the elements of literature, awareness of genre conventions, adopting a sufficiently skeptical stance when reading nonfiction—in the classroom develops and hones critical reading skills.

The most important tool for teaching literature is simply this: strive to instill a love of close reading. Young Adult books, such as those by Julia Alvarez and Gary Soto, hook readers during their formative years, turning them into avid readers—and conferring upon them the cognitive benefits of reading. The teacher's task is to then forge minds kindled in the furnace of reading for pleasure into fine-honed instruments that can also read critically. And that requires close reading skills: paying careful attention to the language of the text, formulating questions as one reads, learning to distinguish significant details—such as allusions, metaphors, and symbolism—from trivial ones.

It also means cultivating the habit of looking up any words the reader doesn't know— including those in Spanish—and developing an appreciation for the nuts and bolts of language, sentences, and texts. Even punctuation and grammar are interesting when one realizes that a single comma can change the meaning of a sentence ("let's eat Grandpa" is quite the plot twist compared to "let's eat, Grandpa") or that a sentence rendered in the active voice as opposed to the passive construction ("mistakes were made") can mean the difference between assigning agency and evading responsibility (who, exactly, made those mistakes?). Through textual and linguistic nuance we craft more thoughtful, sophisticated responses to our most pressing moral, political, and existential challenges. Supreme Court decisions—the hermeneutics of which center on a written document, the U.S. Constitution, and are not too far removed from literary interpretation—routinely balance on fine distinctions of word choice and the delicate shadings of meaning. Given the social importance of skillful interpretation, and given, furthermore, that literature introduces us to other points of view, makes us more culturally aware, and expands our empathy for others, one can't help thinking that a global community with more close readers would be a more reasonable and compassionate world.

The elements of literature

The first set of tools consists of the elements of literature, which readers expect to encounter in works of fiction but frequently overlook when reading nonfiction. Despite this tendency, awareness of literary devices is often even more important when reading nonfiction because, to take the example of tropes, its metaphors are employed not simply to entertain us but more pointedly to persuade. The following schematic gloss of the elements of literature is by no means exclusive, limitations of space precluding going into details or providing a glossary of terms, and so I refer teachers to the plethora of readily available handbooks and resource guides on writing, literary analysis, and the teaching of both—including those by Aldama, Corbett, Gottschalk, Graff, Griffith, and others listed in the Resources for Teaching Latino Literary Nonfiction section at the end of this chapter.

Let us begin with tropes and **analogies** (see Corbett; Griffith) of various kinds: metaphor, simile, metonymy, and synecdoche. These are not just literary flourishes, but tools for thinking, both through association and by logical connection. Likewise essential to cognitive functioning is **imagery**, its powerful effect in literature reflecting the dominance of vision in human perception. It should be noted, however, that the best writing evokes sensorial impressions that appeal to the other senses as well: smells, tastes, sounds, and descriptions of touch and textures. A similar principle holds for **symbolism** (something standing for something else), which, given its inherent ambiguity, may challenge the literal-minded, who might be surprised to learn that the logic of symbolism is not only indispensable to their own thought processes but also makes human language possible.

A good way to introduce the fundamental elements of literature is by performing, early in the semester, a close reading, or unpacking, of a poem in class. Poetry is ideal for priming students to become close readers, as it is not only the most condensed literary form but also the one in which the elements of literature are most ubiquitous. Poems give teachers an opportunity to point out **poetic devices** (see Vendler)—rhyme, meter, rhythm, assonance, repetition, alliteration, and musicality—which are also used in fiction and nonfiction.

The **classical rhetoric tradition** (see Corbett and Connors 1999) identifies and catalogs such rhetorical devices and figures of speech as irony, ellipsis, litotes, syllepsis, anaphora, hyperbole, oxymoron, parallelism, personification, onomatopoeia, and antimetabole.

At the macro level (see Griffith 2014) are such standbys as theme, setting, and characterization.

Narrative devices (see Aldama 2009) include plot, focalization (of time, the dilation or compression of narrative time, and point of view: who is speaking, and whose consciousness the narrative is filtered through), and the presentation of situations that prompt readers to make moral judgments. Voice and tone can function like a genre. For instance, we interpret a text differently if the voice is ironic and the tone is humorous rather than literal and leaden with gravitas.

Texts, therefore, must be read and appreciated through overlapping interpretive frames: genre (memoir, novel, epic, lyric), context (social, political, historical, ethnic, and more), voice (satire, for example), tone (ludic, tragic, sentimental), and point of view (is the story told from the farm owner's perspective or the farm worker's?)—just to name the more salient starting points. A particularly important interpretive frame concerning literary nonfiction is whether a word or passage should be read literally or figuratively. Wars have been waged over interpretive matters such as these, particularly when the text in question is considered sacred (including secular scripture—witness the example of civil wars fought over the interpretation of a sovereign nation's constitution) to a large number of people.

Other significant interpretive contexts and frames multiply from the above examples as one delves into the text. This is what I mean by the irreducibility of literature. Though their words are fixed to the page, texts are capable of assuming countless permutations. The meanings that one derives from a text depend significantly on the knowledge, beliefs, and experiences one brings to the text, and which interpretive frames one chooses (or, through passive reading, unthinkingly assumes or subconsciously adopts) to view the text through. Each text is a cosmos, the most luminous of which perpetually inspire a sense of wonder in readers. To read more perceptively is to more fully experience the awe and mystery of that cosmos, a spiritual and intellectual journey that not only expands the mind but also makes us more fully human. This is the spirit that I strive to instill in my students when teaching literature, hoping, as every teacher does, that intrinsic motivations will supplant extrinsic ones and that each student will come to her own realization that simply increasing her awareness of common narrative devices and the interpretive frames she is using will not only make her a better close reader but also a better thinker—and, through greater empathy with other points of view, perhaps even a better person too.

Nonfiction genres

There are several different subgenres within the larger rubric of Latino/a literary non-fiction. Among the most popular of these are memoir (Cantú, Chávez), essays

(Anzaldúa, Rodriguez), historical narrative (las Casas, Cabeza de Vaca), and journalistic books (Tobar, Urrea). The examples provided in parentheses will prove far more useful to understanding each genre than will any attempt at a rigid definition for each. A **genre** (see Culler) is essentially a set of conventions and expectations (some more tacit than explicit) framing any piece of writing identified with that form (whether tacitly or explicitly). Readers learn the conventions not by reading a rulebook for each genre, but by reading books belonging to that genre. No rulebook could ever be complete, since genre is not an entity but a category, or set, and because genres are always evolving.

Sometimes the book's predominant genre (though genre is the primary or initial interpretive frame through which a book is typically read) is not immediately apparent. For example, Oscar "Zeta" Acosta's *The Autobiography of a Brown Buffalo* (1972) and its sequel, *The Revolt of the Cockroach People*, are labeled by the publisher as autobiography. However, the protagonist seems more persona than real person; the account reads more like a novel than personal memoir; and the narrative tone is so over-the-top that even descriptions of historical events feel embellished. This is all quite confusing until the reader realizes that the book is also written as **satire** (see Bogel).[3] Reader recognition that the book is satirical brings with it a different set of genre conventions, thus changing the interpretive frame through which readers make sense of the narrative.

As with Acosta's autobiographical satires, many books are **hybrids** of more than one genre. Judith Ortiz Cofer's collection *Latin Deli* (1993), for example, includes a mix of poetry, fiction, folklore, vignettes, epistolary fiction, and personal essays. Jimmy Santiago Baca's *Working in the Dark: Reflections of a Poet of the Barrio* (1992) intermingles essay, poetry, and the poet's journal entries. Gloria Anzaldúa's monumental *Borderlands/La Frontera: The New Mestiza* (1987) seamlessly weaves together myth, poetry, history, Spanglish, scholarship, song lyrics, and the personal essay.

Following is a brief list, in addition to those already mentioned, of exceptionally teachable titles from the Latino/a literary nonfiction canon. (I have only included the subtitle when it elucidates the essence of the book):

Life writing/memoir/autobiography:

Always Running: La Vida Loca by Luis J. Rodríguez
Before Night Falls by Reinaldo Arenas
Canícula: Snapshots of a Girlhood en la Frontera by Norma Cantú
César Chávez: An Organizer's Tale by César Chávez
Heading South, Looking North by Ariel Dorfman
Nobody's Son: Notes from an American Life by Luis Alberto Urrea
Silent Dancing: A Partial Remembrance of a Puerto Rican Childhood by Judith Ortiz Cofer
Waiting for Snow in Havana by Carlos Eire
When I was Puerto Rican by Emeralda Santiago

Prison memoir:

A Place to Stand by Jimmy Santiago Baca
The Man Who Outgrew his Prison Cell: Confessions of a Bank Robber by Joe Loya

Essays:

Brown, Darling, and *Days of Obligation* by Richard Rodriguez
Gritos by Dagoberto Gilb
The Effects of Knut Hamsun on a Fresno Boy by Gary Soto
Zapata's Disciple by Martín Espada

Historical narrative:

Chronicle of the Narváez Expedition by Álvar Núñez Cabeza de Vaca

Exposé (also a historical narrative):

The Devastation of the Indies by Fray Bartolomé de las Casas

Literary journalism:

Translation Nation: Defining a New American Identity in the Spanish-Speaking United States by Héctor Tobar
The Devil's Highway and *Across the Wire: Life and Hard Times on the Mexican Border* by Luis Alberto Urrea

Toolkit for reading life writing

The largest category of Latino/a literary nonfiction is life writing—including memoir, autobiography, and, with varying degrees of overlap, the personal essay—which is why I include a special section dedicated to it here. Conveniently, much of the close reading advice that applies to life writing (see Fuchs and Howes 2007; Smith and Watson 2010) also applies to literary nonfiction more broadly. As when reading any work of nonfiction, a certain level of skepticism is called for since our propensity to read the book as a true account also predisposes us to be persuaded to the particular view of reality that the book presents.

Here are some things to keep in mind when reading life writing:

- All memoirists are liars. (No story can render the whole truth of reality. Literature corresponds in various ways to the real world but does not duplicate it. Memoir and other forms of life writing show the world through the narrow keyhole of one person's subjective point of view.)
- Memoirists privilege story truth over literal truth, though conscientious memoirists strive to remain faithful to historical truth (itself a form of narrative truth) to the extent that it can be determined.
- Life writers are guilty of sins of omission, shaping the narrative through the selection of detail. Ask yourself: what is missing? What facts and details would you have included if trying to be fair and honest in telling the story?
- Ask yourself the investigative reporter's question: why is this person lying to me? What are the writer's motives? What are their presuppositions and hidden agendas? Almost nobody, for instance, is going to present oneself as the bad guy, or as a habitual jerk.

- Never forget: every story is somebody's story, told from a particular point of view. We all have our biases, preconceptions, unexamined assumptions, and the like.
- The people in the memoir are characterizations.
- The literary self of memoir is a persona, the author's biological self rendered as a literary character.
- For similar reasons, whenever the author writes in the first-person voice—and this is even more important in fiction—we must also distinguish the narrator from the flesh-and-blood author.
- Dialogue is reconstructed. (Did you really think that the writer was able to remember every word of a conversation that took place more than 20 years ago?)
- **Dialect** is rendered. (Rather than a strictly phonetic approach to reading dialect aloud, aurally picture what a real person from that region, social location, or linguistic background would actually speak like.)
- Remember, there are different modes of reading. Sometimes we read for pleasure, other times for information or to critically analyze a text.

Finally, to make the learning all the more tangible, as a teacher you might ask your students to write their own memoir, or something like it—even if it is nothing more than keeping a journal. After assigning autobiographical writing to your students, you might have them discuss the techniques they found themselves using when dealing with the challenges of autobiographical writing.

Notes

1 This is because "readers frame their readings of texts based on what they know, or think they know, about the ethnicity of the author" (Garcia 2014: 18). Stated more broadly: "The ways in which works of fiction are meaningful to readers are also informed—as is autobiography—by what readers think they know about the author. Among the more visible of such features, as I have been arguing, is the author's ethnicity" (2014: 168–69).
2 See Garcia 2014: xii, 18–26, 49–54.
3 On Acosta's narratives specifically, see Hames-García 2000.

Resources for teaching Latino literary nonfiction

Abrams, M. H. and Geoffrey Galt Harpham. *A Glossary of Literary Terms*. 9th edn. Boston: Wadsworth, 2009.

Aldama, Frederick Luis. *The Routledge Concise History of Latino/a Literature*. New York and London: Routledge, 2013.

——. *A User's Guide to Postcolonial and Latino Borderland Fiction*. Austin: University of Texas Press, 2009.

Bogel, Fredric V. *The Difference Satire Makes: Rhetoric and Reading from Jonson to Byron*. Ithaca: Cornell University Press, 2000.

Cantú, Norma E. "Memoir, autobiography, testimonio." In Suzanne Bost and Frances R. Aparicio (eds) *The Routledge Companion to Latino/a Literature*. New York: Routledge, 2013.

Corbett, Edward P. J. and Robert J. Connors. *Style and Statement*. New York: Oxford University Press, 1999.

Culler, Jonathan. *Literary Theory: A Very Short Introduction*. Oxford: Oxford University Press, 1997.

Fuchs, Miriam and Craig Howes, eds. *Teaching Life Writing Texts*. New York: MLA, 2007.

Gonzalez, Juan. *Harvest of Empire: A History of Latinos in America.* New York: Viking Penguin, 2000.

Gottschalk, Katherine and Keith Hjortshoj. *The Elements of Teaching Writing: A Resource for Instructors in All Disciplines.* Boston: Bedford, 2004.

Graff, Gerald and Cathy Birkenstein. *They Say, I Say: the Moves that Matter in Academic Writing.* 3rd edn. New York: Norton, 2014.

Griffith, Kelley. *Writing Essays about Literature: A Guide and Style Sheet.* Boston: Wadsworth, 2014.

Hogan, Patrick Colm. *Cognitive Science, Literature, and the Arts: A Guide for Humanists.* New York and London: Routledge, 2003.

Markus, Hazel Rose and Paula M. L. Moya. *Doing Race: 21 Essays for the 21st Century.* New York: Norton, 2010.

Nealon, Jeffrey and Susan Searls Giroux. *The Theory Toolbox: Critical Concepts for the Humanities, Arts, and Social Sciences.* Lanham, MD: Rowan and Littlefield, 2003.

Richter, David H., ed. *Falling into Theory: Conflicting Views on Reading Literature.* 2nd edn. Boston: Bedford, 2000.

Smith, Sidonie and Julia Watson. *Reading Autobiography: A Guide for Interpreting Life Narratives.* 2nd edn. Minneapolis: University of Minnesota Press, 2010.

Stavans, Ilan, ed. *The Norton Anthology of Latino Literature.* New York: Norton, 2011.

Velasco, Juan. "*Automitografías*: The border paradigm and Chicana/o autobiography." *Biography* 27.2 (2004): 313–38.

Vendler, Helen. *Poems, Poets, Poetry: An Introduction and Anthology.* 2nd edn. Boston: Bedford, 2002.

Part II

Teaching parts that make up the Latino/a whole

8 Teaching Mexican American/Chicano authors

Christopher González

Works by Mexican American or Chicano[1] authors comprise the largest block of writings in the United States by any single Latino group. Perhaps this should not be too big a surprise. According to the 2010 U.S. Census nearly three out of every four Latinos in the United States are of Mexican heritage; 31.8 million Mexican Americans comprise 63 percent of all U.S. Hispanics (United States). This straightforward statistic, coupled with the growing number of Mexican Americans, suggest that a course concentrating on Mexican American literature is a viable offering to secondary and post-secondary students.[2] In particular, such a course offers students the chance to further their understanding of Mexican American culture and literary production. However, because an intense examination of Mexican American literature can be used as a means of purely historical, sociological, or political forays, at times these kinds of literature courses can lose sight of the fact that the literary component of Mexican American literature is just as important an aspect of this tradition of writing as anything else. Indeed, because it is the form that gives shape to the content, studying the formal aspects of Mexican American literature can be an important entry point for discussing overarching thematic issues that reach beyond the text.[3] Teaching Mexican American literature, then, requires a two-pronged approach: one that considers important contextual matters (historical, social, political) and another that focuses on how a given author uses formal devices (point of view, voice, temporal play, even syntax) to give shape to the content of their literary product.

The core problem one faces in teaching Mexican American literature, a point which I will expand on momentarily, is that teachers invariably contend with entrenched stereotypes held by students. To make matters worse, these students often rely on stereotypes without their realizing it. Though it is easy to point to Warner Brothers character Speedy Gonzales as an exemplar of these potent stereotypes, let us not fail to forget how American literature and Hollywood have been complicit in creating the one-dimensional image of the siesta-seeking, serape-wearing, shifty Mexican, the spicy bombshell, or more recently, the gangbanger/narco kingpin. Alternatively, when these outrageous caricatures are absent from the literature we read and teach, the truth is that Mexican Americans remain invisible and without voice in American literature—a literature that, echoing Lincoln, ought to be of, by, and for all Americans. Hoping to reverse this trend and give Mexican Americans a stake in the American literary landscape, authors have worked hard to publish their work in the hopes that it would reach a willing readership. A course in Mexican American literature should strive to facilitate this critical goal.

Although there are several universities that have worked hard to establish departments in Chicana/o Studies, such as UCLA, the vast majority of institutions of higher learning do not yet have readily accessible resources for teaching a course devoted to

Mexican American or Chicana/o literature. This is changing, but some instructors and professors at institutions of higher learning may have the opportunity to teach this kind of course as part of a traditional English or Comparative Studies program without the anchor of a Mexican American Studies program. I imagine most readers of this chapter, and indeed this entire volume, may not necessarily have the resources of a program or department devoted to the study of Chicanos and Mexican Americans but nevertheless want to conduct a literature-based course on the subject.

Initial tips

There are several considerations I outline below that may save you from headaches and frustrations later on in your course. Keep in mind that students enrolled in this sort of class may have very little experience with Mexican American culture beyond what they have seen in the popular American imagination, to say nothing of Mexican American literature. As the instructor of such a course, you must prepare to grapple with a lack of cultural knowledge among your students. Indeed, part of the goal of a Mexican American literature course is to address this lack of knowledge. Remember to reassure your students that they need no prior experience in Mexican American culture in order to take the class. Also, please be aware of the following pedagogical concerns as well:

1   Students with little background knowledge on the topic will naturally have the impulse to read works of Mexican American literature as indicative of *all* Mexican American culture. They may feel like they really *know* the culture after just a few readings. Therefore, you must strive to provide a wide array of thematic content in your readings and to emphasize the diversity within Mexican American literature. Constantly remind your students that while the class readings strive to be a diverse sample, they are not one-for-one correspondences to all of Mexican American culture. For instance, not all Mexican Americans have recently arrived to the United States.
2   The same holds true when it comes to formal considerations of the readings. If students only read works that employ, say, Spanglish in heavy doses, they may associate *all* works of Mexican American literature with this characteristic. You must endeavor to present students with a variety of literary readings—from poetry to short stories; from fiction to memoir; from film to comic art.
3   You may have students who are of Mexican American heritage in your class. If you have a few such students enrolled in your course, other students may look to these students as the "experts." While they may indeed have more detailed knowledge than their non-Mexican American classmates, one should always put a stop to such pressure being placed upon these students. This is especially difficult when the student wants to volunteer this information. You should strive to validate their knowledge, but still remember that it is not fair for them to become the embodiment of all things Mexican American for the class. I recommend discussing the issue with these students privately during office hours and formulating a plan of action with them.
4   It is impossible to discuss the thematic content of the vast majority of Mexican American literature without raising the politics associated with it. Invariably you will have students at different ends of the political spectrum. You must be prepared to facilitate these discussions and avoid shutting down students with unpopular views. Foster a healthy dialogue whenever possible. This is best accomplished by modeling questions, responses, and discussion points. As in discussing matters of

religion in the literature classroom, I advise presenting all positions equally and then testing them against scholarly, rigorous argument and analysis. Above all, when discussions seem to be going down rabbit holes, stop the discussion and return to an analysis of the text at hand.

5 Some students who may have very limited knowledge of Mexican American culture may hold many controversial, stereotypical notions. Remember that the purpose of your course, in addition to attending to the literature, is to help dispel misinformation. Thus, you must work to establish a risk-free environment in order to discourage embarrassment and encourage students to voice their ideas. In return, ask that your students keep an open mind and entertain the possibility that their views and opinions might need reconsideration.

These suggestions are not comprehensive, but being aware of them when preparing for your course will be helpful. With these things in mind, the remainder of this chapter will lay out a number of approaches to Mexican American literature in the classroom. Understand that I will focus on what I think are the more significant formal features of Mexican American literature. Attention to other aspects outside of textual form such as issues of representation, identity, gender, ideopolitical considerations, and resistance are also key areas that will illuminate the readings, but those are not what I will discuss below.

Language

A preponderance of Mexican American/Chicano literature is concerned with the interaction between the English and the Spanish languages. Because this is a reality in the lives and experiences of a multitude of Mexican Americans, and an early concern in their lives as well, the subject is often a relevant topic in this area of literary production. The intersection of these two languages as a site of trauma is at the fore of the writings of such writers as, for instance, Richard Rodriguez's *The Hunger of Memory* (1982) and Gloria Anzaldúa's *Borderlands/La Frontera: The New Mestiza* (1987). Each of these writers concentrates on how Spanish, a familial, private language, found little welcome in English-speaking grade schools in California and Texas, respectively. Rodriguez and Anzaldúa explored the subject of language for the rest of their careers.

But the interplay between English and Spanish is not only a thematic concern for authors such as Rodriguez and Anzaldúa, it is also a central formal aspect of the narratives they create. Related to this issue of language is also the materialistic reality that publishers work to enhance sales of their books rather than hinder them. This fact, especially during the middle of the twentieth century, resulted in Mexican American authors who were highly aware of their use of Spanish.[4] Some of the early novels such as José Antonio Villarreal's *Pocho* (1959) and John Rechy's *City of Night* (1963) use only the slightest amount of Spanish. Yet as Mexican American literature developed through the twentieth century and into the twenty-first century, authors continued to press the boundaries for the use of Spanish and have employed a heightened level of code-switching in the creation of their storyworld. As a consequence, readers needed to be able to translate varying amounts of Spanish in order to fully reconstruct the inscribed storyworld. In short, there has been a shifting obligation from the author to the reader that has steadily occurred throughout the development of Mexican American literature. Where authors were once obliged by audiences and publishers to exercise linguistic restraint in their narratives, Mexican American authors are more and more leaving it to readers to do the work of going outside of the text to gather the information needed to reconstruct storyworlds.

Rodriguez and Anzaldúa are the Mexican American authors who most overtly take up the issue of language and the clash of bilingualism. But this tension between English and Spanish in Mexican American literature is almost always a salient feature. That is to say, the tension is evident even when it does not overtly announce itself. Most often this occurs in the form of **code-switching**. Indeed, the political and ideological imperatives in this tradition of literature are only arrived at by careful decisions for when to switch codes, and especially, how far these authors can push the interchange of languages as they construct their storyworld blueprints. As noted above, it is important to remember that authors of Mexican American/Chicano literature have had, for much of their history, little freedom to adopt a bilingual approach in creating their narratives. The result is an ever-present disparity between an ideal reader—one that can handle the narrative in any language or code—and an actual reader who may only understand English.

Many students in the typical English literature classroom are often frustrated or otherwise bothered by the presence of Spanish words in a work of Mexican American literature. At times these students take code-switching as a personal affront. They become frustrated and may come out with a bold declaration such as, "Why doesn't this author write in English when clearly he or she can?" I tend to pre-empt these sorts of surface-level criticisms at the start of the course and reserve addressing the issue until after we have read a few of the required readings. I remind my students to remember that the greater percentage of a typical novel-length work by a Mexican American author is written with an English-only speaker in mind. This means that the students' own sense for how much Spanish appears in the text is most likely overstated. I encourage them to work to discern the Spanish using context clues, and for those students who are not satisfied by this, to use online resources.

The question of *why* an author chooses to incorporate a second language has the potential to yield a productive discussion or a banal one. Banal answers to the question are simply that the author has majority control for what appears on the page. End of story. But any good teacher or professor will resist such an easy accounting of the author's use of language by the student. The following observations will facilitate valuable discussion on how language is used in Mexican American/Chicano literature:

- The use of Spanish in an English language text is rarely used willy-nilly, which indicates that the author has made a purposeful decision to switch to Spanish. Because of the history of the struggle for civil rights by Mexican Americans, and specifically the Chicano Movement, bringing Spanish to bear on what is essentially English discourse hearkens to the political nature of language in the United States. Ask students to identify those moments when Spanish is employed and to draw relevant conclusions and to attempt to address the question, "Why Spanish *here*?"
- When authors of Mexican American/Chicano literature decide to deploy Spanish in their texts, they tacitly announce certain assumptions about their readers. In addition, not all instances of code-switching are equal. Some authors code-switch and then immediately translate what was just said in Spanish; others code-switch and provide ample context clues to orient a reader; still others refuse to imagine a reader who is not bilingual. Attending to these differences will help students understand that it is not simply a matter of an author deciding to use Spanish at a whim. Rather, such

a decision has significant implications. Ask students to analyze these different types of code-switching moves and discuss how they interact with the story the author tells and the students' reception of the story.

- It is important to recognize not only when code-switching occurs in a text but also what aspect of the narrative is connected to these changes in language. For instance, consider a novel where a heterodiegetic (third-person) narrator doesn't use Spanish but the dialogue of certain characters does. Or consider a homodiegetic (first-person) narrator that uses heavy doses of Spanish. Each of these instances of code-switching reveal something significant to the narrative. Thus, encourage students to attend to the narratological constructs such as narrator and reported speech when coming to terms with the language of the texts. (See also Heather Alumbaugh's important insights concerning translation and student exercise of mapping narrative devices used in a given Latino/a literary text.)

- Once your students have had an opportunity to read several examples of Mexican American/Chicano literature that employ code-switching, have them read an excerpt of Chapter 3 of Cormac McCarthy's *All the Pretty Horses* (1992) that features code-switching, preferably during class. The key is to withhold McCarthy's identity until after preliminary discussion. This excerpt has relatively long passages in Spanish (more than just a few words) and may thwart students who cannot read Spanish with some fluency. Ask them what they make of the excerpt and its use of Spanish. Then reveal that a well-respected white author wrote the passage. Some key questions: Is McCarthy allowed to be more aggressive in his use of Spanish than Mexican American authors? How would a publisher react to an author of a Chicano novel with such heavy doses of Spanish in the story? How might a double standard be at work here, and what are the implications of that double standard?

Diversity of form and genre

A course concentrating on Mexican American/Chicano literary production, because it may be the only sustained opportunity for study some students may have, should strive to provide wide coverage based not simply on thematic content but rather on form and genre. The overarching aim for such a course is to demonstrate to the students the diversity within Mexican American literature. While a focus on several novels can be an excellent way of exploring the thematic concerns of Mexican American literature, a course that wishes to highlight diversity of form and genre will need to rely on excerpts and selections. *The Norton Anthology of Latino Literature* (2011), edited by Ilan Stavans, is an outstanding choice that also provides excellent historical and contextual material. If you wish to expose students to several novels, you might have them select a novel from a list provided to them and present on it during the final week or two of the semester. You may choose the parameters of their presentation to fit your learning objectives.

For instance, an excerpt from María Amparo Ruiz de Burton's *The Squatter and the Don* (1885) serves as an important historical reminder to students that Mexican American writing has been around for a minimum of 130 years. Further, Ruiz de Burton's style incorporates the traditions of European romanticism with American realism. Even in this early example of Mexican American literature, *The Squatter and the Don* evinces an amalgam of many literary traditions rather than being something that is hermetically sealed. As students will discover, Mexican American literature has always engaged with other traditions and forms. There is the comedy found in Daniel Venegas's *The*

Adventures of Don Chipote (1928)—originally written in Spanish, Ernesto Galarza's autobiographical *bildungsroman Barrio Boy* (1961), and Américo Paredes's scholarly and seminal *With His Pistol in His Hand* (1958), a folkloric exploration of the legendary Gregorio Cortez. Even from this early range of texts, students will get a sense of the diversity of form in these writings, allowing them to recognize the literary qualities that enable the construction of these particular narratives and essays in the first place.

It is important to remember that students enrolled in this sort of course will most likely have an understanding of British and American literature as diverse in form. That is to say, a good deal of an English major's fundamental knowledge of literature asserts that there have been phases of development within the tradition. They may have learned of the Novel (British), the Romantic period of poetry (British), Walt Whitman's championing of Free Verse poetry, the American Slave narrative, and so on. In other words, students have been trained to see American and British literature as constantly innovative in both content and form. Mexican American literature, until very recently, has been at the margins of the American tradition of literature. As evidence, consider that The Library of America, whose motto reads "America's best and most significant writing in durable and authoritative editions," has yet to devote a single edition to a Mexican American author or poet. Therefore, it is crucial that students are led to see similar development in literary style, form, and technique within the Mexican American literary tradition as they have in American literature. Indeed, that Mexican American literature is a significant part of American literature.

Also, one finds that Mexican American literature truly begins to take all manner of formal techniques in the early 1970s, and specifically in 1972, what I designate as the beginning of a true Mexican American literary tradition. Oscar "Zeta" Acosta's irreverent *The Autobiography of a Brown Buffalo* (1972), Rudolfo Anaya's *Bless Me, Ultima* (1972; a book that has never been out of print), and Rudy Acuña's *Occupied America: The Chicano's Struggle toward Liberation* (1972; a reconsideration of American history) all were published in this watershed year. As a result, a flowering of Mexican American writings is found in the lead up to 1972, a flowering that has continued as the decades have passed.

I mention 1972 as an epicenter of Mexican American literature because it helps contextualize for students why Mexican American novels were relatively late in the literary game in terms of abundance and formal diversity. I remind students that 1972 was at the height of the Chicano Movement, and political and ideological dissent could be found all across the United States. During this time period, many of the barriers to publishing were beginning to crack under the pressure of an activist movement, and smaller presses such as Aunt Lute and Quinto Sol provided an outlet and distribution point for historically marginalized voices. I urge my students to dispel the notion that Mexican American authors and poets were incapable of creating literary works, but rather to imagine the difficulties presented by a publishing industry that had in mind a purchasing readership that did not want to read stories by and about Mexican Americans.

In my class, once we identify the genre of a selected reading, which is another way of saying once we identify the intended audience, there are two simple questions I use to prepare students to grapple with formal elements in the selected readings. The first is, "Who is speaking?" This question is the first question I have my students ask themselves no matter what they are reading for any of my courses. The second is, "Who is being spoken to?" The relevant **narratological** term here is "**narratee**," or the narrator's audience or listener. I have my students create a character sketch of the narrator and the narratee. I also remind students of the basic but oft overlooked distinction between the narrator and the author. Similarly, the narratee is not the actual reader. Doing this helps students feel less alienated when the narrator, for example, speaks in Spanish. The narrator clearly has in mind a narratee who understands Spanish. Since Mexican American literature is often rooted in the life experiences of the author, though fictionalized, it is important that the narrator/narratee relationship be established early in the course. Otherwise, students may have the tendency to read *all* Mexican American literature as memoir or autobiography. Authors like Acosta and Anzaldúa rupture the neat divisions of fiction and autobiography for specific reasons. Indeed, this brings me to my next area of consideration.

Did that really happen, and does it matter?

It is a supposed truism that many writers, regardless of their cultural heritage, write about things they have experienced in life. Take for instance the dictum imposed on creative writers to "write what they know." But at times it seems that readers of Mexican American literature subscribe to the notion that the authors "write only what has happened to them." As suggested by Michael Nieto Garcia in his chapter "Literary Nonfiction" in this volume, I recommend that instructors do away with their students' too-ready adherence to this idea. Reading every work of Mexican American literature as autobiographical, rooted in verifiable fact, deprives the authors of the power and ingenuity of creating fictional **storyworlds**. In other words, we want to encourage students to see Mexican American literature as more than just a set of documents—chronicles and reportage of a life lived as a Chicano or Chicana.

That is not to say that there are no works by Mexican Americans that adhere to facts. Luis Alberto Urrea's *The Devil's Highway* (2004), for instance, is a work of investigative journalism that examines the plight of 26 Mexicans who struggled against brutal hardships to cross the border into the unforgiving Arizona desert. *Enrique's Journey* (2006), by Sonia Nazario, traces the story of a young Honduran boy's search for his mother in America. And Héctor Tobar's *Translation Nation* (2005), too, reveals the struggles of actual, as opposed to fictional, Mexican Americans. These works call out to be read as documents of verifiable fact, yet they are more than simple chronicles. Each of these authors uses the tools of storytelling to bring the reader into the worlds of marginalized people. Through narration and focalization, they bring their subjects to their readers in ways that are not possible otherwise.

Even here, in this style of reportage and investigative journalism, it is important for students to recognize how the facts are organized into a narrative. This holds true even in other works of literary non-fiction such as Galarza's *Barrio Boy*, Rodriguez's *The Hunger of Memory*, and others. Galarza employs conventions of the novel in order to tell his memoir, draping certain parts of his narrative with the veil of fiction. Rodriguez makes great use of the essay form. And there are those works that play with the conventions of life writing. Tomás Rivera's *And the Earth Did Not Devour Him/y no se lo tragó la tierra* (1971), is a significant novel that is structured as a series of interconnected vignettes. Through his use of modernist techniques, Rivera's novel feels like autobiography but is not. Acosta's *The Autobiography of a Brown Buffalo* purposefully misdirects readers by invoking the anything goes "gonzo" style of storytelling. And Anzaldúa's *Borderlands/ La Frontera* may be the most challenging text of all. Not only does it weave multiple languages without consideration of a reader, it comprises short chapters based on life experience, quasi-theoretical philosophy, fantastical thought experiments, as well as a section of poems. None of these works ought to be read as simple retellings of life events. They are carefully designed, complex works of literature.

Of course, there are Mexican American novels that rely heavily on their author's life experiences. But I consistently remind my students that such an approach to literature ought to be but one approach amidst a host of considerations. It is true, for example, that an understanding of James Joyce's life may enrich our enjoyment of *Ulysses* (1922), but if we only attend to considerations for how his life manifests in his novel, we are doing Joyce, *Ulysses*, and ourselves a disservice. Arturo Islas's *The Rain God* (1984), John Rechy's *City of Night* (1963), Luis Urrea's *The Hummingbird's Daughter* (2006), the short stories in Dagoberto Gilb's *The Magic of Blood* (1993), for instance, all tender some aspect of their lives that has been extruded through the wringer of fiction. And they call out to be read as works of fiction.

Thus, it is important to acknowledge the impact that certain events have had on a writer's life and how that makes its way into his or her fiction, but students must not lose sight of the fact that these are works of fiction and not documents. Failing to recognize this diminishes the artistry and literariness of these works. In short, do not let a focus on the author's biography become the dominant thread of exploration in this sort of a class. This becomes easier if students read something like Salvador Plascencia's *The People of Paper* (2005), which indulges in postmodernist narrative technique, or Sesshu Foster's *Atomik Aztex* (2005), an alternate history that ponders what the world would be like if the Aztecs had driven back the Spanish Conquistadores. Since these novels overtly push against a "realistic" setting, students have less of a tendency to attempt to read them as autobiography. Ana Castillo's *So Far from God* (1993) infuses its storyworld with elements of magical realism, defying a reader's understanding of the natural world. Manuel Muñoz's *What You See in the Dark* (2011) employs a second-person narrator as a means of drawing the reader into its Hitchcockian storyworld. And Manuel Gonzales's collection *The Miniature Wife* (2013) features stories that incorporate zombies, faux-science reporting, and an airline jet that has been circling Dallas, Texas for dozens of years. It is precisely these sorts of stories and novels that help students see Mexican American literature as a multifaceted tradition of American letters.

Invariably, these texts will challenge students' prior understandings of Mexican American literature. One narratological concept that helps reinforce the distinction between the narrative as a construction and the author as a person is what Wayne Booth identifies in *The Rhetoric of Fiction* (1961) as the "**implied author**," best thought of as a writing persona or creative projection of the actual author. Put in another way, the idea of the author we construct as we read the text may not necessarily align with the living person who wrote the text. When students recognize the difference, they are more apt to think of the narrative as a strategic and aesthetic blueprint of a narrative rather than a document of facts. The result is that students begin to engage with the text as something that is designed to provoke and evoke specific thoughts and emotions within them, rather than thinking of it as sociological or anthropological writing. You may then begin to ask students questions such as, "Why does Anzaldúa include poetry in *Borderlands/La Frontera*?" "Why does Acosta include elements of fiction in what he titles an autobiography?" "How do we read Urrea's novel, *The Hummingbird's Daughter*, when we know the characters are based on actual members of his family?" In other words, present questions that compel students to confront the *how* of the text and not just the *what*. Always ask your students how the text does what it does—how it is that words on the page can make them feel a range of emotions and ponder substantive issues.

Final words

Teaching a course on Mexican American and Chicano literature is not easy. Not because the subject is daunting or inherently difficult. Rather, a teacher or professor must contend with the little cultural knowledge students may bring with them to the class. The old adage that "a little knowledge is dangerous" is particularly insightful here, precisely because some students may have arrived at that small bit of knowledge through the media, which, as William Nericcio has explored in *Tex[t]-Mex* (2007), revels in stereotypical and racist depictions of Mexican Americans. Because most students are unaware of how problematic their understandings of Mexican American culture might be, care must be taken to leave certain preconceptions at the proverbial door. Additionally, even students of Mexican American heritage may not be familiar with their own history. Therefore, one must never assume.

I always encourage my students to conduct research on the historical contexts of course readings and then share them in class where applicable. But during class lectures and discussions I always emphasize the formal elements of the readings and posit how they refer us back to the historical contexts as well as our current political climate as well. When teaching Mexican American/Chicano literature, it is not enough to simply present an assembly of readings and focus on thematic story ingredients. As teachers of literature, we must attend to the study of Mexican American/Chicano literature as an artistic literary endeavor with the same sorts of rigor that is applied to any other tradition in the literature classroom. With careful analysis of how these works are willfully constructed to move readerships emotionally while forcing them to reconsider, or consider for the first time, how Mexican American/Chicano authors create complex stories, students will leave the course with a nuanced understanding of Mexican American literature and culture.

Notes

1 Despite the title of this chapter, the terms "Mexican American" and "Chicano" are not interchangeable. Many writers, scholars, and activists continue to view "Chicano" with the politics of resistance and it is most associated with *El Movimiento*, or the Chicano Movement. The term was met with immediate resistance from many women who felt left out of the Chicano Movement. Thus began the rise of Chicana Feminism. In more recent years, some writers of Mexican descent who came of age after the Movement do not have the same affinity for the term "Chicano." And some authors such as Salvador Plascencia, born in 1975 in Guadalajara, Mexico and moved to the United States at a young age, is quite literally Mexican American. In this essay I will use Mexican American generically and Chicano when tied specifically to the politics of resistance.

2 According to the 2010 Census, more than half of the total population growth in the United States from 2000 to 2010 was attributable to the increase in the Hispanic/Latino population (United States).

3 For more on how one might teach the use of the formal devices used to give shape to the content of the fiction, see Aldama's *A User's Guide to Postcolonial and Latino Borderland Fiction* (2009) and "A scientific approach to the teaching of a flash fiction" (2014).

4 One readily notes this discomfort of using Spanish when reading José Antonio Villarreal's 1959 *Pocho*. One of the striking features of this novel is Villarreal's decision to not only translate conversation and dialogue within the narrative that take place in Spanish within the

storyworld, but to render these moments into translations of literal English. The result is an odd, markedly stilted English that gives the impression that the novel's characters are speaking in antiquated idioms.

Resources for teaching Mexican American/Chicano authors

Abbott, H. Porter. *The Cambridge Introduction to Narrative*. 2nd edn. New York: Cambridge University Press, 2008.

Aldama, Frederick Luis. *A User's Guide to Postcolonial and Latino Borderland Fiction*. Austin, TX: University of Texas Press, 2010.

——. *The Routledge Concise History of Latino Literature*. New York: Routledge, 2013.

Brown, Ruth. "Telling the story of Mexican migration: chronicle, literature, and film from the post-gatekeeper period," PhD thesis, 2013. Available from: http://uknowledge.uky.edu/hisp_etds/11 (accessed February 4, 2015).

Calderón, Héctor. "Chicano/a literature." In *The Routledge Companion to Latino/a Literature*. Eds. Suzanne Bost and Francis R. Aparicio. London: Routledge, 2013.

——. *Narratives of Greater Mexico: Essays on Chicano Literary History, Genre, and Borders*. Austin: University of Texas Press, 2004.

Contreras, Sheila. *Blood Lines: Myth, Indigenism, and Chicana/o Literature*. Austin: University of Texas Press, 2008.

Gallego, Carlos. "Introduction: migration and movement(s) in Chicano/a literature," *Arizona Quarterly: A Journal of American Literature, Culture, and Theory* 70. 2 (Summer 2014): 1–7.

Gilb, Dagoberto. *Gritos: Essays*. New York: Grove, 2003.

Martín-Rodríguez, Manuel M. *Life in Search of Readers: Reading (in) Chicano/a Literature*. Albuquerque, NM: University of New Mexico Press, 2003.

Rodríguez, Richard T. *Next of Kin: The Family in Chicano/a Cultural Politics*. Durham, NC: Duke University Press, 2009.

Saldívar, Ramón. *Chicano Narrative: The Dialectics of Difference*. Madison: University of Wisconsin Press, 1990.

Stavans, Ilan, ed. *The Norton Anthology of Latino Literature*. New York: Norton, 2011.

Tatum, Charles M. *Chicano and Chicana Literature: Otra voz del pueblo*. Tucson, AZ: University of Arizona Press, 2006.

9 Teaching the Hispanophone Caribbean

María Acosta Cruz

The main objective of my courses on the Hispanic Caribbean islanders and their migrating brethren is two-fold: First, I want to familiarize students with the central themes presented by well-known first-, second-, and third-generation authors from Cuba, the Dominican Republic and Puerto Rico. (I use the category of author expansively to include not just writers but also artists, musicians, and filmmakers who migrated from one of the three islands and who live[d] and/or publish[ed] in the United States.) Second, I want to have them explore the different linguistic and other formal choices these authors make in giving shape to these themes.

To teach the Hispanic Caribbean I find it necessary to give the students an overview of the area's sociohistorical panorama in order to ground the creative works in their cultural and historical heritage. This includes discussion of what cultural (national) "baggage" these communities bring with them; which themes from history are remembered, and which appear to be forgotten. I also find it absolutely necessary to include discussions of language use. For instance, students focus on the use of devices such as code-switching as a way to understand better how authors, filmmakers, artists, and musicians interact with at least two cultures at once: their island and the United States. I draw attention to the fact that in the writer, artist, musician, filmmaker's choice to use Spanish, English, and/or Spanglish they make a statement about attitudes to homeland, new land, and adaptation. I make clear how their language preference connects to the issue of nationality: for instance, on the islands Spanish has traditionally been regarded as the only "real" language for literature; and in the United States the choice of Spanglish is sometimes criticized as being alienating to a mainstream audience. In an ideal world, students would read Spanish and English (making Spanglish easier to understand) but that frequently is not the case for undergraduates. So that when preparing the syllabus for an undergraduate course one has to learn which works, particularly those of the early writers, are available in translation. (See also Christopher González and Heather Alumbaugh's discussion of language choice as an expression of a Latino/a worldview in their respective chapters in this volume.)

Historical background

When I begin my courses I always try to get a sense of how familiar the students are with the Hispanic Caribbean region and its **diasporas** to the United States. Even when the students are familiar with the area (mostly through family heritage) I still like to begin with a review of historical background because the students often have the context of only one island—that of their family of origin. In any case a historical review encourages critical thinking about which stories they have heard in their family environment and which they have not. Other students, who do not have a family background in the area, have at best a touristy notion of the Caribbean.

There is more in common between the three islands than most students realize, which becomes apparent when we review the shared colonial history of the Antilles. The Hispanic Caribbean was, is, and always will be a meeting place of cultures and peoples. The Greater Antilles—as the Spaniards called the group—first became globalized in 1492 in the harshest way possible when Spain "discovered" the islands and their different communities of native inhabitants. From then on Europeans (mostly, but not exclusively, from Spain) started settling in those three islands—after the early extinction of the **Arawak** tribes and **Caribs** (the native inhabitants) due to war, disease, and forced labor. The islands belonged to Spain until the nineteenth and early twentieth centuries when two became independent: the eastern half of the island of Hispaniola became the Dominican Republic first; later, Cuba did. In 1898, when the United States won the Spanish-American War, Puerto Rico was transferred over. A picture emerges of a region that has, during close to 500 plus years, seen waves of colonial and neocolonial turmoil and to-and-fro migrations.

For twenty-first-century undergraduates in the United States it is also important to clarify how and why Cubans, Puerto Ricans, and Dominicans have been migrating to (mostly) the East Coast of the United States. It is useful to sketch how the reasons for migration have changed.

In the nineteenth century independence-minded intellectuals immigrated to the United States fleeing Spain's repression. Cubans in the mid-twentieth century sought refuge for political reasons as well. Dominicans have also come to the United States for political reasons—during the times of dictatorship on the island—but later frequently for economic reasons. Puerto Ricans were encouraged by their government to come to the United States starting in the 1940s as a safety valve for the island's troubled economy and to provide labor for U.S. industry; for economic reasons also Puerto Rican numbers have increased in the last decade and shockingly, during the last decade, Puerto Ricans in the United States surpassed in number the island's inhabitants. The U.S. Census website provides useful information on when and where Latinos from the Hispanic Caribbean have settled. I have found that showing the documentary *Harvest of Empire* allows students to see the links between many of these migration movements as well as the aftereffects of U.S. interventions in Latin America. It is available free online.

Students sometimes regard the Greater Antilles as one isolated cultural block composed of three discrete Spanish-speaking nations: Cuba, the Dominican Republic, and Puerto Rico. In order to explore the pre-Columbian background (and to shake up the students' preconceived assumptions about modern nationhood) I use an image of the hemisphere before the Europeans came. The map of the Americas in Charles C. Mann's *1491: New Revelations of the Americas Before Columbus*, shows our well-known hemisphere but the islands are labeled not under their present national monikers, having instead the names of the peoples who resided there before Columbus: "Guana-Hatabey," "Taino Chiefdoms" and "Caribs." Furthermore, North America shows the "Algonkian Alliances" in place of the East Coast, the "Caddo Confederacies" where one expects the Midwest and "Nomads" where the West Coast states are now. This powerful visual reminder sets up a discussion not only about those **pre-Columbian** cultures but also about how what we think of as timeless nations were really created rather recently.

Also in conjunction with the map, I deploy visual materials and other data about the forced African migrations to the islands during the era of the slave trade. Google

Images has many but make sure they come from reputable sources and that they are about the Caribbean specifically, since much of the material concerns slavery in the United States. Data on the languages and religions that the slaves brought with them is also fascinating. The nations of the Spanish-speaking Antilles would only come into existence much later—as well as all the nations of the hemisphere. I then go into general historical summaries of the birth of those Hispanic Caribbean nations, two of them independent sovereign entities (Dominican Republic in 1844, Cuba in 1902) and one still a dependent associated commonwealth (Puerto Rico). All this background can be illustrated using symbols (such as the ubiquitous national flags), stories, allegories, and images that refer back to specific island events.

The history of the islands' colonial relations with Spain, of course, will foreground any analysis of Hispanic Caribbean/Latino culture because the **Iberian** heritage left essential points of reference such as Spanish language and Catholic religion. Also useful is an overview of the points of contact between these three islands and other Caribbean cultures. For instance, French Caribbean notions of *négritude* antecede and inspired the afro-Antillean cultural movement (which was a game changer during the 1930s because it reassessed the islands' African heritage). Another indispensable example of the connections between the Spanish-speaking islands and the Francophone Caribbean is the fraught, contentious relationship that the Dominican Republic has had with Haiti since the early nineteenth century, when Haiti invaded the part of Hispaniola then known as Santo Domingo (which later became the name of the Dominican Republic's capital city). To this day this troubled past bleeds over into Dominicans' multifaceted racial attitudes. The impact of the Haitian revolution (and later the Cuban revolution) marks a historical touchstone for the entire Caribbean. For background on that incendiary event—which changed the course of the Caribbean in the nineteenth century—send students to the *Khan Academy*'s section on the Haitian revolution of 1791–1804 (this useful, free website is better known for its mathematical and scientific lessons).

Cultural background

I teach the students that the *specific* national origins and histories of the three islands are *indispensable* for Hispanic Caribbean/Latino identity. However, it is also important to teach the students that there is a Greater Antilles and Caribbean supra-identity that acts as an overlay, like a color filter on a group photo. A very fun way to teach this unity is to point out how much of the region's popular music is cross-pollinated (**salsa, Afro-Cuban music, merengue, reggaeton**, etc.). Food is another obvious, common cultural factor (the primacy of plantains, which were an African import, is clear to anyone familiar with the cuisine of the islands). Another common point was the dream of an Antillean political Confederation, a shared aspiration of the region in the nineteenth century. Absolutely necessary for students to know is the background historical information on the multiple connections of these territories with the United States, including American interventions (militarily and financially) in (largely) unwelcome ways in the last two centuries. Data on recent migrations from the islands serves us well to illustrate to the students the geographic areas where one finds Hispanic Caribbean immigrants.

Culture itself constructs and highlights each country's identity and differentiates the things that are considered "authentic" and important to each island's separate heritage. I recommend using YouTube videos of the three national anthems and discussing their symbols, images, and messages to illustrate notions of what constitutes national heritage; anthems also show how music shapes shared views of the nation. This leads again to stressing the differences between the three nations. For example, the racial legacy of the Dominican Republic's tense sharing of the island of Hispaniola with Haiti, the confrontations between the United States and the Cuban communist government, Puerto Rico's long-standing electoral record of choosing dependence over independence, etc. But some commonalities are also striking and are worth discussing: the common thread of slavery and its aftermath, the impact of the sugar industry on the economies and social dynamics of the three islands, and migrations to the United States.

Latin America in general has influenced the islands' intellectual history since before the three nations became distinct cultural entities. This can be illustrated with a powerful and luminous essay written about Latin America by Cuban luminary José Martí (a necessary writer when teaching the intellectual history of Cuban Americans), "Our America" (published in 1894 in New York's *Revista Ilustrada*; reprinted in Martí 2010). He wrote for *all* the Spanish-speaking countries of the hemisphere and defined the intellectual history of the time; he also tackled that 800-pound gorilla, the threat posed by the United States to Latin America. In general, Martí's cultural footprint is so pervasive that you could use only works that he published while in New York City or in American newspapers.

Exploring the Hispanic Caribbean

When exploring the theme of Hispanic Caribbean connections to the rest of the globe it's always interesting to point out the presence of more far-flung cultures in the area. There was, for example, a contingent of laborers from China into Cuba in the early twentieth century and they made their mark in literature (see for instance Cuban writer Severo Sarduy's novels—an author more suitable for graduate level courses). In the twenty-first century, the most famous Puerto Rican novel, *Simone* (2012) by Eduardo Lalo, which won the prestigious Latin American Rómulo Gallegos prize, features as the protagonist's romantic interest a girl of Chinese extraction, and Lalo discusses current Chinese migration into Puerto Rico.

Of course, what concerns us is the presence of people from the three islands in the United States, an influx that started in significant ways in the nineteenth century and rose throughout the span of the twentieth and twenty-first centuries in a series of crests: after the Cuban revolution, from Puerto Rico due to the economic troubles starting in the 1940s and from the Dominican Republic starting in the mid-twentieth century.

For primary texts, *The Norton Anthology of Latino Literature*, edited by Ilan Stavans (2011), is an essential tool. This anthology provides many indispensable materials; however, it is arranged chronologically and contains many Latino writers from other regions, not just the Caribbean (particularly the larger Mexican American contingent). It also offers expansive background pop culture items: sayings, songs, cartoons, legends. It provides colonial literature including Juan de Castellanos's "Revolt of the Borinqueños" (about Borikén, Puerto Rico's native name) and Bartolomé de Las Casas, the earliest human rights advocate in the Americas whose "The Devastation of the Indies" berated the Spanish conquest of Hispaniola. Despite its vast scope, the Norton anthology is a very useful tool since it provides translations of key Hispanic Caribbean writers in the nineteenth century, who wrote in Spanish only. There are other useful anthologies, among them *Herencia*, edited by Nicolás Kanellos (2002). The most famous writers, such as Martí, have readily available translated works.

Nationalism is taken for granted by most people and as much as any other force has shaped the Hispanic Caribbean and its diasporas, and must be *interrogated* at every turn. Despite the common name "Latino" that we use for people who have as their heritage one of the three separate nations, the primary way people identify is as Cuban American, Dominican American or Puerto Rican/Nuyorican. Migrants defend their background passionately and it is best to not confuse one with another. Despite the pressing need to provide historical background for the three nations, I find that a thematic approach to crafting syllabi is more useful because undergraduates are put to sleep by strictly nationalist chronologies—that is to say by sequencing main authors and cultural movements from the nineteenth, twentieth, and twenty-first century by each culture in turn. This does not mean that one shouldn't enhance discussions by going back to specific events in the nations and their histories, since these affect the symbols, images, and stories of Latinos.

Nevertheless, I usually mix and match writers from the three islands and tie them thematically while continuing to compare and contrast. As a theoretical opening for discussion of what the Caribbean means I use selections from Cuban writer Antonio Benítez Rojo's trans-Caribbean *The Repeating Island* (1992); particularly the introduction of his essay that explores vividly the significance of the birth and development of the Caribbean as a region central to and a repository of global cultures. He casts the Caribbean as a protagonist in the oceanic and cultural gyres of peoples, technology, commodities, and information that make up the globe, particularly since the era of so-called discovery.

To the syllabus

While the first layer for a possible syllabus might be more bound to nations, other layers might consider highlighting additional possible topics such as gender, race, class, and ethnicity. For instance, the poetry of Martí (considered the forefather of Caribbean nationalists) can be used as a launch into themes of transnationalism. Other themes you might consider exploring with your students include:

- The greater Caribbean: I have the students compare and contrast Hispanic-based writers with writers who come from the so-called Lesser Antilles: French, English, Dutch, and American Caribbean nations.
- The legacies of **colonialism** and **neocolonialism**: my students tackle colonialism based on the many ways it has impacted the area's socioeconomics; they consider the multiple scars of slavery (illustrated by images of slave bodies and tales and legends from African and native cultures) or the sugar industry and its human and environmental impact (frequently depicted in landscape art). I use works that have subject matter focusing on:
  - the colonial presence of Spain in the Hispanic Caribbean;
  - the neocolonial influence of the United States in the three islands, and, of course, the matter of the Soviet Union in Cuba.
- Gender and minority studies: students read women writers, **GLBT** authors, and those of workers' movements to interrogate gender norms and machismo.
- **Eco-criticism**: students learn how the islands' particular ecosystems are memorialized by Latino culture and become symbolic of Latino connections to the homelands. The omnipresence of the sea, for instance, is notable in poetry. The flora

and fauna of the islands is the subject of manifold representations in graphic arts. Also we explore the opposite in images of despoiled islands overcome by colonialism, rampant overdevelopment, and governmental lack of oversight in the Dominican Republic and Puerto Rico during the late twentieth and twenty-first centuries. Google Images is a great resource for art and imagery from the Caribbean.

- Stereotypes of Latinos in urban environments in the United States: we discuss the different stereotypes of Latinos, including views of the islands as seen through the lens of the tourist industry.
- The impact of politics on culture: probe examples of nineteenth-century movements for independence. For instance, we explore Puerto Rico's non-sovereign political status and how people overlook that voters on the island have chosen for the past half-century to remain tied to the United States. We also consider other political topics such as the aftereffects of revolution (Cuba) and dictatorships (Cuba and the Dominican Republic). We also consider the political participation of Latinos in the U.S. electoral system.
- Race and class matters: The students compare and contrast constructions of race and class on the islands and in the United States.
- Religion and social status: The students gain an understanding of Catholicism and its symbols, and its Caribbean **syncretic** variants such as the cult of the Virgen del Cobre in Cuba and *santería*. These first arose in the Caribbean when colonial authorities censored native and African religious traditions. The incursion of the charismatic Christian faiths and Protestant denominations in the twentieth century; religious representations in culture.
- Migrations and diasporas: The students consider how many Latino cultural producers use the theme of the journey to represent the joys and challenges of migration, assimilation, and adaptation.
- Latina autobiographies and memoirs: students read Puerto Rican authors such as Esmeralda Santiago, Judith Ortiz Cofer, and Justice Sonia Sotomayor.

My syllabi always have explicit goals, including that students discover their own Caribbean Hispanic media and arts supplements besides those already assigned. Students are particularly good at finding music videos that illustrate larger class topics and famous historical figures and movements. It also gives them a sense of investment in their learning. I help guide them to link their chosen media and arts supplements to the topics and main themes of the course. Comparatist in nature, I have the students compare and contrast works from different eras and backgrounds to see how topics are reinterpreted and how sociopolitical and historical shifts in time and place change attitudes towards race and gender.

[Tip: If you use a blackboard, as I do, keep a record of those discussions by taking pictures of the notes on the blackboard at the end of each class (or at least before you erase it—I use an iPad). Make these pictures accessible to the students if you have a moodle or online class site. The photos also give you a semester-long summary of class discussions.]

Possible Cuban texts

The necessary starting point for Cuban culture is José Martí (Cuba 1853–95). His style of writing is *sui generis* so there's no one to compare him to, really. I mentioned his essay

"Our America" but his poetry is also among the most anthologized and widely available and should be taught not just for historical background but to look at his inventive use of what amounts to a new, deceptively simple language. His seemingly straightforward poems are easy to teach as well as thought provoking: for instance selections from *Ismaelillo* or *Free Verses* as well as his letters from New York. Even though he wrote in Spanish, all his works are available in translation and he often wrote about U.S. culture (e.g., Ralph Waldo Emerson). His biography is also worth teaching in order to illustrate the main currents of thought in nineteenth-century Hispanic Caribbean culture as well as the heroism that a public intellectual such as Martí can have. Both sides of the bitter Cuban political divide (on the island and in the states) appropriate his work and regard him as a forefather. His treatment of racial minorities and women is also interesting and speaks to our contemporary values in many ways, although his Catholicism has not been very popular with culture critics in the twenty-first century.

The theme of exile is primary for Cuban American culture and the distinct waves of migrations are worth looking at in detail because the incomers were very different in their ideology and class distinctions. Those who came earlier were often intellectuals who favored independence from Spain. You can foreground nineteenth-century Cuban exilic themes using either Martí's poems or José María Heredia's Romantic angst in his famous poem "Ode to Niagara." Right after the Cuban revolution of 1959 most exiles were people of the middle and upper classes fleeing political instability. On the other hand, the Cubans who came during the *Marielito* boat lift in the 1980s were a motley crew; many, such as homosexuals, had been encouraged by the government to leave the island after being labeled as undesirables. The theme of exile appears in the works of important writers such as Reinaldo Arenas, Gustavo Pérez Firmat, and Cristina García. You can also cover a wide range of repercussions of exile by using the writing of Heberto Padilla, José Koser, Silvia Curbelo, Achy Obejas, Ana Menéndez, and performances by Coco Fusco. Cristina García's fiction, such as *Dreaming in Cuban* (1992), is accessible to all levels of students.

For an example of how Cubans have been depicted (often as caricatures) in popular culture in the United States, I show clips from *I Love Lucy* or *Scarface*. A far more serious cross-cultural endeavor is Julian Schnabel's film of Reinaldo Arenas's *Before Night Falls* (as well as the book of memoirs itself). Besides the displacement and pain of exile in the United States, Arenas shines a light on the Cuban government's repression of homosexuality during the early 1970s (this situation has since changed). Pérez Firmat's observations about Cuban life in the United States appear in creative, genre-busting works, such as *My Own Private Cuba* (1999); he mixes fiction and cultural analysis in *Life on the Hyphen* (1994).

Another important theme repeated often in Cuban/Latino literature is the divide between generations. This theme features in a gendered way in Garcia's *Dreaming in Cuban* where it is represented by mother-daughter Lourdes and Pilar's differing adaptation to the United States. Achy Obejas explores the same theme in a humorous way, especially her *Memory Mambo* (1996). Richard Blanco also explores how family generations clash and adapt to life in exile. There have only been five inaugural poets in the United States, Blanco served as President Obama's in January 2013 and his recitation of that poem, "One Today," is on YouTube; in the eponymous book he mixes poems and narration in a tender tour-de-force exploration of generational differences and assimilation.

The category of performance is also worth exploring. By teaching Carmelita Tropicana and Alina Troyano's film *Carmelita Tropicana: Your Kinst Is Your Waffen* (1994) one can have students explore notions of Cuban national identity—and their vital recreation.

Possible Dominican Republican texts

In the last decades, Dominican migration to the United States has intensified so much that by the twenty-first century their numbers outstripped both Puerto Rican and Cuban cohorts. They are now, for example, the largest Latino population in New York. In relation to the Dominican Republic we can study the legacy of strong women writers, starting in the early twentieth century with the essayist Camila Henríquez, who studied and taught at the University of Minnesota and belonged to the island's most prominent literary family. She was, in turn, the daughter of a famous nineteenth-century poet, Salomé Ureña de Henríquez, and sister to three famous literati. Julia Alvarez uses Camila's story in her novel *In the Name of Salomé* (2000); this sequence offers the opportunity to connect three generations of Dominican women writers. One of the best-known names of the Hispanic Caribbean Latino contingent, Alvarez's *How the García Girls Lost Their Accents* (1991) and other popular fictions, stress the interconnectedness of the island with the lives of émigrés. *In the Time of the Butterflies* (1994) is a historical novel that offers a gripping account of the lives of the Mirabal sisters during the Trujillo dictatorship. The life of Dominicans in the United States appears in her *Yo!* (1997). Alvarez's works provide another opportunity to examine gender roles for Hispanic Caribbean Latinos as well as highlighting women heroes. Rita Indiana is another twenty-first-century daughter of the Dominican female writerly tradition; a writer and performance artist, her video oeuvre is available on YouTube. For her, some national distinctions become permeable because, while the island context is still important in her works, her videos deal with globalized topics. For instance in "Maldito Feisbú" she tackles the ubiquitous presence of Facebook in Latin America but she also offers a serious message of racial healing in "Da Pa Lo Do," which presents the inter-connectedness of Dominican-Haitian identity. Indiana's novels have received less attention; *Papi* features experimental prose. Josefina Baez's best known performance/ texts are more traditionally theatrical; they include themes of race and ethnic identities in *Dominicanish* (2005) and others.

Other notable *Quisqueyano/a* figures are Fabio Fiallo (who strides the nineteenth and twentieth centuries), Sherezada "Chiqui Vicioso" and Franklin Gutiérrez, who are also accessible in translation or write in Spanglish. Junot Díaz, who came to the United States as a teen, is perhaps the most acclaimed Hispanic Caribbean/Latino writer and critic. His works garnered a Pulitzer Prize (he has since gone on to serve on Pulitzer-awarding juries) and a MacArthur Prize. Readily accessible are his novel *The Brief Wondrous Life of Oscar Wao* (2007) and collections of short stories, *Drown* (1996) and *This is How You Lose Her* (2012). Díaz's originality and the verve of his oft-imitated prose style, dazzle with their masterful code-switching practice of Spanglish—a sign of how he gets the better of the two cultures. Díaz's works also feature a mix of literary language and popular culture. Above all, though, they are hysterically *funny*. In terms of historical context, his characters constantly shuttle to-and-from the Dominican Republic and the United States (mostly New Jersey, where the characters live out stark class, gender, and race issues). The fallout of the brutal Trujillo dictatorship also follows the characters to the U.S. The introduction to *Oscar Wao* is worth teaching for its tour-de-force mix of high-and-low brow allusions commixing nerd fan boy references (Tolkien) alongside Dominican history (Trujillo, or, as Díaz refers to the dictator, "Fuckface"). Stories from the dictatorship of Rafael Leonidas Trujillo have fired up some of the most powerful contemporary Dominican fiction.

For a selection of translated Dominican texts you might reproduce for your students the interviews, stories, and poems by Julia Alvarez, Annecy Baez, Jeannette Miller, Pedro Mir, Sherezada Vicioso, José Alcántara Almánzar, Junot Díaz, and others in the summer 2000 journal *Callalloo* (volume 23, no.3).

Possible Puerto Rican texts

Puerto Ricans started coming to the East Coast of the United States in the nineteenth century during the independence fights with Spain. Clearly, the ease with which Puerto Ricans (who have been American citizens since 1917) come and go from the island to the United States has resulted in interesting uses of interlinked cultures. From the earlier age, Eugenio María de Hostos, the writer/moralist "Citizen of America," from the late nineteenth century, still holds interest. Also important from that earlier era are poems by Lola Rodríguez de Tió and William Carlos Williams as well as memoirs of life in New York City by Francisco Gonzalo "Pachín" Marín, Arthur A. Schomburg (especially useful for racial issues) and Bernardo Vega. These and other writers portray the experience of Puerto Ricans in the United States as one of clashing cultural values, nostalgia, and lives subject to discrimination and poverty. The Nuyorican Poets Café movement, which started in the late 1960s, has some of the most important later writing and presents clear examples of the search for national identity that bedevils many Nuyoricans. Among the top names of that gritty generation are Miguel Algarín, Piri Thomas, Miguel Piñero (whose life was the subject of the film *Piñero*, directed by León Ichaso, 2001), Tato Laviera and Sandra María Esteves. Pedro Pietri's *Puerto Rican Obituary* (1973) is a raw and gripping catalog of the challenges of *Boricua* life in the United States. Julia de Burgos is the de facto poet laureate of the Puerto Rican nation and her poems are easily available in translation as well as poems she wrote in English while in New York.

Island-based writers from the mid-twentieth century also represent the experience of migrating *Boricuas* facing the challenges of life in the United States. Life in New York City is at the center of René Marqués's play "The Oxcart" (1953) and José Luis González's short story "The Night We Became a People Again" (1973). Luis Rafael Sánchez's essay "The Airbus" (1994) is particularly important because it represents the nation of Puerto Rico up in the air, in an airplane, transitioning back and forth between the island and New York, the latter of which has become, because of the circular migration, another Puerto Rican "pueblo."

Also among the many important Puerto Rican/Latino writers are Nicholasa Mohr, whose "Nilda" (1973) features a teenage Puerto Rican girl in New York during the World War II era. Mohr's *Bronx Remembered* (1975) also has stories set in New York. Island writer Rosario Ferré writes fiction in both Spanish and English, such as her novel *The House on the Lagoon* (1995). Víctor Hernández Cruz is one of the most distinguished contemporary poets. Other well-known poets are Martín Espada, Willie Perdomo, and María Teresa "Mariposa" Fernández. I also add a selection from a cultural artifact such as *West Side Story* to show how Puerto Ricans were stereotypically portrayed.

The introduction to Esmeralda Santiago's memoir *When I Was Puerto Rican* (1993) is useful for teaching notions of national "authenticity" since in it she uses the image of the guava to represent the authenticity of the lost homeland. Teaching memoirs is a particularly valuable approach when it comes to Latino literature in general. For Puerto Ricans, for instance, you could contrast and compare selections from

Esmeralda Santiago, Judith Ortiz Cofer's *Silent Dancing* (1990) and Justice Sonia Sotomayor's *My Beloved World* (2013).

For a broader outlook of how Puerto Rican themes connect to the wider Latino contingents you might include a selection from Ed Morales's *Living in Spanglish* (2002). Available online, Adál Maldonado's photographs can allow students to see how language and the arts express the dream of Puerto Rico as a free nation.

Resources for teaching the Hispanophone Caribbean

Beidler, Philip D. *The Island Called Paradise: Cuba in History, Literature, and the Arts.* Tuscaloosa, AL: University of Alabama Press, 2014.

Bost, Suzanne. *Mulattas and Mestizas: Representing Mixed Identities in the Americas, 1850–2000.* Athens, GA: University of Georgia Press, 2003.

De Ferrari, Guillermina. *Vulnerable States: Bodies of Memory in Contemporary Caribbean Fiction.* Charlottesville, VA: University of Virginia Press, 2012.

Halloran, Vivian Nun. *Exhibiting Slavery: The Caribbean Postmodern Novel as Museum.* Charlottesville, VA: University of Virginia Press, 2009.

Harrison, Rebecca L., and Emily Hipchen, eds. *Inhabiting La Patria: Identity, Agency, and Antojo in the Work of Julia Alvarez.* Albany: State University of New York Press, 2014.

Moreno, Marisel C. *Family Matters: Puerto Rican Women Authors on the Island and the Mainland.* Charlottesville, VA: University of Virginia Press, 2012.

Orlando, Valérie, and Sandra Cypess, eds. *Reimagining the Caribbean: Conversations among the Creole, English, French, and Spanish Caribbean.* Lanham, MD: Lexington Books, 2014.

Romero, Channette. *Activism and the American Novel: Religion and Resistance in Fiction by Women of Color.* Charlottesville, VA: University of Virginia Press, 2012.

Sánchez, Marta E. *Shakin' Up Race and Gender: Intercultural Connections in Puerto Rican, African American, and Chicano Narratives and Culture (1965–1995).* Austin: University of Texas Press, 2005.

Socolovsky, Maya. *Troubling Nationhood in U.S. Latina Literature: Explorations of Place and Belonging.* New Brunswick, NJ: Rutgers University Press, 2013.

Torres-Padilla, José, and Carmen Haydée Rivera. *Writing Off the Hyphen: New Perspectives on the Literature of the Puerto Rican Diaspora.* Seattle: University of Washington Press, 2008.

Valdés, Vanessa K. *Oshun's Daughters: The Search for Womanhood in the Americas.* Albany: State University of New York Press, 2014.

10 Teaching Boricua literature

Lisa Sánchez González

On the alchemy of teaching

Teaching well, in any subject, is alchemy. The elements in the admixture for the alchemist are basic: expertise in the subject matter, knowledge of the context in which the subject matter evolves, and an understanding of the dynamic created by the students in the classroom. What is complicated about alchemy is, of course, properly measuring the basic elements for a specific moment, a specific experiment, a specific classroom, a specific institutional culture. Sometimes the experiment will fail. Other times there will be an explosion. Constant calibration of these elements is therefore crucial.

Expertise is, as Aristotle explains in *The Nichomachean Ethics* (1926), not merely technical skill, though ironically the root of the English word "technical" in ancient Greek is "techne," which Aristotle uses to mean "expertise." Expertise is a combination of training and experience in doing well what you've been trained to do. For those who teach **Boricua** literature, this training and experience is very hard to come by. Few universities have undergraduate courses in this subject area. Fewer still offer any semblance of graduate study in this field. Despite the curricular ground gained on public college campuses in the wake of the Civil Rights movement, and despite the Puerto Rican diaspora's standing as the nation's second-largest Latino community, the study of Boricua literature is rare in the field of Latino studies, which is dominated by Chicano studies. Compounding this lack of curricular representation is the more recent usurpation of Latino studies by Latin American studies programs. At a variety of universities in states where the Puerto Rican diaspora is a significant demographic, such as Illinois, New York, and Connecticut, Latino studies curricula (and faculty lines) have been folded into, and often made to disappear by, Latin American studies curricula and hiring priorities. Expertise in Boricua literature, in other words, is very hard to come by at public universities in the United States, even in states where Boricuas have historically settled.

How then does one acquire this expertise, since it is essential to teaching this crucial story of the American experience? As one highly committed bilingual education teacher who retired from a Connecticut school district with a huge Boricua demographic once put it, "I couldn't find any Boricua literature to teach my Boricua students for a long time." Indeed, very little is available in print for younger readers, and much less in bilingual edition. Even highly motivated autodidactic teachers have a hard time simply finding the material that will give them the texts and historical contexts of the lives of stateside Puerto Rican students. At the college level, there are clearly more resources, although the deliberately orchestrated confusion between Latin American and Latino studies can make finding those library resources difficult. Adding to this confusion is the colonial condition of all Puerto Ricans. Whether born on the island or in the diaspora, all Puerto Ricans are U.S. citizens by birth. **The Jones Act**, approved by the U.S. Congress in 1917, imposed U.S. citizenship on the entire population. Therefore Boricuas born on the island who move to the U.S. mainland are not immigrants, but migrants, and their children are not sons and daughters of immigrants either. Given the pervasive practice of cataloging books on or by Latinos using the descriptors "immigration" or "emigrants," merely trying to find the proper search terms can be very difficult for a novice interested in the field.

Studying historical context is key to gaining expertise in Boricua literature. Granted, some literary texts can be taught in a historical vacuum, and certain Boricua authors lend themselves well to this. William Carlos Williams, for example, has enjoyed a huge international following and there is a burgeoning body of research exploring his global influence on modern poetry. Theoretically, then, a class could meaningfully study some of his work without historical grounding by focusing strictly on his poetic form, which is what so many others have found so compelling around the world and in translation. However, most Boricua literature needs to be historically contextualized because it is deeply entrenched in social, political, and intellectual movements. Teaching this material therefore requires knowledge of the colonial history of Puerto Rico and the social history of the colonial **diaspora** in the continental United States. It may be possible for a monolingual English-language reader to get an approximation of these histories, but Puerto Rico has a recent and vibrant new historicist wave of scholarship, so an understanding of Puerto Rican history in its fullest form requires fluency in reading Spanish as well.

It cannot be stressed enough that teaching Boricua literature requires mastery of the historical context of this tradition. This is true for purely intellectual or factual reasons. For example, understanding the work of Jesús Colón, one of the earliest figures in this literary tradition, means understanding the internationalist radicalism of the 1930s in New York City, where he arrived as a stowaway in 1917. It also means learning about the fin-de-siècle labor movement in Puerto Rico, where he was born and gained a political consciousness of the world around him as a child, not to mention the migration of that labor movement stateside with the migration of political organizers to Florida and New York. Colón spent many years working as the editor of the Communist Party USA's newspaper, *The Daily Worker*, and many of his vignettes, which were anthologized by Masses and Mainstream in 1961 (and are still in print as the International Publishers edition of 1982), were published in this venue. Yet to understand the breadth of his writing, one must also read his contributions to Spanish language newspapers in New York, which are housed at the NYPL, as well as socialist newspapers in San Juan. Simply put, to comprehend Jesús Colón's ethical investments and aesthetic innovations as a writer, one cannot ignore his politics, the historical context of those politics, and the history of small newspapers in New York and Puerto Rico. There is also a wealth of information about him in his archives, some of which have been digitized and made available on the Center for Puerto Rican Studies' (Hunter College, CUNY) website. Much the same could be said for Luisa Capetillo, an **anarchist** and **feminist** who lived, loved, and agitated not only in New York City, but in Florida and Cuba as well, and who read internationally and whose books and articles were read internationally by a wide anarchist and socialist audience. Like Capetillo and Colón, Pura Belpré and Arturo Schomburg, two other extremely important figures in this literary tradition, were autodidacts. Therefore understanding the literary contributions of some of the earliest

Boricua writers also entails a grasp of the history of public libraries in New York City, which was one of the foundational public library systems in the world, as well as the history of the bibliophilic organizations to which they belonged, such as the American Library Association (Belpré) and the American Negro Academy (Schomburg).

Teaching Boricua literature in the college or high school classroom also requires mastery of the historical context of this literary tradition for another crucial reason; the ignorance of students about the history of Puerto Rico and its colonial diaspora as well as their intense curiosity once they start learning a bit about it and, in the process, unlearning a lot of misinformation they have been taught to believe. Part of the colonial design for centuries has been the erasure of the colonized in the colonizers' histories. We all know that, and the same can be said of the difficulties of teaching in other fields of ethnic American literature too.

Perhaps the closest parallel to Boricua literary studies is Native American literary studies because of the sheer wall of ignorance a teacher faces as well as the sheer tonnage of stereotyping that fills the void of that knowledge. Students, including Latino students, presume they know a lot about "ethnic diversity," and unfortunately their false assumptions are often confirmed or even created in courses they take and the ritual performances of "diversity" they experience in school—perennial Day of the Dead parties for Halloween, the pilgrims and Indians skits for Thanksgiving, taco night to "celebrate diversity," and so forth—which only serve to exoticize and flatten the perception of ethnic and racial difference while twisting the historical record in the interests of safeguarding white hegemony. As a result, common assumptions that students bring to the Boricua literature classroom include the notions that all Latinos speak Spanish as a first language, speak English with an accent, were born elsewhere, are extremely poor, and therefore come from a cultural ghetto. The negative sociological view of Latinos, and Boricuas especially in the Northeast, is dehumanizing. Often it is hateful too. The mythic view of the Latino existential ghetto has to be debunked carefully and quickly in the classroom if students are to learn anything at all about the subject. The goal in this should be to teach students, whatever their background, that the individual and collective lives of the culturally othered are just as complex and sophisticated as their own.

In the process of peeling back these layers of misinformation and half-truths, a teacher will inevitably encounter episodes of **cognitive dissonance** in the classroom. Students comfortable with their worldviews do not always appreciate the opportunity to revise them with new knowledge, and a host of strange and hostile behaviors can ensue. Debate and divergent opinions should always be welcome in a learning environment, however the aggression and microaggression that erupts in an ethnic studies classroom can be very difficult to manage. Students may throw verbal tantrums, give dirty looks to others for the entire class, refuse to believe the facts presented, refuse to do the reading, or simply stop showing up for class (yet expect a pass grade for the course). Other behaviors are more subtle though no less pernicious to the learning that is supposed to be the purpose of education. This can include persistent misapprehension of a simple fact that a student forgets over and over again. Insisting on calling Boricuas "immigrants," is one example, after a lecture explaining why they are not; calling Boricuas "Latin Americans" after a lecture explaining the difference between a Latino and a Latin American is another. Habits of thought are difficult to undo, even in young people. And when perceived racial difference is in the mix—especially if the teacher is non-white in a predominantly white classroom—it can be even more difficult. In those situations, one of the best solutions is to simply take the time to put the issue on the table without personalizing it.

"Why is this class having such a hard time learning this fact?" for example, or "why am I seeing so much negative body language in the room today? What's wrong?" Depending on the teacher's personality, there are other ways to confront the dissonance as well. Humor is very effective. Analogies are helpful too when discussions swerve into stereotypes; I've often turned the tables on such discussions by describing other groups of people in the same unfortunate ways Boricuas are being described, which often relieves the tension in the room with laughter. Ultimately, in my experience, the best way to minimize cognitive dissonance and to cope with it when it inevitably erupts is to acknowledge that it exists and to encourage the students themselves to talk candidly about it as something that has serious meaning.

The alchemy of teaching Boricua literature may not be entirely different from the alchemy of teaching other subjects, but the tasks of mastering the field, mastering the history surrounding this literary tradition, and guiding class discussions and pedagogical strategies to suit the human beings taking the course is intense work. The field is always evolving too, so a syllabus for such a class must constantly evolve in tandem with it.

Teaching tips from a tenured radical: anarchism and pedagogy

While I have suggestions and ideas for those who are not teaching at a university along with suggested reading for those who do not have the opportunity to study this field in any formal way (in the last section of this essay), my teaching strategies and tactics obviously come from my location as a tenured professor of English at the University of Connecticut. Some may consider this location to be highly privileged. Perhaps it is. Yet I think that solid pedagogy translates across the many institutional spaces and cultures that teachers occupy. I also believe good teaching methods are valuable in and of themselves.

My pedagogy is **anarchistic**. I put that on the table the first class day. Students often laugh when they hear that, mistakenly thinking that anarchism means lawlessness and chaos. But once the course gets rolling they soon realize that an anarchist pedagogy can be extremely rigorous. Every student in my Boricua literature classes has to do independent research. Every student is responsible for contributing to the class discussions. No one is off the hook, in other words, in producing new knowledge. Kropotkin's *Fields, Factories, and Workshops* (1912) as well as the anarchist pedagogy of Luisa Capetillo, specifically her educational work in the protest movement Cruzada del Ideal at the turn of the twentieth century in Puerto Rico, inform what I do in the classroom and why I do it. Most simply put, my pedagogy derives from my conviction that it is just as important for all workers to produce knowledge on their own as it is to produce whatever their labor creates for pay. Translated into the twenty-first century, true north on my anarchist pedagogy's compass points to developing habits of critical thought in students who, along with whatever career they choose after college, should be actively and critically thinking for themselves and aware of how knowledge is produced *for* them or, to borrow a brilliant way of putting it from Noam Chomsky (2002), how contemporary media manufactures their consent. No matter what my students' backgrounds are, they all understand and appreciate why this kind of critical thinking matters. In a profound way, it not only levels the playing field for everyone in the class, since few if any have enjoyed that freedom before, but it also gives them a shared purpose and a sense of intellectual adventure that is contagious. As Ivan Illich persuasively argued in *Deschooling Society* (1971), learning is not a result of instruction, but rather the result of being free to explore something in a meaningful environment. I also believe that this holds true for the teacher in a class. I shudder at the thought of how boring my work life would be if I were simply rehashing, year after year, the same lecture notes and PowerPoint presentations in class.

Teaching courses for over 25 years now in critical race studies, Latina feminism, Chicano literature, Caribbean literature, and Boricua literature, along with surveys of classical and American literature, I have seen not so much the "dumbing down" of the students as much as the rise of a certain alienated behavior they perform in class. It is not merely their constant fussing with smartphones in class either; it is the culture of instruction into which all but a very few have been indoctrinated. The basic rules of this culture are straightforward. Only do the required reading, and only as much of it as will make it possible to succeed in exams. Take notes and regurgitate the information the teacher gives you in those exams. Sit quietly in class and try to seem alert as you absorb that information. If you have a question, email the professor. If you don't get an A, interrogate the professor as to why. And at all costs, maximize your leisure time. After all is said and done, *that* is what the college experience is supposed to be about.

Perhaps it is a function of standardized testing, perhaps it is caused by grade inflation, perhaps it is the message that administrators in the corporate university deliberately cultivate, or perhaps it is a byproduct of the non-stop media blitz in their lives. Whatever the root causes, this is not a culture of instruction conducive to actual learning. Granted, some disciplines may benefit from rote memorization and regurgitation, but I cannot think of any discipline in the Humanities, besides foreign language instruction, for which that might be the case. My anarchist pedagogy requires engagement in class; students must come prepared with their own questions and observations. With a few ground rules about not launching personal attacks and the necessity of mutual respect, my classroom is a free speech zone, which I carefully curate so the students actually feel free to voice dissent and all manner of inquiry. I let them know that any position is valid as long as they have a reasoned argument (not merely anecdote) to back it up and as long as they are open to critique. All of the written assignments are open topics, so the student can center their own interests, and they revolve around doing research and close textual analysis of the assigned books. I set the bar very high. If I do not see evidence of independent thought, critical analysis, and careful writing, then very early in the semester their grades send that message loud and clear.

Sound like tough love? No, not at all. Frankly, it feels more like revolution. While my students are often stunned by these new (and high) standards, once they get their feet wet it is exhilarating. The transformation I see in my students is a wonder to behold. Students who have found the same article independently but have a very different view of its merit will debate like seasoned scholars. Others who have never done such research before go from shrinking violets to confident and intellectually mature young adults in the classroom. Plus it is so much more interesting to grade papers that the students themselves are excited about writing. Their excitement stems from their genuine engagement with and personal investment in the topics they choose. I am often astonished at what they pursue and I learn a lot in the process too. If I handed them prefabricated prompts, this transformation would never happen. Often, by the end of the semester (and by design), the students themselves are teaching the course to themselves and to each other.

A huge part of making this pedagogy work in my Boricua literature classes stems from training the students in information literacy. While younger students today are born into digital culture, that does not mean they know how to do online research in library databases and catalogs, though they learn those tools very quickly since browsing digital data is in their instinct. After introducing the course, the first order of business is discussing how to define a research topic and how to search for reliable secondary sources. Frequently, getting them up to speed with research methods involves a class session with a research librarian. While Boricua literature is the subject, and students roam far and wide in the databases for the information and analyses they seek, the research skills they learn in this class make them genuine intellectuals capable of researching any topic. One of the most frequent comments from students in these classes is that this is the first time in their lives when they have done research on their own. And they love it.

Of course, when students are given free rein to discover the scholarship on Boricuas for themselves, some will inevitably find sources that are highly problematic. A lot of social scientific research on Boricuas is indebted to Oscar Lewis's "culture of poverty" theory, which, though it has been widely critiqued and discredited, is still a rather popular frame for analyzing this community. While scholarship in this poisoned vein is often irrelevant to the primary texts we are studying, some students believe that litera-ture is a reflection of reality and justify that path of inquiry as such. Academic freedom is sacrosanct in my classroom – it applies to students as well as the professor. Since my students are active participants in the class discussions, the more problematic scholar-ship gets aired and critiqued along with all the other scholarship. Asking students to present their research opens the floor for other students to offer criticism and for the presenter to respond. Sometimes the debates become heated and that is OK. The dia-lectical engagement produced by debate, of whatever temperature, can be one of the most profound sources of learning for everyone involved if the teacher is on her toes and moderates the discussion skillfully.

Boricua students in my classroom are as diverse as any other demographic group, but when they learn—always for the first time—that our community has an intellec-tual and literary history, it often dramatically affects them in unique ways because it belies the messages they have absorbed about themselves for a long, long time. We might call this kind of cognitive dissonance "**decolonial** shock." Despite the fact that most of them come from public school districts with a vast majority of Puerto Ricans, African Americans, and other Latino, Native, and Caribbean students, they have never been exposed in any meaningful way to the full scope of these communities' literary contributions before college. The upending of internalized racism—yet another colonial malaise—is to be expected. Helping these students specifically—to cope with the shock of unlearning what they thought they knew about themselves and their community's history—is difficult work, but some of the most rewarding work of all in a Boricua literature classroom. Decolonial shock can produce anger, sadness, euphoria, and all sorts of emotions in between. I employ a host of tactics and strategies for these students in particular. Channeling the affective force of their learning experience into productive lines of research is the strategy I use the most, but some-times it just takes a sympathetic ear in office hours or after class to help them process one-on-one what they have learned. Though my role as a teacher who is herself Boricua plays a part in this (and also entails its own challenges), the baseline of this interaction is mutual respect, empathy, and trust, which any teacher in the Humanities can and should achieve with students struggling with a radical change in their worldview.

Creating literary canons of the Puerto Rican diaspora

For a view of the work being done to create a literary canon of the Puerto Rican diaspora, there are a few monographs, anthologies, and encyclopedias that are useful. A recent title, *In Visible Movement* (2014), aims to chart the history of Nuyorican poetry of the past five decades. For the outline and major figures of the intellectual and literary history of the Puerto Rican diaspora, with a focus on narrative genres, *Boricua Literature* (2001) is a foundational text. For other scholarly sources that are out of print but relevant, the bibliographies of both these works are invaluable. Anthologies are rare and some classics are out of print as well. In print, Roberto Márquez's *Puerto Rican Poetry* (2007) is a treasure. While the translations of insular Puerto Rican poetry into English are sometimes difficult for students to follow, the book surveys Puerto Rican poetry from pre-colonial times to the present and offers brilliant introductions to each section and author. Myrna Nieves's *Breaking Ground* (2012) is a bilingual collection of the work of 46 contemporary women poets on the Nuyorican scene. For younger readers, *The Stories I Read to the Children* (2013) is a volume of storyteller and librarian Pura Belpré's selected work, recovered from rare books and her archival papers, and recently published by the Center for Puerto Rican Studies at Hunter College. This Center's journal, *Centro*, is also a great resource for reviews of recently published titles in Puerto Rican studies and their online samples of archival papers and author guides lend themselves well to use in the classroom. Two reference works I would recommend are *The Routledge Companion to Latino/a Literature* (2013) and *Latino and Latina Writers* (2004).

The classic text on Puerto Rican history, Fernando Picó's *Historia general de Puerto Rico*, has been translated into English under the title *History of Puerto Rico* (2006). Although the book has a rather unflattering view of and dismissive posture toward the island's colonial diaspora, and more or less ends its rigorous treatment of the subject matter around 1950, it is still the most authoritative book on the subject in English. Another classic, James Dietz's *Economic History of Puerto Rico* (1986), is a tremendously useful book for understanding the economic legacy of colonialism on the island, past and present, and the economic causes of the massive migration that has emptied the island of over half the Boricua population. Virginia Sánchez Korrol's *From Colonia to Community* (originally published in 1986 then revised and reprinted in 1994) is the only major study that explores the history *qua* history of the Puerto Rican diaspora in New York City. Sociological books abound on Boricuas but are rarely useful in a literature class.

As students have nearly a blank slate of true knowledge about Boricuas when they start a course on Boricua literature, giving them an overview of the history and identity politics of the diaspora can be challenging. One resource I have found helpful in getting started is the English-language film *¡ Yo soy Boricua, pa'que tu lo sepas!* (2009: 86 minutes), which is directed by and features Rosie Perez. While the tone of the documentary is light and funny for the most part, Perez delves into many of the heavy issues—Puerto Rican nationalism, political persecution, racial identity politics, the forced sterilization of Puerto Rican women, and the naval base on Vieques—that students tend to be curious about. Puerto Rican radicalism, in the strict political sense, is something students also find fascinating. Though it is out of print, Ronald Fernández's *Los Macheteros* (1987) is an excellent and straightforward history of Puerto Rican armed revolutionary struggle on the island and in the diaspora, and his 1996 book, *The Disenchanted Island*, is also a great companion to it. On the Young Lords and Civil Rights era Boricua organizing history, Haymarket Books has reissued the classic 1971 book *Palante: Voices and Photographs of the Young Lords, 1969–1971* (2011) and there is a companion video with archival footage as well.

The most recent topic of intrigue in my Boricua literature classes has been the indigenous heritage of Puerto Rico. Currently the debate is raging over whether or not Boricuas are authentically native American (Taíno) and, if we are, what that might mean. Sentiment on both sides of the debate is so dismissive of the other (and so polemical) that the scholarship being produced in English is not very helpful in sorting out even provisional answers to those questions. But since students, including Boricuas themselves who are very invested in Taíno identity, will invariably bring up the topic, it makes sense to read up on it. The best sources on early colonial Puerto Rican history are in Spanish and the two I would recommend for teachers are both by the historian Jalil Sued Badillo: the revised edition of *La mujer indígena y su sociedad* (1979, 6th edn 2010) and his more recent and truly remarkable study entitled *Agüeybaná El Bravo* (2008).

One of the boons of teaching Boricua literature as a course every year is that I can stay in touch with what young people find most urgent in Puerto Rican studies along with the issues that I, as a veteran scholar, find important too. Race, racism, the history of U.S. military involvement in the Americas, hip-hop, salsa music, reggaetón—all of these topics and more erupt as counterpoint to literature in my anarchist classroom. Pedagogically, whatever the philosophy behind it, it is crucial to design these courses so that students co-produce what they learn. After all, it is their futures at stake in what we teach.

Resources for teaching Boricua literature

Bost, Suzanne, and Frances Aparicio. *The Routledge Companion to Latino/a Literature.* New York: Routledge, 2013.

Noel, Urayoán. *In Visible Movement: Nuyorican Poetry from the Sixties to Slam.* Iowa City, IA: University of Iowa Press, 2014.

Perez, Rosie, and Liz Garbus, dir. *¡Yo soy Boricua, pa'que tu lo sepas!* Magnolia Home Entertainment, 2009.

Picó, Fernando. *History of Puerto Rico: A Panorama of its People.* Princeton, NJ: Markus Weiner Press, 2006.

Sánchez González, Lisa. *Boricua Literature: A Literary History of the Puerto Rican Diaspora.* New York: New York University Press, 2001.

——. *The Stories I Read to the Children: The Life and Writing of Pura Belpré.* New York: Centro Press, CUNY, 2013.

Sánchez Korrol, Virginia E. *From Colonia to Community: The History of Puerto Ricans in New York City.* Berkeley and Los Angeles: University of California Press, 1994.

Sued Badillo, Jalil. *Agüeybaná El Bravo.* San Juan, PR: Ediciones Puerto, 2008.

——. *La mujer indígena y su sociedad.* 6th edn. Río Piedras, PR: Editorial Cultural, 1975. Rpt. 2010.

West-Durán, Alan, ed. *Latino and Latina Writers.* 2 vols. New York: Scribners/Gale Group, 2004.

11 Central American U.S. Latinos

Ana Patricia Rodríguez

When Héctor Tobar first published his novel *The Tattooed Soldier* in 1998, a literature on **Central Americans** in the United States and by *Central American U.S. Latinos/as* seemed to have arrived on the scene of what was then being hailed as the U.S. Latino literary boom. For many of us who had been hungry to read texts on Central American topics, or by U.S. Central American writers, *The Tattooed Soldier* was nothing less than earthshattering. While we had been bereft of critical representations of Central America and Central Americans in the United States, here was a novel set in Guatemala and Los Angeles, linking the **Guatemalan civil war** (1960–96) and the Los Angeles Riots (1992). In the novel, the two main characters—an ex-Kaibil soldier turned death squad killer named Guillermo Longoria and his victim, a former university student by the name of Antonio Bernal, whose family had been massacred by the same Jaguar-tattooed soldier—encounter one another in the streets of Los Angeles. Upon recognizing the telltale tattoo on a chess player's arm in MacArthur Park, Bernal's mind immediately "spun in the flux between decades and countries, time and space distorted. He was in a park in Guatemala, a park in Los Angeles. The present, the past, somewhere in between" (79). In this significant psychic and historical clash of memories, readers were given a full frontal view of the violence that forced the characters to migrate to the United States and the violence homebred in the United States that pulled them into a narrative of historical reckoning.

On a larger scale, the novel served as an indictment of U.S. political and economic interventions in Central America in the nineteenth through twenty-first centuries, which to this day are a great source of ongoing migrations. Thus, the uncanny meeting of the Central American victimizer and victim in Los Angeles's MacArthur Park, the epicenter of Central American migrations in the region and now home to the Monseñor Oscar A. Romero Memorial Plaza, is symbolically fitting. A chance meeting of the Central American diaspora could not happen in a better place than Los Angeles, or, for that matter, San Francisco, Houston, Washington, D.C., and other unnamed translocations of the Central American diaspora. Facing eviction from his apartment and the prospect of homelessness and life on the streets, Bernal reflects on his diasporic condition: "*There must be a hundred people living here, chapines and guanacos too, living here as if it was the most normal thing in the world, as if they'd been here for years and years*" (Tobar 1998: 13; emphasis in original). Although this quote refers to Bernal's undocumented status, and thus stateless and unhomely condition (Bhabha 1992) in Los Angeles, the quote also serves herein as a point of entry into a discussion on approaches to teaching the literatures of the Central American diaspora in the United States in the twenty-first century.

In this chapter, I identify a growing body of literature by Central American U.S. Latino/a (U.S. Central American) writers[1] and map out an approach to teaching U.S. Central American literatures in historical context, at the intersection of Central American and U.S. Latino/a Studies, and as an interdisciplinary or intersectional practice. I draw primary and secondary texts from literary, film, and cultural studies and scholarship on history, oral history, anthropology, sociology, migration, diaspora, trauma, gender, among others. I provide a context for understanding the most salient issues and topics to be covered in courses on this literature as well as sample modules that may be incorporated into U.S. Latino/a literature classes, or classes focusing on Central Americans in the United States. My pedagogy is student-centered, community-based, and motivated by a **social justice** agenda that attempts to sensitize students to social struggle, **migration**, and displacement, especially in the context of Central Americans in and outside of the **isthmus**.

Initial considerations on teaching U.S. Central American literatures and cultures

To start the discussion, I would ask any instructor or student embarking on the study of U.S. Central American literatures and cultures to ponder what we mean exactly when we refer to Central American diasporas, Central American transnational migrations, and U.S. Central American literary and cultural productions. These days, rather than discussing the potentially reified "invisibility" of Central Americans in the United States, or naming their cultural formation as "Central American American" (Arias 2007), I suggest that we more fully explore, especially in the classroom, the historically situated, produced, circulated, and consumed cultural tropes, narratives, and imaginaries of Central America and Central Americans in the isthmus and in their multiple diasporas. In the 1980s, Central Americans, especially those from the war zones of El Salvador, Guatemala, Nicaragua, and their adjoining neighbors Honduras, Costa Rica, Belize, and Panama, were cast as war refugees.[2] In the twenty-first century Central America continues, for the most part, to be represented as a hotbed of crisis, violence, and criminality (Benz 1997), and its people as refugees, criminals, and victims (see most representations of Central Americans in mainstream media and political discourse today).

It is imperative that through literary and cultural studies we learn about Central America and its diasporas in more historical context, critical depth, and transnational linkages and that we bring to the fore counter narratives and representations such as those produced by U.S. Central American cultural producers. Herein, then, I will map out approaches to teaching works by U.S. Central American cultural producers. The geographic and cultural diversity of the field makes a comparative study a fruitful task by which we can teach students to see and make connections and interrogate neocolonial isolationist and **neoliberal** integrationist (economist) tropes. How does narrative creation interrogate systems that create tropicalized, impoverished, and criminal images of Central America? How can we counter these with other resilient images, visions, and stories of Central America and its **diasporas**? How do we teach students to challenge representations of Central Americans as disease-ridden refugees, welfare-needing anchor-baby mothers, and threatening gang members and build empathy for people fleeing conditions produced by wider global forces? These are some considerations that guide much of my curricula building on all things Central American and that might serve other instructors as roadmaps and guideposts through the minefield of U.S. Central American literary and cultural production.

As a U.S. Central Americanist writing and teaching, for some time, on Central American history, culture, literature, and diasporas in the United States and Central America, and critically engaged with both Latin American and U.S. Latino/a Studies, I cross multiple disciplinary borders, intersect various bodies of scholarship, and use diverse texts, not necessarily identified as "literature," in my teaching of U.S. Central American cultural production. In fact, my concept of Central American diasporan literatures is very fluid and hybrid, drawing from the traditions (and critiques) of *testimonio,* engaged **resistance literature** (*literatura comprometida*), historically based concrete **poetics** (*exteriorismo*), oral history and tradition, and more social science literature. Central American literatures, as I suggest elsewhere, require reading "outside of categories that up to now have elided larger regional [and transnational] complexities" (Rodríguez 2009: 2). In teaching U.S. Central American literatures, I suggest that we need to challenge, if not break, the boundaries of genre, nation, borders, and most of all literary conventions in order to draw and incorporate materials into our classes from the wider fields of narrative, poetry, testimony, social science literature, digital media, and oral and visual texts such as music, film, and painting, among others. I borrow this idea from lessons learned when I spent time during graduate school teaching English at the Universidad of El Salvador (UES) and doing research on Salvadoran literature and *testimonio* in 1990 before the end of the civil war.

Under the duress of civil war and limited and liminal conditions, I observed how professors and students read, discussed, and wrote about massacre, disappearance, death, and violence from a wide array of sources such as interviews, word-of-mouth narratives, oral tradition, newspaper articles, mimeographed material, and testimonial texts clandestinely covered in birthday wrap. To learn, for them, was to use all materials at-hand without access to the knowledge capital of a well-stocked library. In one particular class on Salvadoran literature which I sat in, we discussed social realism, the theories of Lucien Goldman, the engaged poetry of Salvadoran poet Roque Dalton and others, the testimonial genre, and the latest episodes of *Telepirata* (Pirate TV), a comedy show that ran on national TV casting actor Julio Yúdice as La Tenchis Céliber, a raunchy, socially minded, and outspoken *pupusa* (stuffed corn tortillas) maker and mother of 16, and La Niña Tula, the Salvadoran aristocrat for whom La Tenchis worked. In the show, La Tenchis often mentioned her children who lived in the United States and sent her money, yet she always stopped short of expressing her desire to migrate to the United States. She lived out the civil war in her *canton* (village). Where most spaces for social commentary were hidden, if not silenced during the civil war in El Salvador, *Telepirata* satirized the military, the government, and the violence experienced by the Salvadoran people. In class at the UES, we drew from all these at-hand, makeshift literary and cultural materials that made education relevant, challenged the power structure, and critically explored the relationship between a society at war and its narrative production. Hence, learned in the warfront so to speak and a product of my conditions as a Salvadoran raised in diaspora, my pedagogy seeks to draw from the wealth of materials at my students' reach and their own funds of knowledge.

U.S. Central American literary and cultural production

My classes these days on U.S. Central American diasporic literatures are tempered by the legacy of war and its postwar aftermath. The literary critic Beatriz Cortez has called contemporary postwar Central American literature a literature of cynicism. Although the claim, perhaps, may not apply to U.S. Central American diasporic texts, an overview of the latter would highlight the prevalent themes of violence, criminality, displacement, dispossession, migration, transnationality, and living in the in-between of diaspora, time, geopolitics, migratory status, and memories, as Tobar has suggested. Across a wide range of narrative, poetic, visual, and oral texts produced by U.S. Central Americans, these themes are repeated and re-elaborated, like traumas needing to be worked on, even across and despite diasporic spaces and separations. Indeed, Central American U.S. writers have found niches writing novels and stories set in war, massacre, and ongoing violence (Bencastro; Castañeda; Joya; Pineda; Sirias); political thrillers connected to civil war intrigues (Goldman; Tobar); detective novels alluding to past violations (McPeek Villatoro; Unger); true crime fiction investigating unresolved deeds (Goldman); historical novels reconstructing the past (Goldman; McPeek Villatoro); narratives of memory, trauma, and recovery (Barrientos; Escobar; Galindo; Sellers-García; Goldman; Henríquez); personal memoirs and *testimonios* (Cowy et al.; Mendoza; Olmos; Perera); and narratives of transnational migration, resettlement, and (non)belonging (Bencastro; Goldman; Henríquez; Nelson; R. Quesada; U. Quesada; Tobar). Poets and spoken word artists have explored similar themes in a growing corpus of collections and recordings (Ambroggio and Parada Ayala; Aragón; Archila; J. Argueta; Avilés; Chinchilla; Chinchilla and Oliva-Alvarado; M. Cortez; Escobar; Gonzales; Hernández-Linares; Monge; Oliva-Alvarado; Pleitez-Vela, Regalado, and de Sola).

While the study of the Central American diasporas and the nascent field of U.S. Central American literatures has tended to focus mostly on texts produced in the context of the civil wars in the 1980s and thereafter, I suggest that we must go back—further back to recuperate more archival material documenting the presence of Central Americans in the United States. To that end, I am working on a project engaged in the recovery and incorporation of what Kirsten Silva Gruesz has called Transamerican "ambassadors of culture," whose works can be identified as part of the larger U.S. Central American literary and cultural corpus. I seek to re-situate and think beyond minimalist definitions of transnational literature to incorporate the work of Central American cultural sojourners such as Máximo Soto Hall (1871–1944), Salomón de la Selva (1893–1959), José Coronel Urtecho (1906–94), Salvador Efraín Salazar Arrué (Salarrué, 1899–1975), Margarita del Carmen Brannon Vega (Claudia Lars, 1899–1974), Claribel Alegría (1924–), Manlio Argueta (1935–), and many others, whose presence and writings while in the United States have left deep imprints in Central American diasporan literatures and cultures (see Rodríguez, forthcoming).

My hypothesis is that Central Americans have resided or sojourned in the United States since at least the mid-nineteenth century. Central American historians even claim that during the colonial period native peoples of the isthmus were removed from the region and enslaved in Spanish ships and territories. Others have studied the long migration patterns, for example, of the Garifuna and Creole peoples who have worked in shipping and ports all along the Atlantic seaboard from Central America to New York, while still others have indicated that Central Americans have served as laborers and braceros in U.S. banana and coffee plantations, sea ports and shipping centers, and other industries and imperial projects such as the construction of the Panama Canal (Dalton 1974), which made early transnational migrations possible especially to sites such as San Francisco, New Orleans, and New York. Recent research, moreover, shows that Central Americans migrated to the goldfields of California, mostly likely experiencing the exclusionary acts that targeted Chinese, Mexican, Chilean, and other non-white miners (Hayes-Bautista, Chamberlin, and Zuniga 2009). Along these historical lines, there is a need to train our students who are interested in the presence of Central Americans in the United States to conduct and excavate archival material in and outside of the United States. I have found valuable archival materials on Central American migrations, for example, in national and private archives in Costa Rica, El Salvador, Guatemala, Honduras, and even Buenos Aires, Argentina, not to mention the rich materials to be found across libraries, personal holdings, and other sources in the United States.

Framing U.S. Central American literatures in U.S. Latino/a studies

Having now identified an expansive and growing corpus of U.S. Central American literary texts, I ask us to think critically about how we approach the study of U.S. Central American literatures and cultures and how we position ourselves in relation to and incorporate Central American diasporic texts into our syllabi and curricula, mindful of the particular histories, contexts, traditions, and scholarship in Central American Studies. In particular, I ask that we think about:

- The conscious and conscientious inclusion of U.S. Central American subjects, topics, and texts in U.S. Latino/a Studies;
- Our nearly clichéd and unpacked uses of the tropes "Central American American" and "Invisibility" in regards to Central Americans (Arias 2007);
- The almost absolute association of Central America and Central Americans with crisis (e.g., civil war, natural disasters, violence, gangs, undocumented migration, child migration);
- The pressing need to challenge representations of Central Americans in the media, popular culture, and, yes, in our classes and course curriculum design, and to study the larger contexts, conditions, and locations in and from which they are produced;
- The important training of students to do original research, pose critical questions, and produce new knowledge in regards to Central Americans in the isthmus and in the United States;
- The productive intersections of community-based and -engaged research, collaborative learning, community partnerships, and production of knowledge in undergraduate and graduate education.

In this context, I suggest the need to produce community-based and engaged research in Central American diasporic contexts and to engage in service-learning with local Central American immigrant communities in order not only to produce research with and about a highly underrepresented Latino population but also to build a greater understanding of contemporary flows of transnational migration embedded in larger histories of U.S. imperialism and occupation. To make relevant connections between North and South and "the present, the past, somewhere in between" (Tobar 1998: 79), it is important to give full coverage to the histories, politics, economics, cultures, literatures, and current issues in Central American Studies.

Incorporating U.S. Central American texts into courses on U.S. Latino/a literatures and cultures

At my current institution, I have had the opportunity to develop and teach graduate and undergraduate courses focusing exclusively on the transnational histories, literatures, and cultures of Central America as well as the Central American diasporas. These courses have included Latino/a Transmigration and Transnationalism (El Salvador); El Salvador and Its Diaspora: Politics of Representation; Central American Diasporas; Central American Literatures: Violence, Trauma, Memory; Central American Isthmus: Transnational Cultures; Central America: From Caficulturas to Revolutions; and Central American Literatures, Cultures, and Histories. I have also had the opportunity to create modules on Central American diasporic texts for my classes on U.S. Latino/a Literatures and Cultures in the Department of American Studies and my home Department of Spanish and Portuguese. Many primary and secondary and supplementary critical materials can be found in both Spanish and English for use in classes.

In what follows, I outline sample teaching and learning modules for classes on U.S. Central American literatures and cultures. These modules could also be incorporated into classes on U.S. Latino/a literatures and cultures, depending on the topic. Each module might be taught over a period of two weeks and require completion of assigned readings, film and documentary screenings, discussions, short critical reflections and papers (four pages), and community-based research and service-learning activities such as coordinating participatory visits of high school students to the university, organizing student-led and -run symposia and forums on topics, public screenings and discussions of films on and off campus, participating in literary and cultural exchanges at local schools or organizations, and producing oral histories, auto/ethnographies, and digital stories based on materials. I have tried all these activities with students in my U.S. Latino/a and Central American diaspora classes. Learning assessments might include short critical reflections/papers, midterm and final exams, electronic discussion posts on films and documentaries, and digital storytelling projects.

Module 1: Central American Civil Wars, Migration, Social Networks (Guatemala)

- Héctor Tobar, *The Tattooed Soldier*
- John A. Booth, Christine J. Wade, Thomas W. Walker, *Understanding Central America*
- Rigoberta Menchú, *I, Rigoberta Menchú: An Indian Woman in Guatemala* (excerpt)
- *Guatemala Never Again! Recovery of Historical Memory Project (REMHI)* (excerpt)
- Cecilia Menjívar, *Fragmented Ties* (excerpt)
- *Men with Guns* (Dir. John Sayles)
- *Discovering Dominga* (Dir. Patricia Flynn)
- Short critical reflection/paper

Module 2: Inter/Intra-Latino/a Solidarity Activism (El Salvador/Chicana)

- Demetria Martínez, *Mother Tongue*[3]
- Manlio Argueta, "Lengua e identidad en la novela *Lengua Madre*, de Demetria Martinez"

- Carlos Córdova, *The Salvadoran Americans* (excerpt)
- Héctor Perla and Susan B. Coutin, "Legacies and Origins of the 1980s U.S.-Central American Sanctuary Movement"
- Ana Patricia Rodríguez, "The Fiction of Solidarity: *Transfronterista* Feminisms and Anti-Imperialist Struggles in Central American Transnational Narratives"
- *My Family/Mi Familia* (Dir. Gregory Nava)
- Short critical reflection/paper

Module 3: Postwar, Diaspora (El Salvador)

- Mario Bencastro, *Paraíso Portátil/Portable Paradise*
- John A. Booth, Christine J. Wade, Thomas W. Walker, *Understanding Central America*
- Robin Cohen, *Global Diaspora* (excerpt)
- *Innocent Voices/Voces inocentes* (Dir. Luis Mandoki)
- *El lugar más pequeño/The Tiniest Place* (Dir. Tatiana Huezo)
- Short critical reflection/paper

Module 4: Violence, Child Migration (Honduras)

- Sonia Nazario, *Enrique's Journey*
- John A. Booth, Christine J. Wade, Thomas W. Walker, *Understanding Central America*
- Leisy Abrego, *Sacrificing Families: Navigating Laws, Labor, and Love Across Borders* (excerpt)
- *Which Way Home* (Dir. Rebecca Cammisa)
- Twitter feed on child migrant crisis
- Short critical reflection/paper

Module 5: U.S. Central Americans, Inter/Intra-Latinidades (Panama, Guatemala, Nicaragua, Mexico, Dominican Republic, Puerto Rico, Colombia, Venezuela, Paraguay)

- Cristina Henríquez, *The Book of Unknown Americans*
- Quique Avilés, "Latinhood"
- Frances Aparicio, "Cultural Twins and National Others: Allegories of Intralatino Subjectivities in U.S. Latino/a Literature"
- *Estamos Aquí/We Are Here* (Teleduction)
- Short critical reflection/paper

Module 6: U.S. Central American Trans-identities

- Maya Chinchilla, *The Cha Cha Files: A Chapina Poética*
- Maya Chinchilla and Karina Oliva-Alvarado (eds) *Desde el EpiCentro: An Anthology of U.S. Central American Poetry*
- Yajaira Padilla, *Changing Women, Changing Nation* (excerpt)
- Horacio Roque Ramírez, "In Transnational Distance: Translocal Gay Immigrant Salvadoran Lives in Los Angeles"
- Short critical reflection/paper

For lack of space, I will only elaborate on possible discussion points for Module 1: Central American Civil Wars, Migration, Social Networks (Guatemala). Héctor Tobar's novel, *The Tattooed Soldier* (1998), with which I began this chapter, has become one of the foundational texts of the Central American diaspora, along with the work of Francisco Goldman and Mario Bencastro. In 1992, Francisco Goldman published *The Long Night of White Chickens* (1992), which was awarded the Sue Kaufman Prize for first fiction from the Academy of Arts and Letters and nominated for a PEN/Faulkner award. Tobar's, Goldman's, and Bencastro's respective texts allow us ways not only to discuss the content matter of Central American histories and diasporas but also the formation and canonization of a new sub-literature within Latino/a literary studies. In discussing more recognized U.S. Central American texts like Tobar's and Goldman's, one might examine the historical and discursive conditions that make the publication and circulation of these texts possible as well as the intertextualities between Central American texts produced in the isthmus and in diaspora and the linkages forged in diaspora, or what Frances Aparicio has called "intra-latinidades," which might be explored more fully in Module 5.

Tobar's *The Tattooed Soldier* and Goldman's *The Long Night of White Chickens* might be read intertextually as they are among the first U.S. Central American texts published by mainstream presses and incorporated into the U.S. Latino literary boom. Both deal with the Guatemala civil war but more generally are about Central American diasporic subjects shaped by war, violence, and trauma. While Tobar's novel resituates the Central American crisis in the United States, Goldman's *Long Night* returns to the scene of genocide in Guatemala. In *Long Night,* Roger Graetz, born and raised in Boston of mixed Jewish and Guatemalan parentage, visits Guatemala in search of his "adopted" sister Flor de Mayo, only to discover that she has been murdered for her work at an orphanage. The novel brings Graetz and readers face-to-face with the violence and terror raging in Guatemala during its long civil war.

Goldman's novel is also notable for a little-known fact. It served as the inspiration for the production of the film *Men With Guns* (written, directed, and edited by John Sayles). Released in 1998, the same year as the publication of the human rights report titled *Guatemala, Never Again! Recovery of Historical Memory Project* (*REMHI*) and Tobar's *The Tattooed Soldier*, the film tells the story of the last days of Dr. Humberto Fuentes, who three years previously with the aid of an internationally funded humanitarian program had sent his medical students to the war-ravaged regions of Guatemala. Attempting to find them, he learns that one by one they have been murdered and that his comfortable middle class life and unengaged work have not only made him blind to the genocide but also complicit in the production of violence. His search for his students morphs into a search for the reality of Guatemala and for his last resting place called *Cerca del Cielo* [Near Heaven]. At the end of the film while the credits are running, a caption gives tribute to *Long Night*: "The character of Dr. Fuentes was inspired by the character of Dr. Arrau who appears in the novel *The Long Night of White Chickens* by Francisco Goldman" (*Men with Guns*).

I use this example to show that when teaching on Central America and the Central American diasporas it is worth recreating "the scene of the crime," so to speak, with students. Through readings, films, documentaries, and critical reflection, students and instructor can learn about the civil wars in Central America and the reasons for migration to this day. U.S. interventions can be presented through films on the School of the Americas and websites such as the one for the Center for Justice and Accountability

(CJA). Literary genres such as *testimonio*, journalism, and **auto/ethnographies** can be discussed as strategic discursive productions while questioning their assumed "truth" value (see Arias 2001). Furthermore, together, we can reflect and challenge the boundaries between fiction and fact, reality and representation, literature and social sciences, and *testimonio* and truth(s), to name only a few areas that require hybrid ways of reading and analysis. These genre and disciplinary crossings, bendings, and blendings provide fruitful spaces in successive modules to interrogate Western phallogocentric epistemologies and ways of knowing, seeing, and explaining the world. In this case, one may build a learning module in which students can study the fine workings of intertextuality and heteroglossia by reading side-by-side Tobar's *The Tattooed Soldier*, excerpts from Rigoberta Menchú's *I, Rigoberta Menchú: An Indian Woman in Guatemala*, the REMHI, and Francisco Goldman's true crime exposé *The Art of Political Murder: Who Killed the Bishop?* and screening *Men with Guns* and/or the documentary *Discovering Dominga* (directed by Patricia Flynn 2002).

Conclusions

While in my book *Dividing the Isthmus: Central American Transnational Histories, Literatures, and Cultures*, I sought to map out the transnational crossings and intersections of culture *in situ* and in the diaspora of Central Americans, I have become increasingly interested in how Central America/ns are included and interpellated into hemispheric and transnational geopolitical discourses, debates, maps, and curricula. In this chapter, I have sketched ideas for teaching an interdisciplinary course on Central American diasporic texts.[4] Primarily, I draw critical materials from scholarship on diaspora, transnational migration, cultures of U.S. imperialism, hemispheric/Americas, and Central American Studies, critical race, ethnic, and gender theories, among others. As explained in *Dividing the Isthmus*, I am less interested in constructing a unilateral area studies of the Central American diaspora through consideration of its literatures and cultures, but more concerned with exploring and reconstructing "the ever-shifting literary, cultural, and historical configurations of the Central American isthmus [and its diasporas] as an in-between discursive space linking regions, peoples, cultures, and material goods" (2). I would like us to think about how the Central American diasporas in the United States and elsewhere figure into the constant re-mappings and constructions of Central American cultural formations, which I have called the *transisthmus*—"an imaginary yet materially [grounded] space" that travels with Central Americans to make "home" in the most inhospitable and ghastly "unhomely" sites as Bhabha would have it. In that light, there are multiple points of entry into the discussion of the Central American diaspora as well as approaches to teaching and learning about the region and its people, histories, cultures, and texts.

Notes

1 I use the terms *Central American U.S. Latino/a, U.S. Central American*, and *U.S. Central American diasporic* interchangeably to discuss Central American literatures and cultures in the United States. I acknowledge that there are connotative differences in the use of each term.
2 See my article "Refugees of the South: Central Americans in the US Latino Imaginary."
3 For other U.S. Latino/a solidarity and Central American-identified writers, see Benítez; Castillo; Culture Clash; Fernández; Gaspar de Alba, Herrera-Sobek, and Martínez; García; Limón;

Martínez; Moraga; Murguía; Rodríguez Barron; Villanueva; Viramontes. Instructors may wish to use and vary any of these U.S. Latino/a texts, which address Central American issues or content. In "Cultural Twins and National Others: Allegories of Intralatino Subjectivities in US Latino/a Literature," Frances Aparicio discusses the intralatino identity negotiations of hybrid Latino/a subjects as well as intralatino/a relations, solidarities, and pan-identities as represented in specific novels.

4 For a more comprehensive discussion of U.S. Central American literatures please see my chapter "Literatures of Central Americans in the United States" in *The Routledge Companion to Latino/a Literature* (2013), edited by Suzanne Bost and Frances Aparicio.

Resources for teaching Central American and U.S. Latinos

Aparicio, F. "Cultural twins and national others: allegories of intralatino subjectivities in U.S. Latino/a literature." *Identities: Global Studies in Culture and Power*, 16.5 (2009): 622–41.

Arias, A. *Taking Their Word: Literature and the Signs of Central America*. Minneapolis: University of Minnesota Press, 2007.

Booth, J. A., C. J. Wade, and T. W. Walker. *Understanding Central America: Global Forces, Rebellion, and Change*. Boulder: Westview P, forthcoming.

Córdova, Carlos B. *The Salvadoran Americans*. Westport, CT: Greenwood P, 2005.

Goldman, Francisco. *The Art of Political Murder: Who Killed the Bishop?* New York: Grove P, 2007.

Menjívar, Cecilia. "Immigrant art as liminal expression: the case of Central Americans." *Art in the Lives of Immigrant Communities in the United States*. Ed. P. Dimaggio and P. Fernandez-Kelly. New Brunswick: Rutgers University Press, 176–96, 2010.

Padilla, Yajaira. *Changing Women, Changing Nation: Female Agency, Nationhood, and Identity in Trans-Salvadoran Narratives*. Albany: State University of New York Press, 2012.

Perla, Héctor and Susan B. Coutin. "Legacies and origins of the 1980s US-Central American Sanctuary Movement." *Refuge* 26.1 (2009): 7–19.

Rodríguez, Ana Patricia. *Dividing the Isthmus: Transnational Central American Histories, Cultures, and Literatures*. Austin: University of Texas Press, 2009.

Tobar, Héctor. *The Tattooed Soldier*. New York: Penguin Books, 1998.

Part III

Teaching poetry, theatre, and performance arts

12 Teaching U.S. Latino/a poetry in the age of social media

Urayoán Noel

A *performalist* pedagogy

When teaching U.S. Latino/a poetry I seek a balance between **close reading** and social analysis, between **formalist** and **culturalist** approaches. In teaching the formalist approach, I have found Michael Meyer's *Poetry: An Introduction* (2001) helpful for its division into sections (Word Choice, Word Order, and Tone; Images; Figures of Speech; Symbol, Allegory, and Irony; Sounds; Patterns of Poetry; Poetic Forms, etc.), its wide range of poems (including works by a number of U.S. Latino/a poets), and its reading strategies and studies of particular poets. In teaching the culturalist approach I often refer to Maria Damon and Ira Livingston's *Poetry and Cultural Studies: A Reader* (2009), which includes work by so-called precursors such as Wordsworth, Adorno, Benjamin, and Du Bois alongside a multicultural and transnational variety of more recent selections, among them two essays that are key to the study of U.S. Latino/a poetics: Américo Paredes's "Some Aspects of Folk Poetry" (1964) and Miguel Algarín's "Nuyorican Language," his introduction to the anthology *Nuyorican Poetry: An Anthology of Puerto Rican Words and Feelings* (1975). I also find Jonathan Culler's *Literary Theory: A Very Short Introduction* (1997) to be useful in framing a field of reading practices, critical traditions, and institutional histories.

I emphasize to my students that poetry was central to New Criticism's project of institutionalizing literary study as a formal exercise attuned to the specialization imperatives of the modern research university; in this context the difficulty or complexity of poetry was a value in itself, inasmuch as it demanded a formal rigor and an avoidance of facile historical and/or biographic readings. Conversely, I go on to underscore how within Latino Studies the complexity of poetry has often been linked to its cultural and historic specificity, its rootedness in personal and social experience, its ethnographic and sociolinguistic significance (see Paredes and Algarín), and its role in helping shape our understanding of essential terms such as *border* and *diaspora*.

Latino Studies scholars have stressed poetry's relationship to expressive cultures, and especially to folk, oral, and musical forms such as the *corrido* (Limón) or the *bomba* (Flores); they have also looked to vernacular practices such as code-switching and the use of Spanglish (Aparicio, Stavans) both as a way of close-reading interlingual forms (Bruce-Novoa) and as a cultural metaphor (Morales). Accordingly, I briefly introduce students to these expressive practices and vernacular forms, and I ask them to think about how their decisive presence in U.S. Latino/a poetry challenges conventional formalist assumptions. At the same time, I make sure that we also engage with the formal features that might help us mark these texts as poems (figures of speech, sound, tone, etc.), and I ask us to consider what it might mean to close-read with an eye for the differential forms of Spanglish or the corrido.

In the classroom, then, I attempt to bridge formalist and culturalist approaches while complicating both, in an effort to nurture what might be called a *performalist* pedagogy at the intersection of literary text and expressive culture. Mine is an expansive conception of performance that does not refer solely to discrete poetry events but also to a poem's life on and off the page across space and time, to what Peter Middleton calls the "long history of the poem" (its circulation, distribution, reception, and so on) that close readings typically sidestep. To describe this necessary counterpoint to close reading, Middleton uses the term **distant reading**, which is also the name Franco Moretti gives to his own networked, global, and data-friendly approach to literary study. Whereas Middleton is calling for a long history attuned to the "aggregative textual archive that composes the textual memory of the poem" (2005: 23), Moretti argues for the mapping and graphing of data as a means of visualization, as a way to "literally *see* literary history in a new way" (2013: 76, italics in the original).

Following Middleton, I might ask my students to reflect on all the ways in which we are distant readers when we engage with Rodolfo "Corky" Gonzales's "I Am Joaquín" (see Gonzales 2010) or Pedro Pietri's "Puerto Rican Obituary" (1973), two foundational epic poems from *el movimiento* (or social movement) of the 1960s. Not only are we far removed from the movimiento era, we are also arriving at these poems in latter-day versions, some of them significantly revised and with eccentricities streamlined. Even with the benefit of the thoroughly annotated versions included in Stavans's *Norton Anthology of Latino Literature* (2011), we are missing a sense of such poems' often fascinating and sometimes confounding publication and performance histories: from their appearance in community newspapers and activist publications to their audio and video recording, which involved the poets themselves (as in Pietri's poetry LPs from the 1970s) as well as various cover versions and adaptations by poets and non-poets alike (as in Luis Valdez and El Teatro Campesino's iconic stage and screen versions of Gonzales's poem).

In class I might ask students to research and present one of these alternative versions of "I Am Joaquín" or "Puerto Rican Obituary," to describe their research process and to reflect on what we are missing by engaging primarily with the *Norton Latino* version of these poems. When describing their research process students will typically mention web searches, and many of them will end up finding their alternative versions through social media such as YouTube or Tumblr. Following their presentations, I try to ask us to think about what it means to *read* in the digital age. Can the laptop or tablet or e-reader screen retain the intimacy of close-reading a print text, or does the proliferation of social media, e-books, blogs, and online publications force us to grapple with an expanded and seemingly unmanageable textual field thereby leading us farther away from any stable notion of reading?

In asking students to consider these questions my aim is not to generate definitive answers but to have them reflect on their own reading practices, especially as they are shaped by the problematics of what Jay David Bolter and Richard Grusin (1999) call "**remediation**" (how new media repurpose old media) and what N. Katherine Hayles (2008) calls the "intermediation" between humans and computers that increasingly shapes our experience of the literary, from word processors and digital slide shows to e-readers and blogs. While movimiento poets like Gonzales and Pietri were invested in a countercultural politics that was fundamentally anti-technocratic (Roszak), our own contemporary experiences of their poems are inevitably enmeshed in the problematics of remediation and intermediation; as I tell my students, in that sense were are all distant readers and remedial learners.

Poetry as a social medium

From my performalist perspective, poetry is a social medium (and, of course, all media are social), and in fact one might argue that the social impact of a poem such as "I Am Joaquín" was shaped and is evidenced by its numerous and ongoing media lives (as a Teatro Campesino play and a Valdez film and in countless popular performance and mimeograph versions). One might add that the *Norton Latino*'s canonization of the poem as a staple of U.S. Latino/a literature hinges on the bracketing off of these other media versions in the name of its textual stability and proper close reading. (Although, to its credit, the *Norton Latino* helpfully includes a concluding section called "Popular Dimensions" that features jokes, cartoons, legends, songs, and other non-traditionally literary texts, we are given little sense of the long history of "I Am Joaquín.") To remedy (and remediate) this situation in the classroom, I have often resorted informally to YouTube when seeking out video of various versions of "I Am Joaquín," and I know that many of my colleagues use YouTube in similar ways.

I began thinking in earnest about these issues after witnessing a colleague whose work I respect and admire crowdsource Facebook friends for a link to a video of a performance by poet Willie Perdomo that had been deleted from YouTube. I sent my colleague a link to the performance from another site, but I could not help wonder if we, as teachers, did not need to do a better job of addressing and problematizing this ad hoc use of social media in the classroom. It is not that YouTube cannot function as a community resource, provisional archive, and teaching tool (in fact, many of us have been using it in these ways for years); it is that its aims and logic were and remain unabashedly commercial and its value to participatory culture is what Jean Burgess and Joshua Green call "an unintended and often unsupported consequence of the practices of its users" (2009: 76). For instance, YouTube limits video uploads by unverified users to a maximum of 15 minutes, so that longer videos may appear in problematically decontextualized form, while its move toward the embedding of advertisements within videos creates political and pedagogical problems, as well as problems of form (how do we close-read a video with embedded advertisements?). Lastly, there is a problem of attribution, since we may not know who posted these videos, where they were taken from, if they were manipulated in some way, or what rights might be in play.

By addressing the messiness of "reading" poetry on YouTube, I try to get students to think about the promise and the pitfalls of social media; as with all sorts of *spreadable* media (Jenkins, Ford, and Green), YouTube functions from above and from below: it reinforces corporate interests (it is advertising-driven and owned by Google) but it also allows for decentered alternative uses by artists, activists, and others. Could it be that one result of teaching poetry in the social-media classroom is to make us sensitive to how poetry is also a spreadable medium defined not just by the (necessary) institutionalizing imperative of the *Norton Latino* but also by a social history of cross-media circulation? Given their brevity (at least compared to the movimiento-era **Bildungsroman** exemplified by *Autobiography of a Brown Buffalo* (1972) and *Down These Mean Streets* (1967)), their relationship to music and the spoken word, and their rich cross-media life, "I Am Joaquín" and "Puerto Rican Obituary" emerge as works whose status as defining social texts of the movimiento era is tied to what might be called a poetics of spreadability.

But how do we read spreadable media, and what role can close-reading play? When I teach these two poems I ask students to close-read them and to pay attention to distinctive formal features such as their short lines and their use of typography for dramatic emphasis (all uppercase words, exclamation marks). I then ask us to think about these formal features in the social context of movimiento politics by reading "El Plan Espiritual de Aztlán" and the Young Lords' Party's "13 Point Program and Platform." We discuss the tensions between both documents' programmatic politics and the more open-ended and eccentric vision encoded in the two poems, but we also consider the significant role these poems played in their respective (Chicano, Puerto Rican) movimiento contexts. Building on Lorenzo Thomas's conception of the Black Arts poem as a score for a future performance, I ask students to think about the poems' short lines and dramatic cues as pointing to a future performance inasmuch as they link their composition to the breath and voice. The spreadability of these two poems is partly a matter of social history (they were performed, published, and adapted in various ways) but it is also a matter of poetic composition (of the vernacular force of their short lines and long stanzas, their urgent tone, their dramatic address), so that a proper reading of the poems would require the type of performalist pedagogy I am sketching: attuned to formal intricacies and to broader social and cultural contexts.

Perhaps unsurprisingly, these two poems have a particularly strong presence on YouTube, where we can find everything from Valdez's film version of "I Am Joaquín" to a snippet from Pietri's performance of "Puerto Rican Obituary" on the Young Lords' Newsreel film El Pueblo Se Levanta, to a variety of cover versions of both poems by a variety of users. As part of an ongoing project on Latinidad in the age of social media, I am writing about these YouTube cover versions of "I Am Joaquín," which range from a choreographic version done by students for their Latin American History course at UCLA to a hip-hop version by Denver-based group 2MX2 to amateur kitchen-table readings and adaptations by community poets and activists.

As a way of getting students to reflect on U.S. Latino/a poetry as a social medium, I might jettison the typical research paper and instead ask students to undertake their own social-media project, which might take the form of a creative project or response (as in the UCLA students' cover version), a YouTube playlist or Tumblr page or Twitter mobilization inspired by the poetry we have read, an interactive blog, or the creation or editing of a relevant Wikipedia entry ("Puerto Rican Obituary" is still in need of an entry while the one for "I Am Joaquín" could use some developing). Because I do not want students to merely reproduce the logic of social media but also to reflect on their own close and distant reading practices, I would ask them to also submit an essay describing their project, its methodology and aims, and its relevance to the course topic. (When I have done something along these lines in the past, the length and complexity of this essay has depended on the level of the course and on how much we have already covered in class; in one case, I gave students the typology developed by Leah A. Lievrouw in her book *Alternative and Activist New Media* (2011) for a framework to keep in mind as they wrote about their projects.)

Existing critical literature on the use of social media in the classroom has tended to stress its potential to help us problematize traditional pedagogical assumptions; in their essay on the use of online videos in the classroom Nick Pearce and Elaine Tan emphasize how their use dovetails with a "constructivist approach to teaching and learning" (2013: 145) that is not limited to content delivery and that stresses discussion, including discussion about the use of videos and the teaching and learning process.

I share Pearce and Tan's investment in fomenting self-reflexive learning through the use of social media in the classroom, but I also wonder about their characterization of online videos as "free content" that allows staff to not have to worry about "the generation of new content" in a "climate where resources are scarce" (145).

While YouTube is (for the moment at least) free, it relies on the unfettered monetization of data and on the work of vast numbers of willing uploaders; furthermore, I wonder what message we send our students when we simply embrace the logic of corporate out-sourcing as a reaction to the politics of scarcity—is that not a classic neoliberal move? From my vantage point social media does not resolve the politics of archive, if anything it makes things more complex by facilitating all kinds of access while raising numerous political, pedagogical, and pragmatic questions. Will university administrators further slash funding for libraries and dedicated archives because all these materials are sup-posedly now available for free via YouTube? What are the pedagogical implications of relying on YouTube, where, as Burgess and Green note, decontextualization and recontextualization are common and constant inasmuch as "it is often very difficult to determine what regimes of truth govern different genres of user-generated content" (2009: 122)? My sense is that these sorts of questions need to become part of our classroom discussions, even as we embrace the constructivist potential of social media with a healthy dose of criticality.

To have my students finesse their thinking on social media as they prepare their essays, I might have them read short essays spanning a range of ideological positions, from Tim O'Reilly's defining "What is Web 2.0: Design Patterns and Business Models for the Next Generation of Software" to Felix Stalder's "Between Democracy and Spectacle. The Front and the Back of the Social Web," both included in Michael Mandiberg's *The Social Media Reader* (2012). Stalder distinguishes between "the front-end, the social web, or Web 2.0, [which] may well advance semiotic democracy" and the back-end, which "may just as well turn into Spectacle 2.0, new forms of control and manipulation, masked by a mere simulation of involvement and participation" ("Between Democracy and Spectacle"). I think it is important for students to engage critically yet creatively with their relationship to social media, partly since one might argue that we are living in a new social media-driven movimiento era: from the online mobilizations of the Librotraficante project to the DREAMers' YouTube *testimonios* to the Facebook group Poets Responding to SB1070, activists and artists (and, of course, poets) are turning to social media as an alternative to the mainstream political culture around such issues as immigration and education.

There are some important similarities between this new movimiento and the 1960s–70s one, and a number of these new artists and activists specifically connect their work to movimiento histories, figures, and traditions, but there are also significant differ-ences; we do a disservice to our students if we do not ask them to work through some of those differences. For those of us who are trained and invested in literary study, the differences are formal as much as political: how do the cross-media lives of "I Am Joaquín" lead us (or not) to the new media art and activism of Web 2.0; how does the community-specific address of these movimiento epics survive (or not) its screening and de/recontextualization; and how can these epics matter in a meme-driven culture characterized by what Carol Vernallis calls in her analysis of YouTube, music videos, and digital cinema "intensified audiovisual aesthetics" (2013: 33)? There is no one answer to any of these questions, but to ask them is to begin thinking about poetry as a social medium in a way that might help bridge the movimiento era and our own.

The performalist pedagogy I have in mind could be applied not only to movimiento-era poems but also to contemporary poems that underscore their own terms of address or that would appear to require distant readings of some sort. It might even help us engage with a ceremonial poem such as Richard Blanco's "One Today" (2014), written for and performed at the 2013 swearing-in ceremony for President Barack Obama. A close reading of "One Today" might highlight how the poem's enjambments create a tension that belies its democratic vistas, the ceremonial togetherness seemingly demanded by the formality of the inaugural poem: "apples, limes, and oranges arrayed like rainbows / begging our praise. Silver trucks heavy with oil or paper" (Bruce 2014). While the poem is relatively straightforward in terms of language and syntax, the unpredictable enjambments make it tricky to read aloud; whereas the movimiento epics scored a future performance, Blanco's poem reads, in keeping with its title, like a snapshot of an unrecoverable present.

There are various user interpretations of "One Today" on YouTube, and it is instructive to experience the poem as read by students, fans, and recitation contestants, and even as a soundtrack for an online photo slideshow. These interpretations would appear to destabilize or trivialize the scene of address, as there are now many *todays*, but they also make us experience the rhetorical weight of the poem's enjambments, whose difficulty does not disappear, as well as its balancing act between the ceremonial and the quotidian. Looped between the poem as a poetic text and a metapoetic event, a performalist reading of "One Today" might consider its seeming understatedness (again, at least compared to Gonzales and Pietri's epics) as both a ceremonial convention and as tied to its problematic shareability, especially as terms such as "Cuban American" and "gay" frame the text that accompanies some of the YouTube videos in their media ecosystem.

In a YouTube environment that prizes "intensified audiovisual aesthetics," the understated enjambments of "One Today" mark the complex social capital of the poem, its ceremonial elegance, but also its modest visibility in such a memetic context: the more than 75,000 views the ABC News upload of "One Today" has received are undoubtedly a lot for a poem on YouTube, but they are far from meme-worthy. One question that social media can help us ask our students is: what can poetry (and literature more generally) do in the age of memes, and what are its modes of shareability on- and offline? When we have these sorts of conversations in class we are likely to get to the question of what exactly counts as poetry, and we might note that the status of poetry looks very different if we count popular music and spoken word as poetry (and, following Paredes, maybe we should). The point is not to engage in philosophizing or gatekeeping as to what is or is not poetry, but to get students thinking about the study of poetry across and along this formalist and culturalist continuum.

In other words, in teaching U.S. Latino/a poetry I aim to expose students to a broader conception of **poetics** where form does not merely refer to the conventions of genre or to classical forms (sonnet, sestina, etc.) but also to media contexts past and present. A renewed attention to poetics in this broad sense might afford us what Markku Eskelinen calls in *Cybertext Poetics* "a more nuanced and pragmatic understanding of the types of relations texts may have with one another, and more precisely towards changes in these relations due to changes in the mechanics of textual machines" (2012: 50).

Reading networks

In a sense, I am using poetry—in its various print/performance and offline/online iterations—as a way to get students to think about the complexity of social texts. This may seem obvious, but in my experience teaching upper-level undergraduate courses that draw students from both English/literary studies and Latino Studies, it is a key pedagogical move: while one might expect that the former students will be at least minimally trained in the intricacies of close-reading texts, they may struggle with social and cultural contexts, while the latter students may have the opposite problem (they may have a solid background in ethnic and/or cultural studies but little or no familiarity with the close reading of literary texts, and especially poetry).

Developing this type of hybrid reader seems key to me given the richness and complexity of contemporary U.S. Latino/a poetry. As Nicolás Kanellos suggests, in recent decades many Latino/a poets have emerged through university creative-writing programs, and their work may well be steeped in formal languages and traditions far removed from *movimiento* histories. At the same time, countless U.S. Latino/a poets work outside or at the margins of these institutional contexts, many of them in open mics, community readings, and/or activist circles. With the transnational rise of hip-hop culture and the popularization of poetry slams, Latino/a poetry circulates in global networks far beyond the U.S. literary corpus, and poets such as Tomás Riley and the aforementioned Willie Perdomo fuse a hip-hop sensibility with nods to Chicano/a and Nuyorican traditions and histories, often reflecting on contemporary issues such as globalization, the so-called War on Terror, and the gentrification of historic *movimiento* neighborhoods such as New York City's Loisaida and San Francisco's La Misión. The fact that such poets engage communities across a local-global matrix while in some cases achieving mainstream visibility (Perdomo's new book is published by Penguin) means that we as teachers need to rethink the binary opposition between a formalist elite conception of poetry and a culturalist/populist one, just as we must rethink questions of form as they evolve in or against emerging media landscapes.

While arguing for a networked approach to form that reads and teaches poetry across media, I am also arguing for a networked approach to questions of identity and belonging. Some of the most engaging contemporary Latino/a poets draw poetic and political inspiration from distinct community-specific histories and poetics even as their work evolves across a range of formal constellations. To properly read books such as Eduardo C. Corral's *Slow Lightning* (2012) or Aracelis Girmay's *Kingdom Animalia* (2011)—two celebrated books by emerging Latino/a poets—would require not only an intersectional approach attuned to vectors of race, class, gender, and sexuality, as well as a subtle revisiting of key terms such as *border* and *diaspora*, but also an understanding of how these poets respond to and remediate earlier poets such as José Montoya and Martín Espada.

Returning to Moretti's conception of distant reading, we might add that digital technology can play an important role in helping students visualize these networked histories. In his intriguing essay "Revenge of the Nerd: Junot Díaz and the Networks of American Literary Imagination" (2013), published in the online journal *Digital Humanities Quarterly*, Ed Finn argues that "we need to expand 'close' reading by looking carefully at the full context of a literary network at a particular point in time, particularly the new dynamic influences of algorithms and digital reading, and to mark that expansion with the term 'middle ground'" (Finn 2013).

Finn's middle ground is, of course, the one between traditional close reading and Moretti's distant one, between "the individual text and the distant reading of thousands of texts, exploring the emerging space of cultural distinction for a particular author's work at a particular time" (Finn 2013). Accordingly, Finn aggregates user reviews and algorithmic recommendations from the websites Amazon and Library Thing along with reviews by professionals and other materials in an effort to map and reflect on the circulation of Díaz's epochal novel *The Brief Wondrous Life of Oscar Wao* (2007). While acknowledging the novel's already canonical status—it won a National Book Critics Circle Award and the Pulitzer Prize for Fiction, and a portion of its first chapter appears in the *Norton Latino*—Finn mines its eccentricity as a social text, using Amazon recommendations and a range of distant-reading strategies to link this bestseller to a range of communities (Caribbean, Latino/a, multi-ethnic, postcolonial, etc.) and genres and forms (comic books, science fiction, hip-hop, Spanglish). Finn's middle ground grants *Oscar Wao* its canonical status as a literary text while allowing us to visualize its quirky status as a social one.

I think we teachers could do more to help our students reflect on, as Finn (2013) puts it, "how books are contextualized and discussed not just among critics and scholars but also among a general readership online," and I think we can start by acknowledging what Finn calls the "digital traces of book culture" but also by looking at all the ways in which poetry happens outside or on the margins of book culture. For instance, when teaching Carmen Giménez Smith's book *Odalisque in Pieces* (2009), I might show students a short YouTube video that accompanies the book, a slightly surreal slideshow backed by ambient electronic music and featuring works of art depicting women (presumably odalisques), many of them reclining, naked, or disguised. The video was not uploaded until 2010 (presumably by Giménez Smith herself, as the uploader's name is carsmi71) and it is not linked to on the publisher's webpage for the book. While I discovered this video by chance while web-browsing, at this point it feels essential to my reading of *Odalisque in Pieces*, a book that is memorable for its savvy and forceful interplay between the fragmentary nature of culture and identity and the fissuring and recovery of the woman's body. Even the video's lo-tech feel and the fact that it has Google ads on it all somehow underscore to me the poignancy of the book's meditation on the fragility and malleability of bodies.

Similarly, when teaching *Slow Lightning* and *Kingdom Animalia*, I might direct students to *Kingdom Animalia*'s Amazon page, which informs us that customers who bought Girmay's book also bought *Slow Lightning* along with Natalie Diaz's *When My Brother Was an Aztec* and Terrance Hayes's *Lighthead*; following Finn, I would ask my students to consider how Amazon's use of algorithms to maximize sales also allows us to locate Corral and Girmay's books in a multi-ethnic network alongside a Native American poet (Diaz) and an African American one (Hayes). Are Amazon's algorithmic recommendations borne out by a comparative analysis of the books (of the kind students might do for a final paper), and what does it mean that Amazon is monetizing multi-ethnic reading networks for emerging U.S. Latino/a poets while scholars of contemporary U.S. Latino literature remain largely silent as to the work of emerging poets and as to pan-Latino/a and multi-ethnic approaches to poetry and poetics?

Finally, when teaching "I Am Joaquín" from the *Norton Latino* I might give students a Google Ngram featuring the terms *Chicano* and *Latino*. (A Google Ngram is an online graph of words and phrases from books digitized by Google.) This Ngram would show them that the term *Latino* booms in the 1980s and 1990s, after the Chicano Movement heyday. Noticing this, students might begin to reflect on the implications of calling "I Am Joaquín" a work of Latino literature given its Chicano-specific associations, and maybe they would also think about the limitations of the book-centric Ngram as applied to a history of remediations. Using visualization tools in this Moretti-esque manner, I might get students to undertand poetics and cultural history in a new and deeper way. Turning back to close reading, I might point out to the students that "I Am Joaquín" in fact includes the term *Latino*, albeit among a list of terms that appear subordinated to an essentialized personal-social identity that defines itself in opposition to assimilation:

> we start to MOVE.
>
>   La Raza!
> Méjicano!
>   Español!
>   Latino!
>   Hispano!
>   Chicano!
> or whatever I call myself,
>   I look the same
>   I feel the same
>   I cry
>   And
>   Sing the same.
>
> I am the masses of my people and
> I refuse to be absorbed.
>   (Gonzales 2010: 798–99)

Referencing Moretti, I might ask students to create a map or graph of these terms as they are used in the poem, and I might point out the importance of lists to Moretti's project. Continuing with the performalist reading, I might ask students to think about movimiento poetics here in terms of the personal-social shift between "we" and "I" but also in terms of the movement of the lines on the page, with their short bursts of text, the centripetal tug of their layout, and the dramatic uses of exclamation marks and uppercase words (the "MOVE" that performs the very movimiento politics the poem thematizes). I might conclude by asking students to compare Gonzales's use of the term *Latino* to Ilan Stavans's in his introduction to the *Norton Latino*. Whereas Stavans's framing of the term is largely binary, relying on the conflict between "Anglo" and "Hispanic" cultures (2010: liii), Gonzales's Latinidad is inseparable from the proliferation of identities, the negotiation of personal and social space, and the tensions between the biological, the cultural, and the affective embodied in his invocation of "La raza" and his performative "whatever I call myself" (Gonzales 2010: 798–99).

One might argue that it is this performative negotiation of personal and social space that makes "I Am Joaquín" such an intriguing text for YouTube interpretations: with its mixture of lyric intensity and epic breadth it resonates on YouTube, a site designed for individual users (the amateur yet monetizable "you" in its name) that, like its social-media brethren, has become a resource for alternative and activist participatory culture even as it risks "new forms of control and manipulation" (Stalder). My performalist poetics is ultimately an attempt to approach poetics in an expanded sense as an embodied language embedded in media networks.

What does movimiento look like in the digital age? We tend to think of social movements in Diana Taylor's terms, as siding with expressive repertoire of the body against the regulatory power of the archive, and Gonzales's and Pietri's epics make their anti-technocratic politics explicit: Pietri laments the fact that his fellow Puerto Ricans did not turn off the television and "tune into their own imaginations" (1973: 11). How, then, are we to read a movimiento 2.0 in the tensions between social movement and social media? The question is not merely political; it has real classroom implications, as students and teachers alike seek to find their way through a neoliberal university in the shadow of privatization, the rise of massive open online courses (MOOCs), and the defunding of the humanities. Could poetry, the most arcane and abstract of genres, show us a new (and not that new) way of reading: on- and offline, in print and in performance, in and against a formal and cultural network of remediations? Here's to a new remedial education!

Resources for teaching U.S. Latino/a poetry

Aldama, Frederick Luis. *Formal Matters in Contemporary Latino Poetry.* New York: Palgrave, 2013.

Aparicio, Frances R. "La vida es un Spanglish disparatero: Bilingualism in Nuyorican Poetry." *European Perspectives on Hispanic Literature of the United States.* Ed. Genevieve Fabre. Houston: Arte Público, 1988, pp.147–60.

Aragón, Francisco, ed. *The Wind Shifts: New Latino Poetry.* Tucson: University of Arizona Press, 2007.

Bernstein, Charles, ed. *Close Listening: Poetry and the Performed Word.* New York: Oxford University Press, 1998.

Bruce-Novoa, Juan. *Chicano Poetry: A Response to Chaos.* Austin: University of Texas Press, 1982.

Culler, Jonathan. *Literary Theory: A Very Short Introduction.* Oxford: Oxford University Press, 1997.

Damon, Maria, and Ira Livingston, eds. *Poetry and Cultural Studies: A Reader.* Urbana: University of Illinois Press, 2009.

Dowdy, Michael. *Broken Souths: Latina/o Poetic Responses to Neoliberalism and Globalization.* Tucson: University of Arizona Press, 2013.

Flores, Juan. "Nueva York, diaspora city: Latinos between and beyond." *Bilingual Games: Some Literary Investigations.* Ed. Doris Sommer. New York: Palgrave, 2003, pp. 69–76.

Kanellos, Nicolás. "An overview of Latino poetry: the iceberg below the surface." *American Book Review* 24.1 (2002): 5–10.

Limón, José E. *Mexican Ballads, Chicano Poems: History and Influence in Mexican-American Social Poetry.* Berkeley: University of California Press, 1992.

Luis, William, ed. *Looking Out, Looking In: Anthology of Latino Poetry.* Houston: Arte Público, 2013.

Meyer, Michael, ed. *Poetry: An Introduction.* 7th edn. Boston: Bedford, 2012.

Middleton, Peter. *Distant Reading: Performance, Readership, and Consumption in Contemporary Poetry.* Tuscaloosa: University of Alabama Press, 2005.

Morales, Ed. *Living in Spanglish: The Search for Latino Identity in America.* New York: St. Martin's, 2003.

Moretti, Franco. *Distant Reading.* London: Verso, 2013.

Noel, Urayoán. "Bodies that antimatter: locating U.S. Latino/a poetry, 2000–2009." *Contemporary Literature* 52.4 (2011): 852–82.

——. *In Visible Movement: Nuyorican Poetry from the Sixties to Slam.* Iowa City: University of Iowa Press, 2014.

Padgett, Ron. *The Teachers and Writers Handbook of Poetic Forms.* 2nd edn. New York: Teachers and Writers, 2000.

Seo, Kay Kyeong-Ju, ed. *Using Social Media Effectively in the Classroom: Blogs, Wikis, Twitter, and More.* New York: Routledge, 2013.

Sommer, Doris. *Bilingual Aesthetics: A New Sentimental Education.* Durham: Duke University Press, 2004.

Stavans, Ilan, gen. ed. *The Norton Anthology of Latino Literature.* New York: Norton, 2010.

13 Theater in the Latino/a literature classroom

William Orchard

Drama is disappearing. Or, so it would appear after a quick, informal perusal of online syllabi for recent classes on Latino/a literature. Poetry joins drama in the retreat from reading lists, and what rises in their place is fiction, which increasingly dominates the teaching of post-1960s Latino/a literature. This may be attributable to more general shifts toward narrative within literary studies. As literary critic Dorothy Hale notes, since the 1980s, we have seen an "explosion everywhere of the novel," which has surpassed poetry to become the "vital object of interest to scholars both within and outside of English departments" (2006: 453). With the novel's rise in prestige, narrative fiction has come to define the "literary." In the classroom, especially the Latino/a literature classroom, which often draws students from outside of literature departments, fiction also proves more accessible when compared with poetry and drama, which are often laden with specialized terms that make them seemingly less approachable. This chapter, however, will explore how theater also renders aspects of literary study and historical contextualization more accessible by enlisting the creative energies of students to imagine how texts can be staged.

Of course, drama is not disappearing at all. If one were to repeat the informal survey of online syllabi, instead searching for syllabi that contained the names of well known Latino/a dramatists like Cherríe Moraga, Miguel Piñero, Dolores Prida, or Luis Valdez, one would discover that these works enjoy a vibrant life in fields beyond literature: in queer studies, gender studies, ethnic studies, and, especially, performance studies. The movement of Latino theater from literature classrooms to these interdisciplinary fields highlights more than just a shift in drama's status in literary study. It also suggests how various forms of Latino theater bump up against other performance traditions, and, as a result, often look distinct from dramatic works that populate the canon of American literature. Writing about Chicano theater, Tomás Ybarra-Frausto has termed the aesthetic of this work "**rascuachi**," in order to highlight both how artists are inventive with limited resources and how they confront "the world from the perspective of the downtrodden, the rebel, the outsider" (1984: 52). The rascuachi aesthetic—which might also describe theatrical work by other Latino groups—reminds us that, although Latinos were excluded from many of the mainstream institutions that produced theater for mass audiences, they were successful in building their own institutions in order to give voice to their stories and respond to the popular and political sentiments of their regional audiences. Because of this ability to create local publics, Latino theater has been especially attuned to the pulse of marginalized lives, even those marginalized within Latino communities themselves. Additionally, in comparison to poetry and fiction, which often required engaging an exclusionary publishing marketplace, theater provided more accessible venues for Latino/a writers and artists, from the nineteenth century through the present. Indeed, of the three major genres of literature, theater is the one that has most significantly engaged Latino/a voices, resulting in a large—if disjointed—body of work that challenges standard literary conceptions of authorship and history, that responds to political issues as they arise, and that cultivates the talents of not only writers but also actors, directors, and production designers.

When dramatic works do appear on Latino/a literature syllabi, they have often been reduced to a set of familiar figures that represent what Jon Rossini calls the "decadal understanding" of Latino/a theater. In this schema, the 1960s mark an era of community-based collectives, while the 1970s see the emergence of individuals and theatrical institutions. The 1980s produce a new generation of professionalized playwrights, while the 1990s and 2000s see the rise of a third generation that problematizes Latino/a identity and attains national acclaim (Rossini 2013: 276). There is much value to this taxonomy, not the least of which is that it provides a legible, if contestable, account of major shifts in Latino/a cultural production that connect with the history of writing and cultural work in other literary genres. However, as Rossini also notes, the decadal understanding of Latino/a drama effaces many of its more eccentric characteristics. Since this approach to incorporating drama is more well known, this chapter will turn toward two familiar, though still eccentric, works: Josefina Niggli's *Soldadera* (1936) and Maria Irene Fornes's *The Conduct of Life* (1986). Taken together, these two short plays share an interest in the ways in which war and political violence impact Latino/a lives, but here they will be considered individually for how they open up ways of thinking about history and how they offer ways of pushing beyond identity to imagine Latino/a political life in new configurations. Key to arriving at these issues is engaging the works *as theater* by inviting students into the process of imagining how a given work might materialize on stage and how a given actor might develop a character.

Staging history

Josefina Niggli's 1936 play *Soldadera* is an effective vehicle for understanding not only the **Mexican Revolution** as an event that transformed Mexican American communities in the United States, but also how this event marked a crucial flashpoint in the development of Mexican American theatrical productions. The period of the Revolution, spanning from 1910 to 1920, is often a difficult one to confront in the Latino/a literature classroom because many of the best known works that emerge from and address that historical moment—like Leonor Villegas de Magnon's *The Rebel* (c. 1920s) and Josefina Niggli's *Mexican Village* (1945)—are long and would take up several weeks on the syllabus.[1] In contrast, *Soldadera* is a mere 30 pages and could be assigned for a single class session, but is probably best studied over two class sessions that combine a reading of the play with short dramaturgical assignments that direct students to investigate aspects of the play's historical context.

Soldadera tells the story of a band of soldier-women who have been charged by their male leader to guard a mountain pass where some ammunition is held. In the course of their watch, they detect and capture a Federal spy, whom they call the Rich One. Through a series of manipulations, the Rich One secures a mirror from one of the soldaderas and uses it to inform his Federal colleagues of his whereabouts. When Concha, the leader of the soldaderas, discovers the Rich One's actions, she makes a plan to save their cherished ammunition by bombing the mountain pass that the Federal soldiers must travel through, even though that action will force her to sacrifice one of her soldier-women. While the play offers a gripping drama on its own, it also provides an opportunity for students to consider the historical forces that shape the dramatic conflict in the play.

A week prior to our discussion of the play, I divide the students into groups that are each charged with researching one of the following topics: the author's biography, the causes and conflicts of the Mexican Revolution, the role of soldaderas in the revolution, and Adelita as she is produced in song and in visual images. Together, the groups report their findings to the class. Although the research is informal, there are a few important sources to which they could be directed. Paula W. Shirley's 1980 biographical entry on Niggli in *The Dictionary of Literary Biography* (1981) accurately reports the details of Niggli's life, as do the opening pages of my and Yolanda Padilla's introduction to the *The Plays of Josefina Niggli* (Niggli 2007). Elizabeth Salas's *Soldaderas in the Mexican Military: Myth and History* (1990) discusses Niggli's play specifically but also, in its introduction, frames some of the key debates about the tensions between the representation and reality of soldaderas. Moreover, Salas provides several photographic images of soldaderas that could help the students in this group make recommendations about how to costume the play's soldaderas. Indeed, when I assign the groups, I also provide them with narrowing questions that help them manage the material or connect it to an aspect of theatrical production, like costuming. For instance, the Mexican Revolution has an immense and complicated history, but students can navigate it when tasked with specific aims, such as identifying the principal causes and considering how the Mexican Revolution impacted Mexican Americans. Those researching Adelita are asked to describe, compare, and contrast how that figure has been produced in song and image. What historical factors account for the change in how Adelita is represented? How should we situate Niggli's Adelita in this range of representation?

The first class begins with a quick round of reports from the groups. As the discussion unfolds, we refer back to this foundation of knowledge. After these reports, we begin discussing the performance context and history of the play. Specifically, in a short lecture, I provide students with some of the history of Mexican American performance during and in the wake of the revolution.[2] This history emphasizes how the flood of Mexicans fleeing into the Southwest in the wake of the war's violence spurred the growth of a variety of performance and theatrical forms, including **carpas** (tent theater), **teatros de revistas**, and **zarzuelas**. These works didn't resemble fully wrought plays in the ways that students are accustomed to thinking about them, but rather consisted of a number of short skits, many performed by noteworthy, charismatic actors and singers. These skits played to regional, popular tastes and were, as one would expect, performed in Spanish.

After establishing this general history, we then consider how Niggli's work fits with this description of Mexican American performance during the period of the revolution. Students who research Niggli's biography often say that Niggli's family fled Mexico for San Antonio as the violence of war encroached upon their home in Monterrey, Nuevo Leon, Mexico. Mention of this often also provides an opportunity to examine a map of Mexico to demonstrate the proximity of Monterrey to Texas as well as to identify Saltillo, the setting of *Soldadera*. Students will sometimes mention Niggli's claim to have been "the most produced one-act dramatist" of the 1930s and 1940s, drawing connections between the one-act form and the short works that constituted Mexican American popular theater. As we begin to explore the differences between Niggli's play and the Mexican American performance tradition, one difference immediately emerges: that the play is written in English. This allows us to consider who the audience of the play was, which bridges the discussion of performance history to a consideration of this work's particular production history.

After noting that the play was written in English, students quickly surmise that, unlike the popular Mexican traditions discussed earlier, Niggli's audience was not primarily Mexican American. The students who researched Niggli's biography sometimes note that Niggli imagined her work as correcting faulty representations of Mexicans in U.S culture. Thus, the primary audience for the play is the Anglo viewer who may have mistakenly imbibed stereotyped representations of Mexicans and accepted them as truth. The text itself hints at some other dimensions of the play's real and imagined audiences. For instance, focusing on the footnotes helps us understand what kinds of information the play imagines its audiences won't know. The footnoted explanations of mescal and the maguey plant suggest the audience is unfamiliar with products that Mexicans might consume as well as with the flora that appear on the Southwestern landscape. The lack of regional knowledge about the Southwest reminds us that the play was produced in North Carolina, at a theater in Chapel Hill where Niggli was a graduate student. On the one hand, Niggli's status as a graduate student mark her, as Alicia Arrizón notes, as part of a Mexican American middle class emerging after the revolution (1999: 43). On the other, her graduate student status connects her with a number of contemporary writers like Sandra Cisneros, Angie Cruz, Junot Díaz, or Helena María Viramontes who also pursued their craft within Master of Fine Arts creative writing programs during what Mark McGurl has recently termed "the Program Era."[3]

Although we don't have many details about *Soldadera's* performance history, there are a few that could be productively used in the classroom. First is the cast list, which lists the names of the actors who originated the parts in North Carolina. Students are quick to note that, with the exception of Niggli, the cast members are all Anglo-Americans. The second readily available pieces of the play's performance are a pair of photographs that show the play being staged in North Carolina.[4] The photographs sometimes surprise students because, despite Niggli's avowed aims to counter the stereotypes about Mexicans that prevailed in the United States at the time, the set and costumes look stereotypical. The players don serapes and large sombreros against a background of cutout cacti and tan hills. These images typically incite two lines of discussion. The first considers why Niggli would represent the Mexicans in this way, which forces students to understand how dramatists sometimes had to conform to audience expectations even as they sought to challenge them. The second line of questioning asks students to think about how they would construct the stage, fashion the costumes, and cast the play now. The ensuing discussion often engages how audience attitudes and expectations have changed in the interval between 1936 and the present, how realistic representation is one way to circumvent the hold of the stereotype, and how race and ethnicity might play a role in casting decisions.

While the first class session on *Soldadera* ends by using some of the context that the students discovered on their own in order to imagine how they might stage the play in the present, the second day turns to some of the major conflicts in the play by examining characters and their motivations. We begin briefly with a discussion of the soldaderas en masse, recognizing them as figures who were radicalized by violence and who are in search of vengeance, and then turn to the more rounded characters of the Rich One, Concha, and, especially, Adelita, who is described in the play's stage directions as "the poetry of the Revolution, and the beauty" (158).

The characters are best discussed in pairs in order to highlight how they relate to each other. The discussion between the Rich One and Concha upon her return to the camp (176–81) dramatizes many of the main conflicts of the revolution, providing an opportunity to refer again to the research that students did for the first day. Since this section of the play is short, it is ideally suited to an informal, in-class staged reading. Before the play is read, though, we discuss how each role should be performed and why. The stage directions tell us that the Rich One is called that "by the women, since he represents the hated upper-class which has held them in subjection for so long" (160). Given this information, would his voice be assured and confident? Condescending? And, if the dialogue between the Rich One and Concha is meant to convey the class conflicts that motivate the revolution, how could the performance of each character foreground this conflict for the audience?

Unlike Adelita and the Rich One, whom the text refers to as "symbols," Concha initially resists such symbolization. However, Concha can be viewed as a symbol of the revolution in its realistic sense. She inhabits authority not only as the group's leader but also in her unflinching acceptance of the revolution's violence and cruelty. As students imagine how she should be portrayed, they could consider how her voice differs from that of the other women, and what other kinds of tensions emerge with the Rich One as she debates the revolution and attempts to discern what he knows. What comes into focus is how the class conflict that is readily apparent in the discussion between the Rich One and Concha is undergirded by a gender conflict, one that also recalls earlier conversations in the play about whether the soldaderas were demoted by their leader Hilario when they were asked to simply guard ammunition. With class and gender on the table as topics for discussions, students who did their preliminary research on the Mexican Revolution sometimes ask about race. This leads to a number of questions: Why would Niggli avoid discussing race in 1936? How could a performance of the play now incorporate an attention to the racial dynamics of the revolution? By asking students to think about and compare performances—real and hypothetical—we provide them with the opportunity not only to learn about history but also to understand how historical representation is affected by the moment when that representation is undertaken.

One of the key moments of contention between Concha and the Rich One concerns the appropriate singing of "La Adelita." In response to the Rich One's weak rendition, Concha declares, "Stop! You have no heart! What do you know of the song of the Revolution? It has fire! It has life!" (177), and then she proceeds to perform her own impassioned version. The contest over the song also correlates with a contest over who gets to control the revolution and its representation. The play is invested in this contest, offering its own statement in the form of the character Adelita. Here, students who reported on Adelita can remind the class that, in comparison to the musical and visual representations of this figure, Niggli's Adelita is naïve and innocent, a figure who is not an object of desire but who believes in the revolution as an ennobling activity. Seen from this vantage, her death in the play's final moments signifies the death of revolution's idealism—its "poetry," to use Niggli's term—in the face of an increasingly violent reality. The play thus evinces the disillusionment that Mexicans and Mexican Americans were beginning to feel as the revolution was reaching its end.

The discussion concludes by considering two performances at the end of the play. The first asks students to consider how Adelita delivers her final lines, "This is the Revolution! The sun will be in my face! Long live the Revolution!" (191–92). Does she deliver these lines forcefully, with the conviction of a true believer? Or, does she do so haltingly, resigned to her fate, even as she voices optimism? How do these different deliveries of Adelita's final lines impact the play's meaning and its effects on the audience? The second performance to discuss is the final performance of "La Adelita" by the soldaderas. Comparing it to the earlier instances when it was sung, students often see that Niggli has, in the course of a short one-act play, transformed the song from something that is celebratory and inspirational into a dirge, mourning the passing of an ideal.

Beyond identity/mapping power

If considering how to stage Niggli's *Soldadera* contributes to students' understanding of history and how it is represented, attending to the staging and performance of Maria Irene Fornes's *The Conduct of Life* forces students to consider how subjects—including the reader and audience—are positioned, and how the relations of power embedded in those positionings not only reveal something about Latino/a experience but also produce a more expansive vision of power's operations that connect Latino/a concerns to those of other groups. As John Rossini notes, Fornes is a "figure often elided in accounts of Latino/a theater" (2013: 279) However, beginning in 1981, Fornes led the Hispanic Playwrights Workshop at New York's International Arts Relations (INTAR), where she helped develop the work of a generation of acclaimed Latino/a playwrights, including Nilo Cruz, Migdalia Cruz, Josefina López, Cherríe Moraga, and Caridad Svich. In Latino/a literature classes, Fornes, if she is mentioned at all, is more likely to be cited as an influence than have one of her plays discussed.

In their valuable book on Latina drama, *Stages of Life* (2001), Alberto Sanchez-Sandoval and Nancy Saporta Sternbach see this generation that Fornes fostered as pursuing a "politics of identity," defined as "the process by which a speaking subject constitutes herself in given social relations of power and discursive formations, while at the same time positioning herself in the dialectical 'give and take' of a subjectivity-in-process" (5). Their focus on identity may be strange because Fornes herself resisted identity politics in her work. The phrase "subjectivity-in-process" recalls Norma Alarcón's "identity-in-difference," a concept inclusive of both the processual nature of identity and the fact that it remains marginal to the norms around which full citizenship is articulated. José Esteban Muñoz builds on Alarcón's concept, arguing that "[w]hat unites and consolidates oppositional groups is not simply the fact of identity but the way they perform affect, especially in relation to an official 'national affect' that is aligned with the hegemonic class" (2010: 205). Moreover, Muñoz offers Fornes as an example of a playwright who "eschews identity labels such as *Latina*" while still "represent[ing] a Latina/o affective reality" (210). This is consequential because, by moving away from conventional understandings of identity, we are able to catch a glimpse of the various ways that Latinas and Latinos inhabit and make their worlds, and those affective realities open up spaces for connecting to similarly oriented minoritarian subjects. With a play like Fornes's *The Conduct of Life*, one wants to find connections—aesthetic, political, social—with other types of Latino/a cultural production while also remaining alert for the new conceptual terrain that it offers us.

The Conduct of Life was the first play that Fornes wrote after she began presiding over the Hispanic Playwrights Lab (López 2003: 78), and is therefore one of her works that is most overtly in dialogue with the Latino experience, even though, aside from being set in an unnamed Latin American country, there are no other discernible Latino markers. Like Niggli's *Soldadera*, *The Conduct of Life* is a short play, comprising 19 brief scenes, which can be assigned for one class section but is best discussed over at least two, in part because of its difficult subject matter and in part because of its complicated aesthetics.[5] The play centers on four characters: Orlando, a lieutenant who quickly rises to lieutenant commander as a result of his efficiency as a torturer and interrogator; Nena, a 12-year-old orphan that Orlando brutalizes and rapes in his home; Leticia, Orlando's wife whose growing awareness of her husband's activities presages the play's final standoff; and Olimpia, Leticia's servant who tries to comfort Nena.

As this brief sketch of the play suggests, *The Conduct of Life*, although written in the 1980s, connects easily with late twentieth and early twenty-first century works like Junot Díaz's *The Brief Wondrous Life of Oscar Wao* (2007) and Hector Tobar's *The Tattooed Soldier* (1998) that confront the legacies of dictatorship and state violence on Latino subjects, especially their gendered aspects. However, I also have students consider how by removing it from a specific national context, Fornes distills how power circulates in such scenes of political violence, providing an account that is more inter-subjective than psychological. As Diane Lynn Moroff notes, in Fornes's drama, "action is about interaction" (1997: 114).

In order get to track how power circulates in the play, I ask students to focus on theatrical space in two ways: the space of the stage, which Fornes describes at great length in the opening stage directions, and how each scene is its own play with actors and spectators embedded within it. Students are divided into groups and asked to draw maps of the stage from the stage directions. This invariably leads to some disputes and a few discoveries. For instance, students will often remark that the dimensions of the stage seem unusually deep, which indeed they were when the play was originally staged (Cummings 2012: 113). Before thinking about the alterations one might need to make for various venues, we think about the ways in which the various rooms—living room, dining room, basement, warehouse, hallway—relate to each other. What kinds of activities are associated with these rooms? What are their relationships to publicness or privacy, the national or the domestic? Given the set's unique structure, what can the audience see, particularly when looking at action that is taking place upstage in the basement or the warehouse? This line of questioning is building to W. B. Worthen's argument that the stage "provides a visual emblem of the hierarchy of power in the play" (1999: 75). What he calls the "spaces of sociability" are downstage: they are what the audience must look through in order to see the play's first acts of violence and they are gradually infiltrated by that violence (75). State violence becomes domestic violence.

The remainder of the first session is spent closely reading several of the play's opening scenes in order to model a short writing assignment that students will submit on the second day that we discuss the play. The writing exercise asks them, in a typed single-spaced page, to analyze the relations of power in one of the scenes from the play that we will discuss on the second day. As we look through the first four scenes from the play, I highlight several ideas that are contained in the prompt. As we spent the first half or more of the class session discussing the physical space of the stage, the first thing that they are prompted to think about is who is the actor and who is the audience in any given scene. Often, Fornes works scenes in such a way that there is a speaker who delivers information to a listener. For instance, in the second scene, Alejo, a lieutenant commander, sits between Orlando and Leticia, listening to their argument. If he is a spectator, he is not entirely passive: he questions Leticia's desire for an education, and both of the scene's principal speakers direct their language toward him, as though he were a judge. When he rejects Leticia's plan to educate herself, does Alejo fulfill his spectator role? When we see something, when we witness a testimony, do we have an obligation to act in a particular way? In this environment, it becomes unclear where power resides. Is it with Leticia, who speaks the most words, opening and closing the scene? Or is it with her husband and his comrade who undo her claims with their quick dismissals? The concerns with language and literacy that Leticia raises connect the second scene with the third, which is mostly devoid of language, as Orlando assaults Nena for the first time. Although power clearly tilts toward Orlando in this early scene, we have to consider the force of gesture, and the audience's relationship to the power that it sees. Do we dismiss Nena's pain, as Alejo casually sweeps away Leticia's concerns? Or do we take a stand, showing that power also flows toward us? If these attempts at close reading go as planned, students are equipped to consider looking at relations between characters, the ethics of witness, and the force of language and gesture as they analyze the relations of power in their chosen scene for the second class.

The aim of the assignment is to help students grasp the theatricality of these scenes, and, in the process, de-dramatize some of the more emotional content by emphasizing its artifice. In the second class, we discuss what students discovered as they looked closely at scenes. The students typically develop a more sophisticated sense of power as something that permeates a social body and moves in unexpected ways. This conception of power can be carried forward into discussions of more overtly Latino texts, such as the ones mentioned above. The discussion ends with a consideration of why Leticia is finally moved toward violence at the end of the play, and why, sharing a similar kind of oppression rooted in the nation, the military, and patriarchy, the women fail to achieve the kind of solidarity that the audience yearns for. To use Muñoz's language, is there a feeling that binds these women together? And if not, what are the blockages to those kinds of connections?

These two plays by Niggli and Fornes demonstrate that theater can be a powerful vehicle for students to understand complicated concepts in literary study. One of the reasons why it is useful for students to build knowledge about historical processes or power relations is that it enlists the creative energies of the student as well as his or her intellectual skills. By inviting students not only to analyze the works but also to imagine the possibilities of the worlds that are being staged, we allow students to create their knowledge as they perform it.

Notes

1 In the seventh edition of the *Heath Anthology of American Literature* (2012), Yolanda Padilla has nicely excerpted these works and placed them alongside other textual material in order to provide a manageable account of the effect of the Mexican Revolution on American literary history.

2 This history is recounted neatly in Alicia Arrizón's excellent chapter on Niggli and La Chata Noelesca in *Latina Performance* (1999), Nicolás Kanellos's *A History of Hispanic Theatre in the United States: Origins to 1940* (1990), and Tomás Ybarra-Frausto's "I can still hear the applause: La Farándula Chicana: Carpas y Tandas de Variedad" (1984). The Ybarra-Frausto and Arrizón texts contain images that could be used to help students visualize what this material looked like on the stage.

3 Interestingly, several of the figures in the University of North Carolina's MFA program in playwriting helped establish the University of Iowa Writer's Workshop, which, for McGurl, is the key institution of the Program Era.

4 These photos are available in the 1938 edition of Niggli's *Mexican Folk Plays*, which is still held in many university libraries. Some of the images are also reprinted online and in some of the scholarly monographs listed above.

5 The pedagogy section of Tiffany Ana Lopez's excellent chapter on Fornes in *Reading U.S. Latina Writers* (2003) offers some tips for grappling with the play's graphic sexual violence, among which are knowing the support services at your institution for helping students and providing

students with a deep contextualization of the various debates about fascism, feminism, and political violence with which the play responds (82–85). Despite the text's difficulty in this regard, Lopez sees it as indispensable to her classes on Latina drama, often beginning the course with this challenging work. Lopez's article is a useful, comprehensive essay on teaching the play in a Latina drama course.

Resources for teaching Latino/a theatre

Arrizón, Alicia. *Latina Performance: Traversing the Stage.* Bloomington: Indiana University Press, 1999.

Broyles-González, Yolanda. *El Teatro Campesino: Theater in the Chicano Movement.* Austin: University of Texas Press, 1994.

Danielson, Marivel T. *Homecoming Queers: Desire and Difference in Chicana Latina Cultural Production.* New Brunswick, NJ: Rutgers University Press, 2009.

Huerta, Jorge. *Chicano Drama: Performance, Society, and Myth.* New York: Cambridge University Press, 2000.

Kanellos, Nicolás., ed. *Hispanic Theatre in the United States.* Houston: Arte Público, 1984.

——. *A History of Hispanic Theatre in the United States: Origins to 1940.* Austin: University of Texas Press, 1990.

López, Tiffany Ana. "Maria Irene Fornes, *The Conduct of Life.*" *Reading U.S. Latina Writers: Remapping American Literature.* Ed. Alvina Quintana. New York: Palgrave Macmillan, 2003, pp. 77–89.

Muñoz, José Esteban. "Feeling Brown: Ricardo Bracho's *The Sweetest Hangover and Other STDs.*" *Gay Latino Studies.* Ed. Michael Hames-Garcia and Ernesto Martinez. Durham: Duke University Press, 2010, pp. 204–19.

Ramírez, Elizabeth C. *Chicanas / Latinas in American Theatre: A History of Performance.* Bloomington: Indiana University Press, 2000.

Rossini, Jon. "Teatro." *The Routledge Companion to Latino/a Literature.* Ed. Suzanne Bost and Frances Aparicio. New York: Routledge, 2013, pp. 285–98.

Sandoval-Sánchez, Alberto, and Nancy Saporta Sternbach. *Stages of Life: Transcultural Performances in U.S. Latina Theater.* Tucson: University of Arizona Press, 2001.

Yarbro-Bejarano, Yvonne. *The Wounded Heart: Writing on Cherríe Moraga.* Austin: University of Texas Press, 2001.

14 Teaching U.S. Latino/a performance

Marivel T. Danielson

In this chapter I will offer a discussion of a variety of different approaches to integrating Chicano/a and U.S. Latino/a performance texts and tradition into a college or university classroom at the undergraduate level. Each of these texts and approaches might be easily altered to accommodate a more advanced graduate level course, as well. I conclude this chapter with a description and analysis of one student project that emerged from one of my courses which I believe illustrates some of the exciting potential that performance studies offers to both students and instructors engaged in critical and creative thinking around issues of race, class, ethnicity, gender, sexuality.

The coming together of teaching and U.S. Latino/a performance in this chapter seems especially appropriate given the nature of most higher education settings: an educator, an audience of eager learners, and the classroom where, for a quarter, semester, or an academic year, the intellectual journey is staged. Like performance art, these educational encounters are ephemeral, spontaneous in many regards. Though an instructor may start each day with a detailed lesson plan, she can never know exactly what her students will bring to the stage on any given day, nor what circumstances in or outside the classroom doors will shape these students' views of the world, each other, and the texts or activities laid before them. In her work defining what she calls "engaged pedagogy," bell hooks elucidates this unique parallel between educator and performer:

> Teaching is a performative act. And it is that aspect of our work that offers the space for change, invention, spontaneous shifts, that can serve as a catalyst drawing out the unique elements in each classroom. To embrace the performative aspect of teaching we are compelled to engage "audiences," to consider issues of reciprocity. Teachers are not performers in the traditional sense of the word in that our work is not meant to be a spectacle. Yet it is meant to serve as a catalyst that calls everyone to become more and more engaged, to become active participants in learning.
>
> (1994: 11)

While hooks' call for a more participatory learning environment might certainly be beneficial for a wide range of topics, it seems particularly useful to think about performative pedagogies when the subject is, in fact, performance. How might educators harness the unique elements of performance as practice in order to provide students with innovative ways to engage with and build upon the extensive body of U.S. Latino/a performative texts? It is with hooks' critical gesture towards the performative within an invocation of engaged pedagogy that I begin this discussion of teaching U.S. Latino/a performance.

Defining the terms

When introducing U.S. Latino/a performance texts into the classroom for the first time, I generally begin with an interrogation of the key concepts that shape the course: What and who do we mean by U.S. Latino/a? What do we mean by performance? What does identity have to do with art? While these queries are far too broad to address comprehensively here in this brief chapter, one can find quite compelling and useful work within the field of Latino/a and theater/performance studies that serves to define and contextualize the intended scope of study for students at all levels of study.

Latin/o American performance scholar Diana Taylor posits that, "[Performance] signals various specific art forms common both to Latinos and Latin Americans (from performance art to public performance) [and also] encompasses socialized and internalized roles (including those associated with gender, sexuality, and race) that cannot really be analyzed as 'theatrical discourses'" (1994: 14). From scholar to artist, Cuban American performer Carmelita Tropicana declares that: "Performance art changes the way you look at the world. Your perceptions are changed; an object is no longer what it seems" (177). At the intersection of these two models we find an art form with the potential to interrogate the middle spaces between these identity categories and perhaps even create new modes of being and expression. In most of my course offerings I focus thematic readings and activities on issues of identity formation and expression. I find these issues generate discussion that introductory level students can relate to as well as acquire broader perspectives through class engagement.

The genre of performance also begs the question of temporality. While an instructor can encourage or even require students to see live performances[1] in their local community—this is something I require in my performance-focused courses—the bulk of engagement for students and instructor will take place in the classroom setting and most likely will not include live spectacles, but rather video recordings and written performance scripts. Alicia Arrizón reminds us of Peggy Phelan's observation that "performance's only life is in the present," yet Arrizón adds that "it is a very particular present, which can be transformed and modified once its spatiality has been recorded either as a visual or written text. It is a significant present with a memorable past in which future stagings or readings become the grand possibility of documentation" (1999: 356). Therefore one of the issues with which to contend is how to confront the absolute ephemerality of performance art. This becomes even more of an issue for marginalized artists, Chicano/a, Latino/a, and/or queer performers who don't routinely tour their work, and may not have access to the resources necessary to document and archive their work. Given these limitations, we as scholars and students must "make do" with the traces we have of that "memorable past." Students must learn to read between the lines, to address and envision stage directions and playwrights' notes, to research and document the economic, political, and physical circumstances surrounding a given production.

Initial engagements

In introductory level courses broadly focused on cultural expression, popular forms of performative expression, like music, provide the easiest access for novice students of both performance studies and Chicano/a and Latino/a Studies. For example, an instructor might introduce Selena Quintanilla Pérez's musical and popular culture legacy alongside a chapter or two from Deborah Parédez's *Selenidad: Selena, Latinos, and the Performance of Memory* (2009) and even Lourdes Portillo's documentary films *Corpus: A Home Movie for Selena* (1998) or *A Conversation about Selena with Academics* (1999). These texts offer an accessible view of mainstream performance and reception for a Chicana artist and present interesting connections to contemporary U.S. Latino/a artists like Jennifer Lopez, Shakira, Selena Gomez, or Ariana Grande. Scholarly work on musical performance and U.S. Latino/a representation in a broader body of popular music can be found in the recent work of María Elena Cepeda (*Musical ImagiNation*, 2010), Angharad Valdivia (*Latino/as and the Media*, 2010), Mary Beltrán (*Latino/a Stars in U.S. Eyes*, 2009), or Deborah Pacini Hernandez (*Oye como va!*, 2010).

Integrating discussion on the music genre of reggaetón at the university level can also be productive as it enables complex conversations about gender representation, sexuality, and patriarchy. Critical discussions of popular musical expression can include analysis of the ethnic and gendered stereotypes embodied in artists' performances. For even lower division courses a basic critical framework for stereotype as seen in the work of postcolonial theorist Homi Bhabha (*The Location of Culture*, 1994) and film scholar Charles Ramírez Berg (*Latino Images in Film Stereotypes, Subversion, Resistance*, 2002) can be useful to mapping the functionality of these representations.

Because of its heavy reliance on and early roots in collective work and improvisational technique, I integrate the work of Luis Valdez and Teatro Campesino as representative of the performative genre (via an extensive collection of videos along with artist information, interviews, and lectures that is accessible online through New York University's Hemispheric Institute Digital Video Library)[2] into my introductory level courses on transborder Chicano/a and Latino/a culture. The 2001 recording of *La carpa de los Rasquachis* engages the experiences and history of **transborder culture** in myriad ways. We see the journey of Jesus Pelado Rasquachi, played by Rubén C. González struggle with the decision to leave his mother and sister to journey to the United States in search of more opportunity for himself and his family. From discussions of the intricate choreography employed to represent agricultural workers to the ingenious use of performers' bodies and minimal props to construct complicated living portraits of the border spaces between the United States and Mexico, heaven and hell, life and death, the visual spectacle and deep political and cultural significance of Teatro Campesino's work transcends language and time. Living and studying so near the U.S.–Mexico border, these issues come alive to students who have themselves crossed these borders, or live with and love individuals who have.

Thus, geographical and political context can inform an instructor's selection of primary performative texts in powerful ways. In Texas, an instructor might utilize the work of Chicana solo performer Laura Esparza, whose work "I DisMember the Alamo" stages the human struggle to negotiate conflicting Texas histories, one mainstream version from textbooks and Hollywood films and the multiple generations and layers of memory emerging from her Chicana and Tejana family. Similarly, the Loisaida narrative—a Latino/a reinscription of New York's Lower East Side—found in the representations of Alina Troyano's performance alter ego Carmelita Tropicana.

Bodies in motion

Paramount to any discussion of the art of performance is the body. As a creative tool, corporeality becomes even more powerful when harnessed by historically marginalized subjects—racial, ethnic, gender fluid, and queer subjects. The diverse legacy and continually growing body of Chicano/a and U.S. Latino/a performance represents one such area where questions of power and privilege take center stage and provide audiences—researchers, students, educators, and activists among others—with the material to generate important conversations and invaluable teaching moments that extend far past the theater or the classroom.

College, university, and even high school students are generally quite versed in engaging with the written word. Narrative on the page becomes a familiar part of most students' training from their first lessons with the alphabet. Analyzing visual texts and cues can be foreign to learners who have spent years reading, memorizing, and annotating books and essays. (See also William Orchard's discussion in his chapter in this volume of the seeming primacy of the novel over theatre.) This visual element is something that educators can address from the very first moments of the class. What can we learn about each other based on the way we sit—our posture, placement of limbs or feet—or the way we move from one side of the room to the other—our gait, spinal alignment, or gaze? How can we translate this knowledge of the body and its movement through space to our interpretation of the performing body moving on stage? This visual analysis can be applied in effective ways to public performances or demonstrations where individuals use their bodies to confront power inequalities and reclaim space. In performance texts, one might screen John Leguizamo's 1992 solo performance of *Mambo Mouth*, and focus a subsequent discussion on mapping out how the performer uses movement to build multidimensional characters on stage. From numerous Latina characters played in drag to a young Latino man trying to pass as Asian to shed the stigmatized role of ignorant Latino thug, Leguizamo's physicality enables rich discussions of corporeality—the significance of the body in motion on stage to portray subjects engaged in a wide range of geopolitical, linguistic, gender, and ethnic border crossings. When Leguizamo holds a set of metal bars the size of a small window in front of his face, how does his movement with and against this prop help construct the reality of a locked immigration detention center? How does his body perform the devastation and survival instincts of an undocumented immigrant in police custody? This type of close visual analysis enables students to grasp the power of performance to tell complex stories with the simplest of resources.

In addition to reading the visual on a stage or screen, I find it quite compelling to integrate improvisational movement exercises into beginning level discussion of performative texts—particularly when they exist solely in written form. Frequently I will invite students to select pivotal scenes from a particular performance script to collectively re-enact in the classroom, focusing on the visual representation of power dynamics, emotional arcs, and diverse characterization. These activities strengthen the students' directorial instincts and help them to envision the performance released from a static page in a book.

Transborder queer performativity

In Spring 2008 I conceptualized a course on U.S. Latino/a performance that I was able to offer to upper division undergraduate students at Arizona State University. Though the total enrollment was just four students during that first semester, I was able to refine the course focus, evaluate components, and define objectives in a way that served to strengthen the course moving forward. Because of this course's overlap with the topic of this chapter, I will share some observations and insight from my experience teaching Transborder Queer Performativity over the last six years.

In this course I define the concept of the performative broadly as both theatrical or staged work as well as daily, lived movement through this geographical and political space, and the narratives that retell this experience. In this way, "performativity" became a more useful and relevant term than the more limiting genre specific "performance art." The more abstract concept also came with a dizzying array of theoretical lenses with which to examine identity, from Judith Butler's gender performativity to Karen Christian's ethnic and cultural identity as drag. I believed the flexibility of the term would stimulate student interest and multiple perspectives.

Given my academic home in ASU's School of Transborder Studies, I also chose to engage with the notion of borders and crossing as they offer fascinating lenses from which to discuss gender fluidity, sexuality, and desire in addition to race, ethnicity, and migration. Employing Gloria Anzaldúa's tropes of los atravesados and la mestiza, and her poetic theorization of aliens, alienation, monstrosity and crossing over, we begin the course by mapping the processes through which subjects/performers stage the perceived excessive monstrosity of difference in the representation and reception of transborder cultural identities.

In her foundational work *Borderlands: La frontera* Anzaldúa posits a borderlands space and its inhabitants:

> A borderland is a vague and undetermined place created by the emotional residue of an unnatural boundary. Los atravesados live here: the squint-eyed, the perverse, the queer, the troublesome, the mongrel, the mulatto, the half-breed, the half dead; in short, those who cross over, pass over, or go through the confines of the "normal."
>
> (2012: 25)

Anzaldúa's conceptualizations of Borderlands and los atravesados (the crossers) yield a valuable critical framework for thinking about the performance of marginalized difference as a collective form of resistance. Anzaldúa throws historically pejorative, racist, and homophobic terms into a space where these beings ultimately shift from exile to autonomy—claiming and defining this borderlands space as their own. Because Anzaldúa engages the literal and metaphorical borderlands as both a specific and abstract concept, it is fairly simple for students to follow her transition from crossing between nations to languages, to genders, and back again.

I list the following learning objectives in my syllabus for Transborder Queer Performativity at Arizona State University:

> By the completion of this course successfully you should be able to.

- Identify key performers, works and themes in transborder Latin@ and/or queer solo and collaborative performance,
- Understand issues key to performance production, reception, and analysis.
- Interpret and analyze written performance scripts, video, and live performance.
- Explore basic elements of improvisational technique.
- Create a brief original performance script and either perform from memory and/or serve as director for a classmate's performance piece.

My bottom line as a professor: to truly engage performative texts in any kind of depth, students must also write and perform. For all the borders we discuss in this Transborder Studies course, the line from audience member to performer is perhaps the most significant for the students to cross. In addition to reading texts, viewing performances—both live and recorded—and writing critically about all of this, you must be willing to stand in front of the class and share your stories. I reassure students on the first day of class, you don't have to tell the truth—though the truth helps write itself. Make something up! But be ready every single week to walk to the front of the room, turn to face your classmates, and share something of yourself. This is a powerful and hugely vulnerable act for most students, but as bell hooks reminds us, "To hear each other (the sound of different voices), to listen to one another, is an exercise in recognition" (1994: 41). These moments are the first for many students to hold their own creative voices up for scrutiny. Largely they are not theater majors. In fact, they are majors in things like Women's Studies, elementary education, sociology, or political science. The stage does not call them. But something happens when a group of non-performers is made to repeatedly perform for each other. They take the leap each week together. They share far more personal, tragic, poignant, and intimate stories than I ever expect, and they take these leaps, carve their histories into notebook sheets, stand before strangers becoming family, not for a grade—for my eva-luation of these weekly assignments is more of a "done/not done" assessment. They perform because, as hooks would say, they are engaged, committed to the task of sharing, to the brilliance of being "recognized" and to the cultivation of a learning environment where cultural expression and individual identity produce critical collective knowledge.

In addition to weekly short writing/performance exercises, each undergraduate student enrolled in my Transborder Queer Performativity course writes an original 3–5 minute performance script and performs and/or directs a piece for a public showcase staged in a campus theater space. I have produced a showcase each year since 2008 when I first cre-ated and offered the course. In addition to producing and promoting the event, I arrange for students to work in a black box theater space for several weeks, give them opportunities to engage with sound, visual, and lighting design, as well as movement, timing, and expression—all concepts integral to performance studies and production. One student from the Spring 2010 class stated that the performative aspects of the class were "powerful tools in gaining perspective on others and learning about the different aspects of the per-formance process." Another student in the class remarked that "the performative aspect made it super engaging and directly applied all of the scholarly material we covered," while another noted that the class "taught me to open up, public speak, use my body. Both prac-tical and artistic." I integrate multiple creative components to my performance studies courses in order to provide students with opportunities to engage the genre from the plat-forms of both scholarship and practice. In an ideal classroom experience, the students will find their way to a comfort somewhere in between these two approaches—creating critically informed performance pieces or scholarship with a more comprehensive understanding of the multiple layers that factor into the performance(s) they analyze.

My experience creating a hybrid course with scholarly and creative components has been transformative, particularly because my students challenge the limits of the course in powerful and illuminating ways. In the closing section of this chapter I'll offer a recounting of a particularly significant student project that emerged from this Transborder Queer Performativity course.

Restaging the cage

The performance, "Aliens in the Cage" (2008), was conceptualized by Silvia Rodríguez Vega in a Chicano/a Latino/a Performance course I taught at Arizona State in Spring

2008. Facing the reality that she may not have the funds to complete her undergraduate education, Rodríguez Vega calmly revealed her then undocumented status to me, her professor, as well as the handful of other students in the class. Collectively we all spoke about ways to utilize performance as resistance to the alienation she felt on and off campus because of the ongoing anti-immigrant narratives so prevalent in Arizona at that time. After an in-class screening of a film documenting a particular performance, Rodríguez Vega became inspired to adapt the artists' framework for her own self-expression.

The film, *The Couple in the Cage: A Guatinaui Odyssey*, emerged in 1992 as a response to the Quincentennial anniversary of Columbus's discovery of the Americas. Coco Fusco and Guillermo Gómez-Peña conceptualized a traveling installation in which the two performers play the roles of the last undiscovered Amerindian man and woman. Anglo curators encouraged audience members to interact with the performers within the scene for a small payment. Fusco and Gómez-Peña staged their characters within what seemed to be extreme realms of excess—from their Fusco's coconut bra and converse sneakers to Gómez-Peña's hybrid Spanish/English/Guatinaui tongue and Mexican **Lucha Libre** mask, however they were surprised to find that many audiences members failed to "get the joke"—responding with seemingly genuine curiosity about the couple, their history, and their customs.

While not what the performers had originally anticipated, the audience responses laid fertile ground for the artists' critique of Eurocentric alienation and objectification of indigenous peoples from colonial to contemporary times. Certainly as a performative strategy, the piece—known to students largely through the documentary film—continues to resonate with young scholars who seek alternate modes of intervention into dominant discourses of marginalization, silencing, and erasure of queer brown and female bodies and experiences.

The students in my class initiated their performance at lunchtime, staging a procession through a part of campus frequented by students eating, studying, and socializing in a large bank of outdoor seating. The collective, consisting of ASU students and community members Silvia Rodríguez Vega, Dulce Juárez, Renato Ramos, and Shianna Hines among others, marched up the library steps to a popular plaza where they circled a large fountain and ended by depositing the two prisoners in a wire mesh cage adjacent to the Student Union.

Two women perform as prisoners, wearing black clothing, white paint smeared across their exposed brown skin, thick black barcodes and serial numbers inscribed upon their chest and back. The initial spectacle of their bodies is punctuated by a drummer who leads the group, and claims a sense of aural ownership of the vast and noisy public space. Though the two prisoners are silent, they plead with directed gaze to any observer to intervene. This directorial choice, to cast these roles as silenced but not submissive, allows the prisoners to perverse a semblance of agency—their humanity as they actively seek out allies among the crowd of onlookers.

But like Fusco and Gómez-Peña's *Couple*, "Aliens" did not elicit any engagement beyond the paid polaroid photos, recitations, and feedings. No one attempted to open the cage or challenge the women's confinement. Certainly, an easy interpretation here would be that students accepted the spectacle as such, and felt no need to respond. But even so, one might wonder why the mere presence of shackled women led around campus on leashes, accompanied by a beating drum and a circus ringmaster/barker figure would not elicit more play from the many young people walking blankly past the cage.

For more than an hour in the intense Arizona midday sun, Rodríguez Vega and her comadre paraded around the mall in front of the Student Union or sat silently within the confines of the cage. They were extricated for brief periods to entertain the gathering crowd, a poem, a polaroid, a quick protest and back to the cage. For the latter half of the performance a police squad car pulled up to within 50 feet of the cage. The theatricality of the piece, including a ringmaster/auctioneer in full circus garb, served several functions. First, the sideshow atmosphere created a sense of spectacle—it was loud, colorful, exciting—and satire—the exaggerated portrayal suggested a clear critique of existing legislation and public practices. The heightened drama also provided a buffer of sorts, suggesting that this was a fictional account; that these were characters to play with. The truth of Rodríguez Vega's status was still tucked within the layers of her artistry and dramatic persona.

Rodríguez Vega was enrolled in a theater class the same semester she created this performance for my course. That professor attended the performance and interacted with the performers—something I could not bring myself to do, squatting for a polaroid, writing on their flesh with wide tipped markers. Though I wanted to support them, I could not stop seeing the women as brutalized, and though the experience was empowering for them—the students wrote the script, designed the set and props, and directed the entire piece, I could not cross even an imaginary border long enough to "play" the other side. I see Rodríguez Vega's work as a powerful deployment of Anzaldúa's Mestiza consciousness—reconstructing a border and potentially liberatory space on the very campus where she felt persecuted and demonized, the dangers of crossing remained for some of us who were spectators rather than players in the scene. This, too, was a significant finding within the performance. Though some of us remained silent, Rodríguez Vega, under the layers of paint, shackles, and chain link, found a way to speak, to talk back.

So to conclude, I return to Anzaldúa's mapping of Mestiza consciousness and the "new meanings" given to binary conceptualizations. Utilizing a framework of performance and performativity alongside the fluidity of Mestiza movement and perspective, I find exciting opportunities to map out borders and crossings in everyday interpersonal exchanges as well as more formalized theatrical productions. When does a performance of difference begin? Who casts the roles, and who directs the action, where does the stage begin and end? Might the notion of performance allow for a ludic space of consciousness shifting, where play with borders and crossing, venturing beyond safe limits and speaking unrehearsed roles open paths to increasing intersectionality and self-reflection for students and educators alike? Could we invoke performance in the name of Gloria Anzaldúa and find new ways to talk back, move forward, and cross over—to enact and embody a **critical** *travesía*—to these new meanings and ways of seeing the world?

Notes

1 These types of activities offer multiple benefits, as the students increase their understanding of live performance, and local performance artists and venues gain new audience members and support. Performance isn't something to be studied in books, it's happening in powerful ways within the students' very communities.
2 The video archive along with artist information can be found at: http://hemisphericinstitute. org/hemi/en/hidvl

Resources for teaching U.S. Latino/a performance

Alfaro, Luis. *Downtown*. Lawndale, CA: New Alliance Records, 1993.
——. *Straight as a Line*. Beverly Hills, CA: Audrey Skirball-Kenis Theatre, 1994.

Anthony, Adelina, and Cherríe Moraga. *Las Hociconas: Three Locas with Big Mouths and Even Bigger Brains.* San Francisco: Kórima Press, 2013.

Anthony, Adelina, Dino Foxx, and Lorenzo Herrera y Lozano. *Tragic Bitches: An Experiment in Queer Xicana & Xicano Performance Poetry.* San Francisco: Kórima Press, 2011.

Anthony, Adelina, Marisa Becerra, Linda Yvette Chávez, and D'Lo. *La Hocicona Series: An Original X-X-Xicana Comedic Triptych.* [Burbank, CA]: Comediva, 2011.

Anzoategui, Karen. "From *SER: L.A. Vs. B.A.*" *Chicana/Latina Studies* 13.1 (2013): 174–91.

Biggs, Denis, John Leguizamo, Spike Lee, and Malik Sayeed. *John Leguizamo Freak.* [S.l.]: HBO, 2010.

Esparza, Laura. "I DisMember the Alamo: A Long Poem for Performance." *Latinas on Stage.* Ed. Arrizón, Alicia and Lillian Manzor. Berkeley, CA: Third Woman Press, 2000, pp. 70–89.

Gomez, Marga. "From *Marga Gomez Is Pretty, Witty & Gay.*" *Out, Loud, & Laughing: A Collection of Gay & Lesbian Humor.* Ed. Charles Flowers. New York: Anchor Books, 1995.

——. "Excerpts from *Memory Tricks, Marga Gómez Is Pretty, Witty & Gay* and *A Line Around the Block.*" In Perkins, Kathy A., and Roberta Uno. *Contemporary Plays by Women of Color: An Anthology.* London: Routledge, 1996, pp. 194–98.

——. *Hung Like a Fly.* Westlake Village, CA: Uproar Entertainment, 1997.

——. *jaywalker* (excerpts). *Extreme Exposure.* Ed. Jo Bonney. London: Nick Hern, 2000, pp. 367–70.

Gómez-Peña, Guillermo, and Isaac Artenstein. *Border brujo.* New York: Third World Newsreel, 1991.

Gómez-Peña, Guillermo, Adrienne Jenik, Phillip Djwa, Roberto Sifuentes, and Rubén Martínez. *El Naftazteca: Cyber-Aztec TV for 2000 A.D.* Chicago: Video Data Bank, 1995.

Gómez-Peña, Guillermo, and Elaine Peña. *Ethno-techno: Writings on Performance, Activism, and Pedagogy.* New York: Routledge, 2005.

Grise, Virginia, and Irma Mayorga. *The Panza Monologues.* Austin: University of Texas Press, 2014.

Leguizamo, John. *Mambo Mouth: A Savage Comedy.* New York: Bantam Books, 1993.

——. *Spic-o-rama: A Dysfunctional Comedy.* New York: Bantam Books, 1994.

——. *The Works of John Leguizamo.* New York: Harper, 2008.

Leguizamo, John, Thomas Schlamme, Jeff Ross, and Martin Bregman. *Mambo Mouth.* [S.l.]: Island Visual Arts, 1992.

Palacios, Monica. "Describe Your Work." *Puro Teatro: A Latina Anthology.* Ed. Alberto Sandoval-Sánchez and Nancy Saporta Sternbach. Tucson, AZ: University of Arizona Press, 2000a.

——. "Greetings from a Queer Señorita." *Out of the Fringe: Contemporary Latina/Latino Theatre and Performance.* Ed. Svich and María Teresa Marrero. New York: Theatre Communications Group, 2000b, pp. 369–90.

——. "Latin Lezbo Comic: A Performance about Happiness, Challenges and Tacos." *Latinas on Stage.* Ed. Alicia Arrizón and Lillian Manzor. Berkeley, CA: Third Woman Press, 2000c. (Out of print)

Parédez, Deborah. *Selenidad: Selena, Latinos, and the Performance of Memory.* Durham, NC: Duke University Press, 2009.

Sandoval-Sánchez, Alberto, and Nancy Saporta Sternbach. *Puro Teatro: A Latina Anthology.* Tucson, AZ: University of Arizona Press, 2000.

Troyano, Alina, Ela Troyano, Uzi Parnes, and Chon A. Noriega. *I, Carmelita Tropicana: Performing between Cultures.* Boston: Beacon Press, 2000.

15 Performance pedagogy in the Latino literature classroom

Guillermo Gómez-Peña's La Pocha Nostra

Paloma Martínez-Cruz

La Pocha Nostra (LPN) was founded in 1993 by Guillermo Gómez-Peña, Roberto Sifuentes, and Nola Mariano in Los Angeles, California as a way to provide a formal framework for Gómez-Peña's collaborations and experiments with other artists. In 2001, the company became a non-profit organization. Artists Violeta Luna, Michéle Ceballos, James Luna, Erica Mott, Dani d'Emilia, and Saul Garcia Lopez figure among the core members who joined the founders in the years since the company's inception, with a slate of over 30 associates collaborating in performances throughout the world. Projects range from solo or duet performances to large-scale multi-media productions that often solicit the participation of audience members. A MacArthur fellow, prolific writer, and indefatigable artist and activist, Gómez-Peña has collaborated on, or been the single author of over ten books. Pocha Nostra videos, image archives, publications, DVDs, booking information, and dialogues with collaborators on art practices and performance pedagogy (including performances mentioned below) are located on the expansive Pocha Nostra website: www.pochanostra.com. For a minimal selection of background readings that provide a roadmap of my engagement with La Pocha Nostra's contributions, Diana Taylor, Paulo Freire, and Elizabeth Bell's publications are listed in the "Resources" section at the end of this chapter.

While there are many ways to engage with La Pocha Nostra's performances and texts, I submit that the company's most valuable contribution that transfers to our own performances as Latino studies educators are the various strategies they offer to help erode the hierarchical divisions between artist/spectator and teacher/student. Aligned with the mission of Paulo Freire's pedagogy of the oppressed, La Pocha Nostra's performance techniques foster emancipatory learning opportunities that promote new relationships between teacher, student, and society. The sections of the present pedagogical reflection discuss how I teach Gómez-Peña's *Dangerous Border Crossers* (2000) and how I have employed performance exercises developed by La Pocha Nostra in my classes in order to engage student-centered knowledge flows so that they become more accountable and empowered actors in the planetary condition.

Although the term "performance" is heavily contested, performance scholars are mainly concerned with interpreting social and cultural *live actions* (Bell 2008: 17–18). Definitions of performance will emphasize the process of transmission, rather than the production, of a circulatable object. The transactional, communicative, "doing a thing" process is the baseline for what can be defined as performance. As a hemispheric undertaking, performance inquiry takes on a **decolonial** valence. In *The Archive and the Repertoire: Performing Cultural Memory in the Americas* (2003), Diana Taylor challenges the Western consolidation of power through the privileging of textual knowledge:

My particular investment in performance studies derives less from what it *is* than what it allows us to *do*. By taking performance seriously as a system of learning, storing, and transmitting knowledge, performance studies allows us to expand what we understand by "knowledge." This move, for starters, might prepare us to challenge the preponderance of writing in Western epistemologies.

(Taylor 2003: 16)

Performance scholarship in Latino studies allows us to "do" alternative epistemologies by resisting the privileging of lettered over non-lettered cultures. Taylor further posits that the repertoire, rather than the archive, is where we must turn to interpret "acts of transfer," reminding us that, "not everyone comes to 'culture' or modernity through writing" (xviii). The inclusion of marginalized **epistemologies** is a core prospect of the Latino studies discipline and **border knowledge**, which, as Walter Mignolo has written, provides the opportunity to learn *from* rather than *about* people who experience the consequences of colonial oppression.

In my teaching, the inclusion of performance practices and performance texts assert the body as a locus of knowledge. For example, in Latin American literature classes, we analyze pre-conquest Aztec rituals, shamanic poetry, and ceremonies of traditional indigenous healers. In U.S. Latino/a and gender studies classes, I develop exercises that help students understand the performative nature of gender and language in the everyday "scripts" of how we inhabit social space.

Why is this so important? To emphasize the body as a site of knowing countermands the Western conception that the mind is supreme, and the body is little more than its temporary receptacle. This kind of thinking results in "disposable" approaches to natural resources, because the belief is that mind is superior to matter, and after the body dies, the soul is supernaturally transported to a superior plane. The it-doesn't-matter-what-happens-to-the-body-or-planet disposition has its roots in the rise of textual knowledge in Europe. In *The Spell of the Sensuous* (1996), David Abram shows that ancient Greek thinkers proposed a realm of ideas communicated through letters. Later, Christian doctrine furthered the notion of a non-physical extra-terrestrial heaven. "Bodilessness" progressed in lockstep with alphabetic literacy: "In the absence of writing, human utterance, whether embodied in songs, stories, or spontaneous sounds, was inseparable from the inhaled breath" (254). Bodily knowledge flows, such as those transmitted by pagans and shamans, became markers of all that was deemed uncivilized, even demonic, as the Western project increasingly professionalized intellectual authority, making it the exclusive realm of its readers and writers.

When we include embodied cultural production in Latino literature courses, and discuss with our students the ways that textual, archival knowledge has consolidated Western hegemony, we not only reassess the value of knowledge forms coming from non-lettered societies, we also contribute to the re-estimation of the terrestrial world. Americas-based performance pedagogy has the potential to foster new kinds of stewardship of the body and the social and ecological environments we inhabit.

Opening Pandora's box

My first live engagement with Pocha Nostra took place when I was a graduate student at Columbia University. I attended the first Hemispheric Institute of Performance and Politics Encuentro held in Rio de Janeiro, Brazil, in the year 2000. Guillermo Gómez-Peña and

Roberto Sifuentes invited me to participate as one of three docents in their production of *El Mexterminator*, an interactive performance installation that activates extreme cultural hypertypes driven by fears of the Chicano "Other." Manifesting their personae as "El Mexterminator" (Gómez-Peña) and the "Cyber-Vato" (Sifuentes), audience members were invited to interact with the living "specimens." Participants fed, groomed, and occasionally harassed the performers, who established an interactive relationship with the audience. Performers were simultaneously menacing and vulnerable; sensual yet detached. Dim, dance club lighting, an apocalyptic-Tijuana-on-amphetamines soundtrack, and a hapless chicken's cadaver hanging in the middle of the performance zone all worked in concert to create the feeling of a world without rules.

As participants warmed to the different ways they could interact with Gómez-Peña and Sifuentes, a particularly eager Brazilian participant perched himself on el Cyber-Vato's lap, turning Sifuentes into a playground for his amusement and making full use of the various implements arranged around the set. The participant liberally painted the specimen with green paint, kissed him on the mouth with a probing tongue, and slowly sliced open his white tank top with a large carving knife.

On the day after the *Mexterminator* production, the artists led a conference-wide discussion of their performance practices. Turning the conversation to the previous evening's spectacle, an incensed participant demanded to know how such violent behavior could be tolerated. Her strongly held belief was that the audience member who had taken such license with Sifuentes' persona needed to be held accountable for his transgressions and sanctioned by his peers.

As a docent, I had been assigned a specific role. I was to help audience members in the performance zone engage with Gómez-Peña's and Sifuentes' personae. It was not my task to try to place a limit on the desires of the audience members, or the communication of these desires, with the bodies that were on active display, and so I knew that I had not been personally indicted by these remarks. Instead, what troubled me about this angry participant's disgust was that, for the duration of the performance, all the audience members had been invited to intervene in any way that they chose. They had been made aware that they were at complete liberty to chart their own actions in space. They had been welcomed by the docents—I recall reading the welcoming remarks in English, Spanish, and Portuguese—to explore the **dystopian border imaginary**, and position themselves in the way that suited them best. So why did the angry participant deem herself to be powerless, and why did she feel that the alleged offender held more agency in the simulated border zone than she? In a rarified atmosphere of permission, why hadn't she given herself the permission to intervene? Why did she think it was safe to critique, but not to engage or transform?

Since 2000, I have consistently inaugurated my courses by assigning the performance texts of Gómez-Peña's and Sifuentes' La Pocha Nostra in order to answer these questions about positionality and identity in our own lives. In particular, Gómez-Peña's book publication *Dangerous Border Crossers: The Artist Talks Back* (Routledge, 2000), and *Exercises for Rebel Artists* (Routledge, 2011) prepare my students to enter into critical dialogue that cuts across cultural assumptions and scripted social identities.

Dangerous Border Crossers as frame tale

Having taught U.S. Latino literature courses for over a decade, I have found that I can consistently rely on *Dangerous Border Crossers: The Artist Talks Back* to set the tone for the semester. Like Gómez-Peña's other published performance diaries, the volume constitutes an amalgam of poetic interventions, performance narratives, and travel chronicles with his collaborators, revealing what it is like to be a Chicano border artist in diverse contexts. The "Performance Documents" section consists of excerpts of the performance pieces *BORDERscape 2000*, *Temple of Confessions*, "ethno-techno" art experiments, and *The Mexterminator*. The "Migrant Provocateurs" section brings together commentary and images from travel to regions as diverse as Chiapas, Wales, Montana, and Helsinki. The "Conversations Across the Border Fence" section assembles discussions about Pocha Nostra's pastiche creative process and the allegiances that emerge from shared forms of artistic insurrection. "In Search of a New Topography," the volume's final section, provides a series of talks and reflections on the iconographies of radicalism in the information age. From the historical view, *Dangerous Border Crossers* deals specifically with initial responses to **NAFTA**, **Zapatismo**, and mass media flows in ways that mark its specificity as a contribution to millennial radical art. Formalistically, the text works as a genre-bending performance diary, opening an awareness of the code- and register-switching that characterize border reality. At the same time, the work continues to be evocative and fresh, since the Americas must still cope with the imprint of the border, and grapple with art's potential to exorcise colonial ghosts.

Dangerous Border Crossers frequently provides the "frame tale" for my Latino literature classes. A frame story is a literary technique that sometimes serves as a story within a story. The film *The Titanic* is framed by the elderly Rose who talks about her first love, sending us back in time where we see her as a young woman who narrowly escapes death, and then concludes with Rose as an elderly woman once again. *One Thousand and One Nights* and *The Decameron* are classic works that employ frame tales. Similarly, I present *Dangerous Border Crossers* as a frame: it is the first introduction that students have to the content and goals of the course, and then we revisit the work again at the end when students are required to create their own performance project based on the work of La Pocha Nostra.

For their first assignment, students read, interpret, and discuss the *Temple of Confessions* project. Debuting in 1994, in *Temple of Confessions*, Gómez-Peña and Sifuentes exhibited themselves in Plexiglas boxes as a cross between living religious icons and sideshow aberrations. Audience members were invited to confess their fears to the saints, and later added an Internet confessional to the project. Gómez-Peña writes, "Once the project was over, sharing the actual confessions with our readers was perhaps the best way we could contribute to the understanding of the dangerous territory of intercultural and interracial relations in contemporary America" (2000: 35). My students open what Gómez-Peña describes as a Pandora's box of identity, otherness, borders, and the routes they have traveled into the worlds of cultural Others that were both liberating and destabilizing at the same time. They gamely begin their Latino literature course by excavating their own responses to the poetics of border imagination, and quickly capture the idea that they must bring their whole selves to the exploration of Latino cultural production.

The selection of confessions, fears, and desires that appear in *Dangerous Border Crossers* from live and virtual audience participants are extreme. I require students to read out loud in class from the section, voicing excerpts in class such as "Chicanos scare me. The men, they scream at me. When I see them, I think 'rape.' I feel this is wrong, but I can't help it," or "My smart, sensitive, attractive, vivacious 17 year old daughter is attracted to Latin boys. She now has herpes. These Latin boys need to learn some respect." As a group, we unpack the assumptions about the cultural Other that lurk in these remarks, and students begin to confess some of their own biases or those of their families. Students from different cultural and national backgrounds begin to develop a vocabulary of cultural difference that they build from a place of radical honesty. By reading the confessions of audience members, they are emboldened to give language to their own cultural position rather than grasp for the "correct" one. As the way to introduce the border realities of Latino authors, *Dangerous Border Crossers* works as a container that creates a compassionate space for building a cohesive, yet multi-vocal, learning community.

We revisit *Dangerous Border Crossers* again at the end of the academic term, when students are required to create a group performance based on La Pocha Nostra's *Temple of Confessions*. The assignment is to create an original intervention that deals with the notion of positionality, and elicits audience participation. I have warned students at the beginning of the term that they would be seeing Gómez-Peña and Sifuentes again. Now it is their turn to be the instructors, think critically about the parameters of exclusion and inclusion communicated by body and language, and create an interactive spectacle for the rest of the class.

With enrollments typically numbering 20 to 30, groups of four or five students have never failed to come up with presentations that reveal deep appreciation for the ways we perform our identities, and new insights about their own continuum of agency and acquiescence. One group set up temporary "shower stalls" in the classroom with different cultural personae hiding behind each shower curtain. We were asked to step into each of the stalls and write down our first impression of the specimen we saw. The impressions were then read out loud to the group. Other performances have consisted of auto-ethnographic testimonies, while some have opted to closely interpret scenarios from the works we have read during the semester. Because the first assigned reading had been a performance text voicing extreme examples of fear, desire, and anger, by the end of the semester my students are ready to enter the dangers of the performance zone and ready to critique their own positionality. *Dangerous Border Crossers* helps my Latino literature classrooms become laboratories for testing new social imagination, which is a core objective of the transformational project of Latino studies.

La Pocha Nostra pedagogy in a planetary republic

In the information age, it is easy for students to conflate "information" and "knowledge." Border performance techniques shake students from the passivity of being at the receiving end of information flows, and provide routes to becoming accountable and empowered citizens of the planetary republic. To help educators and artists move away from bodiless, extra-terrestrial learning modalities that are privileged in the West, and move toward sensuous, terrestrial learning that is associated with non-lettered and/or colonial conditions, La Pocha Nostra has developed significant pedagogical offerings that can be adapted for a range of teaching contexts. In this section I limit my remarks to the ways I have recently used *Exercises for Rebel Artists: Radical Performance Pedagogy* (Routledge, 2011) in my courses. I draw on conversations and written communications with Pocha Nostra core members as well as reflections as a participant in the summer intensive workshop held in Athens, Greece in June of 2013 to develop practical tools that are appropriate for the Latino cultural studies environments where most of my teaching takes place.

When *Exercises for Rebel Artists: Radical Performance Pedagogy* appeared in 2011, the volume emboldened me to apply more practical performance techniques in my instruction of Latino and Latin American literature. The material included in the compendium was honed in workshops around the world, but its roots were in the Los Angeles **borderlands**. According to Sifuentes, a formal Pocha Nostra pedagogy received its baptism by fire. He and Gómez-Peña had been working with students as mentors and instructors in various capacities throughout the 1990s, but the Pocha Nostra initial practical workshop took place at California State University at Long Beach when the two were invited by Juan Felipe Herrera to give a presentation in his radical art workshop in July of 1996. Herrera was a foundational figure in Chicano poetry and their highly esteemed creative mentor. He asked the duo to provide a practical workshop, but they respectfully declined. However, when they arrived on the day of their talk prepared to provide an audiovisual discussion of their work, Herrera had something else in mind.

"He refused to take no for an answer," Sifuentes recalls. "We had requested a projector for us to show and talk about our work. There was no projector. There was just this group of students wearing exercise clothes. He told us that he had already warmed them up. We couldn't say no because how do you say no to your Chicano elder? And it coincided with the demand that we were hearing over and over. The art world had been demanding a border pedagogy—a language to transfer what we did to art and activist groups. So after that we acknowledged the need and desire to do it." In our conversation, Sifuentes emphasized that the exercises that made their way to publication came from the modular structures that they had been using in collaborations around the world to incorporate artists of different nationalities into their performance projects. But it was a "how do you say 'no' to your Chicano elder?" moment that literally forced Gómez-Peña and Sifuentes to commit to developing a pedagogical playbook that could be adapted for arts practitioners, educators, and activists across various disciplinary backgrounds. From the beginning, their pedagogy was border-generated, but planetary in scope.

When *Exercises for Rebel Artists* came out, I had already been employing performance techniques in my courses for over a decade, primarily featuring exercises I had learned in Augusto Boal's Theatre of the Oppressed workshops and experiments in critical auto-ethnography alongside the *Temple of Confessions*-based assignment that I describe above. However, with *Exercises for Rebel Artists* in hand, I now had the chance to try out Pocha Nostra exercises straight from their own playbook.

The perfect opportunity to get my hands dirty soon arose. In January 2013, I held a one-semester visiting appointment at Columbus State University in Columbus, Georgia as the Elena Diaz-Verson Amos Eminent Scholar in Latin American Studies. While there, I taught two courses in Spanish in the Department of Modern and Classical Languages, and gave talks hosted by the Department of Art and the Center for International Education. Members of the Art and Theater Departments encouraged my interdisciplinarity as a scholar-artist, and provided support for me to create a public, end-of-term performance with my upper level Gender and Power in Latin American literature class.

Because the Spanish program at CSU was much smaller than those I had worked in previously, the enrollment of six students did not lend itself to a classroom performance as a culminating project for the course. I determined that I would perform with the students, and create a persona that would serve as a docent of the live art exhibit that we titled *Americas Situation Room Exploratorium Experience*. The students quickly proved that they had both enthusiasm and aptitude for performance. There were a few students who, for various reasons, did not feel they could commit to the conceptual performance format, and non-performing students supported the production by creating publicity, helping to design the set, and providing technical assistance.

To prepare students for this work, I initiated the course with *Dangerous Border Crossers* as I had done in the past, but for the first time I also used *Exercises for Radical Artists*, which gave me a template for the series of workshops and rehearsals that led to the *Americas Situation Room* production. Obviously, some of the exercises were not going to work for a group of non-performance artist Spanish students. Exercises that had participants touching, smelling, or in other ways sensorially exploring each other's bodies were summarily rejected. But Pocha Nostra's methods for establishing a performance zone, prop and costume stations, and event flow remarks proved extremely useful in helping me translate what had long been an intimate, for-class-members-only structure into a public performance conceived and presented by non-performers.

To get non-performance artists to develop cultural performance, I asked students to bring two sets of costumes to our first practical workshop. One was "my madness," and the second was "my stereotype." These two outward representations of identity were eventually synthesized to create a final persona that they activated in the performance space. A white, female student performed a racist antebellum woman in a *Gone-With-the-Wind* style dress. Blindfolded, with her hair in front of her face like a veil, she clumsily arranged plastic flowers in front of her, from time to time using the flower like a dart to stab photocopied images of Aunt Jemima and Pulman Porter-style African Americans in different postures of gleeful subservience, as though the act of puncturing blacks were a party game, or part of appropriate regional etiquette. Another student played the role of a blindfolded Catholic schoolgirl. Her attendant taped black tape across her body in horizontal lines, evoking the image of censor bars. The Latina student played with multiple identities, first as a mother in a wheelchair selling her infants in the global marketplace, and then as a possessed **santería** priestess who joins the military. The white, male student in the group played the role of "American Guy." He sat on a sofa in a collegiate cap and gown and played Grand Theft Auto on a gaming console for the duration of the performance. I assumed the persona of an "illegal alien" by dressing in a classic Star Trek style silver lamé dress, green face paint, and a silvery helmet with tall antennae that looked like a cross between an insect and a vintage television set. I introduced myself as "Lady Olmec" to the gathered audience members outside the performance zone, explaining that I was an illegal alien, but they shouldn't worry because I would self deport "once the floors and toilettes were cleaned." I then led audience participants into the performance zone and ensured that they engage with the various specimens on display. Audience members fed cheese puffs and sips of Coke to American Guy and Catholic Schoolgirl. They read Bible passages and racist children's literature to Southern Belle, and accepted small objects from Wheelchair Latina that represented the children she loses to migration and exploitative industries.

The audience was composed of my colleagues in the Art and Modern and Classical Languages Departments, family members of performers, community members, and students of other classes who were there to see friends or win a few extra credit points. I provided all audience participants with programs and distributed slips of paper for them to write confessions and deposit them anonymously into a confessional box. After I had collected confessions from all participants, I read a selection of them that were pulled from the box at random, announcing that absolution had been granted. Belle and Catholic Schoolgirl both had attendants that helped them transform into brides, who then made their way toward American Guy in a slow, stylized choreography led by their attendants. The piece concluded with an audience singalong to the saccharin voice of Merrilee Rush's version of "What the World Needs Now," while the two brides, finally freed from their blindfolds, stare vacantly at the screen and American Guy continues to kill as many characters as he can in his Grand Theft Auto game. During the reception following the performance, I read the remaining confessions to friends and performers, and audience members claimed authorship of many of the cultural confessions I read to the crowd.

Both students and faculty members appreciated the chance to be exposed to a performance approach to cultural criticism, and I was honored and humbled by my students' willingness to jump into the unknown with me and create stylized displays of our exaggerated cultural identities that are often suppressed and silenced. *Exercises for Rebel Artists* provided more than a series of activities to try, but a borderlands framework for exercising colonial demons and forging an environment of radical safety.

I am currently teaching a course at the Ohio State University in the Department of Spanish and Portuguese that emphasizes the cultural production of Central and South American and Caribbean groups that are less represented in Latino studies curricula. We have been conducting a rigorous examination of pan-Latino identity, paying particular attention to José Martí's seminal essay "Nuestra América," and also delving into social margins and the notion of the Other. With the curricular mandate to focus on works by U.S. Latino authors other than those of Mexican, Cuban, and Puerto Rican descent in mind, the frame tale of *Temple of Confessions* did not seem appropriate. I decided to base their final presentation requirement on the human altar exercise that I learned with Pocha Nostra in the summer intensive of 2013 and is featured in *Exercises for Rebel Artists*. Divided into groups of five or six, students will create two live art installations on the theme "El hombre americano" as described by José Martí in "Nuestra América," and on the theme "Santa Otredad" ("Saint Otherness"). The installations will be mounted either in a public or non-public space, and documented by the group members. Groups will create an audiovisual presentation in Spanish on their installations (rather than installing live art in the classroom) of ten minutes in length. I require students to write an in-class self-evaluation detailing how they contributed to the installations, how they contributed to the group's efforts, and the critical connections they were able to make between the installation and the themes of pan-Latino identity and the cultural Other.

Moving beyond individual course design to the broader curricular needs of students in Latino studies programs and the humanities writ large, Latino literature classes have a unique responsibility to insist on the inclusion of **Americas-based epistemologies** characterized by live acts of transfer. When the repertoire is considered alongside the archive, an entire hemisphere of knowledge flows comes to life to be embodied, restored, and interpreted by students. La Pocha Nostra offers daring exercises in radical hope: they activate a world in which practitioners are empowered not only to critique—but also to engage and transform—the planetary circumstances they inherit.

Resources for teaching Americas-based performance studies

Bell, Elizabeth. *Theories of Performance.* Thousand Oaks, California: Sage, 2008.
Denzin, Norman K. *Performance Ethnography: Critical Pedagogy and the Politics of Culture.* Thousand Oaks, California: Sage, 2003.
Freire, Paulo. *Pedagogy of the Oppressed.* New York: Continuum, 1993.

Gómez-Peña, Guillermo. *Dangerous Border Crossers: The Artist Talks Back*. New York: Routledge, 2000.

Gómez-Peña, Guillermo. *Ethno-Techno: Writings on Performance, Activism and Pedagogy*. Elaine A. Peña, ed. New York: Routledge, 2005.

Gómez-Peña, Guillermo, and Roberto Sifuentes. *Exercises for Rebel Artists: Radical Performance Pedagogy*. New York: Routledge, 2011.

Martinez-Cruz, Paloma. *Women and Knowledge in Mesoamerica: From East L.A. to Anahuac*. Tucson: University of Arizona Press, 2011.

Mignolo, Walter. *Local Histories, Global Designs: Coloniality, Subaltern Knowledges, and Border Thinking*. New Jersey: Princeton University Press, 2000.

Muñoz, José Esteban. *Disidentifications: Queers of Color and the Performance of Politics*. Minneapolis: University of Minnesota Press, 1999.

Schechner, Richard. *Performance Theory*. New York: Routledge, 2003.

Stucky, Nathan, and Cynthia Wimmer, eds. *Teaching Performance Studies*. Carbondale: Southern Illinois University Press, 2002.

Taylor, Diana. *The Archive and the Repertoire: Performing Cultural Memory in the Americas*. Durham: Duke University Press, 2003.

Part IV

Other Latino/a forms and spaces

16 Teaching comics by and about Latinos/as

Frederick Luis Aldama

Whether teaching graduate, undergraduate, or high school students (as I do in the Humanities and Cognitive Sciences High School Summer Institute at Ohio State University), when I teach comic books by and about Latinos, I constantly remind my students to keep the following questions in mind: (1) Why is a respective comic book made? (2) What is it conveying? (3) How is it conveying this? (4) Does it succeed on its own terms? These seemingly simple questions allow me to keep the students focused on issues such as the difference between formal techniques (and structures) and themes (and characterizations). It helps them see how the formal techniques (layout, panel size and shape, ink, letters, colors, among others) and structures (point of view, temporal play, among others) shape the content. It helps them see all the cognitive and emotive processes involved when an author/artist makes real in comic book form something originally imagined and felt. Finally, it helps the students step into the shoes of the "ideal" comic book reader who picks up on all the signposts built into the respective comic book's design. As a given course unfolds and more comic books by and about Latinos are read, in discussion and lecture I give nuance to each of these aspects. This approach becomes more and more a part of an intuitive analytical framework that they use to study comic books by and about Latinos/as.

Almost without knowing how deeply they have come to understand the first question (why a respective comic book is made), by the end of the course, whether it is a one-week, ten-week, or fifteen-week module, students understand that the author-artist's choice to create a given comic book reorganizes and gives shape to the intellectual and material building blocks we recognize as coming from a reality that is increasingly made up of Latinos. They come to understand that this given comic book also adds something *new* to the world. That is, while comic book author-artists use natural, social, and biosocial features of reality as building blocks in the making of their **storyworlds**, comic books are a special kind of *addition to* reality. Students understand how to approach and even answer questions 2 and 3, realizing that the subject matter, theme, and characterization in Latino comic books are actually few. And so what gives Latino comic books their amazing variety and abundance is not their content but their form. Students understand that each comic book studied is fresh and new because it has gone through the formal shaping device of the discourse, that is, the series of formal and technical means used by the author-artist to guide her shaping of the story. Finally, the students learn to put at arm's length idiosyncratic taste and thus step into the shoes of the ideal reader-viewer when evaluating a given Latino comic book.

In framing my classes with these questions and following through with specific pro-positions and pedagogical directives, I enter into a journey of discovery *with* my students.

It's a journey that brings alive the Latino comic book encounter through attentive close readings and viewings. It is a journey always attuned to the cognitive and emotive processes involved in the work of authors-artists creating and readers co-creating. Hence, the journey also expands their knowledge of the nature of creativity, embodied in author-artists' imagination and skillful use of device in the making of a comic book—and in the *re-creative* processes the students as reader-viewers use to complete the texts by inference.

Foundations

I would like to share with my fellow teachers details of the foundational propositions that I keep in mind when teaching Latino comic books. I don't teach these precepts directly and verbatim to the students. Indeed, I find it more pedagogically efficacious to keep the students in the mode of close reading and viewing. However, by always having this foundational framework in my peripheral view, I can guide the students to come into a richer understanding of the comics. The propositions are as follows:

First, my students and I keep in mind that Latinos have been and continue to be present in comic books in the United States—both as creators of comics and also in the **storyworld** contents. In the Marvel and DC universes there are over 50 Latino superheroes (and supervillains) that first began to appear after the Second World War. (See Aldama's *Your Brain on Latino Comics* 2009.) The students come to realize that the presence of Latinos in comics and in the making of comics can be accounted for because Latinos have been and very much continue to be a significant presence in the United States. And, our numbers have been increasing exponentially.

Second, this storytelling media is especially attractive to Latino makers of narrative fiction. As a storytelling format it offers a resplendent and infinite variety of ways one can choose to give shape to a story, allowing for all kinds of tensions and harmonies between its visual and verbal elements. It costs little to make. It offers the possibility of a grassroots-style distribution—web, word of mouth, and expos, for instance. (See the annual Latino Comics Expo.) It appeals to all variety of reader-viewers: children, teens, adults as well as women and men, Latinos and all others. Its consumption can take place in short bursts and on the fly.

Third, with Latinos increasingly pushed into urban settings to scratch out a living came an urban lifestyle and psychological outlook—especially among the newer generation of Latinos. Alienation and anonymity associated with urban life that was especially prevalent among the older generation began to transform into a sense of cultural renewal, especially for a newer generation—a generation not working in the factories 24/7 and that had more time and access to all variety of entertainment. This led to the developing of tastes for consuming and desire to participate in making all sorts of cultural products, including the reading and creating of comic books.

Fourth, Latinos making comics in today's independent and mainstream marketplaces are actively *transforming* this comic book world, just as their imagination, tastes, skills are transformed by this newly and constantly transforming world. The Latino comics created are complex and multidimensional in ways that reflect the increasingly diverse range of Latinos that make up *and* give shape to the culture of the United States.

Fifth, the history of Latinos in comic books is a living archive of sorts. It is an archive that is growing and changing day by day as author-artists create comics about Latinos—and as scholars excavate what has come before. It is an archive that reflects just how the Latino population in the United States itself has changed: from a minority within a minority and rural to a majority within the minority and urban. Today, Latinos are the largest minority population in the United States. Second only to Mexico City, Los Angeles has the largest Latino population. The trend in mainstream and independent comics has been increasingly to reflect this reality by creating compelling Latino comic book characters.

Sixth, not all comic books are made equal. When a student learns to step into the shoes of the ideal reader-viewer, they also learn to evaluate the comics on their own terms—and some just don't measure up. The quality of imagination and visual and verbal storytelling skill varies from one comic to another. I use the example of DC's Paco Ramon as Vibe. Introduced in 1984 DC's creators had no problem identifying him with the pejorative "Paco" and to build his identity out of all sorts of stereotypes and clichés: He's a former gangleader, sprinkles his dialogue with truncated Spanglish phrases like "watchu doin," and is preternaturally good at dancing (breakdancing, in this case). Moreover, the students come to see how line, perspective, panel layout, and other formal features do little to energize the story.

Background

Given that most students know little about the history of comics generally and absolutely nothing about Latinos in comics, I provide lectures that give them this history. (This history is available in the first section of *Your Brain on Latino Comics*.) I talk about the independents such as Los Bros Hernandez—first out of the gate in the early 1980s. I then move into discussion of the work that followed in the late 1980s and 1990s by the likes of Richard Dominguez, Ivan Velez, Laura Molina, Carlos Saldaña, Rafael Navarro, Javier Hernandez, Rhode Montijo, Wilfred Santiago, Anthony Oropeza, Lalo Alcaraz, among others. With the exception of Los Bros Hernandez (Mario, Jaime, and Gilbert) these author-artists struggled long and hard to get their work into the hands of readers. Most continue to create comics but still hold other jobs to make ends meet. These first wave creators opened doors and role-modeled possibilities for new waves of younger generation of Latino *and* Latina comic book storytellers such as Graciela Rodriguez, Liz Mayorga, Anthony Aguilar and Luke Lizalde, Christian Ramirez, Crystal Gonzalez, and Daniel Parada, among others.

I also provide a history of Latinos creating and represented in the DC and Marvel mainstream comic book world. DC and Marvel have been creating Latino superheroes since the mid-1940s. While they were identified in written character descriptions as Latino, they often appeared in the visuals less with **mestizo** and more with European features. DC's introduction in 1946 of the Zorro-styled vigilante Rodrigo "Rodney" Elwood Gaynor is a case in point. Marvel's introduction of Hector Ayala as the White Tiger in 1975 introduced another, more complex way to represent Latinos. At the hand of Latino visual artists George Pérez and storyteller Bill Mantlo not only was White Tiger solidly rooted in his Puerto Rican (Boricua) heritage, but the skillful use of the visuals gave the story and character tremendous energy. There were many other Latinos that followed, including Latinas such as DC's Beatriz "Bea" Bonilla da Costa as Fire, Marvel's Bonita Juarez as Firebird in 1981, and also supervillains like DC's El Papayago in 1977. I bring them up to the present, discussing some of the more recent Latinos such as the Santerians, Araña, Ms. America Chavez, Spider-Girl and the Blatino Spider-Man in Marvel's Ultimate Comics series as well as the new Blue

Beetle, the new Latina White Tiger and the new Vibe. In PowerPoint presentations that outline the history of Latinos in the DC and Marvel universes, the students learn to discern between those made with a great will to style when it comes to representation and the visual elements carefully geometrizing of the story—and those with little will to style that rely on stock stereotypes and formal techniques that do little to energize the stories.

Genres

By assigning a number of different kinds of comics (from science fiction to noir to autobiographical, among others) the students learn about the wide spectrum of genres chosen by author-artists in shaping Latino identity and experience. Here's a sampling of comics that I use:

- History: Ilan Stavans's (writer) and Lalo Alcaraz's (artist) *Latino USA* (2000) provides students with a deep social, historical, and cultural knowledge about Latinos.
- Science Fiction: Several comics that show students how comics set in the future can imaginatively extrapolate from the present condition of Latinos in new and innovative ways. These include Frank Espinosa's *Rocketo* and Los Bros Hernandez's *Citizen Rex* (2011) as well as the slightly harder to come by *Spider-Man 2099* by Peter David (writer) and Rick Leonardi (artist); the latter features a mixed Irish and Mexican Miguel "Mig" O'Hara as Spider-Man. For instance, when teaching *Citizen Rex* the students begin to explore issues of class and different forms of otherness (cyborgs and robots). They explore how formal techniques such as line style and the use of black and white contrasts give weight and dimension to the objects, buildings, and characters that make up the storyworld. When teaching Frank Espinosa's *Rocketo* I have students read my interview with Espinosa (*Your Brain on Latino Comics*) as a *map* of sorts for reading how this comic book functions as an allegory of the Latino exilic experience. The interview also provides the students with keys to unlocking other riches; they learn to see how Espinosa transforms many of his visual and verbal influences including German Expressionism, Japanese art, *Flash Gordon*, and *Heart of Darkness*.
- Noir: Several Latino comics that use (and reform) the generic shaping structures of noir can deepen the students' understanding of the present as well as the past—the deep mythological past. Comics I've used include those from Rafael Navarro's *Sonambulo* series as well as those from Gilbert Hernandez's stand-alone graphic novel series such as *Chance in Hell*, *Speak of the Devil*, *Troublemakers*, and *Maria M.* When I teach *Sonambulo* I provide a brief lecture on pre-Columbian myth (including especially Mictlan) and the history of **lucha libre**. This background enriches their understanding of how Novarro recreates both in the making of his **luchador**-mask wearing Latino detective protagonist, Sonambulo. When I teach any one of Gilbert's stand-alone graphic novels I excerpt passages from the beginnings of any of the noir novels of Jim Thompson, David Goodis, James Cain, and Elmore Leonard. This leads students to see how Gilbert uses the generic conventions of noir as the framing device for storyworlds that contain erratic, seemingly inexplicable eruptions of violence. He does so to creatively construct a fatalistic storyworld that reflects our present day social tissue increasingly ripped apart and that predetermines a futureless world for younger generations—Latino or otherwise.

- Coming of Age: I like to assign Latino coming-of-age and *coming out* comics such as Graciela Rodriguez's *Lunatic Fringe*, Rhode Montijo's *Pablo's Inferno*, and Ivan Velez Jr.'s *Tales of the Closet*. For instance, when I teach *Pablo's Inferno* I provide information about European conquest of the Americas so students can see how Rhode uses visuals and textual means to *recreate* pre-Columbian history and myth in the making of his coming of age story of Pablo. Students learn to identify how Rhode uses perspective and also a careful use of geometric shapes in the making of the protagonist that pulls the reader-viewer into the story and asks that they align themselves with the child protagonist. They learn to better understand the emotions triggered by Rhode's choice to filter the horrors of the Euro-Spanish genocide and conquest of the Americas through the myth-inspired character Quetzal and the innocent Pablo. When I teach Ivan Velez's *Tales of the Closet Vol. 1* (2005) the students come to understand how simple panel layout can be used to richly texture the Latino teen experience, doubly complicated when coming out as gay and lesbian.
- **Bildungsroman**: One of the most successful education-of-the-senses comics that I assign is Wilfred Santiago's *In My Darkest Hour*. Students learn to grasp just how important the visual devices are in shaping the journey of the Nuyorican protagonist, Omar, during a time that leads up to the events of 9/11 by attending to Santiago's use of color wash (to indicate an extended flashback, for instance) and stretched and distorted photographs (to indicate how capitalism and consumer culture distort reality). They learn, too, how Santiago conveys through visual and verbal means moments when one's emotion system is shaped dramatically by social and historical events: panel layout, color scheme, and style blur the boundary between Omar's interiority as a Nuyorican and a pre- and post-9/11 American social psyche.
- Superhero: I assign comics from the superhero genre for students to see how capacious it can be for conveying Latino experiences and identities. For instance, in teaching Javier Hernandez's *El Muerto* they learn how a superhero can be made within a Mesoamerican mythic structure—and not those we conventionally see with the DC and Marvel superheroes. When teaching Laura Molina's *Cihualyaomiquiz, the Jaguar* and George Peréz's *White Tiger* students learn that Batman is not the only self-constructed superhero—and that self-made Latino superheroes fight different kinds of injustice, including those that grow out of racism and sexism. (I also provide biographical details on Peréz, including that it wasn't until he mastered his geometry that he came into his own as a comic book creator. Students learn of the importance of the tool of geometry and the learning of how to *geometricize* the story.) In teaching Joe Quesada's *Santerians* students learn about the history of cultural syncretism in the Hispanophone Caribbean. With Orson Scott Card's *Ultimate Iron Man* they learn how a comic book can turn upside down stereotypes of Latinos as all body. With Michael Bendis's (writer) and Sara Pichelli's (artist) *Ultimate Spider-Man Comics* and Miles Morales as a Blatino Spider-Man students learn just how complex cultural and biological *latinidad* can be. With Steve Ross's *Chesty Sanchez* students learn that one can also have fun in superhero comics. His Latina superhero, Chesty Sanchez, brings down corporate villains with her sidekick Torpedo. His deadly weapons are his *pedos* (farts).
- Autobiography: In teaching Latino comic books in the autobiographical mode I sometimes choose Inverna Lockpez's (author) and Dean Haspiel's (artist) *Cuba My Revolution* and Wilfred Santiago's *21: The Story of Roberto Clemente*. With *Cuba* students learn how visuals (brown, gray lines, sepia washes, splashes of red,

regular and irregular panel layouts) convey a topsy-turvy experience of the Cuban Revolution. With *21: The Story of Roberto* (2011) students learn how a narrative framing structure (the biography unfolds as an extended flashback) intensifies our sense of Clemente's at once breaking of the color line in baseball and his confinement within a racist society; no matter what, he remains confined and within this confinement separated and alone. Students also learn of the importance of speech balloons. Santiago uses white for their background when Spanish is spoken and shades of brown as the background when English is spoken, flipping readerly expectation that English is the language of whites (Anglo) and that Spanish is the language of those who are shades of brown (Latinos). In all they learn how Santiago's will to style leads to the careful use of geometry and perspective give the story rhythm and energy.

Geometrized storytelling

When teaching Latino comics I provide students with the formal concepts and tools that are used to give shape to stories in comics. Whether of the superheroic or everyday earth-bound variety, comic books by and about Latinos demand a great concentration of visual and verbal narrative devices and plot to hit their mark and realize their intended effect on the reader-viewers.

I find Will Eisner's *Expressive Anatomy* (2008) and Stan Lee's *How to Draw Comics* (2010) to be excellent primers for students to learn about the devices and structures used to geometrize stories about Latinos. They teach the students a geometric vocabulary that includes: panel layout, line (thin or thick), color, perspective, object shape, balloon shape and placement, lettering, and gutter size and width. They show students just how *crucial* these geometric shaping devices are in the making of comic book stories that *move* and in the creating of Latino protagonists that *pop*.

I sometimes ask the students to compare the art in Alcaraz's and Stavans's *Latino USA* with, for instance, Peréz's *White Tiger*. They figure out that when there is an abundance of text and where the story isn't sufficiently geometrized, the author-artists are not taking full advantage of the rich palette of devices available to the comic book storytelling format. The students come to realize that unlike Stavans and Alcaraz, who seek to *illustrate* the history of Latinos, Pérez creates a compelling and rich Latino superhero comic book not just in plot and theme but also in the kinetic energy Peréz invested in the visuals. Indeed, they begin to see just how the layout, lettering, and use of bubbles function integrally to the plot and push the story forward.

The students also learn about how our minds work to fill in gaps left strategically by author-artists. For instance, when Frank Espinosa creates *Rocketo*, he draws a figure or scene and erases unnecessary lines to create the minimum of direction for the reader-viewer to fill in the rest (movement, objects, reactions) in their imagination. That is, students learn about how the author-artists' willful use of space design (layout and panel size and shape) can create different kinds of movement within and between the panels *in the imagination* of the reader-viewer.

Along with the willful use of technique and storytelling comes a responsibility to subject matter. Students come to realize that there is a difference that makes a crucial difference between comic book author-artists who particularize Latino experience in places *in* time with a clear will to style and those who abstract character experience in places *out of* time. They learn to attend to the formal features involved in making comics as well as how author-artists particularize features of *latinidad* contained in the subject matter (themes, places, and time).

Creating in time and place

It is important for my students to understand that Latino comics are not created out of thin air. They need to know that there are material, social, and historical contexts that shape the production and consumption of comics by and about Latinos. Historically, with imagination, skill, pen, and paper Latino author-artists with limited means have been able to create stories in the comic book format. They have been able to maintain a total control over their artistic product. However, there remains the need to get these stories into the hands of reader-viewers—and, the hope that one might even be able to make a living doing so. I discuss with students the history of distribution and the problems with monopolies like Diamond that do get comics out to readers, but that also eat into profits so scarce for the independent Latino author-artists. I might assign an interview or two by those Latino author-artists like Ivan Velez who worked for Marvel and DC but were forced into straightjackets that suffocated their creativity. I talk about the history of other, less restrictive publishing venues for Latino author-artists such as Seattle's Fantagraphics, Montreal's Drawn & Quarterly, Berkeley's Image Comics—and the significance of technologies that have allowed for web publication and distribution.

In spite of the distribution obstacles, we have seen a steady increase in the production of comics by and about Latinos. As they continue to be made, so too a scholarship around Latino comics continues to grow. When teaching Latino comics students come to realize that they are helping shape an incipient field of study and with this a Latino canon of comics. Framing the assignment of excerpts from the growing body of scholarship on Latino comics gives them a wide-angle sense of how this field is being shaped. I assign *Your Brain on Latino Comics* (Aldama 2009) as well as the essays and chapters collected in Héctor Fernández L'Hoeste's and Juan Poblete's *Redrawing the Nation* (2009), those included in *Multicultural Comics* (Aldama 2010), as well those in Christopher González's (2013) special issue of *ImageText* on Los Bros Hernandez. By reading the scholarship on comics by and about Latinos, students deepen an understanding of comics both within national and historical contexts as well as see first-hand how the canon of Latino comics is being shaped by the making of such comics and their interpretation and analysis.

Wrap up

When teaching Latino comics, I seek to provide the students with: a sound sense of the living archive of comics by and about Latinos; a conceptual and technical grammar for analyzing these comics; and a sense of the biological mechanisms and sociohistorical contexts involved in creating and consuming comics by and about Latinos. That is, as teachers, I see our task as guiding and encouraging students to acquire a historical knowledge of comics by and about Latinos as well as to discover how individual comics are built and how they are consumed. Finally, in the teaching of comic books by and about Latinos I hope that students will come to understand that *latinidad* in the Latino comic book world can come in any shape and any size: from Saldaña's superheroic, bilingual Burrito who wears a *sarape* to save the day and Navarro's post-Mictlan detective hero Sonambulo to Frank Espinosa's post-apocalyptic world mapper, Rocketo.

In all, what I hope the students will learn is just how resplendent the craft of comic book storytelling is when it comes to giving shape to the Latino experience.

Resources for teaching comics by and about Latinos

Aldama, Frederick Luis. *Your Brain on Latino Comics*. Austin: University of Texas Press, 2009.
——"Characters in comic books." In *Characters in Fictional Worlds: Understanding Imaginary Beings in Literature, Film, and Other Media*. Eds. Jens Eder, Fotis Jannidis, Ralf Schneider. Berlin: De Gruyter, 2010, pp. 318–28.
——, ed. *Multicultural Comics: From Zap to Blue Beetle*. Austin: University of Texas Press, 2010.
——, ed. *Latinos and Narrative Media: Participation and Portrayal*. New York: Palgrave, 2013.
Eisner, Will. *Expressive Anatomy for Comics and Narrative: Principles and Practices from the Legendary Cartoonist*. New York: W.W. Norton, 2008.
Espinoza, Mauricio. "The alien is here to stay: otherness, anti-assimilation, and empowerment in Latino/a superhero comics." In *Mind the Gap: Latino Comic Books Past, Present, and Future*. Eds. Frederick Luis Aldama and Christopher González. Austin: University of Texas Press. [Forthcoming.]
Foster, David William. "Latino comics: Javier Hernandez's *El Muerto* as an allegory of Chicano identity." In *Latinos and Narrative Media: Participation and Portrayal*. Ed. Frederick Luis Aldama. New York: Palgrave, 2013, pp. 225–40.
Frank, Kathryn M. "Everybody wants to rule the multiverse." In *Mind the Gap: Latino Comic Books Past, Present, and Future*. Eds. Frederick Luis Aldama and Christopher González. Austin: University of Texas Press. [Forthcoming.]
González, Christopher. "Turf, tags, and territory: spatiality in Jaime Hernandez's 'Vida Loca: The Death of Speedy Ortiz.'" *ImageTexT: Interdisciplinary Comics Studies* 7.1 (2013). www.english.ufl.edu/imagetext/archives/v7_1/gonzalez/ (accessed June 15, 2014).
Hatfield, Charles. *Alternative Comics: An Emerging Literature*. Jackson, MI: University Press of Mississippi, 2005.
Hetrick, Nick. "Chronology, country, and consciousness in Wilfred Santiago's *In My Darkest Hour*." In *Multicultural Comics: From Zap to Blue Beetle*. Ed. Frederick Luis Aldama. Austin: University of Texas Press, 2010, pp. 189–201.
Lee, Stan. *How to Draw Comics*. Berkeley: Ten Speed Press, 2010.
L'Hoeste, Héctor Fernández and Juan Poblete, eds. *Redrawing the Nation: National Identity in Latin/o American Comics*. New York: Palgrave, 2009.
Millán, Isabel. "Anya Sofía (Araña) Corazón: the inner webbings & Mexi-Ricanization of Spider-Girl." In *Mind the Gap: Latino Comic Books Past, Present, and Future*. Eds. Frederick Luis Aldama and Christopher González. Austin: University of Texas Press. [Forthcoming.]
Nama, Adilifu. "Staking out a *Blatino* borderlands." In *Latinos and Narrative Media: Participation and Portrayal*. Ed. Frederick Luis Aldama. New York: Palgrave, 2013, pp. 131–42.
Risner, Jonathan. "'Authentic' Latina/os and queer characters in mainstream and alternative comics." In *Multicultural Comics: From Zap to Blue Beetle*. Ed. Frederick Luis Aldama. Austin: University of Texas Press, 2010, pp. 39–54.
Rodriguez, Richard T. "Revealing secret identities: gay Latino superheroes and the necessity of disclosure." In *Mind the Gap: Latino Comic Books Past, Present, and Future*. Eds. Frederick Luis Aldama and Christopher González. Austin: University of Texas Press. [Forthcoming.]

17 Crowdsourcing Latino literary study

Participatory learning and enhanced e-books

Ellen McCracken

As humanities education transforms itself in the early twenty-first century, participatory models of learning increasingly involve digital interfaces. The traditional binary that separates the professor as expert from the student who imbibes the expert's knowledge becomes even more dysfunctional as portable computer technology reaches more and more learners across the United States. This empowering access to digital interfaces invites professors and students to engage in more broadly participatory knowledge creation, moving beyond the traditional model of the "sage on the stage" who presents lectures, answers a few questions from students, and encourages some discussion. (Urayoán Noel's chapter in this volume identifies a *performalist* pedagogy that also carves a path for the teaching of different, twenty-first-century digital formats in the Latino/a literary classroom.)

This is not to deny the need for expertise, guidance, and professional responsibility but rather to broaden the modes of accessing and creating knowledge now possible in the digital age. How might the study of U.S. Latino literature transform itself for more participatory learning models that employ digital interfaces? Here I will not focus on the valuable new strategies of computational analysis of literary texts such as visualizations, word trees and clouds, term frequencies, patterns of code-switching or social network analysis—charting relational networks between characters, networks of cultural allusions and dialogues, and directional paths through which readers are encouraged to move through the novels.[1] Instead, I will focus on enhanced e-book creation as a strategy for participatory research, creation, and dissemination of knowledge about U.S. Latino literature. Here, literary analysis is "crowd sourced" among the students who combine their efforts of research, design, and implementation to create digital books that help to democratize knowledge in a wider public arena. By developing digital enhancements for printed literary texts, this participatory mode of Latino literary study highlights new elements of texts to pay attention to and new ways to do so.

Early twentieth-century Russian Formalist theorist Viktor Shklovsky argued that literature makes the ordinary strange, allowing non-routinized perceptions and alternate cognitive engagements with the world. Classroom crowdsourcing of literary analysis facilitates a similar pattern of positive *estrangement* (that is, alternate perceptions of the usual and everyday) of both literary texts and extant literary criticism. The printed text to which we have become accustomed over centuries is "made strange" with a new network of multimedial augmentations in the enhanced digital edition. A double estrangement occurs—in today's terminology, a meta-reading of the author's initial strategies of estrangement. In this sense, the author's original rhetorical and thematic techniques of making the ordinary strange are expanded digitally and taken in additional directions. This self-conscious, analytical trajectory in turn opens numerous unexpected paths for further analysis.

Michel de Certeau theorized that literary texts are fundamentally unstable because readers introduce plurality and difference into them, functioning as nomads poaching their way across the fields they did not write. Readers perform advances and retreats, playing various tactics and games with the text. Crowdsourcing of analysis in courses on Latino literature encourages and brings to light some of this plurality. The work of designing enhanced e-books invites both the creators of the digital editions and other readers to engage with new paths and trajectories across literary texts that the designers perceive to be exciting and valuable. Crowdsourced e-books create new and different modes of paying attention to texts.

Cathy Davidson has noted that "[h]ow we perceive the world, what we pay attention to, and whether we pay attention with delight or alarm are often a function of the tools that extend our capabilities or intensify our interactions with the world" (2011: 16). Enhanced e-books offer both creators and readers alternate tools with which to perceive and pay attention to literary texts. The augmentations of textuality employ various media—from additional words, to pictures, sounds, 3-D images, videos, motion-enhanced photos, street-views and many others. When a careful balance is constructed between the literary text and the new enhancements, the reader experiences new capabilities in engaging with the text and intensified interactions with it.

Enhanced electronic books

With the proliferation of portable electronic devices such as the iPad, the Kindle Fire, and smartphones since 2010,[2] the enhanced e-book has blossomed as a new genre. Portability, accessibility in multiple locales, and quick downloading of books have attracted wider audiences to literary texts, and the new digital capabilities of these devices have spurred content creators and publishers to develop textual enhancements to attract audiences and increase sales. Unlike experimental digital literature created and read on computers with multiple directional paths and game-like sensibilities, enhanced e-books adapt printed texts or create new works by adding easily consumed extra material such as video clips, voice-overs, maps, documents, photos, interviews, and performances to augment the reading experience and increase knowledge about the text. Brad Inman pioneered Vooks in 2009 as mobile applications for the web, and other publishers began to produce enhanced e-books in spring 2010 because of the iPad's huge success and the possibilities for new forms of embedding that it offers. By May 2012, nearly 1,500 enhanced e-books were available in the iBooks store, with over 700 titles from Vook, and thousands continue to be published. As of August 2013 Amazon listed 1,254 Kindle books with audio and video and by June 2014 the inventory in this category had increased to 2,025 titles.[3]

In January 2012, Apple released the free iBooks Author software through which people can create enhanced books themselves, and by May that year the iBook Store listed over 3,200 titles made using the software. Most are very short "how to" books, children's titles, travel books, classroom publishing experiments, and a few literary works. This easy-to-learn software offers innovative participatory opportunities for classes engaging with U.S. Latino literature. How might professors and students work together to create such enhanced editions? Striking models for such enhancement have become available for authors such as William Styron, Jack Kerouac, T. S. Eliot, and hundreds of other texts.

Enhanced e-books span a range of minor, relatively unobtrusive augmentations to cross-media enhancements that profoundly alter the book so that it is transformed into a multimedia text. At the less intrusive end of the enhancement spectrum, Open Road Integrated Media introduced editions of novels by writers such as William Styron and Pat Conroy in 2010. In order to avoid interrupting the experience of reading the text of the novels, a video clip is placed at the beginning, and at the end are biographies with text, photos, memorabilia, and videos. In this way, readers may choose to focus solely on the literary text or to view the enhancements when they desire. Similarly, Vook published an enhanced excerpt of Bernhard Schlink's *The Weekend* in 2010. This "video-book" opens with Schlink explaining the background of the book, with close-ups that allow us a sense of intimacy with the visually present author rather than only the implied author. Subsequent chapters open with graphic video clips of the Baader-Meinhof group's violence, the group's psychological and political mindset, and links to maps and other background material. However, although these are only minor enhancements, some students told me they would rather read the text themselves before hearing the author's explanations. Nonetheless, various modes of engagement are available in enhanced books, and readers may choose to open the links later if desired.

In June 2011, Penguin introduced a rich amplified edition of Jack Kerouac's *On the Road*. The application opens with visual/verbal links to the text of the novel and four categories of enhancements on the "front cover," surrounding the title and author lines. The amplified material includes videos, photos, audio of Kerouac reading, his essays on the Beat Generation and other writing, maps, and sketches of his late 1940s trips across the United States and Mexico, textual comparisons between the scroll and the first edition, commentary, memos and letters, and photos and brief biographies of the members of the Beat Generation. Throughout the digital text of the novel are links in the margins to the corresponding biographies of the people various characters represent. Although "The Book" link to the text itself appears in the upper left-hand corner of the opening screen, the other attractive visual links to the amplifications most likely draw readers in first. These lead to extensive paratexts where readers can spend hours engaging with fascinating information before even beginning to read the novel. For some, the word-only text of the novel must wait while they engage with the glitzy new enhancements Penguin provides. In contrast, readers often skip standard introductions of books, anxious to begin reading the text proper. When and if one clicks in the upper left corner and decides to spend time with the novel itself, the reading experience is relatively uninterrupted. Discretely placed sidebar links may be tapped for information on who the characters represent and other cultural references. Despite its richness, this enhanced e-book raises key issues that students need to discuss about balancing the extra material they add to Latino literary texts.

Among the dozens of noteworthy enhanced editions of literary texts are Penguin's amplified edition of Steinbeck's *Of Mice and Men* (www.penguin.com/static/pages/features/of_mice_and_men.php), T. S. Eliot's *The Wasteland* by Touch Press (https://itunes.apple.com/us/app/the-waste-land/id427434046?mt=8), and Globe Education's enhanced editions of *Romeo and Juliet* and other Shakespeare plays in the iBookstore. Particularly useful for the project of participatory learning in classes on U.S. Latino literature is *Digital Dubliners*, a 2014 iBook made by students at Boston University with Professor Joseph Nugent.

The 15 students in Nugent's class were each responsible for thoroughly researching one of the stories in Joyce's *The Dubliners*, constructing an annotated bibliography of key secondary sources, writing a critical essay on it, and creating a related chapter for the enhanced iBook. The students were subdivided into four peer-editing groups, supporting and critiquing one another as they worked on their essays for over a month. They also participated in five operational subgroups related to the technology of iBook creation: layout and design, editing, marketing, technology, and audio. This collective effort, combined with the expertise of Professor Nugent and other Joyce scholars, resulted in an extraordinary enhanced e-book in which the whole is greater than the sum of its parts.

The students glossed many words in Joyce's book, listing some of these annotations in sidebar links that readers who so desire may tap to access a text box with extra material about the person, term, or context. Many sidebars contain pictures that can be enlarged and examined in more detail when tapped, revealing an explanatory caption. Sometimes the images are interleafed between pages of the stories, interrupting the narrative flow. The students also created video "office hours" with two Joyce scholars that appear at various points in the book. In short videos before each story, the student who is responsible for the chapter introduces the text, previewing their critical essay and annotated bibliography and inviting readers to enjoy the story. Among the enhancements in each chapter are maps showing the location of each story's setting, explanatory videos and interviews, visualizations, artworks, contemporary ads, photographs, music, newspapers, books, magazines, and other related elements of Irish material culture (see Figure 17.1).

The group's creativity is evident not only in the usefulness and scope of the enhancements but in the students' use of the innovative formatting of iBooks Author software.

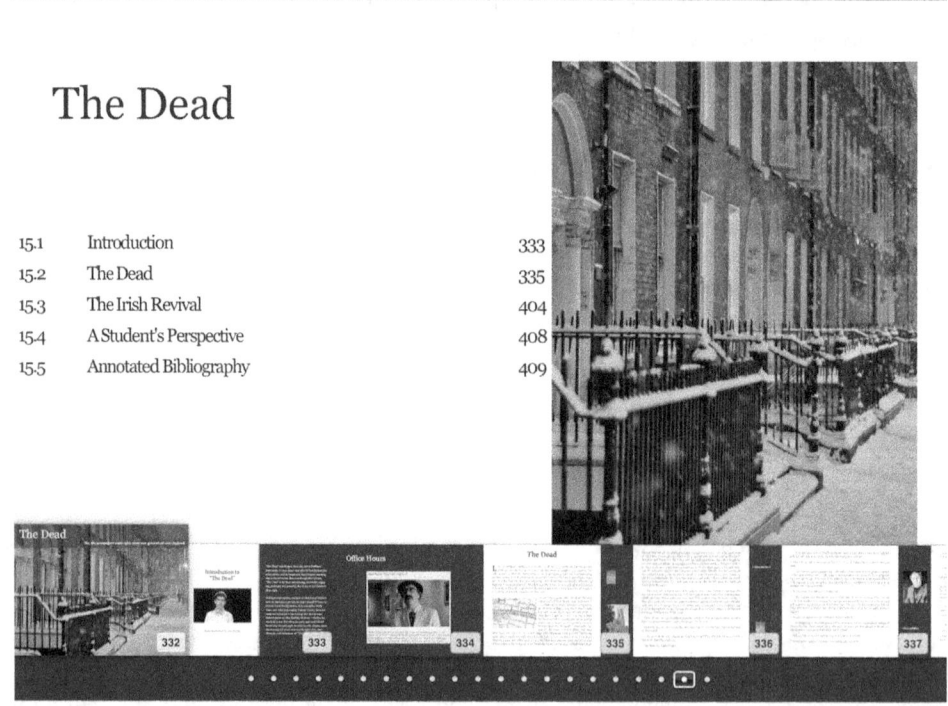

The Dead

Figure 17.1 "The Dead" screenshot, *Digital Dubliners*

Photo boxes sometimes contain several related pictures that can be swiped to view one by one, and camera shots move across still archival images to create a sense of motion. Joyce's death mask is included in one chapter as a 3-D image that can be examined from several viewing angles when manipulated by touching the iPad screen. The students were able to obtain an archival video of the 1903 motorcar race in Ireland on which Joyce based the story "After the Race." All of the enhancements reflect painstaking research, excitement about the literary texts, and insightful analysis. How might similar projects be designed for U.S. Latino literature?

Enhanced U.S. Latino books

In early 2011, about a year after enhanced e-books began to appear, I approached Sandra Cisneros and her agent Susan Bergholz about editing an enhanced edition of one of the writer's stories. Although Cisneros seemed quite interested, her agent politely denied the request, noting that she wanted to wait to see the direction digital books would take. Publishers such as Penguin, Open Road, and Vook have experimented with enhanced digital versions of books that are out of copyright or to which they hold the rights. Similar work on contemporary Latino literature faces copyright restrictions and difficulties obtaining permission from agents and publishers. The participatory class work I discuss here therefore takes a two-pronged approach. The first option is that students work with the literary texts studied that are under copyright protection, designing enhanced e-books that they do not immediately upload to the iBookstore for public consumption but rather share with each other as a class or conference presentation. (The software allows authors to preview their work with the iBooks app.) Subsequently, this work can be shown to publishers, agents, and authors and will perhaps entice them to agree to the digital publication of the attractive educational editions. A second option is the creation of a critical iBook containing the same enhancements without the literary text that can be uploaded and made available to the public in the iBookstore and will serve as a digital companion to the printed literary work. Both projects have great educational value, excite students about the literary works we study, and teach new research and digital skills.

Such class projects follow the methods of publishing houses that have begun to create enhanced e-books. Small editorial and production teams carefully design enhancements that augment the literary text without overwhelming it. The creation of enhanced e-books often involves teamwork and as a learning strategy in the classroom helps to counteract the dominant American ideology of individualism. These new digital research projects not only teach the cooperation and teamwork that students will find useful in their careers but also allow them to master a software interface, a skill that they can add to their resumés.

In more specific terms, how might Chicano/a/Latino/a literature be enhanced? To remedy the gaps in knowledge of the basic history of most U.S. readers, for example, (the result of what Junot Díaz terms the "mandatory two seconds of Dominican history" in American education) a novel such as Julia Alvarez's *In the Time of the Butterflies* (1994) should have electronic enhancements such as a map of the Dominican Republic and the Caribbean; photos and film clips of Trujillo, pictures of the Mirabal sisters and others who fought to overthrow the dictator and were assassinated by his forces, and the family home, now a museum; further material could include a video clip of an interview with the surviving sister, and a timeline of the diegetic and historical events recounted since the novel is narrated non-chronologically. The publishers of the print book used the form's limited possibilities of enhancement to move in this direction by creating a wall of names on the inside front and back covers, listing those assassinated by Trujillo's forces, with the book's protagonists in boldface, drawings by the youngest sister, and a prison diary with censored words blacked out. The new opportunities for enhancement available on such devices as the iPad can extend these initial narrative gestures that try to expand the static print medium.

For another enhanced e-book, imagine hearing the exuberant notes of Lalo Guerrero singing "La minifalda de Reynalda" as you read Patricia Preciado Martin's "Amor Prohibido" in her story collection, *Amor Eterno: Eleven Lessons in Love* (2000). The teenager Lola blows into town one summer dressed like the go-go dancer Reynalda in the song, whose miniskirt allows everyone to see "hasta la espalda" when she bends over. Or what if we could hear the poignant strains of Juan Gabriel or Rocío Durcal singing "Amor Eterno" as we read about the widow who still sets a place at the table for her deceased husband in the story "Amor inolvidable."[4] While the print book includes the song lyrics as epigraphs to each story, and this allows readers to construct some degree of interrelated meaning, only after having heard the songs or seen a YouTube video performance can readers adequately understand Preciado Martin's narratives. The gestures and facial emotions visible in a performance video would more fully carry over the interrelationship the author intended in pairing the epigraph to the story. What if readers could tap a link on a tablet or smartphone touchscreen to hear the music so essential to the author's narrative utterances?[5] What if they could tap to see a map or Google street-view of the ten-mile pilgrimage that Dona Eloisa Contreras makes through the barrio in Tucson to pray for the safety of her son and the community's sons fighting in the Korean War? How might images of the church of San Xavier del Bac that she journeys to, with its **bulto** of San Francisco and grotto to the Virgin enhance the narrative experience? (see Figure 17.2).

I pair Demetria Martínez's *Mother Tongue* (1994) or Graciela Limón's *In Search of Bernabé* (1993) in the classroom with Luis Mandoki's powerful film *Voces Inocentes* (2005), asking students to think about the strengths and limitations of both genres for learning about the civil war in El Salvador. But what if new enhanced versions of these novels could include links to video clips from the film, maps, timelines, images of Archbishop Romero, the military's air attack on his funeral, the assassinations of Maryknoll nuns and the Jesuits at the Universidad Centroamericana, information on liberation theology, the Sanctuary Movement, and interviews with refugees? This material could appear both unobtrusively at the end of the digitized novels, and very selectively in links throughout the text. Publishers might be able to work out small royalty payments to copyright holders of this material who in turn might see the enhanced novel as an additional advertising venue for their work. Viewers of film clips from *Voces Inocentes* might then pay to view the entire film later, having had their interest piqued (see Figure 17.3).

I have always been frustrated that Sandra Cisneros's entirely verbal story "Little Miracles, Kept Promises" (1991) does not include any images of the predominantly visual traditions of the **ex voto** and the **manda**. These strong forms of popular religious culture among Latinos on both sides of the border are unknown to many mainstream U.S. readers and the story cries out for their inclusion. An enhanced version would include links to images of **retablos**, **santos**, and other key visual intertexts necessary to properly understand the narrative. Readers could quickly tap links to images or 3-D renditions of **milagritos**, the imitation metal miniature figures that petitioners pin to the

Figure 17.2 Church of San Xavier del Bac, Tucson

Figure 17.3 Memorial crosses at Santa Clara University for victims killed at the Universidad Centroamericana, El Salvador, 1989

states of saints in churches requesting "little miracles," showing the saint visually what they need; *retablos*, visual and verbal *ex-voto* paintings left at shrines in thanksgiving for favors received; images of the religious figures Cisneros's characters pray to such as the Santo Niño de Atocha, the black Peruvian, San Martín de Porres, the Guatemalan Black Christ of Esquipulas with contemporary devotions in New Mexico and San Antonio, Texas, El Niño Fidencio, the Seven African Powers who syncretize ancient Yoruban gods with Catholic saints, the Virgin of Guadalupe, and Chicana artist Yolanda López's contemporary rearticulation of that image which parallels the protagonist's development in Cisneros's story. This literary text cries out for enhancements to explain these key popular religious traditions that spill into the north from the south as migration flows. Such enhancement would not only augment the cultural competence of readers unfamiliar with the traditions but would open new paths of engagement with the visual expression so fundamental to these popular practices.

Luis Alberto Urrea's 2009 novel *Into the Beautiful North* offers key opportunities for an enhanced edition. Urrea humorously and poignantly employs techniques of estrangement and reversal to reconfigure the common migratory journeys of Mexicanos from south to north. The initial narrative disequilibrium in the text is the loss of nearly all the men in the Sinaloan village "Tres Camarones" who have gone north to find work. A group of young women, thoroughly versed in U.S. mass culture, decide to journey north as warriors to recruit disillusioned Mexican migrants in the United States to come to their village to replenish the supply of men in the town. The protagonist Nayeli decides this in an epiphanic moment watching John Sturges's *The Magnificent Seven* in the Pedro Infante movie theatre in Tres Camarones. She and two other women will journey to San Diego with the town's gay restaurant owner to recruit men to fight the bandidos (an ex-cop and a drug lord) who threaten the town's safety. "We can repopulate our town. We can save Mexico. It begins with us! It's the new revolution!. Isn't it time we got our men back in our own country? ... We are going ... to bring home the Magnificent Seven!" (56–57). Nayeli is driven by a double desire to reconnect with Matt, a handsome blond missionary who previously came to Tres Camarones, and to find her long-lost father who deserted the family years ago.

This quest narrative that reverses gender roles and migratory journeys relies throughout on allusions to Sturges's 1960 film. The novel's first line, "The bandidos came to the village at the worst possible time," the bandits' subsequent violent visit, and their failure to pay for their food at the restaurant corresponds to the opening of the 1960 film. Readers unfamiliar with this key intertext will miss the force of Urrea's politically laden role reversals, humor, and cultural commentary. An enhanced version of this novel would have a link to the first scene of the movie, or a trailer with various scenes—links that might also encourage readers unfamiliar with the film to then view the entire movie.

The enhanced novel would also need a link to a YouTube clip of the pre-text of the 1960 film, Kurosawa's 1954 *The Seven Samurai*. The novel frequently alludes to both films and requires readers' cultural competence to decode the allusions. Urrea's description of the mountain of trash where **pepenadores** in Tijuana have erected shrines to their dead loved ones is a quotation of the mounds with samurai swords displayed in tribute in Kurosawa's film. From these Tijuana mounds the colorful figure Atómiko surfaces, a reincarnation of Kurosawa's Toshiro Mufine, the rough Ronin warrior. Urrea's character protects the group on their journey north.

There are dozens of references that an enhanced novel could choose to incorporate. Maps of the bus journey to Tijuana from Tres Camarones and the subsequent trip across the United States would help to situate readers geographically. Images of the border fence, Google street views of downtown Tijuana, the low-rent sections of Clairemont in San Diego, and Camp Guadalupe in north San Diego would make the novel's settings visually present. Tía Irma insists that Yul Brynner is a Mexicano because he lives in Acapulco but few students today (most born in the 1990s) know what this movie star looks like. There are references to Pedro Infante, Cantinflas, Antonio Banderas, the scandal newspaper, *Alarma!,* and many popular songs that need glosses. When the characters sign into hotels as Mr. & Mrs. Vicente Fox, Mr. P. Villa, and Mrs. S. Hayak and the innkeepers see nothing amiss, captioned pictures might help some understand the humor. An enhanced novel should gloss Urrea's neologisms such as "Los Yunaites," Pachuco slang, and other bilingual word play. An allusion in the beginning to fathers taking their sons to see the ice trucks in 1936 would be enhanced for many readers through a link to the intertext from García Márquez.

In working with longer novels, student teams may decide to enhance only one chapter or an important excerpt for these initial projects. They might design, plan, and record Google Hangouts with one another in which they discuss important issues in the text. They might decide to interview one or more scholars who have published important work on their author using Google Hangout software or an in-person interview that a team-member films. In some cases, the Latino author may agree to a short video interview or reading and allow it to be included in the enhanced digital book.

For enhanced e-book projects, paratexts such as these must be carefully designed to take readers only briefly away from the primary literary text when they desire more information and quickly back to it. A link to a video or photos of dictator Rafael Trujillo in Junot Díaz's or Julia Alvarez's novels, for example, must be a brief informational visual enhancement from which readers can quickly return to the text, rather than a series of hyperlinks taking them on endless paths from which return is sometimes impossible without starting over again. The literary text should remain predominant, with enhancements designed as supplemental enriching forays, sharing some characteristics of a classroom PowerPoint presentation that aids rather than distracts from the reading of the text. In reading the extremely well designed *Digital Dubliners* e-book, for example, I nonetheless found the strategy of sometimes inserting entire pages of enhancements between the story's pages disruptive to reading. Similarly, the strategy of alerting readers to key images and themes before and during the reading process sometimes interfered with the joy of discovery in one's own reading process. Perhaps a few "spoiler alerts" need to be included in the enhanced editions students prepare. Various potential audiences need to be taken into account in selecting and placing the enhancements.

Practical issues

While students should not be expected to have their own iPads, university computer labs have Mac computers that can download the iBooks Author software for them to use. Since the 2013 Mavericks OS update, iBooks can now be read on Mac computers, but students should also have access to iPads to experiment with the full functionality of the books they design and create. Private universities may have more funding to make iPads available to students than large public universities (Santa Clara University and Oberlin College are two private schools that I am familiar with that provide iPads for students to check out of the library).[6] I encountered many difficulties in obtaining the free software and iPads for students to access at my large public university when I taught a course in

2013 on enhanced e-books. The central library would not agree to put the iPads my department purchased on reserve for students to use. The computer lab was reluctant to download the free iBook Author software to its computers. Finally, the digital media lab agreed to let the students use the iPads there but its Macs were too old to download the new book creation software. Budgetary limitations made well-intentioned IT staff reluctant to order Apple computers because they are much more expensive than PCs. After numerous visits to instructional technology staff, I was finally able to arrange an adequate workspace for my students.

The issue of copyright is an important factor affecting the design and creation of enhanced e-books. Writers, agents, and publishers derive income often needed to survive (excluding, of course, media conglomerates such as Bertelsmann AG, which owns Cisneros's publisher, Random House). Some writers are now struggling to retain the digital rights to their printed work and to reach fair agreements with publishers who wish to increase profit by paying paltry royalties for digital republications that cost them very little to produce. Since professors' salaries compensate them for research and teaching, and students receive course credit for working on such projects, enhanced e-books such as *Digital Dubliners* where the original work is now out of copyright can be made available to the public for free through the iBookstore. Contemporary U.S. Latino writers would most likely need royalties from any enhanced e-book editions of their work. However, some might be willing to allow a small portion of their writing, such as a story or a poem to be made available in an enhanced edition in the iBookstore as a means of advertising their work and thereby promoting future sales.

This occurred, for example, in the case of Vook's 2010 title, *On Writing the Weekend*, an ad for the English translation of Bernhard Schlink's novel *The Weekend* disguised as an enhanced e-book. The excerpt of four short chapters from the novel with introductory videos and a new short story by Schlink is a clever ad that, like many consumer products, disguises less as more. The four short novel chapters are augmented with professional videos of Schlink talking about the novel and photos and contemporary news footage of the Baader-Meinhof group, the subject of the novel. Together with the extra short story, this enhanced e-book claims to offer readers more when in fact only a sample of the novel is presented, much like the use of a larger container for a reduced amount of a food product. Nonetheless, suggesting to writers, agents, and publishers that the enhanced e-books our classes create might function as advertising paratexts at the same time that they increase knowledge, might make these parties more amenable to granting rights for these digital editions to be available free in the iBookstore.

Another key aspect of copyright is obtaining permission for the material used in the enhancements. Here the benefits of crowdsourcing this research among the course participants comes into play: students work together in small groups with the professor on the labor-intensive task of obtaining appropriate available material and permissions where needed. Apple lists several sources of non-copyrighted media for use in iBook Author projects such as Flickr Creative Commons and Wikimedia Commons. (See www.apple.com/education/create-with-ibooks-author/). Joseph Nugent's project at Boston University employs dozens of such images from sources such as the Internet Archive (archive.org) and other public resources. As part of the creative process, student teams can also take their own digital photos of relevant cultural phenomena when possible.

Other practical concerns involve time constraints in adding these labor-intense projects into a single course's curriculum. One strategy is to design a two-term course that allows one term for studying the course material and beginning the research for the selected project and another term (or portion thereof) for further research, design, and execution of the enhanced edition of the literary text(s). This might involve a second-term course with fewer credit hours than the first.

The choices about which texts to enhance should be made by the students after reading the course material. The class should decide if they wish to concentrate their joint efforts on a single literary work with thematic chapters designed by various subgroups, or if they would rather work in separate groups on several literary texts. In this case, the projects can be published either as separate iBooks or as separate chapters of an anthology for a group publication. Class size is an important factor here.

It is also important to be aware that we are at the beginning stages of a major technological change in the way in which books are created and consumed. In these early years, excitement about new possibilities of adapting printed books to digital formats must also be tempered with consciousness of the transitory nature of technological innovations. Sylvia K. Miller (2012) terms the enhancements now possible in e-books "magical": pictures move and speak, music on the page can be heard, and paths take readers virtually to other spaces, collections, and publications. She notes that enhanced e-books can take two forms currently: (1) embedded multimedia files are contained in the e-book itself or (2) the e-book contains live links to multimedia content that is hosted separately. The latter requires an Internet connection and runs the risk that hot links may eventually cease to function. The former makes a very large e-book that uses up limited memory on the iPad or other tablet device. Both forms run the risk of software obsolescence, just as the VHS video format and CDs are now being replaced with other media.

Enhanced e-books also raise important questions about the digital divide, class inequities in U.S. society, and which audiences might be reached through these new transmedial texts. Although e-reading is growing, large sectors of society do not have access to iPads or Mac computers on which to read enhanced iBooks. In my view, this is not sufficient reason to forgo the valuable software as a learning tool in the classroom, since the primary aim of the project is to teach university students about Latino literature and involve them in an active learning process with the best technology we have at this moment.

Another concern to be pondered is the changing nature of literature from entirely word-based creations to glitzy, visually enhanced hybrid textuality. By engendering new expectations about creativity in the digital age, do enhanced e-books contribute to the decline of interest in the artful writing that has enriched our culture for centuries? Will multimedia enhancements become a necessity for cultural communication in decades to come—a new audience-driven demand placed on writers? Or do enhanced e-books instead lead readers more deeply into the written word, revealing the subtleties and genius of great works of literature?

Despite the limitations in this early stage of the transition from print to digital publication, iBook Author software for creating enhanced e-books is, in my view, a valuable strategy for participatory research, creation, and dissemination of knowledge about U.S. Latino literature. Enhanced e-books can help to remedy cultural lacunae among readers through quick links to allusions in the text that would no longer require leaving it to look up a definition, reference, or image. I am hopeful that larger sectors of society will be allowed more consistent access to these digital devices as prices inevitably decrease. By collaborating on enhanced versions of Latino literary texts together, scholars and students will then be even more successful in democratically extending their research, expertise, and educational privilege to a wider public.

Notes

1 See, for example, Ed Finn.
2 As of June 2014 the most widely used tablets were Apple's iPad and iPad mini, Amazon's Kindle Fire HD, the Google Nexus, the Barnes & Noble Nook HD, the Samsung Galaxy Note, and the Microsoft Surface. In late June, Barnes & Noble announced that it would spin off its struggling Nook division from its bookstores because of poor sales. The iPad and Kindle Fire are the most widely used tablets. In October 2013, Apple CEO Tim Cook announced that 217 million iPads had been sold to date, while Amazon's CEO Jeff Bezos is more secretive about sales figures, noting only that "there are tens of millions of Kindle tablet owners" at the Amazon Live Event in Seattle, June 18, 2014. A Pew Foundation study in January 2014 found that 42 percent of American adults own tablets, and one half of adults own either a tablet or other e-reading device. Smartphones continue to be released with larger screens that facilitate the reading of e-books. With much fanfare on June 18, Jeff Bezos introduced the Amazon Fire Phone with a 4.7 in. screen that integrates Kindle reading enhancements such as highlighting, note-taking, "X-Ray" information on books including notes and highlights others have made, "immersion reading" with audio while one reads, device synchronization, and individualized automatic page scrolling activated by tilting the phone while one reads. See, Amazon Live Event; Apple Live Event; de la Merced; and Zickuhr and Rainie.
3 See "Kindle Editions with Audio and Video."
4 See, for example, Durcal's performance of *Amor Eterno* at: www.google.com/search?q=rocio+durcal+amor+eterno&ie=utf-8&oe=utf-8&aq=t&rls=org.mozilla:en-US:official&client=firefox-a&channel=sb (accessed June 14, 2014).
5 One prototype of this is *Beethoven, His Life and Music* by Jeremy Siepmann (Naxos Books, 2011) in the iBooks store, which contains two and a half hours of music embedded in the text. No connection to the Internet is necessary for playback.
6 See Grim and Gallagher (2012).

Resources for teaching e-books in the Latino classroom

Amazon Live Event. June 18, 2014. http://techcrunch.com/2014/06/18/here-is-the-full-video-of-amazons-fire-phone-launch-event/ (accessed July 2, 2014).
Apple Live Event. Oct 22, 2013. www.apple.com/apple-events/ (accessed July 2, 2014).
"Create with iBooks Author." www.apple.com/education/create-with-ibooks-author/ (accessed July 2, 2014).
Creative Commons. http://search.creativecommons.org/ (accessed July 2, 2014).
de la Merced, Michael J. "Barnes and Noble spins off Nook as sales continue to fall." *New York Times.* June 25, 2014. http://dealbook.nytimes.com/2014/06/25/barnes-noble-to-spin-off-nook-unit/?_php=true&_type=blogs&_r=0 (accessed July 2, 2014).
Digital Dubliners. http://digitaldubliners.com/.
"Donna Seamen interviews Sandra Cisneros," Oct. 20, 2003. *Internet Archive,* https://archive.org/details/DonnaSeamanInterviewsSandraCisneros (accessed July 2, 2014).
Eliot, T. S. *The Wasteland for iPad,* London: Touch Press Limited and Faber and Faber Limited, 2013. www.touchpress.com/titles/thewasteland/ (accessed July 2, 2014).
Finn, Ed. "Revenge of the nerd: Junot Díaz and the networks of American literary imagination." *Digital Humanities Quarterly,* 7.1 (2013) www.digitalhumanities.org/dhq/vol/7/1/000148/000148.html#yworks201 (accessed Apr. 12, 2014).
Google + Hangouts. www.google.com/+/learnmore/hangouts/ (accessed July 2, 2014).
iBooks Author software. www.apple.com/ibooks-author/ (accessed July 2, 2014).
"Kindle Editions with Audio and Video." June 29, 2014 www.amazon.com/s/ref=sr_pg_1?rh=n%3A133140011%2Cn%3A154606011%2Ck%3AKindle+editions+with+audio+and+video&keywords=Kindle+editions+with+audio+and+video&ie=UTF8&qid=1404082086 (accessed July 2, 2014).
McCracken, Ellen. "Expanding Genette's epitext." *Narrative* 21.1 (Jan. 2013): 105–24.
McKesson, Nellie, and Adam Witwer. *Publishing with iBooks Author: An Introduction to Creating Ebooks for the iPad.* New York: O'Reilly Media/Tools of Change, 2012. (Available to

download free in multiple formats—computer, iPad, Kindle, Nook, Android devices, and smart phones at: http://shop.oreilly.com/product/0636920025597.do (accessed July 2, 2014).)

Steinbeck, John. *Of Mice and Men: Amplified (Enhanced Edition)*. New York: Penguin, 2011. www.penguin.com/static/pages/features/of_mice_and_men.php (accessed July 2, 2014).

Zickuhr, Katherine, and Lee Rainie. "E-Reading rises as device ownership jumps," Pew Research Internet Project. Jan 16, 2014. www.pewinternet.org/2014/01/16/e-reading-rises-as-device-ownership-jumps/ (accessed July 2, 2014).

18 Latino/a young adult and children's literature

Jackie K. White

Throughout the 1990s Avon and Harper Books released a series of *Growing Up* anthologies addressing and edited by major Asian-American, Black, Chicano, Native American, Puerto Rican, and Latino/a writers, respectively. In his foreword to Ana López's edited *Growing Up Chicana/o: An Anthology*, Rudolfo Anaya reminds us that "growing up is one of the universal themes of literature [because i]t is where our values are formed" and how we come to "understand our place in the world" (1993: 5). In her introduction to this edited collection, Ana López states, "When I was growing up, I never read anything in school by anyone who had a *z* in their last name. No Gonzalez, no Jiménez, no Chávez, no López. And I grew to accept this and eventually to stop looking" (17). These two statements express the value of Latino/a, Young Adult (YA), and Children's Literature and the powerful impact of either providing or withholding that literature from developing readers, particularly those in the United States who come from backgrounds other than the historically dominant microculture.[1] While the identifying of various U.S. ethnic literary canons has been taking place for some time now, their respective YA components continue to be disparaged by English Language Arts (ELA) teachers (grades 6–12, middle to high school). They are considered too controversial or useful only for low-ability students—even though courses in these literatures are increasingly offered and often required for those studying to become ELA educators (Tomlinsen 5, 13). Furthermore, although Latino/a YA and children's texts remain especially disproportionately underrepresented and somewhat invisible in the classroom and in publishing houses, the number of texts available in these categories is growing exponentially and will continue to do so if educators and others more actively demand a greater supply.[2]

Given our students' need for this literature and that the majority of grade 6–12 teachers continue to be white females[3] (as am I) who, thus, may be unfamiliar with or hesitant to use Latino/a literature, this chapter aims to provide all teachers at all levels educating all populations of students with: (1) a brief background to these fields; (2) an introduction to some major Latino/a literary YA and children's authors and texts; and (3) an overview of teaching strategies and curricular approaches to making these literatures a more integral part of any curriculum, from pre-K to graduate school. It is my hope that, as more educators extend their familiarity with, deepen their appreciation of, and introduce students to the unique features and universal themes of Latino/a YA and Children's Literature, there will be fewer students who, as many of my undergraduates have done, nod their heads sadly in agreement when they read López's words.

While the value and validity of Latino/a literature for Latinos/as should be obvious, explaining its benefits for non-Latinos/as continues to seem expected. A survey of the most prominent YA and children's literature textbooks over the last 20 years, and the numerous scholarly sources that they cite, reveals that multicultural literature can diminish stereotyping (Athanases 1998), "raise the consciousness and awareness of differences between and among people across contexts, continents, and culture" (Boyd 2002: 89), and allow readers to "identify and collaborate with the perspectives and practices of opposi- tional subjects," experience shifts in perspective, and come to challenge "the workings of prevailing power systems" (Philion 2001: 56). White students in particular are often sur- prised by the historical *and contemporary* mistreatment that non-whites face (Bauman 1996: 105) who, in turn, are surprised to discover that they are not alone. Common sense, as well as a wealth of literacy theory, tells us that children develop as skilled readers the more that they read, and they are more likely to keep reading if they find relevance and pleasure in the content, language, and style of what they read. That relevance and pleasure come from seeing one's self and one's experiences reflected in the text and from making connections with others (Landt, 2006). Therefore, from picturebooks[4] and YA series to crossover works from the Latino/a literary canon, Latino/a YA and children's material has the potential to create lifelong readers from all microcultures and, thus, a more empathic, informed, and critically thinking citizenry (Leland *et al.*, 2013).

Young adult literature

I begin with young adult literature (YAL) because it is newer, less familiar, more overlooked, and undervalued. In textbooks and scholarly works, it is often included under (and somewhat obscured by) "Children's Literature," and it has received scant critical attention (Brady 2013 and Cappella 2010). The history of YAL—previously called "Adolescent Literature"—as an independent category is considered to have begun with S. E. Hinton's 1967 novel, *The Outsiders* (the title itself speaks to the liminal or **borderland sensibility** most adolescents feel in being neither children nor adults—a primary theme addressed in much *Latino/a* YA literature, as well). From 1904, when G. Stanley Hall introduced the term and life-stage of "adolescence," through the 1960s era of expanding civil rights and eroding social taboos, which contributed to the expansion of the YAL market, the literature taught to adolescents was almost exclusively "classic" adult literature, albeit with an adolescent (but predominantly white male) protagonist—*Romeo and Juliet, Great Expectations, Huckleberry Finn, Lord of the Flies, Catcher in the Rye*, and the like—works that continue to dominate high school curricula (Gilmore, 2011). From the 1970s on, however, the YAL field burgeoned, aided by the foundation of the American Library Association's YALSA (Young Adult Library Services Association) and NCTE's ALAN (Assembly on Literature for Adolescents)[5] and the establishment of several prizes for notable YAL, including those expressly for works by and about Latinos/as.[6]

The basic definition and chief characteristics of YAL as literature are the following:

- Features a young adult protagonist who matures as s/he drives the actions and resolutions of the plot and engages with relevant socio-political and moral-ethical issues
- Uses language, dialogue, and point of view authentic to adolescents
- Is marked by parental absence or conflicts
- Is written expressly for 11–18 year olds and marketed as YA literature by the publisher
- It resists firm and happy endings (http://highered.mcgraw-hill.com/sites/dl/free/ 0073525936/664244/Sample_chapter.pdf)

210 Jackie K. White

The criteria for Latino/a YAL awards are as follows:

- Require that the books exhibit exceptional literary quality
- "Authentically and engagingly portray Latin American, the Caribbean, or Latinos in the United States" (The Américas Award for Children's & Young Adult Literature, 1993: http://claspprograms.org/americasaward)
- "Authentically reflect the lives of Mexican American children and young adults in the Southwestern region of the United States" (The Tomás Rivera Mexican American Children's Book Award, 1995: www.education.txstate.edu/c-p/Tomas-Rivera-Book-Award-Project-Link.html)
- Be written or illustrated "by an author of Latin American descent and have as a central theme Latino cultural experience" (The Pura Belpré Award, 1996: www.ala.org/alsc/awardsgrants/bookmedia/belpremedal)

Nearly all of the texts I teach and that I will reference here have been awarded these and other prizes,[7] and among the earliest prize-winners are crossover[8] writers Puerto Rican Judith Ortiz Cofer's short story cycle, *An Island Like You: Stories of the Barrio* (Belpré 1996), and Mexican American Juan Felipe Herrera's *Crashboomlove: A Novel in Verse* (Américas 1999). Indeed, three prevalent trends in YAL are the increase in adult authors, hybrid genres, and diversity of characters (Collier 2012). Ortiz Cofer also offers the historical novel, *The Meaning of Consuelo* (2003), whose protagonist becomes the guardian of her schizophrenic sister during the Operation Bootstrap-era; *Call me María: A novel in letters, poems, and prose* (2004); and the realistic novel *If I Could Fly* (2011) which revisits *Island* characters, including the seemingly gay Arturo and the Afro-Puerto Rican Yolanda as part of the coming-of-age of Doris who learns to "fly" by embracing her acting and vocal talents even as they make her more like her parents. Herrera's *Upside Down Boy/El niño de cabeza* (2000) has been adapted into a musical, and his *Cinnamon Girl: Letters Found Inside a Cereal Box* (2005) presents the 9/11 tragedy through the perspective of a young Puerto Rican girl. Mexican American Gary Soto, who has also produced a range of YA and children's texts from his middle-grade short story collection, *Baseball in April* (1990) to his fantasy *Afterlife* (2003) narrated by the teenage ghost, Chuy, is another prominent example of these trends.

Highlights of other renowned adult writers adding prestige and diversity to the field includes Chilean-exile Isabel Allende, with her trilogy of middle-school fantasy-quest novels—*City of the Beasts* (2002) set in the Amazon; *Kingdom of the Golden Dragon* (2004) set in Himalaya; and *Forest of the Pygmies* (2004) set in Africa—which feature co-protagonists, Anglo-U.S. Alexander Cold and Brazilian Nadia Santos who repeatedly thwart adults' abuses of power and fight to protect native cultures and their environments. Dominican American Julia Alvarez likewise covers an extraordinary range of themes and microcultures beginning with her historical novel *Before We Were Free* (2002) about the De la Torre side of the García family who stayed in the Dominican Republic told in part through 12-year-old Anita's diary-written-in-hiding (à la Anne Frank); her contemporary realist novel *finding miracles* (2004) narrated by 16-year-old Milly Kaufmann adopted as a newborn from an unnamed Latin or Central American country who initially wants to be, and passes as, "100% American," but later journeys south to search for her birthmother; and *Return to Sender* (2009), a middle-school novel told in chapters that alternate between two 11-year-old co-protagonists—the French-Canadian-U.S. farm boy, Tyler Paquette, from a third-person perspective, and the first-person letters of undocumented Mexican Mari Cruz whose father and uncles work on Tyler's farm. In addition to Alvarez's Vermont, readers can experience Cuban American Oscar Hijuelos' Wisconsin farm to which white-Cuban Rico Fuentes runs away, to join his lottery-winning, college-bound mentor, in *Dark Dude* (2008).

Other noteworthy crossover YA novels include Cuban American Cristina García's middle-school story of Japanese-Jewish Cuban Yumi Ruíz-Hirsch, *I Wanna Be Your Shoebox* (2008b) and her 1970s boarding school transnational novel *Dreams of Significant Girls* (2011) featuring the alternating voices of Jewish-Cuban, German-Canadian, and Iranian teenagers; or Mexican Americans Benjamin Aliere Sáenz's bildungsroman of two gay boys, *Aristotle and Dante Discover the Secrets of the Universe* (2013), and Luis Albert Urrea's poem *Vatos* transformed into a book with black-and-white photographs, celebrating Latino masculinity. All these texts present fresh, nuanced, fast-paced, provocative, and entertaining complexities of the Latino/a adolescent experience that have resonance for all adolescents searching for who they are, where they belong, how to develop acceptance of peers and parents, and how to negotiate inevitable personal changes and unavoidable sociopolitical legacies. The range of genres available from these writers suggests how Latino/a YA literature can contribute to many curricular goals, and the blurring of genres reflects an attribute historically pronounced in Latino/a literature, as in the works of Gloria Anzaldúa and Cherríe Moraga.

Another attribute of this literature is, of course, the use of varieties of code-switching, which functions doubly in Latino/a YA texts given the "coded" language adolescents often create and use. (See also Christopher González's discussion of code-switching in his chapter in this volume.) Perhaps the best known work that educators have for years treated as a crossover text and that exemplifies generic blurring and lyrical polyphony is Chicana author Sandra Cisneros's *The House on Mango Street* (1984). I foresee the same happening with Dominican American Junot Díaz's *Drown* (1996) and *The Brief Wondrous Life of Oscar Wao* (2007), which are already being explored as accounts of adolescence as it occurs within both Dominican and U.S. sociopolitical contexts and in genres of "dirty realism" and hip historical footnoted-sci-fi fantasy. All of these writers build on now-classic 1970s' autoethnographic bildungsroman: Afro-Cuban-Puerto Rican Piri Thomas's *Down These Mean Streets* (1967), Mexican American Rudolfo Anaya's magical realistic novel, *Bless me, Última* (1972), and Puerto Rican Nicholasa Mohr's *Nilda* (1973). Their successes perhaps contributed to the recovery of Pura Belpré's *Firefly Summer*—written in the 1940s but not published till 1996—a middle-grade chapter book about seventh grader Teresa Rodrigo's summer in the idyllic Puerto Rican countryside and her suspenseful search for teenage Román's real parents.

Additional successful writers who became known first for their YA *and* Children's books include Mexican Americans Francisco Jiménez—famed for his migrant childhood and adolescence memoir-trilogy of *The Circuit* (1997), *Breaking Through* (2001), and *Reaching Out* (2008)—Pam Muñoz Ryan, whose *Esperanza Rising* (2000), often paired with *Grapes of Wrath*, presents a poignant Depression-era story of a Mexican girl's downward mobility after her father's murder forces her to move to the United States; and Matt de la Peña who emerged on the YA scene with *Ball Don't Lie* (2005), novel and film, which takes issue with white privilege even as the white protagonist struggles to overcome a traumatic, foster-care childhood with the help of his African American friends and half-Vietnamese girlfriend. De la Peña's *Mexican White Boy* (2008) examines la migra-border and father-son identity issues of the bicultural, non-Spanish but Spanglish speaking, baseball-playing, inner-city Danny López,[9] and, like

Muñoz Ryan, de la Peña also authored a middle-grade novel, the Mayan time-travel quest, *Infinity Ring: Curse of the Ancients* (2013) with an interactive online adventure game. As with the YAL by canonical Latino/a writers, these works also participate in a range of crossings that challenge stereotypes of what "Latino/a" literature can be and of what YAL is—from realistic fiction to fantasy, from nonfiction to poetry, and from the Latino/a microcultures into many others, addressing ethnicity, social class, race, region, religion, gender, and sexuality. As they demonstrate the universal values and appeal of Latino/a YA literature while inviting exploration of its cultural and linguistic unique-ness, these works are thus powerfully applicable to the crossing-overs all adolescents must negotiate.

Children's literature

In her chapter on "Children's Literature" for *The Routledge Companion to Latino/a Litera-ture*, Mary Pat Brady (2013) presents an analytical history of Latino/a children's literature beginning with the 1889 Spanish language periodical *La edad de oro* of Cuban nationalist exile José Martí, the 1932–78 illustrated folktales of Puerto Rican/Nuyorican Pura Belpré, and Mexican immigrant Marí Cristina Mena's 1940s' adaptations of her adult works into children's stories. While noting different critiques to which these early works are subject, Brady emphasizes their positive cultural and anti-imperialist messages that address the complexity and diversity of Latinidad through content that includes indigenous and African, urban and rural, United States and original homeland, class and gender, tropicalization and assimilation dynamics. The following decades were ones of relative silence for Latino/a children's literature; then, as with YAL, the publishing pace started up again in the 1970s, with Puerto Rican Cruz Martel's picturebook *Yagua Days* (1976) a contemporary, realistic story that moves from an initial *el barrio* setting to the island and home again to New York's Lower East Side, demonstrating both the circular migration of many Puerto Ricans and the motif of connecting second generation puer-torriqueños with their cultural roots. Similarly, Chicanos Victor Ochoa and Alurista (not children's authors per se) published their *Tula y Tonán* Spanish language picturebook series foregrounding indigenous influences on Mexican American culture, and publisher Hill and Wang presented the "La Raza: Challenger" series, three volumes of which are still available (Vol. 3, *Return to Ramos* by Leo Cárdenas; Vol. 4, *Tejanos* by Ed Foster; and Vol. 5, *Viva La Patria* by Camilla Campbell) (Brady 2013: 377–78).

Two prolific and renowned voices from the late 1980s on into the new millennium are Mexican Americans Gary Soto and Pat Mora, with more than 40 children's books between them, including the now "classic" picturebooks *Too Many Tamales* (Soto 1996), a heart-warming snowy Christmas tale of middle-class Latina, Teresa, learning about honesty and humor, and *Tomás and the Library Lady* (Mora 1997b), a partial biography of Tomás Rivera whose love of reading is supported by his abuelo, an oral storyteller, and a white librarian. Other prominent twenty-first-century Latino/a children's authors include Mexican Americans Diana Gonzales Bertrand, Ofelia Dumas Lachtman, Spanish-exile Alma Flor Ada, and Salvadoran-U.S. René Colato Láinez. These writers continue the crossover trend, having ventured into YAL, while adult and YAL writers venture into picturebooks—from Cisneros's companion to her *The House on Mango Street*, *Hairs/Pelitos* (1994), Herrera's migrant worker childhood memoir, *Calling the Doves/ El canto de las palomas* (1997), and Alvarez's four volume (so far) *Tía Lola* series, to de la Peña's *A Nation's Hope: The Story of Boxing Legend Joe Louis* (2011) and Muñoz Ryan's range of alphabet and counting books, biographies of Marian Anderson and Amelia Earhart, and a geography of California. As these latter examples suggest, crossovers into subjects beyond one's own ethnicity also occur here, contributing to a cross-cultural trend.

Non-Latino/a children's authors also are crossing cultural borders, recognizing both the diversity within Latinidad and Latinos/as' artistic and other contributions. For example, Dana Goldberg's anthology, *On my Block: Stories and Paintings by Fifteen Artists* (2007), includes three Chicanas/os, one Cuban, and one Puerto Rican. A fresh example of intercultural dynamics is the subject of African American Nikki Grimes' *Oh, Brother!* (2008), the story of a blended Latino/a and African American family told from the perspective of Xavier in free and fixed verse, while another African American picturebook, Debbi Chocolate's *El Barrio* (2009; Chicago's Humboldt Park, specifically), presents a young Latino celebrating his sister's quinceañera, a topic variously presented for YA readers in Nancy Osa's *Cuba 15* (2003), Gonzales Bertrand's *Sweet Fifteen* (1995), Sharon Weil's similarly titled made-for-TV drama, and the critical text/ memoir, *Once Upon a Quinceañera* (2008) by Alvarez. Latino/a picturebooks notable for nuanced treatments of race, gender, and sexuality are Afro-Puerto Rican Eric Velasquez's autoethnographic picturebook, *Grandma's Gift* (2010), which normalizes Latino racial differences by focusing solely on young Eric's discovery of artist Juan de Pareja and can be paired with repatriated Mexican Elizabeth Borton de Treviño's middle-grade biographical novel *I, Juan de Pareja* (1965; Newberry Winner, 1966); Mexican Americans Daniel Olivas's *Benjamin and the Word* (2005), whose protagonist is bullied for being Chicano *and* Jewish, and Rigoberto González's *Antonio's Card/La Tarjeta del Antonio* (2005), whose protagonist loves words but struggles to find those to celebrate his two moms on Mother's Day; and Colato Laínez's *I am René, the boy/Yo Soy René, el chico* (2005) and *From North to South/Del Norte al Sur* (2010) in which a young boy deals with the deportation of his mother (Brady 2013: 381).

To introduce all students, at any level, to the diversity of Latinidad, I would recommend Ada's free-verse and nonfiction *Yes! We are Latinos* (2013), which opens with the literal question, "What makes someone Latino?" and then presents 13 free-verse, first-person poems, each entitled "My Name is. I am [multiple 'Latino' and other identities]. I live in [U.S. state or city]. I am Latino/a." Each poem is followed by three pages of socio-political and historical context that explain the interplay between these multi-ethnic speakers and the United States, and address indigenous and African roots; issues of conquest and colonization, slavery and war, migrants vs. immigrants; Asian Latinos; Catholic and Jewish faiths; the connections between Latinos/as, land, and biodiversity; and Latino/a contributions to the United States, beginning 200 years before the United States existed as a nation. In the final chapter, the rousing end of Román's poem—"I realize the strength of my heritage / the contradictions of our history. We have been mixing for centuries. / into a greater reality, / a larger identity, / one that is now called Latino. / Yes! We are Latinos." (Ada 2013: 87)—is reminiscent of Corky Gonzales's 1967 dramatic monologue-manifesto "I Am Joaquín" (see Gonzales 2010) which could be brought into the upper grade classroom for further discussion.

As with Ada's book, nonfiction, and particularly biography, is another growing area of Latino/a children's book production, one that supports the new Common Core State Standards and often gestures toward transnationalism; for example, Muñoz Ryan's biography of Pablo Neruda, *The Dreamer* (2010), told in his voice as the child, Neftalí, and Mora's *A Library for Sor Juana* (2002), which blur Latin Americans into the Latino/a community. Exploring common topics of family and gender roles, these picturebooks also contribute to the emphasis on making explicit the universality of themes in Latino/a children's literature. Thus, Carmen Bernier-Grand's *César: Sí, Se Puede/Yes, We Can!* (2011) poem and prose biography lists on its back cover the "core values" that Chávez modeled—learning, service to others, self-sacrifice, respect, acceptance, etc.—while her acknowledgments invite young readers to celebrate "not just La Raza but la raza humana" and to find "the champion" in themselves and their lives. This affirmative sentiment returns us to the primary goals and benefits of children's and YA literature, and of Latino/a literature generally: to delight, inform, *and* prompt change. First, the experiences of Latino/a readers (students, teachers, parents) are validated when they see themselves reflected in literary characters and as potential artists and writers. Second, Latinos/as and non-Latinos/as alike are invited to experience and appreciate the unique (micro)cultures of Latinidad. Third, readers gain insights into themselves and into the dynamic complexity of our multicultural world by drawing comparisons, contrasts, and connections with others (Beach 2006).

Let me also briefly note that whether bilingual, as indicated by many of the titles above, or English-dominant with nearly universal code-switching, Latino/a children's and YA books almost always include glossaries and pronunciation guides, even when the Spanish is immediately translated.[10] One value of these language-rich texts is that children love repetition, and repetition makes the content more memorable. These linguistic variations also acknowledge the importance of validating the bilingual or Spanish-as-a-First-Language student while encouraging and supporting those students in the acquisition of English and English-only students in the acquisition of some Spanish. Furthermore, texts such as *Pepita Talks Twice/Pepita habla dos veces* (Dumas Lacthman 1995) and *Uncle Rain Cloud* (Johnston 2001) also take as their theme the issues of bilingualism from the perspectives of the child translating for adults and the adult struggling with language acquisition, respectively.

Many of these YAL and children's authors are published by Arte Público's Piñata Books, Cinco Puntos Press, and Children's Book Press, whose catalogs offer hundreds of other titles and whose websites provide excellent teaching guides. Well-known non-Latino specific publishers also support this literature—from Holt and Knopf to Scholastic and Simon & Schuster—though not as extensively as one would hope, with statistics showing that less than 2 percent (roughly 100) of children's books published annually have Latino/a content (Terrero). Nevertheless, given the prestige of all these presses, the increasing number of crossover authors, the prizes awarded to Latino/a children's and YA books, and the increasing number and availability of resources for them, their relative dearth is no reason for not including these quality works in every curriculum.

Teaching strategies and concluding remarks

From the preceding literature review, I hope that educators will arrive at their own epiphanies of how these texts could be integrated into their curricula, and I will provide just a few "best practices." While at the college level, discrete or specialized courses, such as Latino/a Literature, serve to provide students with the breadth and depth of sustained "focused study" and are part of specializations that may make graduates more marketable, for K–12 programs, in order to avoid "tokenizing" this literature, it is important to integrate (normalize) the full variety of Latino/a YA and children's authors within—that is, *as*—U.S. American literature typically taught to high school juniors, for example, or as part of units on genre or themes in an elementary or middle school curriculum. As those who teach K–12 are aware, students at all levels benefit from (1) having choice, balance, variety, and in-class reading time; (2) hearing texts read aloud; (3) engaging in both experiencing and responding activities; and (4) a curriculum structured in a "text set" approach—a collection of five to eight works across all genres (one to three for whole-class reads and others for individually selected choices) addressing a central topic.[11] *Combining* these pedagogies offers students a rich comparative experience that leads to greater critical thinking through attention to the nuances and complexities within and across cultural experiences that shape how we see ourselves and others.

Integrating Latino/a children's and YAL is also a fun, non-threatening way to increase literacy for older students who may struggle with or resist reading, a non-confrontational introduction to an "other" culture for non-Latinos/as of all ages, and an opportunity to validate and promote cross-cultural bilingualism. Picturebooks offer a more efficient, creative, and memorable means of "teaching" contexts by bringing historical events and figures to life. They also prompt reflection by filling in much of our untold national story, while the blend of visuals and words lend themselves to increasingly sophisticated levels of analysis. Therefore, as noted at the outset, even in schools with no Latino/a students, these texts are needed to show students more of the world they live in and to let them *see and experience* the achievements, contributions, and cultural practices of this fastest-growing segment of our national population with roots throughout our hemisphere.

Finally, using Latino/a Children's and YAL presents older students with a continuum of Latino/a literature and younger or less-experienced readers with an engaging segue to "grown-up" texts. Imagine, for example, the enrichment and excitement for an older student encountering *The House on Mango Street* to have read *Hair/Pelitos* in grade-school, or reading Tomás Rivera's *… y no se lo tragó la tierra/And the Earth Did Not Devour Him* having read Mora's *Tomás and the Library Lady,* or pre-viewing a text-set of García and Hijuelos adult and YA books by reading aloud Edie Colón's *Good-bye Havana! Hola New York!* (2011). Might it be possible that a middle grade class reading Belpré's *Firefly Summer* could "teach" one of her folktales or Martel's *Yagua Days* to their younger peers? The possibilities for pairings within and across levels of our curricula and institutions is endless, and developing such pairings could be an effective assignment for students of all ages; teacher candidates and graduate students could conduct pedagogical and archival work by exploring the available books by Belpré, Mena, and the La Raza series, for instance.

The aims of this chapter have been to make more visible Latino/a young adult and children's literature and its value for teachers and students. Among the critical roles it plays is as a counter to the continuing "Whitening" of Children's Literature and other multicultural "backlash" attitudes and policies in our current national climate.[12] Unless educators take the initiative to embed Latino/a (and other multicultural) children's and YAL as "standards" in their curricula, non-Latinos will continue to misunderstand and target Latinos/as even as their numbers and roles in the United States continue to grow, and, like Ló, Latino/a children will continue to search for voices and faces like their own to authenticate their sense of self and to propel them into lifelong reading. As we are well aware, ethnocentrism and other prejudices are learned; therefore, they can be unpacked by engaging all students, pre-K through graduate school, Latinos/as and non-Latinos/as, in the critical and creative thinking that the early, integrated, repeated, and full reading of Latino/a YA and Children's literature provokes.

Notes

1 This term comes from the work of Banks and Banks (1993) who offer a way to move out of the "dominant culture"–"multicultural" paradigm by asking us to consider the prevailing white, male, middle class, able-bodied, heterosexual Christian, English speakers as one among many micro-cultures that make up the larger U.S. macroculture (Tomlinson and Lynch-Brown 2007). See also Hintz and Tribunella (2013) for a discussion of the problematic term "ethnic" given that Caucasians also belong to ethnicities.
2 According to University of Wisconsin-Madison's annual tracking, of 5,000 children's books published in 2013, only 1.8 percent featured any Latino/a characters (see Terrero 2014).
3 Bucher and Hinton 2011, citing Hill (38), and Bushman and Bushman (1993: 139).
4 See Bond (2010) on the use of the conjoined term "picturebook" to indicate the integration of words and images and that genre's ability to expand "the aesthetic consciousness of the reader in both spatial and temporal ways" (2010: 85). For analysis of the use of picturebooks with older students, see Bond (2010) and Hintz and Tribunella (2013).
5 The websites for each of these organizations offer reading lists, teaching guides, and useful links.
6 Mark Aronson critiques the establishment of these prizes as "balkanizing" the literature, while Andrea Davis Pinkney notes the dearth of award recognition previously given to non-white texts/authors (Hintz and Tribunella: 273–75).
7 These prizes include Victor Martínez's National Book Award for his YA novel, *Parrot in the Oven: Mi Vida* (1996), and three Caudill Awards for Pam Muñoz Ryan, Newberry's and others.
8 This trend for renowned writers of adult literature to have begun writing expressly YA books is noted by Cappella (2010). I discuss this trend among Latino/a authors at length in an article on Latino/a YAL and *concientización* forthcoming in *alter/nativas*.
9 For a fuller discussion of these de la Peña novels, see Hughes-Hassell (2013) on counter-storytelling.
10 For the many Spanish-only books available for YA's and children, see Schon (2004).
11 Excellent examples of text-sets and other activities can be found in the textbooks provided in "Other Resources."
12 The 2010 policies in Arizona to remove and ban multicultural, particularly Latino/a literature, from classrooms and curricula are perhaps the most egregious example. See also Atkins (2014) and Terrero (2014) and Nancy Larrick's 1965 groundbreaking article, "The All-White World of Children's Books."

Resources for teaching Latino/a young adult and children's literature

Atkins, Laura. "What's the story? Reflections on white privilege in the publication of children's books." https://sites.google.com/site/tockla/ (accessed May 29, 2014).

Augenbraum, Harold, and Margarite Fernández Olmos. *U.S. Literature: A Critical Guide for Students and Teachers.* Westward, CT: Greenwood, 2000.

Beach, Richard, Appleman, D., and Hynds, S. *Teaching Literature to Adolescents.* 2nd edn. New York: Routledge, 2006.

Bond, Ernest L. *Literature and the Young Adult Reader.* Boston: Pearson, 2010.

Herz, Sarah K., and Donald R. Gallo. *From Hinton to Hamlet: Building Bridges between Young Adult Literature and the Classics.* Westport, CT: Greenwood Press, 2005.

Hintz, Carrie, and Eric L. Tribunella. *Reading Children's Literature: A Critical Introduction.* Boston, MA: Bedford/St. Martin's, 2013.

Hughes-Hassell, Sandra. "Multicultural young adult literature as a form of counter-storytelling." *The Library Quarterly* 83.3 (July 2013): 212–28.

Leland, Christine, Mitzie Lewison, and Jerome Harste. *Teaching Children's Literature: It's Critical.* New York: Routledge, 2013.

Terrero, Nina. "Kid's lit primary color: white." *Entertainment Weekly* (11 April 2014): 68–69.

Tomlinson, Carl M., and Carol Lynch-Brown. *Essentials of Young Adult Literature.* Boston: Pearson, 2007 and 2010.

York, Sherry. *Children's and Young Adult Literature by Latino Writers: A Guide for Librarians, Teachers, Parents, and Students.* Worthington, OH: Linworth, 2002.

Zimmerman, Marc. *U.S. Latino Literature: An Essay and Annotated Bibliography.* Chicago: March/Abrazo Press, 1992.

19 Teaching matters of class and style with chica lit

Tace Hedrick

This chapter examines how one might teach a U.S. Latino/Chicana cultural studies course through an **intersectional**[1] framework of socioeconomic class. To do this, I propose a sketch for a course which would, while maintaining those oppositional readings I believe are fundamental to Latina/Chicano studies, open our teaching to texts (and authors) that explicitly imagine *and* privilege middle-class lives, ideas, and values for their Latina/Chicano characters. The middle-class fictions I am specifically thinking about here go by the popular designation "**chica lit**." In particular, chica lit, written by and about self-identified assimilated, middle-class Latinas, elevates and naturalizes a commodified class status and concomitant sense of "style" as an essential component of its characters' very life trajectories. Here I read class-related style not merely as a question of clothing or accessories but also of gesture, language, stance, and even values. As such, as I hope to briefly show, it is also central to more traditionally accepted texts, which engage in representations of working-class, immigrant, or exiled Latino/a subjects.

Indeed, important theorists of class, as Tom Nesbit notes in his "Class and Teaching," lay out for us a much more complex notion of relations between class structures, one which I extend to the relations between people's active engagement with style:

> The sociologist Max Weber, for instance, argued at the turn of the twentieth century that class is better defined by including notions of culture, politics, and ... style. People who fall within the same economic class may occupy different social class positions and have differing opportunities ... Weber discussed a system of social stratification with many different classes that sometimes overlap. Such less deterministic concepts of class take into account other stratifying factors, such as gender, race, ethnicity, place of residence, and age ... More recently, class has come to be regarded as a relation that is constantly changing ... Thus, class structures are not predetermined or imposed from without but subtly reproduced through people's actions.
>
> (2005: 16)

In designing a Latino/Chicana cultural studies course through an intersectional framework of socioeconomic class one could profitably use a wide variety of Latina/Chicana texts, including chica lit. Such a course could take as its overarching theme the way "style" manifests complications of class. Critical and theoretical ideas about socioeconomic class would act as the critical framework through which issues of race, gender, sexuality, and especially the construction and commodification of Latino "identity" might be illuminated.[2] Most importantly, such a framework would allow for seemingly unusual comparative readings between mid-twentieth and twenty-first century Latino/a texts. Taking a hint from Erin Hurt's most excellent essay on the first-ever chica lit novel, Alisa Valdes-Rodriguez's 2003 *Dirty Girls Social Club*, I might call such a course "From Zoot Suits to Manolo Blahniks: Reading Class and Style in Chicana/Latino Texts."

Since chica lit is my touchstone inspiration for thinking about teaching class and style in Latina/Chicano studies, I will be taking my cues from it throughout this chapter. Chica lit itself is easily consumable, pleasurable to read, and consumer-oriented—think comparisons with Terry McMillans' 1992 *Waiting to Exhale* or Helen Fieldings' 1996 *Bridget Jones' Diary*, and Candace Bushnell's 1997 *Sex and the City*. A broad range of U.S. 20- to 30-something women characters populates these fictions: Dominican American, Puerto Rican, Cuban American, Mexican American, and so on.[3] I have shown elsewhere[4] that chica lit is written by Latinas and peopled with Latina characters, and shaped largely by the same genre formulae, and publishing and consumption constraints of "fast fiction"[5] as those romance genres directed principally at white women consumers. Its characters are class and economic strivers and arrivers, embracing the largely conservative tenets of individual success and material wealth in the late modern, neoliberal economic and social landscape of the beginnings of the twenty-first century. Oppositional commentary on racist or sexist characters or situations in these Latina fictions is truncated, if not deliberately undermined, and what passes as ethnic resistance is often no more than window dressing. As I have noted, for chica lit characters, a keen sense of named fashion—and its knowing consumption—is reified as class status. Most notably, material wealth in the form of luxurious style is all-important in transforming these chicas from Latina "stereotype" to Latina "American."

Along with other Latina/Chicano scholars, I contend that scholarly thinking about and canonizing of Latino/Chicano texts often operates on a couple of unquestioned assumptions. First is the assumption that all Latinos/Chicanas share the same life experiences of a working-poor, working-class, or lower-class status; second is the assumption that such a class status, when narrativized in Chicano/Latino texts, will of necessity be oppositional to what feminist theorist bell hooks calls "white supremacist, capitalist patriarchy" (2000: 52). Thus, it would seem at first glance that teaching chica lit in the Latino/a studies classroom might raise some concerns. After all, even though my classes are often majority Latino/a students, I teach Latino/Chicana studies with the aim to raise their critical awareness and consciousness about structural racism, heterosexism, capitalism, and oppression, via a close examination of the ways Latino/a cultural artifacts imagine and negotiate such material issues. In contrast, chica lit openly celebrates middle-class, neoliberal "Latina American" subjects, who not only reject but actively seek to displace the oppositional stance embodied in, as Erin Hurt puts it, "the likes of Edward James Olmos [in *Zoot Suit*]" (2009: 148). These are *chicas* who furthermore proudly adopt commodified romantic imaginings of heterosexual and material class bliss generally not available to those without white/class privilege: "In the place of zoot suits and raised fists, [*Dirty Girls*] substitutes Manolo Blahniks, purchasing power, and the performance of (upper-)class identity" (Hurt 2009: 139–40).

In the past, I have taught chica lit largely through the intersection of **genre theory** with critical discussions of race, commodification, and gender. Yet it is chica lit's foregrounding of (interlocking) matters of socioeconomic class as well as "style," concretized as class identity, which suggests to me that the reading of texts that privilege a middle-class Latino/a subject can be useful in discussing often-unexamined issues of class in the Chicana/Latino studies classroom. Using this theme, my students and I can work to illuminate how these texts imagine and negotiate a variety of ways Latino/Chicana identities are imagined, and why, through representations of socioeconomic class.

I find that using an overarching theme accompanied by a critical and theoretical framework or lens, to be a useful way of teaching students how to read comparatively the often-disparate texts[6] I teach in my Chicano/Latina studies courses. The questions around which I often make my choice of texts—questions of oppression, marginalization, resistance, citizenship, commodification, gender, race, sexuality, and *latinidad*—can profitably intersect with a course-long emphasis on socioeconomic class and the linkages with its concomitant component, taste and style. My students come from a mix of established middle-class (especially Latinas/os and white students, many from Miami) to lower middle and working-class families (especially my African American and Afro-Latino/a students). Yet all of them are often unconsciously themselves embedded in a **commodified** world that works in large part through **visual rhetorics of style**, so that young women and men alike are steered toward what appear to be individual stylistic choices but which often are part of larger discourses of *life*styles. Are you an Android or an IPhone? Is Starbucks, and its lifestyle choices of music, online news, and "sustainable" beverages, your "third place"? Is JLo or Marc Anthony your go-to music choice?

Such a world seems "natural" to most of my students. In *Modernity and Self-Identity*, sociologist Anthony Giddens notes that the seemingly endless choices of (life)styles promoted by consumer capitalism have much to do with making stratified relationships of power and privilege seem natural, saying, "as [Pierre] Bourdieu has emphasized, lifestyle variations between groups are also elementary structuring features of stratification, not just the 'results' of class difference in the realm of production" (1991: 3). For my students, then, paying attention to, and questioning, the willing embrace of class aspirations, **heteronormativity**, and consumer culture in chica lit could serve as a kind of comparative touchstone with other texts, themselves invested in other negotiations with style, class, and consumption in their envisaging of different ways of thinking about *latinidad* and *chicanismo*. Comparative work can illuminate for students how, across different texts and different subject-positions, socioeconomic class is part of a structural web which holds in place and naturalizes access to privilege or the lack thereof and often illustrated in discourses—both resistant and complicit—of style. In this sense, we connect the lessons of style as material negotiation with hegemonic dominance. Here, we as a class would be looking for a more fine-grained analysis of the ways Latina/Chicano texts have imagined, resisted, embraced, and negotiated both dominant and marginal, self-constructed and hegemonic, representations of ethnic "identity" and sense of self from the 1960s through to the present day. In particular, reading texts through Latino histories and changing Latina/Chicano regional presences can show them the ways a sense of (ethnic, racialized, gendered) selves has transformed in places and through times.[7]

Although the privileging of working-class subjects is often one of the implicit determining factors in reading/canonizing/teaching Latina/Chicano texts, prominent scholars have noted that what such a privileging means for thinking about how *latinidad* and *chicanismo* are constructed is not always explicitly discussed. Indeed, I suggest that poverty, marginalization, and oppression—as real as they are in Latino/Chicana populations across the United States—can be thought about in comparative ways alongside the marketing and policy imaginaries as well as realities of upwardly mobile Latinas/os. Otherwise, our choice of texts and lenses through which to read and teach Chicano and Latina texts can create, in the minds of our students, what Arlene Dávila calls a monolithic "imagined working-class" Latino/a subject (2012: 9). Although in their

"Mapping Latino Studies" Antonia Darder and Rodolfo Torres (2003) are more engaged with studying the material class realities of Latinos/as, their argument for a conscious scholarly re-engagement with class and consumer culture can also resonate with the question of textual readings. They argue forcefully for an

> explicit focus on class in Latino/a studies, looking at the political economy and the ways it structures the social conditions of institutions and community life, to impact on class formations; the increasing significance of class; and the specificity of capitalism as a totalizing system of social and political domination and exploitation.
> (308)

I would take their argument to emphasize that in Latino/a cultural studies, the same focus gives students and teachers a way to think about how Chicano/Latina fictions and other cultural work imagines and negotiates such material realities.

The cultural nationalist underpinnings of early Chicano and Puerto Rican politics, research, and canonization of texts have been re-thought through sustained examination of their assumptions of monolithic, masculinist "nations." Yet traces of these assumptions continue to contribute in unexamined ways to a Latina/Chicano imagined unity of cultural experience, lived somehow outside the boundaries of **U.S. hegemonic** constraints. In an interview about Latino/a popular culture, Juan Flores firmly maintains that there is no "cultural space *outside* of and untouched by the workings of the 'culture industry,' not in our time, and by now nowhere in the world." At the same time, he expresses optimism about the "productive agency in people and communities as they articulate their experiences in creative and innovative ways" (1997: 144).

Yet this is a relatively new way of thinking about Latina/Chicano cultural work. As Frederick Aldama notes, the upheavals of the 1960s and the complex, nationwide web of events and struggles of the Chicano *movimiento* called for a "move to identify a common ground" particularly "in the face of a common experience of racism and class discrimination" (2013: 41). Out of these struggles came often heavily contested incursions into the university in the form of Chicano and Puerto Rican Studies programs, where the sense of common ground served to maintain a sense of unity among students, teachers, and communities. In the "Editor's Foreword" to their edited *A Companion to Latina/o Studies* (2007: xxi), Juan Flores and Renato Rosaldo remind us, these programs (much like Women's and African American studies) were born out of "social movements and political struggles." They reiterate that within such programs, strong ties to their various communities "has remained a central philosophical tenet of the field to the present day"; in this sense, they call for Latina/Chicano studies scholars and teachers to be "committed and oppositional." Thinking about Latino/a (popular) culture as *interior* (though not completely subject) to the workings of what Max Horkheimer and Theodor Adorno (2002) called the "culture industry," indeed assuming that there is no "cultural space" outside such an industry, seems a far cry from Latina/Chicano "imagined nations" as a separate cultural space apart from U.S. hegemony.

Yet the concomitant emphasis on an oppositional scholarship can unconsciously privilege those cultural *texts* within which scholars most easily find oppositional or resistant characters and subjects. Such a privileging, conscious or not, can lead to under-theorizing both the oftentimes-ambiguous nature of resistance itself, as well as the intersectional differences in socioeconomic class and attitudes toward class advancement amongst Latinas/Chicanos themselves. Indeed, as Flores notes in "Latino Studies,"

> Both Chicano and Puerto Rican Studies have relied, for their foundational narratives, on the national concept ... The boundedness and relative uniformity of their original territories went largely unquestioned, particularly in demarcating each Latino group from an "American" nationality, mainstream or otherwise ... no new sociological terminology has surfaced that can account for the class relations resulting from the ... intricate transnational alignments and restructurings of present-day capitalism
>
> (1997: 215–16)

As Aldama also reminds us, the growing integration of certain members of Latino and Mexican American groups into the middle class (and I would add into white privilege) means that "class divisions ... [within Latina/Chicano populations] became more apparent." Citing David G. Gutiérrez, Aldama notes that "Given that poverty within the Latino/a population is 'double that of the general population' (Gutiérrez 2004: 23), it is more plausible—and even historically verifiable—that gains will be made based on class identification more than a pan-ethnic Latino category" (43).

Such class identifications depend of course on the varying socioeconomic landscapes of the United States, and are more and more dependent on the stratifications of a consumer culture. Indeed, in the last 15 years or so, there is widespread acknowledgment among scholars of Latina/Chicano Studies that, as Raphael Dalleo and Elena Machado Sáez put it, "Latino/a literature stands at a crossroads, a moment of consolidation and institutionalization for a field that has historically thought of itself as oppositional" (2007: 1). Dalleo and Sáez maintain that much critical reception of what they call post-1960s Latino/a literature, which appears more and more in mainstream markets, names its success as evidence of a move away from concerns with social justice (3). In their readings of such successful texts, they too, like Flores, read evidence of "productive agency" within the commodified spaces of mainstream publishing and popularity. In this sense, as we will see, Latina/Chicano studies itself has been forced to undergo changes in the most basic frameworks within which scholars research and teach. A brief look at writing from some of the most influential theorists in the field calls for more attention to sometimes-radical change in this work. In "(Re)Constructing Latinidad" Frances Aparicio names the early 1990s as the starting point for

> cutting-edge knowledge that responds to the historical shifts witnessed by our communities ... If identity is defined by the dialogic struggles between notions of the self and the constructions imposed from the outside ... then Latino/a identities need to be understood at the interstices of both.
>
> (2007: 40)

Flores also delineates some of this new scholarship yet notes at the same time that "updating the *class* critique ... is less visible within Latino studies" ("Latino Studies" 312, my emphasis). Antonia Darder and Rodolfo Torres make the most explicit argument that the "explosion" of new scholarship on Latino/a populations and work requires a "post-disciplinary approach to our teaching and research in the field," particularly in the areas of class and political economy (2003: 304):

> In the past, the retreat from political economy and class within African American and Latino Studies scholarship was stirred by a response to the narrowness of reductionist economic arguments. And rightly so, for many of the early Marxist

scholars tended to focus on class, without rigorous attention paid to questions of racism, sexism, or heterosexism. However ... such forms of analysis [can] engage class as intrinsic to all social relations, and thus, view all social arrangements as configured, dialectically, within the context of contemporary capitalist social formations.

(306)

This brings me back to my contention that adding texts like chica lit fictions, with their almost-obsessive attention to class status, to Latina/Chicano cultural studies scholarship and teaching will aid us in re-examining assumptions about the workings of socioeconomic class across a broad range of texts.

The remainder of this chapter, then, covers two main sections. First, I briefly look at the often still-unexamined privileging in Chicana/Latino studies of that "monolithic 'imagined working-class community' of the late 1960s and 1970s" identified by Dávila. The fact that the assumed coherence of such a community can no longer be imagined, as Dávila puts it, "in the present landscape" means that we are forced "to recognize how differences along the lines of region, class, citizenship, place, and race may be emphasized or eluded" (2008: 9). In the second section, I turn to textual and theoretical suggestions and examples for my suggested course that will provide myself and my students both the explanatory value of certain theoretical terms and ideas and the close readings which will allow us to think critically—emphasize, rather than elude—through some of the differences Dávila outlines.

Their Wal-Mart pants smell like tamales

One of the many changes since the 1990s which has demanded a re-thinking of Latina/Chicano work along socioeconomic class lines is the small but growing presence, in policy making, marketing, and even cultural work, of Latinos and Mexican Americans who are solidly middle-class.[8] In her *Latino Spin* (2008), Dávila brilliantly traces some of the ways that a presumably new Latino/a middle class has been "uncovered" by middle-class Latino researchers who themselves have become increasingly intolerant "with [what they see as] the stereotypical and unilateral portrayal of Latinos as poverty-stricken." Such researchers' own experiences, "at odds with dominant representations of Latinos as needy and poor" has meant that these particular researchers "have been especially prone to the 'corrective image mode' in order to correct images in which they simply do not recognize themselves, and that many [of them] blame for their subordination" (32). As she continues,

> After the disbanding of social welfare for Welfare to Work Programs in 1996, public policy think tanks saw poverty literally fall from grace as a policy issue that would garner funding support ... [thus] by the 1990s, the "legitimate," though equally filled-with-spin world of policy think tanks, would join marketers in producing influential studies and exposés on the Latino middle class.

(33)

A particularly influential voice on the Latino middle class would be that of "the Los Angeles-based pundit and commentator Gregory Rodriguez," who in 2001 authored "The Latino Middle Class: Myth, Reality and Potential" for the Tomás Rivera Policy Institute (33). Dávila notes that the fact is that while these studies' executive summary and conclusions on the Latino middle class highlight progress and upward mobility, upon closer scrutiny they all show a more complex picture, because the story is unavoidably more complex. However, this is not at all how these studies were received and covered by the mainstream press.

(34)

The mainstream press, eager for evidence of that seemingly rare beast, the Latino middle-class subject, flattened and generalized what is in reality a much more complex view of a Latino middle class. Indeed, Dávila notes, Rodriguez's own study "was intentionally focused on middle-class Latinos in Southern California and was not meant to provide a picture of Latinos nationwide"(33–34).

Similarly, William Clark noted in a 2001 policy paper for the Center for Immigration Studies[9] that Rodriguez's findings in another study on the assimilation and upward mobility of Latino/a immigrant families were also rosy. "Based on an analysis of citizenship, homeownership, language acquisition, and intermarriage, he concludes that immigrants are assimilating today, in the same way that they did in the past." Yet, as Clark continues, "In contrast to the sanguine views in the Rodriguez studies, a new analysis of Latinos in California raises questions about the progress of Latinos ... Perhaps the most surprising conclusion is the finding that low levels of education continue into the third generation [of Latino immigrant families]." Finally, Clark notes that "inequality ratios [which differ from region to region] are evidence of a bifurcating Hispanic population [into] two nations, unequal and increasingly separated" (np). One of the more interesting findings in University of Southern California sociologist Jody Vallejo's recent book is what she calls, in an interview, the "divergent paths" of two distinctly different kinds of Mexican American middle class families:

> The first is a pathway into the "white" middle class where Mexican Americans view themselves, and are seen by others, as much closer and similar to middle class whites ... more common among those raised in middle class households and white neighborhoods. They are often more individualistic ... they are not strongly tied to Mexican ethnic communities, and their Spanish language ability might be limited ... they are often able to disappear into the white middle class. The other pathway is a route into a minority middle class where your ethnic identity as Mexican American is more salient in your everyday life because you retain strong ties to poor relatives and the ethnic community and you have more opportunities to speak Spanish. Even the socially mobile second and third generations retain a more salient ethnic identity than their generational counterparts raised in solidly middle-class households.

(Rojas np)

Chica lit fictions see themselves as doing something like the same kind of "corrective" work as that done by middle-class Latino researchers, though without many of the complexities. One can indeed read chica lit as fulfilling a didactic function, in that it clearly attempts to wrest the question of what it means to be a modern "Latina American" away from what are perceived by authors and characters alike as class- and culture-based "stereotypes" of Latinas/Mexican Americans. At times chica lit complaints about stereotypes have the ring of truth, though these are nearly always undercut by a clear disdain for poorer

Latinos. For instance, Lauren, narrator of *Dirty Girls* and a columnist for a newspaper, notes one of the many ways her co-workers "other" her:

> First week on the job an editor strolled past my desk and said in the deliberate, too-loud English they would all come to use on me, "I'm so glad you're here representing your people". My people, as far as his people are concerned, are stereotypes: brown of face and hair, uniformly poor and uneducated, swarming across the border from "down there" countries with all their belongings in plastic grocery bags.
>
> (7)

Needless to say, neither Valdes nor her characters want anything to do with these stereotypes *or* with actual people whose material realities engender such images.

The Mexican American heroine of Kathy Cano-Murillo's 2010 *Waking Up in the Land of Glitter*, Estrella Esteban (who eschews her Mexican American heritage to the point of calling herself "Star"), also balks, early on in the novel, at embodying "stereotypes":

> Even though her parents owned one of the valley's top Mexican restaurants, Star nixed anything that didn't come between two slices of nine-grain bread. Not that she disliked Mexican food (*she had yet to explore it*), but as a second-generation Mexican American, it irked her that people assumed she spoke Spanish, knew how to make tamales, and smashed piñatas at all her birthday parties. She didn't want to be lumped into those stereotypes.
>
> (13 my emphasis)

The notion that Star's parents own a Mexican restaurant but she had never actually *eaten* Mexican food might boggle some minds, but that is apparently beside the point in this narrative. Such stereotypes, continually (re)constructed in the realm of the U.S. cultural and market imagination, are bound up with a vision of *all* Latinas/Chicanos as simultaneously "illegal, tax burden, patriotic, family-oriented, hard-working, and model consumer" subjects (*Latino Spin* 1). Yet chica lit narratives often insist that at least in part, these stereotypes actually *derive* from the outdated rhetoric of Latina/Chicano civil rights; Star's father, for example, was an "old-school" Chicano but has now abandoned that stance in favor of his love for Jamaican reggae. The modern *chica* must not only disassociate herself from such "old-school" ideas and values, but also actively work to undermine them.

In my next section, then, I look at how these fictions' entanglements of Latina identity with consumer culture, socioeconomic class, and style can suggest other fictions, theoretical readings, and approaches to the course I am proposing. In particular, Valdes's snarky and thinly veiled references to other Chicano/Latina cultural works provide rich fodder for comparative discussions across a variety of texts.

Our pachuco realities will only make sense if you grasp their stylization

The very marketability of chica lit itself—its own publishing success—is bound up with its heroines' ability to learn how to enact a properly modern and "American" style. Among other things, their taste is, or will be, inextricably intertwined with questions of marketing strategies and consumption: for example, wealthy, conservative *Dirty Girls*

New Mexican character Rebecca Baca's life revolves around making sure her style matches perfectly with her sense of her own class and professional position. She takes notes about proper style at business etiquette seminars, and her personal shopper buys all Rebecca's clothes at Talbots or Lord & Taylor's. She translates her conservative Latina style into her magazine, *Ella*, an obvious stand-in for the real magazine *Latina*, itself marketed to middle-class Latinas (and sister magazine to *Essence*). Finally, she will leave her bad marriage for a millionaire British-born, upper class African man whose style and values exactly match her own; the confluence of class, style, and proper heterosexual coupling will teach the reader that financial independence must be paired with the appropriate heteronormative capstone.

In one of the most oft-repeated citations from *Dirty Girls*, Valdes makes thinly veiled references to New Mexican feminist writer Denise Chávez's 1994 *Face of an Angel* and 2001 *Loving Pedro Infante*:

> In reality, we *sucias* are all professionals ... We're not ... like those down-trodden chicks in the novels of those old-school Chicana writers, you know the ones; they wait tables and watch old Mexican movies ... they drive beat-up cars and clean toilets with their fingernails coated in Ajax; their Wal-Mart polyester pants smell like tamales.
>
> (2001: 11)

Yet choices in men complicate the lives of both the *sucias* as well as the characters of the despised "old-school" Chicana novels against which chica lit like Valdes's constructs its class narratives. In comparing fictions like *Dirty Girls* and *Loving Pedro Infante*, superficial similarities often become points of difference in the imagining of Latino/a lives through class. Both novels, for example, describe at various times what Werner Sollors called "ethnic rooms": rooms whose decorating style combines "American," "ethnic," and "old country" objects together. Although Sollors contends that such rooms "reflect the conflicting realms of new country and old" (*Beyond Ethnicity* 1986: 16), the style of *Loving*'s bar, La Tempestad, represents instead the ordinary everydayness of inhabiting, without comment, all these realms at once: the main character, Teresa, can see that the bar's mirror

> reflected ... what I would call early Mejicano Mercado bar décor: lots of old serapes from the market in Juárez made into accordions that fanned out on the walls, neon Budweiser and Coors signs ... and a mishmash of old stained sombreros, posters of Baby Gaby and Al Hurricane, a signed photo of Trini López and one of Willie Nelson with a crew cut.
>
> (30)

Such an "ethnic room" combines Willie Nelson, neon beer signs, and Mexican serapes again without comment save for the main character's own humorous naming of its décor. Although the bar's décor is obviously "classed" for the reader, it is not defamiliarized so as to function as a representation of the bad taste of working-class Chicanas/os.

In contrast, the restaurant where *Dirty Girls'* Lauren waits for her *sucias* is indeed foregrounded and defamiliarized so that its own tacky style and class pretensions will alert the reader that it and its denizens represent *undesirable* places and lives. These are the places and life-experiences from which *sucias* like Afro-Puerto Rican Usnavys have "moved on up," or which the well-off family backgrounds of Cuban-American Jewish ("Juban") Sara or New Mexican "Spanish" Rebecca would protect them from ever having to inhabit in the first place, *gracias a Díos*. In other words, the El Caballito restaurant serves as the working-class foil to foreground the *sucias'* class distance from its greasy décor and depressed waitresses:

> I'm here … slouched in an orange plastic window booth seat at El Caballito … a Jamaica Plain dive that serves Puerto Rican food but calls it "Cuban" in hopes of attracting a more upscale clientele. It hasn't worked. The only other customers tonight are three young *tigres* with fade haircuts, baggy jeans, plaid Hilfiger shirts, gold hoops flashing on their earlobes … It's hot in here. Humid, too. The air smells of cheap men's cologne and fried pork. Someone in the kitchen sings off-key to a popular salsa song while dishes crash and clang.
>
> (2)

"Ethnic" rooms, art, styles of dress, music, classed tastes, and even consumer markets are clearly important in both fictions. Yet careful and informed comparisons might allow students to understand the ways in which these representations imagine the Latina/ Chicano subject quite differently.

In our course, one or several class periods might involve comparing the ways the characters, life trajectories, and values of Lauren and Tere are imagined, both of whom make—and endlessly discuss—bad decisions about men. We would quickly discover that that is where the similarity ends. Lauren's continual pointing to her own class status coupled with her "crap" love life symbolizes, in the world of the chica lit fiction, the need on the part of independent, sexually free women to have their lives rounded off by a heterosexual coupling with a man who has, or will have, the same class values and aspirations for material luxury as does the *chica* in question. On the other hand, the fact that Chávez's main character Tere is named after Teresa de Ávila, the spiritual mystic whose writings inspired Gian Lorenzo Bernini's statue of Ávila's body writhing and contorting in ecstatic communion with the divine, is only the beginning of Chávez's sly, feminist commentaries on Tere's life as a divorcée in Cabritoville. Her focus on recording the styles of Cabritoville's places and inhabitants mostly elides class aspirations; none of the characters are yearning for Harvard educations or six-figure salaries. Though it's obvious that Tere will never make much money, the novel instead is a kind of extended meditation on who exactly Tere might be, as a Mexican American woman, *without* a man in a small, largely Mexican American town. Chávez uses the style—romantic, sentimental, machista—of the Pedro Infante movies (Infante being the ultimate Mexican *mero macho*) as a foil for Tere's own negotiations with the reasons she keeps on seeing her married lover, Lucio. On the night they first get together, "Aquella Noche," Lucio invites Tere for a drink; she realizes, too late, that he means to take her to his well-used motel room

> at the Sands Motel, No. 17. His home away from home.
> Bueno pues. Ni modo.
> It was already over before it was over.
> And that, Tere girl, you puta cabrona, was the beginning of it all. Try and listen this time, girl. Just this once.
>
> (63)

This is the kind of down-to-earth self-examination with which neither Lauren nor her *sucias* engage. Rather, Lauren's problems with men (which, unlike Chávez's novel, the reader of *Dirty Girls* knows will be happily resolved by the end of the novel) are put aside for the moment when her *sucias* finally show up for their yearly reunion—each one described in detail by her name-brand clothing, bearing, regional ethnicity, and class status. When they are finally gathered, Lauren makes reference to and simultaneously attempts to undermine the importance of yet another "old school" text as she dismissively thinks, "the chicks be here, Eddie [Olmos], so move your tired old zoot suit over" (12).[10] The reference, as "insiders" will know, is from Luis Valdéz's play *Zoot Suit*. This play was made into a movie in 1982, starring Edward James Olmos as the figure of El Pachuco, platonic ideal of the zoot-suited, street-wise *vato loco*, a kind of one-man Greek chorus to the events surrounding the 1943 "zoot suit riots" between Chicanos and white sailors on shore leave in Los Angeles. Far from being "tired," the sartorial splendor of the zoot suit is refreshing both in its in-your-face attitude as well as in the main character's clearly ambiguous feelings about being a zoot suiter. Beginning the movie, Olmos slinks onto the stage in his "chuco stroll," wearing a fabulous black-and-red zoot suit, his pockmarked face a mask of *machista* pride and disdain. The movie, though it cuts lines from the play, gives students the visuals they need to read the play, where the Pachuco addresses the audience, directing their attention to his *trapos*, and making it clear that his *buenas garras* symbolize an entire worldview:

> Pachuco: ¿Que le watcha a mis trapos, ese?
> ¿Sabe' qué, carnal?
> Estas garras me las planté porque
> Vamos a dejarnos caer un play, ¿sabe?
> Watcha mi tacuche, ese. Aliviánese con mis calcos, tando,
> lisa, tramos, y carlango, ese.
> The Pachuco Style was an act in Life.
> precursor of revolution
> Or a piteous, hideous heroic joke
> deserving of absolution?
> The Pachuco was existential
> for he was an Actor in the streets
> both profane and reverential.

Again, in the movie, Olmos's lines underscore the "mythic" aspects of the zoot suit in its symbolizing of desires for, and resistance to, white masculine power: is the Pachuco Style a "piteous, hideous joke" or a "precursor of revolution"? Either way,

> It was the secret fantasy of every bato
> in or out of the Chicanada
> to put on a Zoot Suit and play the Myth
> más chucote que la chingada.
> ¡Pos órale!

(25–26)

Ironically, the main character of *Zoot Suit*, Henry Reynas, has already signed up for the Navy, though he takes one last night on the town to don his threads and dance with his *ruca*, or girlfriend. When, in the movie, Reynas is arrested on suspicion of murder, El Pachuco ridicules Reynas for his desire to be a Navy sailor, hissing his heavily accented disapproval in his best *caló* style: "They were going to cut off your DA, carnal. Put you in those tight puto pants, make your ass look like an apricot" (*Zoot Suit*). Each style— zoot suit or sailor suit—represents a different worldview and different aspirations, with Henry stuck in the middle of conflicting desires for access to privilege—or at least patriotism—via the military, or for *barrio* street resistance.

In contrast, as *Dirty Girls*' Lauren informs us, her Afro-Puerto Rican *sucia* Usnavys' own "ghetto" background (before leaving for the mainland United States, her mother named her after the U.S. Navy fleet stationed in Puerto Rico) has not infused her with a sense of resistance to class oppression, but driven her to attain a successful career. Lauren's first description of Usnavys bears citing at some length:

> Usnavys ... just slid up to the curb out front in her silver BMW sedan (leased), driving super slow ... so that all those poor women with all those kids and shop- ping bags from the 99-cent store hunching away from the wind and the snow at the bus stop could stare at her ... Knowing Usnavys, I would bet the Neiman Marcus tag is still attached inside [her fur coat] so she can take it back tomorrow ... Now she's taking her Tiffany key chain out ... triggering the little alarm whistle. It peeps three times, as if to announce: *Bo-RI-cua*! ... All the Dominican women working the deep-fry vats behind the front counter look over at her with their tired horse- eyes, and slip a little lower in their despair ... As she tiptoes toward me, I notice she's wearing sharp little Blahnik pumps.
>
> (12–14)

Although Usnavys "drinks in the attention, plays it up like a star," her class insecurities manifest themselves in her desire to force everyone "back home" to recognize her escape from this space of economic despair and her current success through over-the-top name brand luxuries, no matter that some of them are only on loan. She is also the only *sucia* whose lover, Juan, is "poor"; for this reason, she refuses to marry him until the end of the narrative. The ways in which her character is imagined, the only Afro-Latina in the novel and the only one from a genuinely poor background, might both compare and contrast in interesting ways with that of *Zoot Suit*'s Henry Reynas, different in time and place as they are, yet marked as they both are with conflicting desires made material in their "styles."

Here, I've suggested how in the space of a few chica lit pages one could provide our course's cultural studies syllabus with several fictions, a play, a movie, and even an examination of the class appeals of a magazine such as *Latina*. Naturally, other texts would be chosen as well: Michelle Serros's *How to Be a Chicana Role Model* (2000) suggests itself as a collection of stories which feature the aspirations and lives of what Vallejo calls "minority middle-class" characters; in particular, the short story "Seek Support from Sistas" where the main character's encounter with JLo is anything but supportive. Serros's *Honey Blonde Chica* (2006) ups the class factor with the encounter of two solidly California suburban Mexican American girls with another Mexican American friend, recently returned from Mexico and reborn as a *fresa*—a wealthy Mexican chica, as the Amazon blurb says, "complete with tight designer threads, freaky blue contacts, and that signature blonde hair" (Amazon.com). These are merely suggestions, and many other texts would fit the bill.

Conclusion

In reading, through disparate works, the function of style through the framework of socioeconomic class, critical and theoretical work is necessary for students to have at least a basic grasp of terminology and ideas. I suggest that such a course would center on scholarship that helps illuminate the often-slippery ideas of what constitutes, and keeps in place, class and status both across Latina/Chicano groups as well as across white, capitalist hegemony. Work on the marketing and commodification of *latinidad* in the writings of scholars like Puerto Rican Frances Negrón-Muntaner and Nuyorican Arlene Dávila would be invaluable; on the other side of the coin, fundamental discussions of class and aesthetics would have to include both Luis Valdéz's and Tomás Ybarra-Frausto's discussions of working-class *rasquachismo*. Basic discussions of what the term "class" means, as well as its intersections with ethnicity, might include Tom Nesbit's excellent chapter on "Class and Teaching" as well as Zulema Valdéz's "Intersectionality, Market Capacity, and Latino/a Enterprise," in which she examines differentials in access to class and cultural capital amongst Latinas/os in different regions of the United States. Her book, *The New Entrepreneurs: How Race, Class, and Gender Shape American Enterprise* (2011) is useful for other ways of thinking about "Americanness," class, and social mobility.

One might also venture the more accessible writings of sociologists such as Max Weber and Pierre Bourdieu, particularly Bourdieu's work on (cultural) capital and the hegemonic privilege accorded various uses of "taste." These are of course merely suggestions, and other theoretical work, along with other Latino/a criticism, could be chosen. No matter the material, the point would be to provide students with a critical vocabulary to recognize and discuss the fashioning of sometimes competing, sometimes similar conversations around wealth and poverty, opposition and complicity, immigration and citizenship in Latina/Chicana work.

These suggestions for the Latina/Chicano classroom operate on the basic assumption that Latina/Chicano "identities" are in some sense fictive—that is, consensual constructs that themselves express both internal complexities and contradictions. This is not to say that Latina/Chicano lives are not materially real, nor that class inequities do not have material consequences, but that such realities are constantly being negotiated and re-imagined in the cultural work that the lives of Latinas/Chicanas have produced. In this sense, the work of largely marginalized peoples should constantly be undergoing a process of being re-read, re-theorized, and generally paid close attention to. In this sense, such processes of re-visioning are about not just the construction of canons but about the *stretching* of canons; it is at the breaking-point of what are considered "real" or "representative" texts that some of the most interesting course work can be done, especially in approaching the histories, assumptions, and ideological discourses in which all texts are embedded. The middle-class, neoliberal Latino/a text such as chica lit must be, in my view, taught with the same kinds of attention to fine-grained differences, locales, and histories as we use to read and teach working-class, immigrant, or exile Latina/Chicano texts. It is a question of paying close attention as well to processes of **disidentification**—as the late queer theorist José Muñoz used it—that is, *simultaneous* identification with, resistance to, and residence within structures of power, privilege, and dominance (1999: 11). Chica lit is especially salient in this regard, in that students (especially my women students), fully, and mostly uncritically, immersed in neoliberal, masculinist, and romantic narratives can have a difficult time not being seduced into an identificatory reading. Yet the powerful seduction of Latina fictions like Valdes's or Cano-Murillo's—funny, absorbing, easy to read—only means that emphasizing the immensely varied and intersectional nature of Latina/Chicano histories of subject-formation—themselves often histories of disidentification, in the sense above, with late capitalism and its markets—should be important in teaching *all* Latino/a texts.

Finally, the critical rigor and vigilance we must bring to fiction like chica lit may re-awaken the ways we teach more canonical Latina and Chicano texts. In turn, such vigilance may open up the idea of what "belongs" in the Latina and Chicano Studies classroom to an examination of those ongoing processes of social, economic, and cultural changes which have always put pressure on how Latinos/as imagine themselves, and are in turn imagined.

Notes

1 In her essay "The Complexity of Intersectionality," Leslie McCall (2005) defines the term as "the relationships among multiple dimensions and modalities of social relations and subject formations," adding that there are "distinct and frequently conflicting dynamics that shaped the lived experience of subjects" (1771). That is, subjectivity is never merely the product of one or two material, formative "categories" such as race and gender. Instead, it is an enormously complex product of larger social patterns of hegemonic discourses of power, privilege, and inequity, in conjunction with what I think of as "on the ground" social and personal relationships. It is of course impossible to map out the fullness of all determining factors, but attention must be paid to such "multiple [intersecting] dimensions" (1772).

2 My own position as teacher of Latino/a and Chicano/a studies is as a feminist Latino/a cultural studies scholar. My upbringing as an only child by white, well-educated parents gave me middle-class cultural capital (we read books; television was not allowed in the house). Yet my parents' peripatetic search for a socially liberal Christian community took us not just to live in Pakistan, Mexico, and Guatemala, but on a downward economic slope as my father in particular gradually gave up interest in having or making any more money than was absolutely needed for a roof over our heads (though sometimes without running water). Still, I was situationally and not generationally poor. In the United States, my white privilege and cultural capital got me through where I didn't have economic means. By the time I began college at the age of 27, my grasp of Spanish, my training in literary exegesis, socially oriented values, and a lifetime living with what others would think of dismissively as "poor brown" peoples would eventually make me deeply invested in the teaching of Latin American and United States Latina/Chicano studies. Since then, my work as a scholar has been an ongoing process of learning and teaching both close readings and consciousness-raising, textual strategies and critical thought, theoretical terminologies and decolonization of the mind.

3 In this chapter, I switch between the use of the term "Chicana" and "Mexican American" because chica lit novels do not for the most part use the term "Chicano/a." Their rejection of the term "Chicano" derives from the fact that this term implies a resistant, politically aware stance having its roots in the Chicano/a *movimiento* of the 1960s and 1970s. In some novels, in fact, "Mexican" becomes interchangeable with "Mexican American" despite the fact that for most Americans of Mexican descent there is (naturally) a clear difference between the two. In other fictions, like those of Venezuelan-American author Lara Rios, "Latina" itself becomes, confusingly, interchangeable both with "Mexican" and with "Mexican American."

Importantly, in part because chica lit authors are by and large self-described as assimilated, at least second- if not fourth- or fifth-generation, Spanish accents for authors' and characters' proper names are often dropped as well; I follow their self-adopted usage in this regard, with the understanding that such changes often denote a deliberate change "up" in socioeconomic status.

4 See Tace Hedrick, "From *House on Mango Street* to *Becoming Latina*" (2011), "Chica Lit" (2013) and her forthcoming book, *Chica Lit: Popular Latina Fiction and Americanization in the Twenty-first Century* (2015).

5 Fashion marketers, economists, as well as feminists and ecologists have discussed the economic, social, and environmental impact of what is called, after fast food, "fast fashion"—cheap but

fashionable clothing made quickly, as well as made to turn over quickly and be easily consumable. The worldwide fashion giant Zara, as well as Forever21, are only two of the many (multinational) companies who depend on fast fashion. With "fast fiction," I extend the analogy to certain genres of fiction, beginning with romance fiction, but extending into chick lit and chica lit, which authors for multinational publishers produce as quickly as possible. The ethos of the easily consumable, pleasurable text extends into these genres' own characterization of worlds and characters that embrace consumption as part and parcel of a heteronormative, success-oriented, modern life.

6 That is, not just written texts but other cultural artifacts such as visual art, music, movies and television, content on the Web, advertisements, and comics.

7 I follow theorists of modernity such as Frederic Jameson and Anthony Giddens in positing the self-replicating and deeply pervasive structure of global capital itself as a central actor in interpellating, that is "hailing," a late modern subject into being. It is tempting to speculate that, as the State was a privileged actor in the formation of subjectivities for Luis Althusser, and the capitalist and proletariat for Karl Marx, in a fully "developing" late modern capitalism like that of the United States we would have to go even farther than Antonio Gramsci's notion of hegemony and/or Foucault's decentralizing power. Rather than Althusser's "hey you!" of the policeman, then, it is the seductive promise of a commodified and seemingly magically, ever-available manmade object-world via which we are called into subjectivity. Rejecting history as "the passed," the market-realm of the ever-new structures a hegemony wherein the subject is required to move only in one direction: toward that of the life of the utopic material world of instantaneous being-everywhere. The anxiety produced by the "promise" of such a world versus the privilege one must have to live in it is sharply outlined by the relatively new social media acronym "FOMO." "Fear of missing out" is shaped by this absorptive yet exclusive sphere and sharpened by social media itself, which helps to drive desires for access, privilege, mastery, and control in what black feminist bell hooks identifies in *Teaching to Transgress* as a "dominator culture" (1994: 86) about which, she warns, we must be ever-vigilant.

For Giddens, the "self," now, is at least partially constructed through the questions "What to do? How to act? Who to be?" (301). Thinking of such questions as animating the "self" of late modernity may allow us to move away from totalizing theories of ethnic and racialized "cultural identity" especially in an older anthropological sense, while still understanding that modernity brings its own re-toolings of inequity and lack of access to resources both for the self and its changing "communities." Indeed, Giddens posits that the processes of "late modernity" (what Marxist theorist Frederic Jameson calls "late capitalism") have radically changed how a sense of identity and self is constructed: now, "globalising influences intrude deeply into the reflexive project of the self, and conversely … processes of self-realisation influence global strategies" (214). For Giddens, a "traditional" sense of belonging to communities where one's self is more or less stable and situated according to distinctly bounded cultural values and norms has been unraveling, the coherence of narratives of the self, its "place," and its relations with others "disembedded."

Besides its institutional reflexivity, modern social life is characterized by profound processes of the reorganization of time and space, coupled with the expansion of disembedding mechanisms—mechanisms which prise social relations free from the hold of specific locales, recombining them across wide time-space distances (5).

8 Again, as I have stated before, the term "Chicano/a," with its connotations of a politicized and socially aware sense of raced and ethnic Mexican American self, is not necessarily used by middle-class people of Mexican descent. Indeed, many working-class Mexican Americans do not necessarily self-identify as "Chicanos" either, depending on their class allegiances, state, region, politics, and even proximity to the Mexican border.

9 A conservative-leaning think tank, this center describes itself as being "animated by a unique pro-immigrant, low-immigration vision which seeks fewer immigrants but a warmer welcome for those admitted" (np).

10 The zoot suit has its origins in Harlem, where African American men first designed and wore them. Interestingly enough, where I live in Florida, one can still see solid church-going men wearing a modified type of zoot suit in beautiful bright colors and flashy ties. "Sunday go to meeting" hats for the women—some of them entering the land of fantasia—can also be glimpsed.

Resources for teaching chica lit

Aldama, Frederick, ed. *Latinos and Narrative Media: Participation and Portrayal*. New York, NY: Palgrave, 2013.

Bourdieu, Pierre. "Distinction: a social critique of the judgement of taste." In *Food and Culture: A Reader*. Ed. Carole Counihan and Penny Van Esterik. New York: Routledge, 2013.

Butler, Pamela, and Jigna Desai. "Manolos, marriage, and mantras: chick-lit criticism and transnational feminism." *Meridians: Feminism, Race, Transnationalism*, 8.2 (2008): 1–31.

Connell, R.W. "Hegemonic masculinity and emphasized femininity." In *Gender and Power: Society, the Person, and Sexual Politics*. Palo Alto, CA: Stanford University Press, 1987.

Dávila, Arlene. *Latinos Inc: The Marketing and Making of a People*. 2nd edn. Berkeley, CA: University of California at Berkeley Press, 2012.

Hall, Stuart. "Stereotyping as a signifying practice." In *Representation: Cultural Representations and Signifying Practices*. Thousand Oaks, CA: Sage in association with the Open University, 1997.

Hedrick, Tace. "Chica Lit." In *The Routledge Companion to Latino/a Literature*. Eds. Suzanne Bost and Frances R. Aparicio. New York: Routledge, 2013, pp. 342–50.

hooks, bell. *Feminist Theory: From Margin to Center*. Cambridge, MA: South End Press, 2000.

Philips, Deborah. "Shopping for men: the single woman narrative." *Women: A Cultural Review*, 11.3 (2000): 238–51.

Ramírez, Catherine. "The end of Chicanismo: Alisa Valdes-Rodriguez's *Dirty Girls*." UCLA Chicano/Latino Research Center. n.d. Research Report #2, 1-41. Web.

Stillo, Monica. "Gramsci: concept of hegemony." *Theory.Org.UK: Media/Identity/Resources and Projects*. www.theory.org.uk/index.htm (accessed June 13, 2014). Web.

20 Teaching the suburbs

Randy Ontiveros

Students love talking about themselves. We all do, if we're honest. But while pundits worry that social media is breeding a generation of narcissists and preeners, good teachers know that the confessional desire can be a pedagogical tool.[1] Used wisely, it can foster great class discussions and can ultimately help students better understand literature, the self, and the world. When I teach "The Literature of the **Chicano Movement**," I like to start the course by asking students to write a one-page poem or a piece of short fiction about a moment from their youth that gives insight into their cultural identity. The first goal of the exercise is to bring students closer to realizing that they have such a thing, since many of them—usually white students, but not always—wrongly think otherwise. The second goal is to persuade them that while "**Chicano**" and "**Chicana**" are rooted in the particularities of America's entanglement with Mexico (and vice versa), the experiences these words signify have resonance across the globe.

First-person writing also helps when teaching about the suburbs. Surprisingly, scholars have only recently made suburbia a sustained topic of academic writing and teaching; for decades the subject was too philistine.[2] Students, though, show no such hesitation. They love to think, read, and write about suburbia, a fact that makes for an energetic and illuminating classroom environment. As in our society more generally, student opinion about the suburbs is divided. Some of those who grew up in a split-level house on a leafy cul-de-sac are eager to flee a world they have come to see as dull and deceiving. Many of these disenchanted young suburbanites look to college as a ticket to a more exciting life. Other students are drawn to suburbia's promise of the good life. They may have grown up in the city or the country and quietly envied the suburbs they saw on television, or they may have been raised in the suburbs and now hope to give the same pastoral childhood to their offspring. Still other students—the majority, I suspect—are conflicted. Mass media has taught them that suburban existence is mindless, soulless, and, worst of all, sexless. At the same time, they have seen the suburbs represented as a place of refuge from an **urbanized** world of greed and estrangement.

Taking note of this contradiction and exploring its origins during the first week of class or at the start of a unit on suburbia is a good way to get the attention of the students and to frame major questions. There are as many ways to do this as there are teachers, but one exercise is to have the students screen *El Norte* (1983). Gregory Nava's celebrated independent film tells the story of two teenage siblings, Rosa and Enrique, who are forced to flee the war-ravaged countryside of Guatemala for what they hope will be a more comfortable life in the United States. Early in *El Norte*, on the night that Rosa and Enrique's father leaves for an abandoned hacienda to make plans for a peasant uprising, the family sits down together for a meal with their *compadres*. It's a warm scene of love, humor, and good food. Were it not for the threat of violence hanging over the table—a threat made apparent by a jump cut to the soldiers preparing to foil the peasants and by a close-up shot of the father's machete—the sequence could fit comfortably in a suburban ad or sitcom. The threat of violence, however, has the family dreaming of leaving for *el norte,* where according to the mother Lupe (played by Alicia del Lago) "hasta el más, más pobrecito tiene un escusado igualito de Don Rodrigo, igualito ... Uno puede mear a la moda" ["even the poorest have a toilet like Don Rodrigo, just like it ... you can pee in style there"]. She knows this because Don Rodrigo's cook has been giving her old copies of *Buen Hogar,* or *Good Housekeeping,* for ten years, handed down to her perhaps from the boss's travel, or perhaps from the migratory circuit between the United States and Guatemala. The mother's association of *el norte* with material abundance, and of material abundance with domesticity, reflects the success of American mass media after the Second World War in marketing the suburban ideal as a way of stimulating global demand for U.S. consumer goods.[3] It is an extension of the logic behind Richard Nixon's 1959 "kitchen debate" with Nikita Khrushchev. However, in keeping with the law of unintended consequences, the strategy brought not just capital but people northward, where ironically much of the repression in Guatemala and other parts of Latin America and the Caribbean was funded and equipped.

Shortly after this scene, Rosa and Enrique's father meets his death when he and his *compañeros* are sabotaged by the army. Traumatized by the violence and afraid of what will happen next, the siblings decide they must leave. They make the long journey through Mexico, and when the two finally reach Tijuana, they are met at their bus by *coyotes* competing for their business with promises of safe passage and an easier life. One of the men promises Rosa and Enrique a better life in the United States, "donde va a encontrar usted unas casas bien bonitas, carros bien, bien grandes ... ¡Es el Norte! Es lo mas lindo de la vida, ¿me entiendes?" ["where you're going to find beautiful houses, big cars ... It's the north! It's the most beautiful thing in life, understand me?"]. As he talks, the viewer sees a quick succession of jump-cut shots of what a $300 crossing can buy. The first frames in the sequence show a Mexico of dirt streets, buckling fences, trash-filled yards, and dilapidated homes. The second set shows America, or at least part of America: ranch-style houses with picture windows that face quiet, paved streets; neatly manicured lawns and gardens that are kept green by plentiful water; and cars, all of them in good repair, parked on exclusive driveways.

El Norte's representation of suburban abundance gets its emotional power from long-cherished myths of the United States as a garden in the "new world" of the Americas, an Eden before the fall. There are a number of works one can excerpt to put these myths in a historical context, including Annette Kolodny's *The Lay of the Land: Metaphor as Experience and History in American Life and Letters* (1975), Jackson Lears's *Fables of Abundance: A Cultural History of Advertising in America* (1994), and Sacvan Bercovitch's *American Jeremiad* (1978). Many movies and books about the suburbs are entirely cynical toward the mythologies of American exceptionalism, but *El Norte* is not one of them. When Rosa finds housekeeping work in a wealthy suburb of Los Angeles, she appreciates the neighborhood's natural beauty. It brings to her mind the verdant splendor of Guatemala, something that's worth pointing out to students as a way of challenging stereotypes about Latin American ecology. Rosa also admires the modern comforts of her employer's home, even after the comic confusion she faces when first trying to operate the buttons and dials on the family's expensive washer-dryer set. However, she realizes soon enough that the *coyote* in Tijuana was telling her and her brother a half-truth: the United States can be a paradise, but only for those who can afford to pay the mortgage.

Nava's film captures a second contradiction at the heart of the story of Latinas/os and suburbia. Suburban domestic workers—especially the women who work as house-keepers, nannies, or caregivers—are often required to be both intimate and stranger, family and servant. In the film, there is a geniality between Rosa, her friend Nacha (played memorably by Lupe Ontiveros), and their suburban employer Mrs. Rogers, or "Helen" as she too quickly asks to be called. They are all women made to do a woman's work in a man's world, a dynamic attested to in the film by the fact that the prestige of the man of the house is everywhere visible, but he himself never appears on screen. Sisterhood only goes so far, though. As Mary Romero argues, "Developing personal relationships with the women of color whom they employ functions, for some white middle-class women, to affirm their self-image as nonracist" (1992: 11). It's clear from her body language that Mrs. Rogers takes a self-conscious satisfaction in her kindness toward her employees. At the same time, by distancing herself from Rosa and Nacha with her professional attire—we see her wearing an early-80s-era skirt suit—and her commanding tone, Mrs. Rogers can distance herself from the stigma of housewifery. As Romero pointedly puts it, women of color who work as paid domestics provide their employers with "the self-enhancing satisfactions that emanate from having the presence of an inferior." They vindicate "the employer's lifestyle, ideology, and social world, from their familial interrelations to the economically and racially stratified system in which they live" (Romero 1992: 112). The film's sophisticated treatment of the gender politics of suburbia makes for an engaging introduction to a theme that recurs in the literature.

The body of literature on Latino/a labor in the suburbs is diverse and growing. Perhaps the most widely read work is T. C. Boyle's "Honorary Chicano" novel *Tortilla Curtain* (1995). Written in the realist style of Steinbeck, Oates, and Updike, Boyle's tale of two couples—one Mexican and one American—whose lives tragically intersect in a Los Angeles suburb is a lyrical meditation on themes of work, environmentalism, globaliza-tion, and media. It's especially good for getting students first to see and then to think about the day-labor sites that dot the suburban landscape nationwide and that have become "ground zero" in the debates on immigration.

Other works that focus on Mexican American experiences of suburban work include Richard Vasquez's epic novel *Chicano* (1970) and Héctor Tobar's more recent *Barbarian Nurseries* (2011). When reviewing the syllabus at the start of the semester, I pitch Vasquez's novel as a Chicano *Grapes of Wrath*. (The comparison admittedly works better for some students than for others.) Hortensia and Jilda, young daughters of the fictional patriarch Hector Sandoval, find their first work in America as maids for "an old Cali-fornia family" that can "speak pretty good Spanish" (Vasquez 1970: 78). The house is described as having "a spacious lawn with well-trimmed shrubs and trees, and with stone walks neatly circling the house and leading to the street … of shingle siding with a brick chimney at each side, with freshly painted green trim around the windows and doors. French windows opened onto tiny balconies on the upper floor" (79). As often happens in suburban narratives, though, this well-manicured exterior hides a dark interior. The reader learns that a deliveryman raped Hortensia when she was home alone. When the "patrón" (as Hortensia evocatively calls him) finds out about the assault he chases off the deliveryman and begins raping her himself, until the wife catches her husband and blames the young woman. Hortensia's story presents an opportunity to teach students the conventions of consensual and nonconsensual sex in the suburban bildungsroman and to discuss the painful realities of sexual assault in domestic work—a literary theme that goes back to Samuel Richardson's *Pamela* (1740). *Barbarian Nurseries* explores similar subjects as it tells the story of Araceli Ramirez, a sophisticated *chilanga* (or native of Mexico City) forced to play the stereotypical role of traditional "Third-World Nanny" for a wealthy family collapsing under the weight of recession. Tobar's novel is longer than many students are accustomed to reading, but nuanced characterization and several plot twists draw them in. The man Araceli works for is an upwardly mobile Mexican American named Scott Torres. Asking students to give formal attention to the dialogue between these two characters and to the omniscient narrator's sympathies is a way of exploring class differences among Latinos/as. The book also affords an opportunity to teach about the causes and effects of the 2008 economic downturn, including the real-estate speculation that led up to it, its unequal impact on blacks and Latinos/as, and the dramatic changes it has triggered in labor policy—changes that many students experience firsthand but often have little vocabulary for interpreting (Lewis 2010; Reyes 2010; Ross 2010; Taylor *et al.* 2011).

Mexican Americans are the largest of the several subgroups that together make up the Latino population of the United States, and for decades scholars focused on their histories and traditions. Recently, though, there has been a welcome push within Latino/a studies to give greater attention to the experiences of Central Americans, Puerto Ricans, Cubans, and South Americans. The suburbs are an especially useful geography for developing a sophisticated pan-Latino/a perspective, because they throw into relief the material conditions that give rise to similarities and differences between various Latino communities. Esmeralda Santiago's *América's Dream* (1996) is a case in point. This riveting novel tells the story of América Gonzalez, a Puerto Rican woman who finds work as a live-in housekeeper and nanny in Westchester County after she flees the brutality of her boyfriend on the island of Vieques, a place the U.S. Navy used for weapons testing between 1941 and 2003. Santiago's meticulous emplotment of América's traumatic story tears the ideological veil that so often separates the quiet streets of American suburbia from conflicts in other parts of the world, especially those with U.S. involvement. The book also shows better than any sociology could how the law shapes the everyday lives of Latino/a immigrants. Suburban novels frequently have a crucial play-ground scene. When América meets a Guatemalan nanny at the park, she is "fascinated by the sound of Adela's voice" because she has been starved of Spanish (Santiago 1996: 209). However, tensions emerge later when the protagonist's new friends—women from El Salvador, Paraguay, and the Dominican Republic—express resentment about her legal status: "We don't have a choice when we come here," Adela persists. "We have to take whatever work we can find. But you, an American citizen. And you speak good English" (219). The law's power in their daily life makes it all but impossible for them to realize that while legal citizenship does indeed confer on Puerto Ricans specific advantages that undocumented immigrants lack, it doesn't give them the full set of rights that come with cultural citizenship. Santiago's novel is a powerful representation of what it feels like to inhabit the contradiction of being "foreign in a domestic sense."[4] All immigrants experience this contradiction to an extent, but for Puerto Ricans the contradictions surrounding Latino/a citizenship have been codified in law.

During the last two or three generations, Latinos/as have succeeded African Americans as the major source of paid domestic labor in the suburbs of the South and the East. In much of the Southwest and West, they have provided domestic labor of one sort or another since the 1800s. The subject is apparent as early as María Amparo Ruiz de Burton's *The Squatter and the Don* (1992 [1885]), which is among other things a novelization of the *californio* elite's downward mobility from a landed gentry into a servant class. In the twentieth century, Latino/a domestic labor is often represented in fiction, film, and television as a specter, a force not fully present in the suburbs but not fully absent, either. In truth, paid domestic labor—including but not only Latino/a domestic labor—has been vital *since the very beginning* to the creation, maintenance, and reproduction of the suburban ideal. Cindy I-fen Cheng's research on Asian Americans and Cold War domestic politics includes language from a restrictive covenant at the heart of a major civil-rights case in South Los Angeles. The contract read as follows:

> It is Hereby Mutually Covenanted and Agreed … That no portion or part of said lots or parcels of land ever shall be used or occupied by … any person not of the White or Caucasian race … but if persons not of the Caucasian race are kept thereupon by such Caucasian occupant strictly in the capacity of servants or employees of such occupant, such circumstances shall be permitted.
>
> (Cheng 2013: 29)

Note the force of the word "kept." This is not a model of keeping minorities out of the suburbs so much as it is a model of keeping them in their place.

Raymond Williams's *The Country and the City* (1973) explains how landscape poets and painters of the eighteenth century aided the transition from an exploitative feudal system to a more rationalized system of exploitative agrarian capitalism. Commenting on Thomas Crabbe's anti-pastoral poem "The Village," Williams says the work is unique among many of its contemporaries because it gives "an alteration of landscape, by an alteration of seeing" (87). Literature, more than most things, is able to effect this "alteration of seeing" because it renders through the imagination a point of view that is different than our own. The novels described above do this work, and so do poems like Billy Collins's "Her" and Urayóan Noel's "En los suburbios lejanos" ["In the Faraway Suburbs"]. Collins's contemporary anti-pastoral turns the traditional image of the suburb on its head with a startling opening line: "There is no noisier place than the suburbs." The observation feels wrong, but the reader is given as "fresh evidence" "the chain saw, the leaf-blower … the garbage truck equipped with air brakes, reverse beeper, and merciless grinder." In the geography of industrial capitalism, cities are characterized predominantly as sites of labor, the suburbs as sites of leisure. Sometimes the relationship is more explicit, with suburbs promoted as just reward for work done in the metropolis. Collins's poem insists on hearing the labor so often obscured by the suburban pastoral. The verse ends with the sound of two men laying flooring at the home next door: "Otherwise, all quiet for a change, / just the clicking of tiles being handled and their talking back and forth in Spanish / then one of them asking in English / 'What was her name?' and the silence of the other." Noel's poem similarly challenges readers to re-examine the political and cultural economy of suburbia. Composed as a décima, a poetic form with deep roots in Puerto Rican verse, "En los suburbios lejanos" is sung by a sub-urban flaneur who travels from the island to New York to California and observes, among other things, the "chalets con detalles dóricos / y sirvientes bolivianos / donde juegan los hermanos" ["There are Doric-style chalets / With South American servants / Where the little brothers play"] (2004: 22–23).[5]

Noel's poem is original in many ways, not least because it ponders the significance of Latino/a labor as part of a larger meditation on the American dream, which historically has been associated with the decision to live in the suburbs. This is important because Latinos/as increasingly make their homes in the suburbs. According to demographer William H. Frey's (2011) analysis of census data from the 1990 to 2010 censuses, African Americans, Hispanics, and Asian Americans now make up 35 percent of the suburban population in the United States, roughly equal to their share of the population nationwide. Over half of minorities living in large metropolitan areas live in the suburbs; for Hispanics, the number is 59 percent (1). These "melting pot suburbs," as Frey calls them, are forcing commentators to question basic assumptions about the culture, politics, and sociology of American suburbs. Statistical reports by Frey and other demographers and geographers are an essential tool when teaching about the suburbs because they teach students how to think across disciplines and because they allow for historical specificity. I have found that presenting them in the first week of class challenges outdated myths that many students bring to class regarding whiteness in suburbia, and also reveals nuances in the literature that would likely otherwise go unnoticed. For example, demography attunes students to the complex issues raised by the reality of a small-but-growing Latino/a middle class, as well as the momentous "great inversion" that is driving poor minorities into the suburbs and wealthier professionals and retirees into gentrified cities (Ehrenhalt 2012).

There is a growing body of recent literature that features Latinos/as living in suburbia. The women of Alisa Valdes-Rodriguez's *Dirty Girls* series come from diverse class backgrounds and inhabit different spaces. Their narrative frame that Valdes-Rodriguez uses to tell their story both reflects and reinforces common strategies navigating class differences among Latinos/as. Students in my classes have reacted rather negatively to Valdes-Rodriguez's writing, but the books allow for frank discussion of the publishing industry's hot-and-cold relationship to Latino/a writers and Latino/a narratives. Martha Sherrill's *The Ruins of California* (2007) is a more complex and more original representation of Latinos/as living in suburbia. It tells the story of Inez Garcia Ruin as she navigates the pleasures and pains of family during the strangeness of 1970s California. Another worthwhile text to consider is Patricia Engel's *Vida* (2010), a memorable **bildungsroman** about a young woman named Sabina who feels as much an outsider in her wealthy New Jersey suburb as she does in Colombia, where her parents are from.

The relationship between Latino/a communities and the American suburb is changing rapidly. However, any study of the suburbs in Latino/a history and culture must take as its starting point the recognition that Latinos/as are not *recién llegados* (or recent arrivals), as journalistic accounts too often suggest. They have been part of the story of American suburbia from the very beginning, at times by dispossession, at times in their labor, at times through exclusion, and at times as inhabitants. Historian Andrew Wiese has shown that blacks have inhabited "the outskirts of town" since the 1870s, though unlike the middle-class white suburbs that exploded after World War II these early suburbs were "unplanned, unregulated, and unpretentious working-class communities" (17). The question of what makes a suburb a suburb is surprisingly hard to answer, but one working definition that is both flexible and specific is a physical geography that combines aspects of the urban with aspects of the rural. If we have in view this more inclusive and more accurate image, and not just the prosperous single-family homes of *Father Knows Best* or *Desperate Housewives*, then we find historical and cultural evidence of Latinos/as living long ago on the outskirts of metropolitan centers in much the same way that African Americans did in places like Atlanta, Memphis, and Chicago.

José Antonio Villareal's *Pocho* (1959) can be read as a suburban novel. The same argument can be said of *Hoyt Street* (2006), Mary Helen Ponce's memoir of growing up in the San Fernando Valley during the 1930s and 1940s. Pacoima, or "Pacas," as the Mexican majority called their town, was located "in the shadow of Los Angeles," the city "twenty odd miles to the south" (3). The agricultural labor market that supported Ponce's family was tied to the financial and transport networks of downtown L.A., but her neighborhood had many of the physical and social characteristics of life in the *campo*. Goats and chickens were in nearly every yard, worn goods were put in "el yonque," or the junk pile, for recycling, and family went beyond the nuclear household. Of her elderly neighbor, Ponce says "Doña Luisa, though not a blood relative, was considered family; *entre familia* there was no need for fences" (13). Pacoima residents loved their homes because they reminded them of the homes they had left, most of them as refugees during the Mexican Revolution: "On Hoyt Street most residents had once lived in Mexican ranchitos and had a greater need for land" (7). Yet their houses had also acquired some of the outward signs of the "suburban ideal" (to use Kenneth Jackson's famous phrase) that took shape in the United States during the last half of the nineteenth century. Here is her description of the landscaping at 13011 Hoyt Street:

> My father's pride and joy was the white picket fence. It faced Hoyt Street and was his original design, or so he liked to think ... I often thought that perhaps my father's family had not owned property in Mexico. It was important for him to fence, to secure the right of ownership. Or perhaps, unknown to us, my father was an artist who liked to express himself in works of cement, wire, and wood.
>
> (13–14)

Hoyt Street helps us better understand Latino/a history because it points to material and cultural worlds not fully knowable with the traditional paradigm of **barrio** and **colonia**. Ponce's memoir also presents an opportunity to rethink a truism of suburban studies by showing that the suburbs are not everywhere and always a geography of assimilation; they have in times past served as sites of cultural preservation and self-defense for the Latino/a communities living in them, and they continue to do so today in places like Langley Park, Maryland, Commerce, California, and Long Island, New York. The book serves as an example of how teaching the suburbs in Latino/a literature and film makes it possible for students to make lasting intellectual and political connections across a range of pressing questions.

Notes

1 Fellowship support for this essay came from a 2014 Research and Scholarship Award from the University of Maryland's Graduate School. My thanks to Laura Halperín for introducing me to the story of América Gonzalez.

2 The definitive history of the American suburbs is Kenneth T. Jackson, *Crabgrass Frontier: The Suburbanization of the United States* (New York: Oxford, 1987). Jackson's work is worth assigning because its prose is accessible and the argument brilliant. Most students love reading it. Other sources to consider include: Eric Avila, *Popular Culture in the Age of White Flight: Fear and Fantasy in Suburban Los Angeles* (Berkeley: University of California Press, 2004); Robert Bruegmann, *Sprawl: A Compact History* (Chicago: University of Chicago Press, 2005); Herbert J. Gans, *The Levittowners: Ways of Life and Politics in a New Suburban*

Community (New York: Columbia University Press, 1982); Dolores Hayden, *Building Suburbia: Green Fields and Urban Growth, 1820–2000* (New York: Pantheon Books, 2003); Wei Li, *Ethnoburb: The New Ethnic Community in Urban America* (Honolulu: University of Hawai'i Press, 2009); Becky M. Nicolaides and Andrew Wiese, eds., *The Suburb Reader* (Routledge, 2006); Becky M. Nicolaides, *My Blue Heaven: Life and Politics in the Working-Class Suburbs of Los Angeles, 1920–1965* (Chicago: University of Chicago Press, 2002); Adam Rome, *The Bulldozer in the Countryside: Suburban Sprawl and the Rise of American Environmentalism* (Cambridge: Cambridge University Press, 2001); Karen Tongson, *Relocations: Queer Suburban Imaginaries* (New York: New York University Press, 2011); Jody Agius Vallejo, *Barrios to Burbs: The Making of the Mexican-American Middle Class* (Stanford: Stanford University Press, 2012); William Hollingsworth Whyte, *The Organization Man* (Philadelphia: University of Pennsylvania Press, 2002).

3 Three highly teachable overviews of the relationship between gender, consumption, and geography are Lizabeth Cohen, Elaine Tyler May, and Vicki L. Ruiz.

4 The infamous phrase comes from Supreme Court Justice White's opinion in the Insular Case *Downes v. Bidwell* (1901). The helpful distinction between cultural citizenship and legal citizenship is developed in Renato Rosaldo (1997: 27–38).

5 Noel includes Spanish and English versions of the poem in this code-switching collection.

Resources for teaching the suburbs

Cheng, Cindy I-Fen. *Citizens of Asian America: Democracy and Race during the Cold War*. New York: New York University Press, 2013.

Cohen, Lizabeth. *A Consumers' Republic: The Politics of Mass Consumption in Postwar America*. New York: Knopf, 2003.

Ehrenhalt, Alan. *The Great Inversion and the Future of the American City*. New York: Vintage Books, 2012.

Frey, William H. *Melting Pot Cities and Suburbs: Racial and Ethnic Change in Metro America in the 2000s*. Washington, DC: Brookings Institution. May 2011, 1. www.brookings.edu/research/papers/2011/05/04-census-ethnicity-frey (accessed May 23, 2014).

Jackson Lears, T. J. *Fables of Abundance: A Cultural History of Advertising in America*. New York: Basic Books, 1994.

Kolodny, Annette. *The Lay of the Land: Metaphor as Experience and History in American Life and Letters*. Chapel Hill: University of North Carolina Press, 1975.

Lewis, Michael. *The Big Short: Inside the Doomsday Machine*. New York: W. W. Norton, 2010.

May, Elaine Tyler. *Homeward Bound: American Families in the Cold War Era*. Rev. and updated edn. New York: Basic Books, 2008.

Nava, Gregory. *El Norte*. Irvington, NY: Criterion Collection, 2008.

Nicolaides, Becky M., and Andrew Wiese, ed. *The Suburb Reader*. New York: Routledge, 2006.

Noel, Urayoán. *Kool Logic = La Lógica Kool*. Tempe: Bilingual Press/Editorial Bilingüe, 2005.

Ponce, Mary Helen. *Hoyt Street: An Autobiography*. Albuquerque: University of New Mexico Press, 2006.

Reyes, Paul. *Exiles in Eden: Life among the Ruins of Florida's Great Recession*. New York: Henry Holt, 2010.

Romero, Mary. *Maid in the U.S.A.* New York: Routledge, 1992.

Rosaldo, Renato. "Cultural citizenship, inequality, and multiculturalism." In *Latino Cultural Citizenship: Claiming Identity, Space, and Rights*. Ed. William V. Flores and Rina Benmayor. Boston: Beacon Press, 1997, pp. 27–38.

Ross, Andrew. *Nice Work if You Can Get It: Life and Labor in Precarious Times*. New York: New York University Press, 2010.

Ruiz, Vicki L. "'Star struck': acculturation, adolescence, and Mexican American women, 1920–1950." *Unequal Sisters: An Inclusive Reader in U.S. Women's History*. 4th edn. New York: Routledge, 2008, pp. 363–78.

Santiago, Esmeralda. *América's Dream*. New York: HarperCollins, 1996; New York: Rayo, 2003.

Sherrill, Martha. *The Ruins of California*. New York: Penguin, 2006.

Suro, Roberto, and Audrey Singer. *Latino Growth in Metropolitan America: Changing Patterns, New Locations*. Washington, DC: Brookings Institution, Center on Urban and Metropolitan Policy in collaboration with the Pew Hispanic Center, 2002.

Taylor, Paul, Rakesh Kochhar, Richard Fry, Gabriel Velasco, and Seth Motel. *Wealth Gaps Rise to Record Highs between Whites, Blacks, Hispanics*. Washington, DC: Pew Research Center, July 26, 2011. www.pewsocialtrends.org (accessed May 23, 2014).

Tobar, Héctor. *The Barbarian Nurseries*. New York: Farrar, Straus and Giroux, 2011.

Vallejo, Jody Agius. *Barrios to Burbs: The Making of the Mexican American Middle Class*. Stanford: Stanford University Press, 2012.

Vasquez, Richard. *Chicano: A Novel*. 1970. New York: Rayo, 2005.

Williams, Raymond. *The Country and the City*. New York: Oxford University Press, 1973.

21 Defamiliarized bodies

Disability studies in the Latino/a literature classroom

Julie Avril Minich

Working at the intersection of Latino/a and **disability studies**, I often find colleagues interested in my research but skeptical of its practicality in the classroom: "That sounds trendy! But how do you *teach* it?" Behind this question lie two assumptions. The first is that a pedagogical approach combining Latino/a literature and disability studies would focus exclusively on texts by or about Latinas/os with disabilities. The second is that such an approach must appeal to few students. At a time when many of us in the humanities are concerned with enrollment numbers, people wonder: *Who would sign up for a course on disability in Latino/a literature?* In what follows, I hope to offer an expanded sense of what might constitute Latino/a disability studies and make a case for the generative potential of including disability perspectives in the Latino/a literature classroom. The first half of this chapter will review major premises and debates in disability studies that align most productively with Latino/a literary study, while the second half looks at how this alignment manifests in specific texts. For these case studies, I have chosen texts covering a range of genres by Puerto Rican, Chicano/a, and Cuban American writers: "Class Poem" by Aurora Levins Morales (1986), "The Moths" by Helena María Viramontes (1985), "Above All, A Family Man" by Achy Obejas (1994), and *Still Water Saints* by Alex Espinoza (2007).

This chapter begins from the (perhaps predictable) premise that an intersectional understanding of disability, race, gender, and sexuality benefits students with diverse career goals, academic experiences, and cultural backgrounds. Less predictably, it also assumes that many scholars of Latino/a literature already approach their teaching from a perspective compatible with disability studies. Therefore, my goal is not solely to convince readers to incorporate Latino/a texts about disability into their syllabi, but also to offer some ideas for engaging with concepts of disability studies that may already circulate in their classes. By naming and addressing these concepts directly, teachers of Latino/a literature can offer fresh perspectives on familiar texts and more effectively help their students to develop the reading, writing, and critical thinking skills that are at the heart of literary study.

Disability studies and Latino/a literature

My argument requires making a case for disability studies, like **feminist/queer studies** and **critical ethnic studies**, as a *mode of analysis* rather than an *object of study*. For this reason, as my case studies will show, I have chosen to look at texts that examine bodily conditions and experiences that are not always viewed as disabilities. Disability scholars seek to unsettle normative expectations for the movement, appearance, shape, and function of bodies, not simply to study people with disabilities. (Indeed, many would say that people with disabilities have been "studied" quite enough!) As a result, a Latino/a disability studies perspective could emerge from the study of any text that meaningfully engages with the cultural and political significance of Latino/a embodiment. As teachers of minoritized literatures, literary critics working in Latino/a studies regularly argue that people of color are not the only people for whom issues of race are salient, just as feminist/queer studies scholars are accustomed to showing students why gender and sexuality are not the exclusive concern of women and **LGBTIQ** people. Yet it is still rare for students and scholars who believe themselves to be non-disabled to see non-normative forms of embodiment as relevant to them. As a result, asking students to take seriously the sociopolitical, **epistemic**, and ethical implications of bodies—their own and those of others—can open up class discussions in surprising and exciting ways.

When including disability perspectives in my Latino/a literature classes, I often rely upon Tobin Siebers's notion of the *ideology of ability*, which reveals how forms of oppression apparently unrelated to disability (like racism, sexism, and homophobia) work by portraying oppressed groups as mentally or physically defective. (For instance, my recent book, *Accessible Citizenships*, contains a chapter exploring how the ideology of ability undergirds contemporary public rhetoric about the U.S.-Mexico border.) Siebers writes:

> The ideology of ability is at its simplest the preference for able-bodiedness. At its most radical, it defines the baseline by which humanness is determined, setting the measure of body and mind that gives or denies human status to individual persons. It affects nearly all of our judgments, definitions and values about human beings, but because it is discriminatory and exclusionary, it creates social locations outside of and critical of its purview, most notably in this case, the perspective of disability.
>
> (2008: 8)

My research addresses how Latino/a literature unsettles the alignment of Latino/a populations with physical and mental disabilities. I believe that this is accomplished most effectively when, instead of simply denying that Latino/a bodies and minds are deficient, Latino/a writers place under critical scrutiny the concept of deficiency itself, thus exposing and undermining the ideology of ability. Furthermore, I believe that critical disability perspectives can help students of Latino/a literature not only to contest harmful representations of Latinos/as but also to dismantle the **rhetorical** conditions that make these representations possible.

One useful starting point in this work is to examine the distinction often made by disability scholars between a "medical model" of disability (defining disability as a physical shortcoming of the human body that can or should be treated by medical intervention) and a "social model" (understanding disability in terms of the social environment that fails to accommodate bodily variation, such as a lack of ramps on a building with stairs). I discuss medical and social models of disability in Latino/a literature classes when explaining to students the principles of **social constructionism**, or the idea that race, gender, sexuality, and ability are social (not biological) entities. Susan Wendell explains the cultural specificity of disability in terms that students quickly grasp:

> I, who can walk about half a mile several times a week but not more, am not significantly disabled with respect to walking in my society, where most people are not

expected to walk further than that in the course of their daily activities. But in some societies … , where women normally walk several miles twice a day to obtain water for the household, I would be much more severely disabled.

(1996: 14)

Including Wendell's point in an introductory Latino/a literature course—one in which, for example, students may not know how race is enacted differently in the United States and Latin America, or may not understand the significance of how these different racial formations register in Latino/a texts—can help illustrate how the identity categories that students believe to be natural and unchanging are, instead, shifting, fluid, and variable. Just as "disabled" means very different things in different social contexts, so too do racial categories and gender norms.

Of course, the constructedness of identities like race and gender does not alleviate their effects. Race may not be "real," my students rightfully argue, but it *matters*—and Latino/a literature offers many examples of how and why it matters. Just as I believe that students of Latino/a literature need to understand Latino/a identities as constructed, I also believe that it is important to teach social constructionism critically. Scholars in disability studies who probe the limits of the social model of disability offer tools for discussing these nuances with students. For instance, Alison Kafer writes:

[T]he social model … erases the lived realities of impairment; in its well-intentioned focus on the disabling effects of society, it overlooks the often-disabling effects of our bodies. People with chronic illness, pain, and fatigue have been among the most critical of this aspect of the social model, rightly noting that social and structural changes will do little to make one's joints stop aching or alleviate back pain. Nor will changes in architecture and attitude heal diabetes or cancer or fatigue. Focusing exclusively on disabling barriers, as a strict social model seems to do, renders pain and fatigue irrelevant to the project of disability politics.

(2013: 7)

Critiques of the social model are particularly fruitful for exploring identities as both materially grounded and socially constructed. For instance, a text like Piri Thomas's *Down These Mean Streets* (1967)—a memoir about growing up dark-skinned in a Puerto Rican family that denies its African ancestry—demands that students understand blackness as both a visible attribute of the body and a socially constructed racial identity. Understanding how scholars in disability studies see features of the body as "real" *and* constructed can help students engage with the unsettling of dominant racial categories that takes place in many Latino/a texts.

My discussion up to this point has focused on how concepts developed by scholars of race and those developed by scholars of disability can provide mutual reinforcement in the classroom. However, as I argued at the beginning of this section, disability theory is also an optic for examining a wide range of social issues. When introducing students to the idea that disability studies can be brought to bear on questions not always immediately understood as "disability issues," I often mobilize Abby L. Wilkerson's description of disability theory:

Disability theory and activism deal with embodied variation and vulnerability as definitive features of human existence, social landscapes shaped by hierarchies of mental and bodily functioning and morphologies, and landscapes that influence our experiences in countless ways … Disability studies illuminates the normalization of bodies in ways that extend far beyond what might seem to be unambiguous or obvious manifestations of disability.

(2012: 184–85)

Wilkerson moves past a medical/social binary to examine the contexts in which bodily features are normalized and hierarchized. Her capacious approach to disability is particularly helpful for teaching texts that deal with experiences—like aging, fatness, or **HIV/AIDS**—that students may not identify as disabilities. Furthermore, because non-normative bodies often populate Latino/a literature (due, in large part, to healthcare disparities that unjustly affect Latino/a populations), Wilkerson's broad understanding of the concerns of disability studies reveals why so many Latino/a texts benefit from a disability analysis.

In considering the normalization and hierarchization of bodies, some teachers (as I do) feel an ethical imperative to move past the passive voice ("*are* normalized;" "*are* hierarchized") to talk about social systems in which *we all* participate. (This is especially important to me because my students often tell me that reading literature by people from marginalized groups awakens their awareness of injustice but leaves them demoralized. "What can we *do* with this knowledge?") When discussing how we might remake the social world that Latino/a literature makes visible to us, I often invoke the concept of "doing race," as developed by social psychologist Hazel Rose Markus and literary critic Paula M. L. Moya. Markus and Moya write:

> Contrary to what most people believe, race and ethnicity are not *things* that people *have* or *are*. Rather, they are *actions* that people *do*. Race and ethnicity are social, historical, and philosophical *processes* that people have done for hundreds of years and are still doing. They emerge through the social transactions that take place among different kinds of people, in a variety of institutional structures (e.g. schools, workplaces, government offices, courts, media) over time, across space, and in all kinds of situations.
>
> (2010: 4, original emphasis)

Considering how this concept might translate to identity categories other than race, we can ask students to discuss how we all (disabled or not) *disable* others—and how literature exposes instances of disablement *as acts* (and not innate bodily attributes). Furthermore, following the idea that race is something "we can all learn to do … differently" (Markus and Moya 2010: 5), we can ask our students how the study of Latino/a literature helps us to *enable* one another.

Of course, to claim that the study of Latino/a literature helps us build a social world that fosters enablement over disablement relies upon an assumption that the study of minoritized literatures can yield tangible social benefits. To understand how and why this is the case, I turn to the work of literary critics like Moya and Lee Bebout, who in different contexts elaborate the importance of Latino/a literature in contemporary curricula. In "What's Identity Got to Do With It?" Moya describes why students need to understand diverse viewpoints:

> Insofar as preparing students to be good citizens of a functioning democracy is an important goal of education, it must provide students with opportunities to

exercise their critical capacities by reflecting on the convictions that guide their judgments about the best way to structure our common society.

(2006: 104)

Bebout, meanwhile, explores how the study of Latino/a literature can facilitate this kind of reflection. He argues for the role of Latino/a literature in producing what he calls *defamiliarized identification*, in which literary texts produce "a funhouse mirror, simultaneously reflecting, reshaping, distorting the world into a new defamiliarized image" that "allows the reader to see herself anew" (2014: 351). Following Bebout and Moya, I suggest that including disability perspectives in Latino/a literature classes can produce defamiliarized identification for all students—Latino/a and non-Latino/a, disabled and non-disabled—and that, as a result, it can create an environment in which students view the world from unfamiliar perspectives. This is because, as Suzanne Bost observes in *Encarnación*, bodies are "significant not as individual models of socially recognized identifications but for the often unpredictable ways in which they interact with their environments and with others around them" (2010: 5). In what follows, I will discuss how students can concretely engage with the issues discussed above through the study of Latino/a texts of diverse genres.

"Class Poem" (Aurora Levins Morales)

"Class Poem" (1986) by Puerto Rican Jewish writer Aurora Levins Morales offers a concise introduction to ideas such as social constructionism; disability as a mode of analysis rather than an object of study; and hierarchies of bodily normalization. Included in the collection *Getting Home Alive*, which Levins Morales co-authored with her mother Rosario Morales, "Class Poem" begins by producing the defamiliarization that Bebout describes: "This is my poem in celebration of my middle-class privilege" (45). For readers who do not identify as middle-class, this line signals that the text will not reflect their experience; however, even for middle-class readers, subsequent lines of the poem defamiliarize their class experiences. The second stanza describes Tita, the speaker's childhood friend, who once longed to become a scientist, "but instead she bore six children ... and who works in a douche bag factory in Maricao" (45), while later stanzas memorialize "Norma / who died of parasites in her stomach when she was four" (46) and "Angélica / who caught on fire while stealing kerosene for her family / and died in pain" (46). The poem thus brings readers into the life-worlds of four characters with different relationships to the healthcare system: the speaker, who grows up with good medical care; Tita, who works manufacturing a pseudo-medical product marketed to wealthy women; and Norma and Angélica, who are denied care. As a result, although "Class Poem" does not have a disabled character, it relies for its emotional impact upon an interrogation of health inequities that deny care to those whose bodies are constructed as disposable in the larger social imaginary (Norma and Angélica), employ others in exploitative working conditions (Tita), and over-medicate privileged women taught to see their bodies as unclean (the bourgeois consumers targeted by the douche bag factory where Tita works).

When teaching this poem, I start by asking why the speaker and Tita have such different outcomes as adults, despite demonstrating similar intellectual curiosities during childhood, when Tita "wanted to know the exact location of color / in the hibiscus petal, and patiently peeled away the thinnest, / most translucent layers to find it" (45). What, I ask my students, does this poem teach us about how some bodies come to be socially valued while others are reduced to the value of the labor they perform? If we see the uneven distribution of health care as a material consequence of bodily norms and hierarchies, how does that deepen our understanding of what it means to say that bodies are socially constructed? Finally, I point students to the moment in the poem when the speaker determines that "not to use the tongue, the self-confidence, the training / my privilege bought me / is to die again for people who are already dead" (1986: 47), suggesting to them that their own act of thinking critically about the society depicted in the poem is also a refusal to "die again" and thus an act with profound political consequences—an act of enablement rather than disablement.

"The Moths" (Helena María Viramontes)

Chicana writer Helena María Viramontes's story "The Moths" (1985) depicts a gender-nonconforming teenage girl who is called upon to care for her dying grandmother. With its achingly beautiful images of the grandmother's body, the story testifies to the disability activist slogan that everyone who lives long enough will become disabled. "The Moths" begins with the narrator stating why she will be the one to help Abuelita die: "[I]t seemed only fair. Abuelita had pulled me through the rages of scarlet fever by placing, removing and replacing potato slices on the temples of my forehead; she had seen me through several whippings, an arm broken by a dare-jump off Tío Enrique's toolshed, puberty, and my first lie" (27). Except for the first lie, each of these deals with a physical transformation or injury, so that from the outset the story takes an approach to embodiment that aligns with Wilkerson's notion of "embodied variation and vulnerability" (2012: 184) as central to human experience. Throughout, "The Moths" powerfully contests the ideology of ability by presenting human bodies as interdependent, in constant transformation, and requiring care and healing at all stages of life. (See also Paula Moya's "Teaching Helena María Viramontes" in this volume.)

The narrator's hands are a recurring image throughout the story, initially introduced as the reason why she "just couldn't do the girl things" (27). They are "too big to handle the fineries of crocheting or embroidery" (27), and her sisters call them "bull hands" (27). After Abuelita rubs the narrator's hands with a balm made of dried moth wings and Vicks, "shaping them back to size" (27) and causing her to feel her "bones melting" (27), the narrator begins to feel a new intimacy with her grandmother. Although readers might initially see this as an attempt to "cure" the narrator, bringing her body in line with social norms, the text is clear that Abuelita does not, in fact, change her hands, as later the narrator helps crush chile, tomatoes, and garlic in a molcajete "until they turned into liquid under my bull hand" (30). Instead, Abuelita's application of the balm to her granddaughter's hands demonstrates love for these non-normative hands, treating them as worthy of affection and attention; Abuelita follows this act by giving the girl tasks that are appropriate for her "bull hands," like pounding nail holes into coffee can planters and crushing chile. Abuelita teaches the narrator to see her bull hands as socially valuable.

Teaching "The Moths," I ask students to talk about the bodily experiences that characterize the narrator's transition from childhood to adulthood and Abuelita's transition from old age to death. I ask them to contemplate why the text presents two women experiencing these bodily transitions in a way that is so intimately aligned, and to discuss how this presentation might change the way we think about bodily vulnerability, aging, and death. In addition, I ask students to closely read the narrator's "bull hands" (as I did above), examining how Abuelita gives the narrator—who initially experiences her body as a poor fit for the world she inhabits—tools to imagine a different relationship between her body and her social environment.

"Above All, A Family Man" (Achy Obejas)

The story "Above All, A Family Man" by Cuban American lesbian writer Achy Obejas documents the early years of the U.S. HIV/AIDS pandemic. Included in Obejas's 1994 debut short story collection *We came all the way from Cuba so you could dress like this?*, the story depicts a road trip from Chicago to Santa Fe, undertaken by the narrator, Tommy Drake, a (presumably) white man who is dying of AIDS-related causes, and his married, (ostensibly) heterosexual Mexican lover Rogelio. Although it includes Tommy's memories of how he and Rogelio met and discusses his diagnosis, the story primarily focuses on a stop the two men make at the Arch in Saint Louis. At the base of the Arch, Tommy and Rogelio encounter two women in wheelchairs who are unable to go to the top; these women inform them that the "Arch isn't accessible" (63); at the top, Tommy grows nauseous and faint, and Rogelio ignores his distress after encountering some family friends. (Rogelio, who gives the story its title, is "above all, a family man" [53].) At the time the story was published, HIV/AIDS was still most prevalent among gay men in the United States, and dominant representations of the crisis tended to focus on white gay men. Today, the pandemic remains as serious as ever in the United States, although it does not carry the same public urgency, and the fastest-growing rates of infection are among young black and Latino/a women and men who have sex with men (MSMs). As a result, teaching this story today is an especially difficult and poignant experience, as it provides an opportunity to explore the social, ethical, and political dimensions of an ongoing public health crisis whose media image continues to change.

Reflecting the continuing nature of the pandemic, my approach to teaching "Above All, A Family Man" is much more open-ended than my approach to teaching "Class Poem" and "The Moths." First, I ask students to explore the consequences of the author's choice of narrator. What does it mean that the story is narrated from the perspective of a white, seropositive man? Chris Bell observes that the "oft-maligned and rarely discussed wishes of HIV-positive individuals" (2012: 226) are rarely heard; "Above All, A Family Man" provides a rare (if fictional) seropositive perspective. Reading a story from the perspective of an HIV-positive man who has sex with a man who assumes himself to be HIV-negative can be uncomfortable for some students, even as Tommy is careful to state: "For the record, I've never been around Rogelio without a parachute. In spite of all his efforts to the contrary, we've never engaged in anything but the safest sex" (55–56). (Other students are uncomfortable with the fact that Rogelio is clearly engaged in an extramarital affair and putting his wife at risk of acquiring HIV.) Rather than seeking to alleviate students' discomfort, I ask them to think about the effects of imagining HIV-positive people as sexual beings. What changes about our understanding of HIV/AIDS when we attend to the complexities of sexual desire instead of rushing to offer prescriptions about what constitutes "responsible" and "irresponsible" sexual behavior? I also ask students to think about the role of the women in the wheelchairs. If students are in a position to think beyond a binary of social/medical models of disability—or beyond socially constructed vs. "real" identities—the story offers rich opportunities for contrasting the women's socially recognized disabilities and Tommy's much more invisible disability. Here it is fruitful to ask students to think about the fact that the women are disabled by a lack of wheelchair-accessible elevators while Tommy is disabled by pejorative social attitudes. Both are disabled by attitudes and environments, not their bodily attributes, but in differential and highly specific ways.

Still Water Saints (Alex Espinoza)

Alex Espinoza's remarkable 2007 novel *Still Water Saints* includes characters with a wide range of bodily conditions relevant to disability studies: fatness, infertility, polio, drug addiction, depression, and post-traumatic stress disorder; these characters are all clients of La Botánica Oshún, a store outside of Los Angeles run by the faith healer Perla, and each is the narrator of a short vignette about an encounter with Perla and the botánica. While I have published a full analysis of this novel elsewhere, here I will discuss my strategies for teaching the novel as they center on one of the novel's most compelling characters: Rosa, a fat teenager whose mother pressures her to lose weight. Rosa initially comes to the botánica with her mother to purchase a weight-loss tea, but after she begins dating a young man who tells her that she is beautiful the way she is and that her tea smells "like cat piss" (26), she decides to stop drinking it. At the botánica, Perla tells her that her mother buys her the tea because she doesn't want to see her hurting, and Rosa replies: "I'm not hurting" (28), at which point Perla gives her back her money and tells her to stop drinking the tea. Rosa's story is the first of the customer narratives in the book, and it is striking because it depicts a moment when the act of healing involves denying a cure. Instead of helping Rosa to alter her body to comply with social norms, Perla helps Rosa learn to love her body the way it is.

Rosa's story often stirs controversy in my classes. Some students—particularly those who identify as fat, and/or who are aware of fat-positive activism—appreciate a text about fatness in which the happy ending is not correlated to weight loss. Other students, influenced by medical discourses about what is often called the "obesity epidemic," worry that the story valorizes unhealthy behaviors. Teaching Rosa's story, I often rely upon the work of April Herndon, which focuses on "exposing and illustrating why … medical rubrics cannot successfully account for the stigma associated with fat embodiment" (2011: 247). In my classes, I emphasize that Rosa's story is not about denying the benefits of eating healthy food or engaging in physical activity (indeed, Rosa herself is quite physically active, dancing cumbia with her boyfriend) but is rather about rejecting the idea that bodies must all conform to a certain size, even to the point of consuming questionable weight-loss remedies in order to achieve this goal.

Conclusion

I will conclude with a line from an author whose position on the Latino/a literature syllabus is unassailable: the heterosexual, male, purportedly non-disabled Dominican writer Junot Díaz. (I say "purportedly" because Díaz—like his primary narrator Yunior—lives with chronic back pain but has not publicly identified himself as a person with a disability.) Near the conclusion of his Pulitzer Prize-winning novel *The Brief Wondrous Life of Oscar Wao* (2007), the fat Afro-Dominican Oscar de León comes to a profound realization: "Every day he watched the 'cool' kids torture the crap out of the fat, the ugly, the smart, the poor, the dark, the black, the unpopular, the African, the Indian, the Arab, the immigrant, the strange, the feminino, the gay—and in every one of these clashes he saw himself" (264). While the novel's narrator, Yunior, places more narrative weight on the moment when Oscar finally gets laid, I like to ask my students what happens if we read this as the novel's climactic scene. It is telling that this passage merges adjectives that describe non-normative bodies and minds (fat, ugly, smart, dark, black, strange) with those designating marginalized racial, gender, and sexual identifications (African, Indian, Arab, immigrant, feminino, gay), revealing how the ideology of ability is deeply imbricated in both white supremacy and heteropatriarchy.

More importantly, however, by depicting Oscar's recognition of himself in "every one of these clashes" (including those that name identity categories, like Arab, to which he does not belong), the novel frames these "clashes" as social justice struggles with implications not just for those being tortured under these names but for everyone who lives in the social world that makes this torture possible. Within the defamiliarized body of Oscar de León, in other words, Díaz gives us a perspective from which to reimagine our social world. Like the other writers discussed here, Díaz uses an unconventional representation of a defamiliarized body to force his readers to imagine a social world that enables instead of disabling.

Resources for teaching disability studies in the Latino/a literature classroom

Bost, Suzanne. "Gloria Anzaldua's Mestiza pain: Mexican sacrifice, chicana embodiment, and feminist politics." Aztlan 30.2 (Fall 2005): 5–31.

——. "Illness." *The Routledge Companion to Latino/a Literature.* Abingdon, Oxon; New York: Routledge, 2013, pp. 88–94.

Danielson, Marivel T. *Homecoming Queers: Desire and Difference in Chicana Latina Cultural Production.* New Brunswick, NJ: Rutgers University Press, 2009.

Esquibel, Catrióna Rueda. *With Her Machete in Her Hand: Reading Chicana Lesbians.* Austin: University of Texas Press, 2006.

James, Jennifer C., and Cynthia Wu. "Race, ethnicity, disability, and literature: intersections and interventions." MELUS 31.3 (Fall 2006): 3–13.

Lewiecki-Wilson, Cynthia, and Cellio, Jen. *Disability and Mothering: Liminal Spaces of Embodied Knowledge.* Syracuse, NY: Syracuse University Press, 2011.

Minich, Julie Avril. "Disabling La Frontera: disability, border subjectivity and masculinity in 'Big Jesse, Little Jesse' by Oscar Casares." *MELUS* 35.1 (Spring 2010): 35–52.

Rebolledo, Tey Diana. *The Chronicles of Panchita Villa and Other Guerrilleras: Essays on Chicana/Latina Literature and Criticism.* Austin: University of Texas Press, 2005.

Part V

Snapshots: Case studies in Action

22 Teaching Oscar "Zeta" Acosta

Christopher González

When I teach Oscar "Zeta" Acosta I begin by providing the students with some biographical context. Self-proclaimed Chicano lawyer who interacted with many of the Chicano Movement's key players in the late 1960s and early 1970s, who appeared in Hunter S. Thompson's *Fear and Loathing in Las Vegas* in 1971 as "Dr. Gonzo," who set important legal precedents in the courtroom, Acosta must be the most enigmatic figure in all of Latino/a literature. I explain to the students that while in recent years there has been a concerted effort by Frederick Luis Aldama, Manuel Luis Martinez, Ramón Saldívar, Ilan Stavans, and other scholars to illuminate the Brown Buffalo and his work, Acosta remains a stubborn phantom of the Latino/a imagination. There is good reason for this. Acosta disappeared in Mexico in June of 1974, and his two published novels, which fell out of print soon after they appeared, were at one time in danger of disappearing as well. Fortunately, the novels were reissued in 1989 and have subsequently enjoyed a renewed scholarly interest. It is unavoidable that Acosta's disappearance leaves one wondering what might have been. The lack of closure regarding what happened to him has cast the life he lived with something akin to a mythical quality, an **ethos** he certainly cultivated while alive. One wonders what books he might have produced and how he might have further shaped Latino/a letters. In life Acosta continually projected a larger-than-life persona, while simultaneously adopting the mantle of sacrificial lamb for the Chicano cause, believing, as Hunter S. Thompson states in the introduction that appears in both of Acosta's novels, that he would die at the age of 33, like Jesus Christ. As a person and as an author, Acosta maintained a series of dualities: champion/martyr; adult/child; fiction/nonfiction. I establish these dichotomies at the beginning of a module on Acosta to identify for the students a compass direction for reading and analyzing his two novels.

The Autobiography of a Brown Buffalo (1972)

The most important consideration when teaching *The Autobiography of a Brown Buffalo* is that it is *not* an **autobiography** per se. Students must recognize that the book is a novel that poses as an autobiography. In other words, it is a fiction that masquerades as something authentic. The narrator, a persona of Acosta, unfolds his narrative with caustic wit, ironic distance, and satiric seriousness. So much of the power of the book lies in the narrator's voice and worldview that it is crucial to distinguish him from the biographical author. Because the narrator, Oscar, is a literary construction, he must be read as a narrative device rather than as the flesh and blood Acosta. Again, engage with the book as a novel rather than an autobiography. Doing so will allow students to uncover many of the book's intricacies.

Another notable aspect of the narrator's voice is his mock-confessional tone. He is so brutally straightforward in his narration that the situations in which he finds himself— e.g., masturbating in the shower, arguing with a hallucination of his psychiatrist, obsessively musing about Procol Harum's song "A Whiter Shade of Pale," seem all the more offensive and absurd. Ironically, though he is quite an unreliable narrator, his impulsive penchant for saying what he feels ameliorates whatever duplicity we may suspect in him. The novel makes great use of internal **focalization**, which allows readers access to Oscar's sensory engagement with his world, and also makes what would normally be an outrageous gargantuan of a character more sympathetic. Whereas the people in Oscar's world see him as an overindulgent, subpar attorney, the internally focalized narration reveals a sad and emotionally wracked, self-deprecating man-child. This interaction both invites and repulses readers. I encourage my students to examine this in greater detail.

Above all, the crowning achievement of *The Autobiography of a Brown Buffalo* is the character of Oscar Acosta and the power of his voice to shape the world (and himself) as he sees fit. Within Latino/a literature, there is nothing like Acosta's character narrator until Junot Díaz writes *The Brief Wondrous Life of Oscar Wao* in 2007—a pairing I often make in my classes on Latino/a literature. Díaz's novel is well-respected for its character narrator, Yunior de Las Casas, appearing nearly 35 years after Acosta's novel. To be sure, Acosta's playful engagement with the tradition of the autobiography and his linguistically unrestrained narrator are arguably evidence that *The Autobiography of a Brown Buffalo* is a novel before its time. Within its own historical time, Chicanos weren't interested in what seemed a self-serving, mock-serious book when the "real" political work was being done by Rubén Salazar, César Chávez, Dolores Huerta, Rodolfo "Corky" Gonzales, among others who were doing the hard work of activism. Near the end of the novel, someone asks Oscar if he's ever heard of Corky Gonzales. When he's told that Gonzales "got busted with a bunch of Chicanos during some demonstration in Denver" (177), Oscar replies, "What are the Mexicans protesting?" and through his narration, reveals that he wasn't "really concerned about the answer." Though Acosta, too, was engaged in the political fight for Chicano rights—fights revealed in his next novel, his first novel's playful irony interested very few people at the time of its publication.

Given these aspects of character narration, **focalization**, and voice, students should be urged to explore how these techniques of fiction helped Acosta's pursuit at self-definition and his own relationship to the Chicano Movement.

The Revolt of the Cockroach People (1973)

If time in the curriculum permits, I will also teach *The Revolt of the Cockroach People*—a novel that continues the adventures of Oscar Acosta, here adopting the moniker of Buffalo Zeta Brown. Like its predecessor, this novel borrows heavily from Acosta's lived experience, such as his involvement in the landmark "Trial of the St. Basil Twenty-One." Unlike the meditative and self-indulgent tone of extreme discovery that infuses *The Autobiography of a Brown Buffalo*, the political struggles of Chicanos dominate *Revolt of the Cockroach People*. Despite this, Acosta's second novel is arguably even more critically ignored than his first.

Though Acosta employs what is basically the same character narrator here as he did in his first novel, here called "Brown," I point out to the students several crucial differences. For instance, rather than the **self-reflexive** nature of his narration and his personal journey to better understand who and what he is, in *Revolt* Brown has taken on the challenge of being a champion for his "cockroach" brethren. Oscar also freely adopts the language reflecting his **Mesoamerican** heritage as signaled by the novel's opening line: "It is Christmas Eve in the year of Huitzilopochtli, 1969" (11). I help guide the students to also see a change in the protagonist's sense of self as well as his engagement with the world. I point to how internal focalization is still used but in such a way that it reveals fewer of Oscar's thoughts, musings, and hallucinations. Instead, the device is used to draw the reader's attention to the treatment of Chicanos during this turbulent period in American history. I also guide the students to see the shift from *Autobiography* Acosta where the persona is mock-hero, to the *Revolt* where Brown actually participates in events in a heroic manner. This can be most clearly identified for students in his physical change: from obese and indulgent in *Autobiography* to "tough and hard" (22) in *Revolt*.

Ideally, one would teach both novels together. This way the students can see the changes Oscar undergoes as demonstrated in the way he chooses to construct narrators for each novel. Unlike the Oscar of *Autobiography*, Brown narrates his outrage concerning the deaths of two Chicanos: Roberto Fernandez (a fictional character, in reality) and reporter Roland Zanzibar (based on the actual murder of *L.A. Times* reporter Rubén Salazar). The narration here should remind students that, despite Brown's attempts at being a folk hero for his people, he is ultimately a fallible man rife with shortcomings.

Finally, I seek to open the students' eyes and ears to the way each of Acosta's novels revels in linguistic freedom as a central ingredient to the characterization of both protagonists. A lawyer by trade and an aspiring writer, Oscar/Brown is endowed with the kind of freedom of speech few characters in Latino/a novels enjoy. My aim: that students studying these two novels examine how Oscar's linguistic freedom resonates differently in each novel, as well as how it serves the overarching design of the character; that students reflect on how Oscar's freedom to say what he pleases actually bestows upon him a certain authority that is demonstrable in the fact that he is our only conduit into these **storyworlds** about identity, equality, resistance, and power; that students understand just how the formal elements used to create *The Autobiography of a Brown Buffalo* and *The Revolt of the Cockroach People* are just as important as the content conveyed, providing an inroads to understanding the profundity of this Chicano author and his work.

Resources for teaching Oscar "Zeta" Acosta

Acosta, Oscar "Zeta." *The Autobiography of a Brown Buffalo.* 1972. New York: Vintage Books, 1989.
——. *The Revolt of the Cockroach People.* 1973. New York: Vintage, 1989.
——. *Oscar "Zeta" Acosta: The Uncollected Works.* Ed. Ilan Stavans. Houston, TX: Arte Público Press, 1996.
Aldama, Frederick Luis. *Postethnic Narrative Criticism.* Austin: University of Texas Press, 2003.
Bruce-Novoa, Juan. "Fear and loathing on the Buffalo Trail." *MELUS* 6.4 (1979): 39–50.
Carrasquillo, Marci L. "Oscar 'Zeta' Acosta's American odyssey." *MELUS* 35.1 (2010): 77–97.
Lee, Robert A. *Multicultural American Literature: Comparative Black, Native, Latino/a and Asian American Fictions.* Jackson, MS: University Press of Mississippi, 2003.
Martinez, Manuel Luis. *Countering the Counterculture: Rereading Postwar American Dissent from Jack Kerouac to Tomás Rivera.* Madison: University of Wisconsin Press, 2003.

Saldívar, José David. *Dialectics of our Americas: Genealogy, Cultural Critique, and Literary History.* Durham: Duke University Press, 1995.

Sánchez, Marta E. *"Shakin' Up" Race and Gender: Intercultural Connections in Puerto Rican, African American, and Chicano Narratives of Culture (1965–1995).* Austin, TX: University of Texas Press, 2005.

Stavans, Ilan. *Bandido: Oscar "Zeta" Acosta and the Chicano Experience.* New York: HarperCollins, 1995.

Thompson, Hunter S. *Fear and Loathing in Las Vegas: A Savage Journey to the Heart of the American Dream.* New York: Vintage, 1971.

23 Teaching Gloria Anzaldúa and Cherríe Moraga

Ellen M. Gil-Gómez

I routinely teach the works of Gloria Anzaldúa and Cherríe Moraga within my normal teaching load, singly, in combination with other authors, and from numerous approaches. This is due in no small part to the nature and scope of the works themselves. The specific classroom context wherein these authors appear influences how students contend with them. In my usual teaching assignment, I offer them most often in the introduction to Chicano/a Literature, which I teach online at least twice every year.

The institutional context, the audience for the class, and its relation to both department and university curricula have done much to affect the way I encourage students to approach these materials. While there are a number of other courses in the English Department that include Chicano/a or Latino/a literature this course is the only named course in the subject that is offered each year. Its main function is to provide English majors with a solid background in the literary area, its major authors and texts. In addition, the course is part of the Liberal Studies major curriculum (focused on preparing students planning a profession in Education) and can be taken also by majors in World Languages and Literatures. Any General Education student can select the course to fulfill their Humanities and Literature requirement and lastly any student may select it as an elective.

Even with all of these possible audiences, the usual student make-up is one-third English majors, one-third General Education students (primarily students from the Social Sciences), and one-third Liberal Studies students. No matter the major distribution, easily half are of Chicano or Latino heritage and the remaining half are not. Regardless, the vast majority have no prior experience with Chicano/a literature outside perhaps reading Sandra Cisneros's *The House on Mango Street* sometime in high school. Consequently the overriding goal of these diverse students is to learn the history, subject matter, and nature of Chicano/a literatures. My main goals for the course are that students can (1) explain how Chicano/a histories and culture have both influenced, and been influenced by important authors and literary texts; (2) how authors have conceived of, and represented, Chicano/a identity over time and in differing ways; and (3) how Chicano/a authors use varying language traditions—English, Spanish, **Caló**, and varied forms of bilingualism—differently within diverse literary genres.

To those ends I use a dual organizational approach to present these materials: both chronological and genre-based using the indispensable *Literatura Chicana* anthology along with a variety of additional single-authored texts. Accordingly, I begin the course with some Chicano/a nonfiction essays to introduce students to the main social and political articulations of Chicano identity from the 1960s. In addition, I require that students view and discuss my introductory presentation mainly focused on terminology and an overview of Chicano/a literary history alongside the first hour-long episode of the **PBS** documentary from the *Chicano! The History of the Mexican American Civil Rights Movement* series: *Quest for a Homeland* that nicely overviews the importance of Aztlán within civil rights history. Because the online format is not constrained by the same need for time management as the traditional classroom, the online course can spend a good amount of time encouraging the "deep learning" on introductory concepts that this documentary can offer. Students will understand both the historical and political beginnings of the **Chicano movement** and also consider how literature and the arts played an important role in both defining it and creating its identity for the community. The teaching of this combination of historical and artistic threads continues throughout the course as we move from genre to genre: starting with fiction, then poetry and concluding with Chicano drama. The final week of the course moves back into Chicano/a nonfiction including the works of Gloria Anzaldúa and Cherríe Moraga. I conclude with these and other contemporary essays so that students reflect upon the changes to Chicano/a identity and representations that occurred through the decades from the 1960s to the 1990s and beyond.

I use the **Blackboard platform** for all of my online teaching and in most of my introductory level literature courses I use the same basic approaches/activities for student learning. I use module specific "lectures" (videos or PowerPoint presentations). In this course I include one to introduce identity labels and their histories and a general overview of Chicano/a literary history, and one for each genre included in the class. In addition, each student must complete multiple posts each week on the Discussion Board that contains a number of questions focused on analyzing the weekly reading materials and other course content. Each student must also select, or is assigned, one presentation topic from a list of choices of contextual historical, social, and cultural topics related to Chicano/a literature. For example, topics include the history of the **Mexican Revolution**, the **Zoot Suit Riots**, as well as Chicano/a murals and graffiti art, and **Chicana feminisms**. The presentations are directly connected to the weekly content and each week approximately five revised student presentations are posted on the site for review. In addition all students must complete both a midterm and final exam that include content terms and concepts in short answer form as well as essay length analyses of literary texts. Lastly, each student must complete a final research-based analytical project wherein students must complete close reading analyses of required course texts. This flexibility both requires students to demonstrate a basic level of literary analytical skill but also gives non-literature students the freedom to approach the materials from their own disciplinary view. I have found these assignments and activities best engage the wide range of student backgrounds and experiences within the course.

The autobiographical move

Within these contexts I find these authors' texts particularly helpful to bring numerous threads of the full term's work together and also challenge students' prior expectations for Chicano/a identities and community crosscurrents. The two pieces included in *Literatura Chicana* are "La consciencia de la mestiza: Towards a New Consciousness" from Anzaldúa's groundbreaking *Borderlands/La Frontera* (1987) and Moraga's "La Güera" from her *Loving in the War Years* (1983). Both of these essays use an approach grounded in the autobiographical—also called the *testimonio* in women of color studies—which the two women made most famous in their co-edited anthology *This Bridge Called My Back:*

Writings by Radical Women of Color (1981). Indeed Moraga's essay was reprinted from that volume, and revised for her manuscript *Loving*. One useful focus to present these essays is to emphasize the importance of the autobiographical move within Chicano/a literature as a whole. It is a useful way to propose to students "that all stories are driven by desire, and that radical politics will invest subjugated desires in stories from which they were erased" (Morgensen 2011: 141). In other words, the essay provides the students with a compass direction for analyzing the interrelatedness of autobiography, silence, and political power.

By this time of the term, students can easily recognize the importance of the family and community as both makers and sources of meaning, restrictions to be pushed against, and lifelines to be made safe within. They've seen it represented to both advantage and disadvantage in fiction: Estella Trambley's "The Paris Gown," and Mario Suárez's "El Hoyo." In poetry: Corky Gonzales's "I Am Joaquín," Ricardo Sanchez's "Barrios of the World," and Bernice Zamora's "Notes from a Chicana 'Coed'." And theater: in Luis Valdez's *Los Vendidos* and Cherríe Moraga's own *Giving Up the Ghost*. These texts all, to more or less degree, demonstrate the unique struggle that Chicanos/as have as minorities within the larger American society but also as Americans from a Mexican perspective. What makes these essays most useful at this stage is that they don't just represent concepts, but synthesize and analyze their central ideas as well. They model for understanding how the above representations impact the individual and community and can be challenged.

Moraga begins her essay with "I am the very well-educated daughter of a woman who, by the standards in this country, would be considered largely illiterate. My mother was born in Santa Paula, Southern California, at a time when much of the central Valley there was still farmland. Nearly 35 years later, in 1948, she was the only daughter of six to marry an anglo, my father" (1994: 66). She goes on to analyze these two threads of her identity, one from her working class Mexican American mother, the other from her middle class Anglo father, as they created a unique struggle in her psyche: "I experience, daily, a huge disparity between what I was born into and what I was to grow up to become" (67). Thus, her mixed-race heritage adds a very unique voice within Chicano/a literature complicating the symbol of color—specifically brownness—as it directly connects to the **Mexican Indigenous** tradition and distinguishes Chicano/a identity from whiteness. Moraga's identity as "la güera," or a light-skinned woman, de-essentializes Chicano/a racial/ethnic identity and its use of color as an essential symbol of identity. (For example, the use of **la raza**, the race, as shorthand for the politicized Chicano/a community as Corky Gonzales uses it in "I Am Joaquín": "I look the same/I feel the same" (p. 221, lines 498–99).) Moraga continues by explaining how her sexual identity interconnects with her race and ethnicity: "My lesbianism is the avenue through which I learned most about silence and oppression, and it continues to be the most tactile reminder to me that we are not free human beings" (68). She analyzes these two poles of her identity, as they shaped her connection to her family, and came to know herself as an individual, as both victim of others' bias and guilty recipient of white privilege. As Moraga asks: "What is my responsibility to my roots—both white and brown, Spanish-speaking and English? I am a woman with a foot in both worlds; and I refuse the split" (73).

Gloria Anzaldúa's essay on the other hand, uses a multi-genre approach to the autobiographical rather than a personal narrative. Her essay begins conceptually, relying upon José Vasconcelos' *La Raza Cósmica*, for a racial construct that emphasizes mixture and inclusion rather than purity and exclusion. She argues that this construction of race, and thus identity broadly, is not only a Mexican concept but instead "a consciousness of the Borderlands" (75). From there she includes her bilingual poem "Una lucha de fronteras / A Struggle of Borders": "Because I, a mestiza, / continually walk out of one culture / and into another, / because I am in all cultures at the same time / *alma entre dos mundos, tres, cuatro, / me zumba la cabeza con lo contradictorio. / Estoy norteada por todas las voces que me hablan / sumultáneamente.*" (76) Here, it's her poetry that carries the autobiographical voice, and this pattern of presenting multiple voices in multiple untranslated languages juxtaposed throughout the essay reflects a different *testimonio* approach that is at once individual and communal in nature.

In many ways Anzaldúa herself, unlike Cherríe Moraga, represented the quintessential Chicano/a subject—a dark-skinned farmworker, a first generation American from immigrant parents, who spoke Spanish in the home and was born and raised in the rural Southwest. At the same time, similar to Moraga, she asks a similar series of questions: "Being a tricultural, monolingual, bilingual, or multilingual, speaking a patois, and in a state of perpetual transition, the mestiza faces the dilemma of the mixed breed: which collectivity does the daughter of a darkskinnned mother listen to?" (76) Not of mixed-race heritage, Anzaldúa instead is more cognizant here of a multi-lingual ancestry that comes from "the mixed breed" experience of any **mestiza**. In the series of answers to this question she speaks both from one mestiza's experience and from mestiza culture generally.

This autobiographical move that both of these authors make of speaking both from and against one's own culture challenges those students who may defensively believe Chicano/a literature focuses too much on reaction to those outside the community (i.e., Anglos) in order to find its voice. Both Moraga's and Anzaldúa's essays challenge the Chicano/a community's tradition of consistent sexism as well as its **homophobia**, **classism**, and **colorism**. They both do so, not through reaction or by pointing a finger at one villain (straight men, for example), but with voices that explore the nature of oppression which can enslave any individual. To emphasize this challenge by Anzaldúa and Moraga I remind students of their own first Discussion Board posts from the beginning of the quarter where many will have expressed a concern about Chicanos/as being critical of "whites" in their texts, and also a concern with their perception of the unnecessary "anger" in the "radical" political stances. It's invaluable to have students re-read their own words and impressions, and those of their classmates, on this subject and to begin to unpack the nuances of the philosophies of these two writers.

Beyond binary thinking: "I refuse the split" and "Serpent and eagle eyes"

The other major approach that Anzaldúa's and Moraga's work affords is student engagement in the development of women's views on the nature of Chicano/a identity, more specifically how their approaches forever asserted the interrelatedness of gender/ sexuality and ethnic identity, and moved Chicano/a studies into mainstream academic discussion. Both of these writers grounded their essays in interrogations, and personal and communal explorations, of the limits of binary thinking within their worlds and the Chicano/a community as a whole.

In "La Güera" Cherríe Moraga tracks her own personal history of struggle with multiple binary concepts of identity—in her case "brown" versus "white," lesbian and straight, and middle versus working class—and how her growing personal awareness reflected how these binary oppressions function generally. Her main realization after analyzing all of these binary identities and experiences: "In this country, lesbianism is a poverty—as is being brown, as is being a woman, as is being just plain poor. The danger lies in ranking the oppressions. The danger lies in failing to acknowledge the specificity of the oppression. The danger lies in attempting to deal with oppression purely from a theoretical base" (68). The concepts articulated here are specific examples of the "theory in the flesh" approach that is described in the introductory materials from *This Bridge Called My Back*: "A theory in the flesh means one where the physical realities of our lives—our skin color, the land or concrete we grew up on, our sexual longings—all fuse to create a politic born out of necessity. Here we attempt to bridge the contradictions of our experience" (23). Moraga continually insists upon the importance of lived realities, of physical, emotional, and sexual experience in shaping identity and the extension of those elements to the communal level so as to form political and social movements. This concept consequently found important articulations and further development in women of color and postcolonial feminisms both inside and outside of Chicano Studies.

Moraga's concerns contrast with the majority of early voices defining Chicano identity and consciousness from the 1960s wherein women's lives, and definitely lesbians, were erased from the equation. In the *Literatura Chicana* anthology specifically the two earlier essays from Macías ("The Evolution of the Mind") and Romano-V ("The Historical and Intellectual Presence of Mexican Americans") both originally published in 1969 include no women as examples or within the analyses. While Chicana authors are a major part of the anthology, as are representations of gender oppression, it's Anzaldúa and Moraga that synthesize these concerns so as to challenge prior Chicano/a identity constructs. Some students are mindful and critical of the masculinist emphasis fairly early in the term, while others confront it in the last weeks of class.

Moraga's insistence that "I refuse the split" (73) within the multiple layers of oppression foregrounds that which is not easy to organize around, as she describes: "it is looking to the nightmare that the dream is found ... a vision, yes, born out of what is dark and female" (73–74). Thus, she suggests that every individual and community must explore internal oppressions in order to be liberatory. As she says directly in an interview from *Voices from the Gaps*:

> I believe in the Chicano Nation (the right and longing for "place") and also fundamentally believe that what continues to weaken and sicken us as a "pueblo" is homophobia and an entrenched misogyny. This is not to say I feel these oppressive behaviors are more prevalent among Chicanos than other groups, only that Chicanos are those who I care to cure.

Moraga's approach challenges and encourages students to think critically about how Chicano/a literature has reflected its defining ideals, and how transforming definitions of identity altered literary representations.

Anzaldúa's approach to the same questions—the limits of binary thinking and domination of binary categories—is far more theoretical and broadly metaphorical than is Moraga's emphasis on the physical plane of identity. This important difference ensures that when comparing and contrasting these essays students are not left with the impression that just like there is no one "Chicano" approach there is likewise no one "Chicana lesbian" approach to conceptualizing identity. Anzaldúa is best known for introducing the binary challenging concepts of "mestiza consciousness" (78) and "consciousness of the Borderlands" (75) into mainstream academic discourse. She also delineates historical and cultural concepts that make up oppressive binaries such as: machismo, homophobia, white supremacy, and others. "The struggle is inner: Chicano, *indio*, American Indian, *mojado*, *mexicano*, immigrant Latino, Anglo in power, working class Anglo, Black, Asian—our psyches resemble the bordertowns and are populated by the same people. The struggle has always been inner, and is played out in the outer terrains" (85). Her view increases the connectedness of different identities simultaneously challenging and welcoming diverse students into the conversation in a way that no other essay from the text does. Many introductory students have a difficult time with these complexities and thus I have students first brainstorm what Anzaldúa might mean by mestizas seeing "through serpent and eagle eyes" (77). All students who have reviewed the prior course content are quite familiar with the symbolic power and meaning of these images—from the Mexican flag, a depiction of the founding of Tenochtitlán, later Mexico City, an Aztec origin story—so that they can trace its use and meanings throughout prior representations and finally better comprehend the suggestions that Anzaldúa makes.

These two authors, Gloria Anzaldúa and Cherríe Moraga, mark an important place in the course where Chicano/a thought turned inward to both critique and conceptualize their community and experiences as "inner" struggles as well as "outer" ones. At the same moment, Chicano/a thought moved outside of the "minority" community and into the mainstream academic and literary conversation.

Resources for teaching Gloria Anzaldúa and Cherríe Moraga

Aldama, Frederick Luis. *Spilling the Beans in Chicanolandia: Conversations with Writers and Artists.* Austin: University of Texas Press, 2006.

Esquibel, Catrióna Rueda. *With Her Machete in Her Hand: Reading Chicana Lesbians.* Austin: University of Texas Press, 2006.

Hernández, Ellie D. *Postnationalism in Chicana/o Literature and Culture.* Austin: University of Texas Press, 2009.

Martínez, Ernesto J. *On Making Sense: Queer Race Narratives of Intelligibility.* Stanford: Stanford University Press, 2013.

Martínez-Cruz, Paloma. *Women and Knowledge in Mesoamerica: From East L.A. to Anahuac.* Tucson, AZ: University of Arizona Press, 2012.

Minich, Julie. *Accessible Citizenships: Disability, Nation, and the Cultural Politics of Greater Mexico.* Philadelphia: Temple University Press, 2013.

24 Teaching Ana Castillo

Part 1

Magdalena L. Barrera

My approach to teaching Chicano/a literature is shaped by my institutional setting. I teach in Mexican-American Studies, a small interdisciplinary department with an undergraduate minor at a large, urban university. There is only one Chicano/a literature class on campus; it is one of surprisingly few ethnic literature courses in the entire "majority minority" school. Most students in the course are Chicano/a social science majors who last took a literature class in high school. As first-generation college students, they feel pressured to take "practical" classes and choose the course for leisure. Though drawn in by the content, they hesitate to "read too much" into the texts. In this setting, my goals are to help students (a) develop close reading skills, (b) learn to make an argument about literature, and (c) reflect more deeply on *all* texts, considering not just what they say, but how they say it.

The final two weeks of the course focus on Ana Castillo's *So Far from God* (1993). Castillo's best-known novel presents students with opportunities to explore issues of ethnic identity, histories of struggle and oppression, gender ideologies, sexual and regional identities within Chicano/a communities, religious traditions, folklore and **curanderismo,** and environmentalism. By this point in the semester, students have practiced close readings and are capable of examining the imagery and symbolism in Castillo's writing. I open with a discussion of how Castillo's experience of growing up poor and ethnically marginalized in Chicago runs through her oeuvre; she writes, "My prose and poems are often populated by narrators who also experience alienation and yet make a place for themselves in the world" ("Looking for Mambo" 1996: 3). *So Far from God* engages directly with this theme: Set in the small town of Tome, New Mexico, the novel tells the story of Sofia and her four daughters—Esperanza, Caridad, Fe, and Loca—as they struggle to find love and live in peace. I approach *So Far from God* as a text that invites students to explore, on a number of levels, the meaning of faith.

Faith in Castillo and the process of reading

Guiding questions:

- How does this novel challenge you as a reader?
- How does magical realism enhance the story?
- Who is the narrator, and how do we know?

The first challenge students face is to have faith in Castillo as a writer, as *So Far from God* is a novel unlike any other they have encountered. In the first chapter, Castillo introduces the primary characters, quickly describing their biographies and personalities. Three of Sofia's daughters have names based on Christian ideals—Esperanza (Hope),

Caridad (Charity), and Fe (Faith). Because students confuse their biographical details, I ask students to consider how their names relate to their experiences: "To whom does Esperanza give hope? What does she hope for herself? Where does Fe place her faith?". Such questions allow them to connect characters' names to their roles in the text.

Castillo also uses plot developments that surprise students: Three-year-old Loca springs back to life during her funeral; Fe screams nonstop for weeks when dumped by her fiancé; Caridad is inexplicably restored to perfect health after a brutal attack. These plot points introduce students to **magical realism**, "a storytelling format whereby the narrative in its totality defies the physical, social, and biological laws of nature" (Aldama 2014: 133). I push students to consider how magical realism illuminates Chicano/a community struggles. Students note that Castillo's use of magical realism, which prevents them from predicting what may happen, challenges them to be present with the text.

The narrator's tone is also a point of discussion. Though the narrator uses an omniscient third-person voice, there are brief moments when the first-person emerges: "[L]ike I said, [St. Anthony] is for finding things, not people" (82). At these junctures, I ask students to imagine who the narrator is. Students collect subtle details: First, the narrator uses double negatives—Sofia "couldn't take no more the reality of a permanently traumatized daughter" (34)—a trait that reflects the local idiom (Romero). Second, the narrator is familiar with community gossip: "this all depends on who is telling the story, and as far as anybody has been able to put it all together, it begins something like this" (120). Students surmise that the narrator is likely a local resident of Tome, gossiping with us about Sofia's family saga. Through such strategies, Castillo brings readers into the community of the novel.

Castillo's awareness of the reader's experience also emerges in her chapter titles, such as "What Appears to Be a Deviation of Our Story but Wherein, with Some Patience, the Reader Will Discover That There Is Always More Than the Eye Can See to Any Account" (120). Anticipating readers' confusion—perhaps exasperation—with the introduction of new characters and side plots, Castillo writes, "[W]ith some patience … a few people actually made the connection in the end, like in one of those connect-the-dots games" (120). Students learn that what appears to be an unrelated diversion actually serves to develop the main story. At one point, the narrator explains that like the side plots of *So Far from God*, "this existence of ours has no start and no finish but is the continuance of a journey on an endless, unpaved road" (124). I use this statement as a writing prompt, inviting students to explore this philosophical view and their experience as readers of the text.

Faith in cultural and women's resilience

Guiding questions:

* What cultural traditions are alive in Tome?
* What challenges do female characters face, and what tools do they use to confront them?

A second theme of *So Far from God* related to faith is its rich representation of cultural resilience and women's ability to heal themselves and their communities. Through two minor characters that reflect local traditions, Castillo presents an opportunity to consider representations of ***nuevomexicano* regional identity** within Chicano/a literature. For example, Francisco el Penitente is a santero who carves **bultos**, "a wooden sculpture of a saint" (96). In New Mexico, santeros are believed to be guided by the saints they carve, and by adopting this vocation, Francisco heals from his experience in the Vietnam War. I help students connect to this unfamiliar tradition by showing images of **santero** folk art. Francisco is also notable because the novel's title is embedded in a description of him: Francisco and his uncle "worked together in silence—like their Spanish ancestors had done for nearly three hundred years on that strange land they felt was so far from God" (102). Here, we pause to reflect on why *nuevomexicanos* might feel "so far from God," and how folk traditions mitigate feelings of displacement.

Francisco's godmother Doña Felicia represents another significant folk tradition: Curanderismo, a syncretic blend of physical and spiritual healing based on Christian prayers and indigenous medicinal knowledge. Castillo again shifts narrative perspective and creates a segment of the book that reads as a "how to" manual of curanderismo. In "A Brief Sampling of Doña Felicia's Remedies," readers take the position of Caridad receiving lessons from Felicia on how to cure gastrointestinal obstruction; internal draft; evil eye; and spiritual cleansing (65–71). Just as the comadre-like narrator directly addresses the readers, so too does Castillo invite them to learn this healing tradition and carry on these practices and beliefs.

Castillo thus presents an entry point into a discussion of curanderismo's relation to women's resilience in the novel. Felicia survived the Mexican Revolution and the Great Depression, worked as a nurse in Europe during the Second World War, and faced the violent deaths of two of her eight children. Felicia, who "had nothing but faith left and devoted herself to healing" (62) mentors Caridad, who then develops a reputation as a healer and a medium, a major turnaround from her previously wild life.

Another point of discussion is Sofia's decision to become the mayor of Tome. She begins a collective sheep-grazing and wool-weaving enterprise, and turns her meat market into a cooperative business, actions that heal and revitalize the town. The people of Tome overcome complacency and undertake other collective community efforts, such as confronting the local drug problem. The seeds of these changes, Sofia explains, were sown many years prior by her eldest daughter:

> [Esperanza] always talked about things like working to change the "system." I never paid no attention to her then ... but I see that the only way things are going to get better around here, is if we, all of us together, try to do something about it.
> (142)

Sofia's overdue embrace of Esperanza's activism helps her shed her own complacency in her marriage, leading her to finally divorce her gambler husband. She questions what the point is of being a "good" woman, as defined by mainstream cultural expectations. Students identify such sentiments as reflecting the spirit of **Chicana feminism** that undergirds the novel: the idea that women's perseverance and faith have the ability to transform not only themselves, but also entire communities.

Extremes of faith

Guiding questions:

- What kind of faith is worth keeping?
- What are the consequences of carrying faith too far?

The third form of faith we explore questions the extremes. In this area, we focus on two particular characters: Fe and Francisco. Students are struck by the cruel fate of Fe, the literal *faith* of the novel. Of Sofia's daughters, she is the most conformist, working to distance herself from her roots and striving for mainstream middle-class respectability. She places so much faith in her fiancé that the end of their engagement nearly breaks her. Fe gets a brief glimpse of happiness years later when she falls in love with her cousin Casey and finally may live "a life like people do on T.V." (189). Her happiness ends abruptly when she takes a job disposing of hazardous chemicals. Without proper ventilation and protective clothing, the chemicals seep into her body, and she develops terminal cancer.

Though all of Sofia's daughters die over the course of the novel, the narrator especially mourns Fe, because

> she did not resurrect as La Loca did at age three. She also did not return ecto-plasmically like her tenacious earth-bound sister Esperanza. Very shortly after that first prognosis, Fe just died. And when someone dies that plain dead, it is hard to talk about.
>
> (186)

At this point, I return to one of the earliest questions we pose of the text: In whom does Fe place her faith? Fe blindly follows mainstream conventions, seeking the approval of her white friends and blindly trusting in powerful corporations to pave her way to a happy ending. The novel argues that in following a path so far afield from her cultural traditions, Fe endangers herself. The chemicals and compounds she handles are at the opposite end of the spectrum from those handled by Felicia and Caridad; as a result, she literally is eaten away from the inside rather than nourished and restored.

Meanwhile, Francisco's embodiment of Catholic faith and the santero tradition takes a dark turn. I push students to examine clues about how his santero community is predominated by men "seeking absolution through penance and mortification" (96). Francisco has had only one romantic relationship, which ended in disillusionment when "his angel [was] on to other men" (100). Francisco, in viewing women as heavenly creatures, holds them to impossible ideals. His behavior grows increasingly bizarre; he becomes obsessed with Caridad to the point of stalking both her and her love interest, Esmeralda. His aunt Loretta can see the danger, yet she "knew well enough that it would do no good to laugh nor cry about what she saw the men in her husband's family do in the name of God" (191). In carrying his santero knowledge too far, Francisco becomes a greater threat to Caridad and Esmeralda as time goes on, leading to one of the most challenging moments for students in the novel, described below.

Students' faith in themselves

Guiding questions:

- What—or who—is the malogra?
- Can we finally "connect the dots"?
- How do you interpret what happens to Caridad and Esmeralda at Sky City?

As we near the end of the semester, students read one of the most difficult passages, the novel's climax, in which Caridad and Esmeralda run off the edge of the cliff of Sky City, only to disappear into the earth without a trace, followed by Francisco found hanging from a tree. The narrator opens the door for us to understand when she explains, "*Tsichtinako was calling!*" (211). Knowing that students will not look up Tsichtinako on their own, I distribute a copy of the Acoma creation story, explain the significance of the Sky City location (the oldest continually inhabited settlement in the United States), and instruct them to reread the passage.

Students work to piece together this part of the narrative: Caridad and Esmeralda represent the first two humans, **Iatiku** and **Nautsiti**, while the shadowy Francisco stands in for the disobedient Locust, punished for his transgressions. I encourage students to return to earlier unanswered questions: What is the malogra that attacked Caridad? Understanding that Castillo draws from Native American narratives, students begin to understand the description of the malogra, "made of sharp metal and splintered wood, of limestone, gold, and brittle parchment" (77), as a metaphor for the forces of settler colonialism and genocide. The discussion turns to how the contemporary Chicanas struggle with such painful legacies. After discussing how Francisco carries his faith too far and harbors a simultaneous desire and fear of Caridad (who is in love with Esmeralda), students experience an "a-ha!" moment: They suggest that Francisco may be the maniac who threatens a lesbian couple in an earlier "interlude," a side story that Castillo promised would have an eventual pay-off.

Over the course of the semester, the students move from having no background in Chicano/a literature to being able to interpret the most challenging passages of *So Far from God*. As we complete our discussion of the novel, students no longer preface their comments with, "I don't know if I'm reading too much into this quote, but ... " When I point this out, they are amazed to realize that Chicano/a literature has enabled them to develop faith in themselves as interpreters of literary texts.

This point represents a transformative moment for our classroom community: When students see themselves, their families, and their communities reflected in literature assigned to them, they are willing to make a deeper time investment to read and analyze these texts. Such connection makes a world of difference for first-generation Latino/a students who experience education as an institution that devalues their skills and knowledge. Novels like *So Far from God* present us not only with the opportunity to imagine lively, magically real worlds, but also to rebuild students' confidence and enthusiasm for the humanities—and nothing could have greater "real world" impact.

Resources for teaching Ana Castillo's *So Far from God*

Aldama, Frederick Luis. *Postethnic Narrative Criticism: Magicorealism in Ana Castillo, Hanif Kureishi, Julie Dash, Oscar "Zeta" Acosta, and Salman Rushdie.* Austin: University of Texas Press, 2003.

Caminero-Santangelo, Marta. "'The pleas of the desperate': collective agency versus magical realism in Ana Castillo's *So Far from God.*" *Tulsa Studies in Women's Literature* 24:1 (Spring 2005): 81–103.

Delgadillo, Theresa. "Forms of Chicana feminist resistance: hybrid spirituality in Ana Castillo's *So Far from God.*" *Modern Fiction Studies* 44:4 (1998): 888–916.

Lanza, Carmela Delia. "Hearing the voices: women and home and Ana Castillo's *So Far from God.*" *MELUS* 23:1 (Spring, 1998): 65–79.

Manríquez, B. J. "Ana Castillo's *So Far from God*: intimations of the absurd." *College Literature* 29:2 (Spring 2002): 37–49.

Martínez, Danizete. "Teaching Chicano/a literature in community college with Ana Castillo's *So Far from God*." *Rocky Mountain Review* 65:2 (Fall 2011): 216–25.

Rodríguez, Ralph E. "Chicano/a fiction from resistance to contestation: the role of creation in Ana Castillo's *So Far from God*." *MELUS* 25:2 (Summer 2000): 63–82.

Saeta, Elsa, and Ana Castillo. "A MELUS interview: Ana Castillo." *MELUS* 22:3 (Autumn, 1997): 133–49.

25 Teaching Ana Castillo
Part 2

Nan Tynberg

While Magdelena Barrera focused on Ana Castillo's *So Far from God* (1993), in my snapshot approach to teaching Castillo, I will focus on her hybrid novel *Peel My Love Like an Onion* (2000). I situate the teaching of this novel within a Studies in Literary Diversity course where I also include three other contemporary American writers: Toni Morrison, Sherman Alexie, and Maxine Hong Kingston.

In my 26 years in the English Department of California State University, San Bernardino, I taught upper-division literature courses at the Palm Desert satellite campus. By and large our students transfer from the local community college (College of the Desert), yet represent a diverse demography in terms of ethnic background and age span. (I like to say I teach "ages 28 to 78"!) Our campus attracts a non-traditional college population for a number of reasons: we are a resort and retirement community, an agricultural and light-industrial region, and we are home to a large military base in nearby Twentynine Palms, California. The once-a-week, four-hour schedule for seminar classes was designed to meet the needs of an adult, working population. This mix of students and my back-ground in Comparative Literature lent itself to creating a multiethnic course. I also had to consider other extracurricular factors, such as class size (about 20) and number of weeks in the quarter (ten), when selecting reading material. This snapshot approach to teaching *Peel My Love Like an Onion* in a comparative literary context will reflect on how a diverse group of students, with widely different experiences in reading, writing, and discussing literature, can join forces to illuminate a unique fusion of late twentieth-century American works.

The principal goal of the Studies in Literary Diversity course is to achieve maximum student participation during the four-hour classroom experience. The nature of the reading material encourages student involvement in a number of ways. Along with *Peel My Love*, I include Toni Morrison's *Sula* (1982), Sherman Alexie's *Reservation Blues* (1995), and Maxine Hong Kingston's *The Woman Warrior* (1989). Each is informed by oral and folkloric "performance" structures (song, dance, storytelling) in their themes and organizing features. During the first class meeting, we watch a video of American Indian writer Leslie Marmon Silko, who gossips with friends on her back porch and tells trickster tales to children by the fireside, visually and orally demonstrating "the doing of folklore … involving performer, art form, audience, and setting" (Bauman 1995: 290). We then read a selection from the course packet that includes all required reading tales, legends, stories, and songs. These provide cultural background for each of the novels. As prelude to Castillo's *Peel My Love*, we study the ballad "El Corrido de Gregorio Cortez." There are always a few Spanish speakers in the class who volunteer to read the Spanish version of the verses. One student even asked to sing the *corrido*, making up her own melody to fit the words and rhythms. Because the typical corrido celebrates the exploits of Mexican outlaws on the border, it is an ironic introduction to Castillo's work. The male figures in *Peel My Love* are anything but heroic. The book is about the small triumphs of women, but they are victories nonetheless.

All four works in the course challenge the conventions of the traditional novel. They are, in fact, hybrids, accessible combinations of memoir, testimony, drama, myth, history, and poetry. These open forms tend to draw in the reader and encourage his or her participation in the narrative. Class time is devoted to reading aloud the various forms of spoken language in the works, for example: gossip, arguments, talk-stories, and poetry. In spite of *Peel My Love's* subtitle, "*A Novel*," the book is divided into installments, with melodramatic headings ("uno: I remember him dark"), more **telenovela** than novel. In contrast to the traditional Western fictive heroine and narrator, I draw attention to how Carmen is more like a standup comedienne, or drama queen of soap opera. The further division of "installments" arranges them into arbitrary Spanish-numbered sequences or steps. On one occasion, a student suggested that this pattern mimics a "fractured tango," like crippled Carmen with a bum leg. She has all the passion and beauty of a flamenco dancer, but more often than not, misses a beat.

The rest of the study is devoted to how the class, divided into teams, approaches the three archetypal figures who animate the works of Castillo, Morrison, Alexie, and Hong Kingston: the Trickster, the Ghost, and the Weeping Woman. Team responses to a list of prearranged questions not only engenders class participation, but ensures that students work with their classmates in an informal, less structured setting. For example, each team meets anywhere on campus during the break. For a class of 20, there would be five teams. The teams decide how to apportion any aspect of the question, including that of "reader from text." At any time during the subsequent presentation of answers, students from the class at large can add a comment, or read from their journals relative to the discussion. I include in bold below some typical team day questions.

Trickster: The trickster figure resists a simple definition. All the same, Carmen, Sula, Thomas Builds-the-Fire, and Maxine, our leading characters, are tricksters. They are iconoclasts and oxymorons, pariahs and paradoxes. They are all restless and peripatetic. Mostly they are shape-shifters. Their impairments and bodily markings not only define them physically—conditions that mutate over time—but drive the plot as well. The left leg of Carmen "la Coja" [The Cripple], "a dead gnarled limb, thin and crooked" (13), results from childhood polio. She is driven to defy her status as "disabled" by becoming a renowned flamenco dancer. When post-poliomyelitis sets in during her 40s, Carmen finds another artistic outlet: singing. The innocuous-seeming rose or tadpole or crook above nine-year-old Sula's eye darkens with time. When she returns to the Bottom in her 20s, she brings with her a plague of robins, among other misfortunes. The birthmark is then perceived as a snake or dagger. Goofy-looking Thomas Builds-the-Fire, with his big head and crooked teeth, is a compulsive "narrator" due to neural or spiritual overload. He uses this compulsion to form a hybrid blues band whereby he writes all the song lyrics and appoints himself lead singer. Maxine's mother often repeats an anecdote about how she deliberately cut the frenum of her infant Maxine's tongue. Just as often, though, Maxine's mother (Brave Orchid) retracts the story. Maxine considers that this mutilation was done to promote silence and obedience in a girl child or, paradoxically, to provide a daughter with a sense of liberation. Maxine's squeaky "pressed-duck" voice goes on to describe a first-generation Chinese American childhood and to retell, in her own fashion, Brave Orchid's talk-stories.

> **Question: Throughout *Peel My Love Like an Onion*, Carmen undergoes many physical changes not polio related. What are they?**

Trickster heroes have mythological forebears as well as progenitors closer to home. Harold Scheub explains: "The trickster ... exists both in our time and in myth-time" (2012: 30). Carmen's mother, Amá, and Maxine's mother, Brave Orchid, are antecedent con artists and fabulators. Sula's audacity and preternatural power over others are inherited from her maternal grandmother, Eva Peace. In *Reservation Blues*, Big Mom is not the biological source for Thomas's trickster nature but she is his soul parent. Big Mom is caretaker of all things tribal and musical, and the unassuming Thomas is her only reservation acolyte.

> **Question: Carmen (*Peel My Love*) and Eva Peace (*Sula*) have either unworkable or missing legs. Are they similar in other ways? How are they different?**

In the inscriptive poem that opens *Peel My Love*, Carmen appeals to Tezcatlipoca, "*horned creature to whom / I have given wings, come back*" (10–11). Carmen's shifting physical states and her many-layered psychic identities are connected to the Toltec trickster-god who is "sometimes depicted with a sacrificed leg and a smoking mirror emerging from his stump" (Bost 2010: 161). Carmen is variously labeled "cripple," "Chicago Chicana," barroom dancer, *gaji* (non-gypsy), *calorra* (gypsy), Augustín's woman, Manolo's woman, etc., but the real portrayal is one of resistance to labels. She refuses to be constrained by physical limitations, lovers, family, or cultural identities. While Sula's verbal gymnastics with her grandmother—the "sputin en contendin" (Chandler Harris 2004: 2)—recall African American tricksters Br'er Rabbit and Br'er Fox, her alliance with West African trickster-deity Eshu is paramount. Brian George (2011) writes: "To say that Eshu is destructive is like saying that fire is hot." There are many voices who narrate *Reservation Blues*: the rez news, for example; but it is the journal of Thomas Builds-the-Fire that provides the definition of Coyote, his avatar: "A trickster whose bag of tricks contains permutations of love, hate, weather, chance, laughter, and tears, for example, Lucille Ball" (48). Thomas is what Gerald Vizenor calls a "comic liberator and word healer" trickster, trying to do good, even as he gets under one's skin (qtd. in Rosier Smith 1997: 72). "The tricksterlike image of the elusive, ever-changing dragon appears throughout *The Woman Warrior*, suggesting the impossibility of a single all-encompassing perspective" (34). Maxine and Brave Orchid were born in "dragon years" and are unreliable narrators, although Maxine is the craftier "knotmaker" storyteller (109, 163). Her account of the Fa Mu Lan legend ("White Tigers") reveals a young woman in multiple roles: fearsome warrior one day, the proverbial "wife or slave" the next (19).

> **Question: Both Carmen (*Peel My Love*) and Maxine (*The Woman Warrior*) are, at times, family outcasts. Why? What brings them back into the fold?**

Ghost: As a concept, the "ghost" is as elaborate as everything else in the four novels. In addition to the actual dead, ghosts are: shell-shocked vets; drunks; drug addicts and delinquent dads; wandering lovers and missing husbands. The principal ghosts, however, who serve as agents of change for our main characters, are anything but shadowy figures; they are colorful spirit helpers, unwitting boosters of artistry and potential. Manolo is Carmen's head ghost. He is a dark-skinned gypsy flamenco star, her lover and dancing partner for one all-consuming year. But Manolo disappears, only to resurface as a tired, feckless nobody. Sula's ghost is Shadrack. Fire and water are threads that run through *Sula*, and Shadrack embodies both. Unlike his Old Testament namesake, Shadrack does not escape unscathed from the blast furnace of hell. He is a shell-shocked survivor of the First World War. If Sula has a conscience, his name is Shadrack. She fears no man, with his exception. She is not afraid of Shadrack's ravings, but of the mistaken belief that he witnessed the accidental drowning of Chicken Little for which she was the cause. The only Indian to greet Robert Johnson at the crossroads of the Wellpinit Reservation and an empty highway is Thomas Builds-the-Fire. One doesn't know whether it was Thomas or Big Mom who conjured up the greatest blues guitarist in history; what is important is the black man's role as Thomas's friendly ghost and the bequeathing of Johnson's legendary guitar to the Coyote Springs band. The subtitle of *The Woman Warrior* is "*Memoirs of a Girlhood Among Ghosts*," and hundreds of ghosts—of every stripe—make their appearance. No Name Aunt is the one ghost who most enlivens Maxine's imagination and sense of justice. Maxine resurrects her aunt from family disgrace and obscurity by imagining no less than seven scenarios to explain the woman's out-of-wedlock pregnancy.

> **Question: The so-called friends of Thomas Builds-the-Fire in *Reservation Blues* are Victor and Junior. They are clowns, but also ghosts. Point out language in the text to suggest that the boys are "walking dead."**

Weeping Woman: The La LLorona legend (The Weeping Woman) in the course packet is a traditional version and a cautionary tale: La LLorona drowns her children out of spite, Medea style, against a philandering husband, and is forever condemned to walk the earth wailing for her loss. This cultural and gender stereotype, of woman dependent on her man for identity and direction, at any cost, is challenged in all four novels. Dry-eyed and single, Eva Peace kills her drug-addicted son by setting him on fire to save him from a life of future pain. Similarly, No Name Aunt drowns herself and her newborn in the family well as protection against reprisals from a disapproving family. Androgynous Big Mom, "with fingers as big as [] arms" (204), is tribal leader and healer. This matriarchal role is in keeping with a traditional American Indian worldview, but Thomas Builds-the-Fire is an anomaly, past or present. Neither warrior nor drunk, he houses and feeds the band, a tender-of-the-hearth, a caretaker. Sula's manifesto, "I don't want to make somebody else. I want to make myself" (92) is echoed by Carmen: "In our own skin we can be reincarnated. You don't have to have a baby, reproduce yourself for a new and improved you" (197).

> **Question: Carmen's stoic mother, Amá, cries only once in the novel. When does she weep?**

In this snapshot approach to teaching Ana Castillo's *Peel My Love Like an Onion* I identify the novel as the linchpin to teaching the four other American ethnic novels in a course on literary diversity. These narratives represent an oral tradition and students are encouraged to participate fully in the classroom via reading aloud, performance, and team presentation.

Resources for teaching *Peel My Love Like an Onion*

Aldama, Frederick Luis. *Brown on Brown: Chicano/a Representations of Gender, Sexuality, and Ethnicity.* Austin: University of Texas Press, 2005.

Bost, Suzanne. *Encarnacion: Illness and Body Politics in Chicana Feminist Literature.* New York: Fordham University Press, 2009.

Lopez, Marissa. *Chicano Nations: The Hemispheric Origins of Mexican American Literature.* New York: New York University Press, 2011.

Martin, Rebecca. "*Peel My Love Like an Onion* de Ana Castillo: El amor 'antiromantico' y la audiencia major." *Hipertexto* 8 (Winter 2008): 63–71.

Quintana Millamto, María Esther. "Aprendiendo a amarse a sí misma: Peel My Love Like an Onion de Ana Castillo." *Confluencia* 26.1 (Fall 2010): 120–31.

Rose, Jane E. "Negotiating work in the novels of Ana Castillo: social disease and the American dream." *CLA Journal* 54.4 (June 2011): 387–409.

Soto, K. Sandra. *Reading Chican@ Like a Queer: The De-Mastery of Desire.* Austin: University of Texas Press, 2010.

Tarr, Andrea. "On the literary road with the gypsies." *Library Journal* 129.20 (Dec. 2004): 186.

Villar Raso, Manuel, Maria Herrera-Sobek. "A Spanish novelist's perspective on Chicano/a literature." *Journal of Modern Literature* 25.1 (2001): 17–34.

26 Teaching Sandra Cisneros's *House on Mango Street*

Brant M. Torres

I first encountered Sandra Cisneros's fiction as a college freshman in a class on literary theory. What that experience taught me, and what it did *not* teach me, continues to guide how I approach her work with my own students. Reading Cisneros alongside literary theorists like Julia Kristeva, Helen Cixous, and Judith Butler allowed me to see how a text that could be read as young adult literature could also be read for issues of race, gender, sexuality, and other cultural constructions. In our class on theory, Cisneros's *The House on Mango Street* (1989) acted as a kind of testing ground for the different theoretical approaches we had been struggling with throughout the semester. We discussed how her prose could illustrate *l'écriture féminine* and how her stories could confront the reader with different modes of **alterity**. We talked about the social construction of gender, about race, and about how Cisneros's work gave voice to the ways subjects encounter, struggle with, and come to terms with class, race, sexuality, and gender performativity.

While reading Cisneros as a freshman and being challenged to put her work in conversation with a theorist like Cixous, I was also getting something more from her work, something visceral, more personal, and unarticulated—something I struggled to name, something that the theory I was learning didn't really help me to understand. *The House on Mango Street* (and later, *Woman Hollering Creek and Other Stories* (1991)) exposed me to something strangely familiar. Cisneros's stories were closer to home. In the pages of *Mango Street*, I was reminded of growing up in a Mexican-American community, of being educated in a bilingual school, of being around names like Salcedo, López, and Velázquez, of referring to the women who were my teachers in elementary school as Señora and Señorita. Cisneros's work didn't just capture the language of the neighborhoods I was quick to move away from in my efforts to fit in at college as a first-generation student—but her tone, her style, captured some half-remembered richness.

I open up with the biographical because it directly informs how I now teach a text like *The House on Mango Street*. For many scholars teaching Latino/a literature, our pedagogical investments and goals have roots in our own experiences. Certainly, we must encourage students to think about form, tone, voice, and figurative language in Cisneros. A text like *The House on Mango Street*, with its natural, ingenuous tone and straightforward, simple sentences belies a rich, artful complexity. When students encounter the text it can push them to engage with language, allowing for the opportunity to unpack and critique what they might otherwise register as simple and straightforward. As such, *The House on Mango Street* can also work as an excellent means for students to explore concepts such as how language constructs categories of gender, sexuality, race, class, and ethnicity. And *The House on Mango Street* invites students to think about our personal lives and our own communities. Moreover,

Cisneros beautifully articulates and encourages readers to explore new (sometimes strange and sometimes forgotten) ways of knowing and being in the world.

When teaching Cisneros, I invite students to think about how a culture finds both its voice and its epistemology in smaller moments, be they personal or communal. In my experience as a teacher, while a work like *The House on Mango Street* invites students to listen to a Chicana voice, it also motivates them to find their own voice—something I actively encourage. I know that some teachers move away from doing this in classrooms devoted to literary criticism and not creative writing. When I've asked why, I've been told that they fear the classroom will slant more toward a book club than a space for rigorous close readings, engagement with literary concepts, and cultural criticism. But I don't believe these are mutually exclusive modes of reading, nor should they be.

In fact, with writing that calls so much attention to inner emotional lives, I think it a disservice to students to not allow them to reflect on how their own culture(s) and inner worlds find expression in language. One way I invite students to engage the personal while also keeping larger cultural issues in mind is by opening with a pair of vignettes, "Marin" and "Those Who Don't" from *Mango Street*. Part of the power of Cisneros's vignettes rests in her ability to zoom in and out of personal moments within the larger context of community. In "Those Who Don't" we get a wider view of Esperanza's neighborhood. The vignette hinges on perspectival differences of insider/ outsider to demonstrate not only how race unites and separates communities but also how it creates different ways of knowing. Describing the neighborhood, Esperanza says "All brown all around, we are safe. But watch us drive into a neighborhood of another color and our knees go shakity-shake and our car windows get rolled up tight and our eyes look straight" (28). I encourage students to explore how Esperanza constructs an outsider's perspective of her neighborhood as dangerous in contrast with her own view that is grounded in the intimate relations that create a sense of safety. Moreover, I guide the students to see how this story is also a reflection of how they (as readers) relate to the text. Cisneros writes, "Those who don't know any better come into our neighborhood scared. They think we're dangerous" (28). I remind students that one of our tasks as readers is attempting to "know better." And part of the way we do that is through a more direct and intimate understanding of others' experiences. By carefully reading *Mango Street* students become self-reflexive of their own entrance into a textual neighborhood that asks them to become more familiar with its characters.

While pushing students to think about *Mango Street* globally, I also invite them to relate to it more personally, which is my reason for having students look at "Those Who Don't" and "Marin" as a pair. "Marin" directly precedes "Those Who Don't." In many ways, "Marin" is a story about being stuck: in a bad job, in a specific neighborhood, in a certain class, in a specific body. I find that this story encourages students to think about the larger structures (political and cultural) that either confine or shape identities. While students willingly engage such concepts on a more abstract and impersonal level, it seems that the final lines of "Marin" are where we always end up pausing. Cisneros concludes, "Marin, under the streetlight, dancing by herself, is singing the same song somewhere. I know. Is waiting for a car to stop, a star to fall, someone to change her life" (27). In this final moment, students describe a visceral reaction to a sense of hope and Marin's almost debilitating struggle for agency. Cisneros illustrates Marin's painful hopefulness complicated and shaped by larger cultural and political structures. *The House on Mango Street* is one of the best texts I've encountered that helps students to see that cultural, economic, and political structures are never abstractions; they are felt and experienced in quotidian moments.

Calling attention to the relationship between larger cultural structures and affect allows students to also pause and reflect on the personal as it relates to the literary. How does the literary allow personal experience to become legible in moments where it might remain unknown? How do we approach a text whose language is strange or unfamiliar to us—what relationship might we have to it? Just as importantly they ask: when a text resonates on a personal level, how does one then engage that connection critically while sustaining a fidelity to one's own reactions?

Cisneros's *The House on Mango Street* offers students an entrance into the complexities of language *not* by getting them to engage prose that is particularly difficult, but by asking them to explore how clear, simple language can convey complex issues. As Christina Lopez pointed out to me when we were discussing teaching various texts, "Cisneros is really the kind of work that begs to be discussed after reading, because while on the surface some of her stories are categorized as young adult literature, the subject matter is often incredibly serious, and can be quite heavy."

That heaviness manifests in a text like *The House on Mango Street* in small moments, brief sentences. For example, "The Family of Little Feet," retells a Cinderella like transformation story about shoes. What starts as a simple story about girls playing dress up takes a turn when they encounter a "bum man on the stoop" (41). The story quickly exposes how painful it is to encounter sexuality, gender norms, and power relations—doing so with a single line, "We are tired of being beautiful" (42). Sentences like this distill powerful and complex cultural forces, thus allowing students to pause with the text and unpack its language.

Of course, this doesn't always happen easily. Getting students to critically engage with issues like gender formation, sexuality, and race often involves moving slowly. I've found that one of the best ways to do this, and something for which Cisneros's work is particularly well-suited, is to have students engage in different free writes before we begin discussion of the reading. When introducing Cisneros, I give students ample time to reflect; we spend the first ten minutes of class on free writing. Sometimes we work with prompts, but sometimes I will just have students free write thoughts on the reading. Letting students revisit and write about vivid memories of childhood while encouraging them to find a narrative voice that best expresses these moments has been a very productive exercise when teaching *The House on Mango Street*, and I find that this often allows for a more seamless and comfortable entry into discussing Cisneros's style.

After free writes, we then break up into smaller groups so that students can become comfortable talking about somewhat private experiences with their peers, without feeling called on to perform for the entire class. At this point, I usually go around to each group to get a better sense of their reactions and interpretations. Only after these two activities, do we come back together as a whole class to talk about the relationship of their writing that day to Cisneros's work. The ways students speak to each other in smaller groups differs at first from how they wish to appear to the class as a whole. Nevertheless, I press them to be more forthright with their reactions and take greater risks with their interpretations. Each of these steps helps students to feel more comfortable working with material that frankly deals with sexuality, race, and class. It also helps set an open and engaged tone in the classroom.

In presenting this snapshot of teaching, I realized how important it was for me to not have two classrooms: the idealized and abstracted one I might talk about to demonstrate a pedagogy of Latino/a literature, and one I *actually* teach. For me, teaching Latino/a literature has required that sometimes I be vulnerable and forthright about my own identifications and experiences with race, gender, and class—and sometimes it requires that I stay *very* far offstage. Making this call is never easy, but if I've learned anything teaching Cisneros, it's that private experience is political *and* pedagogical; it deserves sensitivity as well as critical engagement. I try to extend these two qualities to my own students as they share their reactions to the text. Any of us as readers, I tell students, might be "Those who don't know any better" and enter a text a bit confused. Our job as educators and as readers is to make our best effort to know better, and Cisneros's *The House on Mango Street* give us a beautiful space to do just that.

Resources for teaching Sandra Cisneros

Cruz, Felicia J. "On the 'Simplicity' of Sandra Cisneros's *House on Mango Street*." *MFS: Modern Fiction Studies* 47.4 (2001): 910–46.

Grobman, Laurie. "Rhetorizing the Contact Zone: Multicultural Texts in Writing Classrooms." *Reading Sites: Social Difference and Reader Response*. New York: Modern Language Association of America, 2004, pp. 256–85.

Guerra, Ramón J. "Teaching 'Story' as a Component of Fiction in Cisneros's *Caramelo*." *Eureka Studies in Teaching Short Fiction* 9.1 (2008): 147–56.

Harmon, Mary R. "Contact, Colonization, and Classrooms: Language Issues via Cisneros's *Woman Hollering Creek* and Villanueva's *Bootstraps*." *Professing in the Contact Zone: Bringing Theory and Practice Together*. Urbana, IL: National Council of Teachers of English, 2002, pp. 197–212.

Lu, Min-zhan. "Reading and Writing Differences: the Problematic of Experience." In *Feminism and Composition Studies: In Other Words*. New York: Modern Language Association of America, 1998, pp. 239–51.

Olivares, Julián. "Entering *The House on Mango Street* (Sandra Cisneros)." *Teaching American Ethnic Literatures: Nineteen Essays*. Albuquerque: University of New Mexico Press, 1996, pp. 209–35.

Valdés, María Elena de. "The Critical Reception of Sandra Cisneros's *The House on Mango Street*." In *Gender, Self, and Society*. Ed. Renate von Bardeleben. Frankfurt: Peter Lang, 1993, pp. 287–300.

Van Horn, Leigh. "Making Connections, Articulating Discoveries, and Revealing Selves Through Strategic Reading, Talking, and Writing." *Notes on American Literature* 21 (2012): 23–33.

27 Teaching Denise Chávez and Pat Mora

Ellen M. Gil-Gómez

The works of Denise Chávez and Pat Mora can be contextualized in any number of ways in the university classroom: within American literature, within introductions to fiction and drama, or fiction, poetry, and nonfiction respectively; in Chicano/a or Latino/a literatures; women's literature or any combinations thereof. My own experience teaching these authors is primarily within the framework of Latina literatures and criticism and thus my discussion here highlights that context.

These courses come in two differing frameworks: one as introductory students to women's literature, which is generally made up of General Education students, Liberal Studies students (pre-Education) and English majors mainly expecting a traditional course focused on canonical white British and/or American women writers. The other formulation is as an advanced topics course in the English major, the audience for which is solely English majors from three concentrations: creative writing, literature, and linguistics. The difference in these designs is the level of course: the advanced includes more critical approaches; the introductory includes more historical/cultural contexts. The audience for the broader introduction assumes more resistance to the materials themselves: students are inherently challenged by, and some are strongly resistant to, the assumption that a focus on Latina literature is appropriate for a class in "women's" literature at all. Students don't debate that Latinas are women, but that a focus on Latina writers is inherently biased and limited in a way that mainstream American and/or British is not. At least that's the argument made. On the other hand, students in the advanced course warmly embrace the focus on Latina writing and welcome the focus that challenges the assumption that canonical American or British texts are of foremost importance to the study of literature. Regardless of these audience perspectives, I find value in using similar frameworks when teaching these authors, though with dissimilar prominence and for unique purposes.

In the introductory class I must do a lot more work to do my best to ensure that all students begin to challenge their own preconceived assumptions about what defines "women's" literature and why they believe or don't believe Latinas are appropriate subjects of study within this context. In order to do this, I foreground how Chávez's *Face of an Angel* (1994) and Mora's *House of Houses* (1997a) use the trope of the "family tree" as a common Chicano/Latino signifier; how the novels challenge genre boundaries and meanings; how the authors use important cultural and personal markers through narrative experimentation; and how all of these elements allow Chávez and Mora to foreground how Chicana lives and worlds can be transformative and evolutionary both within and without traditional Chicano culture.

Family trees and genre

On one level an author's use of the family tree is self-evident—to visually represent and explain a family's genealogy and lineage, one person's relationship to another—without having to resort to a biblical level of exegesis in their prose. Depending on the genre, fiction, or nonfiction, it can also suggest adherence to historical tradition and meanings. Thus, in Mora's *House of Houses*, which she describes as a family memoir, the tree before the title page indicates a straightforward genealogy, a nod to the reader that the book itself is a family history. The photographs that follow add to this perception of the text more fully. Consequently, early indications within these beginning pages prepare the reader for a historical, biographical, or autobiographical narrative to follow. Chávez's *Face of an Angel* is identified as a novel on the cover, yet it includes a similar family tree after the title page. The unsuspecting reader might make the same assumptions as with Mora's text: the narrative to follow will be historical, biographical, or autobiographical in nature.

Within Chicano/a literature, however, the line between fiction and nonfiction is quite thin and thus these assumptions made by beginning readers are not as firm as they seem. Chicano/a literature is, at least in part, a tradition whose goal was and is to proclaim, document, and represent the lives, communities, and histories of a people with a complex relationship with the United States. As a U.S., Third World, or Postcolonial, tradition the battle for existence and presence within the dominant culture is easily found. It is quite common for Chicano/a fiction to be directly or indirectly historical using many of the symbols and tropes of historical narratives or to be based on actual family or community histories. Or for Chicano/a nonfiction to use many elements of fiction so as to blur the boundaries between the real and the imagined, and the natural or super-natural, as within the tradition of "magical realism." As in probably the most famous Chicano literary text—*Rain of Gold* (1991) by Victor Villaseñor—a narrative that the author has always claimed is a true story, i.e., a family memoir, while the publishers first interested in it insisted it would be marketed as fiction.

Likewise it would be easy to describe Mora's text in a similar manner, that while it is a story of her family's history it also relies self-reflexively on the imaginary. In fact the book begins:

> "How can you be hungry if you're dead?" Aunt Chloe sing-songs her question in the high pitch she reserves for birds, children, spirits. *"Ay, mi Raú, querido,* what do you want?" "I'll get him something, Tía," I say. In my dreamhouse my father returns, dark-skinned, balding, filling the room. "What do you want, Daddy? Coffee?"
>
> (1)

Mora indicates clearly in these opening lines that the space that gives her book its title is a dream space wherein the living and the dead, the past and the present, and memory and history can all coexist. Chávez's narrative begins not with a dialogue conversation, but with the main character and narrator, Soveida Dosamontes, running through the names on the family tree: "Luardo my father. Dolores my mother. Hector my brother. Mara my cousin" (3). Soveida then reflects on the cyclical and repetitive nature of life while repeating the words of her grandmother that "everyone has a story" (3). Soveida ends the first chapter with "I speak for them now. Mother. Father. Brother. Sister. Cousin. Uncle. Aunt. Husband. Lover. Their memories are mine. That sweet telling mine. Mine the ash. It's a long story" (4). Both texts position these two women as family historians as well as subjects in history. Both texts' initial chapters include the protagonist and narrator declaring her search for, role in, and indebtedness to the collecting of stories. Mora states "Rumors of my unending questions alter the pitch and rhythms of speech within these walls I know. All know: I'm after stories, brewed in the bone" (7).

By highlighting these and other parallels in these two texts students can directly engage with the functions of the symbol of the family tree specifically, the role of family and communal history within Chicano/a and women's narratives broadly, and how the presence of ancestors affect the creation of individual identity. Another productive analytical focus is how these elements operate differently within the genre of fiction versus nonfiction. Ultimately, this question helps move students into the broader consideration of how these Chicana authors have reshaped genre through their individual narrative experiments to better shape their story's goals and content.

Experimental narrative structures and frameworks

Beyond the general blurring of genre boundaries both texts also reflect different narrative frameworks and experimental approaches that illustrate how these two authors challenge representations through the use of cultural markers.

In Pat Mora's *House of Houses* she uses the symbol of the family adobe as the central symbol through which she not only finds her family's stories, but also to create their meanings through their locations. She describes her process:

> I struggle to sketch the home we inherited, adobe body to house the spirits I gather, living and dead; mud refuge whose outer skin, the exterior wall, offers the pleasure of being encircled by earth, the poetry of place. Between its layers, the outer and inner walls, grow piñon pines, Mexican elders, yucca, a giant mesquite that arches above the children's swings in the front courtyard.
>
> (3)

She goes on to describe the external surrounding wall, garage, and yard and personifies the house as having knowledge of the Rio Grande. She then endows the river with the geographical, cultural, and social history of place ultimately representing "a border" of multiple meanings from the Spanish and Indian perspective. Mora has said "the border for me, la frontera, is a definite place, the U.S./Mexico border, that space separated by El Río Grande, those two tangled countries, the United States and Mexico rubbing against one another, the friction of languages, histories, values, economic disparity, attraction and revulsion. That constant tension is the geographical/emotional place from which I come" (Interview with Maria-Antónia Oliver-Rotger). Further she juxtaposes the meanings of the house from these two approaches, the way "ancient desert dwellers" believe a house is "living, some feed them, bury caches to appease the hungry spirit in *la casa*" and still a "house of paradox" (3–4). Mora then meditates on dream and time, using the house as a touchstone for a variety of meanings that infuse, and have infused the land and thus her family. She uses it to tell a natural history of her family, their lives, experiences and feelings, and how the home, the garden, and the land reflect the variety of ways they have shaped meaning through the ages. Then, as an author, she recognizes her own part within that same process.

Mora uses the partially imagined moment of reading her aunt's missal to find shape and substance to the text that follows. Reading the missal to other women in the family brings on the importance of women's spaces in the home and culture: "They've all been here, are here, the family of women, nursing one another with teas. sacramental acts for another woman, or husband, father, or child" (11). This foundation of women and service as connected to ritual and Catholicism as reflected in the liturgical calendar find flesh in the narratives chapter headings and focus. As she says "the cycles of Advent, Christmas, Epiphany, Ordinary Time, Lent, Easter, Pentecost, the annual repetition. the religious repetitions—litanies and rosaries, rhythmic as the seasons" (12) stand in for all of these connections. The chapters of the text are labeled bilingually with the months of the year with mainly seasonal descriptors: "*Enero friolero*/Chilly January" and "*Marzo airoso/* Windy March" but also contextualized with proverbs and *dichos* around specific months and seasons: "*Junio*/June: *Huerta sin agua, cuerpo sin alma/*An orchard without water is like a body without a soul" (145). The central image in each heading has some evocation in the chapter that follows but does not directly tie to meaning. Mora also includes an index of dichos included in each chapter. The narrative as a whole interweaves family histories with cultural histories, memories, and dialogue alongside the texts of wedding invitations, recipes, songs, speeches, captions of photographs, gift cards, holy cards, prayers, real and imagined conversations.

All of these elements challenge students who are trying to make meaning from this text as nonfiction, and Mora's insistence upon revelation instead of declaration forces students to identify and question their own forms of interpretation that they bring to bear on it. Within an introductory course on Latina writers it is fruitful to have students consider if these devices are somehow unique to women authors. In an advanced course it is useful to have students explain how Mora's use of these multiple and primarily domestic elements function both as representation and operate as a method of critical synthesis. The last chapter *Deciembre*/December evokes the beginning chapter by again describing the dreamhouse and all of its threads. Mora writes:

> I look around the living room at six generations of desert dwellers now gathered in this dream house hovering near el Rio Grande between El Paso and Santa Fe, between the pass to the North and holy faith, a treacherous pass, the route to faith, all of us immigrants. Made of earth as we are, this nested adobe house, its body inherited and temporary, like ours, is protected by exterior walls we create and construct around the fertile interior, layers of vulnerable beauty. Within the body of the family dwell the homes of the next generation, another nesting, and within each of our bodies, all the selves we've been and are, held together by skin, fragile yet sturdy a paradox. Like the house that's green yet in the desert, visible yet private, unique yet organic, old yet new, open yet closed, imagined yet real, a retreat, private yet communal.
>
> (288–89)

All of these many threads evoke but don't declare meanings through the constant juxtaposition of all of these paradigms within her text. Mora states, "I like writing about the complexity of the juxtapositions" (Interview with Maria-Antónia Oliver-Rotger).

In *Face of an Angel* Chávez uses some of these same approaches but pushes the narrative construction even further. The novel contains more than 60 short chapters or "scenes" as the author calls them. She also insists that her writing style should be seen as a unique combination of dramatic prose and that she is "a performance writer" (Chávez, "Denise" 1994: 30). In addition to this dramatic approach to fiction, there are two "books" within Chávez's novel by main character and narrator Soveida Dosamantes. One is her 12-year-old autobiography, the other a set of instructions/suggestions for aspiring waitresses, called The Book of Service, which consists of 13 chapters interspersed in the final two-thirds of the novel. Other elements that challenge the reader include a chapter focused on the story of her parents' relationship written in dual columns: one her mother's version of the romance and one her father's. What becomes obvious are the differences between their two versions, thus foregrounding a variety of binaries including those of gender, class, and national identity.

Beyond these experimental forms of structure, comes Chávez's use of thematic organizational devices, parallel to Mora's use of seasons and *dichos*. Similarly, Chávez uses an organizational structure based in part on Catholic ritual and meaning; specifically she uses the hierarchy of angels in order to suggest levels of intimacy and meaning between characters and their lives. Chávez describes it thus:

> The angels I am targeting are both universal and ingrained in Catholicism. I have patterned the sections on the hierarchy of angels, from the lowest order to the highest. At the end of the book, I do think Soveida has achieved a state of understanding she didn't have before.
>
> (Chávez, "Denise" 1999: 39)

As with *House of Houses* these meanings are indirect and suggestive rather than direct and overt. In another parallel, Chávez foregrounds and expects juxtaposition from these multiple elements and structures. She says in her interview with Marilyn Meham and AnaLouise Keating that "it's the structure of how the chapters are put together that's jarring for readers. There are also so many voices in that book, perhaps too many voices; the voices intertwine, but I do always go back to each one. Like the rooms that readers can't completely inhabit, they—readers—probably don't ever get to feel that they are completely at home with any one voice, either. I wanted to have those voices in there gloating in the atmosphere in order for readers to get into the rooms; I wanted readers to feel that the spirits were hovering" (Chávez, "Carrying" 2001: 135).

It can be quite challenging for students to directly consider how these two authors use the symbol of the "house" conceptually and as technique in their narratives. While both overtly contextualize from within the Catholic and the spirit planes, for Mora, it is as central symbol for conceiving and telling family and cultural histories and for Chávez, as a guiding metaphor for, and readers' response to, the construction of her multivocal narrative. As with the reliance on juxtaposition of the mainly domestic cultural elements, the question arises if the symbol of the house, the use of Catholic hierarchies, and the calling of the spirit are important ways that Latinas craft narratives or embody meaning within characters.

Women's identity: transforming traditional women

Finally, while I have described above that a number of the approaches within these two texts use fairly traditional female-identified elements—for example, domestic spaces, personal texts, and indirect and circular language—these elements can be misread as creating stereotypical and traditional Chicana characters or identity. In fact, both authors do represent some of their women's worlds stereotypically. Chávez's character Soveida is a waitress who is focused on explaining and celebrating service as part of a fulfilled life, a fairly typical expectation for women. Mora's text is also interested in service, serving the family and the continuation of culture through the mainly female symbols of gardening, cooking, and nurturing. While on one level it's appropriate to point out the ways that these two texts use these stereotypical elements in order to draw and develop their female subjectivities, it is also useful to help students deconstruct how both authors complicate these assumptions through their larger understanding of the nature of service itself.

On the one hand, Pat Mora muses:

> In my experience, women are better at doing for others. Why? History. We emulate much of what previous generations have done and the experience of motherhood or family nurturing which demands that we set ourselves aside a bit. My hope is that men develop their giving side and that women see the psychological value of bringing their spirit and talents into the world for its betterment while developing the capacity for protecting and nurturing. Selfishness is no virtue.
>
> (Interview with Maria-Antónia Oliver-Rotger)

On the other hand, Chávez simply states "I write about life and love and transformation through suffering, and what it means to find the meaning of service in one's life" (Chávez, "Denise" 1999: 35) and more generally "each of us [are] 'servers' on our own pilgrimage" (39). Service from the perspective of these authors is not solely about femaleness but about relationships between human beings, between the self and the spirit, culture and history. Both of these texts insist that readers consider how the individual relates to a broader community. These associations can aid students in unpacking their gendered assumptions, and in particular assumptions about Latina identity, that may presuppose Latinas as submissive and desirous of domination.

The way both authors highlight the individual's indebtedness to ancestors also reveals how these authors create women as evolutionary not static figures that are capable of change. This context brings us back to where we started, with the family tree and genealogy as guiding symbols and structures, but also encourages us to analyze what kinds of knowledge, gifts, and baggage that older generations of women give to or force on our main characters. Mora puts herself directly in conversation with many ancestors describing that "this is a 'world that we can call our own,' this family space through which generations move, each bringing its gifts, handing down languages and stories, recipes for living, gathering around the kitchen table to serve one another" (7) but finding the greatest resonance in finding herself in her female ancestry when she quotes Adrienne Rich saying "It is strange to be so many women" (11). Here types, stereo-types, individuals, collective and all forms of identity are not only possible, they are viable. Soveida addresses this directly through the family tree by contemplating her connections to whom she was named for:

> the name of a dead woman. The other Soveida was a pregnant woman with two small children. She was only twenty-seven years old when she was killed instantly in a car accident. Dolores read about it in the obituary column. She liked the name. It stuck. I, Soveida Dosamantes, am her namesake. Husbandless. Childless. Daughter of. Sister of. Wife of. Mother of no one except herself.
>
> (3)

Although her name comes from her mother, she also compares and contrasts herself with a very specific image of femaleness as well as the numerous expectations of womanhood in society and culture. Chávez explores this throughout the novel and we find Soveida pregnant at the end of the book, when she finally seems able to combine mothering herself with mothering a child. As Chávez states in an interview, the novel also represents Soveida's breaking of behavioral patterns and coming into a consciousness of her existence in the universe (Chávez, "Carrying" 2001: 131).

The insistence that women are not static conveyors of meaning, even though society and culture may desire that they serve this function, but instead are individually complex and subjective, is in itself a liberatory message whether students encounter it within the larger context of women's writing or from within the critical and cultural expectations of comparative Latina literature.

Resources for teaching Denise Chávez and Pat Mora

Aldama, Frederick Luis. *Spilling the Beans in Chicanolandia: Conversations with Writers and Artists.* Austin: University of Texas Press, 2006.

Christian, Marie. "Many ways to remember: layered time in Mora's *House of Houses.*" *MELUS* 30.1 (Spring 2005): 135–148.

Herrera, Cristina. "Comadres: female friendship in Denise Chávez's *Loving Pedro Infante.*" *Confluencia* 27.1 (Fall 2011): 51–62.

Leen, Catherine and Niamh Thornton. *International Perspectives on Chicana/o Studies: "This World is My Place."* New York: Routledge, 2013.

Mehaffy, Marilyn, AnaLouise Keating. *Aztlan: A Journal of Chicano Studies* 26.1 (Spring 2001): 127–156.

Socolovsky, Maya. "Narrative and traumatic memory in Denise Chávez's *Face of an Angel.*" *MELUS* 28.4 (Winter 2003): 187–205.

28 Teaching Jimmy Santiago Baca

Cruz Medina

On the surface, Jimmy Santiago Baca's lyrical prose can in itself provide rich material for teaching. However, the more profound socially conscious messages in his writing go unrecognized unless taught with a **social justice** approach.

From *Working in the Dark: Reflections of a Poet of the Barrio* (1992), Baca's essay "Coming into Language" depicts metaphors of death and rebirth alongside evocative violent imagery; yet, it more importantly transmits an urgent message about the necessary struggle for literacy. To teach "Coming into Language," I argue that the context of Tucson Magnet High School's Mexican American Studies (MAS) curriculum and pedagogy profoundly informs the teaching of Baca's struggle, especially since his writing was a part of the books that were banned when Arizona House Bill 2281 outlawed the MAS program in 2011. Former Tucson MAS teacher Curtis Acosta (2007) highlights his curriculum and pedagogy for teaching Latino/a literature with the thematic inclusion of resistance, referencing the goal of developing students' ability to critically evaluate systems of oppression such as the legislation that outlawed the MAS program. Even though Baca effectively describes becoming literate through metaphors of death and rebirth, the additional context of Tucson's banned theoretical framework grounds his work in a deeply rooted tradition of struggle for education that imparts seeds of knowledge for readers.

As an instructor, I am inspired by liberatory approaches to education that have proven successful for institutionalized students. I have had the good fortune to listen to and speak with Curtis Acosta and teach MAS graduates while at the University of Arizona, so I believe in the power of MAS pedagogy to provoke critical consciousness and engage students in relevant issues for the purpose of effecting change. Previously, I have looked at the culturally relevant writing in Tucson during the period when HB 2281 outlawed the MAS program (Medina 2013). "Coming into Language" provides a culturally relevant literacy narrative that reflects Baca's obstacles encountered in school and prison, ultimately culminating with his discovery of both literacy's liberatory effect and his love of language. As a community and culture-based pedagogy and curriculum, the MAS framework engages students with **Pre-Columbian** concepts that originate "from the Aztec sun stone or *calendario* and the teachings of elders and maestros within our community" (Acosta 2007: 37). Revealing the social inequality connected with Baca's writing, Tucson's MAS program's use of the **Nahuatl** (Aztec) tropes of **Tezkatlipoka**, **Quetzalcoatl**, Huetzilopochli, and **Xipe Totec** serve as a culturally relevant lens for interpreting Baca's essay (Acosta 2007). Translated as self-reflection, precious and beautiful knowledge, the will to act, and transformation, the curricular methodology of the MAS program draws attention to Baca's skillful weaving of resistance, violent imagery, and the agency he realizes through writing.

The metaphoric nature of the MAS framework is fitting for Baca's "Coming into Language" given his use of figurative language related to his impending death before his rebirth after learning to read and write. Baca's self-reflections of working in an "emergency room, mopping up pools of blood and carting plastic bags stuffed with arms, legs, and hands to the outdoor incinerator" appeals to readers with visceral descriptions like "shotgunned, knifed, and mangled kids writhing on gurneys" (3). Not describing violence for violence's sake or to simply entertain, his writing triggers self-reflection—or Tezkatlipoka in MAS terms—thereby recognizing his place in the world and what he could learn about himself by looking inward. In doing so, student readers see how he is impacted by social and economic factors that limit his social mobility. According to former MAS teacher Acosta, *Tezkatlipoka* represents "memory as well as self-reflection" and "the active journey to find our inner self" (37).

Baca's self-reflections reveal layers of pain he experienced in a world that presented education as punishment. He writes of teachers "punishing me for not knowing my lessons by making me stick my nose in a circle chalked on the blackboard" and how this led him to feel as though he were the "target in the cross hairs of a hunter's rifle" and could feel a "hang-rope tighten around my neck and the trapdoor creak beneath my feet ... I felt intimidated and vulnerable, ridiculed and scorned" (4). Baca poignantly demonstrates the negative kind of education that Angela Valenzuela (1999) describes as "schooling," which is devoid of genuine concern for students' well-being. Schooling contributes to the institutionalization that prepares young people like Baca to become wards of the state in correctional facilities. As a narrative about his experience with becoming literate, Baca underscores his feeling of powerlessness without an education.

Weaving in images of resistance, Baca demonstrates how the period of his life marked by suffering changed when he discovered the beautiful knowledge of his culture transmitted in the book *450 Years of Chicano History in Pictures*. At 17, Baca still could not read, but he explains that "those pictures confirmed my identity ... this book told us we were alive" (4). The effects of the descriptions of lynched Mexicans and **César Chávez** leading boycotts juxtaposed with Baca's interest is twofold: the inspiration he experiences from the Chicano/a images reaffirm the notion of precious and beautiful knowledge, or Quetzalcoatl, *and* they provide broad sociohistorical examples of oppression to discuss with students. A part of the concept of Quetzalcoatl, or beautiful knowledge, is reading about experiences that illuminate "the diversity and complexity of life as a member of a historically oppressed population" (Acosta 2007: 39). The context of Tucson's MAS program serves as a contemporary case study that demonstrates how Latinos/as continue to struggle for education and for education that represents Latino/a culture. Without a MAS approach, references such as *450 Years of Chicano History* could be overlooked as merely a part of Baca's early literacy development; instead, through Quetzalcoatl the students' "experiences are the focus of analysis," allowing them to develop their analytical skills on familiar subjects that authorize their meaning-making (Acosta 2007: 38). *Quetzalcoatl* and the interpretation of beautiful knowledge encourage students to engage with reading and writing as they learn about their culture.

From Baca's exposure to culturally relevant books and images, he experiences a pride in his culture that was previously unknown. His early experiences with listening to fellow prison inmates read writers such as Pablo Neruda and Octavio Paz made him feel "that invisible threat from without lessen ... Their language was the magic that could liberate me from myself ... I began to learn my own language, the bilingual words and phrases explaining to me my place in the universe" (4). For Baca, literature motivates him to learn more about both of the languages intertwined in his bicultural identity. For resistant readers and writers, the notion of beautiful and precious knowledge—Quetzalcoatl—calls for students to consider how knowledge can help them to better understand themselves and the world. Supported by a social justice agenda, the MAS pedagogy asks students to develop their critical lens for interpreting their education by following Paulo Freire's (1993) notion of *reading the world* and recognizing relevant systems of inequality.

As in Tucson, AZ, Baca struggles most to become literate after finding inspiration in what he has learned. In the MAS curriculum, Baca's activism for education parallels the trope of Xipe Totec, the will to act. After witnessing police beat up a drunk, Baca steals a policeman's schoolbook as silent protest (5). Later, he actively fights to earn his GED, proclaiming, "I will never do any work in this prison system as long as I am not allowed to get my G.E.D" (8). Baca's civil disobedience parallels the walkouts, marches, and Tucson Unified School District school board takeover by students who had been silenced when attempting to navigate institutional channels of power (Cabrera *et al.* 2013). Although most students reading Latino/a literature such as Baca may not have to struggle to learn from his writing, the contemporary case of Tucson's real-world struggle for Mexican American Studies makes the social injustice that Baca experiences more temporally relevant. I agree with Frederick Aldama's assertion that Baca desires to "make the leap from the private sphere … to the public domain of the communicable, the diversely evaluated, the possibly shared or challenged, and ultimately the socially effective" (Aldama 2005). Since the MAS program effectively raised state test scores and graduation rates of high school students (Cabrera *et al.* 2012), it is important to note how teaching the beauty of knowledge can impact students with previous experiences with institutional schooling.

By the end of "Coming into Language," the MAS theme of transformation becomes clear in the conclusion of Baca's narrative. While students often relate to Baca's remark that "I always had thought reading a waste of time," his description of rebirth counter-argues for the transformative power of education (6). Reiterating the power of literacy, Baca explains that he felt "as if a grave illness lifted from me and I was cured, innocently believing in the beauty of life again" (6). Referring to the child in him "who had witnessed and endured unspeakable terrors," Baca explains that "with the power of language … [t]hrough language I was free" (7). In keeping with Santiago Baca's love of language, Acosta explains that "[w]hether it is love for our cultural heritage and the beauty of our *gente*, a love of learning, or the respect and love within our classroom, it is love that is the seed for the tree" (39). At all levels of education, Baca's love of language can show students the potential for personal transformation, while Baca's experience with incarceration points to larger issues of social inequality. Finally, transformation asks that students see how the author views the world differently and how the worldview of students might be impacted by engaging with texts that provoke discussion of social justice issues.

"Coming into Language" is but one essay in *Working in the Dark*, although Jimmy Santiago Baca's oeuvre includes more on his life (*A Place to Stand: The Making of a Poet*, 2001) and writing (*The Importance of a Piece of Paper*, 2004), as well as collections of poetry (*Black Mesa Poems*, 1989; *Healing Earthquakes: A Love Story in Poems*, 2001; *C-Train and Thirteen Mexicans*, 2002; *Winter Poems Along the Rio Grande*, 2004). Still, Baca's literacy narrative highlights for students the process of self-reflection, recognizing the beauty of knowledge, embracing the will to act, and realizing the strength of transformation. At the same time, educators draw on the pedagogical strength of a program that raised state test scores and graduation rates. Adapting the **Mesoamerican** tropes and meanings Acosta outlines for my writing assignments, I have integrated the "banned" MAS framework into my teaching of first-year composition in summer bridge programs for Latino/a students in Tucson, Arizona over the past five years. Although the Mesoamerican tropes can be most directly linked to the culture of Pre-Columbian Mexico, the alternative framework for reading Baca's writing inspires students to reflect on their relationship with becoming educated, while locating themselves within a rich historical tradition of knowledge in the Americas.

Resources for teaching Jimmy Santiago Baca

Aldama, Frederick Luis. "An interview with Jimmy Santiago Baca." *MELUS* 30.3 (2005): 113–26.
Baca, Jimmy Santiago, Releah Lent. *Adolescents on the Edge: Stories and Lessons to Transform Learning*. Portsmouth, NH: Heinemann, 2010.
Bruno, Paula M. "'Ni miedo de la pinta, ni miedo de la muerte': Jimmy Santiago Baca's prison poems." *GENRE* 35.3-5 (Fall–Winter 2002): 575–98.
Fuss, Adam. "Jimmy Santiago Baca." *Bomb* 84 (Summer 2003): 58–63.
Lynch, Thomas. "Toward a symbiosis of ecology and justice: water and land conflicts in Frank Waters, John Nichols, and Jimmy Santiago Baca." *Western American Literature* 37.4 (2003): 405–28.

29 Teaching Junot Díaz

David A. Colón

I begin the teaching of Junot Díaz by providing my students with biographical context. He was born in Santo Domingo, Dominican Republic on December 31, 1968. Soon before his sixth birthday, he immigrated to New Jersey where he was raised, attending grade school and college there and graduating from Rutgers University in 1992. He received his MFA in Creative Writing from Cornell University in 1995. He is currently the Rudge and Nancy Allen Professor of Writing at the Massachusetts Institute of Technology. His awards and honors include a Pulitzer Prize, a National Book Critics Circle Award, a MacArthur "Genius" Fellowship, a PEN/Malamud Award, a Dayton Literary Peace Prize, a Guggenheim Fellowship, and a PEN/O. Henry Award. Díaz currently serves as fiction editor at the *Boston Review*, and he is a co-founder of the Voices of Our Nation Workshop, a program building community and excellence among emergent writers of color.

I also identify Díaz's publications as well as his main themes. That he has published three long works of fiction to date: the short story collections *Drown* (1996) and *This Is How You Lose Her* (2012), and the novel *The Brief Wondrous Life of Oscar Wao* (2007). All three books raise topics of transnationalism and immigration, *quisqueyano* identity and life in the Dominican Republic, and the gender dynamics of *machismo* and *marianismo*.

To deepen my students' sense of Díaz within biographical—and historical, cultural, and personal—contexts, I assign students research projects on Dominican history, culture, and lifestyle. I ask questions such as: Who was Rafael Trujillo? How has the Dominican Republic's economy changed over time? What are the hallmarks of Dominican Spanish slang? What is **bachata** music? These and others can establish greater student understanding of the contemporary cultural contexts of Díaz's world. When these projects take the form of in-class multimedia oral presentations, the research can be shared with all students and essentially become common ground: to allow contextual analysis, in the spirit of "generative reading," to preface more effective close reading of the fiction.

As the teaching of Díaz's works unfolds, themes between the three books begin to tie together. This is due in large part to the ubiquitous presence of the character Yunior. The central character of *Drown* and *This Is How You Lose Her* as well as the principal narrator of *Oscar Wao*, Yunior is widely considered a projection of sorts of Díaz's own persona. This aspect of Yunior's character—a synecdotal relationship between fiction and biography—is worth exploring in student-based discussion, starting with the narrow, seemingly innocuous question of how to pronounce the name Yunior: in recorded interviews and symposia, Díaz himself has pronounced the name with both the Anglo pronunciation (*Yoo-nior*) and the Spanish pronunciation (*Joo-nior*), and an instructor can expound upon how such a nominal issue in fiction can actually pertain deeply to larger subjects of cultural relativism and audience agency. Moreover, it raises the matter of the author Díaz projecting himself into this character; the name Junot, as it is pronounced in the French manner and not the Spanish, in some ways aligns with the authorial decision to spell Yunior with a Y and not a J.

With students I explore how Yunior's character presents several important themes in these three books: the challenges and freedoms of bilingualism; the relationship between voice, dialect, and realism as a matter of literary form; the curious tension and play between high and low sensibilities; the alienating effect of masculine vulnerability in a **machista** milieu; and the romantic appreciation and pursuit of love. Díaz is deceptively subtle in his presentation of the complexities of these nuances, and thus they are good opportunities to provide premises for structured in-class debates in which students argue their way to different conclusions. For example, a teacher might follow a model I use where I divide a class into three groups, and offer the following three positions: (1) Yunior embraces *machismo*, (2) Yunior resents *machismo*, (3) Yunior is indifferent toward *machismo*. Working collaboratively, students are tasked with finding textual evidence from Díaz's books (or just one book: *Drown*, for instance) to substantiate their group's assigned position, and after an in-group discussion period and a full-class timed debate, the exercise can lead the group to an assessment of the extent to which Díaz designs this character with a spectrum of competing sensibilities representative of contemporary Latino/a cultural discourse.

In teaching *Drown* I identify how it is composed of ten stories with settings that oscillate between the Dominican Republic and New Jersey. Upon reaching the final story, "Negocios," we see how it amplifies the migratory context to the wider Eastern seaboard. Beyond matters of cultural expression grounded in Dominican American experience—a discussion of how "Ysrael" and "No Face" constitute an allegory of postcolonial and decolonial identity politics, engaging with critical theory (Frantz Fanon and Ngugi wa Thiong'o, for instance), is vital—perhaps the two most salient topics to explore, in both discussion and research-based arguments, are the **bildungsroman** and the **picaresque**. An instructor would serve students well by elaborating on these two literary forms in multi-media lectures, offering definitions and histories of major contributions and innovations to these subgenres before turning to related discussion questions applied to *Drown*. As a book of stories all inclined toward Yunior that could be regarded as a near-novel, *Drown* exhibits the classic characteristics of the picaresque: its structure is episodic and its predominantly first-person narrative voice, of a low social standing often speaking in slang and dialect, exudes an attitude resistant to authority. The story "How to Date a Browngirl, Blackgirl, Whitegirl, or Halfie" is rich with satire as well, as the immaturity of the narrator inadvertently puts the *machista* outlook of sexual conquest under a microscope of puerile impotence. The vulnerability of Yunior as a boy becoming a man, at once a reluctant student of *machismo* under the tutelage of his older brother Rafa and his father Ramón, is resonant throughout *Drown*, and ending the collection with a narrative of Papi's travails in attempting to establish a life for himself and his family in the United States lifts the veil from patriarchal authority. Coupled with the reveal that this account was passed on from father to son in the spirit of coming clean, it completes the bildungsroman of Yunior, or at least to the point of establishing Yunior as a fully rounded character that can develop complexity in the books published after *Drown*.

The Brief Wondrous Life of Oscar Wao is also a bildungsroman (the final lines, "Diablo! If only I'd known! The beauty! The beauty!" make this consideration viable) but more ambitious in historical reach and formal complexity. *Oscar Wao* inhabits the generational layers of Latino/a identity and, in a manner akin to a framed story, is composed in what could be considered concentric circles of narrative. Therefore, it is a good idea to spend some classroom time discussing the structure of the novel (as setting moves forward, back, and forward again in time) and focusing the discussion around a collaborative exercise of diagramming its structure—keying on the analogy of concentric circles—either on a whiteboard/blackboard or in software like Prezi. This will engage students who are more visually inclined learners while illustrating for all students an example of a structurally sophisticated novel.

An intriguing dimension that one might choose to teach in *Oscar Wao* is the parallel between the Caribbean and science fiction. The opening pages introduce the premise of *fukú* and *zafa*, curse and counter-curse, as a metaphysical manifestation of the collision of worlds in the colonial era, and this parallel grows into a veritable leitmotif that gathers importance as Yunior narrates the story through analogies borrowed from SF/F (science fiction/fantasy) literature and film (and, notably, occasional explanatory footnotes). While the range of SF/F references in *Oscar Wao* is wide, almost encyclopedic, they gravitate toward two poles: the unlikely superhero with a meek alter ego (evoking Oscar), and the omnipotent demigod supervillain (evoking Trujillo). The effect is that, while transforming Oscar from anti-hero to hero over the course of the story, a greater allegory is developed: that contact zones of far and alien worlds are not immaterial fantasies but rather grounded in our very real past, detectable by observing how we live, speak, love, and hate in the present.

This Is How You Lose Her, as the third and latest of Díaz's books, is so contingent on the prior two that it is the least desirable to teach on its own if one is pressed to choose one Díaz book for a syllabus. However, this also makes it the best book to use to illustrate single-author intertextuality. The vulnerable, neglected Yunior of *Drown*, owing so much of his intellectual maturity to his relationship with Oscar in *Oscar Wao*, becomes subject of a scrutiny of pathos in *This Is How You Lose Her* that is furtive and subtle: as Joe Fassler argued in *The Atlantic*, Díaz "wrote a sexist character, but not a sexist book." This collection of stories serves as a meditation on the emotional solitude of male chauvinism, and a discussion question worth posing at both the beginning and the end of coverage of this novel is: Who is the "she" of *This Is How You Lose Her*? It will yield a variety of considerations that expose the limitations of Yunior's sensibility and pose *machismo* in a new light—that of the tragic flaw.

Resources for teaching Junot Díaz

www.annotated-oscar-wao.com/ (accessed July 3, 2014).

Balée, Susan. "Caves, masks, and code switching: the inventive narratives of Junot Díaz." *Hudson Review* 66.2 (2013): 337–52.

Fassler, Joe. "How Junot Diaz wrote a sexist character, but not a sexist book." *The Atlantic* (Sept. 11, 2012): n.p. Web.

Lanzendörfer, Tim. "The marvelous history of the Dominican Republic in Junot Díaz's *The Brief Wondrous Life of Oscar Wao*." *MELUS: Multi-Ethnic Literature of the U.S.* 38.2 (2013): 127–42.

López-Calvo, Ignacio. "A postmodern Plátano's Trujillo: Junot Díaz's *The Brief Wondrous Life of Oscar Wao*, more Macondo than McCondo." *Antípodas: Journal of Hispanic and Galician Studies* 20 (2009): 75–90.

Loss, Jacquelyn. "Junot Díaz." *Latino and Latina Writers*. Ed. Alan West-Durán. Detroit: Charles Scribner's Sons, 2003, pp. 803–16.

Machado Sáez, Elena. "Dictating desire, dictating diaspora: Junot Díaz's *The Brief Wondrous Life of Oscar Wao* as foundational romance." *Contemporary Literature* 52.3 (2011): 522–55.

Miller, T. S. "Preternatural narration and the lens of genre fiction in Junot Díaz's *The Brief Wondrous Life of Oscar Wao*." *Science Fiction Studies* 38.1 (2011): 92–114.

Riofrio, John. "Situating Latin American masculinity: immigration, empathy and emasculation in Junot Díaz's *Drown*." *Atenea* 28.1 (2008): 23–36.

Weese, Katherine. "'Tú no eres nada de Dominicano': Unnatural narration and de-naturalizing gender constructs in Junot Díaz's *The Brief Wondrous Life of Oscar Wao*." *Journal of Men's Studies* 22.2 (2014): 89–104.

30 Teaching Cristina García

Elena Foulis

Visual narrative as a mode of storytelling embodies ways of knowing—at once relational and highly affective. In today's culture, taking photographs is a preferred way of sharing stories. We view and share pictures on Instagram, Facebook, or Tumblr, looking to reach people, engage in storytelling, and in a sense, claim spaces. By using pictures, a venue well known and accessible to today's generation of students, I discuss how storytelling fosters cultural memory in significant ways. More specifically, by using social media as a model for students to reflect on key thematic elements found in Cristina García's novel, *Dreaming in Cuban* (1992), I foster a reflective and creative environment for understanding Latina literature.

As teachers of Latino/a literature, we often encounter students unfamiliar with the rich historical presence of Latinos in the United States and with a limited knowledge of Latino/a cultural identity. Over the past five years I've taught Latino/a literature to a varied economic and regional mostly white student body. I've also taught this course to more classes with more diversity and presence of Latinos/as; one class was all Latino/a. The white majority classroom required more detailed explanation of cultural practices, terminology. The Latino/a only classroom required little explanation as they were familiar with Latino/a historical and cultural practices as well as language traditions: ***curanderas, santeras, la virgen de Guadalupe, machismo, marianismo***. The mixed classroom needed some guidance, but also created opportunities for the peer exchange of ideas not always directed by myself. What all the students shared in common was the connection they made with family stories and the impact of community and place in shaping their identities. Additionally, they all shared a familiarity with digital media: photographs, short movies, digital comics, and so on. I teach Cristina García with these commonalities centrally in mind.

Dreaming in Cuban's richness in spatial and cognitive dissonance allow opportunities to form new narratives that encourage identification with experiences and histories that happened to someone else, even when students might be unfamiliar with Cuban American history and culture. When teaching this novel, I rely on the idea of spatial and **cognitive dissonance** to explain what happens when two contradictory spaces are present. I help the students identify how these contradictory spaces are built in *Dreaming in Cuban*. First, with the character Pilar who represents the present-younger generation in the United States and second, with the character Celia, who represents the older generation in Cuba. We then explore how these dissonant spaces represented by the characters can be found in the students' own life stories. As students experience the novel's heavy descriptions and multiple points of view of life in Cuba juxtaposed and often in conflict with the life and ideals of the United States, I have the students develop media projects that integrate their experiences with those of the characters of the novel. While one obvious focus would be the granddaughter–grandmother relationship, there are many other pairings such as daughters and fathers, mothers and daughters, conservative and liberal ideals, religious practices, and even the impact of a strong political figure such as El Líder. They might begin to collect and create images that unpack the many layers of Cuban history, politics, society, and culture from the perspectives of Cubans in Cuba and Cubans in the United States. More specifically, students might focus on the images generated by Pilar as she tries to make sense of her family's extreme political ideologies along with her own political identity as a Cuban American woman growing up during the second-wave feminist era. They might explore Pilar's mural of the Statue of Liberty (a celebration of her mother's second bakery and the commemoration of the Bicentennial) as a rebellion against the pressure to embrace or reject communism and conservative ideals. I encourage my students to ask why Pilar paints Liberty's torch as "slightly beyond her grasp"? Why she paints "her right hand reaching over to cover her left breast," completing the mural with "black stick figures pulsing in air around Liberty, thorny scars that look like barbed wire" (141)? And finally, why Pilar writes at the base of the statute "'I'M A MESS' with a safety pin through her nose" (141).

With the vivid picture of juxtaposed ideas that question at once Cuban and U.S. politics, the old and new generations, and even the space of women in the art scene, students can begin to explore images that represent their own quest for identity or their own layers of identities that can sometimes be in conflict with the whole. To get students to generate ideas for this assignment, it is important to start by mimicking a combination of Twitter/Instagram posts. Given that Pilar's experiences are *re*created from Cristina García's own biography, students can use the Twitter/Instagram to ask themselves how the novel asks them to reflect upon who they are, what they think, and their own growing up story. In their post I have the students include an image, a Tweet of 140 characters or fewer, at least three hashtags—including one assigned by the class (i.e., #dreamingincuban)—to send me on Twitter and to make changes if comments or retweets are generated within a day. This exercise allows students to have the freedom to fully explore in a self-reflective or creative piece their own life story as it interfaces the protagonist, Pilar's.

In another digital image-based creative assignment I have students consider the novel's rich and imagistic descriptions of the landscape of New York and Cuba. I guide the students to consider how these two regions directly affect the behavior and experiences of some of the characters. I then ask the students to consider how their own environments have shaped their own identities. I ask students to collect pictures of visited cities that have a stamp of the past with colonial structures or of buildings that represent the passage of time, including abandoned buildings. The *National Geographic* has a Cuban photo collection that can be included as an initial assignment.[1] I then encourage them to consider the ways in which the landscapes in *Dreaming in Cuban* illustrate concepts of alienation and decay. Having the students write a micronarrative based on their reaction to the novel and to the images (those, say, from the *National Geographic*) can prompt them to reflect on issues of aesthetics and ethics. While it is not required or expected that students produce professional quality photo-narratives, it is important that students justify and make a connection with García's text and imagery and students' connection to their life or specific theme studied. Engaging with García's novel through a creative project that involves selecting images of past or decaying structures triggers students to critically and creatively think about the impact of the landscape in the novel and in the lives of others. Such a creative image and micronarrative encourages students to engage with the novel, increase their understanding of Cuban Americans, and contribute to their understanding of growing up in America as a Latina.

By taking advantage of the digital age I have been able to get students to think deeply about *Dreaming in Cuban* both personally and within a global cultural context. By embracing social media technologies like Twitter/Instagram I have been able to teach Latino/a literature in a way that connects personally to a wide range of students as well as to situate it within the larger global digital age.

Note

1 See, http://travel.nationalgeographic.com/travel/countries/cuba-photos/ (accessed June 24, 2014).

Resources for teaching Cristina García

Aldama, Frederick L. *Toward a Cognitive Theory of Narrative Acts.* Austin: University of Texas Press, 2010. Web.

Augenbraum, Harold, and Olmos M. Fernández. *U.S. Latino Literature: A Critical Guide for Students and Teachers.* Westport, CT: Greenwood Press, 2000.

Castillo, Debra A. *Redreaming America: Toward a Bilingual American Culture.* Albany: State University of New York Press, 2005.

Fardman, Jason, ed. *The Mobile Story: Narrative Practices with Locative Technologies.* New York: Routledge, 2014.

García, Cristina. *Dreaming in Cuban.* New York: Alfred A. Knopf, 1992.

Kafka, Phillipa. *"Saddling La Gringa:" Gatekeeping in Literature by Contemporary Latina Writers.* Westport: Greenwood Press, 2000.

Luis, William. *Dance between Two Cultures: Latino Caribbean Literature Written in the United States.* Nashville: Vanderbilt University Press, 1997.

Maitino, John R, and David R. Peck. *Teaching American Ethnic Literatures: Nineteen Essays.* Albuquerque: University of New Mexico Press, 1996.

Marrero, Maria Teresa. "Historical and literary *Santería*: unveiling gender and identity in U.S. Cuban literature." In *Tropicalizations: Transcultural Representations of Latinidad.* Ed. Frances R. Aparicio and Susana Chávez-Silverman. Hanover, NH: Dartmouth College, University Press of New England, 1997.

Mauk, John, Jayme Stayer, and Karen Mauk. *Think about It: Critical Skills for Academic Writing.* Boston: Wadsworth Cengage Learning, 2014.

Stavans, Ilan, ed. *The Norton Anthology of Latino Literature.* New York: W.W. Norton, 2011.

31 Teaching Arturo Islas

Frederick Luis Aldama

Teaching Arturo Islas's *The Rain God: A Desert Tale* (1984) can follow many different paths. I suggest several here that include discussion of its publication history, its influences, and close readings of the text that focus on the way its devices and structures give shape to its content.

Background

I find it necessary to provide the students with information that enriches their understanding of the making of *The Rain God* in the time (history) and place (regions). I do this primarily through the lens of recounting details of Islas's life—one that reached into important social, historical, political, and cultural shifts taking place within and outside the Latino and **LGBT** communities in the later half of the twentieth century.

Born in El Paso, Texas, in 1938 Arturo Islas was raised bilingually and excelled at school. As a child he contracted polio, leaving him with a disability for the rest of his life. (See Julie Minich's essay "Enabling Aztlán".) This left him deeply self-conscious physically, driving him even more strongly into the world of books (especially world literature) and his studies. Graduating valedictorian from El Paso High, he won a scholarship to attend Stanford in 1956.

While learning to live with a differently configured body had led him to study subjects that would feed into a career in medicine, he ultimately chose to pursue a career in writing and teaching. As an undergraduate he studied with the writer Hortense Calisher. As a PhD student also at Stanford, he studied with authors Yvor Winters and Wallace Stegner. In the study of the craft of fiction, he was greatly influenced by Dostoevsky, García Márquez, Faulkner, Colette, to name a few.

After completing his PhD in 1971, Islas was given a professorship in Stanford's English Department. During this period, Islas began writing two related novels, *Day of the Dead/Día de los Muertos* and *American Dreams and Fantasies*. They would become the blueprint for the novel he would publish nearly a decade later titled, *The Rain God* (1984).

Islas became acquainted with the hostile world of publishing. This was not because of a lack of talent on his part, but, as he suspected at the time, because of the novel's experimental form and content (a gay Latino protagonist) that defied editor expectations. In spite of the great gains in queer and brown civil rights in the political arena, the publishing world was still run by editors that were either xenophobic or afraid to take a chance on innovative storytelling formats—especially with ethnic authors. Islas didn't write the immigrant farm worker novel as per José Antonio Villarreal's *Pocho* (1959) nor did he write the urban ghetto novel as per Piri Thomas's *Down These Mean Streets*

(1997). Islas's novel did not fit either mold. It was focused on a cast of middle-class Chicano characters and a young man's coming to terms with his queer sexuality.

By assigning students to read sections from my biography of Islas, *Dancing with Ghosts*, they learn the intimate details of the 32 rejection letters that he received from all variety of publishers—including a publisher that would posthumously publish his novel, *La Mollie and the King of Tears*. Each of these letters is critical, variously, of his fiction coming off as too gay or too Chicano. The criticisms varied from telling him that he used too much Spanish, was too gay, had too few working class and/or farm-worker characters, or wasn't urban and gritty enough. They rejected the novel, blinded to its significance by their homophobic and racist prejudice. Publishers were not ready for a novel by a Latino author that would explore the complex intersection between sexuality, *latinidad*—and disability.

Soon after *The Rain God* was published by Alexandrian Press on October 8, 1984, it began to receive local critical and popular acclaim. The first print run of 500 hardbacks sold well enough for Alexandrian Press to print a larger run: 1,500 paperbacks. The paperbacks sold out almost immediately. Word of mouth along with Islas's ruthless self-promotion helped ensure continued sales. By June 1985, *The Rain God* had sold over 3,000 copies. Its success helped the novel travel overseas, with a Dutch press translating and publishing the novel as *De Regen God* early in 1987. It went on to win the Southwestern American Book Award. Today, it is taught in high school and college classes alike, and remains one of the durable titles in the Latino literary canon.

Emplotting time and place

After giving a biographical overview and publication history, I establish the setting of the novel. The novel follows the ins and outs of the Angel family, who live in an unnamed U.S. town (in the sequel, *Migrant Souls*, it's named Del Sapo) on the Texas/Mexico border. The Rio Grande separates the two. It's a desertscape. Although the majority of the narrative takes place in this fictionalized setting, it also briefly moves to San Francisco. We learn from the character Miguel Grande that the town has a growing Mexican population: "the force, like the town, was more than half Mexican now ... The town seemed ready to accept people of Mexican ancestry in positions of power" (76).

I then establish the historical time referenced in: the narrator mentions JFKs assas-sination (57); the Vietnam War (45); the Mexican revolution of 1910–20 (163 and 165); and the Spanish Civil War 1936–39 (59). From this scant information, I guide students to identify the age of the protagonist (and primary **focalizer** of the events), Miguel Chico. We sleuth out together details that suggest he was born in the mid-1930s, raised in the 1940s in this bordertown, and is an adult in San Francisco in the late 1970s—the absolute present tense time of the narration.

Although history is present, it murmurs in the background of the novel. I draw the student's attention to how the characters are only indirectly touched by historical events: the Second World War, McCarthyism, the Korean War, and the civil rights struggles. Rather, the struggles and tensions that do exist are between the younger and older generation of Latinos.

Once the setting is established, I then provide an overview of the plot—or I call on one of the students to provide this. The plot moves through a series of flashbacks; each chapter moves from a more present to a more distant time frame, providing the reader with a strong sense of where the characters came from and where they are going.

However, the narrative never quite provides a solid temporal footing: the flashbacks are intercut with an unidentified temporal present.

In a PowerPoint I provide students with a chapter by chapter breakdown of the sequence of events:

> "Judgment Day" (Chapter 1): Miguel Chico is in the hospital for an operation related to an unidentified intestinal illness: "His body was being held together by a network of tubes and syringes" (8).

- This allows for the narrator, closely aligned with Miguel Chico, to create a series of flashbacks of his childhood (ages 7–9) that include such events as the death of Maria, and memories of cross dressing and playing with dolls associated with her.
- Flashforward: Miguel Chico living in San Francisco "a few years after his operation" (20–21). Readers see how much Maria influences Miguel Chico's life and get a sense of passion for literature: "Literature had given him another way to examine the mind" (28).

> "Chile" (Chapter 2): The Angel family meal with Juanita and sister Nina and others.

- Flashback to the family's move to the United States and information about their French/Mexican father who worked as a cigar maker, lived in San Francisco in search of work where he loses his first born child, then moves to New Mexico then Texas. The generational presence of *machismo* in the family.
- Nina/Ernesto's son Tony drowns.

> "Comadre/Compadre" (Chapter 3): Miguel Grande and Juanita's wedding anniversary.

- Introduction of a character outside of the family: Juanita's best friend Lola.
- Discovery of Miguel Grande's affair with Lola.
- Discovery of Miguel Grande's gay brother Felix murdered and mutilated at the army base. Consequences: Miguel Grande is not selected as chief of police: "he lost faith in himself" (91).
- Miguel Grande's confession to Miguel Chico then Juanita about his affair with Lola.

> "Rain Dancer" (Chapter 4): Felix goes to the desert with a soldier that leads to his murder.

- Flashback gives sense of Felix's home life; he's a gentle father who excessively dotes on his son, JoEl, and sexually ignores his wife Angie.
- Flashback to Felix's marriage with Angie and the family's upset because she is dark skinned—*una india*.

> "Ants" (Chapter 5): Readers meet the outcast members of the older generation family members.

- Tia Cuca and Mr. Davis, who eloped without family's permission; Learn that JoEl goes crazy.

"Rain God" (Chapter 6): Miguel Chico returns to San Francisco after visiting JoEl.

- Flashback to Mama Chona's death and the gathering together of the family.
- Image of Mama Chona at the end of the novel brings readers full circle back to the image of Mama Chona at the beginning of the novel. The novel's use of her image to frame the novel reminds readers of her matriarchal presence in her absence.

After carefully delineating the plot with all its flashbacks (and flashforwards) I then discuss the *rhythm* of the chapters as they unfold. Each chapter varies in terms of page length. I schematize this for the students as follows: A (26) B (17) C (57) D (35) B (15) A (21). With this in mind, I demonstrate how the novel's structure spins the readers into its center: Miguel Grande's affair with Lola and the discovery of Felix's mutilated body. The novel then spirals the reader back to the end, passing through the shorter, more subordinate chapters. I then show the students how this spiraling in and out movement seen in the novel's structure parallels the internal, psychological movement of the protagonist, Miguel Chico. As the narrative unfolds, his mind moves increasingly from memories of his recent present to the past (the center of the novel) then out again to the recent past. Taken as a whole, I demonstrate how the formal structures of the novel mirror Miguel Chico's psychological journey inward. In this journey the reader discovers a paradox: to become absolutely *present* in the *absenting* of life.

This paradox doesn't come out of the blue, as I explain to my students. I ask the students to read closely the Pablo Neruda (the prologue) and the eponymous chapter by the learned poet-king King of Texcoco (the last chapter). With the Neruda poem I have them especially attend to lines such as: "I come to speak through your dead mouth [and] Hasten to my veins, to my mouth. / Speak through my words and my blood." In the "Rain God" poem (162) I have them attend to the lines: "All the earth is a grave and nothing escapes it"; "Vanished are these glories"; and "Nothing recalls them but the written page." I then ask the students to share stories of family acts as a way to preserve a memory of significant events to give them a more direct sense of what it means to bring to life our ancestors through storytelling (our mouths).

Here I draw attention to the fact of the presence of the protagonist Miguel Chico's focalization (or filtering) presence within the novel's third-person omniscient narration. We see the characters, actions, and events contained within the storyworld as if filtered through his glasses. Miguel Chico is the character who attends the university to write and study literature. He is the character endowed with the power to *preserve* through writing the family's story.

I then move on to discuss another related emplotment: the more a given character *integrates* into the social mainstream, the more they are *alienated* from the family. To explore how integration is synonymous with alienation from the family in the novel, I have students read passages from pages 76, 77, 78, 83, 91, and 119. I have them consider, for instance, the distance that arises between JoEl and his mother Angie in the following: "She spoke English with a heavy Mexican accent and used it only when she wanted to make 'important' statements. After his first year in school JoEl learned to be ashamed of the way his mother abused the language" (119). I also have them consider carefully the ironies that arise in a passage such as:

> In his arrogance, Miguel believed he was finding ways out of it through university education. He had not yet had time to combine learning with experience,

however, and he still felt himself superior to those who had brought him up and loved him.

(91)

Other emplotments that can be discussed include: the role of bilingual education (within the novel and of course that the novel is written predominantly in English); racial discrimination, prejudice, and internalized racism (especially with the characters Mama Chona and Tia Cuca); disintegration (the novel's progression is a progression toward disintegration of the family and of the unity of bilingual English/Spanish); progression toward decay (Miguel Chico as the physical embodiment of decay, kept alive only because of tubes hanging out of his gut, for instance); **machismo** (embodied in the figure of Miguel Grande); gay sexuality within the Latino community; and the virgin/whore dichotomy (embodied in the actions of Juanita and Lola, roles that are complicated in the poet-king's poem "The Rain God"). Along with these themes I like to have students consider supporting leitmotifs that weave their way through the novel. I focus on such as *recovery*: To get well as in one's mental health as well as to *recover* after uncovering family stories heard and then recollected on the page. The novel recovers stories by recovering others ultimately in an act of the protagonist Miguel Chico's mental recovery. Recover in the way the desert exists in the novel to recover and disappear some things and to uncover constantly other things. Recover in the sense of facts uncovered. It is in the desert that the closeted uncle Felix is murdered by a **homophobic** soldier. While family members would like to cover over the facts, they are eventually uncovered and recovered by Miguel Chico.

The structures and topics brought up here can provide teachers with a guide to structure lectures and discussions, as well as springboards for creating assignments. Such lectures and assignments might gravitate around themes of recovery, gender, sexuality, religious iconography, racial discrimination (overt and internalized), bilingualism, paradoxes of making absent to create presence, among others.

Resources for teaching *The Rain God*

Aldama, Frederick Luis. *Dancing with Ghosts: A Critical Biography of Arturo Islas.* Berkeley: University of California Press, 2004.
——. *Brown on Brown: Chicano/a Representations of Gender, Sexuality, and Ethnicity.* Austin: University of Texas Press, 2005.
——. *Critical Mappings of Arturo Islas's Fictions.* Tempe, AZ: Bilingual Press/Editorial Bilingüe, 2008.
Caldrón, Héctor and José David Saldívar. *Criticism in the Borderlands: Studies in Chicano Literature, Culture, and Ideology.* Durham: Duke University Press, 1991.
Cutler, John Alba. "Prosthesis, surrogation, and relation in Arturo Islas's *The Rain God.*" *Aztlan: A Journal of Chicano Studies* 33.1 (Spring 2008): 7–32.
Minich, Julie. "Enabling Aztlán: Arturo Islas Jr., disability, and chicano cultural nationalism." *MFS Modern Fiction Studies* 57.4 (Winter 2011): 694–714.
Padilla, Yolanda. "Felix beyond the closet: sexuality, masculinity, and relations of power in Arturo Islas's *The Rain God.*" *Aztlan: A Journal of Chicano Studies* 34.2 (Fall 2009): 11–34.

32 Teaching Andrés Montoya

Stephanie Fetta

Winner of the American Book Award and the University of California, Irvine Chicano/
Latino Literary Prize, *The Ice Worker Sings and Other Poems* by Andrés Montoya
(1968–99) gives students a unique opportunity to consider the limitations of notions of
beauty, greed, and poetry. I teach *The Ice Worker Sings and Other Poems* in Introduction to US Latin@ Literature, an upper-division class taught in Spanish in a
Languages, Literature, and Linguistics Department of a research university in Central
New York. My classes count toward a degree in Spanish but because I ground our study
of literature by analyzing intersectional relations of ethnicity, class, race, gender and
sexual orientation, legal status, and able-bodiedness, my classes are often cross-listed
in Latino/Latin American Studies, and Women and Gender Studies, counting toward
those degrees.

My students tend to be disproportionately female but generally split between affluent,
East Coast, Anglo-Euro students, and working-class East Coast Latin@s in a costly
private university. These populations approach the course material for Introduction to
US Latin@ Literature from significantly different life experiences. Anglo-Euro students
tend to be somewhat less aware of the cultural perception they have of themselves or
of students from different backgrounds. Latin@ students, however, are quite aware of
how they are perceived by non-Latin@s which in turn rails against how they know
themselves. Latin@ students readily and capably express occasions when they have
experienced oppression, while Anglo-Euro students seldom feel they have been subject
to or have subjected others to discrimination. Interestingly, most urban, downstate
Latin@ students do not necessarily understand their experience with oppression as
similar to that of struggling local Latin@ and African American communities, and
only occasionally do any of my students consider themselves in relation to Anglo-Euro
city residents who range considerably in economic class.

We read Montoya's poetry mid-semester after laying the ground work with essay
selections from Gloria Anzaldúa, chapters from Juan González's *Harvest of Empire*, texts
like José Antonio Villarreal's *Pocho*, Piri Thomas's *Down These Mean Streets*, Sandra
Cisnero's *The House on Mango Street*, and poetry selections from Carolina Hospital,
Carmen Tafolla, and Ana Castillo. When we turn to the poetry of Andrés Montoya,
we are familiar with the valence and durability of racialization, class, and gender, as well as
the particularity of ethnicity and histories of migration to various locations across the
United States over a period of five decades. When we look at Montoya's poetry, we
gain insight into what we as readers consider worthy of poetic address. We engage this
question in Montoya's poetry when we access an intimate level of disclosure regarding
what it feels like to grow up rejecting the very society to which one is bound; while the

poetic "I" loathes those around him, he himself and his are treated as loathsome by members of his community as well as the broader U.S. society.

Surprisingly, intimacy develops from this telluric tension. The poetic I throughout the collection's four parts does not shy away from describing his illegal activities and precarious behaviors to which he concedes moral impropriety. Latin@ students often vocally affirm the reality of such behaviors in the environments from which they originate, grounding the poems in a social reality that opens their classmates' eyes to the social circumstance with which their Latin@ classmates have had to contend. It is at this point when the class starts to act as a whole. Anglo-Euro students begin to see their Latin@ classmates with understanding and admiration, and recognize Latin@ classmates as cultural authorities; Latin@ students begin to feel comfortable with the collective support of their stories and lives, opening up further in class discussions and small group interactions.

As the students' relationships build, I guide the students to notice the aesthetic context Montoya creates even in the midst of brutal events continuing in parts II through IV. I ask the class to pause and reflect on Montoya's use of language, its rhythm, the accessibility of his word selection, and Montoya's poetic diversion of grammar intensifying his experience without exaggeration or falling into the obtuse. Montoya's is a poetry that impels the reader with unflattering personal disclosure but that compels with accessible beauty.

However, the appreciation for lyrical beauty arises piecemeal. My students—Latin@ and Anglo-Euro—must acclimate to Montoya's unbecoming behavior by first acknowledging their initial aversion and discomfort. For, at first glance, as the Latin@ students react to stereotypes they have grown tired of, Anglo-Euro students might initially read confirmation of their assumptive stance. This aversion brings the issue of judgment to the fore, leading me to ask, what does *to judge* mean? The question is technically not difficult to answer, however, when considering how *judging* differs from *observing* (frequently mistaken as a synonym) students quickly produce words to differentiate between the two like the adjudication of right or wrong to an action. Students are sophisticated enough to recognize a degree of positionality to these judgments, and a certain uncomfortable stasis arises. They speak to the difference between what an action can mean depending on the conditions of one's life: we ask, what kinds of opportunities are available to the poetic I? To us? What constitutes sameness and difference of opportunities between the poetic voice and us in class? Students are surprised by similarities of individual struggles in relation to family and community but even more so by the strident social conditions rendering the poetic I's opportunities so dim.

Expressed in single words or phrases, the students substantively arrive at critical terms like class, race (which we contextualize to its more appropriate understanding of racialization), gender, and nonhegemonic forms of sexuality. We appreciate the value of location (Central California and the powerful agribusiness industry there) presenting particular kinds of living and suffering that nevertheless build an understanding of multiple sites of oppression of Latin@s across the United States but with comparable degrees of intensity. Most students have seldom had contact with Chican@s on or off campus and soon begin to appreciate the strife of Chican@s and Mexicans, the majority Latin@ group, but in journal entries they begin to voice feelings of complicity and critique minimizing or disregarding the situation of Latin@s across the United States. The discussions in class and in journals help students understand the personal effect of broad social forces to which we are all subjected. At the same time, awareness grows of the ways that each of us may be subjecting others to such forces.

Which leads to the discussion of, why do we not want to read poetry about such experiences and issues? Students sometimes express their belief that poetry should concern itself with beauty, impart wisdom with the *a priori* goal of broadening appreciation of things that students already found beautiful. These expectations, they worry, are not going to be met in their reading. And while the collection portrays a subtle evolution from part I to part IV toward a transcendent poetic I, each section includes morally challenging scenarios.

However, as we read further, I highlight the plaintive yet powerful phrasing found in the majority of poems throughout the collection, lending a transcendental eye to the I's life. For example, when describing his elderly impoverished probably once-abused grandmother, the "I" describes her face like "a bruised petal of forgiveness" in "Luciana: This Is How I See You" of part III. The phrasing presents us with the gravity of a difficult and highly unglamorous life lived that is countered by Abuela's joy. Abuela's orientation to her life is not only honored by the poetic I but is found endearing.

Additionally, the poem recounts finding his brother slain by his own hand in "a letter to kb." The I, despite feeling some degree of hatred for his brother, who the I sees as weak for having committed suicide, writes him as a humble Christ figure, giving credence again to their social reality despite the torment of loss and redemption experienced in the moment:

> i found my brother, one day, behind a door, arms spread wide
> like Christ on the cross, laid out on the floor over a pile of colorful
> clothes ready for wash, the sad slashes at his wrists weeping
> into the stench of stale cigarette smoke and poverty that held captive
> that room, his eyes deep dark wells wet and begging for the logic of death.
>
> ("a letter to kb", 14–20)

I ask students, thinking about the contentious relationship of the speaker to his world which is met in kind by the world toward him, why does he see his grandmother with such affection? How can his so-called wimpy brother also appear to the I as the Christ?

That is, what happens to the I's engagement with judging? Students comment on the emerging Christian message of redemption, that, while not wholly following a Catholic faith tradition, the I adds *discernment* as an alternative to judgment. The I redeems himself and others by reinterpreting his life and that of his community seeking redemption through a Christological frame amidst it all. We come to understand through the collection that beauty and spirituality may be intrinsic experiences of being alive, not just for the select, or the morally rect.

The poetic prism of Montoya's verse provides the collective ambience for me to ask: Could we be divine just as we are? If so, how would that view of ourselves and of one another challenge our institutions? How might this perspective affect our interpersonal relationships? If generally accepted, would people judge? What value would judging have?

The arc of this discussion occurring over two weeks brings the class to an awareness of how racial politics and economic class affect the way we perceive ourselves and one another. They come to realize that their sense of right and wrong is not immutable but contingent to a degree on their particular socioeconomic situation, and ethnicity, among other coordinates of their particular social location. They begin to notice that they hold preconceptions of what poetry is, who can write it, and what kinds of topics poetry should and should not treat. Furthermore, students realize beauty can exist among ugliness; we can override judgment for discernment, allowing us to simultaneously consider beauty in the unseemly.

Lastly, students become aware of the non-religious sense of our sacredness as a possibility with interpretative power. That is, Montoya proposes the sacred as a way to consider our lives and the lives of others, one that generates radically different readings of our relationship to one another and to our world.

Resources for teaching Andrés Montoya

Buckley, Christopher, David Oliveira, and M. L. Williams. *How Much Earth: The Fresno Poets. California Poetry Series.* Vol 8. Berkeley: Heydey Press, 2001.

Chacón, Daniel, ed. "Special Issue: An homage to Andrés Montoya." *In the Grove: California Poets and Writers* 16 (Spring 2008).

Fetta, Stephanie, ed. *Chicano/Latino Literary Prize: An Anthology of Award-winning Fiction, Poetry, and Drama.* Houston: Arte Público Press, 2008.

Heide, Rick, ed. *Under the Fifth Sun: Latino Literature from California.* California Legacy Series. Santa Clara, CA: Santa Clara University Press, 2002.

Montoya, Andrés. *The Ice Worker Sings and Other Poems.* Tempe: Bilingual Press, 1999.

——. *In Brown America.* Master's Thesis. University of Oregon. 1994.

——. *Jury of Trees: Selected and Posthumous Poems by Andrés Montoya.* Daniel Chacon, ed. Tempe: Bilingual Review Press. Forthcoming.

Yogi, Stan, Gayle Mak, and Patricia Wakida, eds. *Highway 99: A Literary Journey Through California's Great Central Valley.* Berkeley: Great Valley Books / Heyday Books, 2007.

33 Teaching Richard Rodriguez

Juan Velasco

When I teach Richard Rodriguez's *Hunger of Memory* (1982) I discuss with the students how the scholarship on this Rodriguez has dominated Chicana/o autobiographical studies.[1] While I point out that the overwhelming attention dedicated to a single book can be problematic to the analysis of the genre, I also discuss what can be learned from the bibliography dedicated to Rodriguez. How this can shed light on the ideological battles the book was engaged in during the 1980s, and the difficulty of including his work within traditional Chicana/o criticism. An essay that I assign alongside *Hunger* is Tomás Rivera's "Richard Rodriguez's *Hunger of Memory* as Humanistic Antithesis" (1984). This allows students to see firsthand the reception of the book within a cultural and historical context; it allows students to see, too, how his opposition to affirmative action and bilingual education was picked up by the ideological conservatives, turning Rodriguez into a celebrity on the right and a bête noir on the left. The aim: to have students explore how Rodriguez's creative strategies can be analyzed and classified to give us insight into how *Hunger* has been written and read, in what context, and for what reasons.

With this contextual backdrop established, I then have students consider how *Hunger of Memory* (and if time allows in a given course, his subsequent books too) can be resituated within Chicano/a autobiography as a tool less for individual recollection and more as a way of exploring issues of writing and identity, aiming at the reclaiming of the dimensions of cultural survival *beyond* the hunger of memories. I guide the students in their reading of *Hunger of Memory* to consider how Rodriguez's turns "experience" into the "autobiographical effect." I therefore create a pedagogical approach that doesn't dismiss easily Rodriguez's autobiographical acts, but rather seeks to analyze Rodriguez's "I" as a complex technology, intertwined with the de-construction of an ethnic space for Chicano/a expression, and defined by the outlines of a representation that refuses the possibility of a "self" within autobiographical discourse.

To effect such a course with my students I reframe *Hunger of Memory* as one of the most haunting tales of the gay Mexican American experience. I explain to the students that it is about a journey of desolation that culminates in the final scene—a moment of intense silence, the gap beyond words, as he contemplates his Mexican father. By reading closely the ending students see his struggles with "difference" and his profoundly alienating sense of identity as absence and the lack of language to express the "loss" of culture and family. Here I move into a discussion of the political implications of turning "difference" into silence or absence. I do so by reminding the students that the publication of *Hunger of Memory* takes place after the **Chicana/o Renaissance** of the 1970s, and the political activism and hope of the **Chicana/o Movement**. It is after all this that Rodriguez writes the most pessimistic and haunting analysis of that activism, relating the identity politics and cultural constructions of the previous two decades to "hunger." I point out that his experience is "queer" to "I Am Joaquín" (the battle cry poem of the Mexican American Civil Rights Movement) and thus *Hunger of Memory* can also be read as a failure to create a space for queerness within the heteropatriarchal sectors of the Chicano Movement. As we work our way back through the text, the students see examples of just how this queerness is realized as absence and alienation—as a rejection of the more homophobic forms of cultural nationalism. They are able to discover instances by which Rodriguez's attempt to find a language to manifest silence only reaffirms as inevitable the loss of language, the ghostly shell of any memories destined to create a self, and the paradoxical anguish of success and assimilation.

This is most clearly indicated by Rodriguez's loss of Spanish. Here I point out how with this loss comes the loss of its memories as well as a physical erasure. The negation of his body and the tragic attempts at negating *lo mexicano* finds its symbolic representation in the moment where he applies a razor to his skin to scrape off the last vestiges of his ethnicity. I point the students to the following sentence: "I wanted to forget that I had a body because I had a brown body" (126). I point out how homosexuality, like his brown skin and the Spanish language, will also be present as erasure. I indicate to the students how this gesture of expunction turns back against every aspect of his "self" as his sexuality, to the very end, remains a secret.

I teach *Hunger of Memory* as an autobiographical narrative attempting to write the secrets that cannot be told; as an example of refusing to build a "self" by branding loss (absence) as the alternative option against the hope (presence) of a Chicano identity as the ultimate mark of experience operating at the center of the narrative. I also teach it as a warning. How his words cannot shake a pain that is unable to transcend the dualistic division of experience (hope and loss), or detect any "presence" in between, as the voice, ultimately, vanishes in the void of sexual and cultural assimilation.

After discussing the function of presence and absence, to hope and loss in *Hunger of Memory* I situate it within more general discussions regarding autobiographical theory such as that of Jacques Derrida (*Memoires for Paul de Man*) and Gloria Anzaldúa (*Borderlands/La Frontera*). I teach Derrida's concept of **prosopopeia** as that which both defines and kills memory as well as that of Anzaldúa and "making faces"("haciendo caras") as a politically subversive gesture. We explore together how "mask" and "face" might offer useful conceptual models for understanding Rodriguez's versions of truth to offer new options to those inherited repressive values within the community. We also explore Rodriguez within the context of Norma Cantú's "fictional autobioethnography" and Latin American testimonial writing generally to see how *Hunger of Memory* might offer a break from dualistic thinking.

With my students and Rodriguez's text we embark on a journey that explores the tension created by the open-ended quality of a "self" wrestling with personal and communal representation. Along the way we consider how contemporary Chicana/o autobiography offers a critique of Western individualism and its understanding of the person as an individual separable from the collective or communal; how *Hunger of Memory* is itself designed to confront the workings of those coexisting paradoxical terms (communal wholeness and personal particularity) and to foreground the role of Chicana/o culture as an ever-unfolding communal project filtered through the "I."

Along the way we also come to understand how Rodriguez questions the healing performative aspects of self-representation. How he exposes the dichotomy of presence and absence by bringing out the tension between the silencing of his experience and the liberatory potential of the cultural voice assigned to this experience. How his particular process of refusing a self that involves writing as a healing performance and self-empowerment, a specific way of addressing the genre emerges. By understanding the mechanisms of emptiness and absence within self-representation, we can also see other aspects of violence exercised on the Chicano/a community, and analyze the space of erasure created by the configuration of the cultural, political, and literary boundaries of representation in the United States.

If time permits me to teach *Hunger of Memory* along with some of his other books, the students begin to clearly see a pattern: his positioning of his work within discourses of craving and absence that challenge the assumption that all Chicanos/as adopt and negotiate a sense of the cultural past in the same way. That is, the students see the rich and varied ways in which he introduces new strategies and models of expression where multiple interactions between self-representation and erasure occur, building an open-ended notion of self that challenges the genre as both individual self-expression and a voice for the community.

Finally, when teaching Rodriguez's *Hunger of Memory* I hope that my students will see how his text is guided by the attempt to name the topography of absence and craving as a form of representation, and relocate the speakers' voices away from the traditional role of Chicano/a autobiography—"a personal and communitarian response to the threat of erasure", as Genaro Padilla writes in *My History, Not Yours* (1993: x). I hope that they will see his work within the larger context of Chicano/a autobiography whereby the autobiographer searches for a construction that involves the writer's sense of personhood, together with politically and personally charged notions of community and nation. Furthermore, I hope that they will come to understand how the past, present, and future are built by the reconstructed notion of self and culture. In that case, for both student and Rodriguez what is at stake is not only the nature of the "I" as it unfolds in the writing, but also the emerging nature of the communal sense of history itself, as it is reflected in *Hunger of Memory*.

Note

1 This article borrows from some of my previous published articles on the issue of Chicana/o autobiography, and from a book project on the same subject.

Resources for teaching Richard Rodriguez

Aldama, Frederick Luis. "Ethnoqueer re-architexturing of metropolitan space." *Nepantla*, 1.3 (2000): 581–604.

——. *Dancing with Ghosts: A Critical Biography of Arturo Islas.* University of California Press, 2004.

——. *Brown on Brown: Chicano/a Representations of Gender, Sexuality, and Ethnicity.* Austin: University of Texas Press, 2005.

García, Michael Nieto. "The inauthentic ethnic: Richard Rodriguez's Brown and resisting essentialist narratives of ethnic identity." *Prose Studies* 34.2 (Aug. 2012): 129–50.

——. *Autobiography in Black and Brown.* Albuquerque: University of New Mexico Press, 2014.

294   *Juan Velasco*

Hernández, Ellie D. *Postnationalism in Chicana/o Literature and Culture.* Austin: University of Texas Press, 2009.

Perry, Yaakov. "Metaphors we write by: desire's (dis)orientation and the border in Richard Rodriguez's *Hunger of Memory.*" *MELUS* 34.3 (Fall 2009): 155–82.

Rivera, Tomás. "Richard Rodriguez's *Hunger of Memory* as humanistic antithesis" *MELUS* 11.4 (Winter 1984): 5–12.

Rodriguez, Richard. *Las fronteras móviles: tradición, modernidad y la búsqueda de "lo mexicano" en la Literatura Chicana contemporánea.* Monterrey: Ediciones Universidad Autónoma de Nuevo León, México, 2003.

——. "Using Queer Chicana/o Autobiography to Teach Courses on Identity and Solidarity." In *Expanding the Circle: Creating an Inclusive Environment in Higher Education for LGBTQ Students and Studies.* Ed. John Hawley. New York: State University of New York, 2015, pp. 245–59.

Soto, Sandra K. *Reading Chican@ Like a Queer: The De-Mastery of Desire.* Austin: University of Texas Press, 2010.

Velasco, Juan. "*Automitografías*: the border paradigm and Chicana/o autobiography." *Biography* 27.2 (2004): 313–38.

34 Teaching María Amparo Ruiz de Burton

Amelia María de la Luz Montes

Students often place Mexican American or Chicano/a literary history around the mid-twentieth century. They may have some knowledge of the 1960s Chicano Civil Rights Movement, and the literature of the historical period between 1950 and 2000. Lesser known to them may be the fact that a Mexican American novelist/playwright, named María Amparo Ruiz de Burton, was present during President Lincoln's inauguration on March 4, 1861. More surprising to them is finding out this writer is a woman, multilingual, trained to litigate in court, and raised in Mexico at a time when land inheritance was matrilineal. Teaching these facts alone opens a whole new world to students and encourages them to find out more about what it means to be Latina or Latino in the United States. They soon learn that Mexican American literary history really began in 1848 with the signing of **The Treaty of Guadalupe**. (See also Jesse Alemán's discussion of this phenomenon in Chapter 1 in this volume.)

María Amparo Ruiz de Burton was born in 1832 and died in 1895. Her wealthy, upper-class family owned what is now most of Riverside and Orange County in Southern California. Ruiz de Burton was privately tutored. She studied Latin, French, English, as well as Spanish. She was well read. Among her favorite writers, who also influenced her own work, were Victor Hugo and Émile Zola. Her life spans remarkable moments in history: the **Mexican American War** (1846–48), the Civil War (1861–65), the French Intervention and Occupation of Mexico (1861–67). Studying her work, then, is an important way to begin a comprehensive study of Mexican American and Chicano/a history. To use her work within an interdisciplinary context also allows for a presentation of various perspectives. Students majoring in various fields of study (history, literature, sociology, political science, psychology, modern languages, even creative writing, for example) will be able to apply their expertise in classroom discussions about Ruiz de Burton's work.

I have taught Ruiz de Burton's two novels, *Who Would Have Thought It?* (1872), *The Squatter and the Don* (1885), and her play, *Don Quixote de la Mancha: A Comedy in Five Acts* (1876) in a variety of contexts as well as geographic areas. I've taught her at universities in California as well as in the Midwest. I've taught her work to primarily Latino students, white students, and in racially mixed classes. Class also figures prominently within the lecture and discussion format. Students coming from working-class backgrounds will question whether or not Ruiz de Burton should be taught in a Chicano literature course. A lively discussion will ensue. My answer is always "yes" because Chicanos and Latinos represent all class levels. Ruiz de Burton began her life in an upper class family. After 1848, she became the "other," having to battle land claims, and her own position under an Anglo-American society. At the end of her life, she was destitute, dying penniless in Chicago, Illinois.

Her frustrations and challenges as a Mexican American and a woman are recorded in her published writings, and in personal letters she wrote to close friends and family. Her experiences and the way she included these struggles within the art form of fiction and drama lead to myriad considerations for students. Ruiz de Burton's writings provide yet another way to study the nineteenth century and its influence on the literary history of the twentieth and twenty-first centuries.

Ruiz de Burton *In Action*

I usually begin teaching Ruiz de Burton within an American Studies context. I begin with a close analysis of Chicano History. Students read sections from Rodolfo Acuña's *Occupied America: A History of Chicanos* (1972). Acuña's work provides them with the necessary historical context of Mexico and early Mexican American history. His work, coupled with Sonya Lipsett-Rivera's *Gender and the Negotiation of Daily Life in Mexico 1750–1856*, work well together. Antonia I. Castañeda's writings are also key for understanding gender and **Californiana** stereotypes (see resource section below). Students then analyze sections from *The Treaty of Guadalupe Hidalgo* before reading Ruiz de Burton. I not only have them read, analyze, and discuss the Treaty, I also guide them by play-acting situational moments. I place students in pairs and ask them to pretend they are Californianas or Californios.

To play the part, we answer the question, "What does it mean to be a Californio?" In answering this question, we discuss historical facts about land ownership and identity using articles such as Antonia I. Castañeda's, "The Political Economy of Nineteenth Century Stereotypes of Californianas." Then I distribute Article VIII from *The Treaty of Guadalupe Hidalgo*. I ask students to discuss, with their "Californio" partner, the salient points of Article VIII. Most students choose the sentence that reads, "In the said territories, property of every kind, now belonging to Mexicans, not established there, shall be inviolably respected" (190). After discussion, I divide the class in half: Californios and Anglo-American settlers. The settlers fall into two categories: squatters (who settle on land without paying rent or buying from the owner), and those willing to buy land if the land they choose is owned. I ask the Anglo-American squatters to place their desks in close proximity to Californios. I point out that "suddenly" Californios have squatters settling on their land. How will Californios explain to squatters that they cannot settle there— that their lands "must be inviolably respected"? We discuss language problems and students usually figure out that Californios were forced to hire translators. I explain how some Californios may have had legal papers regarding land boundaries, but these papers were written in Spanish. Other Californios may have acquired their land simply with a handshake from a Mexican official generations ago and therefore did not have any way to prove ownership. How will they convince the squatter not to settle on their lands?

The next step is to introduce the formation of the California Land Commission to the students. They begin to understand the frustration Californios experienced when they realize Californios had to hire translators and lawyers, to redraw and write the original papers in English in order to present them to the Commission. They also begin to understand how, while the Californios had to wait five, ten, or sometimes 20 years to have their papers legally confirmed by the Commission, the squatters would be building homes and cultivating agriculture on Californio lands. They learn that Californios had to pay taxes on the squatter settlements, and they had to pay taxes on any profits squatters made on the cultivation of land. Californios soon were facing bankruptcy before ever making it to a hearing with the Commission.

After reading and discussing these historical issues, I distribute copies of a letter written on November 22, 1853 by the lawyer Henry Wagner Halleck, who was representing the Californio Pablo de la Guerra from Santa Barbara. Halleck expresses frustration with the commission. He tells de la Guerra that the commission is rejecting and confirming lands on very faulty premises: "I have no further confidence in this Board, & I am fully satisfied that they are—or at least 2 of them are—Squatters, and were appointed by squatters. I should now not be surprised if all of your father's titles were rejected."[1] After reading this letter, the students experience—in concrete terms—how colonization works in subtle ways, how easily a treaty can be dishonored, and how Manifest Destiny is enacted.

With this background, students understand the passion with which Ruiz de Burton writes, and they are better able to discuss the novels within historical, cultural, social, class, and gender contexts. Antonia I. Castañeda's writings especially assist students in learning how, under Mexican law, upper class Californianas could inherit land and litigate in court. U.S. law did not recognize women within the context of law and litigation. This was all the more frustrating for Ruiz de Burton who drew up her own legal papers, yet because she was a woman, she was not recognized under U.S. law.

This classroom example is especially helpful before teaching *The Squatter and the Don* because the novel focuses on California lands. *Who Would Have Thought It?* is primarily set on the East Coast. I find that Midwest students and East Coast students connect more viscerally with *Who Would Have Thought It?* In both novels, race, and racism are prominent themes. However, in *Who Would Have Thought It?*, Washington politics also plays a prominent role, with President Lincoln making an appearance in more than one chapter. Making sure to assign actual personal letters Ruiz de Burton wrote (which describe Lincoln and Washington politics) can make for exciting classroom discussions (see resources for Ruiz de Burton's letters). The Penguin Edition of *Who Would Have Thought It?* includes, in its appendix, a handful of Ruiz de Burton's personal letters that directly connect with the novel.

In a survey class or a course on Chicano/a and/or Latino/a literature, I usually begin with Ruiz de Burton. Throughout the semester, invariably, students will be able to pick themes and characters in more contemporary works that directly connect with Ruiz de Burton. Her works, at the beginning of a course, create a historical and theoretical scaffolding, which students can then continue to build with each work studied. For example, I include in my resources, a contemporary book by Julie Bettie on young girls and class. Her work consists of interviews she conducted with high school girls primarily from working-class backgrounds. This may seem very far removed from Ruiz de Burton, and yet the connections with class, race, and gender, prompt important discussions. As one student noted last year, "We may feel like the nineteenth-century was so long ago, and that we learned from that period, but sometimes in these writings that were just published, I feel that we haven't learned much. The same issues are here." This is why the teaching of Ruiz de Burton's works continue to be important and prescient.

Note

1 Ruiz de Burton, María Amparo. *Letters to George Davidson*. George Davidson Papers. Box 4, Bancroft Library. University of California, Berkeley.

Resources for teaching María Amparo Ruiz de Burton

Acuña, Rodolfo F. *Occupied America: A History of Chicanos.* 1972 7th edn. New York: Pearson, 2010.

Bettie, Julie. *Women without Class: Girls, Race, and Identity.* Oakland: University of California Press, 2003.

Blumin, Stuart. *The Emergence of the Middle Class: Social Experience in the American City, 1760–1900.* New York: Cambridge University Press, 1989.

Castañeda, Antonia I. "Gender, race, and culture: Spanish-Mexican women in the historiography of frontier California." *Frontiers* II (1990a): 8–20.

——. "The political economy of nineteenth century stereotypes of Californianas." In *Between Borders: Essays on Mexicana/Chicana History.* Ed. Adelaida R. Del Castillo. Encino: Floricanto Press, 1990b.

Griswold del Castillo, Richard. *The Treaty of Guadalupe Hidalgo: A Legacy of Conflict.* Norman: University of Oklahoma Press, 1990.

Gutierrez, Ramón A. and Richard J. Orsi. *Contested Eden: California Before the Gold Rush.* Oakland: University of California Press, 1998.

Lipsett-Rivera, Sonya. *Gender and the Negotiation of Daily Life in Mexico, 1750-1856.* Lincoln: University of Nebraska Press, 2012.

Montes, Amelia María de la Luz and Anne Elizabeth Goldman. *María Amparo Ruiz de Burton: Critical and Pedagogical Perspectives.* Lincoln: University of Nebraska Press, 2004.

Ruiz, Vicki L. *From Out of the Shadows: Mexican Women in Twentieth-Century America.* Oxford: Oxford University Press, 2008.

Ruiz de Burton, María Amparo. *Don Quixote de la Mancha: A Comedy in Five Acts, Taken from Cervantes' Novel of That Name.* San Francisco: Carmany, 1876.

——. *The Squatter and the Don.* Houston: Arte Público Press, 1997.

——. *Who Would Have Thought It?* Ed. Amelia María de la Luz Montes. New York: Penguin Classics, 2009.

Sanchez, Rosaura and Beatrice Pita, eds. *Conflicts of Interest: The Letters of María Amparo Ruiz de Burton.* Houston: Arte Público Press, 2001.

35 Teaching Luis Valdez and *Zoot Suit*

Marilyn Patton

Why begin the study of American drama with the early Shakespeare performances, the bowdlerized versions of *Uncle Tom's Cabin*, or the founding of the Provincetown Players? After an intense look at Luis Valdez's *Zoot Suit* (1992), a different approach suggests itself. Why not connect theater back to the very first theatrical performances in the United States in 1598 (Don Juan de Oñate), then on to the *pastorelas*, heroic dramas, amateur and professional theaters (Kanellos 1983: 17) operating continuously in the Southwest, California, and Texas right up to the present?

Let's teach by tracing American theater back to its Spanish and Latino/a origins as well as to the rituals of Aztlán and the drama associated with the church. William Worthen argues that

> Chicana/o theatre is a deeply hybridized theatre, drawing on a wide variety of formal traditions: Aztec ritual; Spanish and colonial drama; Mexican drama; *pastorelas* and other Church drama; the popular *carpa* and *zarzuela* shows operating in Mexico and the Southwest from the turn of the century through the 1950s; genres like the *novela* drawn from Mexican film and television; and forms derived from European and Euro-American drama, both a realism echoing Arthur Miller or Tennessee Williams and an insistent reworking of formal and ideological "alienation" in the Brechtian mode.
>
> (1997: 101)

Studying theater by starting with *Zoot Suit* opens up the world and opens up drama.

Zoot Suit can easily be used to structure a course in American theater; studying it can also introduce a world drama class or provide a revealing case study within a literature survey.

I begin by suggesting an overall strategy and then turn to action—ideas for (literally) breaking into the world of the play.

Understandings and goals

Teachers can use the study of *Zoot Suit,* placed in its historical and cultural context, to achieve the following understandings and goals.

Understandings:

- Theater began as (and ideally continues to be) a celebratory community event, which helps to define the community and which serves to bring isolated individuals into the larger community (Frye 1957; Barber 1961).

- In drama, the opposing forces come into creative opposition (Levi-Strauss 1963).
- Theater can dramatize and clarify social injustice and be a force for change toward a more equal society (Boal 1985).
- Theater can function both to awaken the audience to the power of media and to critique its failings (Brecht 1964).

Goals:

Students will

- build community within the class.
- understand and appreciate the theatrical, social, political, and personal significance of a people's theater and of *Zoot Suit* within the context of theater history.
- see drama as more than entertainment—as action within the social/ political reality.
- awake, after reading or watching *Zoot Suit*, into awareness of the power of media and to their own conditioned responses.

Zoot Suit as a door into drama

Combining student presentations, lectures, and readings, I like to use the play to point toward the entire history of theater, and to see the sophisticated ways in which Valdez recalls and reworks that history.

The following points are examples of the connections that it is possible to make between *Zoot Suit* and the history of drama.

- The figures of **El Pachuco** and the Press, while absolutely specific to the story, also connect to the stock figures of **Commedia dell'Arte**, to the characters like God and the Devil in the medieval mystery cycles, and to the *actos*, which Valdez himself developed on the picket lines of the 1965 **UFW** (United Farm Workers) grape strike.
- The post-*Zoot Suit* riot scene in which El Pachuco is stripped almost naked connects to the tradition of the *mito*. Jorge Huerta (1992) claims that this scene "suggests the sacrificial 'god' of the Aztecs, stripped bare before his heart is offered to the cosmos" ("Introduction" 14).
- Valdez's filmed version makes use of the Los Angeles theater in which *Zoot Suit* first played and looks backward to the history of theater in North America even before California statehood: Spanish and colonial theater.
- Realistic scenes such as the Reyna family argument over Lupe's dress length or the meeting between George the attorney and his prospective clients (the members of the 38th Street gang) recall the realism developed within the theater, a realism that moved out into film and television, what Worthen (1997) calls genres like "the [*tele*] *novela* drawn from Mexican film and television; and forms derived from European and Euro-American drama" (101).
- The musical numbers that punctuate the entire play point toward the connection of theater to *corridos* and the *carpa* and *zarzuela* shows, as well as opera, operetta, musical theater, and *Saturday Night Live*.
- The "stylization" by which action is halted while Henry and El Pachuco engage in psychological battle points toward the drive within drama from Sophocles on to find a sufficient form that could help the audience see into the soul of the character

and which went through experiments like *Strange Interlude* (O'Neill), *The Verge* (Glaspell) and separation of characters into multiple "selves" (Gao Xingjian).

- Valdez's meta-theatrical moves echo and complicate the theories of Brecht and Boal. "The spectator was no longer in any way allowed to submit to an experience uncritically ... by means of simple empathy with the characters in a play. The production took the subject-matter and the incidents shown and put them through a process of alienation that is necessary to all understandings" (Brecht 1964: 71).
- Furthermore, the multiple possible conclusions to the drama, suggested but not conclusively upheld, make the play post-modern and deconstructionist, a term David Henry Hwang claimed for *M. Butterfly*.

Practical and specific suggestions: studying *Zoot Suit* day by day

Cutting through language: first steps

1 Since the Press becomes the prosecutor in the trial, it is crucial for students to connect to the idea of media as a tool for a vendetta. I tape together at least eight double sheets of newspaper in a floor-to-ceiling curtain and then have one student, dressed as closely as possible to El Pachuco, rip through the papers with a plastic knife labeled "switchblade" and step through, then stop before speaking.

   (a) Ask the students to brainstorm what this action means. Whatever they come up with, they definitely will see anger directed against the Press (newspapers), 40s clothes (setting the action in the past), possibly the idea of cutting through lies perpetrated by the Press, possibly showing what is behind those lies, and possibly thinking about what sort of "switch" El Pachuco is making with his blade.
   (b) Students who know that switchblades were not used in the 1940s may force the class to think about why Valdez would deliberately use this anachronism when the rest of the play is fairly faithful to the period (Broyles-Gonzalez 1994: 183).

2 After the student portraying El Pachuco delivers his lines, ask students to brainstorm in small groups why Valdez begins with Spanish, and exactly what he means by referring to himself as "existential," "profane and reverential," "mas chucote que la chingada," and, of course, the "Myth." What world is created by the language? By the use of Pachuco slang? By the alternatives offered within the lines: "precursor of revolution" or "joke/ deserving of absolution"? A particularly telling story that informs Valdez's emphasis on existential choice comes from an interview with his son, Kinan Valdez:

> Valdez's vision of the pachuco was shaped by those he saw growing up in his hometown of Delano. One pachuco named C.C., a friend of his cousin Billy, stood out from the rest.
>
> "My cousin Billy died a pachuco death, 17 knife wounds to the chest. but C.C. survived," Luis Valdez said. "C.C. went from being a teenager to being a sailor to. desegregating Delano theater to organizing the unions. He became Cesar Chavez. C.C. was Cesar Chavez and that's his picture right there, actually."
>
> With that, Valdez points to a picture of a young Cesar Chavez, long before he became a famed labor leader, standing next to cousin Billy and another young pachuco. The trio look cool and tough at once, the classic pachuco profile.
>
> "Cesar Chavez was a 'chuco," Valdez said with a grin. "It was great." (Cabrera 2007)

3   Focus next on Henry Reyna's name. Knowing that the actual character was named Henry Leyva, ask why Valdez chooses "Reyna." What effect does that name have on the audience? Here, one might use ideas from Northrop Frye and Aristotle's *Poetics* to set up the idea of a tragic hero. Or the students may simply consider the psychology implied by Henry's name and by his family's pride in him—and his own pride.

Taking on the roles

After getting Cesar Chavez's permission, Valdez worked with the striking farmworkers to develop the very first *actos,* realizing that violence could escalate easily on the picket lines of the UFW Grape Strike in Delano, California, 1965. Valdez began with the belief that "Teatro / eres el mundo," that drama could help the farmworkers to deal with the betrayal of the scabs (Esquiroles) and with articulating their own positions, for themselves.

Ask students to act out, in small groups, short scenes from *Zoot Suit* as if they were *actos.* Ask them to bring in costumes that fit the forties or what they consider equivalent costumes for the current year. Ask each group to connect Valdez's goals for *actos* to the scene that they perform: "Inspire the audience to social actions. Illuminate specific points about social problems. Satirize the opposition. Show or hint at a solution. Express what people are feeling" (Valdez and Teatro Campesino 1971: 6). Some students may volunteer to perform their scenes for the whole class but the experience of acting, even within a small group, is in itself illuminating. Examples of scenes that can work well: "Pachuco Yo," "Opening of the Trial," and "The Incorrigible Pachuco."

Follow-ups:

- Writing, possibly online, about the experience of acting the parts
- Developing, in small groups, original actos that respond to current issues
- Debating the use of stereotyped, essentialized characters

Critical thinking

In keeping with the courtroom setting of much of the play, setting up a situation for critical thinking can be accomplished using a courtroom structure.

An example of a possible debate topic is Ashley Lucas's claim about the play:

> In using the same images that stigmatize Chicana/os to promote a positive image of their ethnic identity, Valdez uses the tools of media terrorism, including language and visual imagery, to dismantle the ideology that stigmatized Mexican Americans in the mainstream media of the 1940s and to promote a positive conception of Chicana/o identity in the 1970s through the reworking of previously negative media images. *In effect, he revises the historical memory of the zoot-suited Mexican Americans of the 1940s, transforming these youths from symbols of criminality into heroic icons of radical resistance against cultural oppression.*
>
> (Lucas 2009: 61)

This claim could generate a great deal of research but it is also possible to argue the clause in bold by using lines and images and arguments from the play itself.

Preliminary preparation: Let all the students write down their thoughts and then argue their positions within a small group of four students.

The "Trial" itself:

1 Split the class into characters (witnesses), Judge, Prosecutors (a team), and Defensive Attorneys (a team).
2 Students should ask questions of the characters, including questions asked within the play.
3 Witnesses are questioned by both the prosecutorial and defense teams.
4 Each time a person is named, she or he (including the Press, Alice, and George) must stand up.
5 The entire class is the jury and will vote at the end.

If the Lucas quote does not appeal, then debate

- whether it matters that the play misrepresents some historic facts,
- whether the play reinforces or critiques misogyny,
- why *Zoot Suit* failed on Broadway,
- whether ideas in *Zoot Suit* could apply to the Trayvon Martin case or the Fruitvale Station case.

Latino/a literature

Although I have been contending that *Zoot Suit* is a gateway to all of theater, it is also true that it is a text that connects specifically to Latino/a identity and culture. By focusing on one of the pivotal moments of twentieth-century Latino/a history, and by use of El Pachuco, in all his allusiveness, Valdez's achievement may be seen as a defining moment in Latino/a literature. With his intense examination of the issue of identity, with his tri-lingual dialogue, with his fast-paced action, with his exposure of and satire on the American "justice" system, and with scenes that make visible internal psychological struggle, Valdez set a high standard for Latino/a theater.

Valdez says, "I have always believed that theater is the creator of community and that the community is the creator of theater" (KTEHTV) and he demonstrates that principle through the inclusiveness of *Zoot Suit* with "Jews and Gentiles, Protestants and Catholics" all part of the drama, with tragedy and comedy and music, with Brechtian alienation and heart-wrenching abuse of young men and women. Valdez welcomes the opening up of *Zoot Suit* to students. He embraced the selection of a female high school student to play the Pachuco (KTEHTV).

Follow Valdez's lead. Let students bring in ideas from Anzaldúa's *Borderlands/ La Frontera* or her ideas about oppositional consciousness; let students read the harsh critique of *Zoot Suit* by Ingrid Mundel—then think for themselves; let students bring their own experiences, their own languages, their own cultures to their understanding of the play. Then set them loose to write their own plays, to be actors in the world as well as on stage, to choose the roles they will play.

Resources for teaching Luis Valdez and *Zoot Suit*

Bolt, Julie. "Teaching Los Actos of Luis Valdez." *Radical Teacher* 91 (Fall 2011): 71–73.

Bustos, Roxann and Bette-Lee Fox. "From sleepy lagoon to zoot suit: the irreverent path of Alice McGrath." *Library Journal* 122.10 (1 June 1997): 170.

Garcia Hernandez, Arturo. *Entrevista con Luis Valdez—Origenes de los pachucos: Musica, identidad y racismo.* 29 Apr. 2010. Video. YouTube: 12 June 2014.

Giordano, Ralph G. "Hey Pachuco! 'That Zoot Suit can cause a riot.'" *National Association of African American Studies & National Association of Hispanic and Latino Studies: 2000 Literature Monograph Series.* Houston, TX: 2000.

I Am Theatre: Luis Valdez. 10 May 2012. Video. YouTube: 12 June 2014.

Johns, Janet and Abriendo Caminos. *Zoot Suit Discovery Guide.* Migrant Education. 2009. Web. 28 July 2014.

Ramirez, Catherine Sue. *The Woman in the Zoot Suit: Gender, Nationalism, and the Cultural Politics of Memory.* Durham: Duke University Press, 2009.

Rossini, John. "Teatro." *The Routledge Companion to Latino/a Literature.* Ed. Suzanne Bost and Frances Aparicio. New York: Routledge, 2013, pp. 285–98.

University of California Television (UCTV). *Necessary Theatre: Luis Valdez.* Jorge Huerta interviews Luis Valdez. May 1998. Video. YouTube: 12 June 2014.

"Zoot Suit Riots." *American Experience.* PBS. WGBH, 1998–2002. Television.

"Zoot-Suit War." *Time* 21 June 1943: 20.

36 Teaching the fiction of Helena María Viramontes

Paula M. L. Moya

Helena María Viramontes's richly metaphorical fictional narratives about Mexican Americans in mid-to-late twentieth century Los Angeles and agricultural California can be usefully taught in a range of courses. I myself have taught her fiction in courses like Narrative and Narrative Theory (*Under the Feet of Jesus*, focusing on **characterization**, **narrative perspective**, and **focalization**); Contemporary American Literature (*Under*, focusing on representations of farmworker experience); Growing Up in America (*Under* and *The Moths*, focusing on twentieth-century Chicana girlhood experience); Writings by Women of Color (*Moths,* focusing on gender dynamics); and Chicana/o Literature (*Moths* and *Their Dogs Came with Them*, focusing on mid-twentieth-century Chicana/o experience of racial segregation and economic discrimination). Viramontes's acute attention to interpersonal and social dynamics, her lyrical and allusive descriptions of people and places, and the immense generosity she shows toward her remarkably expansive range of character types make her one of the most important Latina writers to have emerged over the last 30 years.

Currently a Professor of Creative Writing in the Department of English at Cornell, Viramontes is a much-loved and valued mentor to younger writers such as Manuel Muñoz, Alex Espinoza, and NoViolet Bulawayo. An activist at heart, Viramontes engages in fiction writing, academic organizing, and teaching as her primary forms of activism. She has co-coordinated several writers' associations, participated in numerous social justice projects, and organized important conferences featuring the artistic production of Latina/o and Chicana/o artists. She is the coeditor, with Maria Herrera Sobek, of two anthologies that bring together art and scholarship. She is the recipient of a U.S. Ford Fellowship in Literature, the John Dos Passos Prize for Literature, a Sundance Institute Fellowship, a National Endowment for the Arts Fellowship, and the Luis Leal Award for Distinction in Chicana/Latino Literature awarded by UCSB.

Viramontes's preoccupations as a writer and scholar were formed early. She was born in East Los Angeles, California on February 26, 1954. Fifth to the youngest, she grew up as one of six sisters in a family of 11. A self-described "invisible child"—not the oldest, not the youngest, and not a boy—Viramontes spent her childhood as an unremarked witness to the chaotic goings-on of her vibrant, busy, crowded, and ultimately loving childhood home ("Beach Blanket Baja" 2008: np). Listening in from the other side of the door to "late night kitchen meetings where everyone talked and laughed in low voices, played cards, talked of loneliness, plans for the futures, [and] of loves lost or won" she was privy to the dreams, fears, and joys of those around her. "[C]apturing the moments and fleeing with them like a thief or a lover," Viramontes began her "apprenticeship" as a writer "without even knowing it" ("Nopalitos: The Making of Fiction" 1990: 291). This feature of Viramontes's biography perhaps accounts for her facility with representing an impressively wide range of characters, ranging from the deeply depressed 50s-something former housewife in "Snapshots," to the troubled transgender character of Turtle in *Dogs*, to the profoundly responsible but oh-so-tired elderly Perfecto in *Under*, to the romantically yearning but tough young women in both *Under* and *Dogs*.

Viramontes's attention to the class and race dynamics that shaped the affective and material lives of the people she grew up with is an important element of her fiction. With little education, her father labored as a hod carrier to support his large and growing family. Stressed with the responsibility and facing systemic racism at work, he "drank and was mean." Because he was "[I]mpatient, screaming a lot of the time," Viramontes and her siblings often found themselves "trembling in his presence" ("Nopalitos" 292). Viramontes's mother, by contrast, was a homemaker, a woman of "total kindness" and "relentless energy" whose care and domestic inventiveness made her "the fiber that held [the] family together." Viramontes writes: "If my mother showed me all that is good in being female, my father showed me all that is bad in being male" ("Nopalitos" 291). The patriarchal character of her family life, together with the circumstance of growing into womanhood during a time and place of intense political activism around systemic gender inequality (the **Women's Liberation movement**); the substandard education accorded to Mexican Americans (the **Garfield High School Blowouts**), residential segregation (the construction in Los Angeles of freeways that decimated Mexican American neighborhoods), and the Vietnam War (the Chicano Moratorium), inspired Viramontes's strong Chicana feminist outlook.

The temporal—and oftentimes cultural—distance between Viramontes's characters and my Stanford students means that they rarely have access to the range of interpretive schemas they need to appreciate Viramontes's work. This places a burden on me to provide basic historical and sociocultural background. An advantage of Viramontes's fiction is that it opens up to readings on several different levels. Even so, the more students know about the contexts from which Viramontes's fiction emerged, the better their comprehension of her work can be. Consequently, I preface a discussion of her fiction with information about Mexican Americans as a racialized minority group within the United States, the **Chicano Movement**, and the development of **Chicana and women of color feminism**. I draw material from a range of sources; useful historical sources include Garcia, Sánchez, Ruiz, and Muñoz. The two anthologies Viramontes coedited with Herrera-Sobek help situate her work within Chicana feminism, as does Saldívar-Hull. To position her work within women of color feminism, I draw material from Anzaldúa and Moraga and Anzaldúa. In a class focusing on Chicano/a literature or the Chicano/a experience, I may charge my students with doing background research at the beginning of the quarter, allowing them to present their findings to their classmates in multimedia presentations. I ask them to address questions like: What was the socioeconomic situation of Mexican Americans in mid-twentieth-century Los Angeles? What effect did continuing immigration from Mexico have on the development of Mexican American culture? How does language figure into the picture? What and when was the Chicano Movement? What are the basic claims of Chicana feminism? In a class not focused solely on Chicano/a issues, I provide this basic information via lecture.

The class in which I am teaching Viramontes's fiction determines the questions I ask of a given text. Some themes, though, are so ubiquitous that they emerge regardless of the approach I take. These include the inevitably deforming effects of racism and patriarchy; the deep humanity of the dispossessed, homeless, mentally ill, or undocumented person; the relentless struggle on the part of even the most powerless person to resist subordination; the unquenchable desire to find love and beauty in the most unlikely situation; and the existence of multiple perspectives on any given event. In Narrative and Narrative Theory, for example, I teach my students about narrative perspective and focalization in *Under* by asking them to pay attention to how Viramontes's variable character-bound focalization emphasizes the partiality of each character's perspective. Although the novel is narrated in the third person, the perspective shifts among the four main characters so that the world portrayed appears very different—often from one paragraph to the next. Although all the characters occupy the same physical fictional world, they experience and perceive it in ways that are consistent with their ages, genders, and social roles. So, when the members of Estrella's family arrive together at the shack that will be their new home, they each look around and see different things. Where Perfecto sees utility, and Petra sees danger, Estrella, younger and less jaded than both, sees adventure and possibility: Perfecto looks at crates and sees an altar for Petra's religious statues; Petra looks at her children's bare feet and sees the threat of scorpions; Estrella looks at a row of eucalyptus trees and sees dancing girls fanning their feathers (*Under* 8–9; Moya 2002: 185–88).

In Narrative and Narrative theory, or in Women of Color or Chicana/o Literature, I might assign *Dogs* so that my students may consider the relationship between characterization and narrative form. Because characterization is one of Viramontes's particular strengths as a writer, discussions and assignments that encourage students' attention to it are especially fruitful. I begin with a short lesson from Woloch to introduce my students to the concepts of **character-space and character-system**. I want them to understand how Viramontes's character-system represents a narrative innovation on the realist novel. In his book, Woloch (2003) shows that the omniscient, asymmetric character-systems of nineteenth-century realist novels create a "formal structure that can imaginatively comprehend the dynamics of alienated labor, and the class structure that underlies this labor" (27). Minor characters, insofar as they fulfill their narrative function in these novels, are necessarily flattened, distorted, and subordinated in the service of allowing the protagonist to grow, develop, and flourish as a "free human being" (29). By contrast, *Dogs* is a realist novel that, by presenting a character-system of all minor characters, refuses these minoritizing operations. The characters are minor in the sense that they represent marginalized persons (the immigrant, the homeless, the mentally ill, the economically marginalized), but also in the sense that there is no protagonist whose interior psychic development necessitates the flattening and distortion—or minoritization—of the other characters. To make the novel cohere in the absence of a clear protagonist, Viramontes weaves the diverse characters together in an intricate web of associations, relationships, and chance encounters. By creating a character-system that equitably represents the interiority of the kinds of characters that have historically been flattened, distorted, and relegated to the edges and margins of the novel form, Viramontes radically democratizes the character-space of the realist novel.

In Writings by Women of Color or Chicana Feminist Theory, I encourage my students to explore the way Viramontes represents the dysfunction of our sexist and racist society while also imagining other ways to be in the world. We engage in close readings that examine the interactions in her work of theme, plot, and metaphor. In "Moths," for example, I point out how Viramontes's symbolism involving the sun and the moon at the story's climax evokes the Aztec legend of **Coyolxauhqui**. I show how she re-members (both in the sense of bringing to mind, and of putting back together) the moon goddess/sister/daughter, whose physical dismemberment by her brother/sun god **Uitzilopochtli** inaugurated Aztec warrior society and affirmed an ideology of male dominance (Moya 2010). The story's plot narrates a reconciliation between mother and daughter, even as its symbolism enacts that same operation.

The semantic richness and literary artistry of Viramontes's fiction make it appropriate for almost any literature course that one could imagine teaching. I have touched on only a few issues and methods. The essays in Gutiérrez y Muhs (2013) offer other productive suggestions.

Resources for teaching Helena María Viramontes

Anzaldúa, Gloria, ed. *Making Face, Making Soul—Haciendo Caras: Creative and Critical Perspectives by Women of Color.* San Francisco: Aunt Lute, 1990.

Garcia, Alma M., ed. *Chicana Feminist Thought: The Basic Historical Writings.* New York: Routledge, 1997.

Gutiérrez y Muhs, Gabriella. *Rebozos De Palabras: An Helena María Viramontes Critical Reader.* Tucson: University of Arizona Press, 2013.

Herrera-Sobek, María and Helena María Viramontes, eds. *Chicana (W)Rites on Word and Film.* Berkeley: Third Woman, 1995.

——, eds. *Chicana Creativity and Criticism: Charting New Frontiers in American Literature.* Houston: Arte Público, 1988.

Moraga, Cherríe and Gloria Anzaldúa. *This Bridge Called My Back: Writings by Radical Women of Color.* 3rd edn. Berkeley: Third Woman, 2001.

Moya, Paula M. L. "Reading as a Realist: Expanded Literacy in Helena María Viramontes's *Under the Feet of Jesus.*" *Learning from Experience: Minority Identities, Multicultural Struggles.* Berkeley: University of California Press, 2002, pp. 175–214.

——. "Another Way to Be: Women of Color, Literature, and Myth." In: *Doing Race: 21 Essays for the 21st Century.* Eds. Hazel Rose Markus and Paula M. L. Moya. New York: W. W. Norton, 2010, pp. 483–508.

Muñoz, Carlos. *Youth, Identity, Power: The Chicano Movement.* New York: Verso, 1989.

Ruiz, Vicki L. *From Out of the Shadows: Mexican Women in Twentieth Century America.* New York: Oxford University Press, 1998.

Saldívar-Hull, Sonia. *Feminism on the Border: Chicana Gender Politics and Literature.* Berkeley: University of California Press, 2000.

Sánchez, George J. *Becoming Mexican American: Ethnicity, Culture, and Identity in Chicano Los Angeles, 1900–1945.* New York: Oxford University Press, 1993.

Viramontes, Helena M. *The Moths and Other Stories.* Houston: Arte Público Press, 1985.

——. "Nopalitos: The Making of Fiction." In: *Making Face, Making Soul—Haciendo Caras: Creative and Critical Perspectives by Women of Color.* Ed. Gloria Anzaldúa. San Francisco: Aunt Lute, 1990, pp. 291–94.

——. *Under the Feet of Jesus.* New York: Plume, 1995.

——. *Their Dogs Came With Them.* New York: Atria, 2007.

——. "Beach Blanket Baja." *New York Times,* New York edn, sec. Opinion: WK 17. 17 Aug. 2008.

Woloch, Alex. *The One vs. The Many: Minor Characters and the Space of the Protagonist in the Novel.* Princeton: Princeton University Press, 2003.

Glossary

Actos: Playwright Luis Valdez conceived of *los actos* as public street theater that addresses sociopolitical issues faced by Latinos. Along with other cultural production, they worked to empower Chicanos in a symbolic recuperation of lands lost after 1848—lands that were the northern Mexican territories and mythologically known as Aztán. See Luis Valdez's *Early Works: Actos, Bernabe, Pensamiento Serpentino* (1990).

Afro-Cuban music and dance: Includes *son*, *rumba*, and *mambo*, among other sounds and dances. Much of the influences on these dances can be traced back to the syncretism of African with Indigenous music and dance within the Caribbean. Some of these dance and music forms were prohibited by the European colonizers and associated with revolutions. See Olavo Alén-Rodríguez's *From Afro-Cuban Music to Salsa* (1998).

Alterity: In the United States, Latinos have historically been identified as different—as *other*—to the white majority because of various interlaced racial, ethnic, and social race prejudices. See Rocco Raymond's *Transforming Citizenship* (2014).

Americas-based epistemologies: Knowledge (or theories of knowledge) that grows out of non-European, Indigenous concepts and formulations about matters of existence in the Americas. See Paloma Martínez-Cruz's *Women and Knowledge in Mesoamerica* (2011).

Analogies: The cognitive process of transferring information between different subjects. See Dedre Gentner, *et al.*'s edited volume, *The Analogical Mind* (2001).

Anarchism: Advocates the forming of a stateless, self-governed society made up of voluntary institutions. See Emma Goldman's *Anarchism* (1911).

Arawak and Caribs: Amerindians that inhabited the Caribbean archipelago before the European conquest that began in 1492. The Arawak were known as a peaceful tribe whereas the Carib were known to have been violent—even possibly practitioners of cannibalism. See Philip Boucher's *Cannibal Encounters* (2009). See also Yolanda Martínez-San Miguel's "Taino Warriors?" (2011).

Autobiography: Latino authors writing about their own life that includes social, political, historical, and personal facts. The autobiography establishes a pact or contract with the reader that it corresponds to facts. Autobiographies can and do include the use of devices one finds in narrative fiction such as voice, perspective, temporal play, and the like. See Norma Klahn's *Literary (Re) Mappings*. See also Frederick Luis Aldama's *A User's Guide to Postcolonial and Latino Borderland Fiction* (2009).

Autoethnography: Latino scholars inserting themselves in a self-reflective manner into their scholarship. This often comes in the form of a scholar exploring their personal experience as it connects with cultural, political, and social research being conducted. See Kevin Concannon *et al.*'s *Imagined Transnationalism* (2009). See also Frances Aparicio's "Of Spanish Dispossessed" (2000).

Aztecs: Indigenous people who spoke Nahuatl and who inhabited central Mexico. Between the fourteenth and sixteenth centuries, Aztecs ruled large parts of Mesoamerica. See Paul Allatson's *Key Terms in Latino/a Cultural and Literary Studies* (2007).

Aztlán (Nahuatl): The term used in the Chicano Movement to identify the ancestral homelands of the Nahua peoples. Aztlán comprised the northern territories of Mexico we know as the Southwest. Chicanos sought to reclaim materially and symbolically this territory.

Bachata: A type of music that grew from the African presence in the Dominican Republic. It solidified as a genre in the early twentieth century, spreading to other parts of the Hispanophone Caribbean and Latin America generally. See Juan Flores's "Oye Como Va! Hybridity and Identity in Latino Popular Music" (2012).

Barrio: A district or neighborhood populated by Latinos, typically grown in and around urban centers in the United States. See Paul Allatson's *Key Terms in Latino/a Cultural and Literary Studies* (2007). See also Raúl Villa's *Barrio-Logos* (2000).

Bildungsroman: A novel structured as the formation and of education of a Latino protagonist. See Harold Augenbraum and Margarite Fernández Olmos's edited *U.S. Latino Literature* (2000).

Blackboard: An e-learning environment for digitally interactive, centralized course delivery and reception; it includes a system for recording, analyzing and assessing students. See Shu-Sheng Liaw's "Investigating Students' Perceived Satisfaction, Behavioral Intention, and Effectiveness of E-learning" (2008).

Border knowledge: Forms of knowledge recovered from Indigenous archives (oral and written) that identify a "border thinking" and decoloniality that resists the colonizer's practices of epistemological erasure. See Walter Mignolo's *Local Histories/Global Designs* (2000).

Borderlands: American or Mexican culture, Chicana literature provides a voice to the people of the borderlands as reclaimed space of gender, class, race, sexuality, ambiguity, and space of multilingualism. See C. Alejandra Elenes's "Reclaiming the Borderlands" (1997).

Borderland sensibility: Latinos growing a sense of themselves in the world as in-between subjects: neither Mexican nor U.S. American as if living somewhere between Mexico and the United States. This living in-between spatial sensibility pervades life for Latinos in the United States. See S. Villenas *et al.*'s "Chicanas/Latinas Building Bridges" (2006).

Boricua: A person who was born in Puerto Rico or with Puerto Rican ancestry who might not have grown up in Puerto Rico. More than Puerto Rican, the term has a political connotation, recognizing its Indigenous Native and African social, historical, and cultural roots. See Lisa Sánchez-González's *Boricua Literature* (2001).

Bultos: Carved figures of saints seen crafted in Latino communities in the Southwest and the Midwest. See Manuel Martin-Rodríguez's "Aesthetic Concepts of Hispanics in the United States" (1993).

Californiana: Identifies a landed-gentry class of Mexican woman living in the Californian territories of Mexico. Given that they were the holders of titles to land, they were disposed through marital mechanisms by Anglo settlers. See Antonia I. Castaneda's "Gender, Race, and Culture: Spanish-Mexican Women in the Historiography of Frontier California" (1990). See also José Aranda's "Contradictory Impulses" (1998).

Caló: Refers to the slang (or argot) used by Mexican Americans (or Chicanos) and is usually associated with urban *barrios*. It was first associated with pachucos (or zoot-suitors) of the 1940s. See Paul Allatson's *Key Terms in Latino/a Cultural and Literary Studies* (2007).

Carpas (tent theater): Forms of popular entertainment first seen in Mexico in the early twentieth century and later revitalized by Chicano playwrights like Luis Valdez. See Nicolás Kanellos's *Hispanic Theatre in the United States* (1990).

Central America: The geographic region (subcontinent) of the Americas that connects the northern with southern Americas. It includes: Belize, Costa Rica, El Salvador, Guatemala, Honduras, Nicaragua. See Ana Patricia Rodríguez's "Refugees of the South" (2001).

César Chávez (1927–93): A significant civil rights figure known for his fight for human rights, equality, and justice for the Latino community. See Richard Griswold del Castello *et al.*'s *César Chávez* (1997).

Character-space and character-system: Some novels construct a system of characters whereby their interaction reveals social class structures. See Alex Woloch's *The One vs. the Many* (2003).

Characterization: The process by which an author creates the personality of a Latino character. See Lourdes Torres's "The Construction of the Self in U.S. Latina Autobiographies" (1991).

Chica lit: Coming of age, bildungsroman, or romance novels by Latina authors whereby the material success of the characters is emphasized. See Tace Hedrick's "Chica Lit" (2012).

Chicana feminism: Excluded from the Anglo feminist movement and from a male, patriarchal dominated Chicano movement, Chicanas identified a resistance and empowerment to racism and sexism. See Alma M. García's edited, *Chicana Feminist Thought* (1997). See also Sonia Saldívar-Hull's *Feminism on the Border* (2000).

Chicanismo: The celebration of Mexican and Indigenous ancestry and culture seen in the Chicano Movement of the 1960s and early 1970s. See Paul Allatson's *Key Terms in Latino/a Cultural and Literary Studies* (2007).

Chicano/Latino (male) and Chicana/Latina (female): These terms have different histories of usage. Latino and Latina refer to people of Latin American extraction or descent. While first used as a term by the U.S. government, scholars and others use it today as an umbrella concept (a pan-*latinidad*) inclusive of people and culture of Mexican, Puerto Rican, Cuban, Central and South American ancestry. Chicano was used in the early twentieth century to refer pejoratively to Mexicans who had left Mexico for the United States. The term was reclaimed and given a political edge in the 1960s during the Chicano Movement. Chicana was used during this period of reclamation to identify and empower women in the movement. Chicano and Chicana continue to have a political resonance. See Paul Allatson's *Key Terms* (2007).

Chicano Movement: Known also as El Movimiento, during the 1960s and early 1970s Chicanos throughout the Southwest stood in solidarity to fight for equal rights as citizens of the United States; the movement solidified goals of achieving enfranchisement already seen in incipient form in the 1940s and before. See Carlos Muñoz's *Youth, Identity, Power* (1989).

Chicano Renaissance: With civil rights gained as a result of *El Movimiento,* Chicano artists, authors, and scholars began celebrating and affirming their own cultural production—a cultural production that very much had a sense of larger Third World cultural liberation movements. See Paul Allatson's *Key Terms* (2007).

Classical rhetoric tradition: The formulation of an elocutionary, rhetorical canon that includes: invention, disposition, style, and delivery. See James L. Golden *et al.*'s collection *The Rhetoric of Blair, Campbell, and Whately* (1968).

Classism: A socioeconomic-based prejudice and discrimination against Latinos. It includes all those attitudes and behavior as well as all variety of policies and practices that discriminate against Latinos as a lower class to benefit the upper class. See Dolores Delgado Bernal's "Critical Race Theory, Latino Critical Theory, and Critical Raced-Gendered Epistemologies" (2002).

Close reading: The refined fine-tuned, nuanced reading of Latino literature that attunes to use of technical devices as well as style. Conversely, distant reading is one that looks for systems and patterns. See Peter Elbow's "The Cultures of Literature and Composition" (2002). See Franco Moretti's *Distant Reading* (2013). See also Stephen Best's and Sharon Marcus's "Surface Reading" (2009).

Code-switching: When Latino authors use the linguistic phenomenon of combining two linguistic codes (English and Spanish, typically) when moving back and forth between phrases. See Lourdes Torres's "In the Contact Zone" (2007).

Cognitive dissonance: When a reader holds two or more contradictory beliefs, ideas, or values at the same time. This can lead to mental discomfort. See Vasti Torres and Marcia B. Baxter Magolda's, "Reconstructing Latino Identity" (2004).

Colonia: Refers to a community or neighborhood. See Virginia Sánchez Korrol's *From Colonia to Community* (1994).

Colonialism (and neocolonialism): The establishment, exploitation, maintenance, acquisition, and expansion of colonies in the Americas by outsiders—the Europeans. Colonialism in the Americas used military and political procedures to set up unequal (racial, social, economic) relationships that at best disenfranchised the Indigenous populations and at worst led to genocide. We are more familiar today with forms of neocolonialism whereby global capitalists assert influence over countries. Also known as imperialism and hegemony. See Paul Allatson's *Key Terms* (2007).

Colonization: The United States, Mexico, Puerto Rico, Cuba, the Dominican Republic, Central and South America all experienced different histories of colonization as settler colonies, trading posts, mining centers, plantations, and so on. All in all, colonialism in the Americas resulted in the ruling of the existing Indigenous peoples along with those uprooted in the slave trade. See Paul Allatson's *Key Terms* (2007).

Colorism: In 1982, Alice Walker coined this term as a way to encapsulate the multiple registers that make up racism and that violently assign individuals to a racial category. See Alice Walker's *In Search of Our Mothers' Gardens* (1983).

Commedia dell'Arte: Latino theatre uses and reshapes sixteenth-century Italian staging of masked "types" in improvised performances based on sketches or scenarios. See John Rossini's "Teatro" (2013).

Commodify: The process of transforming ideas and real racial, gendered, and other experiences of Latinos into a package for ready consumption by others. This can turn the complexity of the Latino experience into something simplistic. Latino/a authors constantly struggle with this when publishing with mainstream presses. See Frederick Luis Aldama's *Dancing with Ghosts* (2004). See Dara E. Goldman's "Out of Place" (2003). See also Ellen McCracken's *New Latina Narrative* (1999).

Compadre: Refers to a friend but also the system of non-biological relationships within the Latino family structure whereby the *compadres* or godparents are nearly as important as parents (and who become the parents in case of the death of the parents) in the raising of offspring. See Gustavo Pérez Firmat's *Tongue Ties* (2003).

Conquest: 1492 marks the year of the beginning of the conquest (and genocide of the Indigenous) of the Americas. Christopher Columbus's arrival at Hispanola (Cuba today) soon led to the decimation of the Indigenous population both from infectious disease brought by the Europeans as well as the horrors of their enslavement. The genocide of the Indigenous population led to the importing of Africans as slaves. The conquest continued with Hernán Cortés's slaughter of the Aztecs that led to his controlling of the territories that we know today as Mexico and the Southwest United States. See Ilan Stavans *The Norton Anthology of Latino Literature* (2011).

Conscientización: Refers to the coming into a consciousness as a Chicana whose history is tied to both the Indigenous of the pre-conquest of the Americas as well as the post-conquest mestiza. See Susan Thananopavarn's "Conscientización of the Oppressed" (2012). See also Cherríe Moraga's *A Xicana Codex of Changing Consciousness* (2011).

Corrido: Refers to the popular ballads (narratives in song and poetry) that focus on themes of oppression and the daily life everyday heroes. This form of storytelling was popular in the Southwest in the early twentieth century and continues to be popular today in its modern, narco-corrido variant. Narco-corridos tell the stories of everyday heroes but are set within today's drug trafficking and culture. See Paul Allatson's *Key Terms* (2007).

Coyolxauhqui: Refers to the Aztec goddess who was the daughter of Coatlicue and Mixcoatl. She was a warrior and a powerful magician reclaimed by Chicana authors and theorists. See Suzanne Bost's *Encarnación* (2010).

Critical race and ethnic theory: Refers to the critical examination of society and culture, through the lens of race, law, and power. See Dolores Delgado Bernal's "Critical Race Theory, Latino Critical Theory, and Critical Raced-Gendered Epistemologies" (2002). See also Gloria Ladson-Billings and William F. Tate's "Toward a Critical Race Theory of Education" (2006).

Critical travesía: Refers to the formulation of physical, sexual, gendered, and ethnic crossings that result in resistance to norms of existence in Latino literature. See José Quiroga's *Tropics of Desire* (2000).

Culturalist approaches: Critically examines the social construction of value, meaning, and interpretation in the U.S. mainstream vis-à-vis the lived reality of Latinos. See Karen Halttunen's edited volume, *A Companion to American Cultural History* (2008).

Curanderismo: Refers to the folk healing tradition commonly practiced in the Southwest and the Central and South Americas. This has been used as a central theme in novels such as Rudolfo A. Anaya's *Bless Me, Última* (1972). See Melissa Pabón's "The Representation of Curanderismo in Selected Mexican American Works" (2007).

Decolonial: Refers to Latino authors, artists, scholars, people generally taking control of frameworks of interpretation and knowledge making that have traditionally been controlled by the Euro-Anglo colonizer. See Walter Mignolo's *The Darker Side of Western Modernity* (2011). Arturo J. Aldama and Naomi Helena Quiñonez's edited volume, *Decolonial Voices* (2002). See also Emma Pérez's *The Decolonial Imaginary* (1999).

Dialect: Refers to an idiosyncratic form of a language located within a specific region or social group. Some Latino authors choose to code-switch between English and Spanish, where the Spanish is of a particular region within the United States; it could be Spanish spoken by Nuyoricans on the East Coast or Chicanos on the West Coast. See John Christie's *Latino Fiction and the Modernist Imagination* (1998).

Diasporas: Refers to the movement (usually forced) of people with common origins from their homelands across countries, continents, and the globe. See Lisa Sánchez-González, *Boricua Literature* (2001). See also José L. Torres-Padilla's and Carmen Haydée Rivera's edited collection, *Writing Off the Hyphen* (2011).

Disability studies: Scholars, activists, and practitioners examine and formulate theories about the social, political, cultural, and economic factors that define disability. There are two dominant models of understanding of disability: the social and medical. See Lennard J. Davis's edited *The Disability Studies Reader* (2006).

Disidentification: This term coined by José Muñoz refers to how racial and sexual other survive by negotiating and transforming mainstream culture—and not aligning with it. See José Muñoz *Disidentifications* (1999).

Distant reading (as opposed to close or surface reading): Refers to a particular approach to literary study that crunches massive amounts of data from a cluster of fictional texts. It is the mapping and graphing of data to understand better what shapes literary history. See Franco Moretti's *Distant Reading* (2013).

Doña Marina (or La Malinche): Refers to the historical figure who acted as interpreter between the Nahua and the Spaniards. There is an intellectual and historical tradition in Mexico that refers to her as a *malinchista*—a traitor—because she was known as Hernán Cortés's lover. Latina scholars and authors have since reclaimed her as a smart, savvy survivor. See Ana Castillo's *Massacre of the Dreamers* (1995). See also Marta Sánchez's *"Shakin' Up" Race and Gender* (2005).

Dystopian border imaginary: Extrapolated from today's destructive, decrepit capitalism, it refers to an imagined, degraded place in which a life is controlled by a totalitarian regime. See Claire F. Fox's "The Portable Border" (1994). See also Christopher González's "Latino Sci-Fi" (2013).

Ecocriticism: In literary studies this refers to an interdisciplinary approach studying characters as they negotiate experience and identity within different environments. See Glynis Carr's edited collection, *New Essays in Ecofeminist Literary Criticism* (2000). See also Christopher M. Travis's "The Natural World in Latin American Literatures" (2012).

El Movimiento (see Chicano Movement). This refers to the Chicano Movement, or Chicano Civil Rights Movement, of the 1960s and early 1970s that sought to achieve civil rights equality and empowerment for Mexican Americans.

Emigration (immigration): Refers to Latinos who have left their country or region of origin and have settled permanently in another. The movement of Latinos generally is referred to as migration. See Bridget Kevane's *Latino Literature in America* (2003).

Enstrangement: Often mistranslated as estrangement (without the "n"), this is the English neologism used to translate from Russian Viktor Shklovsky's invented term *ostraniene*. It is a concept that describes how Latino authors use different shaping devices (point of view, temporal play, style, for instance) to take readers out of their habituated state of experiencing the world. Readers "acquire a deeper knowledge of the object rather than passing it over automatically" (2009: 36), as Aldama writes in *A User's Guide to Postcolonial and Latino Borderland Fiction*. See Brian Richardson's *Unnatural Voices* (2006). See also David P. Wiseman's and Lorraine López's "Latino Literature's Past and Future" (2009).

Epistemic (episteme): Refers to knowledge and degree of its validation. Latino scholars can investigate the ways that Latino literature critiques Western epistemes. See Román De la Campa's *Latin Americanism* (1999).

Ethos (Greek for "character"): Refers to those guiding beliefs or ideals that characterize a community (and nation or ideology) in Latino literature. Scholars have explored how Latino literature conveys a Latino ethos that seeks validation and self-determination. See Juan Flores and George Yudice's "Living Borders/Buscando América" (1990).

Ex voto (or manda): An ex-voto is an offering to a saint or divinity in fulfillment of a vow. In regions of the Southwest United States and Mexico this vow is known as manda. See Elin Luque and Mary Beltrán's "Powerful Images" (2001).

Exile: Refers to the political or punitive prohibition of people from living in their native country. See Marta Caminero-Santangelo's "Contesting the Boundaries of 'Exile' Latino/a Literature" (2000).

Expansionism: Refers to the political and economic policies of territorial (or economic) expansion that have typically led to negative consequences for Latinos on both sides of the U.S./Mexico border. See Nicolás Kanellos's *Hispanic Literature of the United States* (2003).

Feminism: Refers to an approach to Latino/a literature that puts women's issues front and center, destabilizing restrictive gender normative practices. See Sonia Saldívar-Hull, *Feminism on the Border* (2000).

Focalization: Refers to the different perspective (or point of view) possibilities that Latino authors choose from when creating their narrative fictions: the first person using "I," second person using "you," or the third person using "him" or "her." Stories can be told from different narrating perspectives from outside and/or within the storyworld. See Aldama's *A User's Guide to Postcolonial and Latino Borderland Fiction* (2009).

Formalism: Refers to an approach to the study of Latino literature that focuses on the structures and devices used to give shape to any given text. See Aldama's *A User's Guide to Postcolonial and Latino Borderland Fiction* (2009).

Garfield High School Blowouts (March 1–March 8, 1968): Refers to the approximately 15,000 Latino students that walked out of their classes ("blowouts") to protest racism. Garfield High was one of several of the main schools involved. See Michael Soldatenko's "Mexican Student Movements in Los Angeles and Mexico City, 1968" (2003).

Genre (genre theory): Refers to a set of conventions (and expectations) that a Latino narrative text constructs and frames. Those that use a genre theory approach to the study of Latino literature consider how narrative device structures work together to create identifiable patterns with other narrative texts (emergence of genres) and that also create a specific mood when read. See Aldama's *A User's Guide to Postcolonial and Latino Borderland Fiction* (2009).

GLBT (or LGBT): Is an acronym that refers to Gay, Lesbian, Bisexual Transgender people. It reflects the nuances of GLBT people that earlier terms in use such as *gay* did not capture adequately. See Richard T. Rodríguez's *Next of Kin* (2009) and Lázaro. Lima's *The Latino Body* (2007).

Guatemalan civil war (1960–96): Refers to the war between the Guatemalan government and ethnic Mayan Indigenous and farmworker revolutionary groups. Before and during this six-year war, the government committed genocide against this working poor Mayan population. See Ana Patricia Rodríguez's "Refugees of the South" (2001) and Arturo Arias's "Central American-Americans" (2003).

Haitian revolution (1791–1804): This refers to the revolution of slaves in Saint-Dominique against the colonizing French. After much bloodshed of African slaves, the Republic of Haiti was founded. See Sybill Fischer's *Modernity Disavowed* (2004). See also Roberto González Echevarría's "Literature of the Hispanic Caribbean"(1980).

HB 2281: Refers to the Arizona law (designed by Republican Tom Horne) that bans the teaching of ethnic studies in public and charter schools. See Augustine Romero's "The Battle for Educational Sovereignty and the Right to Save the Lives of Our Children" (2014). See also Arlene Dávila's "To Stop Tip-Toeing Around Race" (2012).

Hegemony: Refers to the use of ideology and implied threat of force by a leader state (*hegemon*) to rule subordinate states. See Mary Alexandra Rojas's "An Examination of U.S. Latino Identities as Constructed In/Through Curricular Materials" (2013).

Hernán Cortés de Monroy y Pizarro (1485–1547): A Spanish conquistador who used brutal military tactics to bring about the fall of the Aztec Empire. See Earl Shorris's *Latinos: A Biography of the People* (2003). See Juan Gustavo Cobo Borda's "Carlos Fuentes en tres tiempos" (2013). See also Dietrich Briesemeister's "Un nuevo poema épico neolatino sobre Hernán Cortés" (2013).

Heteronormativity: Refers to the ideology that there are only two genders and two gender roles: man and woman. It refers to the ideology that seeks to *naturalize* heterosexuality as the sexual orientation and that coupling arrangements and relations exist only between people of opposite sexes. It can and does lead to heterosexism and homophobia. See Mollie V. Blackburn and Jill M. Smith's "Moving Beyond the Inclusion of LGBT-Themed Literature in English Language Arts Classrooms" (2010). See also Ernesto Martinez's *On Making Sense: Queer Race Narratives of Intelligibility* (2012).

HIV and AIDS: Refers to the autoimmune disease that can lead to a person becoming ill and dying as a result of infection. AIDS usually develops eight to ten years after initial HIV infection. See Daniel Contreras's *What Have You Done to My Heart* (2006). See also Daniel H. Castellanos's "Compañeros" (2013).

Homophobia: Refers to fear built on prejudices against non-heterosexual people. See Ernesto Martinez and Michael Hames-Garcia's coedited, *Gay Latino Studies* (2011). See Susana Chávez-Silverman and Librada Hernández's edited collection, *Reading and Writing the Ambiente* (2000). See also Lionel Cantu's "Entre Hombres/Between Men" (2011).

Hybrids (cultural and biological): Refers to the meeting (sometimes by force) of different cultures and people across the Americas that results in cultural and biological mixtures. See José David Saldívar's *Border Matters* (1997). See Néstor García Canclini's *Hybrid Cultures* (2005). See Holly Martin's *Writing between Cultures* (2011).

Iatiku (Life-Bringer) and Nautsiti (Full Basket): An Acoma Pueblo creation myth where the two sister-spirits use seeds and models of animals in their baskets to give life to earth. In their fictions, Latino/a authors such as Ana Castillo have variously recreated this myth. See Ralph E. Rodriguez's "Chicana/o Fiction from Resistance to Contestation" (2000).

Iberian: Refers to a person or cultural product originating from Portugal and Spain. See Patricia Novillo-Corvalán's *Latin American and Iberian Perspectives on Literature and Medicine* (2015). See Frauke Gewecke's "Latino/a Literature in Western Europe" (2013). See also Suzanne Bost's and Frances Aparicio's *Routledge Companion to Latino/a Literature* (2013).

Imagery: This refers to a Latino author's use of descriptive and figurative language in such a way that readers distill then reconstruct the image from the words on the page. Imagery can and does engage all of the senses. See Monica Salazar's "Death Imagery in Paz's Blanco" (2013). See also Martin J. La Roche *et al.*'s "A Content Analyses of Guided Imagery Scripts" (2011).

Implied author: Refers to the image readers construct in their mind of an author by way of the devices, structures, and style used in any given narrative text. This entity and its personality traits is generated from a given text and differs from the biographical author. See Eyal Segal's "Current Trends in Narratology" (2013). See also Astrid Lea Raisanen "Bridging Borders" (2011).

Indigenismo: Refers to a politicized ideology that celebrates Indigenous people and culture as well as identifying racial, social, historical, and political issues that have determined imbalanced relationships between the nation state and Indigenous minorities of the Americas. See Carmen Martínez Novo's "Indigenous Appropriations and Boundary Crossing" (2013). See also Amaka C. Ezeife's "Code-alternation in Strengthening Indigenous Cultures and Languages" (2013).

Industrialization: Refers to the period of economic (and social) change that transforms a human group from a rural-based, farmworker society into an urban, industrial society. Latinos continue to be exploited as *braceros* (arms) but less in the agricultural regions and more in the industrialized urban centers. See Sara Gleave and Qingfang Wang's "Foreign-born Latino Labor Market Concentration in Six Metropolitan Areas in the U.S. South" (2013).

Intermediation: In literary criticism and theory this refers to how computer technology shapes human experience. See Lysa Rivera's "Future Histories and Cyborg Labor" (2012).

Intersectional: Refers to the subject formation (negative and positive) that results from a multiple layered social world. See Emir Estrada's and Pierrette Hondagneu-Sotelo's "Intersectional Dignities" (2011).

Isthmus (and transisthmus): Refers to a narrow strip of land sided by sea and that links two larger areas of land. Ana Patricia Rodríguez uses the isthmus as a concept to understand the "in-between discursive" spaces created between regions, peoples, cultures, and material goods of the Americas. She uses the neologism "transisthmus" to identify an "imaginary yet material space" created by the vast intersections of people and cultural products including narrative fiction. See Ana Patricia Rodríguez's *Dividing the Isthmus* (2009).

Jones Act: Refers to a federal act that controls sea trade within the United States, determining the rules and regulations of trade. See Bridget Kevane's *Latino Literature* (2003).

La Raza: Refers to "the race" and is used as a term of Mexican and Indigenous ethnic and racial pride by Chicanos. As a celebration of non-European heritage and as a push back against celebrating the bloody conquest of Columbus, instead of celebrating Columbus Day, Chicanos will celebrate Día de la Raza. See Juan Bruce-Novoa's "The Space of Chicano Literature" (1975).

La Virgen de Guadalupe: Refers to the image of a mestiza Virgin Mary who appeared to the Indigenous farmer, Juan Diego, in the hills of Tepeyac in the outskirts of Mexico City during the period of the conquest. Her image was used by Miguel Hidalgo as he launched the fight for independence. See Ilan Stavan's and Aldama's *¡Muy Pop!: Conversations on Latino Popular Culture* (2013) and S. V. D. Riebe-Estrella's "La Virgen: A Mexican Perspective" (2013). See also Patrick Bruner Reyes's "Relational Bodies" (2014).

Latinidad: Refers to the shared language, culture, and history (of conquest) of those from Mexico, Central America, the Caribbean, and South America. See Grant Glass's "After Latinidad: Reimagining Latino Identity in the Works of Junot Díaz" (2013). See also Marta Caminero-Santangelo's *On Latinidad* (2007).

Literariness: Refers to the existence of narrative fiction as different from other entities that make up the social and natural world. See Aldama's *A User's Guide to Postcolonial and Latino Borderland Fiction* (2009).

Literary toolbox (narrative theory toolbox): Refers to the devices (point of view, voice, temporality, intertextuality, and so on) used by Latino authors to give shape to their fictions. See Aldama's *A User's Guide to Postcolonial and Latino Borderland Fiction* (2009).

Lucha Libre: Refers to professional wrestling originating in Mexico in which the contestants use hyperbolic acrobatic techniques and wear masks. See Heather Levi's *The World of Lucha Libre* (2008). See also Carolina Abello Onofre's and Christophe Chambost's "El Santo's Legacy" (2013).

Luchador: Refers to a person who competes in wrestling that originated in Mexico known as lucha libre. See Ellen Gil-Gómez's "Wrestling with Comic Genres and Genders" (forthcoming). See also Aldama's *Your Brain on Latino Comics* (2009).

Machismo: Refers to the behavior patterns of being strong, aggressive, brave—protector of the family. It also refers to those who preserve strict gender roles in the family, often denigrating the role of women and gay or lesbian members. See Ray Gonzalez's *Muy Macho* (1996).

Machista: Refers to the behavior patterns that exaggerate physical courage, virility, domination of women, and aggressiveness. See Lionel Cantu's "Entre hombres/Between men: Latino Masculinities and Homosexualities" (2011).

Magical realism: Refers to a form of storytelling whereby the narrative makes no distinction nor discriminates between events that defy the laws of nature (in physics, or genetics, for instance) with those that conform to the laws of nature. See Aldama's *Postethnic Narrative Criticism* (2003) and "Magical Realism" in *Routledge Companion to Latino/a Literature* (2013), eds. Bost and Aparicio. See Lyn Di Iorio Sandín's and Richard Perez's *Moments of Magical Realism in U.S. Ethnic Literatures* (2012). See also Ana María Manzanas, *et al.*'s *Uncertain Mirrors* (2009).

La Malinche (Malintzin and Doña Marina): Refers to the Nahua woman enslaved in 1519 by the Spaniards. She was translator and mistress to Hernán Cortés. She gave birth to his first son, Martín, who is considered to have been one of the first mestizos.

The term "malinchista" in Mexico refers to a traitor. See Andrea Powell Wolfe's "Refiguring La Malinche" (2013). See also Leslie Petty's "The 'Dual'-Ing Images of la Malinche and la Virgen De Guadalupe in Cisneros's the House on Mango Street" (2000).

Marianismo: Refers to the honoring of virtues such as passivity, purity, and moral strength in women. This schema is often held up in opposition to that of being impure and immoral in the virgin-whore dichotomy within Latino culture. Latina authors often complicate this dichotomy in their narratives. See Paul Allatson's *Key Terms* (2007).

Memoir: Refers to first-person, literary nonfictions built out of the author's collective memories anchored in and around public (and private) events. As with the auto-biographical pact, so too does one expect the events recounted to be factual, first-person point of view. See Jamie Campbell Naidoo's edited, *Celebrating Cuentos* (2011). See Harold Augenbraum's and Margarite Fernández Olmos's edited *The Latino Reader* (1997). See also Aldama's *The Routledge Concise History of Latino/a Literature* (2013).

Merengue: Refers to a type of music and dance that originated in the Dominican Republic. It is popular among Latinos in the United States and all over Latin America. See Juan Flores's "From Bomba to Hip-Hop" (2000).

Mesoamerican: Refers to a region and cultural area in the Americas that stretches from central California through Belize, Guatemala, El Salvador, Honduras, and Nicaragua, to northern Costa Rica. Indigenous societies flourished here before the Spanish conquest and colonization. See Arturo Arias's "EpiCentro" (2012).

Mestizaje: Refers to the racial and cultural mixing of Indigenous Amerindian with Europeans during the time of the conquest and colonization of the Americas. It has been claimed as a concept by Latino/a authors and scholars as a resistant decolonial worldview and political practice that seeks to remedy social, economic, and political inequality. See Juanita Heredia's *Transnational Latina Narratives in the Twenty-first Century* (2009). See also Ilan Stavans's *The Norton Anthology of Latino Literature* (2011).

Mestizo: Refers to those born of European and Indigenous ancestry. It was used in the construction of a racial cast (casta) system in Latin America. While mestizos were becoming the dominant group during the colonial period, the casta system ensured that they would have fewer rights than the European born and the white colonial-born. See Paul Allatson's *Key Terms* (2007).

Metaphor: Refers to a figure of speech used to compare as the same one thing with another otherwise unrelated object. See David J. Vázquez's *Triangulations* (2011). See Aldama's *Formal Matters in Contemporary Latino Poetry* (2013). See also Elisabeth Mermann-Jozwiak's "Transnational Latino/a Writing, and American and Latino/a Studies" (2014).

Mexican American War (1846–48): Refers to the war between the United States and Mexico that led to additional annexations by the United States of northern Mexican territories, including Texas, New Mexico, and California. See Cecilia Montes-Alcalá's "Writing on the Border" (2013).

Mexican Revolution (1910–20): Refers to the war that started with an uprising led by Francisco I. Madero against Porfirio Díaz. It is considered one of the most important events in Mexico, leading to important social and political reforms. See Héctor Calderón's *Narratives of Greater Mexico* (2004).

Mexicas (Indigenous Mexicans): Refers to the Indigenous people living in Mexico before the conquest who called themselves the Mexicas—Nahuatl for "In the navel of the Moon." See Marta Caminero-Santangelo's "The Lost Ones: Post-Gatekeeper Border Fictions and the Construction of Cultural Trauma" (2010).

Migration: Refers to the movement of people from one area to another—typically for economic reasons. See Ruth Brown's "Telling the Story of Mexican Migration" (2013). See also Vanessa Pérez Rosario's *Hispanic Caribbean Literature of Migration* (2012).

Milagritos (little miracles): Refers to little objects that often represent different parts of the body that one is asking the Virgin Mary (as Santa Maria de los Milagros) to heal. See Erlinda Gonzales-Berry's "Estampas del Valle" (1980).

Minority writing: Refers to narratives that focus on disenfranchised identities shaped by issues of class, race, and ethnicity. See Robert A. Lee's *Multicultural American Literature* (2003).

Modernism (modernity): Refers to a European worldview and cultural movement that grew out of the alienation experienced in the rapid growth of cities followed by the atrocities of new technologies. It took place among artists, authors, and intellectuals in the early twentieth century who were critical of the modern epoch. Modernity refers to the condition of being modern (contemporary) in thought, behavior, and attitude. See Ramón Saldívar's *Chicano Narrative* (1990). See Elías Domínguez Barajas's "The Postmodern Ethnic Condition in Ernesto Quiñónez's *Bodega Dreams*" (2014). See also José Saldívar's *Trans-Americanity* (2011).

NAFTA (The North American Free Trade Agreement): Refers to an agreement signed by Canada, Mexico, and the United States to create a bloc of free trade between the countries. See Ariana Vigil's "The Divine Husband and the Creation of a Transamericana Subject" (2013). See also Marta Caminero-Santangelo's "Narrating the Non-Nation" (2012).

Nahuatl: Refers to a group of related languages and dialects of the Nahua people of Mexico—especially central Mexico. See Elizabeth Hill Boone's *Cycles of Time and Meaning in the Mexican Books of Fate* (2013).

Narratology: Refers to the systematic study of the devices and structures used in the making of Latino/a narratives. See Aldama's *A User's Guide to Postcolonial and Latino Borderland Fiction* (2009).

Neoliberal: Refers to economic policies that favor privatization, free trade, open markets, deregulation, and reductions in government spending, favoring the role of the private sector. See Arlene Dávila's *Barrio Dreams* (2004). See also Richard Delgado's "Locating Latinos in the Field of Civil Rights" (2004).

Nuevomexicano (or Hispanos): Refers to those in New Mexico who consider themselves descendants of the original Spanish colonists. See Francisco Lomelí and A. Gabriel Meléndez's *The Writings of Eusebio Chacón* (2012).

Orishas (Orisa or Orixa): Refers to a spirit in the Yoruba spiritual system. They are part of the belief system of Santería that is practiced in the Hispanophone Caribbean. See Aida L. Heredia's "Yoruba Cosmology as Technique in Malambo by Lucia Charun-Illescas" (2012).

Pachuco and Pachuca: Refers to a Mexican American (usually urban) who dresses in suits with wide-shoulders and pleated pants. These are known as zoot suits and were a style that came into fashion among Mexican Americans in the 1930s in El Paso, Texas. Pachucos used their flamboyant sartorial style to embrace and celebrate their difference from the Anglo mainstream. A pachuca is a Mexican American woman who is known for transgressing the sartorial taboos by wearing pleated pants in public. See Catherine Ramirez's *The Woman in the Zoot Suit* (2009).

Panethnicity: Refers to the clustering of various ethnicities under one umbrella group. It could be labeling all Spanish speakers as Latino, regardless of their country of origin. See Harold Augenbraum's edited, *Latinos in English* (1992).

Patois: Refers to the language spoken in a region that differs from the standard language of the rest of the country. See Ilan Stavans's *A Critic's Journey* (2010).

Pepenadores ("waste pickers"): Refers to those (many of whom are children) who are forced to live by picking through waste in landfills. Illness and early death are common. See Luis Urrea's *Across the Wire: Life and Hard Times on the Mexican Border* (1993).

Picaresque: Refers to the episodic style of narrative fiction that focuses on the sequentially linked adventures of the *pícaro*, or trickster. This storytelling mode often reveals the underbelly of society. See Aldama's *Postethnic Narrative Criticism* (2003).

Pocho: Is a term used (often pejoratively) by Latinos to refer to assimilated Mexican Americans—those who had lost the culture and language of Mexico. See Marta E. Sánchez's "Pocho en español" (2011).

Poetic device and poetics: Refers to the way authors choose to cluster or juxtapose words to achieve specific effects (from pleasing to disquieting) on the listener/reader: alliteration, cacophony, and euphony. Poetics would be the way that language, techniques, and structures give shape to different literary forms. See Eliza Rodriguez Gibson's edited collection, *Stunned Into Being* (2012). See Urayoán Noel's *In Visible Movement* (2014). See also Aldama's *Formal Matters in Contemporary Latino Poetry* (2013).

Pre-Columbian: Refers to the huge stretch of time from the Upper Paleolithic to before the European conquest of the Americas. See Nicolás Kanellos' *Herencia* (2003).

Primitivism: Refers to a worldview among authors and artists in the beginning of the twentieth century that sought to represent a premodern way of being. We see this worldview also in some strands of Latino art and theory. See Sheila Marie Contreras's *Blood Lines* (2008).

Prosopopeia: Refers to the rhetorical device used by a speaker who speaks as another person or object. See Marcos McPeek Villatoro's "In Search of Literary Cojones" (2013).

Queer Studies (or Sexual Diversity Studies): Refers to the study of issues relating to lesbian, gay, bisexual identity and experience. See Michael Hames-García's and Ernesto Javier Martínez's edited volume, *Gay Latino Studies* (2011).

Quetzalcoatl (the Feathered Serpent): Refers to a major Mesoamerican deity. In the Toltec culture (ninth through twelfth centuries) Quetzalcoatl was known as the god of the morning and evening star. See Karina Oliva-Alvarado's "An Interdisciplinary Reading of Chicana/o and (U.S.) Central American Cross-Cultural Narrations" (2013).

Rascuache/Rasquachismo: Tomás Ybarra-Frausto's term to identify how Latino artists are inventing anew from recycled materials to convey the worldview of the outsider. See Ilan Stavans's "*Nacho Libre*: or, The Inauthenticity of Rasquachismo" (2013).

Reggaeton: Refers to a genre of music with roots in the Caribbean. See Jennine Capó Crucet's "Static Signals" (2014). See also Miriam Jiménez-Román and Juan Flores's *The Afro-Latin@ Reader* (2010).

Relato: Refers to the telling of a tale. Latino authors can choose to give their stories the oral quality of recounting a tale. See Luisa Capetillo's *Absolute Equality: An Early Feminist Perspective* (2009). See also Richard Keis's "From Principle to Practice" (2006).

Remediation: Refers to how new media repurposes old media. See Ellen McCracken's "Expanding Genette's Epitext" (2013). See also Ramón Saldívar's "The Second Elevation of the Novel" (2013).

Resistance literature: Refers to literature that foregrounds themes of resistance and liberation; it can also be fiction that is read as an allegory of political resistance. See Raphael Dalleo's and Elena Machado Sáez's *The Latino/a Canon and the Emergence of Post-Sixties Literature* (2007).

Retables: Refer to painted panels (wood, metal, or stone) with statues or mosaics usually found behind altars in churches. See Alberto González *et al.*'s "Latinidad and Vernacular Discourse" (2014).

Rhetorical device: Refers to the use of devices by authors to communicate persuasively (emotively and cognitively) with readers. In the study of Latino literature it is an approach that considers how any given text has the express purpose of telling readers something for some purpose that something has happened. See James Phelan's *Experiencing Fiction* (2007). See Marta Caminero-Santangelo's "Narrating the Non-Nation" (2012). See also Elisabeth Mermann-Jozwiak's "Transnational Latino/a Writing, and American and Latino/a Studies" (2014).

Salsa: Refers to a genre of music rooted in the Hispanophone Caribbean, especially Cuba. It combines elements of jazz, rock, and soul music. See Delia Poey's *Cuban Women and Salsa* (2010), and Frances R. Aparicio's *Listening to Salsa* (1998).

Santería: Refers to a religious tradition that mixes West African (Yoruban) and Caribbean Indigenous spiritual practices. See Sean Moiles's "The Politics of Gentrification in Ernesto Quiñonez's Novels" (2011). See also Frances R. Aparicio's and Susana Chávez-Silverman's *Tropicalizations* (1997).

Santero/Santera: Refers to an artisan who makes saints and other Spanish-style religious artwork. In the Santería tradition, a santero or santera is an initiated priest of the orisha. See Genaro Padilla's "A Reassessment of Fray Angelico Chavez's Fiction" (1984). See also Frances R. Aparicio's and Susana Chávez-Silverman's *Tropicalizations* (1997).

Satire: Refers to a Latino author's use of irony and ridicule to reveal the tears in the sociopolitical fabric that makes up a given society. See Ellen Gil-Gómez's "Mezclando (Mixing) the 'Facts' and the Power of the Image in Latino USA" (2012). See also Aldama's *Postethnic Narrative Criticism* (2003).

Self-reflexive Latino literature: refers to Latino literary works that openly reflect upon their own artifice—as created artifacts for readers to consume. These works of fiction refer to their own fictional status. See Aldama's *A User's Guide to Postcolonial and Latino Borderland Fiction* (2009). See also Christopher González's *Reading Junot Díaz* (2016).

Simile: Refers to the use of a comparison of one thing with another to describe something more powerfully. See also Horace R. Hall's "Poetic Expressions" (2007). See Carol Jago's *Sandra Cisneros in the Classroom* (2002).

Social constructionism: Refers to an approach to Latino literature that considers it and reality generally as a social construct. See Paula Moya's *Identity Politics Reconsidered* (2006).

Social justice: Refers to an approach to the study of Latino literature that uses the tools and insights from sociology, public policy, and law, among others. It aims to create understanding among diverse groups of readers and seeks to clear a space for creating a world of equality. See Paula Moya's and Hazel Markus's edited collection, *Doing Race: 21 Essays for the 21st Century* (2010).

Sociological approach: Examines literature within the socioeconomic and political context in which it is written and/or consumed. Thus it studies the social context of the author and reader as well as analyzes the representation of such societal elements within the narrative fictions themselves. See Ronald Mize's and Grace Peña Delgado's *Latino Immigrants in the United States* (2012).

Story: Refers to an event or sequence of events. (The discourse gives shape to these events.) See Aldama's *A User's Guide* (2009). See also David Herman's *Basic Elements of Narrative* (2009).

Storyworld: Refers to all the character, setting, dialogue, and other ingredients that create the microcosms of life in fiction. See David Herman's *Basic Elements of Narrative* (2009). See also Christopher González's dissertation, *Hospitable Imaginations* (2012).

Suburbs: Refers to areas in the United States just outside of cities built specifically to house people—usually middle class and, because of racial segregation policies still in play till the early 1970s, largely Anglo. See Jody Vallejo's *Barrios to Burbs: The Making of the Mexican American Middle Class* (2012).

Symbolism: Refers to when Latino authors use objects (natural and human made) places, colors, and the like to represent other things. Such authors rely on the reader's capacity to connect the symbol used with the meaning conveyed by the story. This can lead to a deeper understanding of what's going on in the story. See Gregory Stephens's "'When I Was Puerto Rican' as Borderland Narrative" (2009). See also Sydney Redigan's "Latino/a Literature in the Multicultural English Classroom" (2013).

Syncretism. Refers to the practice of combining different cultural systems (religious or otherwise) to create a new one. When enslaved Africans in the Caribbean would not practice their religion openly, they would disguise their deities as Catholic saints. Over time this lead to the combining of the different cultural systems. See Robert A. Lee's *Multicultural American Literature* (2003).

Teatros de revistas: Refers to a genre of popular theatre whose origins can be traced to Brazil and then Portugal. Its light comedic mode touches on the social and political. See Michelle Habell-Pallán's *Loca Motion: The Travels of Chicana and Latina Popular Culture* (2005).

Telenovela: Refers to soap operas from Latin American countries popular among Latinos in the United States. Some authors like Denise Chávez choose to structure their novels like a telenovela. See Aldama's and Theresa Rojas's "Telenovelas" (2012). See Ilan Stavans's edited, *Telenovelas* (2010). See also Carmen Liliana Medina's and Marea del Rocio Costa's "Latino Media and Critical Literacy Pedagogies" (2013).

Testimonio: Refers to narrative texts that grow out of the social and political upheavals that mark Latin America's history. They are based on traumatic sociohistorical events. They are told from an oppressed individual perspective and speak to a communal experience as a whole. They contain devices we commonly find in literary texts like novels and poetry. They convey a strong sense of an oral tradition. See Stephanie M. Alvarez's "Evaluating the Role of the Spanish Department in the Education of US Latin@ Students" (2013). See also Luis Urrieta's and Sofia A. Villenas's "The Legacy of Derrick Bell and Latino/a Education: A Critical Race Testimonio" (2013).

Tezkatlipoka ("Smoking Mirror"): Aztec god associated with hurricanes, discord, and war among others. See Daniel Espinoza-Gonzalez's "Decolonizing the Classroom Through Critical Consciousness" (2014). See also R.C. Rodríguez's "Tucson's Maiz-based Curriculum" (2012).

Transborder culture: Refers to the two-way flow of moveable cultural objects as Latinos move back and forth across the U.S./Mexico border. The making of a transborder culture also entails a transborder economics. See Carlos Vélez-Ibáñez's *An Impossible Living in a Transborder World Culture, Confianza, and Economy of Mexican-Origin Populations* (2000).

Translation: Refers to the distillation and reconstruction in another language of Latino literary texts. The translation process can lose nuances of language and style. In the book marketing global marketplace where English is the lingua franca, the translation process usually flows from Spanish to English. See Daniel Balderston and Marcy E. Schwartz's edited, *Voice-Overs* (2012). See also Aldama's *The Routledge Concise History of Latino/a Literature* (2013).

Treaty of Guadalupe Hidalgo (February 2, 1848): Refers to the signing of a treaty at the city of Guadalupe Hidalgo that ended the Mexican–American War (1846–48). It also marked the moment of the official U.S. annexation of the northern territories of Mexico. See Héctor Calderón's *Narratives of Greater Mexico* (2004).

Trickster: Refers to an underdog, anti-heroic character in Latino literature who plays tricks and cheats to survive. See José Limón's *Dancing with the Devil* (1994).

UFW (The United Farm Workers of America): Refers to the coalition of poorly paid Latino migrant farmworkers that began forming in 1962 and then grew into a powerful Labor Union that fought to increase wages and improve working conditions for workers. See Frank Bardacke's *Trampling Out the Vintage* (2012). See also Roger Bruns's *Cesar Chavez and the United Farm Workers Movement* (2011).

Uitzilopochtli/Huitzilopochtli ("Hummingbird on the Left"): Refers to the pre-Columbian sun god and god of war in Aztec mythology. See Curtis Acosta's "Huitzilopochtli" (2014).

Urbanization: Refers to the process whereby Latinos are pushed to live in cities as rural, farm life becomes increasingly unsustainable. Because of redlining practices (where urban planners would red-line areas for Latinos to live) and also familial contacts, Latinos tended to aggregate in the same parts of U.S. cities. See Kingsley Davis's "The Urbanization of the Human Population" (1965). See also Mike Davis's *City of Quartz* (2006).

Visual rhetoric: Refers to how the design and aesthetic of visual images can communicate meaning persuasively. See Guisela Latorre's *Walls of Empowerment* (2008). See also Luke Winslow's "The Imaged Other" (2014).

Women of color feminisms: Refers to Latina, African American, Native American, Asian American, Filipina American feminists who are committed to making visible the prejudices that women of color face in the United States and around the world. See Grace Kyungwon Hong's "Existentially Surplus Women of Color Feminism and the New Crises of Capitalism" (2012).

Women's Liberation movement: Refers to the women's struggle to eliminate forms of oppression based on gender with the goal of creating a world of social, political, and gender equality. See Susan Sheridan's "Feminist Knowledge, Women's Liberation, and Women's Studies" (2013). See also Ruth Rosen's *The World Split Open: How the Modern Women's Movement Changed America* (2013).

Xipe Totec ("Our lord the Flayed one"): Refers to the Aztec deity who was known as the curer of sicknesses, the god of seasonal transitions, and the god that represented the transition of boys into manhood. See Tanya Corissa Ball's "The Power of Death: Hierarchy in the Representation of Death in Pre-and Post-Conquest Aztec Codices" (2014). See also Markus Eberl's "Nourishing Gods" (2013).

Zapatismo: Refers to the struggle and fight for social justice as embodied by the Mexican revolutionary, Emiliano Zapata (1879–1919). Notably, Zapata's fight to return of disposed land to Mexican farmers led to the land reforms of Mexico in 1917. The Zapatista movement in southern Mexico also derives its name from Zapata. See Neil Barmeyer's "Zapatismo and the Legitimacy of Indigenous Rights" (2011).

Zarzuela: Refers to Spanish comedic (and satirical) opera that is made up of songs, spoken passages, and dances that focus on everyday life. While it originated in the seventeenth century, it continued to evolve over time and has been used in Latino theatre. See David Thatcher Gies's *The Theatre in Nineteenth-Century Spain* (2005).

Zoot Suit Riots: Refers to the summer of 1942 in Los Angeles when Pachucos (Mexican Americans wearing zoot suits) were attacked by military and police that led to the death of one Latino. The "riots" brought to center stage the racial tensions between Latinos and Anglos in the United States. See Catherine Ramírez's *The Woman in the Zoot Suit* (2009).

Suggested further reading

Acosta, Curtis. "Huitzilopochtli: The Will and Resiliency of Tucson Youth to Keep Mexican American Studies Alive." *Multicultural Perspectives* 16.1 (2014): 3–7.

Aldama, Arturo J. and Naomi Helena Quiñonez, eds. *Decolonial Voices: Chicana and Chicano Cultural Studies in the 21st Century*. Indiana: Indiana University Press, 2002.

Aldama, Frederick Luis. *Postethnic Narrative Criticism: Magicorealism in Ana Castillo, Hanif Kureishi, Julie Dash, Oscar "Zeta" Acosta, and Salman Rushdie*. Austin: University of Texas Press, 2003.

——. *A User's Guide to Postcolonial and Latino Borderland Fiction*. Austin: University of Texas Press, 2009.

——. *Your Brain on Latino Comics: From Gus Arriola to Los Bros Hernandez*. Austin: University of Texas Press, 2009.

——. "Magical Realism." In *Routledge Companion to Latino/a Literature*. Eds. Bost and Aparicio. New York: Routledge, 2013, pp. 334–41.

——. *The Routledge Concise History of Latino/a Literature*. New York: Routledge, 2013.

Aldama, Frederick Luis and Theresa Rojas. "Telenovelas." In *Oxford Bibliographies in Latino Studies*. New York: Oxford University Press, 2012.

Alén-Rodríguez, Olavo. *From Afro-Cuban Music to Salsa*. Berlin: Powerplay, 1998.

Allatson, Paul. *Key Terms in Latino/a Cultural and Literary Studies*. Malden, MA, and Oxford: Blackwell, 2007.

Alvarez, Stephanie M. "Evaluating the Role of the Spanish Department in the Education of US Latin@ Students: Un Testimonio." *Journal of Latinos and Education* 12.2 (2013): 131–51.

Aparicio, Frances R. *Listening to Salsa: Gender, Latin Popular Music, And Puerto Rican Cultures*. Middletown: Wesleyan University Press, 1998.

——. "Of Spanish Dispossessed." In *Language Ideologies: Critical Perspectives on the Official English Movement, Volume I: Education and the Social Implications of Official Language*. Eds. Roseann Dueñas Gonzalez and Ildikó Melis. New York: Routledge, 2000, pp. 248–75.

Aparicio, Frances R. and Susana Chávez-Silverman. *Tropicalizations: Transcultural Representations of Latinidad*. Hanover, NH: Dartmouth College, 1997.

Aranda, José F. "Contradictory Impulses: María Amparo Ruiz de Burton, Resistance Theory, and the Politics of Chicano/a Studies." *American Literature* 70.3 (1998): 551–79.

Arias, Arturo. "Central American-Americans: Invisibility, Power and Representation in the US Latino World." *Latino Studies* 1.1 (2003): 168–87.

——. "EpiCentro: The Emergence of a New Central American-American Literature." *Comparative Literature* 64.3 (2012): 300–315.

Augenbraum, Harold, ed. *Latinos in English: A Selected Bibliography of Latino Fiction Writers of the United States*. New York: Mercantile Library of New York, 1992.

Augenbraum, Harold and Margarite Fernández Olmos, eds. *The Latino Reader: An American Literary Tradition from 1542 to the Present*. New York: Houghton Mifflin Harcourt, 1997.

Augenbraum, Harold and Margarite Fernández Olmos, eds. *US Latino Literature: A Critical Guide for Students and Teachers*. University Park, PA: Penn State Press, 2000.

Avila, Eric. *Popular Culture in the Age of White Flight: Fear and Fantasy in Suburban Los Angeles.* Berkeley: University of California Press, 2004.

Balderston, Daniel and Marcy E. Schwartz, eds. *Voice-Overs: Translation and Latin American Literature.* Albany: SUNY Press, 2012.

Ball, Tanya Corissa. "The Power of Death: Hierarchy in the Representation of Death in Pre-and Post-Conquest Aztec Codices." *Multilingual Discourses* 1.2 (2014): 1–34.

Barajas, Elías Domínguez. "The Postmodern Ethnic Condition in Ernesto Quiñónez's *Bodega Dreams.*" *Latino Studies* 12.1 (2014): 7–26.

Bardacke, Frank. *Trampling Out the Vintage: Cesar Chavez and the Two Souls of the United Farm Workers.* New York: Verso Books, 2012.

Barmeyer, Niels. "Zapatismo and the Legitimacy of Indigenous Rights." *Latin American and Caribbean Ethnic Studies* 6.3 (2011): 329–31.

Bernal, Dolores Delgado. "Critical Race Theory, Latino Critical Theory, and Critical Raced-Gendered Epistemologies: Recognizing Students of Color as Holders and Creators of Knowledge." *Qualitative Inquiry* 8.1 (2002): 105–26.

Best, Stephen and Sharon Marcus. "Surface Reading: An Introduction." *Representations* 108.1 (Fall 2009): 1–21.

Blackburn, Mollie V. and Jill M. Smith. "Moving Beyond the Inclusion of LGBT-themed Literature in English Language Arts Classrooms: Interrogating Heteronormativity and Exploring Intersectionality." *Journal of Adolescent & Adult Literacy* 53.8 (2010): 625–34.

Boone, Elizabeth Hill. *Cycles of Time and Meaning in the Mexican Books of Fate.* Austin: University of Texas Press, 2013.

Borda, Juan Gustavo Cobo. "Carlos Fuentes en tres tiempos (1928–2012)." *Poliantea* 8.15 (2013): 201–213.

Bost, Suzanne. *Encarnación: Illness and Body Politics in Chicana Feminist Literature.* Bronx, NY: Fordham University Press, 2010.

Boucher, Philip P. *Cannibal Encounters: Europeans and Island Caribs, 1492–1763.* Baltimore: Johns Hopkins University Press, 2009.

Briesemeister, Dietrich. "Un nuevo poema épico neolatino sobre Hernán Cortés: la Cortesias del jesuita Pedro Paradinas." *Studia Philologica Valentina* 15.12 (2013): 25–46.

Brown, Ruth. "Telling the Story of Mexican Migration: Chronicle, Literature, and Film from the Post-Gatekeeper Period." Dissertation. (2013).

Bruce-Novoa, Juan. "The Space of Chicano Literature." *De Colores, Journal of Emerging Raza Philosophies* 1.4 (1975): 22–42.

Bruegmann, Robert. *Sprawl: A Compact History.* Chicago: University of Chicago Press, 2005.

Bruns, Roger. *Cesar Chavez and the United Farm Workers Movement.* Santa Barbara: ABC-CLIO, 2011.

Calderón, Héctor. *Narratives of Greater Mexico: Essays on Chicano Literary History, Genre, and Borders.* Austin: University of Texas Press, 2004.

Caminero-Santangelo, Marta. "Contesting the Boundaries of 'Exile' Latino/a Literature." *World Literature Today* 74.3 (2000): 507–17.

——. *On Latinidad: US Latino Literature and the Construction of Ethnicity.* Gainesville, FL: University Press of Florida, 2007.

——. "The Lost Ones: Post-Gatekeeper Border Fictions and the Construction of Cultural Trauma." *Latino Studies* 8.3 (2010): 304–27.

——. "Narrating the Non-Nation: Literary Journalism and 'Illegal' Border Crossings." *Arizona Quarterly: A Journal of American Literature, Culture, and Theory* 68.3 (2012): 157–76.

Canclini, Néstor García. *Hybrid Cultures: Strategies for Entering and Leaving Modernity.* Minneapolis: University of Minnesota Press, 2005.

Cantu, Lionel. "Entre Hombres/Between Men: Latino Masculinities and Homosexualities." *Gay Latino Studies: A Critical Reader.* Durham: Duke University Press, 2011, pp. 147–67.

Capetillo, Luisa. *Absolute Equality: An Early Feminist Perspective: Influencias de Las Ideas Modernas.* Houston: Arte Público Press, 2009.

Carr, Glynis, ed. *New Essays in Ecofeminist Literary Criticism.* Cranbury, NJ: Associated University Press, 2000.

Castaneda, Antonia I. "Gender, Race, and Culture: Spanish-Mexican Women in the Historiography of Frontier California." *Frontiers* 11.1 (1990): 8–20.

Castellanos, H. Daniel. "Compañeros: Latino Activists in the Face of AIDS." *Culture, Health & Sexuality* 15.1 (2013): 117–19.

Castillo, Ana. *Massacre of the Dreamers: Essays on Xicanisma.* New York: Plume, 1995.

Chávez-Silverman, Susana and Librada Hernández, eds. *Reading and Writing the Ambiente: Queer Sexualities in Latino, Latin American, and Spanish Culture.* Madison: University of Wisconsin Press, 2000.

Christie, John S. *Latino Fiction and the Modernist Imagination: Literature of the Borderlands.* New York: Routledge, 1998.

Concannon, Kevin, Francisco A. Lomelí, and Marc Priewe, eds. *Imagined Transnationalism: US Latino/a Literature, Culture, and Identity.* New York: Palgrave, 2009.

Contreras, Daniel. *What Have You Done to My Heart: Unrequited Love and Gay Latino Culture.* New York: Palgrave Macmillan, 2006.

Contreras, Sheila Marie. *Blood Lines: Myth, Indigenism and Chicana/o Literature.* Austin, TX: University of Texas Press, 2008.

Dalleo, Raphael and Elena Machado Sáez. *The Latino/a Canon and the Emergence of Post-Sixties Literature.* New York: Palgrave, 2007.

Dávila, Arlene M. *Barrio Dreams: Puerto Ricans, Latinos, and the Neoliberal City.* Berkeley: University of California Press, 2004.

Dávila, Arlene. "To Stop Tip-Toeing Around Race: What Arizona's Battle Against Ethnic Studies can Teach Academics." *Identities* 19.4 (2012): 411–17.

Davis, Kingsley. "The Urbanization of the Human Population." In *The City Reader.* Eds. Richard T. LeGates and Frederic Stout. New York: Routledge, 2011, pp. 2–11.

Davis, Lennard J., ed. *The Disability Studies Reader.* New York: Routledge, 2006.

Davis, Mike. *City of Quartz: Excavating the Future in Los Angeles.* New York, London: Verso, 2006.

De la Campa, Román. *Latin Americanism.* Minneapolis: University of Minnesota Press, 1999.

Delgado, Richard. "Locating Latinos in the Field of Civil Rights: Assessing the Neoliberal Case for Radical Exclusion." 83 Tex. L. Rev. 489 (2004).

Eberl, Markus. "Nourishing Gods: Birth and Personhood in Highland Mexican Codices." *Cambridge Archaeological Journal* 23.3 (2013): 453–76.

Echevarría, Roberto González. "Literature of the Hispanic Caribbean." *Latin American Literary Review* 8.16 (1980): 1–20.

Elbow, Peter. "The Cultures of Literature and Composition: What Could Each Learn from the Other?" *College English* 64.5 (2002): 533–46.

Elenes, C. Alejandra. "Reclaiming the Borderlands: Chicana/o Identity, Difference, and Critical Pedagogy." *Educational Theory* 47.3 (1997): 359–75.

Espinoza-Gonzalez, Daniel. "Decolonizing the Classroom Through Critical Consciousness: Navigating Solidarity en la Lucha for Mexican American Studies." *The Educational Forum* 78.1 (2014): 54–67.

Estrada, Emir and Pierrette Hondagneu-Sotelo. "Intersectional dignities: Latino Immigrant Street Vendor Youth in Los Angeles." *Journal of Contemporary Ethnography* 40.1 (2011): 102–31.

Ezeife, Amaka C. "Code-alternation in Strengthening Indigenous Cultures and Languages: A Feminist Reading." *Language in India* 13.5 (2013): 243–257.

Fischer, Sybill. *Modernity Disavowed: Haiti and the Cultures of Slavery Revolution.* Durham: Duke University Press, 2004.

Flores, Juan. *Puerto Rican Culture and Latino Identity*. Columbia: Columbia University Press, 2000.

——. "Oye Como Va! Hybridity and Identity in Latino Popular Music." *Latin American Music Review* 33.2 (2012): 266–68.

Flores, Juan and George Yudice. "Living Borders/Buscando América: Languages of Latino Self-formation." *Social Text* 24 (1990): 57–84.

Fox, Claire F. "The Portable Border: Site-Specificity, Art, and the US-Mexico Frontier." *Social Text* 41 (Winter 1994): 61–82.

Gans, Herbert J. *The Levittowners: Ways of Life and Politics in a New Suburban Community*. New York: Columbia University Press, 1982.

García, Alma M., ed. *Chicana Feminist Thought: The Basic Historical Writings*. New York: Routledge, 1997.

Gentner, Dedre, Keith James Holyoak, and Boicho N. Kokinov, eds. *The Analogical Mind: Perspectives from Cognitive Science*. Cambridge: MIT Press, 2001.

Gewecke, Frauke. "Latino/a Literature in Western Europe." In *The Routledge Companion to Latino/a Literature*. Eds. Suzanne Bost and Frances Aparicio. New York: Routledge, 2013.

Gibson, Eliza Rodriguez, ed. *Stunned Into Being: Essays on the Poetry of Lorna Dee Cervantes*. San Antonio: Wings Press, 2012.

Gies, David Thatcher. *The Theatre in Nineteenth-Century Spain*. Cambridge; New York: Cambridge University Press, 2005.

Gil-Gómez, Ellen M. "Mezclando (Mixing) the 'Facts' and the Power of the Image in Latino USA." In *Crossing Boundaries in Graphic Narrative: Essays on Forms, Series and Genres*. Eds. Jake Jakaitis and James F. Wurtz. Jefferson, NC: McFarland, 2012, pp. 152–76.

——. "Wrestling with Comic Genres and Genders: Luchadores as Signifiers in *Sonambulo* and *Locas*." In *Mind the Gap: Latino Comic Books Past, Present, and Future*. Eds. Christopher González and Frederick Luis Aldama. Texas: University of Texas Press, forthcoming.

Glass, Grant. "After Latinidad: Reimagining Latino Identity in the Works of Junot Díaz." *Undergraduate Research Journal for the Human Sciences* 12.1 (2013). www.kon.org/urc/v12/glass.html

Gleave, Sara and Qingfang Wang. "Foreign-born Latino Labor Market Concentration in Six Metropolitan Areas in the US South." *Southeastern Geographer* 53.2 (2013): 157–76.

Golden, James L. and Edward P.J. Corbett. *The Rhetoric of Blair, Campbell, and Whately*. Carbondale: Southern Illinois University Press, 1968.

Goldman, Dara E. "Out of Place: The Demarcation of Hispanic Caribbean Cultural Spaces in the Diaspora." *Latino Studies* 1.3 (2003): 403–23.

Goldman, Emma. *Anarchism: What It Really Stands For*. New York: Mother Earth Publishing Association, 1911.

Gonzales-Berry, Erlinda. "Estampas del Valle: From 'Costumbrismo' to Self-Reflecting Literature." *Bilingual Review/La Revista Bilingüe* 7.1 (1980): 28–38.

González, Alberto, Jorge M. Chávez, and Christine M. Englebrecht. "Latinidad and Vernacular Discourse: Arts Activism in Toledo's Old South End." *Journal of Poverty* 18.1 (2014): 50–64.

González, Christopher. *Hospitable Imaginations: Contemporary Latino/a Literature and the Pursuit of a Readership*. Dissertation. The Ohio State University, 2012.

——. "Latino Sci-Fi: Cognition and Narrative Design in Alex Rivera's Sleep Dealer." *Latinos and Narrative Media: Participation and Portrayal*. Ed. Frederick Luis Aldama. New York: Palgrave Macmillan, 2013.

——. *Reading Junot Díaz*. Pittsburgh: University of Pittsburgh Press, 2016.

Gonzalez, Ray. *Muy Macho*. New York: Anchor Books, 1996.

Griswold del Castello, Richard and Richard A. Garcia. *César Chávez: A Triumph of Spirit*. Oklahoma: University of Oklahoma Press, 1997.

Habell-Pallán, Michelle. *Loca Motion: The Travels of Chicana and Latina Popular Culture*. New York: New York University Press, 2005.

Hall, Horace R. "Poetic Expressions: Students of Color Express Resiliency through Metaphors and Similes." *Journal of Advanced Academics* 18.2 (2007): 216–44.

Halttunen, Karen, ed. *A Companion to American Cultural History.* Malden, MA: Blackwell, 2008. http://onlinelibrary.wiley.com/book/10.1002/9780470691762

Hayden, Dolores. *Building Suburbia: Green Fields and Urban Growth, 1820–2000.* New York: Pantheon Books, 2003.

Hedrick, Tace. "Chica Lit." In *The Routledge Companion to Latino/a Literature.* Eds. Bost, Suzanne, and Frances R. Aparicio. New York: Routledge, 2013, pp. 342–50.

Heredia, Aida L. "Yoruba Cosmology as Technique in Malambo by Lucia Charun-Illescas." In *Critical Perspectives on Afro-Latin American Literature.* Ed. Antonio D. Tillis. New York: Routledge, 2012, pp. 77–98.

Heredia, Juanita. *Transnational Latina Narratives in the Twenty-first Century.* New York: Palgrave, 2009.

Herman, David. *Basic Elements of Narrative.* Malden, MA: Wiley-Blackwell, 2009.

Hong, Grace Kyungwon. "Existentially Surplus Women of Color Feminism and the New Crises of Capitalism." *GLQ: A Journal of Lesbian and Gay Studies* 18.1 (2012): 87–106.

Jackson, Kenneth T. *Crabgrass Frontier: The Suburbanization of the United States.* New York: Oxford, 1987.

Jago, Carol. *Sandra Cisneros in the Classroom: "Do Not Forget To Reach."* The NCTE High School Literature Series. Urbana, IL: National Council of Teachers of English, 2002.

Jiménez-Román, Miriam and Juan Flores, eds. *The Afro-Latin@ Reader: History and Culture in the United States.* Durham: Duke University Press, 2010.

Kane, Adrian Taylor, ed. *The Natural World in Latin American Literatures: Ecocritical Essays on Twentieth-Century Writings.* Jefferson: McFarland, 2010.

Kanellos, Nicolás. *Hispanic Theatre in the United States.* Houston: Arte Público Press, 1984.

——. *Herencia: The Anthology of Hispanic Literature of the United States.* Oxford: Oxford University Press, 2003.

——. *Hispanic Literature of the United States: A Comprehensive Reference.* Westport, CT: Greenwood Publishing Group, 2003.

Keis, Richard. "From Principle to Practice: Using Children's Literature to Promote Dialogue and Facilitate the 'Coming to Voice' in a Rural Latino Community." *Multicultural Perspectives* 8.1 (2006): 13–19.

Kevane, Bridget A. *Latino Literature in America.* Westport, CT: Greenwood Press Group, 2003.

Klahn, Norma. *Literary (Re) Mappings: Autobiographical (Dis)Placements by Chicana Writers.* Durham: Duke University Press, 2003.

Ladson-Billings, Gloria and William F. Tate. "Toward a Critical Race Theory of Education." In *Critical Race Theory in Education: All God's Children Got a Song.* Eds. Adrienne D. Dixson, Celia K. Rousseau and Jamel K. Donnor. New York: Routledge, 2006, pp. 11–30.

La Roche, Martin J., Cynthia Batista, and Eugene D'Angelo. "A Content Analyses of Guided Imagery Scripts: A Strategy for the Development of Cultural Adaptations." *Journal of Clinical Psychology* 67.1 (2011): 45–57.

Latorre, Guisela. *Walls of Empowerment: Chicana/o Indigenist Murals of California.* Austin: University of Texas Press, 2008.

Lee, A. Robert. *Multicultural American Literature: Comparative Black, Native, Latino/a and Asian American Fictions.* Mississippi: University Press of Mississippi, 2003.

Levi, Heather. *The World of Lucha Libre: Secrets, Revelations, and Mexican National Identity.* Durham: Duke University Press, 2008.

Liaw, Shu-Sheng. "Investigating Students' Perceived Satisfaction, Behavioral Intention, and Effectiveness of E-learning: A Case Study of the Blackboard system." *Computers & Education* 51.2 (2008): 864–73.

Lima, Lázaro. *The Latino Body: Crisis Identities in American Literary and Cultural Memory.* New York: New York University Press, 2007.

Limón, José. *Dancing with the Devil: Society and Cultural Poetics.* Madison: University of Wisconsin Press, 1994.

Lomelí, Francisco and A. Gabriel Meléndez, eds. *The Writings of Eusebio Chacón.* Albuquerque: University of New Mexico Press, 2012.

Luque, Elin and M. Beltrán. "Powerful Images: Mexican Ex-Votos." In *Art and Faith in Mexico: The Nineteenth-century Retablo Tradition.* Eds. Elizabeth Netto Calil Zarur and Charles Muir Lovell. Albuquerque: New Mexico, 2001.

Machado Sáez, Elena. "Static Signals: Celia Cruz, Santería, and Markets of Latinidad in Jennine Capó Crucet's *How to Leave Hialeah.*" In *Write in Tune: Contemporary Music in Fiction.* New York; London: Bloomsbury, 2014, pp. 183–196.

Manzanas, Ana María, Jesús Benito, and Begoña Simal. *Uncertain Mirrors: Magical Realisms in U.S. Ethnic Literatures.* Amsterdam, New York: Rodopi, 2009.

Martin, Holly E. *Writing between Cultures: A Study of Hybrid Narratives in Ethnic Literature of the United States.* Jefferson, NC: McFarland, 2011.

Martín-Rodríguez, Manuel. "Aesthetic Concepts of Hispanics in the United States." In *Handbook of Hispanic Cultures in the United States: Literature and Art.* Ed. Nicolás Kanellos. Houston, TX: Arte Público, 1993, p. 109.

Martínez, Ernesto. *On Making Sense: Queer Race Narratives of Intelligibility.* Redwood City: Stanford University Press, 2012.

Martínez, Ernesto and Michael Hames-García, eds. *Gay Latino Studies: A Critical Reader.* Durham: Duke University Press, 2011.

Martínez-Cruz, Paloma. *Women and Knowledge in Mesoamerica: From East L.A. to Anahuac.* Tucson: University of Arizona Press, 2011.

Martínez-San Miguel, Yolanda. "Taino Warriors? Strategies for Recovering Indigenous Voices in Colonial and Contemporary Hispanic Caribbean Discourses." *Centro Journal* 23.1 (2011): 197–215.

McCracken, Ellen. "Expanding Genette's Epitext." *Narrative* 21.1 (Jan. 2013): 105–24.

——. *New Latina Narrative: The Feminine Space of Postmodern Ethnicity.* Tucson: University of Arizona Press, 1999.

Medina, Carmen Liliana and Marea del Rocio Costa. "Latino Media and Critical Literacy Pedagogies: Children's Scripting of Telenovelas Discourses." *Journal of Language and Literacy Education* 9.1 (2013): 161–84.

Mermann-Jozwiak, Elisabeth. "Transnational Latino/a Writing, and American and Latino/a Studies." *Latino Studies* 12.1 (2014): 111–33.

Mignolo, Walter. *The Darker Side of Western Modernity: Global Futures, Decolonial Options.* Durham: Duke University Press, 2011.

——. *Local Histories/Global Designs: Coloniality, Subaltern Knowledges, and Border Thinking.* Princeton: Princeton University Press, 2000.

Mize, Ronald L. and Grace Peña Delgado. *Latino Immigrants in the United States.* Cambridge: Polity Press, 2012.

Moiles, Sean. "The Politics of Gentrification in Ernesto Quiñonez's Novels." *Critique: Studies in Contemporary Fiction* 52.1 (2011): 114–33.

Montes-Alcalá, Cecilia. "Writing on the Border: English y español también." *Landscapes of Writing in Chicano Literature.* New York: Palgrave Macmillan, 2013, pp. 213–30.

Moraga, Cherríe. *A Xicana Codex of Changing Consciousness: Writings, 2000–2010.* Durham: Duke University Press, 2011.

Moretti, Franco. *Distant Reading.* London: Verso, 2013.

Moya, Paula. *Identity Politics Reconsidered.* New York: Palgrave Macmillan, 2006.

Moya, Paula and Hazel Markus, eds. *Doing Race: 21 Essays for the 21st Century.* New York: W.W. Norton, 2010.

Muñoz, Carlos. *Youth, Identity, Power: The Chicano Movement.* New York: Verso, 1989.

Muñoz, José. *Disidentifications: Queers of Color and the Performance of Politics.* Minneapolis: University of Minnesota Press, 1999.

Naidoo, Jamie Campbell, ed. *Celebrating Cuentos: Promoting Latino Children's Literature and Literacy in Classrooms and Libraries.* Santa Barbara: ABC-CLIO, 2011.

Nicolaides, Becky M. *My Blue Heaven: Life and Politics in the Working-Class Suburbs of Los Angeles, 1920–1965.* Chicago: University of Chicago Press, 2002.

Nicolaides, Becky M. and Andrew Wiese, eds. *The Suburb Reader.* New York: Routledge, 2006.

Novillo-Corvalán, Patricia. "Introduction: Medical Humanities Perspectives in Iberian and Latin American Literature." In *Latin American and Iberian Perspectives on Literature and Medicine.* Ed. Patricia Novillo-Corvalán. London: Routledge, 2015.

Novo, Carmen Martínez. "Indigenous Appropriations and Boundary Crossings: Interdisciplinary Perspectives on Indigenous Cultures and Politics in the Andes." *Latin American Research Review* 48.2 (2013): 218–26.

Oliva-Alvarado, Karina. "An Interdisciplinary Reading of Chicana/o and (US) Central American Cross-Cultural Narrations." *Latino Studies* 11.3 (2013): 366–87.

Onofre, Carolina Abello and Christophe Chambost. "El Santo's Legacy: Looking for the Revival of Lucha Libre in Colombian Soap Operas." *Revue de recherche en civilisation américaine* 4 (2013).

Pabón, Melissa. "The Representation of Curanderismo in Selected Mexican American Works." *Journal of Hispanic Higher Education* 6.3 (2007): 227–57.

Padilla, Genaro. "A Reassessment of Fray Angelico Chavez's Fiction." *MELUS* 11.4 (Winter, 1984): 31–45.

Pérez, Emma. *The Decolonial Imaginary: Writing Chicanas into History.* Bloomington: Indiana University Press, 1999.

Pérez Firmat, Gustavo. *Tongue Ties: Logo-Eroticism in Anglo-Hispanic Literature.* New York: Palgrave Macmillan, 2003.

Pérez Rosario, Vanessa. *Hispanic Caribbean Literature of Migration: Narratives of Displacement.* New York: Palgrave Macmillan, 2012.

Petty, Leslie. "The 'Dual'-Ing Images of la Malinche and la Virgen De Guadalupe in Cisneros's the House on Mango Street." *MELUS* 25. 2 (1 July 2000): 119–32.

Phelan, James. *Experiencing Fiction: Judgments, Progressions, and the Rhetorical Theory of Narrative.* Columbus: Ohio State University Press, 2007.

Poey, Delia. *Cuban Women and Salsa.* New York: Palgrave, 2010.

Quiroga, José. *Tropics of Desire: Interventions from Queer Latino America.* New York: New York University Press, 2000.

Raisanen, Astrid Lea. "Bridging Borders: A Rhetoric of Border Narratives." Tucson: University of Arizona, 2011.

Ramírez, Catherine. *The Woman in the Zoot Suit: Gender, Nationalism, and the Cultural Politics of Memory.* Durham: Duke University Press, 2009.

Raymond, Rocco A. *Transforming Citizenship: Democracy, Membership, and Belonging in Latino Communities.* East Lansing, MI: Michigan State University Press, 2014.

Redigan, Sydney. "Latino/a Literature in the Multicultural English Classroom." Research paper. Wayne State University, 2013. http://sydneyredigan.com/wp-content/uploads/2013/07/Latinoa-Literature.pdf (accessed June 23, 2014).

Reyes, Patrick Bruner. "Relational Bodies: Dancing With Latina, Chicana and Latin American Bodies." *Feminist Theology* 22.3 (2014): 253–68.

Richardson, Brian. *Unnatural Voices: Extreme Narration in Modern and Contemporary Fiction.* Columbus: Ohio State University Press, 2006.

Riebe-Estrella, S. V. D. "La Virgen: A Mexican Perspective." *New Theology Review* 12.2 (2013): 39–47.

Rivera, Lysa. "Future Histories and Cyborg Labor: Reading Borderlands Science Fiction after NAFTA." *Science Fiction Studies* 39.3 (2012): 415–36.

Rodríguez, Ana Patricia. "Refugees of the South: Central Americans in the US Latino Imaginary." *American Literature* 73.2 (2001): 387–412.

——. *Dividing the Isthmus: Central American Transnational Histories, Literatures, and Cultures.* Austin: University of Texas Press, 2009.

Rodríguez, R. C. "Tucson's Maiz-based Curriculum: MAS-TUSD Profundo." *Nakum Journal* 2.1 (2012): 72–98.

Rodriguez, Ralph E. "Chicana/o Fiction from Resistance to Contestation: The Role of Creation in Ana Castillo's so Far from God." *MELUS* 25.2 (2000): 63–82.

Rodríguez, Richard T. *Next of Kin: The Family in Chicano/a Cultural Politics.* Durham: Duke University Press, 2009.

Rojas, Mary Alexandra. "An Examination of US Latino Identities as Constructed In/Through Curricular Materials." *Linguistics and Education* 24.3 (2013): 373–80.

Rome, Adam Ward. *The Bulldozer in the Countryside: Suburban Sprawl and the Rise of American Environmentalism.* Cambridge: Cambridge University Press, 2001.

Romero, Augustine. "The Battle for Educational Sovereignty and the Right to Save the Lives of Our Children." In *Raza Studies: The Public Option for Educational Revolution.* Eds. Julio Cammarota and Augustine Romero. Tucson: University of Arizona Press, 2014, pp. 52–62.

Rosen, Ruth. *The World Split Open: How the Modern Women's Movement Changed America.* Tantor eBooks, 2013.

Rossini, Jon. "Teatro." In *The Routledge Companion to Latino/a Literature.* Eds. Suzanne Bost and Frances Aparicio. New York: Routledge, 2013, pp. 285–98.

Salazar, Monica. "Death Imagery in Paz's Blanco." *Plaza: Dialogues in Language and Literature* 3.2 (2013): 34–44.

Saldívar, José David. *Border Matters: Remapping American Cultural Studies.* California: University California Press, 1997.

——. *Trans-Americanity: Subaltern Modernities, Global Coloniality, and the Cultures Greater Mexico.* Durham: Duke University Press, 2011.

Saldívar, Ramón. "The Second Elevation of the Novel: Race, Form and the Postrace Aesthetic in Contemporary Narrative." *Narrative* 21.1 (January 2013): 1–18.

Saldívar-Hull, Sonia. *Feminism on the Border: Chicana Gender Politics and Literature.* Berkeley: University of California Press, 2000.

Sánchez, Marta E. *"Shakin' Up" Race and Gender: Intercultural Connections in Puerto Rican, African American, and Chicano Narratives and Culture (1965–1995).* Austin: University of Texas Press, 2005.

——. "Pocho en español: The anti-pocho pocho." *Translation Studies* 4.3 (2011): 310–24.

Sánchez-González, Lisa. *Boricua Literature: A Literary History of the Puerto Rican Diaspora.* New York: New York University Press, 2001.

Sánchez Korrol, Virginia. *From Colonia to Community: The History of Puerto Ricans in New York City.* Berkeley: University of California Press, 1994.

Sandín, Lyn Di Iorio and Richard Pérez, eds. *Moments of Magical Realism in US Ethnic Literatures.* New York: Palgrave Macmillan, 2012.

Segal, Eyal. "Current Trends in Narratology." *Poetics Today* 34.3 (2013): 414–17.

Sheridan, Susan. "Feminist Knowledge, Women's Liberation, and Women's Studies." In *Feminist Knowledge: Critique and Construct.* Ed. Sneja Gunew. New York; London: Routledge, 2013, pp. 36–55.

Shorris, Earl. *Latinos: A Biography of the People.* New York: Norton, 1992.

Soldatenko, Michael. "Mexican Student Movements in Los Angeles and Mexico City, 1968." *Latino Studies* 1.2 (2003): 284–300.

Stavans, Ilan. *A Critic's Journey.* Ann Arbor: University of Michigan Press, 2010.

——, ed. *Telenovelas.* Santa Barbara: ABC-CLIO, 2010.

——. *The Norton Anthology of Latino Literature.* New York: W.W. Norton, 2011.

——. "Nacho Libre: or, The Inauthenticity of Rasquachismo." In *Latinos in Narrative Media: Participation and Portrayal.* New York: Palgrave, 2013, pp. 111–16.

Stavans, Ilan and Frederick Luis Aldama. *¡Muy Pop! Conversations on Latino Popular Culture.* Ann Arbor: University of Michigan Press, 2013.

Stephens, Gregory. "'When I Was Puerto Rican' as Borderland Narrative: Bridging Caribbean and US Latino Literature." *Confluencia* 25.1 (2009): 30–45.

Thananopavarn, Susan. "Conscientización of the Oppressed." *Aztlán: A Journal of Chicano Studies* 37.1 (2012): 65–86.

Tongson, Karen. *Relocations: Queer Suburban Imaginaries.* New York: New York University Press, 2011.

Torres, Lourdes. "The Construction of the Self in US Latina Autobiographies." In *Women, Knowledge, and Reality: Explorations in Feminist Philosophy,* 1991, New York: Routledge, 1996, pp. 127–44.

——. "In the contact zone: Code-switching strategies by Latino/a writers." *MELUS* 32.1 (Spring 2007): 75–96.

Torres, Vasti and Marcia B. Baxter Magolda. "Reconstructing Latino Identity: The Influence of Cognitive Development on the Ethnic Identity Process of Latino Students." *Journal of College Student Development* 45.3 (2004): 333–47.

Torres-Padilla, José L. and Carmen Haydée Rivera. *Writing Off the Hyphen: New Critical Perspectives on the Literature of the Puerto Rican Diaspora.* Seattle: University of Washington Press, 2011.

Travis, Christopher M. "The Natural World in Latin American Literatures: Ecocritical Essays on Twentieth-Century Writings." *Review: Literature and Arts of the Americas* 45.2 (2012): 257–259.

Urrea, Luis. *Across the Wire: Life and Hard Times on the Mexican Border.* New York: Anchor Books, 1993.

Urrieta, Luis, Jr. and Sofia A. Villenas. "The Legacy of Derrick Bell and Latino/a Education: A Critical Race Testimonio." *Race Ethnicity and Education* 16.4 (2013): 514–35.

Valdez, Luis. *Early Works: Actos, Bernabe, Pensamiento Serpentino.* Houston: Arte Público Press, 1990.

Vallejo, Jody. *Barrios to Burbs: The Making of the Mexican American Middle Class.* Redwood City: Stanford University Press, 2012.

Vélez-Ibáñez, Carlos. *An Impossible Living in a Transborder World Culture, Confianza, and Economy of Mexican-Origin Populations.* Tucson: University of Arizona Press, 2010.

Vigil, Ariana. "The Divine Husband and the Creation of a Transamericana Subject." *Latino Studies* 11.2 (2013): 190–207.

Villa, Raúl. *Barrio-Logos: Space and Place in Urban Chicano Literature and Culture.* Austin: University of Texas Press, 2000.

Villatoro, Marcos McPeek. "In Search of Literary Cojones: Pablo Neruda, US Latino Poetry, and the US Literary Canon: A Testimonio." In *Pablo Neruda and the US Culture Industry.* Ed. Teresa Longo. New York: Routledge, 2013, pp. 163–78.

Villenas, Sofia, Dolores Delgado Bernal, C. Alejandra Elenes, and Francisca E. Godinez. "Chicanas/Latinas Building Bridges." In *Chicana/Latina Education in Everyday Life. Feminista Perspectives on Pedagogy and Epistemology.* Eds. Sofia Villenas, Dolores Delgado Bernal, C. Alejandra Elenes, and Francisca E. Godinez. Albany: State University of New York Press, 2006, pp. 1–9.

Walker, Alice. *In Search of Our Mothers' Gardens.* New York: Harcourt Brace, 1983.

Wei Li, *Ethnoburb: The New Ethnic Community in Urban America.* Honolulu: University of Hawai'i Press, 2009.

Whyte, William Hollingsworth. *The Organization Man.* Philadelphia: University of Pennsylvania Press, 2002.

Winslow, Luke A. "The Imaged Other: Style and Substance in the Rhetoric of Joel Osteen." *Southern Communication Journal* 79.3 (2014): 250–71.

Wiseman, David P. and Lorraine López. "Latino Literature's Past and Future: A Conversation with Lorraine López." *Afro-Hispanic Review* 28.1 (2009): 141–50.

Wolfe, Andrea Powell. "Refiguring La Malinche: Female 'Betrayal' as Cultural Negotiation in the Short Stories of María Cristina Mena." *Label Me Latino/a* 3 (2013): 1–23. http://labelmelatin.com/wp-content/uploads/2013/04/andrea-powell-wolfe-Refiguring-La-Malinche-Female-Betrayal-as-Cultural-Negotiation.pdf (accessed June 26, 2014).

Woloch, Alex. *The One vs. the Many: Minor Characters and the Space of the Protagonist in the Novel*. Princeton: Princeton University Press, 2003.

Bibliography

Abbott, H. Porter. *The Cambridge Introduction to Narrative.* 2nd edn. Cambridge: Cambridge University Press, 2008.

Abram, David. *The Spell of the Sensuous: Perception and Language in a More-Than-Human World.* New York: Vintage Books, 1996.

Abrego, L. *Sacrificing Families: Navigating Laws, Labor, and Love Across Borders.* Stanford: Stanford University Press, 2014.

Acosta, Curtis. "Developing Critical Consciousness: Resistance Literature in a Chicano Literature Class." *The English Journal* 97.2 (2007): 36–42.

Acosta, Oscar "Zeta." *The Autobiography of a Brown Buffalo.* 1972. New York: Vintage Books, 1989.

——. *The Revolt of the Cockroach People.* 1973. New York: Vintage Books, 1989.

Acosta Cruz, Maria. *Dream Nation: Puerto Rican Culture and the Fictions of Independence.* New Brunswick, NJ: Rutgers University Press, 2014.

Acuña, Rudy. *Occupied America.* 1972. New York: Pearson, 2014.

Ada, Alma Flor and F. Isabel Campoy. Pictures by David Diaz. *Yes! We are Latinos.* Watertown, MA: Charlesbridge, 2013.

Alarcón, Daniel. *War by Candlelight.* New York: HarperCollins, 2005.

——. *Lost City Radio.* New York: Harper Collins, 2007.

——. "All Politics Is Local." *Harpers* (Feb. 2012): 35–44.

——. *At Night We Walk in Circles.* New York: Riverhead, 2013.

Alarcón, Norma. "*Traddutora, Traditora*: A Paradigmatic Figure of Chicana Feminism." In *Dangerous Liaisons: Gender, Nation, and Postcolonial Perspectives.* Eds. Anne McClintock, A. Mufti, and Ella Shohat. Minneapolis: University of Minnesota Press, 1997, pp. 278–97.

Aldama, Arturo J., Chela Sandoval, and Peter J. García. *Performing the US Latina and Latino Borderlands.* Bloomington: Indiana University Press, 2012.

Aldama, Frederick Luis. *Dancing with Ghosts: A Critical Biography of Arturo Islas.* Berkeley: University of California Press, 2004.

——. "An Interview with Jimmy Santiago Baca." *MELUS: Multi-Ethnic Literature of the United States* 30.3 (2005): 113–27.

——. *A User's Guide to Postcolonial and Latino Borderland Fiction.* Austin: University of Texas Press, 2009.

——. "Language and Code-Switching." *The Routledge Concise History of Latino/a Literature.* London: Routledge, 2013, pp. 32–37.

——. *The Routledge Concise History of Latino/a Literature.* London: Routledge, 2013.

——. *Formal Matters in Contemporary Latino Poetry.* New York: Palgrave Macmillan, 2013.

——. "A Scientific Approach to the Teaching of a Flash Fiction." *Interdisciplinary Literary Studies* 16:1 (2014): 127–44.

Aldama, Frederick L. and Ilan Stavans. *Muy Pop! Conversations on Latino Popular Culture.* Ann Arbor: University of Michigan Press, 2013.

Alegría, C. *Flowers from the Volcano.* Trans. Carloyn Forche. Pittsburgh: University of Pittsburgh Press, 1983.

Alemán, Jesse. "The Other Country: Mexico, the United States, and the Gothic History of Conquest." *American Literary History* 18.3 (2006): 406–26.

Alexie, Sherman. *Reservation Blues.* New York: Warner Books, 1995.

Algarín, Miguel. "Nuyorican Language." In *Nuyorican Poetry: An Anthology of Puerto Rican Words and Feelings.* 1975. Maria Damon and Ira Livingston, eds. *Poetry and Cultural Studies: A Reader.* Urbana: University of Illinois Press, 2009, pp. 437–46.

Allatson, Paul. *Key Terms in Latino/a Cultural and Literary Studies.* Oxford: Blackwell, 2007.

Allende, Isabel. *City of the Beasts.* Trans. Margaret Sayers Peden. New York: Rayo/Harper Collins, 2002.

——. *Kingdom of the Golden Dragon.* NY: Rayo/Harper Collins, 2004.

——. *Forest of the Pygmies.* NY: Rayo/Harper Collins, 2004.

Alumbaugh, Heather. "Narrative Coyotes: Migration and Narrative Voice in Sandra Cisneros's *Caramelo.*" *MELUS* 35.1 (Spring 2010): 53–75.

Alurista. *Tula y Tonán: texto generativo.* San Diego, CA: Toltecas en Aztl'an Publications, 1973.

——. "El Plan Espiritual De Aztlán." *Aztlán: Essays on the Chicano Homeland.* 1971. Eds. Rudolfo A. Anaya and Francisco Lomeli. Albuquerque: University of New Mexico Press, 1989, pp. 1–5.

Alvarez, Julia. *In the Time of the Butterflies.* Chapel Hill, NC: Algonquin Books, 1994.

——. *Yo!* Chapel Hill, NC: Algonquin Books, 1997.

——. *In the Name of Salomé.* Chapel Hill, NC: Algonquin Books, 2000.

——. *The Tía Lola Series.* New York: Yearling (Random House), 2002.

——. *Before We Were Free.* 2002. New York: Laurel-Leaf (Random House Children's Books), 2004.

——. *finding miracles.* 2004. New York: Laurel-Leaf, 2006.

——. *Once upon a Quinceañera: Coming of Age in the USA.* New York: Plume, 2008.

——. *Return to Sender.* New York: Yearling (Random House), 2009.

——. *How the García Girls Lost Their Accents.* 1991. Chapel Hill, NC: Algonquin Books, 2010a.

——. *Tía Lola: Stories.* New York: Random House Audio/Listening Library, 2010b.

Ambroggio, L.A. and C. Parada Ayala, eds. *Al pie de la Casa Blanca: Poetas hispanos de Washington, DC.* New York: Academia Norteamericana de la Lengua Española, 2010.

Anaya, Rudolfo. *Bless Me, Ultima.* 1972. New York: Warner, 1999.

Anzaldúa, Gloria. "Speaking in Tongues: A Letter to Third World Women Writers". In *This Bridge Called my Back: Writings by Radical Women of Color.* Eds. Cherríe Moraga and Gloria Anzaldúa. New York: Kitchen Table/Women of Color Press, 1983.

Anzaldúa, Gloria, ed. *Borderlands/La Frontera: The New Mestiza.* San Francisco: Aunt Lute Books, 1987; 2007; 4th edn. 2012.

——. ed. *Making Face, Making Soul/Haciendo Caras: Creative and Critical Perspectives by Women of Color.* San Francisco: Aunt Lute Foundation Books, 1990.

Anzaldúa, Gloria and AnaLouise Keating, eds. *This Bridge We Call Home: Radical Visions for Transformation.* New York: Routledge, 2002.

Aparicio, Frances. "On Sub-Versive Signifiers: U.S. Latino/a Writers Tropicalize English." *American Literature* 66.4 (1994): 795–801.

——. "On Sub-Versive Signifiers: Tropicalizing Language in the United States." In *Tropicalizations: Transcultural Representations of Latinidad.* Eds. Frances Aparicio and Susana Chávez-Silverman. Hanover: University Press of New England, 1997, pp. 194–212.

——. "(Re)Constructing Latinidad: The Challenge of Latina/o Studies." In *A Companion to Latina/o Studies.* Eds. Juan Flores and Renato Rosaldo. Malden, MA: Blackwell Publishing, 2007, pp. 39–48.

——. "Cultural Twins and National Others: Allegories of Intralatino Subjectivities in US Latino/a Literature." *Identities: Global Studies in Culture and Power* 16.5 (2009): 622–41.

Aragón, F. *Puerta del Sol*. Tempe: Bilingual Press/Editorial Bilingüe, 2005.
——. *Glow of Our Sweat*. Kansas City: Scapegoat Press, 2010.
Archdiocese of Guatamala. *Guatemala, never again!: REMHI, Recovery of Historical Memory Project*. Maryknoll, NY: Orbis Books, 1999.
Archila, W. *The Art of Exile*. Tempe: Bilingual Press/Editorial Bilingüe, 2009.
Arenas, R. *Before Night Falls*. Trans. Dolores M. Koch. New York, NY: Viking, 1993.
Argueta, J. *Del ocaso a la aborada/From Sundown to Dawn*. Berkeley: Co Press, 1989.
——. *La puerta del diablo/The Devil's Gate*. San Francisco: Editores Unidos Salvadoreños, 1990.
——. *Far from Fire*. San Francisco: Editores Unidos Salvadoreños, 1991.
——. *Love Street*. San Francisco: Editores Unidos Salvadoreños, 1991.
——. *Litany of Love and Hate*. San Francisco: Luna's Press, 1996.
——. *Las frutas del Centro y Otros Sabores/Fruit from the Center and Other Flavors*. Berkeley: Canterbury Press, 1997.
——. *Cerca del Fuego/Close to the Fire*. San Francisco: Luna's Press, 2009.
Argueta, M. *One Day of Life*. Trans. William Brow. New York: Vintage, 1991.
——. "Lengua e identidad en la novela *Lengua Madre*, de Demetria Martinez." *Revista Istmo* 2 (2001). http://istmo.denison.edu/n02/articulos/lengua.html (accessed August 2, 2014).
Arias, A., ed. *The Rigoberta Menchú Controversy*. Minneapolis: University of Minnesota Press, 2001.
——. *Taking Their Word: Literature and the Signs of Central America*. Minneapolis: University of Minnesota Press, 2007.
Aristotle. *Nichomachean Ethics*. Trans. H. Rackham. Loeb Classical Library. Cambridge, MA: Harvard University Press, 1926.
Arrizón, Alicia. *Latina Performance: Traversing the Stage*. Bloomington: Indiana University Press, 1999.
Arrizón, Alicia and Lillian Manzor. *Latinas on Stage*. Berkeley, CA: Third Woman Press, 2000.
Artze, Isis. "Spanglish is Here to Stay." *Hispanic Outlook in Higher Education* 26 Mar. 2001. Web. May 1, 2014.
Asturias, Miguel Angel. *El señor presidente*. Mexico: Costa-Amic, 1946.
——. *The President*. Trans. Frances Partridge. New York: Atheneum, 1964.
Athanases, Steven Z. "Diverse Learners, Diverse Texts: Exploring Identity and Difference through Literary Encounters." *Journal of Literacy Research* 30:2 (June 1998): 273–96.
Atkins, Laura. "What's the Story? Reflections on White Privilege in the Publication of Children's Books." https://sites.google.com/site/tockla/ (accessed May 29, 2014).
Auden, W. H. *Selected Poems*. 2nd edn. New York: Vintage, 2007.
Auer, Peter. *Code-Switching in Conversation: Language, Interaction and Identity*. New York: Routledge, 2013.
Augenbraum, Harold and Margarite Fernández Olmos. *U.S. Literature: A Critical Guide for Students and Teachers*. Westward, CT: Greenwood, 2000.
——. *The Latino Reader*. Boston: Houghton Mifflin, 1997.
Augsburger, Deborah. "Interview." Lewis University, 22 May 2014.
Avilés, Q. *The Immigrant Museum*. Mexico, DF: PinStudio y Raíces de Papel, 2003.
Baca, Jimmy Santiago. *Black Mesa Poems*. New York: New Directions Press, 1989.
——. "Coming into Language." *Working in the Dark: Reflections of a Poet of the Barrio*. Santa Fe: Museum of New Mexico Press, 1992, pp. 3–11.
——. *Healing Earthquakes: A Love Story in Poems*. New York: Grove Press, 2001.
——. *A Place to Stand: The Making of a Poet*. New York: Grove Press, 2001.
——. *C-train and Thirteen Mexicans: Poems*. New York: Grove Press, 2002.
——. *The Importance of a Piece of Paper*. New York: Grove Press, 2004.
——. *Winter Poems along the Rio Grande*. New York: New Directions Press, 2004.
Badillo, Jalil Sued. *La mujer indígena y su sociedad*. Río Piedras, P. R.: Editorial Antillana, 1979.
Baez, Josefina. *Dominicanish*. Alexandria, VA: Alexander Street Press, 2005.

Baker, Mona, ed. *Routledge Encyclopedia of Translation Studies*. London: Routledge, 2001.

Bakhtin, M. M. *The Dialogic Imagination: Four Essays*. Ed. Michael Holquist. Trans. Caryl Emerson. Austin: University of Texas Press, 1981.

Banks, James and Cherry A. McGee Banks. *Multicultural Education: Issues and Perspectives*. Boston: Allyn and Bacon, 1993.

Barak, Julie. "'Turning and Turning in the Widening Gyre': A Second Coming into Language in Julia Alvarez's *How the García Girls Lost Their Accents*." *MELUS* 23.1 (1998): 159–76.

Barber, C. L. *Shakespeare's Festive Comedy*. Princeton: Princeton University Press, 1961.

Barrera, Frankie. *The Diary of Baby Chulo*. Sacramento: Popul Vuh Press, 1999.

Barrera, Magdalena. "Domestic Dramas: Mexican American Music as an Archive of Immigrant Women's Experiences, 1920s–1950s." *Aztlán: A Journal of Chicano Studies* 37.1 (Spring 2012): 7–35.

Barrientos, T. M. *Family Resemblance*. New York: Penguin Books, 2003.

Barthes, Roland. "An Introduction to the Structural Analysis of Narrative." *New Literary History* 6.2 (1975): 237–72.

Bauman, Richard. "Trying to Get Ahead: School Work and Grades in the Educational Advance of African-Americans." Working Paper. Madison, WI: Institute for Research on Poverty, Department of Health and Human Resources, 1996. Cited in *The Black-white Test Score Gap*. Eds Christopher Jenks and Meredith Phillips. Brookings Institute Press, 2011.

——. "Verbal Art as Performance." *American Anthropologist* 7.2 (1995): 290–311. Web. Aug. 20, 2013.

Beach, Richard, D. Appleman, and Susan Hynds. *Teaching Literature to Adolescents*. 2nd edn. New York: Routledge, 2006.

Bebout, Lee. "Skin in the Game: Toward a Theorization of Whiteness in the Classroom." *Pedagogy* 14.2 (2014): 343–54.

Bejarano, V. R. "Necessary Ideas for all Independent People of the Americas." In *Herencia: The Anthology of Hispanic Literature of the United States*. Ed. Nicolás Kanellos. Oxford: Oxford University Press, 2002, pp. 521–22.

Bell, Chris. "I'm Not the Man I Used to Be: Sex, HIV, and Cultural 'Responsibility,'" In *Sex and Disability*. Eds. R. McCruer and A. Mollow. Durham: Duke University Press, 2012, pp. 208–28.

Bell, Elizabeth. *Theories of Performance*. Thousand Oaks, CA: Sage, 2008.

Belnap, Jeffrey and Raúl Fernández, eds. *José Martí's "Our America": From National to Hemispheric Cultural Studies*. Durham, NC: Duke University Press, 1998.

Belpré, Pura. *Firefly Summer*. Houston, TX: Piñata Books/Arte Público Press, 1996.

Beltrán, Mary. *Latina/o Stars in U.S. Eyes: The Making and Meanings of Film and TV Stardom*. Urbana: University of Illinois Press, 2009.

Bencastro, M. *A Shot in the Cathedral*. Trans. S. G. Rascón. Houston: Arte Público Press, 1996.

——. *The Tree of Life: Stories of Civil War*. Trans. S. G. Rascón. Houston: Arte Público Press, 1997.

——. *Odyssey to the North*. Trans. S. G. Rascón. Houston: Arte Público Press, 1999.

——. *A Promise to Keep*. Trans. S. G. Rascón. Houston: Arte Público Press, 2005.

——. *Paraíso portátil/Portable Paradise*. Trans. J. Pluecker. Houston: Arte Público Press, 2010.

Benítez, S. *Bitter Grounds*. New York: Hyperion, 1997.

——. *The Weight of Things*. New York: Hyperion, 2000.

Benjamin, Walter. "The Work of Art in the Age of Mechanical Reproduction." In *Illuminations: Essays and Reflections*. Ed. Hannah Arendt. Trans. Harry Zohn. New York: Schocken Books, 1968.

——. "The Task of the Translator." *Illuminations: Essays and Reflections*. Trans. Harry Zohn. New York: Schocken Books, 1969, pp. 69–82.

Benz, S. "Through the Tropical Looking Glass: The Motif of Resistance in US Literature on Central America." In *Tropicalizations: Transcultural Representations of Latinidad*. Ed. F. Aparicio and S. Chávez-Silverman. Hanover and London: University Press of New England, 1997, pp. 51–66.

Bercovitch, Sacvan. *The American Jeremiad*. Madison: University of Wisconsin Press, 2012.

Berg, Charles Ramírez. *Latino Images in Film Stereotypes, Subversion, Resistance*. Austin, TX: University of Texas Press, 2002.

Bermann, Sandra and Wood, Michael, eds. *Nation, Language, and the Ethics of Translation*. Princeton: Princeton University Press, 2005.

Bernier-Grand, Carmen T. *César: Sí, se puede/Yes, We Can!*. Scholastic: Two Lions, 2011.

Bhabha, H. K. "The World and the Home." *Social Text* 31/32 (1992): 141–53.

——. *The Location of Culture*. London: Routledge, 1994.

Bielsa, Esperança. *The Latin American Urban* Crónica*: Between Literature and Mass Culture*. Lanham, MD: Lexington Books, 2006.

Blanco, Richard, perf. "One Today." *ABC News*. Web. 28 June, 2014.

Boal, Augusto. *Theatre of the Oppressed*. Trans. Charles A. and Maria-Odilia Leal McBride. New York: Theatre Communications Group, 1985.

Bolter, Jay David and Richard Grusin. *Remediation: Understanding New Media*. Cambridge: MIT Press, 1999.

Bond, Ernest L. *Literature and the Young Adult Reader*. Boston: Pearson, 2010.

Booth, J. A., C. J. Wade, and T. W. Walker. *Understanding Central America: Global Forces, Rebellion, and Change*. Boulder: Westview Press, 2015.

Booth, Wayne C. *The Rhetoric of Fiction*. Chicago: University of Chicago Press, 1961.

Borges, Jorge Luis. *Ficciones*. Buenos Aires: Emecé Editores, 1956.

Bost, Suzanne. *Encarnación: Illness and Body Politics in Chicana Feminist Literature*. New York: Fordham University Press, 2010.

Bost, Suzanne and Aparicio, Frances, eds. *The Routledge Companion to Latino/a Literature*. New York: Routledge, 2013.

Bourdieu, Pierre. *Distinction: A Social Critique of the Judgement of Taste*. New York, NY: Routledge, 1984, 2010.

Boyd, F. B. "Conditions, Concessions, and the Many Tender Mercies of Learning through Multicultural Literature." *Reading, Research, and Instruction* 42:1 (2002): 58–92.

Boyle, T. C. *Tortilla Curtain*. New York: Penguin, 1995.

Brading, David A. "Manuel Gamio and Official Indigenism in Mexico." *Bulletin of Latin American Research* 7.1 (1988): 75–89.

Brady, Mary Pat. "Children's Literature." In *The Routledge Companion to Latino/a Literature*. Eds. Suzanne Bost and Frances Aparicio. New York: Routledge, 2013, pp. 375–82.

Braschi, Giannina. *Yo-Yo Boing*. Pittsburgh, PA: Latin American Literary Review Press, 1998.

——. Pelos en la Lengua. Braschi, Giannina. "Sin pelos en la lengua." *Valladolid, Segundo Congreso Internacional de la lengua española*. 2001.

Brecht, Bertolt. *Brecht on Theatre*. Trans. John Willett. New York: Hill and Wang, 1964.

Brickhouse, Anna. *Transamerican Literary Relations and the Nineteenth-Century Public Sphere*. New York: Cambridge University Press, 2004.

Briones, B. "A Glimpse of Domestic Life in 1827." In *Herencia: The Anthology of Hispanic Literature of the United States*. Ed. Nicolás Kanellos. Oxford: Oxford University Press, 2002, pp. 94–95.

Brown, Ruth. "Migration Chronicles: Reporting on the Paradoxes of Migrant Visibility." *Textos Híbridos: Revista de estudios sobre la crónica latinoamericana* 2.1 (2012): 63–86. eScholarship. Web. July 22, 2013.

Brown, Wendy. *Walled States, Waning Sovereignty*. Cambridge, MA: Zone Books, 2010.

Broyles-Gonzalez, Yolanda. *El Teatro Campesino: Theater in the Chicano Movement*. Austin: University of Texas Press, 1994.

Bruce, Mary. "'One Today': Full Text of Richard Blanco Inaugural Poem." *ABC News*. Web. June 28, 2014.

Bruce-Novoa, Juan. "Homosexuality and the Chicano Novel." *Confluencia* 2.1 (1986): 69–77.

Bucher, Katherine and KaaVonia Hinton. *Young Adult Literature: Exploration, Evaluation, and Appreciation.* 2nd edn. Boston, MA: Allyn & Bacon, 2011.

Burgess, Jean and Joshua Green. *YouTube: Online Video and Participatory Culture.* Cambridge: Polity, 2009.

Bushman, John H. and Kay Parks Bushman. *Using Young Adult Literature in the English Classroom.* New York: Merrill/Macmillan, 1993.

Butler, Judith. *Gender Trouble: Feminism and the Subversion of Identity.* New York: Routledge, 1990.

Byrne, Bonifacio. "My Flag." *Herencia: The Anthology of Hispanic Literature of the United States.* Ed. Nicolás Kanellos. New York: Oxford University Press, 2002, pp. 558–59.

Cabeza de Vaca, Álvar Núñez. *Chronicle of the Narváez Expedition.* Trans. Fanny Banelier. New York: Penguin Books, 2002.

Cabrera, Marc. "Wearing His Father's 'Suit': Kinan Valdez Stages a Revival of 'Zoot Suit,' the Iconic Chicano-Themed Play Made Famous by His Father Luis Valdez." *Monterey County Herald.* July 20, 2007.

Cabrera, Nolan L., Jeffery F. Milem, and Ronald W. Marx. "An Empirical Analysis of the Effects of Mexican American Studies Participation on Student Achievement within Tucson Unified School District." UA College of Education, 20 June 2012: 1–19. Web. Nov. 29, 2012.

Cabrera, Nolan L., Elisa L. Meza, Andrea J. Romero, and Roberto C. Rodriguez. "'If There Is No Struggle, There Is No Progress': Transformative Youth Activism and the School of Ethnic Studies." *Urban Review: Issues and Ideas in Public Education* 45.1 (2013): 7–22.

Caminero-Santangelo, Marta. "Narrating the Non-Nation: Literary Journalism and 'Illegal' Border Crossings." *Arizona Quarterly* 68.3 (Aug. 2012): 157–76.

Campbell, Camilla. *Viva La Patria.* New York, Hill and Wang, 1970.

Cancerleo79. "Chicano! PBS Documentary: Quest for a Homeland." YouTube, 19 Sept. 2011. Sept. 26, 2011.

Cano-Murillo, Kathy. *Waking Up in the Land of Glitter.* New York: Grand Central Press, 2010.

Cantú, Norma Elia. *Canícula: Snapshots of a Girlhood en la Frontera.* Albuquerque: University of New Mexico Press, 1995.

Capella, David. "Kicking it Up Beyond the Casual: Fresh Perspectives in Young Adult Literature." *Studies in the Novel* 42.1-2 (Spring & Summer, 2010): 1–10.

Cárdenas, Leo and Nilo Santiago. *Return to Ramos.* New York, Hill and Wang, 1970.

Carpentier, Alejo. *El recurso del método.* La Habana: Editorial de Aete y Literatura, 1974.

——. *Reasons of State.* Trans. Frances Partridge. New York: Knopf, 1976.

Castañeda, O. S. *Remembering to Say "Mouth" or "Face."* Boulder: University of Colorado and Fiction Collective Two, 1993.

Castillo, Ana. *The Mixquiahuala Letters.* Binghamton, NY: Bilingual Press/Editorial Bilingüe, 1986.

——. *Sapogonia (An Anti-romance in 3/8 Meter).* Tempe: Bilingual Press/Editorial Bilingüe, 1990.

——. "Looking for Mambo in Little Italy." *Chicago Tribune* Aug. 30, 1996: 3.

——. *Peel My Love Like an Onion.* New York: Anchor Books, 2000.

——. *So Far from God.* 1993. New York: W.W. Norton, 2005.

Castillo-Speed, L., ed. *Latina: Women's Voices from the Borderlands.* New York: Touchstone Books, 1995.

Cepeda, María Elena. *Musical ImagiNation U.S.-Colombian Identity and the Latin Music Boom.* New York: New York University Press, 2010.

Chametzky, Jules. "Reflections on Multilingualism." In *Multilingual America: Transnationalism, Ethnicity, and the Languages of American Literature.* Ed. Werner Sollors. New York: New York University Press, 1998, pp. 348–50.

Chandra, Sarika. "Re-Producing a Nationalist Literature in the Age of Globalization: Reading (Im)migration in Julia Alvarez's *How the García Girls Lost Their Accents.*" *American Quarterly* 60.3 (2008): 829–50.

Chávez, César. *An Organizer's Tale: Speeches.* Ed. Ilan Stavans. New York: Penguin Group, 2008.

Chávez, Denise. *Face of an Angel.* New York: Warner, 1994.

——. "Denise Chávez: Chicana Woman Writer Crossing Borders: An Interview." Elizabeth Brown-Guillory. *South Central Review* 16.1 (Spring 1999): 30–43.

——. *Loving Pedro Infante.* New York: Simon & Schuster, 2001.

——. "'Carrying the Message': Denise Chávez on the Politics of Chicana Becoming." Interview with Marilyn Meham and AnaLouise Keating. *Aztlán* 26.1 (Spring 2001): 127–57.

Chávez Silverman, Susana. *Killer Crónicas: Bilingual Memories.* Madison: University of Wisconsin Press, 2004.

Chicano Communications Center. *450 Años Del Pueblo Chicano: 450 Years of Chicano History in Pictures.* Albuquerque, NM: Chicano Communications Center, 1976.

Chinchilla, M. *The Cha Cha Files: A Chapina Poética.* Korima Press, 2014.

Chinchilla, M. and K. Oliva-Alvarado, eds. *Desde el EpiCentro: An Anthology of US Central American Poetry.* Oakland: np, 2007.

Chocolate, Debbi. *El Barrio.* Illustrated by David Diaz. New York: Henry Holt, 2009.

Chomsky, Noam. *Manufacturing Consent: The Political Economy of Mass Media.* New York: Pantheon, 2002.

Christian, Karen. *Performing Identity in U.S. Latina/o Fiction.* Albuquerque: University of New Mexico Press, 1997.

Cisneros, Sandra. *The House on Mango Street.* New York: Vintage, 1989.

——. "Little Miracles, Kept Promises." In *Woman Hollering Creek and Other Stories.* New York: Random House, 1991.

——. *Hairs/Pelitos.* Illustrated by Terry Ybáñez. New York: Knopf/Dragonfly Press, 1994.

——. *Caramelo.* New York: Knopf, 2002.

Clark, William. "Immigration and Hispanic Middle Class." Center for Immigration Studies, 2001. http://cis.org/HispanicMiddleClass, accessed June 28, 2014.

Cohen, R. *Global Diaspora.* New York and London: Routledge, 2008.

Colato Laínez, R. *I am René, the boy/Yo soy René, el chico.* Houston, TX: Piñata Books, 2005.

——. *From North to South/Del Norte al Sur.* San Francisco, CA: Children's Book Press, 2010.

Colina, Sonia. "Syllable Structure." In *The Handbook of Hispanic Linguistics.* Eds. Hualde, José Ignacio, Antxon Olarrea, and Erin O'Rourke. Malden, MA/Oxford, UK: Wiley Blackwell, 2012, pp. 133–52.

Collier, Lorna. "YA Literature: Where Teens Go to Find Themselves." NCTE: *The Council Chronicle.* November, 2012, pp. 6–11.

Colón, David. "Other Latino Poetic Method." *Cultural Critique* 47 (Winter 2001): 265–86.

Colón, Edie. *Good-bye Havana! Hola, New York!* Illustrated by Raúl Colón. New York: Simon & Schuster, 2011.

Colón, Jesús. *A Puerto Rican in New York and Other Sketches.* New York: International Press, 1982.

Córdova, C. B. *The Salvadoran Americans.* Westport, CT: Greenwood Press, 2005.

Corona, Ignacio and Beth E. Jörgensen, eds. *The Contemporary Mexican Chronicle: Theoretical Perspectives on the Liminal Genre.* Albany: SUNY Press, 2002.

Coronado, Raúl. *A World Not to Come: A History of Latino Writing and Print Culture.* Cambridge, MA: Harvard University Press, 2013.

Coronel Urtecho, J. *Rápido tránsito (al ritmo de Norteamérica).* Managua: Editorial Nueva Nicaragua, 1985.

Corral, Eduardo C. *Slow Lightning.* New Haven: Yale University Press, 2012.

Cortez, B. *Estética del cinismo.* Guatemala: F&G Editores, 2009.

Cortez, Jaime. *Virgins, Guerrillas, and Locas: Gay Latinos Writing about Love.* San Francisco: Cleis Press, 1999.

Cortez, M. *Nostalgias y soledades.* San Salvador, ES: Editorial Clásicos Roxsil, 1995.

Cortina, Juan Nepomuceno. "Proclamation." In *Herencia: The Anthology of Hispanic Literature of the United States.* Ed. Nicolás Kanellos. New York: Oxford University Press, 2002, pp. 112–13.

Cowy Kim, K., Alfonso Serrano F., L. Ramos, and R. Rocamora, eds. *Izote Vos: A Collection of Salvadoran American Writing and Visual Art*. San Francisco: Pacific News Service, 2000.

Cruz, Angie. *Let It Rain Coffee*. New York: Simon & Schuster, 2005.

Cuadros, Gil. *City of God*. San Francisco: City Lights Publishers, 2001.

Culler, Jonathan. *Literary Theory: A Very Short Introduction*. Oxford; New York: Oxford University Press, 1997.

Culture Clash. "Anthems: Culture Clash in the District." *Culture Clash in America: Four Plays*. New York: Theatre Communications Group, 2003, pp. 151–220.

Cummings, Scott T. *Maria Irene Fornes*. New York: Routledge, 2012.

Cutter, Martha J. *Lost and Found in Translation: Contemporary Ethnic American Writing and the Politics of Language Diversity*. Chapel Hill: University of North Carolina, 2005.

——. "Malinche's Legacy: Translation, Betrayal, and Interlingualism in Chicano/a Literature." *Arizona Quarterly* 66.1 (2010): 1–33.

Dalleo, Raphael and Elena Machado Sáez. *Latina/o Canon and the Emergence of Post-Sixties Literature*. New York: Palgrave Macmillan, 2007.

Dalton, R. "Poema de Amor." In *Las historias prohibidas del Pulgarcito*. 1974. San Salvador: UCA Editores, 1992.

Damon, Maria and Ira Livingston, eds. *Poetry and Cultural Studies: A Reader*. Urbana: University of Illinois Press, 2009.

Danticat, Edwidge. *The Farming of Bones*. New York: Soho Press, 1998.

——. *The Dew Breaker*. New York: Knopf, 2004.

Darder, Antonia and Rodolfo Torres. "Mapping Latino Studies: Critical Reflections on Class and Social Theory." *Latino Studies* 1.2 (2003): 303–24.

Dario, Rubén. *Azul*. Madrid: Biblioteca Rubén Darío, 1927.

Davidson, Cathy N. *Now You See It: How The Brain Science of Attention Will Transform the Way We Live, Work, and Learn*. New York: Viking, 2011. Kindle Edition.

Dávila, Arlene M. *Latino Spin: Public Image and the Whitewashing of Race*. New York, NY: New York University Press, 2008.

Davis, Mike. *Magical Urbanism: Latinos Reinvent the U.S. Big City*. London: Verso, 2001.

de Castellanos, Juan. "Revolt of the Borinqueños". In *Borinquen: An Anthology of Puerto Rican Literature*. Eds. María Teresa Babín and Stan Steiner. New York: Vintage, 1974.

De Certeau, Michel. *The Practice of Everyday Life*. Trans. Steven Rendal. Berkeley: University of California Press, 1984.

De Jesús, Hernández-Gutiérrez and David William Foster, eds. *Literatura Chicana: 1965–1995 an Anthology in Spanish, English and Caló*. New York: Garland, 1997.

de la Guerra de Ord, Maria de las Angustais. "Occurrences in Hispanic California." In *Herencia*. Ed. Nicolás Kanellos. Oxford: Oxford University Press, 2002, pp. 95–100.

de la Peña, Matt. *Ball Don't Lie*. New York: Delacorte Press, 2005.

——. *Mexican Whiteboy*. New York, NY: Delacorte, 2008.

——. *A Nation's Hope: The Story of Boxing Legend Joe Louis*. New York: Dial Books, for Young Readers, 2011.

——. *Infinity Ring: Curse of the Ancients*. New York: Scholastic, 2013.

de las Casas, Fray Bartolomé. *The Devastation of the Indies*. Trans. Herma Briffault. Baltimore: Johns Hopkins University Press, 1992.

De la Selva, S. *Tropical Town and Other Poems*. Ed. S. Sirias. Houston: Arte Público Press, 1999.

de Magnon, Leonor Villegas. *The Rebel* [originally written in the 1920s]. Ed. Clara Lomas. Houston, TX: Arte Público Press, 1994.

de Treviño, Elizabeth Borton. *I, Juan de Pareja*. New York: Bell Books, 1965.

Demby, Gene. "When Our Kids Own America." *NPR: Code Switch*. 2014. Web. 1 June, 2014. http://apps.npr.org/codeswitch-changing-races/ (accessed June 26, 2014).

Derby, Lauren. *The Dictator's Seduction*. Durham: Duke University Press, 2009.

Derrida, Jacques. *Mémoires for Paul de Man*. Ed. Avital Ronell and Eduardo Cadava. Trans. Cecile Lindsay, Jonathan Culler, Eduardo Cadava. New York: Columbia University Press, 1986.

Detwiler, Louise and Janis Breckenridge, eds. *Pushing the Boundaries of Latin American Testimony*. New York: Palgrave Macmillan, 2012.

Díaz, Junot. *Drown*. New York: Riverhead Books, 1996.

——. *The Brief Wondrous Life of Oscar Wao*. New York: Riverhead Books, 2007.

——. *This Is How You Lose Her*. New York: Riverhead Books, 2012.

Diaz, Natalie. *When My Brother Was an Aztec*. Port Townsend, Wash.: Copper Canyon Press, 2012.

Dietz, James L. *Economic History of Puerto Rico: Institutional Change and Capitalist Development*. Princeton, NJ: Princeton University Press, 1986.

Di Iorio Sandín, Lyn and Richard Perez, eds. *Moments of Magical Realism in US Ethnic Literature: Meta-Morphoses and Migrations*. New York: Palgrave Macmillan, 2012.

Dinshaw, Carolyn. *Getting Medieval: Sexualities and Communities, Pre- and Postmodern*. Durham: Duke University Press, 1999.

Discovering Dominga. Dir. P. Flynn. San Francisco: Jaguar House Films, Independent Television Service, and KQED-TV, 2002.

Dorfman, Ariel. *Heading South, Looking North: A Bilingual Journey*. New York: Farrar, Straus, and Giroux, 1998.

——. *Exorcising Terror*. New York: Seven Stories Press, 2002.

——. "The Wandering Bigamists of Language." In *Lives in Translation: Bilingual Writers on Identity and Creativity*. Ed. Isabelle de Courtivron. New York: Palgrave Macmillan, 2003, pp. 29–37.

Dumas Lachtman, Ofelia. *Pepita Talks Twice/Pepita habla dos veces*. Illustrated by Alex Pardo DeLance. Houston, TX: Piñata Books, 1995.

Dussias, Paola E. "Spanish-English Code Mixing at the Auxiliary Phrase: Evidence from Eye-Movement Data." *Revista Internacional de Lingüística Iberoamericana* 1.2 (2003): 7–34.

Eire, Carlos. *Waiting for Snow in Havana*. New York: Free Press, 2010.

El lugar más pequeño/The Tiniest Place. Dir. T. Huezo. Mexico, DF: Centro de Capacitación Cinematográfica/OPROCINE (Fondo para la Producción Cinematográfico de Calidad), 2011.

Engel, P. *Vida*. New York: Black Cat, 2010.

Escobar, M. *Gritos interiors*. Los Angeles: Cuzcatlán Press, 2005.

——. *Paciente 1980*. Turlock, CA: Orbis Press, 2012.

Eskelinen, Markku. *Cybertext Poetics: The Critical Landscape of New Media Literary Theory*. New York: Continuum, 2012.

Espada, Martín. *Zapata's Disciple*. Cambridge, MA: South End Press, 1998.

Espinoza, A. *Still Water Saints*. New York: Random House, 2007.

Esquibel, Catrióna Rueda. *With Her Machete in Her Hand: Reading Chicana Lesbians*. Austin: University of Texas Press, 2006.

Fausset, Richard and Ken Belson. "Faces of an Immigration System Overwhelmed by Women and Children." *New York Times*. June 5, 2014. www.nytimes.com/2014/06/06/us/faces-of-an-immigration-system-overwhelmed-by-women-and-children.html (accessed June 26, 2014).

Feitlowitz, M. *A Lexicon of Terror*. New York: Oxford University Press, 1998.

Fernández, C. *Sleep of the Innocents*. Houston: Art Público Press, 1991.

Fernández, Ronald. *Los Macheteros: The Wells Fargo Robbery and the Violent Struggle for Puerto Rican Independence*. New York: Prentice Hall, 1987.

——. *The Disenchanted Island: Puerto Rico and the United States in the Twentieth Century*. 2nd edn. Westport, CT: Praeger Press, 1996.

Ferré, Rosario. *The House on the Lagoon*. New York: Farrar, Straus and Giroux, 1995.

Ferrer, Ada. *Insurgent Cuba: Race, Nation, and Revolution, 1868–1898*. Chapel Hill: University of North Carolina Press, 1999.

Finn, Ed. "Revenge of the Nerd: Junot Díaz and the Networks of American Literary Imagination." *Digital Humanities Quarterly* 7.1 (2013). Web. June 28, 2014.

Firmat, Gustavo Pérez. *Life on the hyphen: The Cuban-American way.* Austin: University of Texas Press, 2012.

Flores, Juan. "Latino Studies: New Contexts, New Concepts." *Harvard Educational Review* 67.2 (Summer 1997): 208–21.

Flores, Juan and Renato Rosaldo. "Editor's Foreword." In *A Companion to Latina/o Studies.* Eds. Juan Flores and Renato Rosaldo. Malden, MA: Blackwell Publishing, 2007, pp. xxi–xxvi.

Fornes, Maria Irene. *Plays.* Preface by Susan Sontag. New York: PAJ Press, 1986.

Foster, Ed and Bill Negron. *Tejanos.* New York, Hill and Wang, 1970.

Foster, Sesshu. *Atomik Aztex.* San Francisco: City Lights Books, 2005.

Frankson, Marie Stewart. "Chicano Literature for Young Adults: An Annotated Bibliography." *English Journal* 79.1 (Jan. 1990): 30–38.

Freire, Paulo. *Pedagogy of the Oppressed.* New York: Continuum, 1993.

———. "The Friend of Men." "On Behalf of Mankind." In *Herencia: The Anthology of Hispanic Literature of the United States.* Ed. Nicolás Kanellos. New York: Oxford University Press, 2002, pp. 511–17.

Frey, James. *A Million Little Pieces.* New York: N.A. Talese/Doubleday, 2003.

Frye, Northrop. *Anatomy of Criticism.* Princeton: Princeton University Press, 1957.

Galarza, Ernesto. *Barrio Boy.* Notre Dame, IN: University of Notre Dame Press, 1961.

Galindo, M. *Para Amaestrar un Tigre: Cuentos.* San Francisco: np, 2012.

Gallegos, Carlos. "Introduction: Migration and Movement(s) in Chicano/a Literature." *Arizona Quarterly* 70.2 (Summer 2014): 1–7.

Garcia, Alma M., ed. *Chicana Feminist Thought: The Basic Historical Writings.* New York: Routledge, 1997.

García, Cristina. *Dreaming in Cuban.* New York: Ballantine Books, 1992.

———. *A Handbook to Luck.* New York: Vintage, 2008a.

———. *I Wanna Be Your Shoebox.* New York: Simon & Schuster, 2008b.

———. *The Lady Matador's Hotel.* New York: Scribner, 2010.

———. *Dreams of Significant Girls.* New York: Simon & Schuster, 2011.

———. *King of Cuba.* New York: Scribner, 2013.

Garcia, Michael Nieto. *Autobiography in Black and Brown: Ethnic Identity in Richard Wright and Richard Rodriguez.* Albuquerque: University of New Mexico Press, 2014.

García Márquez, Gabriel. *Cien años de soledad.* Buenos Aires: Editorial Sudamericana, 1969.

———. *Autumn of the Patriarch.* Trans. Gregory Rabassa. New York: HarperPerennial, 1991.

Gardner-Chloros, P. "Sociolinguistic Factors in Code-Switching." In *The Cambridge Handbook of Linguistic Code-Switching.* Eds. Barbara E. Bullock and Almeida Jacqueline Toribio. Cambridge: Cambridge University Press, 2012, pp. 97–113.

Garoian, Charles R. *Performing Pedagogy: Toward an Art of Politics.* Albany: State University of New York Press, 1999.

———. *Ethno-Techno: Writings on Performance, Activism and Pedagogy.* Ed. Elaine A. Peña. New York: Routledge, 2005.

Garret, Peter. *Attitudes to Language.* New York: Cambridge University Press, 2010.

Gaspar de Alba, A., M. Herrera-Sobek, and D. Martínez, eds. *Three Times a Woman: Chicana Poetry.* Tempe: Bilingual Press/Editorial Bilingüe, 1989.

George, Brian. "Eshu and Ananse: Liberation by Subversive Knowledge." *Reality Sandwich.* N.P. 26 Aug. 2011. Web. Mar. 2014.

Giddens, Anthony. *Modernity and Self-Identity: Self and Society in the Late Modern Age.* Cambridge, UK: Polity Press, 1991.

Gilb, Dagoberto. *The Magic of Blood.* New Mexico: University of New Mexico Press, 1993.

———. *Gritos!* New York: Grove Press, 2003.

Gill, Lesley. *The School of the Americas: Military Training and Political Violence in the Americas.* Durham: Duke University Press, 2004.

Gilmore, Barry. "Worthy Texts: Who Decides?" *Educational Leadership* 68.6 (2011): 46–50.

Giménez Smith, Carmen. *Odalisque in Pieces.* Tucson: University of Arizona Press, 2009.

——. "Odalisque video." 2010. *YouTube.* Web. 28 June, 2014.

Girmay, Aracelis. *Kingdom Animalia.* Rochester: BOA, 2011.

Godayol, Pilar. "Malintzin/La Malinche/Doña Marina: Re-Reading the Myth of the Treacherous Translator." *Journal of Iberian & Latin American Studies* 18.1 (2012): 61–76.

Goldberg, Dana, ed. *On my Block: Stories and Paintings by Fifteen Artists.* San Francisco: Children's Book Press, 2007.

Golden, Renny and Michael McConnell. *Sanctuary: The New Underground Railroad.* Maryknoll, NY: Orbis Books, 1986.

Goldman, Francisco. *The Long Night of White Chickens.* New York: Atlantic Monthly Press, 1992.

——. *The Ordinary Seaman.* New York: Grove Press, 1997.

——. *The Divine Husband.* New York: Atlantic Monthly Press, 2004.

——. *The Art of Political Murder: Who Killed the Bishop?* New York: Grove, 2007.

——. *Say Her Name.* New York: Grove Press, 2011.

Gomez, Marga. "From *Marga Gomez Is Pretty, Witty and Gay.*" In *Out, Loud, and Laughing: A Collection of Gay and Lesbian Humor.* Ed. Charles Flowers. New York: Anchor Books, 1995.

——. "Excerpts from *Memory Tricks, Marga Gómez Is Pretty, Witty and Gay* and *A Line Around the Block.*" In *Contemporary Plays by Women of Color: An Anthology.* Eds. Kathy A. Perkins and Roberta Uno. London: Routledge, 1996, pp. 194–98.

——. *Hung like a fly.* Westlake Village, CA: Uproar Entertainment, 1997.

——. *jaywalker* (excerpts). *Extreme Exposure.* Ed. Jo Bonney. London: Nick Hern, 2000, pp. 367–70.

Gomez-Barris, Macarena. *Where Memory Dwells: Culture and State Violence in Chile.* Berkeley: University of California Press, 2008.

Gómez-Peña, Guillermo. *Dangerous Border Crossers: The Artist Talks Back.* London; New York: Routledge, 2000.

Gómez-Peña, Guillermo and Isaac Artenstein. *Border brujo.* New York: Third World Newsreel, 1991.

Gómez-Peña, Guillermo, Adrienne Jenik, Phillip Djwa, Roberto Sifuentes, and Rubén Martínez. *El Naftazteca cyber-Aztec TV for 2000 A.D.* Chicago, IL: Video Data Bank, 1995.

Gómez-Peña, Guillermo, Coco Fusco, Paula Heredia, and Daisy Wright, Dir. *The Couple in the Cage: A Guatinaui Odyssey.* New York: Third World Newsreel, 1993.

Gómez-Peña, Guillermo and Elaine Peña. *Ethno-techno: Writings on Performance, Activism, and Pedagogy.* New York: Routledge, 2005.

Gonzáles, Bill Johnson. "The Politics of Translation in Sandra Cisneros' *Caramelo.*" *Differences* 17.3 (2006): 3–19.

Gonzales, Manuel. *The Miniature Wife.* New York: Riverhead, 2013.

Gonzáles, María Dolores. "Crossing Social and Cultural Borders: The Road to Language Hybridity." In *Speaking Chicana: Voice, Power and Identity.* Eds. Letticia Delma and María Dolores Gonzáles. Tucson: University of Arizona Press, 1999.

Gonzales, O. *Central America in My Heart.* Tempe: Bilingual Press/Editorial Bilingüe, 2007.

González, Rigoberto. *Antonio's Card/La tarjeta del Antonio.* San Francisco, CA: Children's Book Press, 2005.

Gonzales, Rodolfo "Corky." "I Am Joaquín." In *The Norton Anthology of Latino Literature.* Ed. Ilan Stavans. New York: Norton, 2010.

Gonzales Bertrand, Diane. *Sweet Fifteen.* Houston, TX: Piñata, 1995.

González, J. *Harvest of Empire.* New York: Viking, 2000.

González, José Luis. "The Night We Became a People Again". In *The Norton Anthology of Latino Literature.* Ed. Ilan Stavans. New York: Norton, 2010.

González, Rigoberto. *Butterfly Boy*. Madison: University of Wisconsin Press, 2011.

González Echevarría, Roberto. "Is 'Spanglish' a Language?" *New York Times*. 28 Mar. 1997. Web. 19 Aug. 2014.

Grande, Reyna. *The Distance Between Us: A Memoir*. New York: Atria, 2012.

Grim, Jessica and Allison Gallagher. "The iPad Loaner Program at Oberlin College Library." In *No Shelf Required 2: Use and Management of Electronic Books*, Ed. Sue Polanka. Chicago: American Library Association, 2012.

Grimes, Nikki. *Oh, Brother!* Illustrated by Mike Benny. Greenwillow Books, 2008.

Grise, Virginia and Irma Mayorga. *The Panza Monologues*. Austin: University of Texas Press, 2014.

Grosjean, François. *Life with Two Languages*. Cambridge, MA: Cambridge University Press, 1982.

Guerra, Erasmo. *Latin Lovers: True Stories of Men in Love*. New York: Painted Leaf Press, 1999.

Gumperz, John J. *Discourse Strategies*. New York: Cambridge University Press, 1982.

Gutiérrez, David G., ed. *The Columbia History of Latinos in the United States Since 1960*. New York, NY: Columbia University Press, 2004.

Gutiérrez y Muhs, Gabriella. *Rebozos De Palabras: An Helena María Viramontes Critical Reader*. Tucson: University of Arizona Press, 2013.

Hale, Dorothy. "Introduction." In *The Novel: An Anthology of Criticism and Theory, 1900–2000*. Malden, MA: Blackwell, 2006.

Hames-García, Michael "Dr. Gonzo's Carnival: The Testimonial Satires of Oscar 'Zeta' Acosta," *American Literature* 72.3 (2000): 463–93.

Hamilton, N. and N. Stoltz Chinchilla. *Seeking Community in a Global City: Guatemalans and Salvadorans in Los Angeles*. Philadelphia: Temple University Press, 2001.

Hanna, Monica. "Chronicling the New Transnational Migrant Experience: An Interview with Daniel Hernandez." *Label Me Latina/o* 4 (Spring 2014). http://labelmelatin.com/wp-content/uploads/2014/02/Chronicling-the-New-Transnational-Migrant-Experience-An-Interview-with-Daniel-Hernandez.pdf (accessed May 3, 2014).

——. "In the Stacks" with a Book in Their Hand: Chicano Readers and Readerships across the Centuries. Ed. Manuel M. Martín-Rodríguez. Albuquerque: University New Mexico Press, 2014.

Harris, Joel Chandler. "Mr. Rabbit Grossly Deceives Mr. Fox," *Uncle Remus Stories. Course Packet*. Comp. Nan Tynberg. Palm Desert: CSUSB, 2004, pp. 1–2.

Hayes, Terrance. *Lighthead*. New York, NY: Penguin Books, 2010.

Hayes-Bautista, D. E., C. L. Chamberlin, and N. Zuniga. "A Gold Rush Salvadoran in California's Latino World, 1857." *Southern California Quarterly* 91.3 (2009): 257–94.

Hayles, N. Katherine. *Electronic Literature: New Horizons for the Literary*. Notre Dame: University of Notre Dame Press, 2008.

Hedrick, Tace. "From *House on Mango Street* to *Becoming Latina*." *La Nueva Literatura Hispánica* 15.11 (Spring 2011): 87–114.

——. *Chica Lit: Popular Latina Fiction and Americanization in the Twenty-first Century*. Pittsburgh: University of Pittsburgh Press, 2015.

Henríquez, C. *Come Together, Fall Apart: A Novella and Stories*. New York: Riverhead Books/Penguin Group, 2006.

——. *The World in Half*. New York: Riverhead Books/Penguin Group, 2009.

——. *The Book of Unknown Americans*. New York: Knopf, 2014.

Heredia, José María. "Hymn of the Exile." In *Herencia: The Anthology of Hispanic Literature of the United States*. Ed. Nicolás Kanellos. New York: Oxford University Press, 2002, pp. 545–48.

——. "Ode to Niagara." In *The Norton Anthology of Latino Literature*. Ed. Ilan Stavans. New York: Norton, 2010.

Heredia, Juanita. *Transnational Latina Narratives in the Twenty-First Century: The Politics of Gender, Race, and Migrations*. New York: Palgrave Macmillan, 2009.

Hernandez, Daniel. *Down & Delirious in Mexico City: The Aztec Metropolis in the Twenty-First Century.* New York: Scribner, 2011.

Hernández-Linares, L. *Razor Edges of My Tongue.* San Diego: Calaca Press, 2002.

——. *Mucha Muchacha.* San Francisco: San Francisco Arts Commission, 2010. CD.

Herndon, April. "Disparate but Disabled: Fat Embodiment and Disability Studies." In *Feminist Disability Studies.* Ed. K. Q. Hall. Bloomington: Indiana University Press, 2011.

Herrera, J. F. *Calling the Doves/El canto de las palomas.* San Francisco, CA: Children's Book Press, 1997.

——. *Crashboomlove: A Novel in Verse.* Albuquerque: University of New Mexico Press, 1999.

——. *Upside Down Boy/El niño de cabeza.* San Francisco, CA: Children's Book Press, 2000.

——. *Cinnamon Girl: Letters Found Inside a Cereal Box,* New York: Joanna Cotler Books, 2005.

Herrera-Sobek, María and Helena María Viramontes, eds. *Chicana Creativity and Criticism: Charting New Frontiers in American Literature.* Houston: Arte Público, 1988.

——, eds. *Chicana (W)Rites on Word and Film.* Berkeley: Third Woman, 1995.

Herz, Sarah K. and Donald R. Gallo. *From Hinton to Hamlet: Building Bridges between Young Adult Literature and the Classics.* Westport, CT: Greenwood Press, 2005.

Hijuelos, Oscar. *Dark Dude.* New York: Atheneum Books for Young Readers, 2008.

Hinton, Susan E. *The Outsiders.* [1967] New York: Penguin, 2012.

Hintz, Carrie and Eric L. Tribunella. *Reading Children's Literature: A Critical Introduction.* Boston: Bedford/St. Martin's, 2013.

Hirsch, Marianne. *The Generation of Postmemory: Writing and Visual Culture After the Holocaust.* New York: Columbia University Press, 2012.

hooks, bell. *Teaching to Transgress: Education as the Practice of Freedom.* New York, NY: Routledge, 1994.

——. *Feminist Theory: From Margin to Center.* London: Pluto Press, 2000. www.youtube.com/watch?v=isPFm9A_xRM (accessed 12 June, 2014).

Horkheimer, Max, and Theodor W. Adorno. "The Culture Industry: Enlightenment as Mass Deception." In *Dialectic of Enlightenment: Philosophical Fragments.* Ed. Gunzelin Schmid Noerr. Stanford: Stanford University Press, 2002.

Hualde, José Ignacio. "Stress and Rhythm." In *The Handbook of Hispanic Linguistics.* Ed. Hualde, José Ignacio, Antxon Olarrea, and Erin O'Rourke. Malden, MA/Oxford UK: Wiley Blackwell, 2012, pp. 153–72.

Huerta, Jorge. "Introduction." In *Zoot Suit and Other Plays.* Luis Valdez. Houston: Arte Público Press, 1992.

——. "Luis Valdez: Overview." *Contemporary Dramatists,* 5th edn. London: St. James Press, 1993.

Hughes-Hassell, Sandra. "Multicultural Literature as a Form of Counter-Storytelling." *The Library Quarterly* 83.3 (July 2013): 212–228.

Hurt, Erin. "Trading Cultural Baggage for Gucci Luggage: The Ambivalent Latinidad of Alisa Valdes-Rodriguez's *The Dirty Girls Social Club.*" *MELUS* 34.3, Racial Desire(s) (Fall 2009): 133–53.

iBooks *James Joyce's Digital Dubliners: For Students By Students: A Multimedia Edition,* June, 2014.

Illich, Ivan. *Deschooling Society.* London, UK: Marion Boyars Publishers, 1971.

Innocent Voices/Voces inocentes. Dir. L. Mandoki. Twentieth Century Fox Home Entertainment, 2005.

Irizarry, Ylce. "An Interview with Cristina García." *Contemporary Literature* 48.2 (2007): 175–94.

Islas, Arturo. *American Dreams and Fantasies.* Stanford Special Collections. Box 12, Folder 1. Approximately 1975.

——. *Day of the Dead/Día de los Muertos.* Stanford Special Collections. Box 13, Folder 1. Approximately 1975.

——. *Migrant Souls.* New York: Morrow, 1990.

——. *La Mollie and the King of Tears: A Novel.* University of New Mexico Press, 1996.

——. *The Rain God.* 1984. New York: Perennial, 2003.

Jacobus, Lee A., ed. *The Bedford Introduction to Drama*, 6th edn. Boston: Bedford/ St. Martin's, 2009.

Jakobson, Roman. *Language in Literature.* Cambridge: Harvard University Press, 1990.

Jay, Paul. *Global Matters: The Transnational Turn in Literary Studies.* Ithaca: Cornell University Press, 2010.

Jenkins, Henry, Sam Ford, and Joshua Green. *Spreadable Media: Creating Value and Meaning in a Networked Culture.* New York: New York University Press, 2013.

Jiménez, Francisco. *The Circuit.* Albuquerque, NM: University of New Mexico Press, 1997.

——. *Breaking Through.* Boston: Houghton Mifflin, 2001.

——. *Reaching Out.* Boston: Houghton Mifflin, 2008.

Johannessen, Lene M. *Threshold Time: Passage of Crisis in Chicano Literature.* New York: Rodopi Press, 2008.

Johnson, Fern. *Speaking Culturally: Language Diversity in the United States.* London: Sage Publications, 2000.

Johnston, Tony. *Uncle Rain Cloud.* Illustrated by Fabricio VandenBroek. Watertown, MA: Charlesbridge, 2001.

Joya, D. *Sueños de un callejero.* San Salvador: Editorial Nuevo Enfoque, 2003.

Joyce, James. *Ulysses.* 1922. New York: Random House, 1986.

Kafer, A. *Feminist, Queer, Crip.* Bloomington: Indiana University Press, 2013.

Kanellos, Nicolás. "Two Centuries of Spanish Theatre in the Southwest." In *Mexican-American Theatre: Then & Now.* Ed. Nicolás Kanellos. Houston, TX: Arte Público, 1983, pp. 17–36.

——. *A History of Hispanic Theatre in the United States: Origins to 1940.* Austin: University of Texas Press, 1990.

Kanellos, Nicolás, ed. *Herencia: The Anthology of Hispanic Literature of the United States.* New York: Oxford University Press, 2002.

Keating, AnaLouise, ed. *Interviews/Entrevistas.* New York: Routledge, 2000.

Kerouac, Jack. *On the Road.* Amplified Edition. New York: Penguin Books, 2011.

Kingston, Maxine Hong. *The Woman Warrior.* New York: Vintage Books, 1989.

Korrol, Virginia Sánchez. *From Colonia to Community: The History of Puerto Ricans in New York City.* Berkeley: University of California Press, 1994.

Kropotkin, Peter. *Fields, Factories, and Workshops.* 1912/rpt. 1993. New Brunswick, NJ: Transaction, 1971.

Kutas, Marta, Eva Moreno, and Nicole Wicha. "Code-Switching and the Brain." In *The Cambridge Handbook of Linguistic Code-Switching.* Eds. Barbara E. Bullock and Almeida Jacqueline Toribio. Cambridge: Cambridge University Press, 2012, pp. 270–88.

La Fountain-Stokes, Lawrence. *Queer Ricans: Cultures and Sexualities in the Diaspora.* Minneapolis: University of Minnesota Press, 2009.

Lafourcade, Enrique. *La fiesta del rey acab.* Santiago: Del Pacífico, 1959.

——. *King Arab's Feast.* New York: St. Martin's Press, 1963.

Lalo, Eduardo. *Simone.* Buenos Aires: Ediciones Corregidor, 2012.

Lambert, Wallace, Richard Hodgson, Robert Gardner, and Samuel Fillenbaum. "Evaluational Reactions to Spoken Languages." *Journal of Abnormal and Social Psychology* 60.1 (1960): 44–51.

Landt, Susan M. "Multicultural Literature and Young Adolescents: A Kaleidoscope of Opportunity." *Journal of Adolescent & Adult Literacy* 49:8 (May 2006): 690–97.

Larrick, Nancy. "The All-White World of Children's Books." *The Saturday Review* 11 (September 1965): 63–65.

Latina Feminist Group. *Telling to Live: Latina Feminist Testimonios.* Durham, NC: Duke University Press, 2001.

Leguizamo, John. *Mambo Mouth: A Savage Comedy.* New York: Bantam Books, 1993.

——. *Spic-o-rama: A Dysfunctional Comedy.* New York: Bantam Books, 1994.

——. *The Works of John Leguizamo*. New York: Harper, 2008.

Leguizamo, John, Thomas Schlamme, Jeff Ross, and Martin Bregman. *Mambo Mouth*. [S.l.]: Island Visual Arts, 1992.

Lejeune, Philippe. *On Autobiography*. Ed. and foreword by Paul John Eakin. Trans. Katherine Leary. Minneapolis: University of Minnesota Press, 1989.

Leland, Christine, Mitzie Lewison, and Jerome Harste. *Teaching Children's Literature: It's Critical*. New York: Routledge, 2013.

Lemus, Felicia Luna. *Trace Elements of Random Tea Parties*. New York: Farrar, Straus, and Giroux, 2004.

——. *Like Son: A Novel*. New York: Akashic Books, 2007.

Lengel, Kerry. "Hot Chica Lit Takes a Sassy Style to Look at Latina Life." *Hispanic Trending: Documenting Latino's Imprint in America*. 18 May 2006. Online. 28 Dec. 2012.

León-Portilla, M. *The Broken Spears: The Aztec Account of the Conquest of Mexico*. Trans. Lysander Kemp. Boston: Beacon Press, 1966.

Levander, Caroline F. and Robert S. Levine. *Hemispheric American Studies: Essays Beyond the Nation*. New Brunswick: Rutgers University Press, 2007.

Levi-Strauss, Claude. "The Structural Study of Myth." In *Structural Anthropology*. Trans. Claire Jacobson and Brooke Grundfest Schoepf. New York: Basic, 1963.

Levins Morales, A. "Class Poem." In *Getting Home Alive*. Eds. A. Levins Morales and R. Morales. Ann Arbor, MI: Firebrand Books, 1986.

Lievrouw, Leah. *Alternative and Activist New Media*. Cambridge: Polity, 2011.

Limón, Graciela. *In Search of Bernabé*. Houston, TX: Arte Público, 1993.

López, Alfred J. *José Martí: A Revolutionary Life*. Austin: University of Texas Press, 2014.

López, Ana. *Growing Up Chicana/o: An Anthology*. New York: W.W. Norton, 1993.

——. "Maria Irene Fornes, *The Conduct of Life*." In *Reading U.S. Latina Writers: Remapping American Literature*. Ed. Alvina Quintana. New York: Palgrave Macmillan, 2003, pp. 77–89.

Lovelady, Stephanie. "Walking Backwards: Chronology, Immigration, and Coming of Age in *My Ántonia* and *How the García Girls Lost Their Accents*." *Modern Language Studies* 35.1 (2005): 28–37.

Loya, Joe. *The Man Who Outgrew his Prison Cell: Confessions of a Bank Robber*. New York: Rayo, 2004.

Lucas, Ashley. "Reinventing the *Pachuco*: The Radical Transformation from the Criminalized to the Heroic in Luis Valdez's Play *Zoot Suit*." *Journal for the Study of Radicalism* 3:1 (2009): 61–87.

Luis, William. "A Search for Identity in Julia Alvarez's *How the García Girls Lost Their Accents*." *Callaloo* 43.3 (2000): 839–49.

Mandiberg, Michael, ed. *The Social Media Reader*. New York: New York University Press, 2012.

Mann, Charles C. *1491: New Revelations of the Americas Before Columbus*. New York: Vintage Books, 2006.

Markus, Hazel R. and Paula M. L. Moya. "Doing Race: An Introduction." *Doing Race: 21 Essays for the 21st Century*. Eds. H. R. Markus and P. M. L. Moya. New York: W. W. Norton, 2010.

Mármol, J. *Amalia*. La Habana: Casa de las Américas, 1976.

Marqués, René. "The Oxcart". In *The Norton Anthology of Latino Literature*. Ed. Ilan Stavans. New York: Norton, 2010.

Márquez, Roberto, ed. and trans. *Puerto Rican Poetry: An Anthology from Aboriginal to Contemporary Times*. Amherst and Boston, MA: University of Massachusetts Press, 2007.

Martel, Cruz. Pictures by Jerry Pinkey. *Yagua Days*. Orlando: Dial Books, 1976.

Martí, José. *Free Verses*. In *José Martí: Selected Writings*. Eds. Esther Allen and Roberto González Echevarría. New York: Penguin Books, 2002: 56–68.

——. "Letters from New York" In *José Martí: Selected Writings*. Eds. Esther Allen and Roberto González Echevarría. New York: Penguin Books, 2002. 89–244.

——. "Simple Verses." In *Herencia: The Anthology of Hispanic Literature of the United States.* Ed. Nicolás Kanellos. New York: Oxford University Press, 2002, pp. 575–77.

——. *Versos sencillos.* Trans. Anne Fountain. Jefferson, N.C.: McFarland & Co., 2005.

——. *Ismaelillo.* Trans. Tyler Fisher. [1882] San Antonio: Wings Press, 2007.

——. "Nuestra America" ["Our America"]. Trans. Esther Allen. In *The Norton Anthology of Latino Literature.* Ed. Ilan Stavans. New York: Norton, 2010.

Martín Alcoff, Linda. "Puerto Rican Studies in a German Philosophy Context: An Interview with Juan Flores." *Nepantla: Views from South* 4.1 (2003): 139–46.

Martín-Rodríguez, Manuel M. *Life in Search of Readers: Reading (in) Chicano/a Literature.* Albuquerque: University of New Mexico Press, 2003.

Martínez, Demetria. "Turning." *Three Times a Woman: Chicana Poetry.* Eds. A. Gaspar de Alba, M. Herrera-Sobek, and D. Martínez. Tempe: Bilingual Press/Editorial Bilingüe, 1989, pp. 101–56.

——. *Mother Tongue.* New York: One World Books, 1994.

Martínez, Rubén. *Crossing Over: A Mexican Family on the Migrant Trail.* New York: Picador, 2001.

Martínez Victor. *Parrot in the Oven: Mi Vida.* New York: HarperCollins Publishers, 1996.

Mayock, Ellen C. "The Bicultural Construction of Self in Cisneros, Alvarez, and Santiago." *Bilingual Review* 23.3 (1998): 223–29.

McCall, Leslie. "The Complexity of Intersectionality." *Signs* 30.3 (Spring 2005): 1771–1800.

McCarthy, Cormac. *All the Pretty Horses.* New York: Knopf, 1992.

McCracken, Ellen. "Postmodern Ethnicity in Sandra Cisneros' *Caramelo*: Hybridity, Spectacle, and Memory in the Nomadic Text." *Journal of American Studies of Turkey* 12 (Fall 2000): np.

McGurl, Mark. *The Program Era: Postwar Fiction and the Rise of Creative Writing.* Cambridge: Harvard University Press, 2009.

McPeek Villatoro, M. *A Fire in the Earth.* Houston: Arte Público Press, 1996.

——. *Home Killings: A Romilia Chacón Novel.* New York: Bantam Dell/Random House, 2001.

——. *Minos: A Romilia Chacón Novel.* New York: Bantam Dell/Random House, 2003.

——. *A Venom Beneath the Skin: A Romilia Chacón Novel.* Boston: Kate's Mystery Books/Justin, Charles & Co. Press, 2005

——. *Blood Daughters: A Romilia Chacón Novel.* Pasadena: Red Hen Press, 2011.

Medina, Cruz. "The Family Profession." *CCC* 65:1 (Sept. 2013): 34–36.

——. "Nuestros Refranes: Culturally Relevant Writing in Tucson High Schools." *Reflections: A Journal of Public Rhetoric, Civic Writing, and Service Learning* 12.3 (2013): 52–79.

Men with Guns. Dir. J. Sayles. Sony Pictures, 1997.

Mena, María C. and Amy Doherty. *The Collected Stories of María Cristina Mena.* Houston, TX: Arte Público Press, 1997.

Menchú, R. *I, Rigoberta Menchú: An Indian Woman in Guatemala.* Ed. Elisabeth Burgos-Debray. Trans. Ann Wright. London: Verso, 1984.

Mendoza, S. N. *America Is My Home: A Guatemalan Emigrant's Story.* Pittsburgh: Dorrance Press, 2007.

Menjívar, C. *Fragmented Ties: Salvadoran Immigrant Networks in America.* Berkeley and Los Angeles: University of California Press, 2000.

——. "Immigrant Art as Liminal Expression: The Case of Central Americans." In *Art in the Lives of Immigrant Communities in the United States.* Ed. P. Dimaggio and P. Fernandez-Kelly. New Brunswick: Rutgers University Press, 2010, pp. 176–96.

Meyer, Michael. *Poetry: An Introduction.* Boston: Bedford/St. Martin's, 2001.

Middleton, Peter. *Distant Reading: Performance, Readership, and Consumption in Contemporary Poetry.* Tuscaloosa: University of Alabama Press, 2005.

Mignolo, Walter. *Local Histories, Global Designs: Coloniality, Subaltern Knowledges, and Border Thinking.* New Jersey: Princeton University Press, 2000.

Miller, Silvia K. "Enhanced eBooks." In *No Shelf Required 2: Use and Management of Electronic Books,* Ed. Sue Polanka. Chicago: American Library Association, 2012, pp. 115–26.

Milroy, James. "The Ideology of Standard Language." In *The Routledge Companion to Socio-linguistics*. Ed. Carmen Llamas, Louise Mullany, and Peter Stockwell. London: Routledge, 2007, pp. 133–39.

Minich, J. A. *Accessible Citizenships: Disability, Nation, and the Cultural Politics of Greater Mexico*. Philadelphia: Temple University Press, 2014.

Mitchell, David T. "National Families and Familial nations: Communista Americans in Cristina García's *Dreaming in Cuban*." *Tulsa Studies in Women's Literature* 15.1 (1996): 51–60.

Mohr, N. *Nilda*. Houston, TX: Arte Público Press, 1973.

——. *Bronx Remembered*. New York: Harper & Row, 1975.

Monge, V. *Pasajeros en el tiempo/Passengers in Time*. Lawrence, MA: Cambridge BrickHouse, 2006.

Monsiváis, Carlos. *Mexican Postcards*. Trans. and intro. John Kraniauskas. London: Verso, 1997.

——. *A ustedes les consta. Antología de la crónica en México*. 2nd edn. Mexico, DF: Era, 2006.

Montejo, V. *Voices from Exile: Violence and Survival in Modern Maya History*. Norman: University of Oklahoma Press, 1999.

Montes-Alcalá, C. "Hispanics in the United States: More than *Spanglish*." *Camino Real* 1 (2009): 97–115.

Montoya, A. *The Ice Worker Sings and Other Poems*. Tempe, AZ: Bilingual Press/Editorial Bilingüe, 1999.

Mora, Pat. *House of Houses*. Boston: Beacon, 1997a.

——. *Tomás and the Library Lady*. Illustrated by Raul Colón. New York: Knopf, 1997b.

——. Interview with Maria-Antónia Oliver-Rotger. *Voices from the Gaps*. University of Minnesota. May and June 1999. 20 July, 2014.

——. *A Library for Sor Juana*. New York: Alfred A. Knopf/Random House, 2002.

Moraga, Cherríe, *Loving in the War Years: lo que nunca pasó por sus labios*. 1983. Cambridge, MA: South End Press, 2000.

——. "A long line of vendidas". In *Loving in the War Years: Lo que nunca pasó por sus labios*. Boston: South End Press, 1983.

——. "Art in América con Acento." In *Negotiating Performance: Gender, Sexuality and Theatricality in Latino America*. Eds. Diana Taylor and Juan Villegas. Durham, NC: Duke University Press, 1994a, p. 32.

——. *Giving Up the Ghost*. Albuquerque: West End Press, 1994b.

——. "Art in América con Acento." In *Latina: Women's Voices from the Borderlands*. Ed. L. Castillo-Speed. New York: Touchstone Books, 1995, pp. 211–20.

——. "City of Desire." Interview by Bridget A. Kevane and Juanita Heredia. In *Latina Self-Portraits: Interviews with Contemporary Women Writers*. Eds. Bridget A. Kevane and Juanita Heredia. Albuquerque: University of New Mexico Press, 2000.

——. *A Xicana Codex of Changing Consciousness: Writings, 2000–2010*. Durham: Duke University Press, 2011.

——. Interview by Maria-Antónia Oliver-Rotger. *Voices from the Gaps*. University of Minnesota. Jan 2000. Web. 18 July, 2014.

Moraga, Cherríe, and Gloria Anzaldúa. *This Bridge Called My Back: Writings by Radical Women of Color*. 1981. New York: Kitchen Table/Women of Color Press, 1983.

——. *This Bridge Called My Back: Writings by Radical Women of Color*. 3rd edn. Berkeley: Third Woman, 2001.

Morales, Ed. *Living in Spanglish*. New York: LA Weekly Books/St. Martin's Press, 2002.

Morgensen, Scott Lauria. "Unsettling Queer Politics: What Can Non Natives Learn from Two-Spirit Organizing." In *Queer Indigenous Studies: Critical Interventions in Theory, Politics and Literature*. Tucson: University of Arizona Press, 2011, pp. 132–52.

Moroff, Diane Lynn. *Fornes: Theater in the Present Tense*. Ann Arbor: University of Michigan Press, 1997.

Morrison, Toni. *Sula*. New York: Penguin Books, 1982.

——. *Beloved: A Novel.* New York: Knopf, 1987.

Moya, Paula M. L. "Reading as a Realist: Expanded Literacy in Helena Maria Viramontes' *Under the Feet of Jesus.*" In *Learning from Experience: Minority Identities, Multicultural Struggles.* Berkeley: University of California Press, 2002, pp. 175–214.

——. "What's Identity Got to Do With It? Mobilizing Identities in the Multicultural Classroom." In *Identity Politics Reconsidered.* Eds. L. M. Alcoff, M. Hames-García, S. P. Mohanty, and P. M. L. Moya. New York: Palgrave Macmillan, 2006, pp. 96-117.

——. "Another Way to Be: Women of Color, Literature, and Myth." In *Doing Race: 21 Essays for the 21st Century.* Eds. Hazel Rose Markus and Paula M. L. Moya. New York: W. W. Norton, 2010, pp. 483–508.

Moya, Paula M. L. and Ramón Saldívar. "Fictions of the Trans-American Imaginary." *Modern Fiction Studies* 49.1 (Spring 2003): 1–18.

Mujcinovic, Fatima. "Multiple Articulations of Exile in US Latina Literature: Confronting Exilic Absence and Trauma." *MELUS* 28.4 (2003): 167–86.

Mundel, Ingrid. "Performing (R) evolution: The Story of El Teatro Campesino." *Postcolonial Text* 3.1 (2007): 1–16.

Muñoz, Carlos. *Youth, Identity, Power: The Chicano Movement.* New York: Verso, 1989.

Muñoz, José Esteban. *Disidentifications: Queers of Color and Performance of Politics.* Minneapolis: University of Minnesota Press, 1999.

——. "Feeling Brown: Ricardo Bracho's *The Sweetest Hangover and Other STDs.*" In *Gay Latino Studies.* Eds. Michael Hames-Garcia and Ernesto Martinez. Durham: Duke University Press, 2010, pp. 204–19.

Muñoz, Manuel. *Zigzagger.* Evanston, IL: Northwestern University Press, 2003.

——. *The Faith Healer of Olive Avenue.* Chapel Hill, NC: Algonquin Books of Chapel Hill, 2007.

——. *What You See in the Dark.* Chapel Hill, NC: Algonquin Books of Chapel Hill, 2011.

Muñoz Ryan, Pam. *Esperanza Rising.* New York: Scholastic, 2000.

——. *The Dreamer.* New York: Scholastic, 2010.

Murguía, A. *Southern Front.* Tempe: Bilingual Press/Editorial Bilingüe, 1990.

——. "Concordia: The San Francisco Bay Area in Central American Literature." Paper presented at the First Annual Conference on Central American Literatures and Cultures, Arizona State University, Tempe, 1999.

My Family/Mi familia. Dir. G. Nava. New Line Home Video/Turner Home Entertainment, 1995.

Nance, Kimberly A. "'Something that Might Resemble a Call': Testimonial Theory and Practice in the Twenty-First Century." In *Pushing the Boundaries of Latin American Testimony: Metamorphoses and Migrations.* Eds. Louise Detwiler and Janis Breckenridge. New York: Palgrave Macmillan, 2012.

Nazario, Sonia. *Enrique's Journey: The Story of a Boy's Dangerous Odyssey to Reunite with His Mother.* New York: Random House, 2006.

Nelson, D. *El regreso de una wetback: Novela testimonial.* Tegucigalpa: Ediciones Guardabarranco, 2006.

Nericcio, William. *Tex[t]-Mex: Seductive Hallucinations of the "Mexican" in American.* Austin, TX: University of Texas Press, 2007.

Nesbit, Tom. "Class and Teaching." In *Class Concerns: Adult Education and Social Class.* Jossey-Bass, New Directions for Adult and Continuing Education, Number 106, 2005, pp. 15–24.

Nieves, Myrna, ed. *Breaking Ground: Anthology of Puerto Rican Women Writers in New York 1980–2012/Abriendo Caminos: Antología de escritoras puertorriqueñas en Nueva York.* New York: Editorial Campana, 2012.

Niggli, Josefina. *Mexican Folk Plays.* Chapel Hill: University of North Carolina Press, 1938.

——. *The Plays of Josefina Niggli: Recovered Landmarks of Latino Literature.* Eds. William Orchard and Yolanda Padilla. Madison: University of Wisconsin Press, 2007.

——. *Josefina Niggli's Mexican Village and Other Works.* Ed. Ilan Stavans. Evanston, IL: Northwestern University Press, 2008.

Noel, Urayoán. *In Visible Movement: Nuyorican Poetry from the Sixties to Slam*. Iowa City, IA: University of Iowa Press, 2014.

NPR. "The Latino Experience in Appalachia." 14 Apr. 2014. Web. 1 May, 2014.

Obejas, Achy. *We came all the way from Cuba so you could dress like this?* San Francisco: Cleis Press, 1994.

——. "Above all, a Family Man." 1994. http://isites.harvard.edu/fs/docs/icb.topic868218.files/Obejas.pdf (accessed June 21, 2014).

——. *Memory Mambo*. Pittsburgh, PA: Cleis Press, 1996.

OED. "criss-cross, v." *OED Online*. Oxford University Press, June 2014. Web. July 2, 2014.

OED. "trans-, prefix." *OED Online*. Oxford University Press, June 2014. Web. July 2, 2014.

OED. "translate, v." *OED Online*. Oxford University Press, June 2014. Web. July 2, 2014.

Oliva-Alvarado, K. *Transverse: Altar de Tierra, Altar de Sol*. Los Angeles: Izote Press, 2009.

Olivas, Daniel. *Benjamin and the Word*. Houston, TX: Piñata Books, 2005.

Olmos, M. *Caminantes de maíz: Una historia guanaca*. Los Angeles: Ediciones M.O. Promotions, 1998.

Orchard, Bill and Yolanda Padilla, eds. *The Plays of Josefina Niggli: Recovered Landmarks of Latino Literature*. Madison: University of Wisconsin Press, 2007.

O'Reilly Herrera, Andrea. "Women and the Revolution in Cristina García's *Dreaming in Cuban*." *Modern Language Studies* 27.3/4 (1997): 69–91.

O'Rourke, Erin. "Intonation in Spanish." In *The Handbook of Hispanic Linguistics*. Ed. Hualde, José Ignacio, Antxon Olarrea, and Erin O'Rourke. Malden, MA/Oxford UK: Wiley Blackwell, 2012, pp. 173–92.

Ortiz Cofer, Judith. *Silent Dancing: A Partial Remembrance of a Puerto Rican Childhood*. Houston, TX: Arte Público Press, 1990.

——. *The Latin Deli: Prose and Poetry*. Athens: University of Georgia Press, 1993.

——. *An Island Like You: Stories from the Barrio*. New York: Puffin, 1995.

——. *The Meaning of Consuelo*. New York: Farrar, Straus, and Giroux, 2003.

——. *Call Me María: A novel in letters, poems, and prose*. New York: Scholastic, 2004.

——. *If I Could Fly*. New York: Farrar, Straus, Giroux, 2011

Osa, Nancy. *Cuba 15*. New York: Delacorte Press, 2003.

O'Shea, Elena Zamora, Andrés Tijerina, and Leticia Garza-Falcón. *El Mesquite: A Story of the Early Spanish Settlements between the Nueces and the Rio Grande, as told by, "La Posta de la Palo Alto."* 1935. College Station: University of Texas Press, 2000.

Pacini Hernandez, Deborah. *Oye como va! Hybridity and Identity in Latino Popular Music*. Philadelphia: Temple University Press, 2010.

Padilla, Genaro M. *My History, Not Yours: The Formation of Mexican American Autobiography*. Madison: University of Wisconsin Press, 1993.

Padilla, Y. *Changing Women, Changing Nation: Female Agency, Nationhood, and Identity in Trans-Salvadoran Narratives*. Albany: State University of New York Press, 2012.

Padilla, Yolanda. "Mexican American Literary and Newspaper Engagements with the Mexican Revolution." In *The Heath Anthology of American Literature: The Modern Period, 1910–1945*. Vol. E, seventh edn. Ed. Paul Lauter. Boston: Houghton Mifflin, 2012.

Palacios, Monica. "Describe Your Work." In *Puro Teatro: a Latina Anthology*. Eds. Alberto Sandoval-Sánchez and Nancy Saporta Sternbach. Tucson, AZ: University of Arizona Press, 2000.

——. "Greetings from a Queer Señorita." In *Out of the Fringe: Contemporary Latina/Latino Theatre and Performance*. Eds. Caridad Svich and María Teresa Marreros. New York: Theatre Communications Group, 2000, pp. 369–90.

——. "Latin Lezbo Comic: A Performance about Happiness, Challenges and Tacos." In *Latinas on Stage*. Eds. Alicia Arrizón and Lillian Manzor. Berkeley, CA: Third Woman Press, 2000. [Out of print.]

Paredes, Américo. *With His Pistol in His Hand: A Border Ballad and Its Hero*. 1958. Austin: University of Texas Press, 2004.

——. "Some Aspects of Folk Poetry." *Texas Studies in Literature and Language* 6.2 (Spring 1964): 213–225.

Paredes, Raymund A. "The Evolution of Chicano Literature." *MELUS* 5.2 (1978): 71–110.

Parédez, Deborah. *Selenidad: Selena, Latinos, and the Performance of Memory*. Durham, NC: Duke University Press, 2009.

Parkinson Zamora, Lois. *The Usable Past: The Imagination of History in Recent Fiction of the Americas*. Cambridge: Cambridge University Press, 1997.

Parkinson Zamora, Lois, and Wendy Faris, eds. *Magical Realism: Theory, History, Community*. Durham, NC: Duke University Press, 1995.

Passel, Jeffrey S., D'Vera Cohn, and Marck Hugo López. "Hispanics Account for More than Half of Nation's Growth in Past Decade." *Pew Research Center*. 24 Mar 2011. Web. 7 Aug. 2014.

Payant, Katherine B. "Alienation to Reconciliation in the Novels of Cristina García." *MELUS* 26.3 (2001): 163–82.

Paz, Octavio. "The Sons of La Malinche." In *The Labyrinth of Solitude and Other Writings*. New York: Grove Press, 1994, pp. 65–88.

Pearce, Nick and Elaine Tan. "Online Videos in the Classroom." In *Using Social Media Effectively in the Classroom: Blogs, Wikis, Twitter, and More*. Eds. Kay Kyeong Ju Seo. New York: Routledge, 2013, pp. 132–46.

Peñalosa, Fernando. *Chicano Sociolinguistics: A Brief Introduction*. Rowley, MA: Newbury House Publishers, 1980.

Perdomo, Willie. *The Essential Hits of Shorty Bon Bon*. New York: Penguin, 2014.

Perera, V. *Rites: A Guatemalan Boyhood*. San Francisco: Mercury House, 1985.

Pérez, Loida Maritza. *Geographies of Home*. New York: Viking, 1999.

Perez, Rosie and Liz Garbus, Dir. *¡Yo soy Boricua, pa'que tu lo sepas!* Magnolia Home Entertainment, 2009.

Pérez Firmat, Gustavo, ed. *Do the Americas Have a Common Literature?* Durham, NC: Duke University Press, 1990.

——. *Next Year in Cuba: A Cubano's Coming-of-Age in America*. New York: Doubleday, 1995.

——. *My Own Private Cuba*. Boulder, CO: Society of Spanish and Spanish-American Studies, 1999.

Peréz Rosario, Vanessa, ed. *Hispanic Caribbean Literature of Migration: Narratives of Displacement*. New York: Palgrave, 2010.

Perla, H. and S. B. Coutin. "Legacies and Origins of the 1980s US-Central American Sanctuary Movement." *Refuge* 26.1 (2009): 7–19.

Philion, Thomas. "Is it Too Late to Get a Program Change? The Role of Oppositionality in Secondary English Education." *English Education* 34.1 (Oct. 2001): 50–71.

Picó, Fernando. *History of Puerto Rico: A Panorama of its People*. Princeton, NJ: Markus Weiner Publishers, 2006.

Pietri, Pedro. *Puerto Rican Obituary*. New York: Monthly Review, 1973.

Pineda, G. *Centauros ciegos: Verdades evidentes*. San Salvador: Talleres gráficos, 2003.

Pizzato, Mark. *Theatres of Human Sacrifice: From Ancient Ritual to Screen Violence*. Albany: State University of New York Press, 2005.

Plascencia, Salvador. *The People of Paper*. San Francisco: McSweeney's Books, 2005.

Pleitez-Vela, T., A. L. Regalado, and L. de Sola, eds. *Teatro bajo mi piel/Theater Under My Skin*. San Salvador: Editorial Kalina, 2014.

Poblete, Juan, ed. *Critical Latin American and Latino Studies*. Minneapolis: University of Minnesota Press, 2003.

Poplack, Shana. "Direct Acquisition Among Puerto Rican Bilinguals." *Language in Society* 7.1 (April 1978): 89–103.

Preciado Martin, Patricia. *Amor Eterno: Eleven Lessons in Love*. Tucson: University of Arizona Press, 2000.

Preston, Dennis Richard. "Whaddayaknow? The Modes of Folklinguistic Awareness." *Language Awareness* 5.1 (1996): 40–74.

Puig, Manuel. *El Beso de la mujer araña [Kiss of the Spider Woman]* Trans. Thomas Colchie. New York: Vintage, 1991.

Quesada, R. *The Big Banana.* Trans. W. Krochmal. Houston: Arte Público Press, 1999.

——. *Never Through Miami.* Trans. P. J. Duncan. Houston: Arte Público Press, 2002.

Quesada, U. *Lejos, tan lejos.* San José, CR: Editorial Costa Rica, 2004.

Radio Ambulante. "Moving." *Radio Ambulante,* June 26, 2012 episode performance, posted July 12, 2012. http://radioambulante.org/en/blog-en/ra-live-moving (accessed July 13, 2014).

Radio Ambulante. "Junot Díaz and Francisco Goldman Live in New York." *Radio Ambulante,* February 5, 2013 episode performance, posted April 18, 2013. http://radioambulante.org/en/blog-en/ra-new-york (accessed July 13, 2014).

Ramírez, F. P. "Editorials." In *Herencia.* Ed. Nicolás Kanellos. Oxford: Oxford University Press, 2002, pp. 109–111.

Ramírez, S. *De Tropeles y Tropelias Con Grabados De Dieter Masuhr.* Managua, Nicaragua: Editorial Nueva Nicaragua, 1976.

Ramos, Jorge. *Morir en el intento. La peor tragedia de inmigrantes en la historia de los Estados Unidos.* New York: Harper Collins, 2005.

——. *Dying to Cross: The Worst Immigrant Tragedy in American History.* Trans. Kristina Cordero. New York: Harper Collins, 2006.

Ramos, Juanita, ed. *Compañeras: Latina Lesbians: An Anthology* [1987]. New York: Routledge, 1994.

Rechy, John. *City of Night.* 1963. New York: Grove/Atlantic, 1984.

Reid-Pharr, Robert F. *Black Gay Man: Essays.* New York: New York University Press, 2001.

Reyes, Rodrigo, Francisco X. Alarcón, and Juan Pablo Gutiérrez. *Ya Vas, Carnal.* San Francisco: Humanizarte Publications, 1985.

Riggen, Patricia, Dir. *La misma luna / Under the Same Moon. Fox Searchlight,* 2007. Film.

Riley, Tomás. *Mahcic: Selected Poems.* National City: Calaca, 2005.

Rivera, Tomás. *And the Earth Did Not Devour Him / y no se lo tragó la tierra.* 1971. Houston: Arte Público Press, 1995.

——. "Richard Rodriguez's *Hunger of Memory* as Humanistic Antithesis." *MELUS* 11.4 (1984): 5–14.

Roa Bastos, Augusto. *I, the Supreme.* Trans. Helen Lane. New York: Dalkey Archive, 2000.

Rodríguez, Ana Patricia "Refugees of the South: Central Americans in the US Latino Imaginary." *American Literature: Special Issue on Violence, the Body, and "the South"* 73.2 (2001): 386–412.

——. "The Fiction of Solidarity: *Transfronterista* Feminisms and Anti-Imperialist Struggles in Central American Transnational Narratives." *Feminist Studies* 34.1/2 (2008): 199–226.

——. *Dividing the Isthmus: Central American Transnational Histories, Literatures and Cultures.* Austin: University of Texas Press, 2009.

——. "Literatures of Central Americans in the United States." In *Routledge Companion to Latino/a Literature.* Eds. S. Bost and F. Aparicio. New York and London: Taylor & Francis/Routledge, 2013, pp. 445–53.

——. "Genealogías transnacionales: De Máximo Soto Hall a Francisco Goldman." *Revista Iberoamericana* 79.242 (2013): 243–56.

——. "Invisible No More: US Central American Literature Before and Beyond the Age of Neoliberalism." In *The Cambridge History of Latina/o Literature.* Ed. J. M. González and L. Lomas. [Forthcoming.]

Rodríguez Barron, S. *The Heiress of Water: A Novel.* New York: Harper Paperbacks, 2008.

Rodríguez de Tió, Lola. "Ode to October 10." In *Herencia: The Anthology of Hispanic Literature of the United States.* Ed. Nicolás Kanellos. New York: Oxford University Press, 2002, pp. 560–63.

Rodríguez, Luis J. *Always Running: La Vida Loca.* Willimantic, CT: Curbstone Press, 1993.

Rodriguez, Richard. *Hunger of Memory: An Autobiography.* Boston: David R. Godine, 1981.

——. *The Hunger of Memory: The Education of Richard Rodriguez.* 1982. New York: Dial, 2005.

——. *Days of Obligation: An Argument with My Mexican Father.* New York: Viking, 1992.

——. *Brown: The Last Discovery of America.* New York: Viking, 2003.

——. *Darling: A Spiritual Autobiography.* New York: Viking, 2013.

Rodríguez, Richard T. *Next of Kin: The Family in Chicano/a Cultural Production.* Durham: Duke University Press, 2009.

——. "Being and Belonging: Joey Terrill's Performance of Politics." *Biography* 34.3 (2011): 467–91.

Rodríguez-González, Eva and M. Carmen Parafita-Couto. "Calling for Interdisciplinary Approaches to the Study of *Spanglish* and Its Linguistic Manifestations." *Hispania* 95.3 (2012): 461–80.

Rojas, Leslie Berestein. "Stereotypes, Coconuts, and Giving Back: Life in the Latino Middle Class." *Multi-American: How Immigrants are Redefining "American" in Southern California.* Southern California Public Radio. 22 Jan. 2013. Web. 27 June, 2014.

Rojo, Antonio Benítez. *La isla que se repite: el Caribe y la perspectiva posmoderna.* Hanover, NH: Ediciones del Norte, 1989.

——. *The Repeating Island: The Caribbean and the Postmodern Perspective.* Durham, NC: Duke University Press, 1992.

Román, David. *Acts of Intervention: Performance, Gay Culture, and AIDS.* Bloomington: Indiana University Press, 1998.

——. *Performance in America: Contemporary U.S. Culture and the Performing Arts.* Durham: Duke University Press, 2005.

Romero, Rolando and Amanda Nolacea Harris, eds. *Feminism, Nation and Myth: La Malinche.* Houston: Arte Público Press, 2005.

Romero, Simon. "An Interview with Ana Castillo." *NuCity* 18 June 1993. Online. www.english.illinois.edu/maps/poets/a_f/castillo/interview.htm (accessed 2 June, 2014).

Roque Ramírez, Horacio. "'That's *My* Place!': Negotiating Racial, Sexual, and Gender Politics in San Francisco's Gay Latino Alliance, 1975–1983." *Journal of the History of Sexuality* 12.2 (2003): 224–58.

——. "In Transnational Distance: Translocal Gay Immigrant Salvadoran Lives in Los Angeles." *Diálogo* 12 (2009): 6–12.

Rossini, Jon. "Teatro." In *The Routledge Companion to Latino/a Literature.* Eds. Suzanne Bost and Frances Aparicio. New York: Routledge, 2013, pp. 275–84.

Roszak, Theodore. *The Making of a Counter Culture: Reflections on the Technocratic Society and Its Youthful Opposition.* New York: Doubleday, 1969.

Rothman, Jason and Amy Beth Bell. "A Linguistic Analysis of Spanglish: Relating Language to Identity." *Linguistics and the Human Sciences* 1.3 (2005): 515–36.

Ruiz, Vicki L. *From Out of the Shadows: Mexican Women in Twentieth Century America.* New York: Oxford University Press, 1998.

Ruiz de Burton, María Amparo. *The Squatter and the Don.* 1885. Eds. Rosaura Sánchez and Beatrice Pita. Houston, TX: Arte Público Press, 1992.

——. *Who Would Have Thought It?* Ed. Amelia María de la Luz Montes. New York: Penguin Classics, 2009.

Sáenz, Benjamin Alire. "Alligator Park". In *Mirrors Beneath the Earth: Short Fiction by Chicano Writers.* Ed. Ray González. Willimantic, CT: Curbstone Press, 1992.

——. *Aristotle and Dante Discover the Secrets of the Universe.* New York: Simon & Schuster, 2013.

Salas, Elizabeth. *Soldaderas in the Mexican Military: Myth and History.* Austin, TX: University of Texas Press, 1990.

Saldívar, José David. *The Dialectics of Our America: Genealogy, Cultural Critique, and Literary History.* Durham, NC: Duke University Press, 1991.

——. *Trans-Americanity: Subaltern Modernities, Global Coloniality, and the Cultures of Greater Mexico.* Durham, NC: Duke University Press, 2011.

Saldívar, Ramón. *Chicano Narrative: The Dialectics of Difference.* Madison: University of Wisconsin Press, 1990.

——. *The Borderlands of Culture: Américo Paredes and the Transnational Imaginary.* Durham, NC: Duke University Press, 2006.

Saldívar-Hull, Sonia. *Feminism on the Border: Chicana Gender Politics and Literature.* Berkeley: University of California Press, 2000.

Salmon, William and Gómez Menjívar. "Whose Kriol is Moa Beta? Prestige and Dialects of Kriol in Belize." *Berkeley Linguistics Society* 40 (2014): 440–63.

Sánchez, George J. *Becoming Mexican American: Ethnicity, Culture, and Identity in Chicano Los Angeles, 1900–1945.* New York: Oxford University Press, 1993.

Sánchez, Luis Rafael. "The Airbus". In *The Norton Anthology of Latino Literature.* Ed. Ilan Stavans. New York: Norton, 2010.

Sanchez, Ricardo. "Barrios of the World." In: *The Ricardo Sanchez Reader: Critical Essays and Anthology.* Ed. Arnolodo Carlos Vento. Academia: Ediciones Nuestro Espacio, 2000.

Sánchez González, Lisa. "Modernism and Boricua Literature: A Reconsideration of Arturo Schomburg and William Carlos Williams." *American Literary History* 13.2 (Summer 2001): 243–64.

——. *Boricua Literature: A Literary History of the Puerto Rican Diaspora.* New York: New York University Press, 2001.

——. *The Stories I Read to the Children: The Life and Writing of Pura Belpré.* New York: Centro Press, CUNY, 2013.

Sánchez Korrol, Virginia E. *From Colonia to Community: The History of Puerto Ricans in New York City.* Berkeley and Los Angeles: University of California Press, 1994.

Sandoval-Sánchez, Alberto and Nancy Saporta Sternbach. *Puro Teatro: A Latina Anthology.* Tucson: University of Arizona Press, 2000.

——. *Stages of Life: Transcultural Performances in U.S. Latina Theater.* Tucson: University of Arizona Press, 2001.

Sankoff, David and Shana Poplack. "A Formal Grammar for Code-Switching." *Linguistic Research* 14.1 (1981): 3–43.

Santiago, Danny. *Famous All Over Town.* New York: Simon & Schuster, 1983.

Santiago, Esmeralda. *When I Was Puerto Rican.* Reading, MA: Addison-Wesley,1993.

Santicilia, Pedro. "To Spain." In *Herencia: The Anthology of Hispanic Literature of the United States.* Ed. Nicolás Kanellos. New York: Oxford University Press, 2002, pp. 551–56.

Sarmiento, Domingo Faustino. *Facundo: Civilización y barbarie.* Garden City, NY: Doubleday, 1961.

——. *Facundo: Civilization and Barbarism.* Trans. Kathleen Ross. Berkeley: University of California Press, 2003.

Scheub, Harold. *Trickster and Hero: Two Characters in the Oral and Written Traditions of the World.* Madison: University Wisconsin Press, 2012.

Schlink, Bernhard. *On Making the Weekend.* Vook, 2010. www.adweek.com/socialtimes/vook-launches-bernhard-schlink-author-app/154945

Schmidt Camacho, Alicia. *Migrant Imaginaries: Latino Cultural Politics in the U.S.-Mexico Borderlands.* New York: New York University Press, 2008.

Schon, Isabel. *Recommended Books in Spanish for Children and Young Adults: 2000 through 2004.* Lanham, MD: Scarecrow Press, 2004.

Seguín, Juan Nepomuceno. "Personal Memoirs of John N. Seguín, from the Year 1834 to the Retreat of General Woll from the City of San Antonio 1842." In *Herencia: The Anthology of Hispanic Literature of the United States.* Ed. Nicolás Kanellos. New York: Oxford University Press, 2002, pp. 106–9.

Sellers-García, S. *When the Ground Turns in Its Sleep.* New York: Riverhead Books, 2007.

Serros, Michelle. *How to Be a Chicana Role Model.* New York, NY: Riverhead Books, 2000.

——. *Honey Blonde Chica.* New York, NY: Simon Pulse, 2006.

Shakespeare, William. *Romeo and Juliet*. Globe Education iPad edition, 2013.

Shirley, Paula W. *The Dictionary of Literary Biography Yearbook, 1980*. Eds. Karen L. Rood, Jean W. Ross, and Richard Ziegfield. Detroit: Gale, 1981, p. 283.

Shklovsky, Viktor. "Art as Technique." 1917. In *Russian Formalist Criticism: Four Essays*. Trans. Lee T. Lemon and Marion J. Reis. Lincoln: University of Nebraska Press, 1965, pp. 5–25.

Siebers, Tobin. *Disability Theory*. Ann Arbor: University of Michigan Press, 2008.

Siepmann, Jeremy. *Beethoven: His Life and Music*. Naperville, IL.: Sourcebooks, 2006.

Silva Gruesz, Kirsten. *Ambassadors of Culture: The Transamerican Origins of Latino Writing*. Princeton, NJ: Princeton University Press, 2001.

Silva Gruesz, Kirsten. "What Was Latino Literature." *PMLA* 127.2 (2012): 335–41.

Sirias, S. *Bernardo and the Virgin*. Evanston: Northwestern University Press, 2005.

———. *Meet Me under the Ceiba*. Houston: Arte Público Press, 2009.

Smith, Jeanne Rosier. *Writing Tricksters: Mythic Gambols in American Ethnic Literature*. Berkeley: University of California Press, 1997.

Smith, Jon and Deborah Cohn, eds. *Look Away: The U.S. South in New World Studies*. Durham, NC: Duke University Press, 2004.

Sollors, Werner. *Beyond Ethnicity: Consent and Descent in American Culture*. New York, NY: Oxford University Press, 1986.

———. "Introduction: After the Culture Wars or, From 'English Only' to 'English Plus.'" In *Multilingual America: Transnationalism, Ethnicity, and the Languages of American Literature*. Ed. Werner Sollors. New York: New York University Press, 1998, pp. 1–13.

Sommer, Doris. *Proceed with Caution, when Engaged by Minority Writing in the Americas*. Cambridge, MA: Harvard University Press, 1999.

Soto, Gary. *Baseball in April and Other Stories*. San Diego: Harcourt, Brace, Jovanovich, 1990.

———. *Too Many Tamales*. New York: PaperStar, 1996.

———. *The Effects of Knut Hamsun on a Fresno Boy*. New York: Persea Books, 2000.

———. *Afterlife*. Orlando: Harcourt, 2003.

Soto, Sandra K. *Reading Chican@ Like a Queer: The De-mastery of Desire*. Austin: University of Texas Press, 2010.

Soto Hall, M. *La sombra de la Casa Blanca*. Buenos Aires: El Ateneo, 1927.

Sotomayor, Justice Sonia. *My Beloved World*. New York: Alfred A. Knopf, 2013.

Stalder, Felix. "Between Democracy and Spectacle. The Front and the Back of the Social Web." *Open Flows*. Web. 28 June, 2014.

Stavans, Ilan. *Latino USA: A Cartoon History*. Illus. Lalo Alcaraz. New York : Basic Books, 2000.

———. "My Love Affair with Spanglish." In *Lives in Translation: Bilingual Writers on Identity and Creativity*. Ed. Isabelle de Courtivron. New York: Palgrave Macmillan, 2003, pp. 129–46.

———. *Spanglish: The Making of a New American Language*. New York: Rayo, 2003.

———. "Translation." In *Encyclopedia Latina: Vol. 4*. Ed. Ilan Stavans. Danbury, CT: Scholastic Library Press, 2005.

———. "Introduction: The Search for Wholeness." In *The Norton Anthology of Latino Literature*. Ed. Ilan Stavans. New York: W.W. Norton, 2010, pp. lxiii–lxxi.

———, ed. *The Norton Anthology of Latino Literature*. New York: Norton, 2011.

Stefanko, Jacqueline. "New Ways of Telling: Latinas' Narratives of Exile and Return." *Frontiers* 17.2 (1996): 50–69.

Steinbeck, John. *Grapes of Wrath*. New York: The Viking Press, 1939.

Suárez, Lucía M. "Julia Alvarez and the Anxiety of Latina Representation." *Meridians* 5.1 (2005): 117–45.

Suárez, M. "El Hoyo." In *Chicano Sketches: Short Stories by Mario Suárez*. Tucson: The University of Arizona Press, 2004.

Sued Badillo, Jalil. *Agüeybaná El Bravo*. San Juan, PR: Ediciones Puerto. (n.d.)

———. *La mujer indígena y su sociedad*. 6th edn. 1975/rpt. 2010. Río Piedras, PR: Editorial Cultural, 2008.

Tafolla, Carmen. "La Malinche." In *Infinite Divisions: An Anthology of Chicana Literature*. Ed. Tey Diana Rebolledo and Eliana S. Rivero. Tucson: University of Arizona, 1993, pp. 198–99.

Taylor, Diana. *Disappearing Acts: Spectacles of Gender and Nationalism in Argentina's "Dirty War."* Durham, NC: Duke University Press, 1997.

——. *The Archive and the Repertoire: Performing Cultural Memory in the Americas*. Durham, NC: Duke University Press, 2003.

Taylor, Diana, and Juan Villegas Morales. *Negotiating Performance: Gender, Sexuality, and Theatricality in Latin/o America*. Durham: Duke University Press, 1994.

Teleduction. *Estamos Aquí/We Are Here*. 2006.

Terrero, Nina. "Kid's Lit Primary Color: White." *Entertainment Weekly* (11 April 2014): 68–69.

Thomas, Lorenzo. "Neon Griot: The Functional Role of Poetry Readings in the Black Arts Movement." In *Close Listening: Poetry and the Performed Word*. Ed. Charles Bernstein. New York: Oxford University Press, 1998, pp. 300–23.

Thomas, P. *Down These Mean Streets*. 1967. Thirtieth Anniversary Edition. New York: Vintage, 1997.

Thompson, Hunter S. *Fear and Loathing in Las Vegas: A Savage Journey to the Heart of the American Dream*. New York: Vintage, 1971.

Tobar, Héctor. *The Tattooed Soldier*. New York: Penguin, 1998.

——. *Translation Nation: Defining A New American Identity In The Spanish-Speaking United States*. New York: Riverhead, 2005.

——. *The Barbarian Nurseries: A Novel*. New York: Farrar, Straus and Giroux, 2011.

Toledo y Dubois, José Alvarez de. "Mexicans." In *Herencia: The Anthology of Hispanic Literature of the United States*. Ed. Nicolás Kanellos. New York: Oxford University Press, 2002, pp. 517–21.

Tolón Miguel Teurbe. "Always." In *Herencia: The Anthology of Hispanic Literature of the United States*. Ed. Nicolás Kanellos. New York: Oxford University Press, 2002, pp. 549–50.

Tomlinson, Carl M. and Carol Lynch-Brown. *Essentials of Young Adult Literature*. 2nd edn. Boston: Pearson, 2010.

Toribio, Almeida Jacqueline. "Spanish-English Code-Switching among US Latinos." *International Journal of the Sociology of Language* 158 (2002): 89–119.

Torres, Lourdes. "The Construction of the Self in U.S. Latina Autobiographies." In *Third World Women and the Politics of Feminism*. Ed. Chandra Talpade Mohanty, Ann Russo, and Lourdes Torres. Bloomington: Indiana University Press, 1991, pp. 271–87.

——. "In the Contact Zone: Code-Switching Strategies by Latino/a Writers." *MELUS* 32.1 (2007): 75–96.

Tovar, Inez. "The Changing Attitude of La Raza Towards the Chicano Idiom." In *Sociolinguistics in the Southwest*. Eds. Bates L. Hoffer and Jacob Ornstein. San Antonio: Trinity University Press, 1974.

Trambley, Portillo. "The Paris Gown." Berkeley, CA: Tonatiuh International, 1975.

Tropicana, Carmelita. *Carmelita Tropicana: Your Kunst is Your Waffen*. First Run/Icarus Films, 1994

Troyano, Alina, Ela Troyano, Uzi Parnes, and Chon A. Noriega. *I, Carmelita Tropicana: Performing between Cultures*. Boston: Beacon Press, 2000.

Trujillo, Carla, ed. *Chicana Lesbians: The Girls Our Mothers Warned Us About*. Berkeley: Third Woman Press, 1991.

Turner, John Kenneth. *Barbarous Mexico*. Austin: University of Texas Press, 1969.

Tynberg, Nan. Comp. *Course Packet for English 319: Studies in Literary Diversity* ("Corridos;" "La LLorona;" Joel Chandler Harris; Zora Neale Hurston; *The Winnebago Trickster Cycle*; Leslie Marmon Silko; Southeast Asian Folktales). Palm Desert: CSUSB, 2004.

Unger, D. *Life in the Damn Tropics: A Novel*. Madison: University of Wisconsin Press, 2004.

United States Census Bureau. "Table 1: Hispanic or Latino Origin Population by Type: 2000 and 2010." *2010 Census Briefs*. Washington: U.S. Census Bureau, May 2011. Web. 1 July, 2014.

Urrea, Luis Alberto. *Nobody's Son: Notes from an American Life.* Tucson: University of Arizona Press, 1998.

———. *Vatos.* Photographs by José Galvez. El Paso, TX: Cinco Puntos Press, 2000.

———. *The Devil's Highway: A True Story.* New York: Little, Brown, 2004.

———. *The Hummingbird's Daughter.* New York: Little, Brown, 2006.

———. *Into the Beautiful North.* New York: Back Bay Books, 2009.

Valdés, Guadalupe. "The Language Situation of Mexican Americans." In *Language Diversity: Problem or Resource.* Ed. Sandra McKay and Sau-ling Wong. New York: Newbury House Publishers, 1988, pp. 111–39.

Valdes-Rodriguez, Alisa. *Dirty Girls Social Club.* New York: St. Martin's Griffin, 2003.

Valdez, Luís. "The Dark Root of a Scream." In *From the Barrio: A Chicano Anthology.* Eds. Luis Omar Salinas and Lillian Faderman. San Francisco: Canfield Press, 1967, pp. 79–98.

———. *Actos-y-el teatro Campesino.* Fresno: Cucaracha Press, 1971.

———. "Soldado Raso." *El Andar* February 1991. N.p.

———. *Zoot Suit and Other Plays.* Houston, TX: University of Houston Arte Público Press, 1992.

———. *Envisioning California: Peoples, Land, and Policies.* 9–11 Feb. 1989. Sacramento: Center for California Studies, Fall 1995.

Valdez, Luis. *Los Vendidos.* Alexandria, VA: Alexander Street Press, 2004.

———. KTEHTV. *This is Us—Luis Valdez.* 10 Jan. 2009. Video. YouTube.

Valdez, Luís and Teatro Campesino. *Actos.* San Juan Bautista: Menyah Productions, 1971.

Valdéz, Zulema. "Intersectionality, Market Capacity, and Latina/o Enterprise." In *The New Entrepreneurs: How Race, Class, and Gender Shape American Enterprise.* Stanford, CA: Stanford University Press, 2011, pp. 63–89.

Valdivia, Angharad N. *Latina/os and the Media.* Cambridge, UK: Polity Press, 2010.

Valenzuela, Angela. *Subtractive Schooling: U.S.-Mexican Youth and the Politics of Caring.* Albany: State University of New York Press, 1999.

Vallejo, Jody Agius. *From Barrios to Burbs: The Making of the Mexican-American Middle Class.* Stanford, CA: Stanford University Press, 2012.

Vallejo, Platón. "Letter to William Heath Davis." In *Herencia.* Ed. Nicolás Kanellos. Oxford: Oxford University Press, 2002, pp. 100–02.

Varela, Félix. "Essay on Slavery." In *Herencia: The Anthology of Hispanic Literature of the United States.* Ed. Nicolás Kanellos. New York: Oxford University Press, 2002, pp. 522–28.

Vargas, Jennifer Harford. "Dictating a Zafa: The Power of Narrative Form in Junot Díaz's *The Brief Wondrous Life of Oscar Wao.*" *MELUS* 39.3 (Fall 2014): 8–30.

Vargas Llosa, Mario. *The Feast of the Goat.* Trans. Edith Grossman. New York: Picador, 2002.

Vázquez, David T. *Triangulations: Narrative Strategies for Navigating Latino Identity.* Minneapolis: University of Minnesota Press, 2011.

Vasquez, Richard. *Chicano.* Garden City, NY: Doubleday, 1970.

Velasquez, Eric. *Grandma's Gift.* New York: Walker & Company, 2010.

Venegas, Daniel. *The Adventures of Don Chipote.* 1928. Houston: Arte Público Press, 2000.

Venuti, Lawrence. "Introduction." In *Rethinking Translation: Discourse, Subjectivity, Ideology.* Ed. Lawrence Venuti. London: Routledge, 1992.

Vernallis, Carol. *Unruly Media: YouTube, Music Video, and the New Digital Cinema.* New York: Oxford University Press, 2013.

Villanueva, A. L. *The Ultraviolet Sky.* Tempe: Bilingual Press/Editorial Bilingüe, 1988.

Villarreal, José Antonio. *Pocho.* 1959. New York: Anchor Books, 1989.

Villaseñor, Victor. *Rain of Gold.* Houston, TX: Arte Público Press, 1991.

Villegas, de M. L. and Clara Lomas. *The Rebel.* Houston: Arte Público Press, 1994.

Villegas, Jr., Richard. *I ♥ Babylon, Tenochtitlan, and Ysteléi.* Los Angeles: Villegas, 2011.

Villoro, Juan. "La crónica, ornitorrinco de la prosa." In *Antología de crónica latinoamericana actual.* Ed. Darío Jaramillo Agudelo. Madrid: Alfaguara, 2012.

Viramontes, H. M. "The Cariboo Café." In *The Moths and Other Stories*. Houston: Arte Público Press, 1985, pp. 59–75.

——. *The Moths and Other Stories*. Houston: Arte Público Press, 1985.

——. "Nopalitos: The Making of Fiction." In *Making Face, Making Soul—Haciendo Caras: Creative and Critical Perspectives by Women of Color*. Ed. Gloria Anzaldúa. San Francisco: Aunt Lute, 1990, pp. 291–94.

——. *Under the Feet of Jesus*. New York: Plume, 1995.

——. *Their Dogs Came With Them*. New York: Atria, 2007.

——. "Beach Blanket Baja." *New York Times*, New York Edition ed., sec. Opinion: WK 17. 17 Aug. 2008.

Ween, Lori. "Translational Backformations: Authenticity and Language in Cuban American Literature." *Comparative Literature Studies* 40.2 (2003): 127–141.

Weir, David. *Anarchy & Culture: The Aesthetic Politics of Modernism*. Amherst: University of Massachusetts Press, 1997.

Wendell, Susan. *The Rejected Body: Feminist Philosophical Reflections on Disability*. New York: Routledge, 1996.

West-Durán, Alan, ed. *Latino and Latina Writers*. 2 vols. New York: Scribners/The Gale Group, 2004.

Which Way Home. Dir. R. Cammisa. HBO Films/Documentress Films, 2009.

Wilkerson, Abby L. "Normate Sex and its Discontents." In *Sex and Disability*. Eds. R. McRuer and A. Mollow. Durham: Duke UniversityPress, 2012, pp. 183–207.

Williams, Raymond. "The Metropolis and the Emergence of Modernism." In *Modernism/ Postmodernism*. Ed. Peter Booker. New York: Longman, 1992.

Wolfe, Tom. *The New Journalism, with an Anthology*. Eds. Tom Wolfe and E.W. Johnson. New York: Harper & Row, 1973.

Woloch, Alex. *The One vs. The Many: Minor Characters and the Space of the Protagonist in the Novel*. Princeton: Princeton University Press, 2003.

Worthen, W. B. "*Still Playing Games*: Ideology and Performance in the Theater of Maria Irene Fornes." In *The Theater of Maria Irene Fornes*. Ed. Marc Robinson. Baltimore: Johns Hopkins University Press, 1999, pp. 61–75.

——. "Staging America: The Subject of History in Chicano/a Theatre." *Theatre Journal* 49.2 (1997): 101–20.

Ybarra-Frausto, Tomás. "I Can Still Hear the Applause: La Farándula Chicana: Carpas y Tandas de Variedad." In *Hispanic Theatre in the United States*. Ed. Nicolás Kanellos. Houston: Arte Público, 1984, pp. 45–61.

York, Sherry. *Children's and Young Adult Literature by Latino Writers*. Worthington, OH: Linworth Publishing, Inc., 2002.

Young Lords Party. *Palante: Voices and Photographs of the Young Lords Party, 1969–1971*. Michael Abramson, Photography. Chicago: Haymarket Books, 2011.

Zamora, Bernice. "Notes from a Chicana COED." *Caracol* 3.9 (1977): 19.

Zavala, Iris M. *Colonialism and Culture: Hispanic Modernisms and the Social Imaginary*. Bloomington: Indiana University Press, 1992.

Zentella, Ana Celia. "Ta Bien, You Could Answer Me en Cualquier Idioma: Puerto Ricon Code-Switching in Bilingual Classrooms." In *Latino Language and Communicative Behavior*. Ed. Richard Durán. Norwood: Ablex, 1981, pp. 109–31.

——. *Growing up Bilingual: Puerto Rican Children in New York*. Maiden, MA: Blackwell, 1997.

Zimmerman, Marc. *U.S. Latino Literature: An Essay and Annotated Bibliography*. Chicago: March/Abrazo Press, 1992.

Index

Sandín, Lyn Di Iorio: *Magical Realism* 75n1
Sandoval-Sánchez, Alberto: *Stages of Life* 146
santeras 56, 279
santería 57, 59, 106, 165
santera 56
Santiago, Danny: *Famous All over Town* 78
Santiago, Emeralda 106; *America's Dream* 221; *When I Was Puerto Rican* 84, 109–10
Santiago, Wilfred 173; *In My Darkest Hour* 175; *21* 175–76
Santicilia, Pedro: "A España" (To Spain) 17, 23
santos 184
Santos, Nadia: *Forest of the Pygmies* 194
Saporta Sternbach, Nancy 146
Sarduy, Severo 104
satire 84, 276, 303
Scarface 107
Schlink, Bernhard: *The Weekend* 181, 188
Schmidt Camacho, Alicia 64
Schnabel, Julian: *Before Night Falls* 107
Schomburg, Arturo A. 109, 112, 113
Scholastic 198
Seguin, Juan: *Personal Memoirs* 18–19, 23, 42
self-reflexive Latino literature 135, 241, 261
Sellers-García, Sylvia: *When the Ground Turns in Its Sleep* 71
Serros, Michelle: *Honey Blonde* 213; *How to Be a Chicana Role Model* 213
sestina 136
Shakespeare, William: *Romeo and Juliet* 181
Shakira 152
Sherrill, Martha: *The Ruins of California* 223
Shirley, Paula W.: *The Dictionary of Literary Biography* 143
Shkovsky, Viktor 179
Siebers, Tobin 228
Sifuentes, Roberto 159; *El Mexterminator* 160–61; *Exercises for Rebel Artists* 164; *Temple of Confessions* 162, 163
Silva Gruesz, Kirsten 14, 21n1, 64, 122
simile 82
Simon 122; *Meet Me* 122
slavery 15–17, 21n2, 21n5, 76n10, 103, 104, 105
Smith, Jon 76n2
social constructionism 228, 229, 231
social justice 8, 66, 76n12, 120, 206, 235, 271, 273, 305
sociological approach 80–81
Sommer, Doris 64
sonnet 136
Soto, Gary 82; *Afterlife* 194; *Baseball in April* 194; *The Effects of Knut Hamsun on a Fresno Boy* 85; *Too Many Tamales* 196
Soto, Sandra K. 32, 36–37, 39n2

Soto Hall, Máximo 122
Sotomayor, Sonia 106; *My Beloved World* 110
South End Press 33
Spanglish 7, 41–50, 92, 101, 108, 131, 132, 195; language attitudes 42–43; speakers 48–49; unpacking 43–47
Spinsters/Aunt Lute 33
Stalder, Felix: "Between Democracy and Spectacle" 135, 139
Stavans, Ilan 131, 239; *History of Latinos* 174, 176; *Norton Anthology of Latino Literature* 14, 41, 95, 104, 132; *The Norton Introduction to Latino Literature* 1–2, 139; *Spanglish* 46
Stefanko, Jacqueline 51, 54
Stegner, Wallace 282
Steinbeck, John 230; *Of Mice and Men* 181
Stepmann, Jeremy: *Beethoven, His Life and Music* 190n5
story 13, 54–55, 59, 81, 85–86; frame 162
storyworlds 93–94, 97, 98, 99n4, 171, 172, 174, 241
Sturges, John: *The Magnificent Seven* 186
Styron, William 180, 181
Suárez, Mario: "El Hoyo" 245
suburbs 10, 218–26; transnational 76n7
supreme Court 82, 225n4
Svich, Caridad 3, 146
symbolism 82, 249, 307, 308; French 24; Mesoamerican theatrical 29
syncretism 106, 175, 251

Tafolla, Carmen 287; "La Malinche" 30
Tafolla, Santiago: *A Life Crossing Borders* 23
Tan, Elaine 134
Taylor, Diana 139–40, 151; *The Archive and the Repertoire* 159–60
Teatro Campesino 29,132,133, 152
teatros de revistas 143
Teleduction: *Estamos Aquí/We Are Here* 125
telenovela 256
Telepirata 121
Terrill, Joey 34, 35
testimonios 1, 18, 64, 74, 75n1, 121, 122, 135, 244, 246
Tezkatlipokia 271, 272
theater in the Latino/a literature classroom 141–49; identity/mapping power 146–48; staging history 142–46
third-person voice 56, 58, 95, 194, 307; omniscient 54, 250, 285
Third Woman Press 33, 39n3
Thomas, Lorenzo 134
Thomas, Piri 109; *Down These Mean Streets* 37, 195, 229, 282–83, 287
Thompson, Hunter S. 66, 239

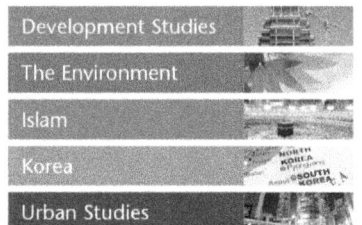

For Product Safety Concerns and Information please contact our EU
representative GPSR@taylorandfrancis.com
Taylor & Francis Verlag GmbH, Kaufingerstraße 24, 80331 München, Germany